"Literchoor Is My Beat"

ALSO BY IAN S. MacNIVEN

Lawrence Durrell: A Biography

"Literchoor Is My Beat"

A LIFE OF JAMES LAUGHLIN,

PUBLISHER OF NEW DIRECTIONS

Ian S. MacNiven

FARRAR, STRAUS AND GIROUX

NEW YORK

Farrar, Straus and Giroux
18 West 18th Street, New York 10011

Owing to limitations of space, all acknowledgments for permission to reprint
previously published and unpublished material appear on pages 581–584.

Library of Congress Cataloging-in-Publication Data
MacNiven, Ian S.
"Literchoor Is My Beat" : a Life of James Laughlin, Publisher of New
Directions / Ian S. MacNiven. — First edition.
    pages   cm
Includes index.
ISBN 978-0-374-29939-2 (hardback) — ISBN 978-0-374-71243-3 (e-book)
    1. Laughlin, James, 1914–1997.   2. Literature publishing—United States—
History—20th century.   3. Publishers and publishing—United States—
Biography.   4. Poets, American—20th century—Biography.   5. New Directions
Publishing Corp.   I. Title.

PS3523.A8245 Z77 2014
811'.54—dc23
[B]

                                                    2014008669

Farrar, Straus and Giroux books may be purchased for educational, business,
or promotional use. For information on bulk purchases, please contact the Macmillan
Corporate and Premium Sales Department at 1-800-221-7945, extension 5442,
or write to specialmarkets@macmillan.com.

www.fsgbooks.com
www.twitter.com/fsgbooks • www.facebook.com/fsgbooks

1   3   5   7   9   10   8   6   4   2

With endless love and devotion to my wife, Peggy Lee Fox, who suggested this book to me and whose detailed knowledge and critical eye made possible its eventual completion

Contents

"Literchoor Is My Beat"

Preface

Born handsome, brilliant, and rich, all his life James Laughlin courted the art of self-effacement. But even as he practiced disappearance, a behind-the-scenes master rather than a public figure, he, more than any other person of the twentieth century, directed the course of American writing and crested the waves of American passions and preoccupations. His life is mirrored in his friendships and in the careers of the many writers he championed.

Laughlin lived eighty-three years and thirteen days, and he was planning, writing, editing, and publishing until the very end. His importance to American and to world literature has been and will continue to be measured by the authors he published under the New Directions imprint, the firm that he founded in 1936 while he was still a Harvard undergraduate—nurturing authors who in many cases would owe their reputations to his early support. He published almost fifteen hundred books by others and wrote more than thirty of his own: poetry, essays, short stories, translations. He developed the Alta ski area in Utah at the very dawn of skiing in America. He loved India and worked there with the Ford Foundation in various publishing ventures over a five-year period. A mere sentence about his relationship with each of the more than two and a half thousand people he corresponded with, entertained, and skied alongside would fill this volume. "Getting around the world as I have done has been a marvelous experience," he wrote to Thomas Merton, "but you pay for it, in a way, in keeping up with all the contacts that you've made in foreign parts."

This story of a life is perforce selective, focused, and yes, arbitrary. It is also the story of the publishing house Laughlin founded. And it is emblematic rather than exhaustive. My greatest regret on committing this work to the publisher is that so many persons significant to Laughlin's life and to the history of New Directions have been accorded mere passing mention, or even omitted entirely. But I have tried to present a true portrait, with the clear outlines of a remarkable personality, a force in publishing, an original voice in American poetry, a visionary in skiing, and a world traveler of discernment and judgment.

More than anything else, perhaps, Laughlin provided a nexus: he brought writers together. He introduced them to other writers whom they needed for their artistic development. Sometimes it was a personal introduction, as when he sent Charles Olson, who needed a mentor, to Ezra Pound, who needed a friend—Pound, accused of treason, had just been committed to St. Elizabeths Hospital. More often, Laughlin furnished books that served as another kind of introduction—to a literary circle that would become vital to a writer then just starting out: "The first person who introduced me to writing as a craft," said the poet Robert Creeley, "was Ezra Pound," whom Creeley encountered in the New Directions editions of *Polite Essays* and *Guide to Kulchur*. Soon Creeley was corresponding with Pound and William Carlos Williams, and he became influenced by others in the extended Laughlin circle: Olson, Robert Duncan, Lawrence Ferlinghetti, Allen Ginsberg, Denise Levertov, Kenneth Rexroth, Louis Zukofsky.

Surrounded by an immense and constantly growing cast, Laughlin himself lived beset by crises. The courage, intelligence, and humor with which he confronted each challenge form the dramatic contours of his life story. Early on, he overcame a physical handicap and injuries; later, he was faced with family opposition to his publishing, public condemnation of some of his authors, marital disruption, and financial constraints. All his life he was threatened by the genetic curse of bipolar illness. In the truest sense, he was a self-created personality. And while he remained, throughout, vitally engaged with the cultural, social, and political being of America and beyond, he was at times the most unhappy of men—lonely and yearning, even when he appeared the most fortunate.

When Laughlin included them in the first of his series of fifty-five anthologies of poetry and prose, Ezra Pound, Wallace Stevens, and William Carlos Williams were virtual unknowns, sometimes driven to self-publishing. Fifty years later, these three would frequently be singled out as the greatest American poets of the twentieth century. No less discerning when it came to foreign literature, Laughlin became either the first or one of the earliest American publishers of a long list of world figures that includes Baudelaire, Borges, Céline, Hermann Hesse, García Lorca, Thomas Merton, Henry Miller, Eugenio Montale, Nabokov, Pablo Neruda, Nicanor Parra, Pasternak, Octavio Paz, Raja Rao, Rimbaud, and countless others. Personally involved in steering his publishing company right up until his death, James Laughlin created the New Directions backlist, a tally of largely modern and modernist authors that is unequaled in American publishing. And he was no mere publishing tycoon, sitting comfortably in a posh office and directing others to scout, edit, print, and sell books. He began as a one-man operation: editing text, selecting type fonts and paper, designing covers, negotiating with printers in America and Europe, driving cross-country to cajole bookstores into stocking his titles.

And while Laughlin's early print runs might be tiny—often only 100 to 1,500 copies—gradually his choices would define the course of modernism. All his life he scanned countless journals for new writing and followed through on recommendations from a great many friends. He was engaged with his authors on the most intimate level: he argued over Fascism and anti-Semitism with Pound, and scolded Henry Miller for his obscenity and his pecuniary fecklessness; he was raucously denounced by Kenneth Rexroth for publishing "fairies like Tennessee Williams," and cursed by Edward Dahlberg for printing nearly everyone but himself; he sought advice from paranoiac Delmore Schwartz, bought ballet shoes for Céline's wife, paid Kenneth Patchen's medical bills, went to the morgue to identify Dylan Thomas, helped Nabokov with his lepidopterology, meticulously arranged into the acclaimed *Asian Journal* the chaos of notes that his friend Merton left behind after his tragic electrocution, dined with Octavio Paz at the Century, and discovered Paul Bowles, Denise Levertov, and John Hawkes.

And he was adventurous physically as well as intellectually. He skied down mountains and broke many bones long before "extreme skiing" had even been named; he climbed up the Matterhorn. When he knew that he would be near trout streams or golf courses, he added fly rods or clubs to his kit; dangled from the end of a lifeline while rock climbing in the Sierras; and punctured a lung scaling a fence to reach a mountain brook.

Born into the wealth of Jones & Laughlin Steel in Pittsburgh, paradoxically Laughlin was forced to run his businesses for decades on tight budgets. The Great Depression still gripped America when he founded

New Directions, and Laughlin grew up with habits of thrift. For this reason, there is a fair amount here about dollars and even pennies in sales figures and book advances; in fact, for many years, Laughlin insisted upon writing out each author's royalty check himself, no matter how small. The reader should bear in mind that these figures need adjustment for inflation. Roughly computed, $100 in 1936, when Laughlin founded New Directions, would be worth at least $1,500 in 2014 dollars. At the peak of his publishing career, Laughlin would list his occupation on his tax return as "Investor," and there was truth to this claim: he never took a salary from either his publishing or his skiing ventures, and aside from inheritances, his substantial net worth on his death was owed in part to prudent investment. The more New Directions achieved publishing successes, the less proud Laughlin allowed himself to appear, although he was always pleased when one of his authors sold well.

However, it was as a poet that Laughlin in his youth hoped to triumph. Then he met Ezra Pound. The best-known tale about Laughlin portrays his giving up poetry under the impact of Pound's alleged disapproval. The account that Laughlin told goes like this: After spending some months studying under Ezra at the "Ezuversity," Pound's informal academy in Rapallo, master and pupil conferred:

> EP: Jaz, you're never gonna be any good as a poet. Why doncher take up somethin' useful?
> JL: What's that, Boss?
> EP: Why doncher assassernate Henry Seidel Canby?
> JL: I'm not smart enough. I wouldn't get away with it.
> EP: You'd better become a publisher. You've prob'ly got enough brains fer that.

Maybe it happened this way. However, the story—a good one that Laughlin relished repeating on the lecture circuit—was told and retold by one of the most self-deprecating yarn-spinners alive, until it became a mythology. And while I like the story very much, I do not believe it, for reasons that I have set down in these pages. And this points to one of the leitmotifs of this volume: the sifting of reality out of the corpus of myth. From time to time I unmask the joker, reveal tricks of the illusionist. That said, I have found that Laughlin was in the main searingly honest, especially in confession. I count it no sin on Laughlin's part if he was occasionally unreliable. He sometimes embroidered not out of malice, but because he was a storyteller in the fine old sense of the word: he loved a good tale, and if he could improve on events by giving them a more dramatic spin, so much the better. Also, he was addicted to a pose of humility, and he often made himself the butt of a joke. He hardly ever invented calumnies about others, although he often did about himself. Sometimes he constructed outcomes from a sentimental need to have episodes turn out *the way he wished them to have happened*—this is one of his most human and endearing traits.

Pound certainly did encourage Laughlin to become a publisher, yet Laughlin continued, by fits and starts, to write poetry throughout his long life. Eventually he blossomed in verse, seeing fifteen volumes of his poems published during his last ten years, and he was inducted into the American Academy of Arts and Letters as a poet. His verse was highly praised by people as varied as Lawrence Ferlinghetti, Guy Davenport, Kenneth Rexroth, and William Carlos Williams. The scholar and author Marjorie Perloff wrote, "Laughlin traces, with the greatest delicacy, grace, and wit, the vagaries of sexual love, the pleasures and pain of memory, the power of literary allusion." He put into his verse those tender and often erotic feelings that his Calvinist reticence forbade him to utter out loud. His best poetry, with a nod toward his master, Catullus, is very fine indeed.

He also wrote hundreds of thousands of letters: missives to authors from Walter Abish to Louis Zukovsky; personal letters to Pound and Jonathan Williams and Tennessee Williams and William Carlos Williams and Henry Miller (an epistolary marathon champion who finally met his match in Laughlin); letters detailing the editing problems of their modernist epic poems or explaining the minutiae of copyright law; letters of gentle rejection ("I have read your manuscript with great admiration, but unfortunately our publishing schedule . . ."); letters of denial to poets wanting to revise poems already in production; letters to his parents, cajoling and scolding them; letters to wives, children, and lovers. To date, seven collections of his exchanges with individual authors—Guy Davenport, Merton, Henry Miller, Pound, Rexroth, Delmore Schwartz, William Carlos Williams— have been published. The year Laughlin died, he did not depart alone among important American literati. As the *Dictionary of Literary Biography Yearbook* proclaims, "1997 was a year that will be noted for the deaths of four major figures: James Dickey, Allen Ginsberg, Denise Levertov, and the poet-publisher James Laughlin." Each of these was towering in accomplishment, yet more than any other figure of his century, Laughlin's decisions shaped English-language modernist poetry.

My wife, who knew Laughlin professionally and personally during a period of more than twenty years, was visited a few years ago by him in a dream: he asked her how the biography was coming along, and then he said distinctly, "I wanted to be free." He made it clear that he had, stubbornly, always done things the way he wanted to do them. Then he wandered off to clear some vines growing over a window. Of course, if he was often ambiguous and contradictory in life, how far can we credit this voice from the world of dreams? Still, it is pleasant to imagine his ghostly presence.

Once, long after his death, I came upon an old pipe in his office at his residence, Meadow House, the dottle still in the bowl, exuding a faintly lingering scent of tobacco. This is an account of a kind of archaeological dig, the story of a publisher and an angler, of a recluse and an adventurer, of a proselytizer and an idealist, of a connoisseur and a Calvinist and a Buddhist, of a writer of letters and an excellent skier, of a lover and a fine poet. It is the story of a man who lived passionately.

—Ian MacNiven,
Gypsy Hollow, Athens, New York,
March 2014

The Ancestors

And when we finally
Made it to Portaferry
Looking for ancestral graves
. . . there was no trace
Left of the old hovel and
Potato patch.
　　　　—James Laughlin, *Byways*

James Laughlin IV walked unsteadily across the stage at the American Academy of Arts and Letters in April 1995, his towering height somewhat reduced by skiing injuries and spinal compression. But Laughlin trembled more from emotion than from the frailty of his eighty years. The novelist John Hawkes stood ready to support him, but he did not stumble. He was to be inducted into the institution as a poet, a recognition that he cherished above all others. He had written poetry all his life in an attempt to understand himself. Finally, he was being called to share this particular honor with the likes of Robert Creeley, Denise Levertov, Ezra Pound, Gary Snyder, and William Carlos Williams, all friends and poets he had published under his New Directions imprint. To Laughlin belonged the achievement of recognizing the promise of Thomas Merton and Tennessee Williams, of championing Henry Miller, Louis-Ferdinand Céline, Octavio Paz, and countless others. Literary modernism would wear a different face in America, in the world, had Laughlin not existed. Such accomplishment would have satisfied most men, but Laughlin yearned above all else to be a poet.

•

The Laughlin family history was in many ways a typical American success story, except that few sons of Ireland succeeded in America quite so handsomely as James's paternal ancestors. In the Old Country the family were farmers on a small scale, with land at Dunover, a tiny hamlet just west of Ballywalter and near Portaferry, looking out over Strangford Lough, County Down, where according to tradition Saint Patrick had commenced his evangelical mission. Various Laughlins tried to trace the family back to Scotland—it was considered more respectable to hail from Scotland than from Ireland—but were stymied by the conflagration that destroyed most of the documents in Dublin's Four Courts building during the uprising of 1916. Nonetheless, the Laughlins, their name also spelled Laghlan, Lachlan, and Loughlin, were in fact descended from a Scottish clan allied to the MacLachlans of Ayrshire. The name itself was Danish and came from Lach-lan, Land of the Lochs or Lakeland, an early name for Denmark. The long-faced, longheaded Scandinavian bloodline remained in their physiognomy. There were Presbyterian Laughlins in Ireland as far back as 1666, and the James Laughlin listed on a rent roll for the Estate of Portaferry in 1738 is very likely the father of old James, who accompanied his younger son of the same name to Pittsburgh, to die there three years later, in 1831. There had been a James in the family for at least six consecutive generations, but not necessarily in a father-to-son succession. The poet-publisher's IV numeral was appended to his name as a courtesy title.

The funds that launched this Laughlin line toward America came from the sale of "the ancestral potato patch." The brothers Alexander and James shared equally with their sister Eliza as required by the deed: "*Dividetus pariter in tres partibus*," which, Laughlin commented, "is bad Latin but this was Ireland." Around 1819, Alexander sold whatever he could, converted the pounds sterling into crockery, and with his wife, Mary Ann Bailey, sailed to Baltimore. He bought a wagon and peddled the dishware to farmers all the way through Pennsylvania, arriving with an empty wagon but enough cash to buy a small house and help fund his father-in-law's grocery store at Fort Pitt at the juncture of the Allegheny and the Monongahela Rivers.

The ancestral James Laughlin left Ireland a decade after his older brother, traveling with his eighty-year-old father. Within ten years after reaching America, he was prominent enough to marry the granddaughter of Major George McCully, who had fought in the Revolution and had assumed command of Fort Pitt. Laughlin became "largely interested" in the Fifth Ward Savings Bank in 1852, later incorporated as the First National Bank of Pittsburgh. National banking was not then a widely accepted concept, but his bank did very well, and James Laughlin would remain its president until his death.

By 1853, James Laughlin had met the Welsh-descended Benjamin Franklin Jones, an impressive younger entrepreneur who had been a builder of canal boats until he realized that the future of transportation lay in railroads instead. The family legend maintains that James Laughlin's eldest son, Henry, wanted to go to Paris to become a painter, so the old man decided to buy into the iron and steel industry and put his four sons to work in it—that would get the art nonsense out of his firstborn's head. Laughlin risked a good deal of bank money in iron production and became an equal partner with Jones in 1856, in what would eventually become the Jones & Laughlin Steel Corporation. When the Civil War began in 1860, the partners, as the main producers of iron rails at the time, were poised to make a fortune.

The partners agreed that any profits would become part of the working capital, not withdrawn for the use of either man, and this was later codified in the bylaws of the company. James Laughlin IV would grow up hearing this maxim: plow profits back into business. And to this there was a stern corollary: *never* borrow. By 1900, Jones & Laughlin was the second-largest steel producer in the United States and would remain privately held until 1923. The J&L employees were a turbulent mix of Irish, Italians, African-Americans, Poles, Welsh, Scots, English, and central-European-descended workers, subdivided into mutually despising "mill hunks" and "cake-eaters"—the white-collar accountants and clerks. Joneses and Laughlins generally figured in equal numbers among the top management, and there was intermarriage between the families.

As James Laughlin IV told the story in the prosaic language of *Byways*, the extensive autobiography in verse that he was still working on at the time of his death, the fortunes of Jones & Laughlin swelled, and his great-grandfather built a mansion where two rivers met to become the Ohio: "Where wide lawns sloped down to the / Allegheny River . . . at the Point where / Once Fort Duquesne had stood." By this time Major George

McCully Laughlin, descendant of the Revolutionary hero, had constructed a sprawling brick-and-stone mansion on Woodland Road in the Squirrel Hill area, where James's parents would later build across the road.

In contrast to the rich of the great East Coast cities, fully a third of whom had inherited their wealth, eighty-one of the hundred Pittsburgh millionaires listed in 1888 possessed self-made fortunes. The city had become known for its disproportionately large number of the very rich. Andrew Carnegie led the pack with a personal fortune of $20 million. James would later characterize his birthplace as tough-minded, practical, and philistine: "The butler passed chewing gum on a silver salver after the coffee."

James's father, Henry Hughart Laughlin, courted Marjory Rea, beautiful daughter of William "Daddy Bill" Holdship Rea, patriarch of another prominent Pittsburgh family. Her pale face and fine features set off by carefully waved dark hair, her slender figure exquisitely clothed, she had the poise of a debutante awaiting the arrival of photographers. Marjory attended the Pennsylvania College for Women on Woodland Road, and her young womanhood was filled with dinners, cotillions, golf, bridge, and dog shows. She was an enthusiastic athlete, won cups at lawn tennis, and played for the Pittsburgh Golf Club. Marjory's grandfather Colonel James Childs had been killed at Antietam while leading the Pennsylvania Cavalry, and his daughter, Adelaide, had married Carnegie's sometime-partner Henry Clay Frick. Hughart Laughlin triumphed in wooing Marjory Rea while singing in a charity production of *The Pirates of Penzance*, and Marjory announced their engagement from the stage. "Each of the contracting parties is worth $20,000,000," stated *The New York Times*. The sum was a bit of an exaggeration.

Hughart's architect brother-in-law, Edgar Viguers Seeler, designed for them an eight-bedroom brick-and-half-timber home with servant quarters at 104 Woodland Road. The same year, Marjory's brother James Childs Rea built a house of similar dimensions next door. Marjory and Hughart were among the gilded people of Pittsburgh, their travels and events featured in the society pages. Their first child, Hughart Rea Laughlin, was born in 1909. Then, on October 30, 1914, came James, born into a world newly at war, exactly twenty-nine years after the poet Ezra Pound had first seen the cold autumn light of Hailey, Idaho. James very nearly did not survive his birth. The somewhat crumpled ears of the adult James resulted from a difficult forceps delivery: the umbilical cord was wrapped twice around his neck and "old Dr. Miller" thought that he was dead, but Bertha

"Mengie" Kaler, the robust German nanny, plunged him into a cold tub and got his breathing started.

As a small child, James was shy, clinging, and rather delicate. His left eye had a tendency to cross and did not focus well on objects close at hand, another likely result of the forceps. This contributed to his sense of insecurity, and he was teased by other children. He would play a persistent solitary game for hours in the nursery with white wooden blocks "that I heaped into piles and built into shapes and masses," he would recall, or remember being told. "My old German Ba," his nanny, sat watching him while she did the family mending.

James's father indulged him, while his mother wielded the hairbrush, the accepted rod of correction. Consequently, he trotted after his father like a puppy and avoided his mother—she seemed to him to prefer it that way. "Wow! wow! wow! wow! wow! Hear the tiger roar," his father, a Princeton man to the marrow, taught him to chant before he had reached four. Princeton was a family tradition, where Grandfather Laughlin, also a graduate, had endowed Laughlin Hall.

The Lord was often mentioned in the Laughlin home, yet as James would write years later, "There was an enormous amount of Bible reading and catechism learning but no inside religious *feeling*." The Laughlins, Reas, and Heinzes, already of the "57 Varieties," were among the benefactors of the Shadyside Presbyterian Church, openly spoken of as the *establishment* church of Pittsburgh. It was no oversight that James's father was not listed in the membership records. Hughart Laughlin was not a professed nonbeliever: he simply left religion alone. Sundays were for boating, hunting, the races.

Marjory, however, was a Presbyterian of the strict-interpretationist school, full to the larynx with religious prejudice. Roman Catholics were Papists to her, and the intricacies of their religion derived from the devil. They were evil, she told James, "because they believed that only other Catholics could go to heaven." There was also an element of class prejudice: most of the steelworkers and some of the housemaids were Catholic. A new housemaid described the Crucifixion to young James in such terms that the boy cried all afternoon. She was dismissed immediately. "The Jews" were simply absent from the Laughlin circle: when they were mentioned, it tended to be as an abstraction usually connected with money. What did stay with the boy from his heavy-handed Calvinistic upbringing was a social conscience that placed wealth second in importance to service. "It was dinned into me from Sunday School days," he said, "that you had a moral responsibility to uplift people[,] to improve the world"—and to assuage a residual guilt at being rich. An uncle, the Reverend Maitland Alexander, preached pounding his fists on the stone pulpit while "shouting / sin sin sin and the / fiery fires of hell."

Hell became linked in young James's mind with the steel mills: on Thanksgiving their father took his boys on their annual tour of the mills, as if to say, "Thank thee, O Lord, for our prosperity!" They donned dark glasses against the searing flare of the furnaces and watched the orange-hot slabs of metal being salted down: "A big cloud of smoke would burst up and the salt would hiss and fizz like bacon frying." The mills both frightened and impressed James: he sensed early that he did not want to enter the family business, that he must escape from "Peeburg."

As a refuge from the soot-heavy air of Pittsburgh, the family bought Big Springs, a farm set amid gentle hills near Rolling Rock. The women and children also retreated there during the Great Steel Strike of 1919, in which tear gas was used against the strikers; this too would become linked in James's mind to wealth-guilt and the need to expiate it through service. His fondest early memories were of the farm, named for its mountain-fed springs. In the front yard there were trout ponds that never froze over, and there were willows, hammocks, a swimming raft. His father would drive up in his elegant Pierce-Arrow—painted fire-engine red to outrage Pittsburgh society—and practice his fly-fishing technique by casting for cigarettes scattered on the lawn as James watched, awed by his quiet concentration. For one of his late volumes of poetry, published in 1995, Laughlin chose as the title poem "The Country Road" and used as a dust jacket illustration an oil painting by his cousin Marjorie Phillips showing one of the roads near the farm that he had walked as a boy: graceful curves, small fields in hay and pasture. The painting, hanging in the old poet's dining room, drew him strongly back to the emotions of his youth:

> As my eyes walk that familiar road, where I walked so often
> > as a child,
> I see things I hadn't detected before,
> Little things of no great importance, but I'm
> > aware of them.

Country was winning the boy's allegiance over city.

Big Springs was a working farm, with the plowing, haying, and milking done by hired men: Lloyd Bunkert—"Bunkert, not drunkard," he liked to say—who had seven children, and Jakes, who lived in a ruinous house on the property. Cream was skimmed in the Spring House, alongside an old stagecoach. In the barn there were vats for boiling maple syrup. The main house was deliberately kept rustic and was not wired for electricity; in the evenings the children were encouraged to work puzzles under oil lamps. When he was old enough, cleaning the soot from the lamp chimneys became James's daily task: "When I had done the lamps I read 'teks' in the hammock"—he favored the decidedly upscale detective fiction of S. S. Van Dine.

Summers the family went to Nantucket, where Grandfather James Laughlin's yacht *Ariadne* was docked, with a crew of twenty and an orange-and-black Princeton pennant at the masthead. George Lister Carlisle, called Uncle Dicky and married to H. Hughart Laughlin's sister, Leila, had inherited from his grandfather, the whaling magnate Henry Coffin, land in Nantucket that included several waterfront "boathouses" and a mansion on the cobbled Main Street. He kept his sloop at one of these Coffin houses, and he would take Hughie, James, and their various cousins sailing. He belonged to the Wharf Rat Club—the very binnacle of Nantucket society.

To flee the gray Pittsburgh winter, the snow darkened with soot from the coke ovens and Bessemer blast furnaces, various Laughlins would board their private railcar for the annual trek to Zellwood, Florida, northwest of Orlando. When James was four, they paused en route to visit his father's cousin Duncan Phillips, the art collector, in Washington. The first night, there was a fire across the street. Thereafter he would plead with his mother, "When can we go back to Aunt Lidie's"—as Duncan's wife, Elizabeth, was called—"to watch the fire engine?"

Zellwood was a small backwoods community inhabited by Georgia crackers and the raffish younger sons of English gentry who for reasons of their own found it convenient to live in a backwater. What the men of Zellwood had in common was a love of hunting, and they ran camps where wealthy Pittsburgh sportsmen could shoot quail and then drink whiskey in log cabins. James Laughlin Jr., James's grandfather, after hunting there for some years, had built in the 1880s what he initially intended as a rustic lodge, named Sidoney for his wife, Sidney Ford Page, on 525 acres of pine and palmetto. When the locals objected to his plans, Laughlin bought Zellwood and moved the entire town a safe distance away. The lodge became a Spanish-style mansion with a broad front veranda with open arches, and it overlooked spring-fed Lake Minore. There were marble foyers, frescoed ceilings, carved mahogany moldings, thirteen bedrooms with canopied beds, a formal dining room with a cut-crystal chandelier, a tiled swimming pool in the basement, and a broad porch surrounded by the front lawn. The acres of garden included trees from all over the world and an aviary filled with rare birds.

Even more than in Pittsburgh, James was surrounded with luxury. However, on the first visit that he could remember, a kidnapping rumor caused panic in the Sidoney community. Young James would try not to fall asleep, sure that he would be killed. Or that he would contract appendicitis or be struck by lightning. "All were acts of God meted out to sinners," he was told. There was also the problem of Grandfather: since 1917 he had lived in a separate house on the property, closely attended by two male nurses. At times gentle and pleasant, he was by turns morosely silent or raging. The boy was frightened when either manifestation of his mental illness was upon him. A figure of dread to his grandson, he died at Sidoney on October 19, 1919.

It was James's grandmother Sidney Ford Page Laughlin whom the boy would know as the matriarch of Sidoney. Everyone called her Danny after young James had tried to say Granny and it came out Danny. Grandmother Danny was quiet, seldom speaking because, as she maintained, "she'd said all she had to / Say," other than to tell tales about ancestors who had served in the colonial British army or who had come from Montserrat in the West Indies to fight in the American Revolution. She did not talk about her husband's strange behavior, except obliquely: "Nobody / Had ever gone potty in her / Family." This pottiness had entered the family when James Laughlin,* the founder of J&L, married Ann McCully Irwin of County Tyrone. And it only af-

---

* With so many James Laughlins in the family, the future poet and publisher would answer patiently to James, Jamesie, Jim, Jimmy, Jas, Jaz, Jay (this one he actively disliked: his mother wrote to him as Jay), and encouraged his familiars to use the shortest of all: simply "J," followed by no period. Since the mature man himself preferred J, thus shall he be designated herein, beyond his youth.

fected the men, she would add with a slightly superior air, giving out "little clucks like a chicken": all three of her sons were "a bit peculiar" at times.

Grandmother Danny had two gray Pierce-Arrows—one was a spare— and a chauffeur in matching gray. She took James, his cousin Marie, and her other grandchildren for drives, the little ones sitting in the rear-facing jump seats. James's father tried to be a companion to him, punting with him on Lake Minore and pointing out the constellations to him. Sirius in Canis Major his father termed "The Big Dog," while Procyon became, whimsically, "Little Dog Peppermint." And he often read out loud to both sons. James responded with ardent affection.

•

People meeting the very tall, handsome, quietly confident James Laughlin of his maturity would have found it difficult to see the future commanding presence in the insecure child. His parents appeared to lavish far more love on his brother, who was held up as a cynosure. At the dinner table Hugh would say, "Mother, James is babbling again, and he's pushing with his fingers." James silently hated him. "Hugh was not a thoughtful person," their cousin Marie Page Edgerton remembered, yet comrades and parents alike doted on him. Hugh's friend and contemporary H. J. "Jack" Heinz invented a construction firm, Hans, Gluppel & Glup, with himself as Hans, Hugh as Gluppel, and James, barely tolerated, as Glup. The firm was based at Big Springs, where there were streams to be diverted, dams and forts to be built. "My purpose was to bring glup," lumps of muck and sod, J would recall, which the older boys used for construction. "More glup, Glup," they would demand. "Get a move on!" It was a profitable firm: "We got paid a dollar per dam."

Young James grew up with a father who by his own choice had no useful job, although he did accept election, along with his neighbor Andrew Mellon, to the board of trustees of the Pennsylvania College for Women down Woodland Road. He had been in charge of the J&L coal mines but had resigned his position and closed his office two weeks after his father's death. He now indulged himself with golf, trout and salmon fishing, polo, horse races, long-hooded cars—and women. He shot game with an English double and patronized tailors and haberdashers in London and in Cambridge, Massachusetts, who fitted him with splendid tailcoats and toppers. And while James decided that he too did not want to make steel, he also knew early on that he did not want to live his father's self-indulgent life.

Back in Pittsburgh, James was sent to Miss Simonson's school for "socializing," where he claimed later to have learned only how to perform "a very slow waltz." Whenever his mother felt that she might not be doing her part to "bring the boy up right," she arranged some new project. One of these twinges of conscience led her to engage a piano teacher, but when James resisted, his mother gave in. His father enjoyed indulging James and bought him "for good behavior" his first bicycle, a Driscoll Glorious that cost $12.

For a more serious introduction to education, James was next enrolled in the Arnold grade school near Woodland Road. The school took its name from Thomas Arnold, headmaster of Rugby. In the junior division the traditional balance of academics and physical development was adhered to, with a nod to the progressive "project method." A hundred pupils were spread among twelve grades. James might be slow at reading and inept athletically, but the Arnold School was for the children of privilege, and there were plenty of awards to go around. Also, he was gaining in self-confidence, and toward the end of his time at the school he was given the female lead in *All-of-a-Sudden Peggy*, an Irish parlor farce imported from London.

James got along better with Uncle Jimmy and with Aunt Leila and Uncle Dicky than with his mother. His father's younger brother, James Laughlin III, lived in Orlando and was married to a second wife, June, who wore her beautiful red hair down her back, billowing in the wind when she and her husband took the boy for fast rides on the St. Johns and Ocklawaha Rivers. Uncle Jimmy had been a noted early automobile racer, had served in the Great War, and was now the fleet captain of the Mount Dora Yacht Club. He "spent money like water when he was high," remembered his nephew disapprovingly. Aunt Leila was fashioned from less supple but tougher metal; she had attended a horticultural college, acted as her father's secretary, and seemed to know everything about Sidoney: crops, outbuildings, water system, staff. In her early womanhood she had been the guest of the American ambassador in Japan, and she had returned with an extensive array of Oriental pottery and statuettes. Young James's interest in Asia began with her. Visits to the Carlisles' home in

Norfolk, Connecticut, were great fun. There was an excellent collection of children's books, and Uncle Dicky would read to him and his cousins for hours on end, *Winnie-the-Pooh* and *The Wind in the Willows*, as well as more serious fare. To the great delight of the children, Annie Dixon, the black housekeeper from Florida, one of the many in her family who served Laughlins and Carlisles, read *Uncle Remus* stories to them in dialect.

Whether in Pittsburgh, at Sidoney or Big Springs, or on Nantucket, James's life moved on as inevitably as the snug existence of a boll weevil. Yes, he was well cared for, but mainly by servants. His older cousin Marie divined his hunger for affection and remembered seeing James, at age ten, climb onto his nanny's lap. When he was eleven, James spent hours lying on a sofa in the main Sidoney living room reading Trollope or Dickens while Grandma Danny worked her embroidery. Her favorite was a Scot named William Edwards, the estate superintendent, who would sit with her for long consultations. "I loved him too," J would write later, "he was / My best friend." When James was only four, his father had outfitted him with kilt, sporran, and dirk. Robert the Bruce became the boy's great hero (he could claim descent from Isabella, the Bruce's sister), and Edwards taught him to recite the Scottish grace immortalized by Robert Burns: "Some hae meat, and canna eat, / And some wad eat that want it."

When Ledlie Irwin Laughlin, later a member of the board of directors of J&L and James's oldest second cousin on the Laughlin side, made up a family genealogy for his bride "to show her what she was getting into," he noted in a neat hand a list of "Skeletons in the cupboard." Some of it was gossip: The Right Reverend Edward R. Laughlin's ex-wife "has been married three times . . . The family with good cause has no use for her." Thomas K. Laughlin "killed himself." All the Laughlins blamed his wife, President Taft's sister-in-law. Others were named with some pride: Irwin B. Laughlin was minister to Greece; Duncan Phillips Jr. (grandson of the first James Laughlin) "is a well-known art critic and has one of the finest private collections in the country." John Page Laughlin, James's uncle, who had once worked for J&L, had gone to the bad: "He studied silver-smithing, sugar raising, music in Rome, and is now raising chickens in Virginia." As if in retribution, Uncle John "suffered early Depression," and his wife had to hire caretakers for him. The implications of Cousin Ledlie's commentary were clear: a Laughlin was expected to excel in respectable work, marry prudently, and stay sane.

•

The family sailed aboard the *Aquitania* for England in 1924. James was taken to the Burlington Arcade in London to buy lead soldiers, his newest collecting passion; he also collected stamps with equal ardor. Left to himself after the shop clerk learned that he could be trusted meticulously to open and reclose each box without tearing the packaging, he would spend hours inspecting the tiny painted figures, in the uniforms of British and Continental regiments.

Not that James was indulged by his parents with *everything* eye saw and heart coveted: money was a teaching tool, and to him it seemed always in short supply. His allowance at first was fifteen cents a week, with bonuses for high marks and good conduct at school. This was what J later called "the poverty of childhood": although he grew up in an opulent household, Calvinist thinking held that unearned money corrupts, and so Hughie and James, and their friend Jack Heinz too, had been restricted to small allowances. This doling out of tiny sums bred in the boys a niggling exactness over expenses. Of his funds James was expected to give a third to "dear Jesus," a third to savings, with only the remaining moiety to be allotted to personal satisfaction. J himself dated his long slide away from conventional piety to his Burlington Arcade visits. In his childhood Eden, "the upswalen [sic] serpent's particular form" was a set of lead cavalry, a mounted Horse Guards Band, which he could purchase only with the addition of funds intended for the collection plate. He bought the set, steeling himself against some dire God-sent punishment. Nothing happened. He enjoyed his sinful booty to the full.

James and his brother once accompanied their father to what he termed his club. They were admitted by a butler into a fine private house and were received by an elaborately dressed lady "[w]ho looked somewhat like the queen." Their father went off with this lady, leaving the boys to be entertained with checkers and ginger ale by Winifred, "[t]he most beautiful girl I had / Ever seen." Young James stared in disbelief when she knelt, in her "rather scanty" gold dress, to knot his chronically untied shoelaces.

James might have seen well enough to notice a girl's beauty, but in truth his vision was seriously compromised. At the Bulstrode Clinic the eminent Dr. Claud Worth, who boasted that King George was a patient, used strange-sounding words like "convergent," "faulty stereopsis," and "hypermetropic." He performed a tenotomy on James's left eye in an attempt to eliminate his squint and counter his amblyopia. As James emerged, parched, from the general anesthesia, he was given a lesson in pronunciation. When he cried out, "Wodder, wodder!" Sister Olive asked sweetly, "Do you mean wotah, dear?" The operation was pronounced a success—prematurely, as it turned out—and four pretty nursing sisters posed with the patient for a snapshot. Wearing corrective lenses, James received a lesson in English prehistory when his father took him and Hugh to see a formation of Druidic standing stones, his brother very much the young gentleman in a bowler, James in shorts and overcoat, with one stocking down-gyved.

•

While James was in Florida in early February 1925, Grandmother Danny died in her sleep at Sidoney, and his old fear of death returned in force. "I went a little bit crazy," he remembered. "It was the end of my / Childhood." Before, death had been an abstraction; this time there was a body he could see. She was seventy-seven, and her heart had simply given out.

Twelve was an age of emotional crisis for James, a time of puberty and of separations. In September 1927, James and his brother were sent to the Institut Le Rosey, the most expensive prep school in Switzerland, in the small town of Rolle on Lake Geneva. The reasons given were various: to escape from strike-ridden Pittsburgh, to "get a taste of Europe," to learn some French, and even, improbably, at James's own request. The main reason was undoubtedly the onset of their father's mental illness: he began to have the violent fluctuations of mood that characterized the strain of manic-depressive psychosis common in the family and from this time on would often be institutionalized. Marjory Laughlin wanted her younger son, especially, not to be witness to his father's distress. Hugh had already been accepted as a freshman at Princeton, but if he spent a year at Le Rosey too, he could keep an eye on James.

French was the language of instruction at Le Rosey, and the masters were very strict in enforcing its use. "I was so unhappy that I studied pretty hard and learned some French," J would recall. If he dozed off, the instructor would yell at him, "Laughlin Deux, la salle de classe n'est pas pour dormir." Part of his unhappiness probably stemmed from the proximity of Hughart, Laughlin One, who was well over six feet tall, handsome, and a fine track athlete. At five feet three and a half inches, and weighing exactly one hundred pounds, James was tall enough for his age but hardly robust. Under "Character" in the school records he was described as "Reserved and rather retiring—clean morally and physically"; also, James was considered "Careless & impetuous—a real student when he is interested & loves competition."

Le Rosey came as a shock to the boy. The staff made no secret of their contempt for these Americans who couldn't speak proper French or German. Nor did their parents' money or social standing impress. There was too much competition along such lines; one schoolmate was a Pahlavi, the crown prince of Iran, and another was a grandson of Metternich. The Latin teacher Laroux, the master at James's dining table, liked to bait him: "Dis donc, Lowgleen, sais-tu que tous les américains sont bêtes? Mais oui, je sais bien qu'ils sont tous des singes"—I know very well that they are all monkeys.

The students from twenty-two different countries did not always mix harmoniously: a group of German boys tried to hang a Belgian from a tree, until his screams brought one of the masters. (James would later incorporate the event in a short story.) A boy from Egypt, assigned to the seat across from James in the dining hall, teased him and kicked him slyly under the table. He did not dare retaliate since any uproar was sure to result in a fine for all, "un franc d'amende pour tout le monde," a serious matter when each boy was permitted only three francs per week pocket money. On the other hand, James seems to have liked his sophisticated roommate, who told him that the gentlemanly way to ask a woman to have intimate relations was to say, "Puis-je vous offrir le bonheur physique?"—May I offer you physical happiness?

James still did not excel athletically. Assigned to pull an oar in a four-man racing shell, in a race he became so excited that he caught his pants in the sliding seat mechanism and capsized the boat. He was banished from the team. However, he took to skiing. With the snows, the main Le Rosey campus closed, and the whole school packed up for Gstaad for the winter term. "Eight days in the mountains are worth eighty days of health," goes an old Swiss adage endorsed by the school. They lived in several large chalets surrounded by firs, below the Hornberg. Skiing,

James Laughlin would later say, is "sexy": "With each turn you send up a cloud of snow-spray. It feels like a sensual rhythmic dance."

Despite his weakness in French, James had done reasonably well academically. On a ten-point scale, at first he received 5s and 6s in Latin, 7s and 8s in French, then rose to 8 in Latin and 9 in French. Hugh outpaced James, taking more courses for credit and receiving 10 in Latin, 9 in French, 7 in German, and 8 in Italian. The boys returned to Pittsburgh.

This experience of Switzerland had been a bitter lesson in estrangement from all that was dearly familiar, yet James had profited. He had learned enough French to speak and read it easily. After the socially homogeneous world of his relatives, he had been thrown together with boys of many nations and cultures. The skiing and the mountains had been wonderful, and he was stronger and healthier. The Old World had given back to the New.

2

Discoveries: The Intellect

The Child is father of the Poet. —Adapted from Wordsworth

A few weeks after his return from Le Rosey in 1928, James was sent away to summer camp in Montana, where his one blazing experience would be a sensual epiphany: off in the woods to relieve himself, he experienced an erection and spontaneous ejaculation of such profound vigor that he noted the date in his diary, recently begun and fitfully kept. He was nearly fourteen, and he would cite this event for the rest of his life as his sexual awakening. It was also a fine awakening to the high country of the American West.

In the fall James matriculated at the Eaglebrook School in Deerfield, Massachusetts, fifty miles from Aunt Leila's home in Norfolk, Connecticut. Eaglebrook was patterned on English boarding schools, with many of the masters and their families living on the grounds, and from the 1920s it had offered the first junior ski program in the country. He remembered it as having a decidedly "homey" atmosphere. Partly in reaction to the pervasive religiosity of the family, James became antireligious during the school year, "though never militantly so."

Coincident with his attending Eaglebrook, James's "parenting [was] . . . almost entirely taken over by . . . Aunt Leila." He liked to give the impression throughout his adult life that he had *chosen* Aunt Leila and Uncle Dicky as his parents, based on their sympathetic understanding and on the location of Norfolk at a safe distance from Pittsburgh. Certainly young James hit it off well with both his aunt and his uncle, but the compelling reason for the change was H. Hughart Laughlin's ongoing psychosis. Marjory Laughlin readily acknowledged the bond between son and father: "This is particularly hard on Jay as he adored his father and misses him dreadfully." Leila Laughlin Carlisle gladly took over the nurture of her nephew.

Aunt Leila and Uncle Dicky had no children, and she had laid down a stipulation that the marriage be childless before she agreed to it. She let it be known that the strain of madness in the family gave her a mandate not to pass on whatever psychotic flaws she might unknowingly harbor. J came to attribute to her a Victorian prudery raised to phobic proportions and speculated that the marriage had never been consummated, a view not shared by other members of the family, privy to the connubial rejoicings that filtered through the uninsulated walls of their summer home in Nantucket. She had first seen her future husband from the deck of the *Ariadne*: the young man had cut a romantic figure, sailing alongside in his slim racing sloop in Newport harbor, and she had resolved at once to marry him. And George Lister Carlisle *did* have an adventurous spirit: he was a Yale engineer who spoke fluent Spanish and had attempted a mining venture in Nicaragua; and he was a skilled deepwater sailor. Quiet and ironic where Leila Laughlin was assertive and opinionated, he considered her a "superlative star," and he both supported and directed her enthusiasms, restraining her with an affectionate "Now, Lily dear!" when he thought she was going too far.

Religion seemed to James an important part of life at Robin Hill, a three-story Neo-Georgian-Palladian mansion designed by Uncle Dicky's cousin the architect Charles Everett in 1927. Although nominally a Protestant, Aunt Leila was not a churchgoer and in her religion was closer to the Catholic mystics than to her ancestral Presbyterians. She was passionately devoted to gardening and good works and loved children—provided they behaved reasonably well. If they did not, if *anyone* misbehaved for that matter, Aunt Leila saw reproof as her duty. "None of my cousins would put up with her," J liked to tell people; it fitted his myth of her as the "Ogre Aunt." She and Uncle Dicky had purchased hundreds of acres of rolling wooded land on both sides of Mountain Road, a mile from Norfolk center and bordering on Tobey Pond, a small private lake shared by half a dozen families. Aunt Leila surrounded Robin Hill with a garden that she laid out in a deliberate asymmetry based on Japanese landscape design. Stands of orange azaleas lit up the springtime plantings. The house was furnished with beautiful antiques and rugs, and her collection of Oriental artifacts and screens gave the place the aspect of a museum. "Jamesie" was given his own third-floor room, and it was understood that he would spend many weekends and school holidays with her. Robin Hill was a youth's paradise: when he was there, life seemed to center on him according to the season, with swimming and boating at Tobey Pond, hiking, snowshoeing, skiing, sledding, and, in the evenings, card and parlor games, and plenty of reading.

Robin Hill was a cosmopolitan house, and the Carlisles read widely in history and other nonfiction, expected good conversation, and entertained frequently. There were many volumes reflecting Aunt Leila's interest in gardening and architecture and a set of John Galsworthy—the Carlisles had named Robin Hill after the family mansion in *The Forsyte Saga*—but very little modernist fiction. Uncle Dicky, although far less possessive than his wife, was equally fond of James and tramped around the estate with him, identifying plants, teaching him to shoot, and telling stories that ranged from Managua to Mombasa, Dar es Salaam to Lake Victoria.

It was also at Aunt Leila's knee that James was given indoctrination in values social and economic, moral and religious. Each morning he was received by his aunt, robed in a Chinese silk peignoir, in her second-floor sitting room. She would have finished her breakfast, a single uncooked egg "downed in a gulp," and was ready for an hour's monologue. These "scholia," as the mature man would call them, covered everything from family stories going back to James-the-Founder, whom Aunt Leila was old enough to remember; the fuliginous mills of Pittsburgh; the early days of Sidoney; the standards of good taste and high social mores; the obligations to philanthropy and the preservation of the natural world; and religion and spiritualism. Philanthropy was integral to her life: in addition to countless other benefactions, she would put more than a hundred people, black and white, through high school and often college. Boston, she said, embodied the best values, the life of the mind; Philadelphia was provincial; New York meant culture, but also an excessive focus on money. Most important, James was included in the adult circle, and it was probably from the Carlisles that he first heard frank discussion of the strain of mental disturbance in the family.

Aunt Leila's admonitory sessions would continue throughout her life. Eager though he might be to begin or resume his own day's work, her nephew listened, not just patiently, but "in thrall to her conviction." He recognized her need of him: above all, her need to re-create in him her idealized conception of her own adored father, for whom he had been named. And J needed his aunt, for guidance, for her living embodiment of family, for her devotion.

•

His illness in abeyance, J's father took him to Europe in the summer of 1929. Perhaps he consciously saw their trip together as a chance to imbue his son with his own cosmopolitan values and to advance his "European education." More likely, he simply enjoyed James's company and seized the excuse to escape from the tensions of Woodland Road. They stayed at London's Burlington Hotel at the end of the great arcade, and his father insisted, as always, on their dressing meticulously for dinner: Hughart had his son measured for a blazer and flannels at his tailors on Savile Row; a craftsman in leather turned out elegant oxfords that conformed perfectly to his long feet. James visited the National and Tate Galleries and lured his father to Covent Garden to see some of the fine Russian dancers, Danilova, Toumanova, Massine.

In Lausanne they lodged at the Hôtel Beau-Rivage and visited a family friend, Mlle Marie-Thérèse d'Authume. Although "Mademoiselle," as they called her, spoke perfect English, she encouraged James to practice his schoolboy French and got him to read some of her favorite poets, which he adopted as his own: Paul Éluard, Lamartine, Max Jacob, and the love sonnets of Louise Labé. To the boy, already dismissive of Pittsburgh society and scornful of the intellect of most of the women he knew, it was a revelation to meet this formidably well-educated woman, witty, charming, and beautiful, who did not condescend to his youth and inexperience. Elegant in a wide white hat and blue parasol, she would walk with him along the lakefront. "Young as I was, I had / Fallen in love with her," he admitted.

While James certainly loved his father, he never felt drawn to the life of a rich playboy. In fact, his own driven industry, already emerging at Eaglebrook, showed his need to do, to make. Gambling was destructive of wealth, drinking of health, dissipation of time: these conclusions came more from the lamentable example of his beloved father than from the exhortations of the Laughlin women and the Presbyterian divines.

Eaglebrook only went through the ninth grade, so James was enrolled at the Choate school in Wallingford, Connecticut, for the 1929–30 school year. His parents had allowed him to choose between two schools, Choate and St. Paul's in New Hampshire. James had opted for Choate because he disliked the religion-centered behavior code of St. Paul's. Choate was a very good private boarding school, but the institution was not quite "It": the sons of New York money went there; the scions of East Coast first families went to older and more prestigious Andover, Exeter, or Milton. John F. Kennedy would graduate from Choate three years after James, and Kennedy wealth like Laughlin wealth was too recently made, the lineage too Irish to be completely acceptable. James was unhappy during his first year and was considered antisocial.

Choate for James came to mean four people: the English master Carey Briggs, who looked like a minute owl, held his honors seminar class in the library and preached respect for books; H. P. "Hup" Arnold, the classics professor, whom the boys called "the Venerable" while they groaned at his puns ("All Choate is divided into three galls"); Clara, wife of the headmaster, George C. St. John; and Dudley Fitts, who would start Laughlin on the road to Rapallo and Ezra Pound. Briggs encouraged the boy to write poetry and planted in the future publisher the idea that a book was something intrinsically fine and could be a work of art. Arnold gave Laughlin an abiding love of the Latin and Greek classics. Clara St. John provided a large measure of the empathy that James felt he did not receive from his own mother. Fitts more than any other challenged him intellectually.

Many years later James would recall his first encounter with Fitts: the delicately boned young master, his Dracula cape flaring, was rushing down the dining hall stairs as James was speeding up. The collision nearly flattened Fitts. Pulling himself together, he said with infinite scorn, "You young puppies who haven't even read Thucydides!" But Fitts was famously accessible, and serious students were welcome to sit reading in his study so long as they kept quiet, and they were encouraged to borrow his books. James would describe Fitts as "handsome but slightly odd-looking" and finally realized that his singularity in appearance stemmed from a brow "an inch taller than any other at Choate," rising above his horn-rimmed glasses. He played the organ in chapel, and soon he enlisted James to sing solos.

James admired Fitts—musician, poet, translator, scholar—but he became a close friend only later. "Fitts is a sort of algae," James would write later to another Choate alumnus, the classicist Robert Fitzgerald: he was inescapable; he grew on you. At the time, young James turned to Clara St. John for inspiration, guidance, and emotional support. Educated in the classics, she had taught Greek at the school before Laughlin's time. During his senior year he achieved a friendship with the highly attractive forty-eight-year-old lady, an early exemplar of the many women he would adulate for their intellectual brilliance and nobility of spirit. "I always knew she was a great woman and was rather afraid of her," Laughlin wrote to Fitzgerald; "now that I approach closer I discover that she is very [sic] charming young gal. Ever so young, and yet full of the wise juice of living." James was a bit wary of George St. John, who liked to say, "We save a boy's soul at the same time we are saving his algebra."

•

In the autumn of 1929, James's father, his bipolar illness still in remission, took him to Daytona, without revealing the true purpose of the trip. They drove from the train station straight to a marina where Hughart gave his son, just turned fifteen, a thirty-foot power yacht, the *Sarsho*, meaning "fish" in Seminole. Together they motored up and down the Florida inland waterway, indulging in nautical talk: James called his father "Skipper" and responded to "Mate." Hughart had designed the elegant boat himself, with a glass-paned cabin, mahogany woodwork, and a powerful inboard engine. It was a happy time of camaraderie.

Indifferent to the business world, Hughart paid attention to the Black Monday crash of October 28 because it substantially affected his disposable funds. James heard much talk at home about money and the shortage thereof, principally from his mother. Whether or not she recognized that bursts of extravagance coincided with her husband's manic episodes, she must have hoped that warnings about financial collapse would have a restraining influence on his philandering. Whatever her motivation, it did not make for peace in the home. In the manic phase Hughart exhibited every variety of excess: in drinking, gambling, spending, pursuit of sexual partners, indulgence in some monomania, wild flourishes in language. Marjory blamed the victim for weakness of will and prayed to God for his reformation. Hughart on his part understood that something was wrong, but he could no more heal himself than could a man with leprosy.

James, meanwhile, increasingly asserted himself as someone out of the ordinary, and for the Christmas recess from Choate he wrote, produced, directed, and starred in a romantic comedy, *The Last of the Holenoffs*, supported by a cast of cousins. His mother, however, did not want him to be *too* out of the ordinary, and on June 13, 1930, he was taken with his brother to join the Shadyside Presbyterian Church "by examination," which meant that he had to answer a few simple religious questions before being confirmed. Howard Heinz and his two sons, Jack and Rust, sat decorously two rows in front of the Laughlins, while Mrs. Heinz was usually too "indisposed" to attend church. It was whispered that she was an alcoholic, and James began to suspect skeletons in everyone's Chippendale.

By his second year at Choate, James realized that he could excel academically. His ambition became to be named top boy. This goal he pursued relentlessly: "[M]arks I hungered and I / yearned and burned for marks / the way other boys / craved girls or being on the / hockey team." He took honors English with Carey Briggs, whom he asked to order books from a New York bookseller for him. One of the barriers across James's route to the summit was the geometry class of "fat old Mr. Kenington," a subject that awoke no resonance in the boy. He decorated the margins of his textbook with sketches of his friends and even of the teacher "scratching his stomach / on the corner of his desk." James conned the figures and diagrams without much understanding, reproducing them on the daily tests, and then during lunch period he would sneak to the teacher's desk and correct any mistakes in his ungraded paper.

During August 1931, James wrote to Frances Steloff's Gotham Book Mart in New York, asking to be put on its mailing list, citing a special interest in modern firsts, and soon he was purchasing books regularly, with a charge account. Fitts was happy to suggest titles, and one of the first volumes of poetry that James bought under his guidance was Archibald MacLeish's *New Found Land*, which thrilled him and helped develop his taste for modern verse. During his senior year he ordered more than fifty books from Steloff, among them Faulkner's *A Rose for Emily*, Kay Boyle's *Year Before Last*, Joyce's *Pomes Penyeach*, Pound's *Poems 1918– 1921*, Gertrude Stein's *Acquaintance with Description*, O'Neill's *Mourning Becomes Electra*, and Blaise Cendrars's *Panama*. He permitted himself an autographed limited edition of E. E. Cummings's *Him* for $7.50, but passed up his *Tulips and Chimneys* as "too high" at $15. His choices were weighted toward poetry with imaginative prose a close second, yet he also acquired essays by Edith Wharton on fiction, Stuart Gilbert on Joyce, and Max Eastman's *The Literary Mind*. He bought a biography of Rimbaud in French, but ordered Proust's *Le temps retrouvé* in translation. A number of the titles were quite obscure, such as the surrealist novel *Murder! Murder!* by Kay Boyle's husband, Laurence Vail, and Charles-Louis Philippe's *Bubu of Montparnasse*, in Vail's translation and with a preface by T. S. Eliot. He also subscribed to Eugene Jolas's *transition*, which featured many new French writers as well as American expatriates. James's growing library showed his discernment, his catholic taste, his wide-ranging curiosity. Sound as most of his purchases would prove as investments, it was not the accrual of value that was a primary motivation: he wanted to read the texts and was willing to accept used copies "if not too dilapidated." Occasionally, given a choice, he bought the limited edition; he already coveted fine printing on hand-laid paper. Some fifty years later when the Gotham sponsored a reception for J, he would be amazed to find invoices for books that he had ordered while at Choate enlarged and tacked to the walls as a display. "Frances, don't you throw *anything* away?" asked J.

Soon he was elected to the board of the *Choate News* and began to spend much of his free time in the room of the managing editor, Hugh Wade, who loaded his mantelpiece with everything from Chaucer and Donne to Joyce's *Ulysses*. Wade spoke on contemporary poetry at the student discussion group, and it was from him as well as, later, from Fitts that James learned to appreciate the poetry of Cummings.

Mr. and Mrs. Briggs had no children, and they opened their home to James and called him Jay. He discussed not only course work, books, and the news with Carey Briggs, but also other boys and masters, problems of education and upbringing, even children's reading. James prided himself on his independence of thought; this and his increasing intellectual achievement encouraged an element of snobbery, which manifested itself in his standing aloof from most of his schoolmates. Nor was he amenable to parental advice: "He is just at the stage now when he considers Mother's opinions old-fashioned," Marjory Laughlin wrote to Briggs. While she was proud of his work at Choate, she was disturbed that he seemed to be developing no "interest in his fellow man." Or woman: "The girl question has not yet entered into the problem," said his mother with terse relief. "I am duly thankful to be spared it for a while." The whole truth was that young James had not confided in his mother: he considered that he had already scored social triumphs at Rosemary Hall, the girls' school near Choate. And he had in fact reached out more to others: he was elected manager of the basketball team, and in March he would be on the school debating team in a contest with Yale freshmen. Briggs was willing to admit that James was "impatient of anything that seeks to set him right," but said that he would take correction where he respected a person's ideas.

An impassioned family row blew up at the beginning of the summer on his return to Pittsburgh, when, full of his wide reading, James said, "I was foolish enough to babble about Cummings, Eliot, et al. to Mother. And whenever I get excited about something, Mother immediately becomes suspicious." She demanded to be shown the "nonsense" that he was reading and pounced upon some passages in *The Waste Land*. James refused to burn "the horrid trash," his mother wept and prayed over him, his brother, Hugh, volunteered that he would never have imagined that his own flesh and blood would read "dirty smut like that," and Aunt Leila invoked the "fine, upright, and clean-minded men" among their Presbyterian ancestors. When James tried to defend his studies by saying that several of the masters at Choate "thought well of 'that rubbish,'" there was unanimous agreement that he should be sent to a military school. In short, discord reigned in this best-of-all-possible households. Only when Mengie, his beloved nanny, intervened was he allowed to go on with his summer reading program, with the understanding that he could return to Choate after all.

James resumed with Joyce: *A Portrait of the Artist as a Young Man*, *Dubliners*, and those portions of the tantalizing Work in Progress that he had been able to lay hands on—"Anna Livia Plurabelle" and "Tales Told of Shem and Shaun." He read the chapter on Joyce in Edmund Wilson's *Axel's Castle* and S. Foster Damon's "Odyssey in Dublin" in Lincoln Kirstein's magazine, *The Hound and Horn*. "I dipped into Eliot, Stein, Hemingway, Ford, Graves, Aldington, and Cummings," he said, "trying in each case to assimilate not so much the actual style or technique as the attitude or philosophy behind each work." He wrote a surrealist sketch with an epigraph from *The Sun Also Rises*, "Road to hell paved with unbought stuffed dogs." He got the "greatest personal satisfaction" from MacLeish's *New Found Land*. MacLeish spoke to him as one who "rebels against the intellectual and spiritual sterility of this country, yet realizes he cannot leave it." Whether James realized it or not, he was articulating the philosophical stance of William Carlos Williams rather than that of Pound, who had chosen exile. It was a program for a writer in embryo, consciously trying to equip himself with the *ideas* of modernism and trusting that he would evolve a style and voice suited to his *American* bent.

During the summer of 1931, James drove regularly in his Model A Ford to Plattsburgh, New York, to see his father in a small private sanitarium that catered to patients from wealthy families. On one of these visits he read D. H. Lawrence's *The Lost Girl* and decided that "the world should be waiting for a power of Darkness to control the evil in the world rather than for a Divine Superman." "At last my Spengler has arrived," the young intellectual concluded, "and I find it way above my head. That is fine; it will give me a real problem to tackle. Mine is one of those natures which must be confronted by an obstacle in order to rise from its self-centered legarthy [*sic*]."

Some of Hughart's companions were also suffering from bipolar disorder; others were afflicted with premature dementia praecox. James saw his father in a straitjacket or "lace[d] into a tub of chilled water," a shock treatment applied in an effort to bring him down from a manic high. At the time, there were sedatives but almost no effective drugs available for the treatment of mental illness. When he was tranquil, as a therapy he was provided with tools for work in leather and sheet metal, and he fashioned for his son a cigarette box with his initials embossed on the lid. "He alone of the family made me regular visits," wrote Hughart of his son, "to one in durance vile, surroundings insane." The plight of his father would haunt James for the rest of his life.

•

In his senior year, James enrolled in Fitts's honors English, where the readings included not only the standard Chaucer, Donne, and Herrick, Samuel Johnson and Hazlitt, Hawthorne and Poe, Pater and Ruskin, but also the Earl of Rochester, Shaw, Eliot, Joyce, Pound, Stein, and William Carlos Williams. "*Kora in / Hell* and *Spring and All* had / Been sacred texts," J was to write in *Byways*. To a great extent, the authors James read under Fitts's guidance would constitute his grounding in English literature, a spread far wider than he would be assigned in college. But Fitts did have arbitrary prejudices, and this resulted in some surprising gaps in James's reading. For instance, Fitts disliked Whitman and did not assign him, so J would only be introduced to his "barbaric yawp" when Edith Sitwell read *Leaves of Grass* to him years later. Thoreau was another writer Fitts ignored, so James bypassed him, as he did Keats and Shelley.

As a teacher, Fitts treated his pupils as his intellectual equals, and he expected a great deal from them. When they wrote about Chaucer, they should be able to discuss his borrowings from Ovid, Boethius, and Guillaume de Machaut. He got J started reading the Loeb Classical Library translations in *The Greek Anthology*. Fitts could be devastating, grading a theme James had thought especially good "Derivative! F." And for an autobiographical sketch, "This is naïveté wch verges on baby-talk. C–." Sometimes he wrote his comments in French: "Beaucoup de bruit pour rien?"— A lot of noise for nothing? Fitts assigned considerable Ibsen to provide a springboard into the study of Joyce. James used the Irishman's play, *Exiles*, as a stalking horse to cover his approach to a pair of his own major concerns: the supremacy of individualism, and the need for freedom within the bonds of marriage. Even more fateful for James was the study of Pound, whom Fitts encouraged him to consider in his relationship to Eliot. Fitts had recently initiated a correspondence with the renegade of Rapallo in Italy, and he handed James the twelve pages of an exchange on the critical reception of the *Cantos*. It was a revelation to James for him to read Pound's forceful lecturing of Fitts: "I doubt if you have enough hate. Impersonal// or if not a hate a sense of sanitation. The drains ought to be cleared; whether it's granny's bonnet or Chimmie's garters that are clogging the trap."

Fitts encouraged his students to see literature as a world entity, and James received an A from him for a translation from the Venerable Bede's *Historiae ecclesiasticae*. There must be no chauvinism in judging writing, Dante stood with Shakespeare, and translation itself could lead to worthy creation: these were dicta Fitts implied rather than baldly stated.

Like most schoolboys, James mined his earlier school experiences and his family life for themes and settings. One of these, "Salle d'étude," described his time at Le Rosey. In another, "Monotone," he portrayed the Laughlins' butler in a manner that mocked not the man, whom he clearly liked, but his own father's university: "Horace laughed in a sing-song way and showed his teeth. They were yellow with many gold fillings. His head was all black and yellow, almost like Princeton colours."

Fitts was a "funny guy," a "bit of a snob" with the "soul of a poet and kindly school-children-crossing policeman," J would recall even as he was publishing his former teacher's work. He wrote to his parents that Fitts had liked his latest "modernistic theme" so well that "he nearly wept on my shoulder." James had received A's in Latin and English, A-plus in both French and history. He had completed a verse translation of Chaucer's "Hymn to the Virgin," and he ended his letter with a passage, quite likely with intended application to his father, in convincing Middle English: "For him that folweth all this world of feres, / Er he be war, is ofte y-lyd ful lowe." "Dear Skipper" had settled on him what the boy called a "join-djure," a monthly stipend that would come to him regularly, like a widow's portion.

By March 1932, James was working on More's *Utopia* and Apuleius's *Metamorphoses* for his Choate classes and reading Mabel Dodge Luhan's *Lorenzo in Taos* for himself. He embellished his diary with a frontispiece photograph of himself in conversation with Fitts, his cherished Model A in the background. He wrote, "My resolve is still determined that I shall learn to dance and crack the social ice," adding cryptically—in case his mother should chance to open his diary—"It seems the best way to calm the green stallion."

Over Easter vacation James and a friend, R. L. Steiner, went by train to Florida. Among the books James brought along was William Carlos Williams's *The Knife of the Times*, "a collection of the world's worst stories." Just because he is a doctor, he thinks he knows human psychology, James fumed. But he found the style in Lawrence's *The Virgin and the Gypsy* and especially in *The Lost Girl* "as swell as ever." In Daytona they were joined by a friend, Francis Matthews, and picked up the *Sarsho*. They had dinner on board between New Smyrna and Eldora, set fire to the galley, got soaked by heavy seas north of Cape Canaveral. Day followed day in idyllic succession; they swam over the side and in the evenings visited friends and distant cousins who entertained them with a tea dance at the Everglades Club, dinners, and excellent sherry. James's father, in reprieve, waved to them from his powerful Marmon sedan as they passed through the Haulover Canal.

On the afternoon of March 25 they left Palm Beach and headed for Fort Lauderdale. James had turned over the charts to Steiner and the wheel to Matthews when the helmsman ran them aground. In the confusion the dinghy line became wrapped around the propeller shaft, and after a badly frightened Steiner had tried and failed to free it, James had to plunge into the muck, wriggle under the boat, and cut the rope from the shaft, guiding his knife by feel.

From the timid and insecure adolescent, James was rapidly emerging as a confident adventurer and a leader. There might be troubles at home, but James's life at Choate went from triumph to triumph, culminating in his graduation at the end of May 1932. He won the nationwide *Atlantic Monthly* essay contest with "Salle d'étude." It was published in the magazine as "The Day Is Over" and earned James a prize of $50. The Wallingford newspaper ran two columns on the Choate Prize Day ceremonies under the boldface screamer "**James Laughlin, IV, Pittsburgh, Receives Highest Choate Rank**," followed in only slightly smaller letters by a summation: "Five Honor Prizes and Three Honorable Mentions for Laughlin, Recent Winner of Atlantic Monthly Essay Contest." His prizes were for the highest academic average in the sixth form, the top scores in English and modern languages, and the best poem and the best prose submitted to the Choate literary magazine, and his honorable mentions were for Latin, history, and debating. James gave the class address.

Three weeks after James's graduation from Choate, his brother, Hugh, received his degree from Princeton with class honors. But James had finally eclipsed him. Had he followed his parents' wishes, James too would have headed for Princeton, yet on July 19, 1932, he received a certificate of admission to the Harvard AB program. Crediting him with "Highest Honors" in English and honors in Latin and French, the document stated that he had "satisfied the language requirements for a degree" in all three subjects. Only the "black sheep," J liked to say, mockingly, "strayed" to Harvard. Fitts was the one who encouraged James to bolt in that direction: Harvard was better, his mentor said, as a nurturer of literati. So he was primed for Cambridge, with wind in his sails. Intellectual snob that he was, James dusted off his copy of *The Decline of the West* as summer reading.

3

Harvard, Part One

... deserting Princeton for the college of the Jews & Beaconhillites.

        —H. Hughart Laughlin on his son

James Laughlin IV's father wept—or so his son claimed—when the youth told him that he had settled on Harvard. A few years later Henry Hughart wrote to Carey Briggs about "J.'s deserting Princeton for the college of the Jews & Beaconhillites." The number of Jews at Harvard might have been limited by quota, but prominent Jews among the alumni included Justice Louis Brandeis (1877) of the Supreme Court and Lincoln Kirstein (1930), already a force in the arts and literature. James's mother probably considered her son's choice in religious terms: Princeton was heavily Presbyterian, and she had hoped that the college might reinvigorate her son's straying faith. Although he credited Fitts with pushing him toward Harvard, the choice was his own. Harvard sealed his escape from Pittsburgh to New England, to the oldest, most richly endowed, and most *intellectual* institution of higher learning in the nation. Harvard also marked the emergence of James's preference for signing himself with the shortened Jay, then to the bare J, and he soon dropped the Roman numeral.

J's father put a good face on the inevitable and escorted him to Cambridge. He would share a two-bedroom suite with Lawrence Angel, a classmate at Choate. Their rooms in Weld Hall in Harvard Yard included a good fireplace, but J's father pronounced the furniture appalling, so at an antiques store they bought two vintage American desks, a pair of bookcases, and a Persian rug with drapes to match. Mr. Lucas, Hughart's English tailor in Cambridge, measured J for a tuxedo, three pairs of dark gray trousers, and three tweed jackets—"suits / Were not worn at Harvard," J said. A supply of striped and plain shirts and the customary white bucks (worn very dirty, commented Mr. Lucas disapprovingly) completed the basic wardrobe.

That evening Hughart took J to Concord to visit cousin Henry Laughlin, then head of the Riverside Press division of Houghton Mifflin. "What a spread!" recalled J. "Twenty acres of meadow, with / Horses grazing." Cousin Henry had bought Castle Hyde in Ireland and rode to hounds. "Plumpish and jolly," with rosy cheeks, he did not strike J as a typical Laughlin: he was a risk taker and a skier, and a horse had "nearly killed him by refusing a stone wall." The Concord Laughlins were useful to J; Henry's wife, Becky, volunteered to get J on the "dance list" so that he would be invited to Beacon Hill debutante balls, where he had heard that the girls were "nonflammable / But very pretty." Becky came from exalted stock, so she could vouch for his being sufficiently wellborn. Though J might be snubbed by the Groton and Milton preppies attending Harvard, he would not, thanks to his cousins, be denied Brahmin society.

There was still the summer between James and Harvard. Hughart relapsed into bipolar dementia, and he was placed in New York under the care of a Mrs. Ottarson for a form of psychotherapy that was strong on "mind-control" and self-help. J spent part of the summer in Montana at Keewaydin Camp for boys and then at the Kelley Ranch in Helmville. A solemn J was photographed towering over his pony. A tan Stetson slanted over his right ear, and his sweater sleeve stopped several inches above his wrist, documenting rapid growth. His whole aspect was satisfyingly western male.

Excused from freshman English, J elected yearlong courses in biology, history, Italian, and philosophy. For history he drew the master of Eliot House, Roger Bigelow Merriman, called Frisky behind his back owing to the thespian exuberance with which he acted out favorite events. J soon discovered that, by and large, "the faculty didn't / Really expect much of us / Freshmen." One exception was P. P. Cram, a section leader in history, for whom J wrote a paper on Spengler, quoting extensively in German. Cram gave J an F. "This is all / Balderdash," he told J, "I want *your* / Ideas, not Spengler's." J was learning the difference between the appearance of accomplishment and the thing itself. So he assessed his instructors, turning in fodder when he thought he could get away with it. Marks, he now said, meant little to him. Being top boy might have counted for everything at Choate; at Harvard he wanted learning, not accolades. He cut many classes, passing often through the neo-Corinthian columns of the Widener Library, where he boasted that he had "conned" an attendant into giving him, a mere freshman, stack privileges. On his own, he began translating Virgil.

J arrived at Harvard with a few friends from Choate, and he soon made others. Joe Pulitzer was a grandson of the great newspaperman. He collected impressionist paintings, performed beautifully on his own grand piano in his suite, and, so J claimed, kept a French mistress at the Boston Ritz. J liked him even though Pulitzer teased him for never having visited St. Mark's in Venice. The future actor John Cromwell, Pulitzer's roommate, seemed to do nothing but contemplate his own bare feet, yet was secretly writing a novel. "Lord Melcarth"—Ba'al Melcarth or Moloch—was the assumed name of a Lebanese painter who wore a monocle and carried a malacca cane topped by a silver devil's head. Melcarth had a friend, Wayne Andrews, who wrote good French, corresponded with Ezra Pound, and knew many of the French surrealists.

Toward the end of his freshman year, J was accepted as a "heeler" for *The Harvard Advocate*, the undergraduate literary journal. Advocate House was a small wooden building in an alley, with tables, chairs, and a worn leather couch, all comfortably scruffy: a den in which serious young writers could play at being bohemian. In fact, he was given more responsibilities than the errand boy designation implied; one of his successful crusades was to overcome the editors' "violent objections" toward publishing Andrews's essay on surrealism.

His time at the *Advocate* was probably the best of J's early Harvard life. Its president when J joined the staff was Cyrus Sulzberger of the *New York Times* family. J would work with Peter Viereck, Arthur Schlesinger Jr., Leonard Bernstein, and Robert Fitzgerald. In 1935, John Jermain Slocum, called Jim, would be elected president: he became a friend for life, as did Fitzgerald. Robert Lowell, although he had been rejected when he applied to become a candidate for the literary board, would drop by the offices. The monthly tried to give voice to serious and even experimental poetry: the undergraduate verse of Eliot, Cummings, Wallace Stevens, and Edwin Arlington Robinson had appeared in its pages. *Dulce est periculum*—Sweet is danger—was the motto, inherited

from a predecessor student publication closed down for opposing mandatory chapel attendance. Originality meant taking risks, and earlier risk
takers on the *Advocate* staff had included Theodore and Franklin D. Roosevelt, the future Scribner's editor Maxwell Perkins, Conrad Aiken, Fitts,
James Gould Cozzens, and Lincoln Kirstein.

J's freshman year coincided with the appointment of T. S. Eliot as
Charles Eliot Norton Professor of Poetry. Eliot was extremely generous in
his efforts, and in addition to his four mandated public Norton Lectures
at Harvard, he taught an undergraduate course on modern English literature. J probably audited the two of Eliot's classes that were specifically
devoted to Pound and Anglo-American poetry. Emboldened by having
studied Eliot's poetry with Fitts, J introduced himself. "Ole / Possum," he
would recall, "Was very amiable for a High / Anglican." When J commented
to Eliot on a plate of cookies on the floor in the middle of the room at the
Eliot House suite that he used for group conferences with students, the
great man explained in his measured tones, "'It's economical,' he / Told
me, 'they're too polite / To go out and grab cookies. / That plate has been
there for / Five weeks.'"

Still, sitting at the feet of the famous was not all J had hoped for
at Harvard. He expected epiphanies. But the classes seemed pedestrian,
the assignments antediluvian. On his drive to Norfolk during the 1932
Christmas recess, J passed through Wallingford to see the St. Johns and
Carey Briggs. While his "good talk" with Clara St. John left him with the
warmest feelings, J was furious at being subjected to a "long skoog" from
"GC" on the "value of being a member of a larger body at certain periods
of life." He hated the condescension. "Screw you, GC, screw you," J did
not say but privately wrote.

J met his mother at the Carlisles', and she wrote to Briggs to sound
him out about her son, who had complained bitterly about Harvard to her:
attitudes were hidebound conservative; the East Coast swells were insuf-
ferably snobbish; the food was bad. Harvard's president, Abbott Lawrence
Lowell, was a bigot: homophobic, anti-Semitic, dismissive or worse toward ethnic minorities. When J said these things to his parents, he must
have realized that their views would be nearer to Lowell's than to his
own. In fact, Lowell hewed close to the American mainstream in 1932: it
was J who was becoming the outsider.

Briggs had known from J's earlier letters that he had "not yet found a settled adjustment to Cambridge," but advised J's parents not to be alarmed because J himself recognized that a freshman year anywhere brought "inevitable disillusionment." Although J did not sense much sympathy in his mother, a year later she would still be writing to Briggs for help in dealing with her son: she was quietly collecting his "literary efforts from the age of five on" and begged his teacher for any examples he might have. In her own way, Marjory Laughlin was as devoted to J as was his father.

On his return from Christmas recess, J took up skiing seriously. The sport did not have varsity status at Harvard during J's first winter in Cambridge, but an early coach of the group of Cambridge enthusiasts had been Otto Schniebs, a German ski instructor who had come to the United States in 1927 from the Austrian Arlberg ski schools. Schniebs had moved on in 1930 to form a powerful team at Dartmouth. In the winter of 1931–32 the unofficial Harvard ski team entered competition, and a Harvard man won the slalom at the Dartmouth Winter Carnival. His victory launched Harvard skiing, and the team would be officially recognized in 1934.

The skiing weekend became part of J's Harvard routine: a six-hour drive to Stowe in Vermont's Green Mountains, slightly less to the New Hampshire ski areas. As he had at Le Rosey, J and his friends climbed with sealskins on their skis. If blizzard conditions permitted, they could make it in two hours, carrying sleeping bags and supplies, up to the Harvard Mountaineering Club hut in Tuckerman Ravine on Mount Washington, New Hampshire.

•

Off the slopes, J's Harvard acquaintance kept expanding. He met John Brooks Wheelwright, a friend to both Fitts and E. E. Cummings. Wheelwright was a Beacon Street bon vivant who had left Harvard without a degree in 1920. Almost forty, Wheels, as he styled himself, was a strikingly handsome man with a prominent aquiline nose and an overbite that aimed his visage like an arrow in flight, and his hair receded rakishly from a widow's peak. He had helped found the Trotskyite Socialist Workers Party, and he gave pacifist lectures to these working-class gatherings, dressed in white tie and tails, often with J as his driver. Wheelwright wrote taut yet discursive poetry characterized by regional identity, blunt language, and typographic devices. He stated in verse that "the New Englander appraises sins, χ finds them beyond his means, χ and hoards."

Influencing both J's politics and his attitude toward sin, Wheels argued that sexual chastity was a perversion of true Christian thought.

Despite such intriguing companions, J poured out his usual discontents to his old mentor, Fitts, who volunteered a letter of introduction to Ezra Pound. Fitts also appeared at the beginning of April in Cambridge to encourage his star alumnus. "Waiting & watching & doing precisely nothing," wrote J in a grumpy mood. "Dudley was in with a few choice words of bull-shit."

It wasn't just Harvard that J was bored with. It was Pittsburgh, Cambridge, Boston, even Norfolk—it was America. He wanted Europe. "We didn't think that one glimpse of an oxcart would turn us into geniuses, but we were sure that things would be different in Europe," J would write after a European trip in 1934, "that barriers inside us that had kept us from writing anything more startling at home than fairly adept imitations would somehow be moved away by the new life." However, J was not quite willing to cut his ties to Harvard and transplant himself to Paris.

During the spring term J's college experience seemed to be engaging him more. Theodore Spencer, an instructor in English, wrote to J in February 1933 that he had gotten his name from Fitts. Spencer was the main Harvard liaison and understudy for Eliot, and his acquaintance helped ease J into the circle around Eliot. Harry Levin, another instructor in English, would become important to J as a future author on James Joyce and as a connecting figure. Levin had been in the first class F. O. Matthiessen taught at Harvard, and like Spencer he had been singled out by Eliot for his brilliance. And when Robert Fitzgerald was asked by Sulzberger to collect material for the next Advocate, he invited J to his room for a consultation. Fitzgerald had graduated from Choate just before J had arrived, but the school bond and their shared love of the Greek classics led to almost immediate friendship.

When Spencer reviewed the April Advocate for the Crimson, he complimented the magazine for "having abandoned at last the repellent format" and especially for having become "a more lively and intelligent periodical." He picked out poetry by James Agee, a sonnet by Fitzgerald, a prose "sketch" by Jim Slocum, and "Forty Days and Forty Nights," a short story by J, for lauding comment. "Mr. Laughlin's description of his travels with an unattractive and [un]sympathetic companion is done neatly," he wrote, "and Mr. Laughlin succeeds in making us share his repugnance for that distressing individual." That month J and Slocum were among the six new members to be added to the literary board of the magazine. Reviewing the May *Advocate*, Matthiessen named J's "The Day Is Over," reprinted with permission from *The Atlantic Monthly*, as "easily the best contribution to this issue." "The effect of the whole piece is authentic," Matthiessen concluded. This was a considerable tribute coming from Matthiessen, whose monumental study, *American Renaissance*, would shortly earn him towering status among scholars of American literature.

At the instigation of a Childs cousin who "owned half of it," J became the Harvard stringer for *The Harkness Hoot* at Yale, a new and short-lived competitor to the venerable *Yale Literary Magazine*. His first article for the *Hoot* was an erudite nine pages on Archibald MacLeish, whose long poem, *Conquistador*, had just received a Pulitzer Prize. When the *Hoot* was also praised for a "saner attitude" and for becoming "a serious journal of discussion," J felt that he had contributed to change at Yale as well.

While J was establishing himself as one of the coming literati of the Harvard-Yale axis, he had been wrestling with his father's fluctuating mental state. Hughart had been recently confined at the Harmon Clinic for psychiatric patients, and J disregarded the advice of Aunt Leila, which was that he try to reinforce the psychoanalytic interventions of Mrs. Ottarson by discussing with his father the progress of his cure. No, J said, he thought that he could help out best "by being as natural with him as possible," treating him as if there were nothing the matter, that he was "quite capable of exerting self-control." J added, "I don't like the idea of talking to my own father as though there were something wrong with him, even if there is." J had a motivation beyond filial concern in involving himself in his father's cure: at age eighteen, he was already keenly aware that heredity might have marked him down for a like affliction. Not that he felt helpless: he believed that his own powerful will could be focused to keep him sane.

In the spring of 1933, J sent his short story "The River" to Lincoln Kirstein, co-founder of *The Hound and Horn*, which Pound usually referred to as "Bitch & Bugle"—the journal's name had come from his own poem "The White Stag." "I'm sorry to say that Lincoln did not like your river story at all," reported Fitts. Kirstein was "one of my idols," J said, a man who used his wealth in service of high artistic values. He was a member of a Thursday evening supper group, as were J, R. P. Blackmur, John Cheever, Fitts, and "dear old Sherry Mangan," that met at the Ararat

Café or the Athens Olympia. J said that he was in awe of Kirstein, seven years his senior and "such a brilliant man . . . doing such great work." Tall and powerfully built, Kirstein was painted, wearing absolutely nothing but a pair of boxing gloves, by Pavel Tchelitchew, one of many artists he championed. Mangan—poet, novelist, and book designer—was as striking an individual as Kirstein. When a friend produced a bookplate for him, the motto on it read, "Everything in Excess," and in his case this meant books, ideas, dinners of curry, chateaubriand, shellfish, and wine, topped with good company in lavish quantities. Although not of great height, his massive, square frame made him seem very big, and a shock of red-blond hair crowned his animated, humorous face. His conversation raced and skipped in jolly flights of wit and invention. New England aristocrat that he was, the Depression had turned him into a passionate Trotskyite.

J was also receiving attention from at least four young women, and with his many extracurricular interests it is hardly surprising that his freshman year record was not outstanding: his grades for his four credit courses were C, B, B, and A. He received an Excellent for the noncredit but mandatory physical training.

The old prejudices lingering from Pittsburgh were crumbling under J's independence and what can best be called his innate sense of fairness. In his admiration for the shy brilliance of Levin and the outspoken if often abrasive idealism of Kirstein, J gradually became ashamed of the anti-Semitic turns of speech accepted without demur by his family. His already quite egalitarian attitudes about race were becoming more liberal as well. A score of years before there was an active movement to integrate public schools, Kirstein was campaigning for an equal representation of black and white students at the ballet school he envisioned. J's friend Wayne Andrews became the first white Harvard student to take a black girl as a date to a freshman dance. And J's friendships had far outstripped in diversity his Pittsburgh circle. Wheels, Mangan, Pulitzer, and Lord Melcarth would easily make any list of notable extroverts, and J had come to the notice of Eliot, Matthiessen, Robert Lowell, and Levin. To most young men, J's intellectual experience and circle of acquaintance would have added up to a highly satisfactory initial year at Harvard. J, however, was yearning to escape. He would make use of Fitts's letter of introduction to Pound.

His departure for Europe was delayed by family visits, but finally, on

June 30, 1933, J's parents drove him to Manhattan, where they dined on the roof of the St. Moritz before his ship, the Holland America Line's *Statendam*, sailed at midnight. For thrift, he traveled third-class on his first solo trip to Europe. The ship carried many other Harvard undergraduates, but J made it clear that he was no casual student tourist: he had a mission.

J disembarked at Plymouth, crossed to Rotterdam, where he visited the great art museums, and then headed for Munich to stay with the Paul Hey family in nearby Gauting north of the Starnberger See. He had arranged to be tutored in German by Frau Hey. "How I / Vexed her because I had / 'Ungenügende Anlegung' / For irregular verbs," he remembered, but she forgave him this lack of aptitude and only asked that he be back before midnight whenever he took the train into Munich for the opera. "I'm learning a lot and having ever so good a time," he wrote in his letters to Aunt Leila. He was careful to combine accounts of how productive his trip was proving with assurances that "letters from home are a necessity for happy living" and that he was already longing for "the peace and warmth of Robin Hill." Brother Hugh had joined Jones & Laughlin, and J even threw in a sentence to the effect that "it gives me no end of a lift to think that a young Laughlin is working out there in the footsteps of all the fine people who have made up our family." He told her how much it meant that she should "stand behind me, even when our judgments as to a specific ethic may differ," and excused his recent "rantings" as stemming from his need to "thrash about" in finding his own direction.

His host, Paul Hey, scraped by painting local scenes for picture postcards. In the frustration of his modest artistic gift, Hey suggested to J the "Herr Professor" of his short story "Melody with Fugue," published in *Story* magazine the next year. Mozart and Wagner festivals were running concurrently in Munich, and J took in *Così fan tutte*, *Figaros Hochzeit*, and *Die Zauberflöte*, as well as *Der fliegende Holländer*, *Parsifal*, and *Tristan und Isolde*, and all but the third opera in Wagner's *Ring* series. At the Prinzregententheater he met Sara Woolsey, a girl from Cornwall, Connecticut, near Norfolk, and they went to concerts and museums together. "You were wearing a blue / Dress and blue shoes with little / White bows on the toes," J wrote later. During the "Liebestod" scene of *Tristan und Isolde*, J turned to Sara and with his finger touched one of hers in a gesture of tender sympathy. Then they traveled in early August to the Salzburg Festival for *Der Rosenkavalier* and another performance of *Die*

Zauberflöte, crossing and recrossing the milky-greenish Salzach that bifurcated the town, "a river fairly blowing its head off to get where it's going . . . It was an excited river, and we were excited too," J wrote in a fictionalized account of his experience of Salzburg, "excited by being face to face with our futures, really alone with our future lives for the first time." They were mad about *Die Zauberflöte* and called each other by the names of the bird catcher and his love, Papageno and Papagena. J was emphatic in his accounts of their time together that they were not lovers but shared rooms for economy, sleeping in separate beds. Once, strangely, J tore the wings off moths and threw them on Sara's pillow. The sensuality, the several threatened rapes, in Mozart's opera allowed J to indulge his seduction fantasies within the frame of an innocent love.

J found himself admiring another vision of the ideal as well. "The people," he said, "are talented, lovely and good." And he wrote to his aunt a strangely biased account that they were well led: "Hitler is as nearly perfect an idealist as could be. His intentions for Germany are even finer than I had imagined. Surely with his leadership Germany may recover from the terrible wrongs done by avaricious powers at Versailles . . . And the Nazis are not violent to the Jews. What we read in our papers was all exaggeration and tabloid falsification of the worst sort. Violence was done only to Communists, no-goods of the worst sort."

The Reichstag fire of February 27, 1933, was blamed on a "Communist conspiracy," and this charge J, instilled with the antilabor, anti-Communist prejudices of capitalist Pittsburgh, was quite willing to swallow. His views were more a testimony to his relatively narrow reading in contemporary politics and to the effectiveness of Joseph Goebbels's propaganda machine than to any deep-seated sympathy for the Nazi cause. While the first official act of the Nazi campaign against the Jews had been the boycott of Jewish businesses announced on April 1, 1933, the murderous horror of Kristallnacht would not burst upon the world until November 1938. Still, anyone who had followed closely the events in Germany during the two months subsequent to Hitler's becoming chancellor on January 30, 1933, would hardly have painted him in such benign terms.

J wrote to Ezra Pound from Gauting on August 21 that he was an American, "said to be clever," and he claimed to be Dudley Fitts's and Sherry Mangan's "whiteheaded boy" in need of advice on "bombarding shits like Canby & Co." and help with the "elucidation" of parts of the

Cantos in order to "preach" them effectively. (Henry Seidel Canby, as the editor in chief of *The Saturday Review of Literature*, was viewed in J's circle as a hopeless reactionary.) J also wondered why Pound "supported" Louis Zukofsky—recognized as a poet although not yet considered an important forerunner of the American avant-garde. J claimed with some hyperbole to be editor of *The Harvard Advocate* and the Yale *Harkness Hoot* and that these positions gave him access to "the few men in the two universities who are worth bothering about." He closed the letter with the same Latin tag that Fitts used to Pound, *Servissimus*. It was a brash letter, calculated to intrigue Pound where it would have offended nearly anyone else. J enclosed a stamped return envelope, and Pound replied with a scrawled note of welcome, "Visability [sic] high." Pound added that he would be in Rapallo until the twenty-eighth or twenty-ninth, and he suggested a meeting with Zukofsky: "You can also have opportunity of slaying the Z. in person. or if you prefer—painfully to pry up the lid of his intelleg." When J arrived on the morning of August 27, 1933, he found a typed note addressed to "Jas Loughlin Esq": "Am probably on the low seas/ Will you come back as soon as you have lunched"—Pound was away for his morning swim.

So that afternoon J entered the arched stone passageway, climbed to Pound's flat on the sixth floor of 12 via Marsala, and stood before "the bearded and cat-eyed man," as Robert Fitzgerald remembered Pound from his own encounter the year before.

If J had thought that his audience with Pound was to be devoted solely to literature and High Art, he was mistaken. It was J's misfortune, perhaps, to hit Pound just as he was turning his main emphasis from literature to economics and politics. Confucius was gaining precedence over Dante, history and good governance over fine arts—except for the music of Vivaldi, which Pound and his violinist mistress, Olga Rudge, were promoting energetically. J was given a generous earful of economic theory, a tirade against "Frankie," Franklin Delano Roosevelt, and a broadside aimed at the "beaneries," especially "Haavud." Pound handed J a typed "CHARGE": "That American 1917/20 [sic] and for ten years after HAD the chance to take over lead in publishing contemporary work. AND DID NOT TAKE IT." As a result, he said, the American young were fifteen years behind European youth in information. J wrote in his notebook the names and addresses of people Pound especially wanted him to contact in America: William Carlos Williams, Zukofsky, and Gorham Munson, who had just founded the Social Credit organ *New Democracy*. Zukofsky had been with Pound for a couple of weeks when J arrived; Zuk would thereafter often tell of their brief encounter in Rapallo, but J would mistakenly place their meeting a year later. J departed with a copy of Pound's *Cavalcanti* and the admonition not to broadcast the news of their meeting.

On August 29, J wrote to his host from Domodossola on the Italian-Swiss border, "without farting about unduly to thank you for pabulum (excellent) and the most vital experience of the summer. The campaign of assassination is launched . . . Remains to be seen how effectively it will blot the university landscape."

The Alps, *Deutschstudium*, Mozart, dalliance, and then the exhilarating and bewildering fulminations of Ezra Pound! As he sailed home, J had much to ponder, but he was sure of one thing: like the Moses of his Sunday school days, he had ascended Mount Pisgah, and his own horizon had exploded to embrace infinity. His dilemma was to decide the part he must play in the cosmos that now stood revealed before him.

4

Correspondence Course in Rebellion: Ezra Pound by Sea-Post

Going to the root is part of his temperament.

—Hugh Kenner on James Laughlin

Back at Harvard for the fall term, J moved into two-year-old Eliot House, modeled on the individual colleges of Cambridge and Oxford, on the Charles River four blocks from the Yard. A dignified four-story red brick Georgian structure facing a grassy courtyard, Eliot was divided into suites for nearly three hundred students and twenty tutors and resident advisers. J met fortnightly with his tutor, Dana Durand, a congenial young scholar who could translate at sight for him from the Greek poets. Living conditions were decidedly posh; each small group of students shared an entrance and a sitting room with a fireplace. There was maid service, and in the dining hall waitresses served a choice of dishes. Over the next decade it would acquire the reputation of being an elite establishment among elites, lair of Yankee aristocrats, Rhodes scholars, rowing champions. "I like it," J wrote to Aunt Leila, "a spirit of work being done that there was not in the Yard." His attitude toward Harvard improved momentarily.

To his friends J reported on his meeting with Pound, garnering Fitts's approval: "Yr sojourn c̃ [cum, with] Ezra sounds nice as you tell it, & it is good to know that he was largient c̃ his wisdom, & gave you to understand that you might count on him." Fitts added as a cautionary note, with a tag from Virgil's Tenth Eclogue, "I think it more likely that he will be counting on you, unless you go into bankruptcy: non illum nostri possunt mutare labores"—our labors can make no change in him. "But let me not be bitchy, even in hexameters." He had some serious advice: "You are writing much less authentically now than you were when you were here, wch is a hell of a Note . . . At the risk of offending you permanently, I shall insist upon raising my fragile yawp if you insist upon striking luffly poses—be they Manganese, or Poundique, or whatever. You shd take a spiritual bromo-seltzer." Fitts directed J toward Stephen Spender and to *The Autobiography of Alice B. Toklas*, "the best english prose for a long time." He closed with a terse postscript: "What are you doing for the Hoot? If you quote from me any more without acknowledgment, I'll have you jailed. Vale."

Meanwhile, J had become a recipient of Pound's blasting, iconoclastic letters, usually couched in the form of the mock hillbilly cum Uncle Remus that Ezra affected, a style all his own that J would later term "Ezratic lingo": "American edderkashun. a process of making slaves and toadies," Pound declaimed. "No prof. expected to know anything he wasn't TAUGHT when a student." What about Auden and Spender? J asked. "Ov all the post Abercrombie/ Post Drinkwater trype!!!!" Pound replied. "Waaal waaal ART AN DACHSHUNDS ARE LONG." J wrote disparagingly about T. S. Eliot, and Pound was quick to defend his old compatriot: "When Joyce and Wyndham L. have long since gaga'd or exploded, Old Possum will be totin' round de golf links and givin' bright nickels to the lads of 1987." J should study Pound's *Active Anthology*—which Homer Pound had found hard going. "My ole farver he sez : Gheez it'z tough," reported Ezra proudly.

J signed up for Dante, Alfred North Whitehead, music, and medieval France—the last with Whitehead's friend Henry Osborn Taylor. "Whitehead ??" queried Pound incredulously, "the scientific bloke ? at Hawwud in purson , because they wdnt feed him in Hengland ??" Whitehead taught a heady mix of cosmology and metaphysics and became one of J's favorite teachers, despite his aversion to the study of philosophy. "My language- / Oriented mind rebels against / It," J would write. He found that he could understand very little of Whitehead's lectures, but Whitehead was radiant with love of learning, and he gave A's most liberally. J decided that he was a "great and lovable man." And J found at least one philosopher with whom he felt a certain kinship: Epicurus. "An eclectic who picked up doctrines to fit his moral urge," J wrote in his study notes. "A feeler more than a thinker. No logical bond between materialism and Epicurean morality."

J aimed toward what he saw as the core of knowledge, the very roots of current literature. He threw himself into a program of research and writing beyond his classwork that added, so he claimed, twelve hours a day to his schedule. In fact, he was marching to at least two different anthems, involving him in such conflicting loyalties that he could hardly admit the one bandleader to the other: Pound and Stein. Pound dismissed Stein as "Gert the ole tub ov guts." To Stein, the bard from Hailey, Idaho, was a trivial talent, a mere "village explainer"; and she demanded exclusive loyalty from her coterie. J excused himself to Pound that "we" were going to "debunk Stein (Toklas)" in the coming issue of the *Advocate*. His pose of irreverence notwithstanding, by November J was writing a monograph about her. By the end of the month he announced that he was about finished with this study. Pound urged J in other directions: get ahold of E. E. Cummings and W. C. Williams. "The Network" is what J termed Pound's "academy by mail." As far back as 1928, Pound had written, "It takes about 600 people to make a civilization. There were umpteen billions of unbreached barbarians in the North woods when Athens etc." Discovering and maintaining contact with this 600 accounted for Pound's major expense, postage. Pound enlisted J as his scout and center of American operations: "Go and see X," he would command, "find out if there's anything in his bean."

In an undated page and a half, typed with purple ribbon and headed "To be watched/ weeklies," Pound set forth his cautions about the American press. The thrust, he continued, should be toward economics and politics: "Most american press/ not question of being in opposition but simply of not understanding vocabulary of Roosevelt administration," and "Marx simply out of date like paddlewheel steamer. the Left is as antiquated as the republican party."

J might still admire Levin, Mangan, and Wheelwright, but clearly he had found a new mentor in Pound. Fitts was disappointing him. "He seems to be settling down quite cosily for a longwintersnap with Auden-Spender-&-where-do-we-stop-from-here," J confided to Pound. "RIP: he was a good man oncet." On his side, Fitts lamented to Mary Fletcher Wardwell, whom J had been dating during the past year, that J was not writing a word about his doings: he sent only photographs. Eager to heal "any estrangement between you," she told J how fond Dudley was of him and urged a reconciliation. Fletch was having her own problem of estrangement with

J, who had just written that his feelings for her were no longer what they had been. No matter, she said bravely, if not with entire honesty, "I have always felt you loved (?) me because I represented many of the things you aren't. I'm a healthy, redblooded, normal little vixen, the essence of simplicity and instinct, sometimes even strength. I have much to give you, Jay, if you'd only osmose without inhibitions." J felt it necessary to drive to Bennington and take Fletch out to dinner. These expenses he entered in the "Luxuries" column in his account sheet: $5.75 for the hotel plus dinner. He was paying his Harvard living expenses out of his own account, $110 for the month. J was also the recipient of less direct if even more passionate letters from his Papagena, but he was determined not to let either girl become a serious distraction.

The day after posting his complaint about Fitts to Pound, J wrote again with a new project: Florence Codman of Arrow Editions would like to publish a fine printing of one or more of the cantos. J could place them first in the *Advocate*, and then Arrow would purchase rights. Pound suggested money-saving ploys, even proposing deferred payment: "I cd. be paid as the woik sells." J offered to pool his own money with whatever Codman could muster, but this Ezra rejected out of hand: "DON'T take your chewing gum and candy money to pay me. That, NO ! the aged shd. not sponge on the next generation."

Meanwhile, J was chafing at everything that was holding back the revolution in teaching that he envisioned. Pound's *Active Anthology* had arrived, but J despaired at interjecting it into the textbook "racket": "The men who are awake suffc. to know the difference don't [choose] the texts as a rule." He would feature Pound's remarks about education in *The Harkness Hoot*, but J insisted that the entrenched pundits were dragging Harvard down: "There are too many fat fools eating up salaries in this shit emporium when men like Mangan are eating their shoes." J laid about him ruthlessly, tuning his theorbo to Pound's diapason. There was, however, a strain of genuine discontent in J's laments. "I don't know how long I can stick out the stupidity, stuffiness, smugness, generally beshitted-pants-ness, of this morgue," he wrote. "What does it cost to live in Italy & would you advise breaking away etc etc?"

Pound dodged the question about the cost of living, and the gist of his advice was probably not what J wanted to hear: "I think you better stick in Hawvud a bit longer. I mean, don't leave the country prematurely/ you might have to return later in life." J agreed to "stick out Harvud," if only "because I need an education & the family will pay for it as long as I get it respectably." Besides, he had plans to wrest control of *The Harkness Hoot* from his cousin and to dominate the *Advocate*, even if he might be too young to be named its head: "They can't get out a decent magazine without me & they know it." He had already persuaded New York bookstores to stock both magazines.

Trying to provoke Pound, J attacked his *Active Anthology*, writing to him: "I need help on Bunting, Zuk[ovsky], [Marianne] Moore? What <u>are</u> they doing? I sense their ability, but haven't the maturity & int. judg. to get at them." Zukofsky was deliberately obscure, his grammar "abominable" to the point of making his writing unintelligible. At Pound's instigation, Harriet Monroe had invited Zukofsky to edit an Objectivist issue of *Poetry* magazine, and he had included in it those poets who shared his propensities—a commitment to eschew "poetic" diction, a "preoccupation with the accuracy of detail in writing"—among them Robert McAlmon, George Oppen, Pound, Carl Rakosi, Charles Resnikoff, Wheelwright, and Williams. J would eventually publish books by each of these authors—but never one by Zukofsky. At present, J was working on an evisceration, to be published in *The Westminster Review*, of Eliot's "last book of thistletwit (*The Use of Poetry*, those terrible lectures he gave last year)," which J called "neatly senile whiffles of pansybreath"; in this judgment, J was decidedly in a minority. Pound replied that he had quoted J "EXACTLY" but anonymously to Eliot and admitted that "Nacherly practically NO poetry satisfies me/ 'not even my own.'" Pound cautioned J, "Don't go on in my erronious vein , by being too god damn uncivil. it defeats its own end. I am prob/ too old to change , but I try . . . oh lllord I try . . . after having typed 'goddblasted son of a siphylitic bitch' I allus TRY to go back and . . . say 'the deviousness of his mind is such that only congenital syphilis cd/ have . . .'" Pound advocated judging Eliot these days for his work in promoting and publishing others more than for his recent verse. Pound was more sanguine about Marianne Moore. The exchange between J and Ezra amounted to a dialogue on quality and editorial judgment. It was not so much that J disagreed with Pound on the criteria for good poetry as that he was testing the soundness of his own judgment against someone he both respected and could count on for honest answers.

J got Pound's "Ignite! Ignite!" into the December *Advocate*. This philippic, on the lamentable state of affairs in the country, caught attention all right, provoking a public response from the Nobelist and prominent conservative Nicholas Murray Butler, president of Columbia University. This convinced Pound that young Laughlin was to be taken seriously, and thereafter Ezra thought of the *Advocate* as a viable organ for political and economic expression. Clearly, it was more important to him to *be heard* than to be paid. Pound was sounding relatively temperate these days, even to the point of admitting that President Roosevelt was "fortunately" not a "complete dithering idiot."

Pound had been riding a tall horse politically at least since early 1933, when he had been granted an audience with Mussolini on January 30, through the agency of the poet's lover, Olga Rudge. *A Draft of XXX Cantos* had lain prominently on Mussolini's immense desk. The poet read a passage from the *Cantos* and presented Il Duce with an eighteen-point synopsis of his economic conclusions. Pound would record the meeting in Canto 41:

"Ma qvesto,"
said the Boss, "è divertente."
catching the point before the aesthetes had got there.

Perhaps Mussolini was merely being the genial, even ironic, host to *il gran poeta* in pronouncing the *Cantos* amusing. Pound had then lectured him on the Social Credit monetary theories of Major C. H. Douglas and Silvio Gesell and had listed books urgently needing translation into Italian, including works by John and Henry Adams, Thomas Jefferson, and William Carlos Williams. Here, finally, was a world leader with a willing ear and the power to enact, Pound thought. Mass production created the goods: now they must be equitably distributed. To accomplish this, Pound proposed paying workers in Gesellist scrip, which would gradually lose its value if not spent. Thus, he argued, money would be kept in circulation, usury would vanish, as would banks as we know them. Mussolini had nodded as if he understood all this, and Pound was enthralled, convinced from then on of the quality of his mind. This scene between poet and dictator, in retrospect, held profound tragicomic undertones.

•

Before leaving Cambridge for the Christmas recess, J wrote his first letter to William Carlos Williams, asking for advice on placing work by Williams, who replied with a friendly note: "Write me again. What plans have you. Where may I fit into them." Williams sent an essay, "The Element of Time," which J lodged in the February 1934 *Advocate*, beginning his long publishing association with the laureate of Rutherford, New Jersey. Williams seconded Pound in calling J's attention to the Objectivist Press group, and especially to Mary Barnard, a young poet from Vancouver. J's network was expanding.

With all the extra work, J's eyes had begun to trouble him: not only the amblyopic left eye, but his good eye appeared to be shifting rapidly from far- to nearsightedness. Before leaving Cambridge, he saw Dr. J. Herbert Waite, who determined that J had only one properly functioning eye and that neither exercises nor corrective lenses would change matters. Years later Dr. Waite would diagnose congenital color blindness in J as well. J admitted his primary vision complaint to his mother and father and said that if he was not permitted to carry on his routine of twelve extracurricular hours per day, then he would simply have to drop out of Harvard in order to pursue his private studies. J was now in control, with an ophthalmologist on his side: he could continue his independent research into Stein, plausibly swerving away from plowing a straight furrow toward an AB. Or he could continue as before. It is noteworthy that the person who quite likely read more manuscripts than any other publisher of his epoch would do it all on one eye. And by his own admission, J was a slow reader, "an every-word reader."

Despite the eye troubles, the visit home was a happy one. J's father seemed fine, "the same sweet and courageous man" as formerly. All was peaceful, and the future augured well.

Soon after the beginning of 1934, J received "a covey of letters" from Pound—one headed "APPY XXX MAS," a "2nd epistle" written the same day, and another of December 31 beginning "Dilectus Filius"—to which the Beloved Son replied, "I am leaving here at mid-years for the time being at least, because, by God, I won't stand it any longer. It all just stinks too much." J planned to request a leave of absence. He needed to strengthen his sight, and he wanted to visit Pound again, but he did not mention these reasons to Ezra: "Don't know where I'm goin', but it will be somewhere where the drainage is better." J would have been pleased to know that he had impressed Pound, who wrote on January 21, his letter crossing J's saying that he was *not* returning to school, to "Binbin," Laurence Binyon, then teaching at Harvard, "There is a savage young man named Laughlin (Jas.) . . . who may or may not be attending yr. lectures. Possibly too diffident to present himself or possibly thinks his opinions too heretical to make conversation agreeable. If you are meeting individual students, he is one worth bothering about." J headed for Norfolk but continued his *Advocate* and *Harkness Hoot* campaigns, having recently been named an associate editor of the latter. Like Scott Fitzgerald's Gatsby, J outlined a program of self-improvement: "Reading: Ec. med. lit. & things on the HOWtoREAD list that I haven't touched yet./ Writin' Pertry (I think I'm getting a bit stronger there) prose & any crit. that will help the KORSE./ Physical Dev.: Skiing, mountains, & ole swimmin hole."

J's allegiances had shifted radically toward Rapallo, and not only in his adoption of some Ezratic orthography. He had committed himself to a campaign for Pound and was expending much energy trying to get him published *and paid* and evaluating possible supporters. R. P. Blackmur in *The Hound and Horn* had shown himself such a "clever detail-critic" that he had missed the big picture—that "the CANTOS are the one non-defeatist poem of the age." Zukofsky "does know what the CANTOS stand for," but writes "in an unintelligible gibble." "Good old Archie" MacLeish was held back by his "credo of criticism," which appeared to be that "one shouldn't say anything about anything because anything is all right because it is." "Wms. could do the most good if only he would," concluded J. "He writes so well you can feel how good it is with your fingers." To Pound himself, the goal of the *Cantos* was utterly clear: to sum up, analyze, and correct the course of civilization.

J still began his letters "Dear Mr. Pound," and he composed in a manner that adapted certain Poundian orthographies and phrasings to his own uses, yet his style remained very much his twenty-year-old own. He would fire a barrage of queries and then interject a tease at his own youth and at Ezra's paternal gravitas: "I am a little girl nine years ole. Will you/ please tell me why grmmer don't have a big/ beard like grn-fer?" He sensed that as "Dilectus Filius" he could get away with a great deal. And while J might say, "I seen your squid [*sic*] in *The Little Magazine*. Good!" he often reported unflattering or ambivalent comments about the Boss: "Writes Gilbert Stevenson of Yhale, Hawaiian Grammarian/

Promoter of Yiddish musick/ Fonetic alfabetist/ 'Pound is filled with shit/
But I laik hit.'"

A certain free hand with the niceties of perlite dialogue crept into
some of J's other correspondence as well. The new Gotham Book Mart
catalog had the temerity to advertise Henry Seidel Canby, and J exploded
to Frances Steloff and her assistant, Kay Steele DuBose. The catalog itself
was "swell," he admitted, "but if you ever again advertise that goddam-
sunofabitch Canby/[Christopher] Morley/Benet I'll severally disembowl
[sic] you each. Putting those swine in the same pages with Ezra and TS is
an unpardonable breach of taste." Steloff and DuBose replied in the same
vein, parodying Stein and then breaking into free verse:

> Names have a way of bouncing off books
>   and sonofabitch is a rubberball
> a rubberball a spitball the saturday review is a spitball
> and don't spit it away until you fall fall until you fall. . . . ,
>   Dear Laughlin, IV

By now J had become Pound's "Respected colleague an fellow sufferer//"
and J wrote to Ezra as "Yr. Eccel." He had ventured to ply Aunt Leila with
the *Cantos*: "Read the Kung canto to me old aunt in me best suede voice
and the old gal done wep," J reported to the author. "She is full of cash &
I'm working on her in your behalf." He was sure of getting a printing press
out of her, "as she thinks that will keep me out of devilment & picket
lines." By mid-March he had found a small used hand-set press.

J was concerned about the weakness of the American poetry market:
"Poetry don't sell over here/ no matter how good it is, unless it's that
Jeffers/ Robinson/ Millay/ Frost/ Masefield/ Sandburg/ stuff./ & MacLeish
sells about 1000 copies usually./ Cous. Henry says 250 is average sale on
poetry book. Anthony Fuckworse now running into 13th milliard"—J was
attacking the popular novel *Anthony Adverse*. As for an American edition
of Pound's *Jefferson and/or Mussolini*, due out the next year in England, J
recognized that it was too long for either the *Advocate* or the *Hoot*. This
was another incentive for him to go into publishing on his own. "I'll set it
up myself on Hays' machine if you like," he wrote to Pound, "and push it
around best 'n I can." Still, J could tot up a few successes: he had published
several of his own poems and two long articles in the *Hoot*, where he had

also crammed in poems by Robert Fitzgerald, Fitts, Dr. Merrill Moore, and Wallace Stevens, as well as Canto 36 and an essay by Pound.

When the term ended in February, J got his Ford out of the Harvard Square Garage and left Cambridge with relief. He told his parents that he had to take a year off to rest his eyes. His mother had thought him too young to go away to college, and she at least said that a year away from Harvard might improve his health. Pound weighed in, having heard from Binyon that J was dropping out on account of his eyesight: "What wd/ please me most wd/ be the Jeff/ Muss getting printed/ but until I know how bad yr/ eyes are, I mean IF the matter is serious , do lay off tootin my horn." J, meanwhile, was still trying to arrange for the periodical publication of individual cantos. "I tried to touch me ole man on your behalf," J wrote to Ezra, "but he says he is agin poetry. He says you would make big money if you were good enough. But you can't tell your ole man to go eat shit." Pound took the refusal calmly. He had refused a few hundred dollars offered by Kirstein for an article the year before. "Don't tell yr/ paw I refused money of Bitch and Bugle," Ezra warned J. "That wd/ CONvince him I oughtn't to be at large."

•

When his mother told him that he could not sit around and do nothing, J wrote to the Gotham Book Mart asking for a job. Steloff replied that she was "most interested" but warned him about "long hours and hard work." She went so far as to announce that James Laughlin IV would be in charge of experimental literature beginning December 1 and that "he will add authors, titles and magazines to make this department most complete." Probing for another option, J wrote within a week to Ezra, stating that "seeing tests" showed that his eyes still had not recovered sufficiently for him either to resume studies at Harvard or to run his newly acquired press. He inquired about lodgings in Rapallo. "Shall be vurry pleesd to see you," Pound replied by return post, adding that Ma Riess could probably put him up. The extent to which Pound already thought of J as one of the family, and one he knew to be discreet, was indicated by his jocular comment: "The aged Yeats"—he was only sixty-nine—had just left, and Pound told J, "I had several seereeyus reflexhuns re/ doing a formal document requesting you to chloriform me before I get to THAT state."

At the end of June, J set sail for England, deliberately leaving his good suit in Pittsburgh. His rejection of sartorial correctness was a declaration of independence from American mores, proprieties, prejudices. He had broken again with Harvard and cut himself off from Pittsburgh. The Dilectus Filius expected that Pound would assume the role of father to him. Ezra might have been joking when he proposed putting his life into J's hands, but his jest would turn into fact.

5

"The Charismatic Pyramid": Gertrude Stein

If every one were not so indolent they would realise that beauty is beauty even when it is irritating and stimulating not only when it is accepted and classic.

—Gertrude Stein

J's crossing was such that he wrote home "scathing remarks about Old Lady Atlantic." The trip had been "boring": J kept to himself aboard the United States Lines *Leviathan*, ate caviar at every meal, swam and exercised in the gymnasium daily. "Nothing much to write about except the state of my mind which wouldn't interest you," he told his mother. He was berthed in first class, courtesy of his traveling companion, Joseph Quattrone, a sophomore at Choate, whose father was an executive with the shipping company; in return, J had agreed to "show Europe" to Joseph. They spent two weeks in London, and J called on T. S. Eliot at Faber and Faber. Immediately, a sea change occurred in J's attitude toward "Papa Possum." "I have been seeing Ole Possum," he wrote to Pound, "what a decent guy he is! I feel very sorry for my tactless review in *Westminster*. It was too personal of a personality of courtesy sans peer."

J told Pound of his eagerness to get at the real business of his life: "I want like hell to clear the decks and write a good lyric—to be done with this indigestion of the intellect, the colic of confused senses—to learn a craft, to make words talk in many voices." His verse was "pickin' up a bit," J thought, a view not shared, apparently, by the American magazines that continued to reject his submissions.

By the end of July, Joseph and J were in Nuremberg to view German High Renaissance religious art—J took seriously his "tutorial" of Joseph—

and by August 1 they had arrived in Munich, seething with unrest over the assassination by Austrian Nazis of Chancellor Engelbert Dollfuss a week before. They were still in Munich the following day when the long-ailing Reichspräsident Paul von Hindenburg died, and J and Joseph sat in the Odeonsplatz watching the black-uniformed *Schutzstaffel*, the SS, assemble in formation. "Torches were lighted that burned late into the night," J wrote, "fiery and red in the night. All the bells tolled in dis-harmony and flags hung draped in black. Standing in the crowd we were driven slowly back by mounted police as far as the Galeriestrasse so that a great empty space lay between civilian herd and sacred soldiery." By chance he ran into his "much loved tutor," Dana Durand, in the city to work on medieval manuscripts at the Staatsbibliothek. They talked about the "financial skulduggery" that the German minister of economics, Hjalmar Schacht, employed to manipulate the value of German bonds, about Dollfuss, and also about the Night of the Long Knives, Hitler's June 30 purge of those leaders of the Nazi storm troopers whom he saw as potential obstacles to his plans. The killing started in Munich and then spread to some twenty other cities in Germany and Austria. The dazzling Schloss Salzburg above the city was filled with the dying, those bayoneted during the Long Knives massacre. Durand had already published a scholarly paper on the early maps of Germany and central Europe and would go on to a career in the OSS and the CIA. His informed insights provided a counterpoise to Pound's views. J was fully conscious of the significance of the events he was witnessing or discussing. Many were saying that Hitler would fall soon: J disagreed. The alacrity with which the German public had accepted the June purge showed how broadly based was his grip on power.

The interesting questions are why J would deliberately leap to the edge of this cauldron and why he would also expose his young compatriot to what was certainly a dangerous and volatile situation. Simply, he was aware that this was an important moment, and he wanted to observe it. Furthermore, he had faith in the protection afforded by an American passport—although he must have realized that this document would be a flimsy shield against a mob of Brownshirts. "I'm very much shocked with the way Germany is again exalting militarism," J wrote to Aunt Leila. "Everywhere one sees parades and drums and uniforms strutting about; it is very disgusting . . . nationalism is always wrong in the long run."

Suddenly J's work on Gertrude Stein took a serendipitous turn. In mid-August, Joseph Quattrone having returned home, J was relaxing beside the Salzburg public *Schwimmbad* when he noticed a dark-haired, sinister-looking man eyeing him. Deciding that the best defense lay in boldness, J walked over and struck up a conversation. It turned out to be Bernard Faÿ, an eminent French authority on American literature and, coincidentally, Stein's closest French friend and the translator of *The Making of Americans*. Faÿ offered to write to Stein, then in Bilignin at her rented *château ferme*, a seventeenth-century fortified farmhouse. Soon J received a "welcome invitation," open-ended, from the lady herself. Faÿ interested J. "A most charming person," he wrote home, a round little man who deliberately wore ill-fitting and outmoded clothes, Faÿ might well emulate Claudel and become ambassador to Washington. His manner was a bit fussy, and clearly he manipulated people, playing upon their weaknesses and appetites to advance his own ends. He appeared to be homosexual, so J was careful to cast himself merely as an admiring litterateur.

Dallying in Salzburg before going to visit Stein and Toklas, J flaunted his seeming-naive charm, his vocation as poet, his serviceable French and his slight German, his spectacular height and medallion profile, his wavy hair and earnest blue eyes, and was invited everywhere—and all without having to exceed his carefully budgeted allowance. "Suddenly without knowing quite how it happened I found myself transplanted from the poet's lonely vigil to a tumultuous whirl of high sassiety," he wrote in an immense letter home. Everyone he met appeared to have a title or be in some way extraordinary. "One princess (the most stunning looking animal you ever saw with golden hair and eyes like a cat and skin so white you would be sure she were dead. You have seen her picture often in Vogue I imagine . . .) She has been . . . very kind to me indeed," he exclaimed—not very reassuringly—to his parents. He exchanged gossip with Baron and Baroness Engel from Vienna about acquaintances from his days at Le Rosey. He saw Ted Spencer and his wife, Marci, and they spent an evening with Olivia Chambers—"My new passion with the bangs" and an absent husband—and Baron van den Branden, secretary of the Palais des Beaux-Arts in Brussels, who argued eloquently with Spencer over Mozart and Beethoven. "Ted was terribly moved and spoke to me with barriers down, as we came home to the Goldene Rose in the late night munching a hot dog. He said 'I wish, Jay, that you had somebody in bed with you, either man or woman,' to which I replied 'that I had for some time had God in bed with me.'"

In fine spirits J set off for his appointment at Bilignin, driven by Faÿ. The serialization of *The Autobiography of Alice B. Toklas* the preceding summer had propelled Stein onto the bestseller lists and the cover of *Time* magazine. As they approached the *château ferme*, Stein appeared suddenly in a second-story window, framed by white shutters and a grapevine, her favorite vantage point from which to greet guests. For a few moments she loomed over him: handsome triangular face, profile of a Roman emperor, warm brown hair, brown skirt, blue brocade vest, coral brooch. She set the tone for the visit at once. "You didn't think I'd ask you here if I didn't expect you to work," she stated rhetorically. He discovered that this work was to write press releases for Stein's coming American tour, to explain in a page of plain language just *what* she was talking about in each of her six planned lectures. Her drafts were in the form of statements, including "What Is English Literature"—the lady detested question marks—and Stein herself admitted that "they are for a pretty intelligent audience and though they are clear very clear they are not too easy." J suggested that she might lecture at Choate and persuaded her to prepare a simplified talk for prep school students. The result was "How Writing Is Written." Each morning when J showed her one of his synopses, Stein would say, "No you haven't got it do it again." As J painstakingly tried once more to transduce Steinese into standard English, Gertrude would sit with her back to the superb outlook and write with great rapidity in a large notebook. J described it as automatic writing, "Zip, zip, zip." "That just ain't art," he recalled much later.

J was not entirely failing in his "work," as he had at first thought, for some days into his visit he heard Stein announce to Faÿ, "I say, the kid hasn't done badly."

Stein liked to walk in the heat of the day, when most life from oxen to insects had gone silent. She kept up a steady patter, "talking about books that had lived and died as we walked along the hot, green hillside," calling to the dogs and lecturing J in a "gay contralto" on what made literature last. "Can you tell which books of your own time will be read in school by your grandchildren? . . . When Henry James was writing how many people thought he would come to be considered America's finest writer?" "Was it," J ventured, "like so many things, a matter of luck?" Stein gave her wonderful hearty laugh and bounded over a wall after her dogs, and his question went unanswered.

Deliberately, J set out to give his letters to his parents a Steinian plain diction and style:

> I like Gertrude very well and she is a great woman but one can never be sure. She knows more about writing and words than anyone else has ever known surely and yet sometimes I think there are things we live which a word cannot tell even when, as in her writing, you give it not its name but the word that makes it be without repeating it. She is very nice to me and very frank . . . and she has a smile in her eyes that is second only to Whitehead's. I have learned more about writing in these few days than ever I have known before. Things that I have felt inside me about the writing of poetry and prose and have never been able to express or fully understand, these things she has made clear to me. I have always had a trouble with my writing that was a bother to me but I could not understand what it was though I knew well that it was. She explained it to me at once. When you write, she said, don't let your hand get ahead of your head. That is what has been troubling me for so long . . . I will always I know want to use words and not be used by them which is the thing that she does.

The purgatorial part of each day that J spent with Stein came during their afternoon drives. "Miss Stein fills the car quite completely though she is not big, but she is like a rock sitting there quite solidly, and she holds the wheel still after driving for thirty years as though it were something she did not quite trust," J wrote to his parents. "She drives very fast and very well and never looks at the road but is never in the wrong place." Gertrude and Alice would sit in the front seats of Godiva, the Model A Ford, while J and Basket, the show-clipped white poodle, and Pépé, the Mexican mongrel, occupied the backseat. The dogs kept licking J, and if he dared to swat one of them, Toklas would turn around and say, "Jay! Be nice to those *dear* dogs!" Mainly, J was intent on learning from Stein: "The landscape . . . is what FOUR SAINTS is about. Miss Stein sat and looked at it for a long time and the things that it always made her think of are the things that you saw in FOUR SAINTS "—J and his mother had seen the

Virgil Thomson/Stein opera six months before on Broadway. One dictum of hers he was determined to apply to his own writing: "I have learned that in the end it is not what you are writing about but what is written, that is the words that are written, that matter."

J felt at once chastened and inspired. "You see all of a sudden it is very wonderful to know that you know a person is a complete person absolutely complete and nothing at all left over or wanting," J summed up Stein— and then himself. "You see it is all a wonderful thing and I am glad that it has happened but of course it would because these things happen to me I am that kind of person. I am the kind of person who is not very amusing and not very dull and things happen to him and he tells about them not very well but he tells about them." He also lowered his own expectations: "It has been very nice to know Miss Stein and also it has its drawbacks. Each time you know a great person you begin to know more and more that you yourself are not a great person and that it would be much more sensible . . . to live in Pittsburgh and work in the steelmill and marry a nice plain girl . . . At present I wouldn't lay much money on my literary success . . . but really I wouldn't lay much money against my still trying to write because really there is only one thing that pleases and that is knowing and when you are writing and trying to write you are knowing things."

Despite her dogmatic pronouncements, J would always speak fondly of Stein, whom he recalled as "certainly—practically—the most charismatic person I've ever met." Stein told J that the test for good books was that they must make the bell ring. This intuitive inner-bell note became J's standard for judgment, rather than a book's adherence to any particular philosophy, style, mode, or ism. And this simple dictum would go a long way toward explaining the eclecticism of the future New Directions, for J, even with his declared intention of publishing "advance guard" literature, would always at heart be an appreciator, not a critic. Ironically, where Stein's writing was concerned, there was no such ringing: J would never ask for a new book of hers to publish. Stein's importance to J lay in her artistic integrity, the purity of her stylistic voice.

J usually trusted his own ear, even as a very young man, but this could get him into trouble. Once Stein discovered him happily immersed in Proust. "Jay, how can you read such stuff?" she demanded angrily. "Don't you know both Joyce and Proust copied their work from my *Making of Americans?*" And when J tried to discuss the Nazi threat at dinner with

Stein, Toklas, and some of their French friends, Baron Robert d'Aiguy told him that he knew nothing about wars, "so please hush until you know what you are talking about." To J, Stein said that Hitler was "a very great man." From the valley below they could hear the rattle of machine guns: a French Moroccan regiment was training. "This is a bad thing but it is a wonderful thing to hear what the war sounds like and not have to be in it," J wrote to his parents. Stein seemed unperturbed by the threat of war. After eight days, J was on his way to Paris, where he planned to complete his work for her.

It might seem at this juncture that two mighty champions were contending for J's allegiance and soul. Stein had become fond of him and saw him as a useful agent in her American campaign. Pound assumed that J was firmly in *his* camp. J might have been fascinated by Stein *as a person*, and saw that a monograph on her would be a good leg up to his reputation as a literary man, but he did not waver in his primary commitment to Pound.

J settled into Paris, "in a windowless cubicle [above] an insurance office," an attic room in the rue des Saints-Pères. After a month he reported to his parents that he was living on $3 per day, bed, board, and entertainment. He certainly did not lack for friends who would feed him, since Mlle Marie-Thérèse d'Authume arrived two days after he did, Faÿ was often in Paris, and Stein and Toklas would come soon. Pound, meanwhile, was tugging J in another direction. Ezra complained of overwork, and he implied that he could use J's help in Rapallo. He would try to make a poet out of J, try to give him a "modus" for writing. Planting the seed of a future anthology for J to found, Ezra also lamented the lack of a magazine that would provide a "forum or vortex for active ideas in AmurikuHHHHHH."

J had set off for Europe with his Stein monograph unfinished, but now he had considerable new material, and Florence Codman promised to publish it. J had finally admitted to Pound that he was writing on Stein: "I suspect Gertrude," he said, "but this seems a good opportunity to bust into print, and so I'm doing what I can for her sad case." He was shoving along his text on Stein in a Sisyphean tedium, writing and tearing up. It was not intended to be criticism, he said, only "an impartial elucidation of her intentions and aesthetic opinions." J visited Shakespeare and Company, where he bought Pound's *Make It New* and paid court to Sylvia Beach, with her

upturned face, short hair, and ruffled appearance of an alarmed but daunt-
less bird. Just as another bookseller, Frances Steloff, was crucial to his early
development in the United States, Beach quickly became one of his vital
windows into European writing.

J's own prose now made him feel desperate. He summed up to Steloff
his main failing by repeating thrice: "My LOUSY critical style." At the beginning of October he wrote to Eliot for advice on finding an English publisher for his "little book on dear old Gertrude Stein," with the caveat that
"it is definitely not up to Faber." Eliot immediately suggested, in vain, that
J send him the typescript and added, "I hope for original as well as critical
work from you."

By the end of the month, J had posted half of his fifteen-thousand-
word typescript to Codman and planned to ship the rest by early November. Then Steloff cabled him offering to publish his text, and J countered
by suggesting a collaboration with Arrow Editions. "The thing to do is not
to hurt Florence's feelings," J explained. He already had a firm, even quixotic, commitment to what he conceived of as the ethics of publishing, as
well as a concern for the individuals he dealt with. However, he felt no
obligation to inform Stein that he was writing about her. Stein, J told Steloff, "likes too well to do her own explaining."

On June 15, J had received word that "Melody with Fugue" had been
accepted by Whit Burnett for the October issue of his *Story* magazine. As
the College Prize Story, it brought J $100. "This is a break for our side," J
wrote to his father, "we may not have to go to work in Allequipa [*sic*] next
fall after all." Hughart was having a bad manic-depressive spell, and J tried
to encourage him at long distance: "I am working for control just as hard as
you are, and though sometimes I make some awful breaks, I know we will
both get there all right."

Meanwhile, J was balancing poetry, writing on Pound and Stein, corresponding, and drafting short sketches for *365 Days*, the daybook calendar of short-shorts that Laurence Vail had proposed. Kay Boyle, Vail, and
J sat talking on the terrace of the Deux Magots, Kay a dramatic study in
black and white, Laurence, her husband, with sharp-edged blond features
gone a bit febrile. Vail accepted two of J's stories." "I don't want to come
home and kick around and get melancholy," J wrote to his parents, "so unless there is something constructive for me to do, I'll stay where I'm not
annoyed. My work goes along and I learn the languages."

J began an autobiographical novel that featured his flawed "bloodmust," but he was easily distracted: he visited the sculptor Constantin Brancusi. "He sure is one swell guy all right," J wrote to Pound. "We had a fine talk and I enjoyed his work wh'ch seems authentic and then some to me." Brancusi plied J with wine and cooked a fine repast on his stone stove, all the while flooding his chaotic studio—forge, anvil, saws, pots of paint—with the warmth of his personality, swinging on a trapeze, mimicking Michelangelo's heroic statuary, invoking Beethoven.

Brancusi's integrity was palpable, and he was a lovable man. Drawing upon his memories of a man in many ways Brancusi's opposite, J sat down to write "Partial Eclipse," based mainly on his encounters with Bernard Faÿ, who appears as Monsieur Beloeil, a glib poseur. J's story is a wicked execution: Beloeil is a talented literary craftsman, not a genius of the first rank. As a foil to Beloeil, J introduces the sculptor Ribischka—clearly modeled on Brancusi. "Ribischka was always refreshing, he was real," thinks Beloeil. Just as Beloeil in the story recognizes that he has taken the easy route to fame, J suspected himself of selling out to his own facility in writing. He also mirrored in the story his relationship with his mother: J might realize now that his mother loved him, but she had seemed not to when he was a child. J moved his character smoothly into an introspective self-portrait: "Had he ever really *loved* the women who had loved him? Or did he merely *make* love to them to sharpen his vanity?"

Stein and Toklas appeared in Paris, and Gertrude called J a "dear boy" and invited him to their apartment at solidly bourgeois 27 rue de Fleurus. On October 17, J saw Stein off for America, Gertrude-the-Monolith carrying her lectures in a specially made leather case and evincing signs of uneasiness. "She is getting just the least bit scared now, going home after thirty years," J realized. The press took a great many photographs of Stein departing, and she turned over all dealings with the reporters to J. "I gave them all they could hold & then some," he said. Whatever apprehensions she might have harbored, Stein's reception in America was stupendous: Eleanor Roosevelt served her tea at the White House, Charlie Chaplin and George Gershwin met with her, and there was great competition for tickets for her forty appearances.

J kept up his efforts on Stein's behalf. "Thanx to yr machinations," wrote Fitts, "Gertrude Stein is lecturing here on the 12th of January, to the vocal despair of Profs Ayres, Wilphongue, Stengel, Maher, et al." Fitts and Mrs. St. John carried the day over strong opposition. It was a triumph for Choate. The lecture committee at Yale had refused Stein, and her lecture at Choate was a "huge success," Fitts said. "Everyone, from the Headmistress down to the heelers of the *Lit*, fell heavily for her gurgling giggle. I drove her and Alice B. down from Springfield," Fitts told J, "and her monologues on Hemingway, her reminiscences of you, and the mentioned giggle, threatened collision c̄ [with] trees every half mile. I never had a more amusing drive; or a more cockeyed set of subsequent letters."

6

The Ezuversity

Literature is news that STAYS news.   —Ezra Pound

Finally it was time to leave Paris, and on November 4, 1934, J turned up in Rapallo. Seductively, the hills pressed the small town close against the sand-and-rock shore of the Mediterranean. The trim beached rowboats and one or two open-cockpit sloops suggested tourist leisure rather than working fishermen. All thought of becoming an employee of the Gotham was forgotten: the draw of Europe and Ezra Pound was too strong. J wanted to write, not peddle others' books. Ezra and Dorothy Pound were warm in their welcome, and the three dined together at the Albergo Rapallo, where the Pounds ate most of their meals. There was a vivid exchange about Paris: J's recent adventures there, the Pounds' life in the city during the early 1920s.

Ezra had found a room for J across town at 12 via delle Americhe with an English widow Pound called Ma Riess. Lucy Mabel Riess was a plump personage who loved to float along the Golfo di Tigullio in an inner tube, her eyes shaded by a tennis visor while she read Tauchnitz paperbacks. She had been married to a Thuringian, and their son, John Holroyd-Reece, had cofounded the Albatross Press, and she was fervently interested in the arts, dance, and spiritualism. She sang Heine's "Lorelei" for J, and in years to come when depression fell upon him, he would hum the tune to recall those joyous times. She quoted Goethe to him: "Edel sei der Mensch, hilfreich und gut"—Humankind should be noble, helpful, and good. In a burst of ruthless introspection, J was to write, "I wish I could have modeled my life on that but I am base clay and use people."

The next day J began his studies at the "Ezuversity," as he would call Pound's completely informal educational institution. Ezra worked on his own writing in the morning, and his "eddycashun" talk—J was the sole pupil at the moment—delivered in loud tones in a voice surprisingly high-pitched coming out of his robust frame, began over lunch at what Ezra termed the "Albuggero Rapallo." The Ezuversity was "a marvelous educational institution." There were no fees, and the classes were "simply Pound's continuous and fascinating monologue," ranging principally across literature, music, art, history, and economics. "Pound's mind always moved sideways, like a crab scuttling across the sand," J said, "anything that occurred to him while he was talking . . . He would go from ancient myth [to] how the Schneider-Creusot people sold arms to both sides" in any conflict. Everything was synchronic. Often the lecture moved to Ezra and Dorothy's penthouse on the narrow via Marsala. Below the seaward windows lay the turquoise sweep of the Gulf of Tigullio. The Pounds lived in a cluster of small rooms, sparely furnished with chairs and tables constructed with some skill by Ezra himself. J saw small statues given them by Gaudier-Brzeska, while Dorothy's money had bought a "beautiful abstraction of two white conch shells" by Max Ernst, and colored drawings by Wyndham Lewis. There were also a number of expert sketches by Dorothy. Gaudier-Brzeska's heraldic bust of Pound reposed in the dining room of the Albergo: it was too heavy to transport up to the Pounds' flat.

Ezra's talk was spiced by irreverence, even for those he admired: "Fat-faced Frankie" was Francesco Petrarch, "Harry-Stop-Her-Knees" was Aristophanes, and so on. Ezra employed, J said, *tapinosis*, colorful slang to highlight serious topics. The many he disliked he skewered with puns and wordplays. The poet laureate Robert Bridges became "Rabbit Britches" who wrote "Worse Libre," bad free verse. If Ezra *really* hated someone, he resorted to innuendo and ribaldry: when he said that "poke-nose" Alfonso of Aragon was "half-bald," he was referring not to his hairline but to his sterility, in sex and in ideas. Colleges did not teach what the young needed to know. These "beaneries," dedicated to cramming useless stuff into one's "bean," had been usurped by professors bent on killing poetry, subsidized by the *mercanti di cannoni* who were in unholy alliance with the bankers to kill people. At the root of human misery was the poverty that starved working men and women, that kept them from the secure possession of homes and family businesses, that deprived artists of the rewards of their masterpieces. This poverty, Pound said, stemmed from "usura," the crippling interest levied by bankers. The draft of his Canto 45, a thundering denunciation of *usura*, was still a year in the future.

Pound was quite at home in most of the modern Romance languages, could read at sight the more difficult Latin authors, could get along in German. He had less Greek, but it was still considerable, and his Chinese was enough for his vers libre "translations" and for his symbolic and ideogrammatic purposes in *The Cantos*. Most important, when he was talking to J or to anyone else he took seriously, he assumed if not their knowledge at least their intelligence and willingness to learn. His erudition was complemented by the most intense and exuberant engagement in the here and now: good food and drink, swimming and tennis, politics and news.

On fine afternoons the lecture might continue on a walk up a *salita* weaving steeply through olive groves and terraced vegetable plots. Sometimes Pound quoted passages from the troubadours in Provençal and in classical Greek about the Eleusinian Mysteries on this natural stage of pastel olive and rock colors, with the incandescent blue of the Mediterranean flashing and wimpling far below. Their progress up the trail became the parade of the Eleusinian celebrants, the δρομενα, or confused wandering, culminating in the achieving of illumination as initiates, with Ezra becoming more and more exalted in his evocation of the great mystery.

After dinner was served at the corner table under the Gaudier-Brzeska bust, Ezra might go to the cinema, taking J along "to improve his Eye-talian." Ezra lounged on a front-row balcony seat, his long legs propped on the railing. The fare was invariably a banal romantic comedy that J found nigh intolerable but that Pound greeted with torrents of laughter.

J, who would come to know many epic talkers—Kenneth Rexroth's roaring excursuses and denunciations, the dipsomaniac Dylan Thomas's Welsh lyricism, Thomas Merton's flights of ecstasy—invariably held up Pound as the standard against whom all other talkers were to be measured. It was partly his delivery, his form of Appalachian cracker-barrel mixed with English upper-class and Cockney accents, done in mockery, alternating with black American slang via Uncle Remus, all salted with profanity and peppered with words and phrases in many European tongues. He was an unparalleled mimic who could recall, seemingly, the speech mannerisms of everyone he had ever heard. J would write much later that he could never read Yeats without hearing "Uncle Willie" in the tones of Pound's ventriloquism, of Ezra affectionately rendering Yeats as "a great Peeeea-cock / in the proide ov his oiye." J also recalled "a Yiddish accent, a middle-European one, an Arab one, and even a lower-class French one as in Canto 16. All these voices were in Pound's head and are part of his humor." It was like hearing the *Cantos* talked out. His method, J thought, was "education by provocation." As one might expect from the synchronism of his mind, his casting was achronistic, and circling with design around a subject until his pattern finally emerged, he could skip without a tremor from Virgil and his patron Augustus Caesar to Natalie Barney riding her horse in the Bois de Boulogne to George Antheil, whose music Olga played and which Ezra persuaded Barney to present in her Paris salon, to con-clude with Djuna Barnes's anonymous pen portrait of Barney in *Ladies Almanack*.

Ezra chose a theme for each discourse: the failure of the universities to educate the young, or the need to rescue Vivaldi's unpublished musical scores from dusty archives, or the desperate lack of good government in most countries. Partly because he would spend twelve years in an insane asylum, it would become fashionable—and not only among Pound's enemies—to be dismissive about his intellect and opinions, but what Ezra *knew* and could recall verbatim was astounding. He had written music under his own name and had employed several pseudonyms, among them B. H. Dias for an "Art Notes" column in *New Age*, music criticism as William Atheling, and polemical verse under the name Alfred Venison. His current passion was economics.

Within weeks J was perplexing the folks back home with all manner of arcane economic theory. He worried to Uncle Dicky about there being no "reliable brake" on "the Roosevelt 'hell-bent-for-bankruptcy-Express,'" now that Senator Frederic Walcott of Norfolk was no longer in Washing-ton. Meanwhile, J said, he was learning Italian with Signorina Canessa, an elderly lady, and Ezra, "our finest American poet," was providing "valuable instruction in versification."

The contrast between life in the Pounds' circle and Pittsburgh or Nor-folk was striking. Pound was fastidious in dress and daily life, conscientious in his symmetrical lifelong relationships with his wife, Dorothy Shake-spear, and his mistress, Olga Rudge. Elitist by choice, he was nevertheless utterly democratic in social discourse and seemed equally pleased to talk *Arbeit*, *Kredit*, and *Gold* in broken German with humble farmers and the same subjects in fluent Italian with Mussolini. Ezra paid personal attention to every domestic detail, buying *olandese* or gruyère cheese here, tomatoes "not too ripe" there. J was drawn to this careful simplicity.

When she was not in Venice, Olga Rudge lived in a rented cottage at Sant'Ambrogio, in an olive grove a mile above Rapallo. Ezra strode up the *salita* regularly to visit, working on musical projects with Olga and sometimes staying overnight. J soon discovered that her status as Ezra's mistress was at least tacitly accepted by Dorothy and that Olga and Ezra had a daughter, Mary, living with a peasant family at Gais in the Italian Alps. Ezra might have been raised a Presbyterian, yet he appeared to have retained no vestige of sexual guilt. Further, J learned that Dorothy had a son, Omar, in England. Ezra acknowledged paternity for the record, but he clearly regarded the boy, more than a year younger than Mary, as Dorothy's affair. Years later Dorothy confided to J that she had been "grateful to Olga" in at least one respect: the beautiful young violinist from Youngstown, Ohio, had taken the burden of "all *that*" out of her relationship with her husband. "I never saw any sexiness" in Dorothy, J would recall.

Because he was ruthless in weeding out works that did not come up to his standard, and because he had an instinct for economy, Ezra did not have endless shelves of books in his study, but those books were in many languages, especially French, German, Italian, and Provençal, as well as English. The core curriculum of the Ezuversity consisted of the books discussed in Pound's *ABC of Reading*, published in London the preceding March, and of economics texts and exposés of the armaments industry. Among the ancients, Homer, Propertius, and Catullus were essential. Ezra gave J Ovid in Golding's translations and the *Aeneid* in Gavin Douglas's to read. He expounded on the superiority of Chaucer over Shakespeare. Acceptable "recent" poets included Villon, Herrick, Rochester, Rimbaud, and Cocteau—the last, Pound's friend. "Ezra was always convinced that Marse Jean was the premier poet of France," J would recall. "I guess Marse Jean had befriended him when he came to Paris and that was that." Flaubert and James were the major novelists; Joyce was good through *A Portrait of the Artist as a Young Man* but suspect in *Ulysses*, and he had gone off his rocker with *Finnegans Wake*. Hemingway could be all right, Ezra told J, but the trouble with him was that he could only keep one idea in his mind at a time.

Pound's immense correspondence was kept clipped together or impaled on spindles behind his desk, while essential tools like scissors and pencils dangled from strings reaching to the ceiling. On the desk was a heavy old manual typewriter that, J remembered, "was played like a percussion instrument (or John Cage at the piano)," depending on Boss Pound's mood. Asked many years later if Ezra had harbored any "Concretist" ideas about the placement of his lines on the page, J thought not. "I just assumed that many of the indentations were more or less accidental, depending on the amount of energy or irritation in his right wrist as he whacked at the typewriter carriage."

During fine weather, the pupil swam or played tennis with Pound and his doctor friend, Elfriede Bacigalupo. Ezra's strategy, especially in a doubles match, was to stand in the center of the court, glare with ferocious concentration, and then slam any ball that came within range in a powerful forehand trajectory aimed at the opposing player. When Pound connected, this stroke was almost impossible to return. Ford Madox Ford said that he played like "an inebriated kangaroo." Ezra's monologue, interrupted perforce by tennis, would continue when they went swimming, when he would rent a pontoon boat and row far out into water cleaner than that near the beach. "He would dive in," J remembered, "surface, his marvelous head bursting from the water, and he would say something like, 'Victor Hugo was an absolute nut, y'know.'" Late afternoon tea might be served by Dorothy, who would read Henry James in her expressive voice so that J could rest his eyes. She was like a character from *The Wings of the Dove*, genteel, principled, "carrying herself delicately with the air, always, of a young Victorian lady out skating." Quiet Dorothy, perfect foil to Ezra, was the unacknowledged—except by J—other faculty member of the Ezuversity. And J was also privileged to see his master from the perspective of his parents, also in residence. Isabel had always encouraged her son to become a poet, but now neither parent could make sense of the *Cantos* and quizzed J about what their son might be up to.

Occasionally, Pound could be persuaded to critique J's verse, which he did with pencil in hand, slashing out words, lines, sometimes whole pages, breaking the lead as if to emphasize his disapproval. Simplicity! Pare it down! "Make it new!" Finally, Ezra in exasperation would scrawl a few lines: "*This* is what you meant to say!" Ezra had already encouraged J, having told him six months earlier "thet yr/ teKneeee/qu iz in verse improvin'." For Ezra this amounted to high praise. He refused to look at J's short stories, saying that he hadn't the time.

"I was still trying to write the Great American Nov.," J would recall. "It was about dreary, philistine Pittsburgh and how an angry young man busts loose 'to forge in the smithy of my soul the uncreated conscience of my race' (Joyce)." One day Pound tossed a crudely produced paperback to J across the lunch table. On the cover was a very recognizable if anatomically inaccurate crab holding a limp girl in its claws. "Waal, Jaz, here's a dirty book that's pretty good," Pound said. "I guess you're old enough to read it." *It* was Henry Miller's *Tropic of Cancer*. The book was corrosive, anarchic. It made J's vision of philistine Pittsburgh look like pale stuff indeed. Pound had told Miller that *Cancer* "out-Ulyssesed Joyce." Reading *Cancer* was another kind of beginning for J and eventually led to one of his major author contacts. *Cancer* also showed J how far he would have to go to compete in the confessional mode.

J found in the Boss, "Grampaw," Ezra, not a replacement for his own father, that warm, troubled being, but an intellectual father, a *soul's* father. Dudley Fitts might be formidable in erudition and intelligence, a good musician, even a fine poet, but he could not reach out to J in quite so many ways. There was something clinical about Fitts: he was Tybalt to Pound's Mercutio. Fitts dueled by the numbers. Ezra, like an errant sun, blazed from within. He did not need others to tell him that a poem he had written was good, great, or poor. He had figured out what ailed civilization, at least to his own satisfaction, and so he set out to change it. Others might dispute his certainties yet not his sincerity in striving toward them. J had never met anyone so driven to act on his ideals.

Fascinating though J found the society of the Pounds, he decided to spend the winter months in the Alps. He would pause in Lausanne, tarry a few days at Le Rosey, the school of his youthful anguish that he now discovered he loved, and then head into Austria for months of skiing. He was sorry to leave Rapallo. Ezra had been "good to me," and he was writing and learning. Still, the skiing would also be "good for me," he said, always careful in his letters home to cast his activities in terms of personal improvement. The tyranny of his Protestant conscience made it necessary for him to convince himself that this was so. The evening before his departure from Rapallo, he allowed himself a flight of lyrical utterance: "The full moon is rising over the mountains. The sea converses quietly with the shore. Night darkens over Europe and the waste of waters."

By December 21, 1934, J was in Lausanne "enjoying Mlle" Marie-Thérèse at her gracious household. He wrote a letter of thanks to the

Pounds, headed simply "Dear Boss" but adding below "and your Mrs.":
"For a great deal of intellectual, amical, and actual B&B I am as grateful
as is possible . . . Old prof. whiskers' course in civilizations and cultured
cussin' is worth any 16 Haavud and Jerusalombia can put together." His
spirits were soaring: "I have seen the snow on the mountains & tomorrow
I'll get skiis [sic] and . . . I'll be comin' down that mountain when I come!"
Before the year ended, he was on the slopes above Gstaad, the mountain
and glacier runs of his youthful initiation, where he and a handful of other
returned Le Rosey alumni were given free room and board in the school's
new chalet. As he looked over his records for the year, he added up eleven
publications in ten different periodicals and little magazines: four poems,
four short stories, a review, and articles in *The Harkness Hoot* and *The Harvard Advocate*.

J traveled on January 8, 1935, to St. Anton am Arlberg in the Austrian
Tirol, the glorious skiing country west of Innsbruck, where he stayed at the
Landhaus Bergheim and took lessons at the world-famous Hannes Schneider Ski School. After becoming St. Anton's youngest ski guide at sixteen,
Schneider had gone on to win the national ski championship of Austria
and subsequently to develop a system for training ski troops during World
War I. Schneider laid out a strict regimen in ascending difficulty—the
snowplow stem, the stem christie, Zdarsky's turn, and so on—and maintained near-military discipline. The Orient Express passed through
St. Anton, and he soon obtained a clientele from Vienna to London and
beyond. By the 1930s he had achieved mythic proportions as the father of
Alpine skiing. Although Schneider no longer taught at his school in J's
time, he held court in the Gasthof *Bierstube*. J openly pleaded poverty, and
Herbert von Karajan, at the beginning of his long career as a conductor,
"took pity on my shortage of cash" and gave J rides up the mountains in
his chauffeur-driven car. J would then ski down with von Karajan and his
private instructor, Luggi Föger, the sixth-ranked skier in the world. By
January 25, J had been moved by Schneider into the master class and had
acquired Föger as his teacher. Now he could concentrate on developing
strategy.

Meanwhile, there were indications that the tensions had worsened
back in Pittsburgh. J was writing to his mother at 104 Woodland Road,
but to his father at No. 100, where Aunt Marianne Hamilton functioned as
the go-between. Partly it was Hughart's manic outbursts, which could be

triggered by the presence of his wife, but the strain between them was attributable to more than mental illness. After both were long dead, J would remark on his father's many skills, adding, "The only thing he wasn't good at was being nice to my Mother. It was a love match but somewhere something went wrong." Always too, these days, there was the money question. Among the projected family expenses for the first month of 1935: St. Francis Hospital, $290; nurses, $500; doctors' bills, "amount unknown"; two Ford cars, "approximately" $1,200—the Model A's were certainly a comedown from the Hispano-Suizas and Marmons of Hughart's palmier days. And there was a tax bill due for $4,200 for the Woodland Road property. For perspective, the average annual family nonfarm income in the United States was then $1,524.

There was an immediate consequence for J: his father had been sending the monthly $100 that supported him in Europe. No one had stepped in when Hughart entered the hospital. Soon J was writing to Aunt Leila that he had not sent her the promised telegrams because he had "eaten them up": his finances were in a delicate condition, and "eating is so important, you know," he explained with heavy irony.

Whatever his European plans, Aunt Leila was laying out temptations for J to return to America. While he was still at the Ezuversity, he had heard from her that Elizabeth Demarest, recently retired head of the Department of History at the Carnegie Institute in Pittsburgh, was staying in Aunt Leila's White Cottage. She had studied at Leipzig and Oxford before earning a doctorate at Radcliffe, and she was just the sort of person to be useful in the book business, J said. "The news of Robin Hill sounds so enticing," J replied to Aunt Leila's suggestions about a publishing venture. "I look forward to our joint efforts in typography and binding. What fun it will be! More and more I come to be thinking that there is really no place for me like Norfolk." Come back to Norfolk and I will help you to indulge your creative bent, implied Aunt Leila; fine, hinted her wayward knight, making his gambit, but then you must compensate me for all I will be missing in Europe. With his parents' finances slipping, J must have looked on a possible inheritance from the Carlisles with growing interest.

In Pittsburgh there were rumblings at Jones & Laughlin: leaders in the local union at the Aliquippa plant were fired, and they complained to the National Labor Relations Board that they had been dismissed because of their union positions. The NLRB agreed and ordered Jones & Laughlin to rehire the men; the company refused. Two years later the Supreme Court would rule in the union's favor. J came to consider his writing and publishing by way of retribution to society for the sins of his family.

Not only was J skiing, he was writing about it as well. On the high slopes of the Silvretta he experienced the joy of new powder snow in the early dawn, the thrill of making "the first track down a long open slope with the snow spraying out in a cloud behind you and your skipoints cutting the fresh surface as a ship's bow cuts the sea; there is no wind, there is no sound, the sky is clear, and in its emptiness the sun, the great sun, the white sun, the sun . . . nothing is like this, nothing you know or can imagine—not the color of water or the color of air at sunset—this is the furthest you can go." He tried to capture the thrilling rush that comes from skiing difficult terrain, traversing a treacherous ravine: "Then your nerves are all alive within you, your whole body is keyed for the run, and you wait . . . wait as you feel the sun and wind on your head, wait as you look across the great valley below to the distant glistening mass of the Silvretta." Despite his recent claim that he did not have time to read J's prose, Ezra wrote approvingly, "A great deal of it is quite good."

J's favorite ski run was the Kandahar racecourse, site of the Challenge Cup in 1911, the world's first acknowledged downhill ski championship. It was savage skiing for a total drop of twenty-four hundred feet from start to finish. J was very honest about his prowess: his legs and ankles were weak, and he considered that he was doing well if he completed the course with only six falls. "I had forty-one falls, I counted / Them," J wrote in a verse draft. "I gradually worked that / Down to three before I went back to / Rapallo."

In the new year J was on a touring party that included Her Royal Highness Princess Juliana of the Netherlands when he took an unlucky fall and split the seat of his pants. HRH took a sewing kit out of her *Sitzpack* and restored him to decency on the spot. J told the story to Ezra, who immediately saw an opportunity to convert the Dutch royal family to Confucianism: he inscribed a copy of the *Ta Hio* for J to send her.

J received startling news from home: during the night of April 7 at his magnificent estate, West End in Orlando, Uncle Jimmy had shot himself through the heart with an automatic pistol. That he was described by a friend as having been "in very good spirits" on his last evening must have suggested to his namesake that James Laughlin III had experienced a violent bipolar mood swing. His wife, June, had been awakened by the shot, found her husband's body at the foot of the bed, and then called not the police but a family friend. There was no inquest because, said the justice of the peace, "it was a plain case of suicide."

•

As the Alpine skiing ended, J asked the Boss for advice: what should he major in at Harvard? A part of him yearned toward Greek, but he wondered whether it would be as useful for a writer as Latin and Italian, with a bit of Old French thrown in. "Don't want to seem yaller," he said, "but it do appear like I would have whiskers before I got through greek verbs." He settled in Lausanne, resolved to resume his writing. He bought a cheap *cahier*, wrote "26-4-35" at the top of the first page, and set down the contents of a planned collection of seven stories to be called "Six Days Have I Labored." On the first day, J outlined a complex story, set in Europe and told from the point of view of one Christl Schindler, but then broke off to draft a review of *Tropic of Cancer*. Soon his diligence flagged, and there were weeklong gaps between entries. He wrote on William Saroyan and composed several sketches that he had promised Kay Boyle for 365 *Days*. Sometimes he incorporated passages in Latin, including phrases from the "Sanctus": "Pleni sunt caeli et terra gloria tua. Hosanna in excelsis"— Heaven and earth are full of thy glory.

J's review of *Cancer*, significantly titled "The Living Word," made clear his admiration for Miller: "The book burns right into you and the heat doesn't soon cool. Miller brands his Paris into your flesh as deeply as Joyce did Dublin, though their techniques have nothing but vitality in common. Joyce is the apotheosis of erudition; Miller had read all the right books but is essentially the man of action (or perhaps violent inaction as he is continually unemployed; the book has a real sociological significance which I pass over). One thinks of Villon . . . His prose has the electricity, the liveliness, the guts of the Elizabethans; his is the living word." J carried on for three pages to outline Miller's skill with words. "Miss Stein," he continued, "has tried to effect such a purging, but her work has small entertainment value because it is pure laboratory science." Nonetheless, J averred, Miller "practices what Stein preaches, the exact arrangement of words." Was he himself a mere technician in the laboratory of language, J wondered, or could he make words live as Henry had?

Although J had not completed the study of Gertrude Stein that he had worked on since 1933, he was still interested in her. He headed a page of his Lausanne notebook "Gertrude tips" and wrote down twelve items, some admonitory, others mnemonic. J had a title for his intended short book: "Understanding Gertrude Stein." "I think now that I am writing for friends and not enemies," he wrote. "America is thorough. For nearly thirty years America thoroughly made fun of Gertrude Stein. And now America is thoroughly enthusiastic about her." Then J articulated a thought that would become a lifelong adage. "The time-lag is inevitable," he said, referring to the time it had taken from her earliest publications to her achieving a wide audience. "Contemporary writing, the work that really expresses its time, is seldom accepted by the generation it mirrors." He hazarded a prediction: "It is reasonable to expect that by 1960 her work will be read in schools."

When J returned to his *cahier*, it was to discuss Stein at length. He cited her lecture "What Is English Literature" on the decay of the English language and the need to dominate it in order to renew it, and he drew a parallel with Cocteau, who said that he alone "had the moral right to smoke opium as he alone could dominate it." The same was true for writers and language. "Have you the 'right' to be a writer?" J challenged his readers, adding introspectively, "Have I?"

Part of the problem that J was encountering was that Stein refused to be compressed into manageable form. And she seemed to need context. He announced "Understanding Gertrude Stein" for publication in the winter of 1936, and he claimed that his book would include "parallel trends in contemporary experimental writing," with chapters on Joyce, Cummings, surrealism, and "Basic English and the Orthological Institute," treating also linguistics and semantics. Having thus painted himself into several corners, J quit. He would never again attempt a work of literary criticism and analysis on this scale.

Both Miller and Stein held temptation before J. Was he willing to cast himself into the lower depths and then make literature out of it? He was able to answer that at once—he wouldn't live Miller's disordered life. Stein's implied offer was more tempting: use the time that wealth allowed him to read "ALL" literature in English, and finally re-create the language. If he could only combine it with publishing and skiing! "No artist needs criticism, he only needs appreciation. If he needs criticism he is no artist," Stein had written in *The Autobiography of Alice B. Toklas*, and this J quoted with approval in his Lausanne *cahier*: it was good advice for a future eclectic publisher as well as for a scholar or a critic or an artist. As for his own art, J stopped mentioning a novel about philistine Pittsburgh.

J met his mother and her "lady-in-waiting," as J called her, in Paris in June 1935 and brought them to Rapallo, where he quartered them in the Hotel Bristol, well upscale from the Albergo Rapallo, where he took a room for himself. Before departing for Venice, the Boss gave him the use of Dorothy's studio, she having left for England. J and his mother planned to stay in Rapallo through most of July, with his mother painting village scenes and J disciplining himself to arise at seven and work on his writing and to study conversational Italian again with Signorina Canessa. He wrote a review of "MURDER in the Kirch"—the Cathedral—as "Mr. Eliot on Holy Ground," in which J praised especially Eliot's "blending of Aristotelian tragedy and Christian Dogma." J was at some pains to analyze Eliot's verse. "There is no fixed metre," he concluded, "but there is metric, in the best sense. Mr. Eliot had been to school and knows his language-tones and sound-lengths as few others do. He can cut a line of sound in time so that it comes off the page to you as a tangible design." J posted a copy to Philip Mairet of *The New English Weekly*, who printed it in July: he was now a published author on both sides of the Atlantic. "As criticism from a literary rather than from a dramatic point of view I think it gave me more pleasure than any other I have had," Eliot wrote in gratitude to J.

Around this time J wrote to Robert Fitzgerald, "Gertrude told me quite candidly the other day for my own good that I was one of those guys who had mistaken sensitiveness for something more and that the sooner I jumped off the poetry boat the better I would later be at making steel." Then J added, "I guess she is about right."

J had doubts about not only his poetry but his fiction and his literary criticism. He had found himself unable to get into his novel or to complete to his satisfaction his monograph on Stein. Under the guise of writing about Stein, he had been probing his own suitability for and commitment to fiction and coming up short.

With his mother, Uncle Dicky, and Ezra urging him in that direction, J decided that it was time to return to Harvard. There is no evidence to corroborate J's story that Ezra had snuffed out his poetic aspirations in favor of publishing others' work. Years later J apparently concocted the story that Ezra had disparaged his poetic ambition and sent him in the direction of publishing, and this became the gospel of the New Directions creation myth. A variation on the theme appeared in J's short story "Melody with Fugue," written *before* J attended the Ezuversity. The story details the futile life of a professor of art, purged by the Nazis from his position and, even worse, in doubt of his calling. The "Herr Professor" nurses an old psychic wound, words spoken to him during his student days by a respected art teacher, words that "had so branded themselves into him": "*No, I am afraid there is no sign of genius, only facility, an aptitude.*" When he had gone back later to beg his teacher for some ray of hope, the old man had told him, "Yes . . . there is always work."

Ezra had made clear to him the difficulty such writers as Williams and himself had in finding good publishers, and he had impressed on J the lack of a "forum or vortex for active ideas." As Pound wrote to Bill Williams about J, "He had the sense to WANT to stay here/ I sez NO go bak be a man and TRY it/ try to see if anything can be did in the sloppy country." J said decades later, in an account that made no reference to the disparagement of his poetic talent, "The diploma from the 'Ezuversity' was Pound's commission to return to the United States and DO SOMETHING about the cultural situation at home." Certainly Pound had suggested what that something might be, including that J should "do something about getting Bill Williams into print," but Ezra managed to combine writing poetry with his own attempts to promote culture, and he would have expected J to do likewise. In 1973, J would tell an interviewer only that Pound had said that it was "time for me to go back to Harvard and do *something useful*. Being useful meant that I should publish books, because at that time publishing was still suffering from the Depression and none of his friends, except Hemingway, had steady publishers." Pound probably did say that if J could learn "to print books right side up"—this has the ring of Ezra—he could become his American publisher, and he would write to his friends and tell them to send manuscripts to "this worthy young man." The conventional story, that Pound had badgered J into entering publishing because he could not otherwise get published, is simply not true, but he knew from experience that there was a definite need in America for a small press that would not be commercially driven. No substantial firm could be counted on to take avant-garde writing, which J would invariably insist on calling by the more American "advance guard."

There was also something ingrained in J that went back well before his meetings with Pound: the obligation to do *useful work*. This he certainly did not get from his father. In J's case it was genetic, ancestral, and also learned. His dear father seemed to do exactly whatever he desired, yet he was clearly unhappy, and crazy to boot. The Protestant ethic might have bypassed H. Hughart, but it had landed squarely on his younger son.

For the rest of his long life J would worry over the Pounds as if they were family. But even as a young man in the 1930s, he saw Ezra entire: vain *and* humble, clear-sighted *yet* prejudiced, "a genius and in some ways a simpleton," patient *and* rash, "an exceptionally good poet and an exceptionally bad diplomat." Mostly, however, J stressed his kindness and his "peculiar gentleness"; he was "hopelessly generous" with his time and, when he had any, his money; "his heart is too good for his own good." Nothing J said or wrote about Pound, beyond the oft-repeated "You're never gonna be any good as a poet," suggests that Ezra was likely thus brusquely to have dismissed someone he too saw as part of his family and someone whose poetry he would continue to hold in regard.

It was on this Rapallo sojourn that J met the German Jewish sculptor Heinz Winterfeld Klussmann, who worked under the pseudonym Heinz Henghes. A year earlier, he had walked most of the way from Hamburg to ask Pound's advice and to see his Gaudier-Brzeska sculptures. Henghes had picked up some pieces of soft slate in the streams as he traveled and with his penknife had carved two birds in flight. From these Pound recognized his talent. With his characteristic generosity, Ezra fed him, bedded him temporarily, borrowed tools, and provided the block of stone from which Henghes carved a rider on a kneeling horse. At Pound's urging, the wife of the head of Fiat bought the statue, and Henghes's career was launched. Ezra had written him into Canto 35 in "The tale of the perfect schnorrer [panhandler]": "a peautiful chewisch poy / wit a vo-ice dot woult / meldt dh heart offa schtone." The story does not end there, for the sketch made for the sculpture would evolve into the future New Directions colophon. But not before J had copied the Henghes drawing as a cover for his review of Eliot's *Murder in the Cathedral*. J bound a typed copy with thread and dedicated it to his father as a "Birthday Fugue."

The wonder was that J was getting any writing done. "Boss, do you know that big beautiful blonde with ten foot boobs that lives in the town?" J complained to Ezra. "Jeez, it is awful, she is taking my mind off my work." Then, five days later: "I don't get very au pres de ma blonde as MADRE sua is always on hand." They had met at a railway crossing, and Lola Avena

was wearing a checked skirt and a "tight white / sweater with nothing on
under it." At this point the seduction was mainly in J's imagination. His
clipped summation to Ezra stated bluntly, "[A]upres de ma blonde/ but
proper, oh very/ ie. no ring/ no cherry!"

So, it was with something like relief that J drove his mother back to
Lausanne and Mlle Marie-Thérèse. Soon Marjory Laughlin departed by
train to Freiburg to visit a Chandler cousin, where J would pick her up days
later. On his way to Freiburg, J visited Stein once again at Bilignin. Not
suspecting J's defection to Pound's orbit, Stein encouraged him to see her
new friend Thornton Wilder while he was in Salzburg. J did not. To Wilder,
Stein described J as "another literary white hope for us." Below the snow-
and-ice line the flowers of summer were open, and he hiked to a meadow
north of Innsbruck with a girl and read to her D. H. Lawrence's lovely
poem "Bavarian Gentians." Later J would write in a poem of his own,

```
You picked a gentian
that day we spent in


the alpine meadow above
Mittenwald and with a


kiss pressed it into
the pages of the book.
```

J lost the flower, but kept the memory.

J had encouraged Ezra and Olga to make a trip to Salzburg, promising
to drive them on to Venice. J's classmate Jim Slocum joined the party—
gifted, athletic, with the features of a matinee idol and the air of having
skipped youth and vaulted into confident manhood. On the way they
paused at Gais in the Italian Tirol to pick up Ezra and Olga's daughter,
Mary Rudge. Mary, aged ten, remembered "the tallest young man in company of the handsomest young man anyone had ever seen." In Venice a
sumptuous breakfast was prepared at Olga's house by a hired cook. Ezra
and Olga presided like the king and queen in *The Rose and the Ring*,
Mary thought, while she cast herself in the role of Angelica, with the tall
young man as Prince Bulbo, her *principe azzurro*.

By August 22, J was in Paris for a good first meeting with Henry Miller.

Two days later he and his mother were aboard the *Statendam*, again, for a quick passage to New York. It had been a glorious time, filled with Ezra's conversation, great skiing, beautiful women, and plans for writing and publishing. Only J's actual writing had fallen far short of his dreams. To judge from his letter to Ezra from the ship, J appeared to be smitten with culture shock. "CHRIST," he exploded. "Already in USA—these marvellous silken legs, legs that make you wince with lust—and on top the assinine [*sic*] blank faces & the whine-whine-whine of their prattling voices." He was resigned to Harvard: "I goes back ready to KICK & BITE thanks to you." He compared Mary to the young American women on board: "Boss, keep that fine gal you got pure of her fatherland! At age 9 [*sic*] she is worth any 9 debutantes on this boat—as to brains & physical grace!"

And so J sailed away from the Ezuversity, carrying with him plenty of advice on writing and publishing, Ezra's benediction, and his British Museum library reading card.

7

New Directions:
From Poet to Publisher

I would sing the American people,

God send them some civilization.

—Ezra Pound, "Redondillas"

J's first priority upon returning to the United States in 1935 was to see Gorham Munson. "He is a very nice chewish chennlmn inteet," J reported to Ezra. "I would trust him about down to the corner in [*sic*] back but not with a nickel." Munson told J that his funding would just about carry *New Democracy* through the following August. They agreed that J would collect material, mainly poetry for a regular column, which Munson would like to see become "the lit'r'y renascence accompanying S[ocial] C[redit]." Munson did not by any means demand that the poetry be strictly utilitarian. J came up with the heading "New Directions," and his section would feature poetry and reviews. Munson wanted J to focus on "New Forms," and he maintained that Social Credit was "the partial manifestation of a renaissance of all creative thought." J found this "a bit thick for me to swallow," but he was willing to mute his skepticism since he *did* want to print new writing. And he joined the American Social Credit Party. It was the contributions from Pound, moreover, that tended to suit the predilections of both Munson and J, in economics and advance-guard writing, respectively. For the short essay "Who Gets It?" J felt that a preface was needed to explain Ezra's method. "Pound has never been able to write a polite essay, probably because he has always had too much to say," J began, "his didactic technic, his 'blasts'—a new direction in English prose. Nothing in it is accidental. The staccato paragraphing, the rough diction, the sound effects, the distorted spelling, the typographic stunts, the anecdotes & allusions, the shouting & swearing are all there for a purpose: to shatter the reader's mental slumber and make him absorb the content." Within a month after the beginning of the fall term, J had already scouted an assortment of material, including "Five Choruses from a Paraphrase of the *Alcestis* of Euripides," a collaborative free verse translation by Fitts and Robert Fitzgerald.

After seeing Munson, J called on William Carlos Williams. The sign at 9 Ridge Road in Rutherford said simply, "W. C. Williams, MD. Please ring bell." The two-story clapboard house was painted an unappetizing dull mustard yellow. Floss Williams opened the door: "You're Jimmy Laughlin. Do come in!" The doctor was seeing a patient, but J was expected. J took in the plain room, the rather shabby furniture. But the modernist paintings! Three Charles Demuths; several paintings by Marsden Hartley; a Charles Sheeler rendering of tulips. Dr. Williams's patients were primarily the Rutherford poor, who often could not pay him: these paintings were gifts from the artists. The tremendous openness of Williams's personality led J to call him "a noncutaneous / Man. No skin separated him from / Others." Williams made him feel instantly accepted as a friend. They spoke about Pound, of course: "What was the old / Nut up to now?" Williams wanted to know. They had a "grand talk," J wrote to Ezra. "He certainly is the goods." J was particularly taken with what he had to say about friendship, especially his with Ezra: "He said, hell what can you do with a friend? You can't fuck him and you can't give him anything, you have just got to have him." Soon the conversation shifted to Williams's difficulties, how he had had to subsidize the publication of his first five books, how he had searched for three years before his friend Zukofsky had agreed to publish his *Collected Poems, 1921–1931*. J asked Williams for advice on the literary column that J was planning for *New Democracy*, "stuff that busts away and shimmies," including "some of your poems." J promised "a little money for the poets, out of my fund, since Munson is broke."

Other visits followed, and Williams walked with J up the hill behind his house, gesturing toward the skyscrapers of Manhattan rising "like / White flowers through the haze" beyond the wetlands of New Jersey. As a young doctor, he had thought of seeking a practice in the metropolis, close to Greenwich Village. But the city, Williams realized, was a "menacing illusion," and his *locus mirabilis* lay in Rutherford and Paterson, among the poor factory workers and along the stinking Passaic River. Williams wrote when he awoke in the night, using time wrenched from sleep. Here was a pattern for J to adopt: to write was a holy thing, but his "work" would be publishing, that vital bridge between the writer and the reader.

Ezra had encouraged J to begin his independent publishing with what would become the first of his annual anthologies, with which J hoped to attract readers to the new in writing. Quick to act on an idea, Pound sent J a list of twenty-five names and addresses, headed, "If you really start/ notice shd/ be sent to." This list included not only such writers as Mary Barnard, Basil Bunting, Hugh MacDiarmid, MacLeish, Oppen, Rakosi, Williams, and Zukofsky but also many who Ezra felt would be useful in publicizing the venture. J outlined his plan to Aunt Leila and Uncle Dicky, who responded with enthusiasm, doubtless thinking that such a substantial occupation as publishing would curb their nephew's wandering tendencies. A press needed an address other than a mere room in Cambridge or Norfolk, and Aunt Leila offered J the White Cottage. It fronted on Mountain Road and was a minute's walk from Robin Hill. Norfolk made a certain sense: it was almost midway between the major publishing centers of New York and Boston, about a three-hour drive to either. J *did* feel great affection for his aunt and uncle, but he was also keenly aware of the practical advantages of the association: free room and board and a source of "loans."

J continued to send Ezra his own verse, hearing from him in longhand in September that "Grandfarver's head is O. K. let it be printed," adding, "Waaal, yuh better come to Venezia and continue the convursashun. or mebbe I can find a wypetriter." Ezra had gone relatively silent: "Dear Jas/ been too busy to write. All out to prevent the British bastids from making it into a European war. Never have they been so rancid." Ezra saw the colonial ambitions of Britain as the greatest threat to world peace, with Communist Russia coming in a close second. At the bottom of it all was the international banking system, centered on England. War led to debt. Here was encapsulated the heart of Pound's theory of the great economic conspiracy: the banking system of the West was geared to debt and interest, and *usura* was the key to its enormous profits. Ezra told J, "The vice regent of the Americ Academy showed me a clippin that said you wuz my sekkertary. I think you cd. sue 'em fer libel on THAT. sekkertary indeed. !!"

Pound did feel overworked: "I ought to have a HELPer/ but you are more use where you are." In his mind this usefulness ranged from placing reviews of books on economics in *New Democracy*, to responding to attacks on his books, to visiting senators and tracking down economists. Ezra continued to approve of Mussolini, but he was wary of Hitler: "Adolph is NOT the woild's Ideal." Ezra began to refer to J's column as "NUDE dye Rectum or the blew behinded barBoon." For Ezra "nude" had become a code word for the bare, unvarnished truth, for the newly created, in this case his contemporary but still unpublished "NUDE canto on USURA," Canto 45, and not merely—although it was also that—irresistible naughty wordplay. "With usura hath no man a house of good stone," Ezra wrote, "each block cut smooth and well fitting / . . . / Usura rusteth the chisel / It rusteth the craft and the craftsman." War meant waste. A tank was not like a tractor that plowed usefully for many years. This was the engine that drove Ezra: he must reveal, educate, warn.

Ezra also urged J to visit Marianne Moore, "the achieved Eliotic poetessa." "A remarkable experience," J said after his trek to Brooklyn, "I have never seen anything like that . . . MaryAnn [*sic*] conversed for two hours, while feeding me orange juice and turkey sandwiches. I have never seen anyone with so much integrity about details . . . Life under magnifying glass. Each little detail of conduct and emotion weighed and weighed. Very educative. She promised to scurry up some good chickens for the ND[*emocracy*]."

J plunged into the sphere of economic reform, opening his first column on November 1, 1935, with an editorial purporting to link Social Credit monetary theory with avant-garde art. J wrote, "The great new direction is, of course, Social Credit, with its changed conception of the means, and the ends, of life." When a painting by Matisse or a tone poem by Stravinsky or verse by Eliot was ridiculed, the freedom of the artist was curtailed. Art and economics responded to the same principles. What was needed was "a renaissance of the principle of liberty." To promote this universal need, his column would "seek to give its readers a picture of what is most vital in the writing of today, of the literature which reflects, though it may not propagandize, the spirit underlying Social Credit . . . the living work of our time *when* it is written, not years later when it has become the fashion." His first offering was William Carlos Williams's "New Direction in the Novel," a laudatory review of John Hargrave's Social Credit fiction *Summer Time Ends*. J identified Williams only as "a great American writer," a judgment that very few apart from Ezra would have then agreed with.

New Democracy turned out to be a valuable launching pad for J's future publishing house. The appearance of two poems, "Rannoch, by Glencoe" and "Cape Ann," contributed by T. S. Eliot simply to encourage the young literary editor, helped give J's column credibility, as he told Eliot. "I wish I thought you wanted my work because you liked it," Eliot told J, "but I am used to people wanting to print work of mine that they don't like merely because I am (as you say) Mr. Eliot of Russell Square." "Don't say things like that crack about Mr. E of R S, because they embarrass me," J scolded, repeating his praise of Eliot's "metric" and "craftsmanship." A new tone came into their correspondence, an element of tease on both sides. Marianne Moore posted J a fine poem and recommended Elizabeth Bishop to him. On Moore's urging, Bishop sent three poems for Munson's journal. Both women would appear in J's first anthology once he got his press going, as would Barnard, Kay Boyle, Emanuel Carnevali, Cummings, Barbara Deming, Fitts, Henry Miller, Lorine Niedecker, Pound, Emma Swan, Vail, and Williams, all contributors to J's column. Pound's Canto 46 would be published in the March 1936 issue of *New Democracy*.

J finally had to put in an appearance at Harvard, complaining vigorously. "It is just awful to be back in this dump, it's just plum awful," he wrote to the head of the Ezuversity. "Eliot House is the same," he wrote to onetime resident T. S. Eliot, "like a birdcage with the cat inside." To sweeten his resumption of his studies, his parents gave him a new Buick.

The September 1935 issue of the *Advocate* rattled considerable teacups. It contained Pound on "the nature of religion," Henry Miller's "Glittering Pie," and J's "A Natural History," a prose excerpt from what he claimed was his novel in progress, "O Beautiful for Spacious Skies." J's first-person narrator, from a self-satisfied ex parte stance, describes a raw scene in which he, Gussy, Hank, Georgia, and Helena drink nearly to oblivion and then drive through a black neighborhood, "plipping" the locals with turtle eggs. "Your piece had at least the excuse of being well-written," wrote Fitts in qualified approval, "although I thought it was all pretty early Hemingway-cum-Faulkner." The Miller he condemned outright as "boarding-school-can trash," invoking Stein: "Gert said that you can always tell from the way a man writes if he is physically, as well as emotionally, impotent. I shd say that particular comrade is both."

Three weeks after the issue hit the newsstands, Chief Timothy Leahy sent the Cambridge police to seize the remaining stock. Bootleg copies went for a dollar instead of the usual thirty-five cents. Five senior staff members, including Jim Slocum but not J, were told to resign their positions, although they were to be allowed to continue to work on the magazine. The assistant district attorney, Frank Volpe, missing J's obvious scorn of his callow subjects, ranted at length about the "crudely written, maudlin" stories, "the product of youths who have made up for a deficiency in experience . . . by too close a study of subjects which were never prescribed by Harvard." Precisely what J so urgently wanted were experiences and subjects that went beyond Harvard's tidy offerings.

J defended his story to *The Bulletin Index* of his hometown: "A Natural History is not obscene. A naturalistic account of common Americans in the American language. A sort of sociological document in fiction form." The event made the Cambridge and Pittsburgh papers, the *Herald Tribune*, the New York *Sun*, and even *The New York Times*. Reached for comment at his office at Jones & Laughlin, Hugh came to his brother's defense: "It's not so bad, is it?" Henry Miller was barely mentioned—leaving J as the principal and unrepentant offender, "dillettantish" and "frail, myopic, uncommunicative" or "serious, gifted," depending on the bias of the journalist. He survived on the staff as the Pegasus, the literary editor, but the affair had been an object lesson in the cost of offending upholders of the status quo.

While the excitement over the *Advocate* was going on, J's father drove to Cambridge, traveling with a companion found for him by his wife. It was around the time of his twenty-first birthday, but J seems not to have anticipated what would transpire. Hughart took his son to a broker and signed over to him securities valued at approximately $100,000—not far south of $2 million in 2014 dollars. J was to use the income to pay for his Harvard education. The dividends came to about $6,000 per annum, three times his college expenses. "He said that this was not my money," J would claim scores of years later, "that I had done nothing to earn it, that it was given in trust to me and that I must use it to help people." Given the deflated economy of the time, J's stock portfolio represented considerable capital, and whatever his father did or did not tell him about helping others, J evidently resolved *at the time* to preserve the *capital* intact: he would not dip into it for personal extravagances or publishing expenses.

Immediately, J began to make specific plans for publishing. He decided to produce an annual anthology of contemporary writing to fill the need that he had discussed with Pound. He proposed to call the collection "New Directions 1936." He would bind it in hard covers and market it as a book. He set out to write to those authors originally suggested by Pound, as well as some of his own choosing. Of those he contacted, all but six sent or allowed publication of material, much of which had already appeared in J's column in *New Democracy*.

J led a busy life off campus. He drove to Wallingford to go over with Fitts the proofs of his poems for the next issue of *New Democracy*. He took the train to New York for editing sessions with Munson and for dinner with the Hilaire Hilers and Robert McAlmon. One evening he motored to Bennington, where he spent the night "conversing with all the 'cuties' and incipient minds." "They are all crazy up there," said the young aesthete, "but very diverting."

"I have a new direction and an increased confidence," J told Aunt Leila. His letters to her were filled with phrases about "the new power and harmony," knowing where his dear aunt stood on the "directed mind." With his aunt's encouragement, he traveled to New York most Thursdays after his classes for tutorials in thought power with Mrs. Ottarson, followed by dancing lessons, and sometimes he flew in a Boston–New York–Hartford–Boston pattern. He had been elected to the Signet Society and ate lunch at the arts and literature club daily. J found "great pleasure" in it, although his description to his mother was more than a little tongue-in-cheek: "The feeling of satisfaction and snobbery is delightful. The boys are quite dull, but they are Boston & New York's best, so I just play dead too and bask in the pompous reflection of Coolidges, Lowells, and one fat Rockefeller."

J acted in the Eliot House Christmas play, which his father came to watch. Hughart had recently returned to Pittsburgh, where he had gone to court to dissolve the guardianship under which he had been restrained. He was "still very shy about his family," blaming his relatives even more than his wife for his enforced confinements, but he felt that J was on his side.

Aunt Leila assembled various Laughlins for Christmas at Robin Hill.

It was wonderful, J said, to see his father once more happy in the family circle, but on the twenty-sixth J left for Jackson, New Hampshire, and some very intensive skiing. He hoped that he could earn a place on the newly accredited Harvard ski team, and soon after New Year's Day he went to Mount Washington for a set of trial races. During the very first race on the narrow tree-lined Sherburne Trail, he took a turn too wide and skied into a tree. "It hurt like all hell and I hollered accordingly," J wrote. His extremities began to go numb, a ranger injected morphine, and he was given the full rescue treatment, down the slope on a stretcher-toboggan. His father, reached in Boston by one of J's friends, hired a car and arrived within seven hours; the next day he wrote to his wife a detailed account of the accident and of J's injuries. Hughart announced himself fully satisfied with the local doctor, experienced in orthopedic trauma, and his rational letter does not support J's later recollection that his father had been, "of course, in a fit." He had moved into a neighboring room in the hospital so as to "keep the boy company."

Soon it turned out that the early assessment of J's injuries had been overly optimistic, as further X-rays showed a crack in the second lumbar vertebra. He would have to spend weeks prone. J was "considerably upset and disappointed" at this news. Hughart had J moved by ambulance to the Brookline Brooks Hospital near Harvard, where a distinguished orthopedic specialist "swaddled" him for two months in a body cast. J had sheared off three "lateral processes (vestigial ribs)" belonging to vertebrae below the rib section, and a corner of one vertebra had broken off on impact. "Don't let them vertebs/ git to settin solid," Ezra advised, "a li'l mASSage . . . to keep you from havin ONE vert/ instead of three when you EEEmerge." Ezra would be proved right: the muscles welded to the processes of the spine deteriorated, atrophied. For the rest of his life J would blame his weakened back on a treatment that had stressed immobility and rest rather than therapy.

The mishap was a good thing for New Directions: with J laid up, he could better concentrate on his editing and publishing responsibilities. He also planned to resume his monograph on Stein. "Ezra thinks I'm a damn fool to fuss over the 'ole tub of guts,'" J wrote to Eliot, "but I must work out my ideas about the nature and habits of language before I can get on to anything else." Eliot sided with Ezra on Stein, stating to J, "but it is up to you to prove to us that we are wrong." J took full advantage of his condition in his dealings with Harvard, in March requesting an extension of his leave of absence.

Still, it was extremely aggravating for J to be hors de combat at such an exciting juncture in American skiing. The first National Downhill and Slalom Championships had been held in 1935 on Mount Rainier, and while an Austrian had won in the open category, the amateur combined trophy had been captured by a young man from Florida, Dick Durrance.

While J was still in the hospital, a bulletin arrived from Boss Pound. Now that his protégé was well launched in the *New Democracy* column, Ezra gave him some good advice: "No real literature will come out of people who are trying to preserve a blind spot. That goes equally for ivory tower aesthetes, anti-propagandists, and communists who refuse to think." He continued, "I suggest, in order not to over balance yr/ pages with EZ/ you take to using a brief like the above in most issues, in black letter if you think advisable." Ezra might want a megaphone, but he made it clear to J that he did not expect exclusivity. Then he entrusted to J negotiations on his behalf with U.S. literary agents. Ezra wanted a personal shove behind his new essays on war and economics, which he hoped to place in the mainstream press. Before long J was acting as Pound's agent and billing him, on Ezra's insistence, for services rendered. Thus began a practice, functioning as agent for certain authors, that J would follow once he became established as a publisher. Pound remained adamant about not sponging off J and tore in two J's latest check, for reprinting a canto, dictating its circular course on the back. In America, only *Esquire* and *New Democracy* would take Ezra's writings on economics, and he asked J to find out where else he could place work for some remuneration. Then, in February, J wrote to Eliot that he was founding a publishing company, both because Ezra had suggested it and because, after Eliot's appearance in the *New Democracy* literary section, poets had begun to send him their best work.

Another principle that J already felt strongly about was the payment of permissions fees for quotations: no charge if for scholarly publications— this came under the rubric of intellectual freedom in his mind—but a substantial charge for anthology or other profitable publications. J himself refused to pay quotation use fees for noncommercial articles that he wrote.

On March 8, J was allowed out of the hospital to go to his father's club for oysters, lobster, and chocolate ice cream. Two days later he moved back across the Charles and resumed boning up on his Latin for the April makeup exams. In addition, he had found good company, a "pretty, charming, & intelygent" Jewish girl. "Her papa is mfr. of whiskies in Kansas," he told Ezra. "Little Esther knows all about Dryden & what Rev. Eliot says about Dryden etc. Also other oriental aptitudes, not common to the species Debutans Bostensis." Clearly, the Hero was coming back to life. "Cant have you espousin no jews," admonished Ezra. "I'se a gwine with her on Monday to Passover and then I quits," J replied.

J became reconnected to family gossip. The most startling rumor was that Uncle Jim had not in fact committed suicide but been shot by his strawberry-blonde wife during a quarrel. Theirs had been a stormy marriage—in fact, multiple marriages, for they had been divorced from and remarried to each other three times. "It was arranged with the coroner that it was an accident," wrote J many years later. Uncle Jim had manifested various symptoms of bipolar mania, further reason for J's apprehension over his own genetic time bomb.

J passed his makeup exams, moved into his old room at Robin Hill, and set out to resume his novel and to put together his first anthology. By July he was sending batches of anthology material to the Otter Valley Press in Brandon, Vermont. The press was the printer for *The Harvard Advocate*, and J had simply asked, "Can you print a book for me?" to which the shop foreman replied, "Sure." With much on his mind, J escaped on a quick trip to Mexico and Cuba with his brother. He sent off a postcard in dubious Italian to Mary Rudge in Gais: "Salute del amico Jas che se trova in Mexico. E une paese molto strano ed interessante. E indata à Venezia quest' anno? Ricorda nostri bagni?"—Greetings from friend Jas who finds himself in Mexico. It is a country very strange and interesting. Are you going to Venice this year? Do you remember our swim?

Back in Norfolk, J worked on the proofs for the anthology, now titled *New Directions in Prose and Poetry*. He sent off the page proofs and wrote the same day to Frances Steloff. "The anthology has been a long time getting itself printed," he told her. "We were held up by Messers Fitts & jolas [*sic*], who took god knows how long to get around to mailing in their stuff." J was amused at being on the other side, in a position to scold his old teacher. He met with Eugene Jolas of *transition* as a diplomatic gesture, aware that the New Directions anthology would be "muscling in on his territory."

Neither Jolas nor his wife made a good impression on J: Eugene he thought "a FAKE, and I say to hell with him. Talking three languages at once." And his "Dam big fat fool of a wife," Maria. Nonetheless, J would dedicate this first anthology to *transition* for having begun the "revolution of the word" with Jolas's manifesto of 1929. Jolas spanned the arts from literature to sculpture and the cinema, and he had a strong messianic impulse: the arts needed to be urged on, and he extravagantly committed his resources and intellect toward this end. J aspired to many of the same goals.

J launched New Directions by publishing Wayne Andrews's *Pianos of Sympathy*, written under the pseudonym Montagu O'Reilly, a jeu d'esprit, a zany flight into the fetishism of hair and pianos, which J thought a "delightful tale." It was to be the first of a series of New Directions pamphlets, which would become one of J's favorite formats for highlighting the work of a writer. A mere sixteen pages in chaste blue paper covers, this booklet was labeled "New Directions Pamphlet No. 1" and sold for fifty cents, at the time a high cost per page, but low for a hand-set volume. In a brief foreword, J proclaimed O'Reilly "the first American Surrealist writer" and his book a "fusion of this world and the next—the *other* world, super-real and dream-deep, which Breton and Dalí have vowed to release."

Andrews became important to his publishing friend more than merely as an author: it was through him that J later met Paul Éluard and André Breton, both of whom he would publish; and it was Andrews who directed him to the French novelist Raymond Queneau, a brilliant language innovator who would come to be called the French Joyce. Andrews was far more deeply immersed than J in French literature, especially in surrealism and the avant-garde. At seventeen he had co-founded a revue, written in French. Andrews was a strange amalgam of a Pierrot harking back to the French Decadence and of Chicago Episcopalian respectability: oval-faced and cheerful, he delighted in an outwardly respectable pose and conservative blue suits, which he then insulted with outrageous cravats. The curtains in his room were Mephistophelean black, and at least once, with his friend Lord Melcarth, he rented seventeenth-century theatrical garb and was served a candlelit dinner in Harvard's Dunster House dining room. The piano was an iconic instrument for Andrews, and on one occasion he incited J and several others—all of them drunk—to beat a piano with rolled-up copies of the *Boston Transcript*.

J printed up "Pianos Cards" to announce the pamphlet, and he sent either these cards or the booklet itself to a long random list of family, friends, and authors he wanted to impress—"Kreymbourg, June, Aunt Jane, Josephine, Mother, Mencken, Pulitzer, Pierre Matisse"—and even to his enemy on the faculty, the poet and critic Robert Hillyer. Zukofsky copied out for J ninety-nine addresses that he had used for his Objectivist Press mailings. Frances Steloff took twenty *Pianos of Sympathy* on consignment for the Gotham Book Mart.

J spent most of September writing articles and reviews for several journals and performing the final tasks on the anthology that would really launch him as a publisher. Sitting in a shoreside cottage at Hancock Point near Bar Harbor, Maine, in September 1936, he drafted an editor's preface, stating that while in preparing his *New Democracy* column he had assumed that the "emphasis of leadership" should be on the economist, he now realized that it was "the poet—the word-worker" who must instead take the lead. If the "paradox of poverty amid plenty" was to be rendered null and economic justice was to be achieved, new thinking was necessary. The key to the required new thinking depends on clarity of language, and "only the writer is in a position to fit the key into the lock and turn it," J wrote. Shaping Shelley's phrase to fit his purpose, J aimed to erase the "*un-*" and make the poet the *acknowledged* legislator of the world. J's preface was directed primarily against the decay of language, the same decay, he said, that had catalyzed Gertrude Stein in her "lonely and valourous [*sic*] career." J's were the words of an idealist, a romantic, and a very young spirit urged on by the incendiary exhortations of Pound. Following Plato and anticipating *1984*, J declared, "Language controls thought."

J designed the first *New Directions in Prose and Poetry* anthology himself. A bold yellow dust wrapper was slashed across with a broad red band, proclaiming, "Indirect Criticism / American Surrealism / Dream Writing." The names of the contributors, listed in alphabetical order, bordered the red band. At the end there were twelve pages advertising publishers and titles. The title page bore the imprint NEW DIRECTIONS / NORFOLK, CT. / 1936.

The anthology of 208 pages was published on November 16, 1936. J paid $396 to print and bind 513 copies, two-fifths in boards, three-fifths in wrappers, priced at $2 each. J's pricing was competitive for quality literature: Random House was offering Faulkner's *Absalom, Absalom!* at $2.50. Although he would later describe his anthology as "an exhibition gallery" for "untested" writers, he was glad to have many seasoned authors, especially his favorites among the modernists. Many of the writers were hardly new to the literati: Pound's first book had appeared in 1908, Stein's and Williams's in 1909. The table of contents included many significant names: Pound—of course!—Bishop, Kay Boyle, Cocteau, Cummings, Fitts, Jolas, Henry Miller, Marianne Moore, Stein, Stevens, Williams, Zukofsky. Many of these fit the Steinian mandate to push out the frontiers of language, but others cannot really be called experimental. They appeared simply because J liked them and their work and ideas. J's sometimes arbitrary but always distinctly personal predilections would define "the New Directions book" for the rest of his life. Most of his contributors might not be untried authors, but all were finding it difficult to gain acceptance, at least for their poetry. Boyle, for instance, had published five novels, as well as a number of short stories in *Harper's Bazaar*, *The New Yorker*, and *Vanity Fair*, but never a volume of verse. Eliot was not represented in the first anthology: J had requested work from him, but Eliot, never prolific, apparently did not have anything new that he wanted to send. J originally planned to reprint several of his poems, but when Harcourt, Brace, Eliot's publishers, demanded $10 for reprint rights, J left them out: he was not paying any of the contributors, and he did not feel that he should make an exception for Eliot.

J knew very little about the mechanics of publishing, and the first of what was to be a long line of annual and sometimes biannual anthologies appeared without pagination—J said later that he simply had not realized that a publisher had to instruct the printer to include page numbers—yet he was hardly concerned: the next two issues would also be unpaginated. Most of the copies of the anthology were distributed, through either sales or free copies sent to contributors, friends, and those J thought sufficiently influential. "Didn't quite pay its way," he said blandly.

In vowing to dedicate his resources to promoting literature, J, while by no means turning his back on social credit, had arrived at a watershed in his emphasis: increasingly, he would pursue art over economics, culture over politics. "My own political activity reached its peak when I was in my twenties," he would recall thirty-four years later. Now, however, he was able to perform an editorial and financial good turn for Pound, by cutting in half his article on the Jefferson-Adams correspondence and selling it to

The North American Review for $175. Ezra saw this as a promising new opening in America, but J cautioned him against trying to use the *Review* "as a flagstaff." John Pell, the editor, was rich, "a society boy from Long Island" who wanted "a nice slick quarterly full of bright ideas, that means half-baked, hair-oil ideas." Ezra should let "Jas or somebody who knows how to squirt hair-oil" rewrite the articles for Pell and take his money. J did not believe that Ezra understood what the country had become: "You see Boss, America is not like what you think it is. There is nobody here who is interested in taking life as seriously as you do."

In the publishing world, a rational glance at the state of American letters and poetry in 1936 should have been enough to discourage even James Laughlin. The 1929 crash and its aftermath had effectively ended many magazines, including *Direction, The Little Review*, and *New Act*, although *New Masses* and Harriet Monroe's *Poetry* still survived, while *Pagany* started up in 1930. The last page of the Gotham Book Mart catalog for 1936 listed twenty-eight periodicals under the ominous heading "Dead Little Mags." The majority were American.

In the midst of this desert J envisioned an oasis, shimmering like a mirage but capable of taking on a real shape, if only he could provide a focus and an outlet for all the talent that he knew was available and persuade readers—who must surely crave it—to buy this nourishment. From the first, he saw New Directions as being in league with, and a natural extension of, the little magazines. J hoped that writers would flow from the little magazines to him, and in the early years New Directions would share with *New Masses* Kenneth Patchen, Muriel Rukeyser, Federico García Lorca, William Saroyan, and William Carlos Williams. What J wanted was something as flexible and as immediate as the little magazines but of such solid weight that it could not be ignored.

If J was concerned that the omens were not positive for a publishing venture specializing in unsalable poetry and experimental prose, he did not express his doubts. The Depression still gripped the world, and nearly everyone conceded that a European war was imminent. J was more immediately concerned with the problems of production and sales. He felt that he could handle the American side with sporadic cross-country trips and personal appeals. Europe was different. Sylvia Beach in Paris was sympathetic, but she warned him that Shakespeare and Company could take only a few copies of *New Directions in Prose and Poetry*: her main customer base, the American and English expatriate intellectuals, had largely departed, and the French were poor, rarely willing to pay as much as a dollar for a book.

The New York Times listed NDPP 1936 under a "Latest Books Received" header as "edited by James Laughlin IV" and described it accurately as "selections from contemporary literature." The fact that the anthology was produced as a hardbound book with quality paper, quality print, and quality binding gave it an impressive appearance and implied a claim to permanency that critics were not yet willing to grant to many of the avant-garde writers who appeared in it. This permanency was precisely what J intended to suggest. And libraries usually bought books only in hard covers. Harking back to Pound's dictum that it might take twenty years for a truly advanced writer to win acceptance, J wanted his anthology to be solid enough to survive for at least that many years. The anthology pointed the way for the New Directions press itself. J included a representation of women generous for the period, one third of the total, and in his inclusion of Carnevali and of Cocteau's essay on de Chirico, "Le mystère laïc," rendered into English by Olga Rudge, he initiated his lifelong commitment to publishing foreign authors in translation.

J obviously hoped for eventual acceptance as a writer himself. He printed his own work, listing his name as an author on the cover. Clearly, he was not about to give up on poetry, whatever Pound and Stein might or might not have told him. And he slipped in a piece of Jabberwocky by Tasilo Ribischka, variously identified in the "Notes on Contributors" of later issues as a "night watchman at an industrial plant" and a "gradecrossing keeper in Melrose." Ribischka was J himself, writing under the first of several pseudonyms, here, a name that he had already used in his short story "Partial Eclipse." Under his own name J included some poems and "A Natural History," the novel fragment that had appeared in the banned issue of the Advocate.

For publicity, J sent out a bright orange circular, crudely printed, proclaiming, "If you are one of a growing number of cultivated readers . . . if you resent the commercialism that promotes 'bestsellers' at the expense of fine writing and poetry . . . if you are this kind of reader, the really intelligent reader, New Directions will interest you." It was an astutely crafted appeal, aimed at the reader with aspirations to culture and a touch of snobbery—not altogether different from the young publisher himself. He had a letterhead printed that stated, in cap sans serifs, "**NEW DIRECTIONS** / NORFOLK, CONN. / JAMES LAUGHLIN IV, EDITOR."

Pound and Williams were jointly, as J realized, the backbone of the embryonic New Directions. It was a brilliant choice of mentors, poets who would eventually be recognized as *the* seminal figures of literary modernism by legions of poets yet unborn. The two writers, in addition to having been friends since 1902, complemented each other. Pound was fiercely cosmopolitan, broadly if erratically polymath, and opinionated. Williams was obstinately American, by no means narrowly educated, and imbued with a scientist's skepticism, and he too was opinionated. Both men suffered from a fault in judgment that Williams's biographer Reed Whittemore referred to as his "inveterate gift for impropriety." Ezra was even more gifted in impropriety, in intemperate and provocative speech. He led J in the direction of European and Oriental literature and Social Credit economics. Williams never ceased to argue for American diction and verse forms, repudiating "English" literature from Shakespeare on, rejecting all that Ezra's friend Eliot stood for in *The Waste Land* with its many allusions to European culture. In Ezra, J found ample inspiration for breadth of scope, for vision. But it would be to Williams more than to Pound that J would turn for models for his own poetry. Like Ezra, J enjoyed the allusive, yet like Williams's, his poetry would become ever more firmly grounded in the mundane image.

With the anthology almost out, J wrote to Williams offering to undertake the novel that its author had been hawking about in vain. Williams's reply was addressed to "Dear God." "You mention, casually, that you are willing to publish my *White Mule*," Williams began. J would pay the costs, and they were to "share, if any, the profits!" The doctor continued euphorically, "My God! It must be that you are so tall that separate clouds circle around that head." He expressed his delight to Ezra—"It sure was a bolt out of the blue of almost despair"—and vowed to rewrite the final chapters "to make this a definite Book . . . It's put ten years on my life." "It does me good to see how happy the Doc is about it," J wrote to Ezra. "Every bastard kike in NYC turned it down like they did the MUTTjeff," Pound's *Jefferson and/or Mussolini*.

J's anti-Semitic remarks were confined largely to his early letters to Ezra, with occasional sallies to the family: more than most, he was a chameleon in correspondence and played to the prejudices of his recipients.

William Carlos Williams was one of the few doctors in Rutherford who would treat blacks, just as he served and admired Italian-Americans, Jews, and Poles, yet his speech and correspondence were speckled with the terms "nigger," "wop," "kike," and "Polack." Pound and his young acolyte employed language, in the unjudging words of Ben Jonson, "such as men doe use." The Jewish villains in Pound's gallery of rogues were in the main bankers—Ezra saw poor Jews as victims, to be enlightened and helped—while for J it was New York publishers, not bankers, who were likely to be branded with the Jew label, even though many, if not most, major American publishing houses were predominantly run by gentiles. In J's mind, bankers fell into a category of predators all their own: it was his neighbor Andrew Mellon, a banker and no Jew, who had profited richly in loaning funds to Jones & Laughlin. And J would always hate debt worse than quicksand.

J would come to be embarrassed by anti-Semitic remarks, and these would gradually disappear from his letters. But an aspect of his nature that would not change with the years was the strong susceptibility to women that he shared with Williams. Once, when Williams was rhapsodizing about a woman of his acquaintance, Floss interrupted her husband: "Bill, do you want to go to bed with *every* woman you meet?" Williams considered this seriously for a moment. "Yes, I do," he responded. In "Remembering William Carlos Williams," J would write nearly sixty years later that Williams's play *A Dream of Love* suggests "That an occasional adultery is / Necessary to renew the fervor / Of connubial love." This too seemed to J a reasonable prescription.

J's publishing venture was now fairly launched. He saw himself as providing a venue for new talent, primarily for advance-guard American poets, and becoming an elevating influence on American culture, in part through introducing his compatriots to the best foreign authors. He also intended to keep alive and encourage fine printing, fine book design. He did not expect to make money, at least for the foreseeable future, yet neither was he prepared to lose large sums. This much he thought he owed to his heredity.

8

Amateur Publisher,
Amateur Ski Impresario

The terrain at Ruapehu is potentially superb, a big sprawling mountain that rolls both ways—rugged ravines that fill with snow, crisscrossed by counterbumps and rolls, which produce a downhill course that can only too justly be called Whackayapapa, which is Maori for I-fall-down-lie-flat.

—James Laughlin, describing skiing in New Zealand

With New Directions in operation, J felt that he had earned some relaxation, and at the end of November 1936 he left by train for the West, traveling in high style with Aunt Leila and Uncle Dicky. They swerved north to take the Canadian route through the Rockies, and J persuaded them to stop for a day in Calgary. His purpose was to report to Pound on the Social Credit movement in Alberta, where William "Bible Bill" Aberhart had formed the Alberta Social Credit League and been elected premier of Alberta in 1935.

By December 4, J was on the slopes at Mount Rainier and Mount Baker in Washington, from which he wrote in telegraphese: "West great place. Great country. Railroads alone enormous." Soon he was in San Francisco, staying at the elegant Fairmont Hotel on Nob Hill. Aunt Leila and Uncle Dicky had preceded him to the city and were visiting the Henry Carlisles. When J made himself ill eating the "marvellous" French cuisine at the Fairmont, his aunt cured him by "thinking" him well: "She puts her hand on my forehead, shuts her eyes, goes into 'the silence' and of course, one feels better at once," he assured his parents. Aunt Leila bought a Chrysler, and they toured the city. There was one drawback, "Leider gibt es hier kein Schnee," no snow, so after Christmas he headed back north, to ski Rainier and Baker again.

J sent home photographs to show how beautiful Rainier was, but Baker was "simply wonderful" because the snow was better: "the slopes are all northern exposure," commented the future ski impresario. "This means that the sun doesn't melt the snow and make it heavy and then frozen the next day." Furthermore, he had won a pair of skis as a race prize. Then, two days later at Mount Baker, J won a slalom run, ahead of an Olympian and the Canadian national champion. He credited "an enormous vorlage"—leaning into the slope from the ankles: for once his long frame worked to his advantage—and a coating of very fast wax. "It was a pleasant surprise to do so well."

After a few days at Mount Hood, where J "bummed rides up the mountain on WPA trucks," he took the Union Pacific Portland Rose to Sun Valley. "The Portland Rose / Goes / pretty slows," he rhymed, adding that his mother should *send money*: "Yeah verily, it might be very well!" J continued on his barnstorming ski tour to Sun Valley, Idaho, just upslope from Hailey, Pound's birthplace. He sounded exuberant despite injuries, including a badly sprained right wrist that had to be put in a cast—yet he kept on skiing. He got no sympathy from Doc Williams, who said only, "Thank God it wasn't your neck, that's what I thought it would be."

Back at Harvard, J moved into new quarters in Claverly Hall, one of the Gold Coast residences that attracted the wealthiest undergraduates, where he was sharing rooms with Jim Field, "a very superior person." For once, he seemed to like his classes. "Catullus seems to me pretty much the RIGHT THING," he decided, and he was "doing some translation into my 'personal metre' . . . for practice." Ezra gave his unqualified approval: "vurry good eggzesize fer yung Jaz." On March 22, J lectured by invitation on experimental literature at Vassar, "about 85 times liver than Harvard," and the "extremely antique" spinster chair of the Department of English had actually read Pound and Joyce. "Around here they wd not admit it if they had," J said of Harvard.

For some months J had been courting the slender and lovely Elizabeth Duval, who "thinks that she wants me to marry her," J wrote to his mother. In his letters, J sounded as if he were trying hard to convince himself that he *should* marry her: the girl harbored "no foolish ideas about my doing any work but my writing"; she wanted to live in Paris, and she was rich and quite willing to support him. Then, after breaking three bones in his left hand while downhill racing in Vermont, the wounded skier pecked out on his typewriter, entirely in lowercase, "i dare say i shall not likely

soon get married however . . . i might easily because really i do like attention very much."

J's focus skipped wildly from Elizabeth Duval to skiing to Harvard to
publishing and back again. "I begin to think maybe I have found my vocation," J proclaimed to his mother. "The books are coming along beautifully
and are going to be terribly handsome . . . almost a justification in themselves for some of our accumulated sins as a family"—Jones & Laughlin
was sometimes called the "toughest anti-union company in America." He
designed title pages and jackets for books by Fitts, Robert McAlmon, and
Yvor Winters, crediting the Winters design to Hiram Handspring, J's first
mention of this particular alter ego.

J wrote his mother a scheme to "'save' Father." "Now listen carefully,"
he admonished her. Father needed to do something "worthwhile and constructive," and he was "perfectly well enough to do a business that doesn't
require personal contacts." J had five "nice" books in mind, beginning with
Williams's *White Mule*, and if he could be talked into the right frame of
mind, Father would enjoy publishing them. At the beginning of March
1937, J demanded $1,000 "right away" to pay the Plimpton Press in Nor-
wood, Massachusetts, to produce *White Mule* in a beautiful design by
Sherry Mangan. *Mule* would be New Directions' first novel. The Henghes-
inspired colophon would make its first appearance on the title page. Miss
Demarest had repeated her offer of help, and in mid-April J's father finally
arrived from Sidoney for his insistent son's tutorial in publishing. "I was
terribly pleased with the way Father took hold of the book business," J
told his mother. "He will really do it much better than I do when he gets
used to it because he is so much more careful than I . . . In a few days I'll
send him . . . the announcements, envelopes, lists etc." J now had two employees, both working for free.

With *White Mule* about to appear, J tried to get Williams's novel some
publicity. He urged Pound to write a "BIG spiel" on the book for *New Democracy*, *The New English Weekly*, and *The Criterion*, but Ezra was too busy
writing on music, politics, economics, and education. J said, "Pop Eliot, yE
pArson, is nibbling at sheets of MULE for hingland"; Eliot nibbled, but
he did not bite. It was going to be up to J to put *White Mule* across. When
he saw a prepublication copy in May 1937, Williams praised J's analytical
"Postscript": "You've done a fine piece of work, of criticism, in focusing the
book." J had written, *"To the editor of* New Directions, WHITE MULE *is*

a symbol—a symbol of his whole hope and will. New Directions *exists only to publish books like this one.*" Included in his afterword was a challenge to and a diatribe against unnamed publishers, *"traitors and enemies of the people,"* who *"have made literature a business."* "This is a rare collaboration between writer and publisher which is almost unheard of today," wrote Williams in gratitude.

Despite this coup, J's mood dipped precipitately in April. The "SHIT floating around this land" was threatening to send "ole Marse Jas" plumb "into the beancoop," he lamented to Ezra. He felt completely inadequate, whether he was writing poetry or prose on banking history; and as to publishing, "I have come recently to think that I am not of much use, except to print people's books for 'em, and the way they squawks about the way I print 'em makes me wonder even if I'm any use for that." In J, depression frequently followed accomplishment.

Meanwhile, J cultivated a family connection in the world of art and culture when he arrived on April 24 at his cousin Duncan Phillips's gallery in Washington. Phillips had the slender height of the Laughlins, but his air of quiet refinement would have made him seem out of place in the boardroom of Jones & Laughlin. He was a favorite of Aunt Leila's, he had written several books on art, and he was a "genuine aristocrat," known for his generosity. The Phillips Gallery, in a Victorian brownstone on Twenty-First Street that had belonged to Great-Aunt Eliza, was acknowledged to be one of the supreme privately held art collections, with many hundreds of paintings running from El Greco to Matisse and Braque. Phillips had his own printing press, and on this visit J spent his time running off the six pages of the first New Directions brochure and printing a supply of rejection slips, helped by his young second cousin Laughlin Phillips. The boy, J wrote to his mother, was "just as smart as I was, and with a much nicer nature."

The brochure proclaimed, in chaste fonts, **NEW DIRECTIONS / NORFOLK, CONN. / "Books of Permanent Literary Value."** The first inside page was addressed "To the Librarian" and proclaimed, "Our first publication was the initial number of an annual anthology devoted to experimental writing—NEW DIRECTIONS IN PROSE AND POETRY, a venture which met with a success so encouraging as to convince us that a need existed for a publishing house concentrating on books of purely literary rather than commercial value." To achieve financial rewards, "the average publisher" must perforce cater to the "poor taste of the masses." New Directions, J stated, would cater to "the cultivated taste of educated readers." Having thus insulted the judgment of the masses and thrown down his gauntlet at the feet of the publishing industry, J offered librarians who ordered direct from ND a "special discount" of 25 percent. The brochure presented the two titles of 1936, plus eight to come, among them Dudley Fitts's *Poems, 1929–1936*, Williams's *White Mule*, and a volume of McAlmon's poetry, *Not Alone Lost*. J announced a collection of his own poems, "I the Eye," described as "Poems only Laughlin could write, in an extraordinary format." This last was never published.

Along with all else, J was still conducting his romance with Elizabeth Duval. The lady was now furious with him, he confided to his mother, for intending to sail on a skiing escape to the Southern Hemisphere instead of marrying her: "I'm having very bad moments with the idea of losing her for good, but I'm too young to get married, and that is that." On the publishing side, J thought that he had New Directions "all highly systematized." In five typed pages, he set out his plans to his mother. His father had responded well to his instructions, and had agreed to help with advertising, address lists, mailings, and other chores. The next day J scrawled a quick note home: he had "about decided" to scrub the antipodean ski trip, leave college, get married, and "stop fooling around and get down to the real business of life"—his writing.

White Mule appeared on June 10, and the following evening J flew to Pittsburgh on the first leg of his ski trip, which was suddenly back on. Because he feared being stuck with a lot of unsold stock that he would not be around to help move, J had ordered the binding of only five hundred of the eleven hundred run of printed sheets. Much to Williams's surprise, there were laudatory reviews in *The New York Times, The Nation, The Saturday Review of Literature*, and *The New Republic*. Carl Van Doren in *The Boston Herald* praised the intensity and honesty of the writing. The lot sold out in weeks. "I thought I was *made*," the author would recall. When the bound copies were gone, Williams tried to contact J, but he was told that his publisher was in New Zealand skiing. Frantically, Williams drove to Norfolk in July, hoping to be able to move the unbound gatherings to the binders, and although he was cordially received by J's father, he was told that nothing could be done until J's return in September. Williams watched in anguish as the opportunities to sell his first commercially successful book receded, his chance to gain profit and expand his readership gone.

J had set off for New Zealand accompanied by Dick Durrance and David and Steven Bradley from Dartmouth. News about initial *White Mule* sales would not catch up with J until August, by which time he was in Australia. J had planned the trip casually, telephoning Durrance at Dartmouth in April to offer to pay his passage to New Zealand and Australia for a season of skiing. Durrance had no idea who J was, but he agreed immediately. Although skiing was not yet a sport with intercollegiate championships, the trio of Durrance and the Bradleys made Dartmouth's the strongest ski team in the nation. "The Dartmouth boys are the real thing of their kind," J wrote to his parents, adding that despite their "carousing" and their standards of dress and hygiene, "I shall likely profit much from them."

Durrance and J were as different in build as they were in personality: Dave Bradley described them as "Brobdingnagian Laughlin, Lilliputian Durrance." Durrance was only five feet seven, incredibly strong, daring, brash; cocksure but not boastful. When J described his new friend as "a wonderful person . . . in his simple, animal way," he intended it as a compliment. J and Dick were able to get the U.S. Ski Association to designate them as official representatives. So the quartet was named the Official U.S. Expeditionary Alpine and Nordic Team, given red, white, and blue uniforms, and assured that they would be guests of the New Zealand and Australian governments. They would be the first American team ever to compete in Oceania. They paused en route at Estes Park near Denver, where Durrance gave J a crash course in slalom, teaching him a fast turn that involved vaulting over a ski pole. Durrance skied in a low crouch that cut wind resistance and added to his speed and control. "Watching him race was like watching a ping-pong ball change directions," recalled Steve Bradley. "You could set up a metronome and see the rhythm."

On their first landfall, Hawaii, they were given a celebrity welcome organized by the Dartmouth Club of Hawaii and the Ski Club, feted at a banquet, and then taken cruising the wave crests in an immense outrigger war canoe. Duke Kahanamoku, the great Hawaiian Olympic swimmer, guided them around. Hawaii was "just too lovely," J wrote. "The vegetation is wild and wonderful and so is the volcanic landscape." Then it was on to Samoa and Fiji.

J arrived at Auckland on July 9, and by the next day, installed in the Chateau Tongariro at the foot of the Ruapehu Volcano, he was ready to assess New Zealand and its people. He found the coastal climate mild and damp, "like Seattle"; the men "over-featured" with "enormous noses, foreheads, chins"; the women "plain as plain," but aggressive: "You have to lock your door at night down here if you don't want things crawling on you." There was "no wealth at all to speak of," no industry, and the architecture was dull, said the son of Pittsburgh. "The people are nice in a way all their own—aloof, abrupt, but friendly."

J and his teammates soon left for Christchurch on the South Island, where they hoped to find better snow. They made their headquarters at the Ball Glacier Hut, high on Mount Cook. J pronounced the hut a fine place, even though they froze at night, ate lamb, potatoes, and apricots three times a day, and didn't wash because there was little water—"naturally I enjoy that," J wrote, to annoy his parents. The mountains were the "most precipitous, icy, and rocky" that he had ever seen. Frequent avalanches thundered down Mount Cook, generating so much electricity that the whole mountain appeared to have taken on a charge, and ghostly blue flames crackled at dusk behind the racers' skis.

So far there had been no official racing, but on the slopes with J's group were the Wigley brothers, members of the New Zealand team. They flew planes and drank great stoups of beer, and their ski technique was "not a source of envy," but J admired their "unlimited courage and spirit." Even in the companionable male athleticism of the Ball Glacier Hut, J maintained his practice of reading quietly in the evenings. For good talk he turned to a young English teacher on leave from India and decided on the spot to "have a look at India some day." And he took notes for "Skiing in New Zealand," the first of many articles that he would write over the years for the *American Ski Annual*.

Finally, on July 26, the competition started, with four events: downhill, slalom, langlauf—cross-country—and jumping. The Americans won easily, "though not thanks to me," J admitted, "who did only medium poor, instead of my usual lousy." Still, J took third in the downhill, behind Durrance and Harry Wigley, fourth in slalom, fourth in jumping—Durrance and the Bradleys were one-two-three in that. The langlauf was scrubbed because of rain, and the downhill turned out to be J's best run of the competition. "The first time I've not done something horrible in a race," he exclaimed. "At high speeds powder snow rolls like the swell of a big sea," J wrote. He had come to doubt that he possessed the basic physique to become a fine skier. "These years I have cared so passionately about ski-

ing," he wrote home, "and now it is crumbling away from under me . . .
I always feel, muscularly, like a scarecrow, made in a dozen sections with
loose hinges between."

To Ezra he poured out his doubts about a subject more important to
him even than his skiing: his writing. Part of it was the example of Bill
Williams's short stories, which J wanted to publish if *White Mule* sold at
all well—"such damn beautiful writing it makes your blood weep." J felt
that his own writing was not improving: "The worse my own writing gets
the more I am driven to do something." "If I can rook Papa again I'll do
other books this fall. I was going to do my own verse but have decided not
to. It's all a lot of bullshit and would be a work of ridiculous vanity." Through
careful economies he had saved enough out of the funds his parents had
provided for his trip to offer Ezra $50 per canto, if he would permit their
publication in the 1937 anthology. He did not, however, wish to lean on
his special relationship with Ezra. "As you know," J wrote to him, "I would
rather have you than any of the other blokes, but want you to print where
it will be best for you."

As far away from his mother as he could be on earth, J wrote to her on
her birthday that he felt that they had drawn closer together during the past
year. Since his own "intellectual empire" had "begun to crumble," he needed
her love and understanding. Each of them had suffered, and he saw "no joy
ahead for either of us," but thought that they could "suffer together." His
father was not turning out to be reliable, and J had written him off: J did
not expect him to recover his equilibrium or his sanity. "I am not afraid of
you anymore as I used to be," J told his mother, "and that is, or can be, the
beginning of love. Let us make it so."

The Expeditionary Alpine and Nordic Team boarded ship for Sydney,
and then on the way to the ski slopes Dave Bradley put his hand through
the car windshield in a freakish accident, and the team was down to three.
Australia, J thought, was "thrilling": the rolling hills and the sheep-cropped
landscape dotted with gracefully formed eucalyptus would make for "grand
painting." The rounded mountains near Mansfield below the ski slopes
reminded J of the Alleghenies, but everything else was wonderfully strange:
in the scrub the kookaburras chuckled, and other birds seemed to talk;
giant tree ferns rose like plumed helms under the towering eucalyptus. "I
haven't felt anything so much for a long time," J said, "not perhaps since
the south of France around Bilignin."

Despite his absorption with Australia, J had an "illumination" about what he wanted to do at New Directions: he would bring out a "reading edition" of the Latin poets to supplant the eighteenth-century Baskervilles, "the last really beautiful printing of the classics." It would not be "fancy" or larded with notes: "just a beautifully designed page." Most important, it would be something to "live for." J's father had sent an accounting of the initial sales of *White Mule*, to which J responded, "I had hoped for more, but am satisfied with the result." J considered publishing the book his major triumph for the year. He would not learn of Williams's anguish over ND's inability to supply reorders until his return to America. He hoped that his father had experienced "the solid, mercenary satisfaction of orders and parcels going out & checks coming in . . . You must have the feeling of motion to enjoy life, the feeling of action," said the young philosopher.

There was plenty of motion in J's life. On August 16, he was entered in the Victorian Downhill on the slopes of Mount Hotham. It was a fast course, ungroomed and uneven. He hurtled downward, dodging marker flags and skittering over icy patches. A small knot of skiers and spectators shouted encouragement, but he tried to block out everything beyond staying upright, and he knew that he was moving well. With mere yards to go, he hit a mogul that catapulted him spectacularly over the finish line, out of control, careening off a tree and into a rock pile.

9

Enter Kenneth Rexroth
and Delmore Schwartz

The miner came in '49,
the whore in '51,
they rolled upon the barroom floor—
then came the Native Son.
—attributed to Mark Twain, on San Francisco

J looked up at a circle of worried faces. He had taken second place, his best finish of the tour. His luck seemed to be holding, even in misfortune. Among the spectators to his crack-up was Dr. Colquhoun, who had worked under the Laughlins' friend Dr. Osgood in Boston, and he taped J up so that he could walk the four hours down the mountain to the nearest road. Then Colquhoun drove J to Melbourne and put him in the same hospital room with Dave Bradley. J's genius for concise speech—when he was paying by the word—did not desert him in his cable to his mother: "SECOND VICTORIAN DOWNHILL BUT BROKE SHOULDER STIVES HOSPITAL MELBOURNE COMFORTABLE EXCELLENT DOCTOR FRIEND OSGOODS PLEASE CABLE FIVE HUNDRED THROUGH COOKS LOVE." A pretty girl on the hospital staff fell in love with J and fussed over him; then he spent a brief time convalescing on Toorak beach, which was "liberally sprinkled with beautiful Australian mermaids." His injuries were more extensive than he admitted initially to his parents and included a cut on the head, a badly fractured shoulder blade, and stretched ligaments joining the collarbone to the shoulder. Old Mengie wrote him a gently scolding letter: "Now that is the 2nd time you have been hurt, you better be careful."

Since he would not be able to ski for months, he decided that he might as well get back to Harvard, especially since required examinations in the Bible, Shakespeare, the ancients, and modern authors were being given the first week of the fall term. Three days later, securely strapped up and "feeling fine," J left the Bradleys and Durrance behind and boarded the SS *Monterey* for Honolulu, where he expected to be joined by his parents—who would stand him up. He upgraded his berth to first class because in Melbourne he had met the daughters of "the richest man in Australia," and they would be on the ship. "How nice," J told his parents, "if I could get interested in one of them." He wouldn't mind living in Australia. Love did not happen, but J won enough from the girls at poker to pay his passage.

J stayed four days in Honolulu, visiting the bookstores to scout out possible sales, before sailing for San Francisco. He asked Miss Demarest to send the accumulated New Directions manuscripts to the Fairmont in San Francisco so that he could attend to them before the school term. On his flight back to Boston, J planned stops in Los Angeles, St. Louis, Pittsburgh, and Philadelphia to become acquainted with bookstores and salespeople. He was developing a card system for targeted sales pitches that would list not only the book buyers' names but notes on their personalities, their special interests, and the "atmosphere" of the shops. J hated selling—"I dread it"—but he told himself he must learn to like it. While he was away, his parents had composed a New Directions advertisement and placed it in *Scribner's Magazine.* "It looked fine," J commended them. "I knew you would manage that all right."

"Welcome home," wrote Doc Williams in September, adding, "I knew it would hit somewhere near your neck and fully expected to have them send you home in two pieces." Ignorant of the fiasco of failing to keep Williams's novel in stock, J wrote calmly to his parents, "I dare say you needed more copies of *Mule* bound and hope Mangan handled that all right." J had already broached to Williams the possibility of a "collected shorter prose pieces," and in November he insisted on the necessity of bringing out *Life Along the Passaic River* in short order. J planned also to produce a limited edition of Williams's *Complete Collected Poems*, boxed and signed. To his parents, he kept stressing that New Directions would become something that "we" would view with "pride and satisfaction."

In Honolulu and again in San Francisco, J had his shoulder x-rayed. He was assured that in a month he wouldn't know the accident had happened. "I certainly have luck," he wrote home. He had every expectation that his body would mend well, far better than it had from the much more serious back injury of the year before. His attitude had changed, however: before New Zealand and Australia, J had let himself hope that through hard work and sheer reckless courage he might turn himself into a skier able to compete seriously with the best. Now he realized, by his close observation of Dick Durrance, that he would never be more than a competent skier. He would continue to ski, but not out of a compulsion to compete. Literature—publishing it if not creating it—would be his main vocation. He was ready to follow Pound's advice to "make it new" in his own way—a new resolve, a commitment to forging New Directions into a major publisher of advance-guard writing. He was prepared to follow the Boss's criteria for judging poetry, as outlined in *ABC of Reading*: phanopoeia, melopoeia, logopoeia. The poem should be visual: "the throwing of an image on the mind's retina." The words must sing, must be a fitting of words to tune. Finally, the poem must engage the reader intellectually.

Probably the most important lesson that J had taken away from the Ezuversity, one that shaped the editorial philosophy for New Directions, was a *method* for literary judgment rather than a set of dicta. Ezra had never demanded that J adopt a Parnassus of immortals named by him. Here was where the Ezuversity stood most distinct from the beaneries, where the student was *told* to revere a pantheon that ran from Homer through Chaucer and Shakespeare to Hawthorne and Hardy and, perhaps, Melville. Pound's method was to encourage the reader to make comparisons, to judge a given writer in part by looking at those who immediately preceded and followed: Did each writer *make something new* out of the corpus that he or she had inherited? Especially in verse, the reader must also listen for the music of language. Most important, content and story line should inform judgment. Pound's method freed J to make his own editorial judgments. His faith in the method gave him the patience to wait until the public awoke, "in the long or short run," to the authors he published.

J kept delaying his return from San Francisco, partly because he had met Kenneth Rexroth, a Pound introduction. While J would discover that he could be "unbearably cranky," on their first encounter "he was on a roll of / Good humor and I found him / Quite irresistible." As Rexroth described their meeting at his Potrero Hill apartment, "a man who looked like he was six foot twelve in height was standing in the doorway with a shy look on his face. I said, 'Gee, you must be Jim Laughlin.'" Finding a ready listener,

Rexroth poured out a flood of facts, theories, and anecdotes from his vast if idiosyncratic self-instruction, and J was hooked. Only Ezra, J thought, was a more riveting talker, and Kenneth seemed free from Ezra's tendency to ride a particular economic or political hobbyhorse. Rexroth saw himself as a pacifist and an anarchist, but he could be more properly termed a contrarian, delighting in opposing *any* stance or creed. He wanted to reform the world, yet he was cynical about virtuous people out to impose their will. He was at contraries in his own nature as well: almost pathologically egocentric, he was also generous and unselfish with his time and his hospitality. Nine years older than J, Kenneth was astonishingly well-read, and he combined extensive erudition with a passionate love for the High Sierras and indeed for the entire natural world. He had arrived in California from Chicago in 1927, seemed most at peace when sleeping under the night sky, and wrote that he was interrelated with "chipmunks and bears and pine trees and stars and nebulae and rocks and fossils, as part of an infinitely interrelated complex of being." From the time of Richard Henry Dana's arrival in 1835 after his "rustication" from Harvard for being too much a rebel, San Francisco had nurtured or attracted writers: Mark Twain, Bret Harte, Jack London, Ambrose Bierce, and Gertrude Stein were luminaries in a long tally. More than these predecessors, Kenneth had set down roots, had become a local literary and political activist. He wrote layered poetry that combined a taut personal meter with a worldwide reference, and he could talk the night through and then spend a morning meditating wordlessly on a stump.

J learned that Rexroth's stories were not always to be trusted. Some years later, with the connivance of the poet Robert Duncan, J laid a trap for Kenneth: at one of Rexroth's Thursday night gatherings, Duncan opened a discussion about contemporary French poets, and J brought up one Auguste Dampière, a complete invention. He was an old friend, Kenneth assured J, they had met in Aix-en-Provence and together had toured a Cézanne site. Soon Kenneth was in the midst of a disquisition on the techniques of the great impressionists. "It was a masterful / Performance," J wrote, "which left Duncan / And me so moved neither of us / Could bring himself to break / The spell by denouncing his / Confabulation."

The personal bond that J formed with Rexroth became his most intense friendship of the 1940s. Throughout his early life, J seemed to be seeking out versions of the relationships that he found unsatisfactory in his immediate family and inamoratas: Aunt Leila was the understanding maternal figure his own mother could not be; Ezra was his spiritual father; and he would look, time after time, outside his marriages for an idealized muse and lover. More than any other person, Kenneth became J's surrogate older brother. Here was someone who was a more accomplished poet, a better talker, a more self-sufficient intellectual, a better outdoorsman. And in so much their thinking ran in harmony: on the relative value of many poets, on the imbecility of the literary establishment, on the war, on the supreme importance of love. The anarchistic and libertarian Kenneth, setting poetics above politics, was quite willing to admit that the best poets of the 1930s were "reactionaries," even that the "Great Writers"—Pound, Eliot, Yeats, Lawrence, Gottfried Benn, and others—were fascists with a lowercase *f*. Rexroth would maintain in his *Autobiographical Novel* that "ski touring and mountaineering have given me some of the happiest moments of my life," and in this he was a reassuring counterbalance to Pound and Williams, who both deplored J's commitment to snow and mountains.

J continued to work on his own poetry, for which he had invented— possibly influenced by Cummings—what he came to call his "typewriter metric": usually in couplets, no capitalization. He would type out the first line of a poem, and then each following line should be within two type-written *spaces* either way from the first line—a mechanical space count in which the spaces between words counted equally with letters. He eliminated punctuation because there was none in the old Greek and Latin manuscripts. "This enables the words to rub against each other," he explained years later, "and produces an effect of semantic continuity in the lines." In any case, J had Ezra's imprimatur: "Verse usually has some element roughly fixed and some other that varies," Pound had written, "but which element is to be fixed and which vary . . . is the affair of the author." J's inspiration for the name of his verse form had come, however, from Bill Williams, a great one for prosodic theory, who called his own "triadic line" "the variable foot." Williams told him early on that "the type-writer was the vehicle of the new age, and that I'd better use it." J would write late in his life, "The point of the screwball metric," of strictly limiting variation, "is that the visual pattern of the couplets works against the sound of the underlying cadences which are from plain speech":

```
like those rabbits the
greyhounds chase round
and round and never any
nearer I follow my beard

and where is it taking
me that's what I'd like
to know just where we're
going tell me beard where.
```

When readers complained that the lack of punctuation prevented them from pausing where sense or cadence suggested it, J refined his metric to include an extra space, a "breath pause," where there might ordinarily have been punctuation. He would continue to use his typewriter metric, which he called "the most artificial metric that man has ever devised," for the rest of his life, although later he would allow himself a variation of three and occasionally more extra space/letter units. And at times he would abandon the form altogether.

J came to appreciate Rexroth's blending of the spectacular western natural world with human love. By 1940, Rexroth had already made his claim to being the poet of the Sierras, celebrating the confluence of high meadows, streams and still lakes, and "impassive snow peaks" with feminine beauty, sensuality, physical love. Stone, iris, "your thighs' exact curve" tied to the undying, the unchanging: "This moment of fact and vision / Seizes immortality." Among Rexroth's obsessions was seeing the evanescent moment against the panorama of ageless flux. His visions might be those of a solitary, but they are strongly rooted in the intimate experience of the lover, the collision of bodies. From Rexroth, J also took the example of incorporated intellect, of a vast learning and developed sensibility. "The obscure cantata / Of tangled water" and the "burning angel" in his "Incarnation" reveal Rexroth not as an unsophisticated mountain whippoorwill but as a poet bringing the lens of high culture to his solitary communings with nature. And his word-love gave him an immense tonal range. Like Pound, Rexroth thought in terms of Greek and Latin masters, of Provençal troubadours and French and Italian Renaissance court poets, of Chinese and Japanese poets. Like Williams, Rexroth celebrated the love and beauty of women. But more than Williams, more than Pound, Rexroth provided the example that J was to follow in his own poetry.

•

J's romance with Elizabeth Duval did not survive his skiing excursion. For this break he gave his mother and Aunt Leila due credit: "You would want to know whether this caused me any pangs. No, very few . . . I am most grateful to you. How admirably you managed that situation . . . I was escaping *to* her." For all of his vaunted independence, J lacked confidence in his emotional life and cultivated a certain coldness to mask his feelings.

J made it back to Harvard in time for his examinations at the beginning of the term. "I exerted my well-known verbal charm and guess I got through them," he wrote to his "Dearest Mum," adding, "How do you like my snappy new paper. I designed it all myself and feel so elegant I nearly bust. Did you ever see anything so snappy?" It was simple and elegant: the Henghes colophon flanked by NEW DIRECTIONS and NORFOLK CONNECTICUT in block capitals, again sans serif, all surrounded by thin double ruling. J would use this stationery, with minor modifications, for the rest of his life. Classical scholar though he was, he would always insist that the colophon displayed a centaur, ignoring the horse's head below the human head: a centaur meant for him the wisdom of Nessus, so to J a centaur it was and would remain.

Looking after his father was growing even more difficult. "Father seems to be holding [h]is own," J reported somewhat doubtfully to his mother. "In fact, he has been a little less embarrassing in the last few days. I guess I can stand it." With Elizabeth Duval gone, J's social life grew in variety. It was the debutante season, the ballet was in town—"my greatest pleasure," he said—and he was taking four different "little debutantes" to performances in as many days, Susan, Lolly, Mary, Patty: "Hugh would approve of any one of them."

Amid distractions, J was trying to compile his second anthology. This time he had no *New Democracy* quarry to mine for material, yet he ignored an unsolicited manuscript from Delmore Schwartz, with a covering note from the author saying that he thought that the five poems and two short stories were just what J wanted for his anthology. By early October, not having heard from J despite a follow-up note, Schwartz offered the story "In Dreams Begin Responsibilities" to *Partisan Review*. This caught J's attention. "As an editor, in defense of editors, of our time & our sanity," he wrote, "I must *give you hell* for disposing of a manuscript which you had offered to me." He "must insist" that Schwartz attempt to get the *Partisan* people to permit New Directions to publish the story. There was no apology from J for not having written sooner: such was his editor's view of the importance of the "principle" involved. *Partisan Review* agreed to let him use "In Dreams," but the magazine published an account of the affair, and a minor tempest ensued. "No I didn't actually think you were wicked," J next wrote in an unrepentant tone. Mild as a dove, Schwartz expressed pleasure that the affair ended "so amiably." Sensitive to the point of paranoia, Schwartz was capable of flying into vituperative rages over unintended affronts while on occasion serenely glossing over serious offenses. Such was the beginning of J's volatile association with the man who was soon to become a vital literary arbiter of New Directions. In person, Schwartz was unforgettable, ardent in conversation, brilliant in repartee. His haunted, expressive eyes were widely set in a squarish face with Tartar cheekbones and topped by rolling waves of light brown hair, his mouth in repose full and sensual.

Another author, William Saroyan, was insisting on page proofs, but J refused firmly: "I'm sorry, but I can't let you have proofs on the stories." Corrections at proof stage cost $3.50 an hour, and if every author were to receive page proofs, it would cost New Directions $150 in corrections per anthology. "I'm sorry, I just can't afford it," J concluded. "You authors will have to realize that we small publishers can print you but can't humour you."

J should have sensed trouble of a different nature when Bill Williams spoke of his need for money and of a libel suit over a short story back in 1926 that had cost the doctor $5,000, his total savings. When Williams wrote in November 1937 that he was thinking of offering a work in progress, *Yes, Mrs. Williams*, his biography of his mother, to "a regular commercial publisher" such as Harcourt, Brace or Simon & Schuster, J had a fit: "You are the cornerstone of New Directions and if you left me I think I wouldn't be able to go on with it." Williams would put ND prominently on the map. "If you stick with me and Ezra perhaps comes in," J continued, "we'll be able to make a machine that can fight the New York machine," the "enemy," those who see literature as "merchandise." J promised to meet any offer Simon & Schuster might make and laid out a program featuring a "steady barrage of Williams." Bill capitulated, writing soothingly that he had not thought that New Directions would *want* to publish a "bulky" book like the biography. Williams was more deeply affected than his rational-sounding letter indicated: he had made an instinctive decision to trust J, trust him because of his obvious commitment to modernist poetry, trust him because he *liked* him. For the emotional Williams, this last was the determining reason.

By the late autumn J had assembled *New Directions in Prose and Poetry* for 1937. Many of the stars of 1936 reappeared, but J added Robert Fitzgerald, as well as Richard Eberhart, Merrill Moore, Kenneth Rexroth, and Delmore Schwartz. He was still paying only "special contributors," he told E. E. Cummings, "of which you are one and Ezra another." Two drawings by Cocteau, one of them a self-portrait, graced "Les mariés de la Tour Eiffel" and marked the introduction of illustrations to the annual. He told Zukofsky that he would have to postpone the publication of the section "A"-8 until next year, pleading financial losses and the difficulty of the poem. He had taken "a hell of a licking" on McAlmon, selling only thirty copies, and "a mild one on the Fitts and Winters." Anticipating Zukofsky's objections, J said that he had printed work not as good as the "A" "movement." "You see quality doesn't make any difference in the marketing problem," he concluded. J's letter, mixing compliments with the appearance of taking the recipient into his confidence, was a masterful performance, one Zukofsky would see repeated in coming years, and he acquiesced, reluctantly, to the delay.

Soon Cummings was suggesting visits, and he wrote J letters rife with ambiguities and evasions. J wanted to publish a volume of his poetry but was waiting until he had enough money to make a reasonable offer. He waited too long, and in the next year Harcourt, Brace would bring out Cummings's *Collected Poems*.

J's most promising new writer was Schwartz, who was immediately hailed by critics as a major talent. Aside from his editor's preface, J contributed an essay, "Language and the Experimental Writer," and, as Tasilo Ribischka, "A Fable." Handspring was credited with having written the rather flippant "Notes on Contributors," in which J's alter ego is himself described: "runs an elevator in the Boston Ritz and designs for New Directions in his spare time. He is slow with his feet but quick with his hands. His eye is on you"—the single eye an oblique reference to J's one good eye.

In his preface, J stated that three things convinced him that his anthology was worthwhile: only a dozen copies of the first issue were unsold; a "flood" of material had come in from prospective contributors; writers, "who know something about writing," were pleased by the volume, but critics, "who don't," were not. It was already an adage with J that most critics merely fill column inches and know very little about literature. New Directions had no political ax to whet, J claimed, although there was a fierce ongoing debate over whether utilitarian values in literature could trump the artistic, between the Far Left—as exemplified by Granville Hicks and Michael Gold of the avowedly Communist weekly *New Masses*—and Philip Rahv of *Partisan Review*. J chose to raise an art-for-art's-sake banner above the fray while still believing, with Ezra, that literature must *mean something*. One of the triumphs of this annual was Harry Levin's brilliant essay on *Finnegans Wake*, which prompted Joyce to write to J that the piece was the "most striking . . . so far" on him; J asked Levin forthwith for a book-length study of Joyce.

J was enjoying laying about him with his battle-ax, for he certainly swung one, despite disclaimers. There *was* a chip on his shoulder, and it would stay there until the "editorial pigsties of Fourth and Madison Avenues" were cleaned out. The "big publishers," in their avid pursuit of "wretched bestsellers," were betraying the "pure writer." Kafka, especially, was the "medicine" most needed to transform the "naturalism" of "American prose fiction." And he touched on Doc Williams: "For one Williams, who can raise his naturalism to the symbolical level, there are a hundred Farrells who can't."

J might have thought that he was being controversial, but his 1937 collection did not strike Ezra that way. The Boss sent a brief note of acknowledgment: "NO my dear boy/ You have so shat in yr/ own bed that it/ will take you hell's own time to clean up./ You may mean well . I dont doubt it/ BUT you have gone/ too far in obscuring essential differences. Too god DAMNED Amy/ble." What had so annoyed Ez? Ezra didn't bother to clarify. "Yr displeasure received," responded the rebuked one. What Ezra *did* approve of was the ND publication of Williams's *Life Along the Passaic River*, which he judged "in most parts as good as W. H. Hudson at his BEST/ so the rest of yr/ mispent life iz fergiven yuh."

The issue also displeased Williams, even though he found Merrill Moore's sonnets "magnificent," claiming that he had abandoned the "stupid formality" of the sonnet while preserving the essential statement-and-rejoinder structure. But Williams thought that the other material "isn't quite as new as it should be." He found the work too reminiscent of *transition* magazine and wanted more J, both editorially and as an artist: "What is new? Answer that next time." Williams was hobbled by being stuck in New Jersey, Ezra said. "Suspect ole Bill's style shows the drag of living back of beyond," he confided to J, "and NEVER having any contact with the present/ as distinct from permanent dulness of the lower orders."

Williams's faith in J appeared to waver. He pleaded for advertising and for adequate "management of sales." "Weeel Jimes, it's up to you to carry Papa across the river," he concluded. "To the future sales! But don't let it slip through your fingers again <—if ever>." J on his part complained about Williams's use of rhyme in the *Paterson* manuscript just received. "I guess I just don't like rhyme," he admitted a year later. "There is something real about your poetry which just doesn't fit with rhyme." He outlined as a publishing strategy "bunching" books to come out in the fall, when people are serious. "In the Spring they're too happy . . . what sells books is catalogue, mailing list, salesman's visits, advertising." J would hear constant complaints that he was "casual" about publishing, but that was hardly the right word. It was more a matter of concentration: for him, there was a time to concentrate on publishing, a time to concentrate on ski development, and there was his private life.

J's father continued to cause worry. For long periods he would be moody, depressed, his behavior erratic and unpredictable. Then for months he would be fine. One of these remissions occurred late in 1937, when he stayed at Sidoney with his sister, Martha Seeler. He reveled in the hunting and fishing, and his family began to hope, as they had many times before, that he had successfully cast off his demon. Then he suffered what seemed a trivial accident: fishing in the Keys, he lodged a hook in his leg, and the wound did not heal, becoming inflamed and locally swollen: septicemia had set in. He traveled north by train and took refuge at Robin Hill. When it was clear that his condition was deteriorating, he was moved to Pittsburgh. Hugh and J were summoned to his bedside, but J soon returned to Harvard and then went to Norfolk for the beginning of the holiday recess. After Christmas, J attempted a new ski jump, landing on his bad shoulder, which "mussed it up." Abruptly, he was recalled to Pittsburgh.

10

Death, Marriage, and Love
Considered and Reconsidered

His worldly possessions—all—are left to Mama, so the renascence of Am Lit is
again delayed.   —James Laughlin, on reading his father's will

Nineteen thirty-eight began with the death from blood poisoning of
H. Hughart Laughlin on New Year's Day. The funeral service was held
during the afternoon of January 3 at 104 Woodland Road.

Among J's emotions was one that he had not expected—blind rage.
His father's body lay in the guest bedroom in his Scottish tweed suit and
orange-and-black Princeton tie, and J's mother told him that he must "say
goodbye." Suddenly J's grief turned to fury. "I raised him / further and
banged his head / against the pillow," J wrote. His anger could perhaps be
explained by the depth of his dependence on his father, "you / the one
who loved me most." Even while his father was alive, J had felt that their
relationship was not entirely satisfactory. "He expected so much of his
father that his father wasn't able to give," J's cousin Marie Edgerton recalled. Another reason for anger came out when the will was read: J had
expected a portion of his inheritance, but the entire estate was left in
trust to his mother, with the stipulation that their two sons would inherit
upon her death. J had no reason to suspect it as he buried his father, but
by November both of his father's surviving brothers would also be dead,
leaving only aunts Leila and Martha on his paternal side—reasons to draw
closer to Aunt Leila and to glance apprehensively at family lifelines.

His comment to Pound seemed callous: "My rev Papa is deceased on
Jan 1st of this year, age 59. 'tristes inferias'"—funeral honors; J was para-
phrasing Catullus. "His worldly possessions—all—are left to Mama, so

the renascence of Am Lit is again delayed." Ezra's *Fifth Decad of Cantos* had just appeared in America from Farrar & Rinehart, and J put in a plug for himself: "Your decad is out and looking lousy as to book production. Why don't you get yourself a decent publisher, like me for instance. What about the Kulcher vollem." His financial picture was not as bleak as he had made out to Ezra, for, writing to Bill Williams twenty days after his father's death, J said, "I have more money at my disposal and I'm beginning to feel strong as hell."

J felt the need to appear solvent, a sound publisher, to Williams, while he wanted to appear *in*solvent to Miller, Schwartz, and others more apt directly to appeal to him for money. J now proposed to initiate the New Classics series, with Pound and Williams as the "backbones." These would resemble the Modern Library series published by Random House and would sell for a dollar. In December 1939, New Directions would publish the first of these New Classics, Williams's *In the American Grain*. In his pursuit of out-of-print classics, J contacted Edward Dahlberg, whose novel *Bottom Dogs* had been published in London in 1929 and had been allowed to go out of print within a year. In his criticisms, Dahlberg could be quite as forthright as Rexroth or Pound: "Your list leans a little too much toward preciosity, that you doubtless know; experimentalism, dadaism, gagaism, all that, is ultimately infantism. Publish six or seven or ten artists, follow them through, and you can create a lasting literature." This publishing philosophy was exactly the direction in which J was moving.

J was prepared to offer continuity of effort and promotion to promising writers who might lack a public to sustain them, and he expected loyalty in return, which meant that an author should stay with ND once committed. Loyalty was a watchword with J, and in this he differed from most publishers. In explaining to Delmore Schwartz his usual request for a three-book option on future titles, J stressed the value of continuity. "I can only do my best work for you if I feel that you are going to be loyal," J wrote. Schwartz signed a contract promising his next three books to ND and offered to dedicate a poem to J, who responded happily, "I am thoroughly sentimental and enjoy all such pleasures to the full."

The impulse that spun off some authors resided in the question of money. J courted avant-garde writers; almost by definition, this meant that they did not sell well, at least at first and usually for many years, yet they had bellies to fill, social lives to lead, and, often, families to support. Once one of J's writers achieved even a modicum of acclaim, he or she was apt to be tempted by offers from other publishers. Everyone knew that J came from a rich family, but not many stopped to think that this did not necessarily mean that he was personally rich. So he was accused of being a skiing dilettante and a miser. He was punctilious about small amounts of money and once sent Schwartz an order to the printer in an addressed envelope, saying that Gertrude Schwartz should "soak off the 3¢ stamp for future use" if Delmore decided against the changes they were discussing. Delmore assumed that J was being serious—he probably was.

Neither, however, did J lack heart or understanding. "I would like to be able to subsidize you right now," he wrote to Delmore in January 1938, "but I simply haven't the cash." Should business conditions improve, he continued, he was prepared to give Schwartz advances comparable to those paid by large publishers. "Right now I'm working by candlelight as the steel business is not paying any dividends," J complained in what was entirely a personal fantasy over the electric bill. A combination of straight talk, kidding, and praise kept many authors if not content at least quiet. To make some money himself, by the end of the year J was writing what he termed "bilge about skiing," on the European ski hut system, for Harry Bull's *Town and Country* magazine. What J himself was not doing was hitting the slopes: he would only ski three days all winter. "New Directions takes a lot of time," he complained to Ezra.

To make time for his other ventures, J delegated various publishing tasks to Dudley Fitts, now at the nerve center of New Directions; a premonitory note, Fitts said, was coming into Doc Williams's dealings with ND, doubtless owing much to his annoyance with J over the *White Mule* supply flap. "Wish you'd tell me Who, exactly, is contracting c̃ Wm C Wms for the collected poemata," Fitts complained to J; "you say you are, Oxford Press says they are, Wms says coyly nothing. It's got us all nuts down here in NHaven County." Fitts appears to have been largely responsible for bringing "Arch" into the third ND anthology, due to Archibald MacLeish's wholehearted approbation of Fitts's *One Hundred Poems from the Palatine Anthology*, published under J's imprint early in 1938.

A note of relief had crept into J's letters to his mother after his father's death. One of the voices that had been urging him to complete his degree studies at Harvard was silenced, yet J had nonetheless resolved to stick it out, not sure whether to do so amounted to "a vice or a virtue." Then he requested another leave of absence for the spring term in order to return to Europe. Perhaps he thought that he had been a bit hard on his mother, for on a narrow strip of paper like a bookmark he wrote out, "Please don't / let it worry / you that I / seem sometimes / to be growing / beyond you in / some ways. I / still and always / will need a / good mother / to take care of / me more than / anything else. / Love J."

Finally, on March 23, 1938, Ted Spencer put J aboard the *Queen Mary*. J's luck soared: he ran into a friend on the dock, who urged him to introduce himself to Martha Gellhorn on the ship. He did that evening, they dined together, she regaled him with stories of Spain and Hemingway—she was about to go with him to Barcelona. In two days J was writing a short story, "The Spanish Beauty," based on one of "Marty's" tales, when he was not working out with her in the gymnasium or reading Williams to her. "Together almost constantly," he wrote in his diary. By the fourth day out J set down, "Resolve to go to Spain"—despite the ongoing violence of the civil war. But by then he had also spoken to an old acquaintance, Duke Dimitri von Leuchtenberg, a Russian émigré descended from Czar Nicholas I, and immediately decided to try to "wangle a trip to the [ski] huts with him." His social life was complicated by the fact that one of his current flames, Patricia, was also on board, "so near but out of reach" owing to another entanglement. "I have worked myself into quite a state," he confessed, and his emotions became even more complicated when, "in spite of talking continuously about Ernest," Gellhorn "kisses me good and proper, which is nice." At Cherbourg they would drink whiskey "and feel sad about Spain" before parting.

To his mother J complained about his brother's prospective bride, Helen Lefebre: "I think she is a very well made little bit, apart from her voice, but I wish Hugh would marry somebody who had some money and position." He continued, "Our family is in a critical position . . . If we don't make good marriages it will drop away into the mass of the middle class and cease to be any thing at all." In fact, J had set his cap for Theodora, daughter of Ellery Sedgwick, owner and editor of *The Atlantic Monthly*: rich family, two hundred years of residence on Beacon Hill. And the girl was beautiful, intellectual, and sweet. Love, of course, posed a problem, but he thought, "Why not fall in love with the right person?" He was not speaking like the modern young man that he thought himself, yet a wealthy marriage seemed to J a perfectly defensible aim.

After a few days in Paris, J headed back to Lausanne and then to

Megève just west of Mont Blanc to visit Kay Boyle and Laurence Vail, taking along Phoebe Davis, a friend dating back to his Choate days. Born in 1902, Kay had come to France in 1926 as the bride of a French aviator, whom she had left to live with another flier, the Irish-American Ernest Walsh, co-founder with Ethel Moorhead of the magazine *This Quarter.* Walsh had died of tuberculosis before he and Kay got around to marrying, and Vail was her second husband, father of four of "Les Cinq Enfants" who had suggested the name of their chalet (two of the children were Vail's with Peggy Guggenheim, two his with Kay, and the fifth was her child by Walsh). Kay might look frail, but she was strong and daring, powered by an unrelenting will, and there was a terrifying element to her intensity. She could hike and ski all day, or, equally, she could shut herself in a room and write for six or eight hours without pause. J and Phoebe hiked with Kay and Laurence to the high cols and skied on the ungroomed slopes of the Rochebrune.

J rendezvoused on April 11 with Duke von Leuchtenberg in Zurich. He was to assist the duke by giving instruction in skiing to the young women who were paying for mountain touring in the Silvretta area. "The mountains fascinate you," J wrote, "because you know they will kill you if you give them the chance." They spent their last two days skiing in a blizzard, making blind runs by compass, floating through the nebulous whiteness with only the wind and the occasional sudden falling away of the snow surface beneath them to give a feeling of speed.

This was J's real introduction to European ski touring using the hut system. In the Austrian Alps there were more than one hundred huts, from primitive cabins to small pensions, at altitudes up to twelve thousand feet. What America needed was a hut system, J decided. He found his German coming back rapidly, and from what he heard the Austrians seemed almost universally delighted with the *Anschluss*—and the prosperity it promised. Children ran out from the farm hamlets to cry, "Heil Hitler!" American papers referred to the "invasion" of Austria: "Is it an invasion when 80% of the population is for it?" J asked rhetorically. "The squawk was put up by the Jews. They were the only ones who suffered and it wasn't their country anyway."

He skied through a snowstorm on the Grosser Vernagt Glacier, and back at the ski hut he finished *The Brothers Karamazov,* "with tears," and commented, "O Incredible genius." Abandoning their skis and roped in two groups, the party ascended the Wildspitze to gaze down upon the Ortler peak, the Grossglockner, the Zugspitze, the Bernina. Here was firmly anchored one pole of his being: the great peaks, snow, pure air, the blood-hot surge of physical release.

At times such as this, J felt that he could forget scribbling, printer's ink, and the drudgery of bookselling and instead give his life to skiing. By the end of the month, sunburned to the hue of a chestnut, he had descended to the plains to eat a quiet lunch in Milan. He went to a service in the cathedral and then bought *The Sun Also Rises*, which he read all the way to Rapallo. "Good & weak," he pronounced it. A fine "reunion w/ the master" followed. "Richness of life. He is glad to see me. More mellow. More calm. Intelligence more shining." The "brazen, sexy maid" at the Albergo Rapallo seemed glad to see him too: "Sex again after the chaste athlete's life in the snow," he entered in his diary.

Inspired, J was working again, "writing well, easily, and with a sense of power," on a long short story, "Mother Told Me to Wait." He set himself a goal of a thousand words per day and kept to it for eight days, then abandoned the story unfinished. On May Day, Lola Avena learned that J was in town and came back into his life "like a ten tun truck": "Plans for taking her to Paris & Boston. Madness?" He and Ezra discussed a job that Ezra was offered at Olivet College in Michigan. A part of Ezra wanted to renew direct contact with America, but he had too many ties to Italy— Olga and Vivaldi, Venice, his daughter, his elderly parents, and Dorothy in Rapallo.

J saw Lola most evenings; like the amorous teenager she was, at the movies she "snuggle bunnied herself against me and called me her tesoro." J told her that he must marry a rich girl, and she replied, "Will you marry me if I win the Lotteria di Tripoli?" With lovemaking came J's self-criticism: "Deux reprises and then my attacks of sadism again," he wrote one day in his diary. "My sentiments on the sea-wall after whacking her ass." There was a reason for J's frustration: Lola might be very free with her petting and even undressed for him, but she denied him a complete consummation, even though she inspected his penis and announced, "Curioso questo." He confessed to his mother that he found her "affected, feminine way" charming, an "inheritance from the hetaire, something that Anglo-Saxons never get." Finally, after two weeks, they became lovers in the fullest sense of the word, although J still had not promised marriage.

Like his father, J divided women into categories: those one made love to and those one married.

J accepted another responsibility when Ezra confided his daughter, Mary Rudge, to his care. "Look after her," Pound urged; he was afraid that her illegitimacy would cut her out of any share in his tangible estate, his manuscripts and the letters received from his now-famous confreres. He wanted to make sure that there would be something for Mary, and for her children, should she marry, and he wanted the trustee to be someone outside his family. He said specifically that all manuscripts, including those already in the New Directions files, were to come to Mary eventually. Ezra must have had some premonition of troubles ahead—troubles that he could have headed off had he taken the trouble to make out a properly attested will.

News from home caught up with J: Elizabeth Demarest was sick, but his mother had "taken over the business"; Uncle Dicky had suffered a heart episode but had recovered; brother Hugh was now officially engaged. This reminded J to lay claim to one of his mother's rings: "I trust if I ever get married you will give me one of yours as I can't see the point of spending on frippery good money that could be put into printing two or three books."

J set out to bend his mother to his will: he wanted her to help produce books during July, even though she had planned to spend the month with her mother. "Import Gammy to the Camp" at Norfolk, J suggested. Aunt Leila could fix her up with a social calendar, and then J's mother would be free to work with him: "I can't see the point of having children do something interesting and not sharing in it." Letters suggesting that Gammy move to Robin Hill Camp, a rustic cabin in the woods on Aunt Leila's property, must have alarmed his grandmother rather badly. She wouldn't budge. Pound's *Culture* and Williams's *Life Along the Passaic River* meant something, J assured his mother. He pointed out that if she would come to Norfolk to share the publishing work with him, it would bring them closer together: "It is somehow the symbol of our new life together." He alternated between bullying his mother and sounding like her suitor.

On learning of Miss Demarest's illness, J had considered returning to America at once to take over the mechanics of running New Directions, but he decided against curtailing his trip, partly because he had planned a London campaign with very specific aims: placing ND books with British publishers instead of exporting them to England, thus avoiding heavy freight charges; and buying sheets of titles published in Britain, which would save about 44 percent over the cost of having them reset and printed in the United States. Then Marjory Laughlin decided to assume Miss Demarest's tasks in person. He had known, J said, that either she or Aunt Leila would come to the rescue of New Directions, but the fact that his mother had done so herself, rather than hire someone, pleased him especially. By early June, Elizabeth Demarest would be in the Winsted hospital, unable even to recognize visitors, and she would die before the end of June.

J was looking ahead to the future of New Directions, and he was angling for another key author. He had been following Dylan Thomas's career since 1935 and finally wrote to him in February 1938, offering to publish him. Thomas, recently married, replied in a desperate-sounding letter. He opened with an acceptance—"I should like you . . . to be my American publisher for good and all"—outlined the dismal publishing fortunes of his three books, and then described his state at length: "I do not mean that we just live poorly; I mean that we go without food . . . I have now less than a shilling; there is no more to come." He did not even name a figure: "I am more than willing to dispense with my future royalties and take whatever sum you can give me for the complete American copyright of all books I shall write." J wrote back that he was trying to raise some money. Again, on April 25, Thomas wrote that he urgently needed the peacefulness of a Welsh village, "without these bloody nagging worries," and that he could rent a fisherman's cottage for less than $5 per week. In return, he said, "you can have all I'll do; & I *must* be paid immediately for it: some advance, I mean." J sent a check at once for $20, and by May 7 another check for a like amount reached Thomas. In early May, J asked for his June allowance, since he was sending money monthly to Thomas. "His books won't make much toward paying the advance," he wrote to his mother, "but I feel more or less that God has put him in my care and I must keep him alive." Dylan turned out to be an excellent investment.

•

On Sunday, May 15, Mussolini made a progress through Rapallo. He was driven slowly under J's balcony in an open car, grinning, waving, obviously enjoying himself. When J left soon after for Paris, Lola Avena slipped onto the train with him, crying and begging to be kissed. "I feel nothing at all," J wrote in his diary. Eight years would pass before he saw Rapallo again.

J moved into the Hotel St.-Romain in Paris and immediately began a round of strategic visits. It was his week for seeing literati, some merely notorious, others already famous. One day was devoted largely to Henry Miller and his circle: first an audience with the compulsive diarist Anaïs Nin on *La Belle Aurore*, her leaking houseboat; then meetings with Henry's satellite, Alfred Perlès, and Jack Kahane, Henry's Paris publisher. That evening J went with Nin to hear the Budapest String Quartet and on other days took in Goethe's *Faust* and attended the centennial revival of *Ruy Blas* at the Comédie-Française. He visited Paul Éluard, a "real man & poet," and Stein entertained J on May 26 while Bernard Faÿ pranced in attendance.

Following Ezra's mandate, J saw Jean Cocteau:

And after we had had lunch at the
Grand Véfour, where there was a
Banquette with his name on a bronze
Plaque, and had dealt at great length
With the topic of flying saucers, in
Which he fervently believed, he took
Me to call on Colette in her rooms
Over the Palais Royal.

Unfortunately, the author of *Gigi* was in bed with a severe grippe, and they departed after four minutes of "charming / Politesse." Ever after, J would speak affectionately of "Marse Jean."

On his last day in Paris, J reported to Ezra, "I called ceremoniously on James Jesus Joyce. He lives very comfortably in a bourgeois interior full of portraits of children. He looks very frail, but trim." The great man had greeted J, "I think Mr. Laughlin that we last met on the battlefield of Clontarf," on Good Friday 1014, and told him that his name derived "from Lochlann which means Norseman in Kelt." "He liked legpulls," J recognized, but Joyce was right enough here. Clontarf, the greatest battle of early Irish history, had turned the tide against Viking expansion in Ireland, and J could certainly pass for a lanky Scandinavian knight. Joyce was very pleased that J's physiology vindicated his philology. "Not senile

I should say—just word-crazy," J said. He had wanted to get Joyce to admit that he had borrowed the concept of the interior monologue from Dujardin, but instead he launched into an interminable story about going to an opera in Rouen with a Siamese prince "who had taken the name 'Ulysse' in his honour."

J's few days in England passed in a whirl. On Sunday, June 5, he went to Cambridge, where he saw John Berryman—ascetic, fragile in body and psyche—and collected three of his poems for the next anthology at the urging of their common friend Delmore Schwartz. J had hoped to visit Dylan Thomas in Laugharne but excused himself to Thomas, unconvincingly, that the railway fare from London was too high. He should have known that this reason, coming from the "Pigiron duke," as Thomas now called him, would not sit well with the impecunious Welshman. While reiterating to J that he wanted New Directions to be his American publisher, to others Thomas spoke of a "disagreement," claiming in contravention of his several letters to J that he had assumed the $40 sent thus far to be a "present," not "his disgusting idea of a business advance." A year later Thomas was still fuming about "the little tyke," claiming that J would have no legal recourse to get his advance back if he should find another publisher.

The trouble for Thomas was that no one else in America seemed to want his poems, so he signed a contract in August 1939 recognizing the accrued $60 as an advance and promising ND first refusal on his next five books. He wrote to J the following month that "it's settled now and that's alright [sic]." And the year after that he felt constrained to accept a "filthy contract" from "dear little Laughlin" offering an advance of $50 for *Portrait of the Artist as a Young Dog*. There was truth, to be sure, in J's consistent stand that, assuming the advance was made up in sales, a small initial figure meant that sooner rather than later the royalty checks would start to come in. Living hand to mouth as Thomas always seemed to do, he was never able to see it this way: money in hand meant glorious sprees and a lordly feeling. "I like drinking," Thomas wrote to the poet Henry Treece, "and when I have money I don't stop." These excesses were precisely what J wanted to spare the Welsh poet.

On June 6, J passed through the doors of Faber and Faber for meetings with Frank Morley ("superb—a powerful engine. What Uncle George calls a $50,000.00 man") and Eliot. Ezra had finally agreed to let J take over his American publishing, and coordinating the production of *The Cantos* with Faber was J's most important mission in London. He also bought sheets or arranged for joint publications of Ezra's *Culture*, the *Ta Hio*, *Polite Essays*, and *ABC of Economics*. He tried in vain to talk Eliot and Morley into taking on Williams, while Eliot recommended *Nightwood* by the largely unknown Djuna Barnes. When J was not consorting with eminent Faberites, he visited agents and authors. Laurence Pollinger made a favorable impression, "a beaming little fat man—hard inside." For the rest of J's life, the Pollinger agency would handle British rights for all authors who by contract turned over these publishing rights to ND. Thanks to Eliot, J spent his final evening with Wyndham Lewis—"the genuine article"—although he failed to acquire the book he wanted for ND and did not buy a painting because Lewis wanted £100 for a major oil. The next day J sailed for New York.

Even though he had just hired James Higgins, a young novelist and former *Advocate* stalwart, as his first full-time paid New Directions employee, J appeared to be spending more time on publishing than on either classes or courtship. He blundered into a contretemps when he decided to print only part of Zukofsky's section "A"-8 in the 1938 anthology, while the poet held out for all or nothing. J countered with a request for $50 in "composition cost," and the poet then demanded $300 for the full text. "Considering your disposition, I can no longer let you have the poem free," Zukofsky wrote angrily. "You come down to earth and return both MS. and galley proof." Finally, J agreed to publish the entire section, and no money changed hands.

In August 1938, J bought a small Vandercook handpress for acquiring some practical knowledge of printing and so that he could run off advertising flyers. His trial effort, a birthday greeting for his mother, was impeccably typeset using two sizes each of italic and boldface fonts:

To DEAR MAMA Upon Her Birthday
Her Odd & Out-size Offspring LITTLE JAMES Offers This Memorial Of His True Affection - Being The First Work Of His Fumbling Fingers On The New Directions Press.

He closed with a tag from Dante: *"Incipit Vita Nuova"*—Here begins the new life. J's ulterior motive was to get his mother to learn to print. That was part of his program for an Unhappy Parent: join the New Directions effort. It was "artistic work and not tiring," he assured her.

On his trip to Boston on Sunday, August 7, J combined New Directions business, reading Dylan Thomas over the radio, and the courtship of Theodora Sedgwick, for J was now openly wife hunting. He had been holding forth to his mother on the subject of an "American Aristocracy" and the admirable virtues of dynastic families. J felt that his own was not such a dynasty but could have been and *might still become one*. He fastened his hopes of building a dynasty on marriage with Theodora. Her mother was a Cabot, and Theo, as he now called her, had a magnificent profile and plenty of what Hemingway liked to call "class." In settling on a fiancée, J was sure that the most difficult consideration was to please Aunt Leila. "I want so much to get one lined up who will really make Aunt Leila happy, because I do think I haven't always been easy on her in the ones I've had about," he told his mother. "Of course I want to please you too, but then you aren't quite as choosey as Aunt Leila." Theodora would not have been flattered to learn that J thought she would "grow up into something just as good as Aunt Leila."

What did please Aunt Leila was the sojourn at Robin Hill Camp of Bill and Floss Williams and their two sons, grown young men. The Williamses made a good impression on Aunt Leila, and Uncle Dicky listened to the poet, J said, "as he does to a republican bank president."

J worked mightily to have his anthology at the printer and still have time for a selling trip before classes started. *NDPP 1938* appeared in October and contained, among other writers new to ND, Berryman, Paul Éluard, Charles Henri Ford, James Higgins, MacLeish, Patchen, Saroyan, and Dylan Thomas—who quickly became one of ND's bestselling poets. The volume included a frontispiece by Kirstein's friend Pavel Tchelitchew, who had suggested the poems of his lover, Ford. One section was headed "Modern Poets of Japan" and featured contemporary poets of the Vou Club, of which Pound's friend Kit Kat, Kitasono Katue, was a founding member. J wrote a preface for the Vou selections, holding them up as proof that "militaristic imperialism" had not eliminated "live poetry" in Japan. A friend from Pittsburgh, Edgar Kaufmann Jr., edited a New Directions in Design survey. Kaufmann had studied with Frank Lloyd Wright, and the cantankerous visionary had built Fallingwater for Kaufmann senior, only a few miles from the Laughlins' Big Springs farm. J printed eight poems under his own name and a bit of surrealist prose signed Tasilo Ribischka: "Last night as I lay in bed I burst. There on the mildewed sheets with the bugs swarming over me and the rotted odour of fecundity sprawling on the room like a gigantic toad squatting, I lay thinking of Talavera."

J's publications list consisted of twelve titles, to make this ND's first year of full operation, and it exemplified the developing credo of New Directions: promote "modern classics" by keeping the major figures of the "revolution of the word" like Pound and Williams in print; publish the influential foreign moderns in translation; print the relatively unknown advance guard; throw together writers from conflicting camps; use good artwork by such figures as Gaudier-Brzeska and Tchelitchew; keep fine printing alive, with boxed, limited editions of Fitts and Williams.

J responded to Pound's diatribe against the previous anthology in his 1938 preface, further defining the role of the annual: "What it does try to do is to print the best work *of a certain kind*—the best *experimental* writing . . . writers whose interest in problems of technique places their work beyond the commercial market." J freely admitted to printing some work that he did not like; it went in nonetheless "because it is obviously authentic experiment." J was coming to view the annual increasingly as *his*, the publication where he could follow his own tastes, instincts, whims, irrespective of the urgings of his various mentors. He did not want the "faddist," the "cultist," those who might confuse mere innovation with quality. Thus, readers should expect both convention and revolt to be represented. Literature was no casual game: "The function of *New Directions* [is] to make all types of literary experiment available to American writers and readers . . . because it is absolutely essential to the healthy evolution of literature." With a clatter of the keys on his Smith-Corona, J typed out bits of his Weltanschauung: "A comparison with politics is not irrelevant; a healthy polity is one in which conservative and liberal forces interact." Conflict burnished the metal of thought.

In his preface, J set out to respond to, anticipate, and challenge his critics. To reviewers who complained that Pound, Cummings, and Stein were no longer "new," he replied that because none had been "assimilated" or widely accepted, they needed to be "kept in current print" so that the value of their innovations would not be lost. Sometimes innovation meant going back to the past, and this is what J claimed Pound had done in *Le Testament*, in which the poet cum composer had attempted *motz el son*, words as sound, the technique of the Provençal troubadours, involving a precise "note-for-syllable" marriage of "vowel-sounds and the pitch and beat of the music." Like many poets, Ezra composed to the musical measure, yet it was more than that. Pound's *Testament* was poetry meant to be sung such as, J maintained, no other modernist was creating, and to support his claim, J reproduced both the text and the musical score—another first for the anthology—of the "Heaulmière" aria from Pound's opera. Ezra saw the *dimensionality* of words. This was one key to the authority of his translations, an authority that transcended questions of literal accuracy: "The River-Merchant's Wife" possessed form, coordinates, mass, velocity, time. Over the years, J would attempt to apply the concept of dimensionality to his own poetry and to his translations of the classics.

For the first time, J's annual included photographic illustrations, in Kaufmann's design portfolio. J defended the inclusion of product design in a literary anthology on the ground that "parallel movements in different arts are complementary" and that there was no publication in America devoted to modern design. "What America needs," said J in barbed conclusion, "is imagination among her writers, by imagination being meant the faculty of going beyond naturalism and realism." J's preface was at once manifesto and exhortation, and it brought him a fan letter and a book order from Jacques Barzun, an influential Columbia professor who would become a close friend. Critical reaction was mixed. Philip Rice attacked in *The Kenyon Review*, and J's new friend the poet Allen Tate found Zukofsky "wholly conventional and timid," yet he endorsed J's overall accomplishment: "To have issued Williams, Dujardin, and Schwartz in one season is a fine record."

During September, J planned to cover "every store in the area lying between Washington [D.C.], Portland [Maine], Chicago, and Cincinnati." While only thirty stores across the United States would order good poetry unpressed, others might if visited personally. So J set off in his new Ford on a selling trip, taking Theodora along for an introduction to the family at Big Springs. On September 16, J left alone to sell books, sending Theo home by train. By September 26 he was back in class at Harvard. In October he visited stores in New York and Connecticut. "Sold every shop I went into," he said, even speculating, "I wonder if I could sell steel as well as I can sell books." J reported to his "Reverend Gent," Fitts, that his *Palatine Anthology* had been easy to sell because "I told them you were as smart as Dorothy Parker." He sold Yvor Winters by announcing that he had held the middleweight boxing championship of California—Winters only claimed to have taught boxing in a mining town. J remarked, "Nobody in this land gives a hoot in hell about poetry."

After all the rushing about, J lamented, "I'm just about dead." Higgins's salary came out of J's allowance; he did not think it fair to New Directions to settle on his company an expense incurred only because school kept him otherwise occupied. J had evolved a complicated double-entry financing for ND, keeping a record of expenses separate from his private accounts but shuffling money around as necessity demanded. For the rest of his life he would separate what he considered legitimate ND expenses from the other expenditures of the "President and Publisher."

J engaged Mary Barnard to come to Norfolk to help Higgins prepare a mailing of catalogs. Barnard's contemporary description belies J's disparagement of his center of operations as a "converted stable":

Norfolk is a beautiful little village of big white houses, pines, a stony brook with a waterfall, a beautiful church with a tall white spire. By contrast the New Directions office might be a Paris attic except for its cleanliness. Abounds in books, photographs (including Cummings and Williams), magazines . . . The building which houses New Directions was built as a caretaker's house. It is of big bricks or stones painted white. The doors are blue, darker than turquoise. It's a three-way affair, including a cottage, what was originally intended for a stable, and a four-car garage. The Carlisles lived in it while they were building their house. They liked it so much that they used it for guests instead of servants . . . they decided a stable was inappropriate so they made the stable into a big living room for the cottage, built a big stone fireplace at one end.

The floor plan included two bedrooms downstairs, as well as a bath and a large kitchen with both wood-burning and electric ranges, and there were more rooms upstairs. There was an alcove with a printing press.

In mid-October, J was on a selling trip when "things busted loose": for the first time, a New Directions book rated a full-page review, a favorable one, in *The New York Times*: Edouard Dujardin's *We'll to the Woods No More*, illustrated by J's cousin Alice Denniston Laughlin. She had a substantial reputation in the art world and had exhibited her stained glass at the Philadelphia World's Fair in 1926. Cousin Alice produced a set of delicate drawings that perfectly complemented Dujardin's prose. J telephoned "all" the bookstores in the city, sold nearly a hundred copies, and had Higgins drive from Norfolk to deliver the copies the very same evening.

All this coursing about, coupled with a full academic load, putting the anthology together, *and* writing for publication, should have been activity enough, but J was still almost obsessively in the marriage market. He attended a "deb party" on the North Shore, going just to "have a look at this year's product. Nothing any good," he decided. Theodora still reigned. A man would not play the field with Theo for wife, J said. He discussed his love life with two mature women—his mother and Mrs. Charles Storey, the mother of J's Harvard roommate—and the latter told him that he would "never be in love with anybody else" but himself. With equal candor, J admitted to his mother, "I suppose that is true, but I certainly do spend a good deal of time thinking about Theodora and just love to be with her." Then he speculated, "I should think if I could get a job in J&L it would be all right to get married, don't you?" With "somebody like Theodora" beside him, he could stand to work temporarily for the firm. J did not seem to grasp the significance of that "somebody *like*": unconsciously, he was seeing her as emblem, as consort, as "Mrs. James Laughlin," not as Theodora the person.

He went so far as to suggest that he and Theodora live with his mother, occupy the third floor, which would save them money and would at least "get some use out of that house since it costs enough to keep it going." He was quite prepared, he said, to "throttle down" New Directions to the annual anthology "and nothing more" for a few years, thinking, naively, that the publishing company would still be there to be claimed ten years along, while surmising, realistically, that Theo would not.

Then there was the Laughlin secret, which J thought might quash his chances with Theodora—or with anyone else of her class. "It probably won't be long until Papa Sedgwick finds out about Father and then he'll put a stop to it," J said. He was concerned not only with the scandal of his father's mental breakdown but with the flawed gene that he himself might be carrying. He had not warned Theodora and did not intend to: "Where would I be if I started letting myself think that I was bound to have the same thing happen to me?" What in a less driven person could simply have become a reason early to despair became in J the motor driving him to produce, to excel. What J did not know was that the Sedgwicks had a better-stocked closet of skeletons than the Laughlins: ten years after J's own death, Theodora's relative John Sedgwick would publish a history of the family, *In My Blood: Six Generations of Madness and Desire in an American Family*.

J convinced himself that he was going through a *crise*. What a "misery" it was that being in love was so complicated! He totted up his abilities in writing—both "good writing and popular writing"—and in selling books. "And still I can never for a moment feel sure that anything I do is the right thing to do," he confessed to his mother, surely expecting reassurance. In his complaining, he lashed out at precisely the direction he had taken as far back as his meeting with Dudley Fitts at Choate: "My literary leanings carried me off into a world where I am not really happy." Now he wanted to "come back," and he saw in Theodora a guide who could lead him back, since "she is completely part of a fixed society," of the mundane, uncomplicated world.

Theodora's birthday was coming up: after considering and rejecting a dachshund puppy and a silver cigarette case, he procured for her a beautiful Nonesuch Press bilingual *Iliad*, which he got "quite cheap on a trade of ND books."

His dead father's reputation presented a more knotty problem. J resolved to create a myth to counter the unacceptable reality of his father's pathology, so he drafted a short story, "This Is My Blood." In it the narrator, MacDonald, submits to a transfusion in which blood passes directly from his veins into his father's, in a desperate attempt to sustain the older man, suffering from blood poisoning. Both men are employed by "MacDonald Steel." J cast the father as the head of the company, "a successful, conventional man," arguing to his mother that "this story will help fix the impression that he was, an impression which will be a great help to me." J claimed that the story "will do me a good deal of good psycologically [*sic*]." Furthermore, although both J and his mother found the story painful to read, J thought that it was "good," and he was going "judiciously" to distribute a few offprints as pamphlets to "people who would assimilate the myth." "And why not have a myth?" J quickly said in justification. "Poor man, it wasn't his fault." There was also an element of expiation: J seems to have felt that he could have, should have, done more to help his father. By

October 3, *Story* magazine had accepted "This Is My Blood" for publication in May of the coming year.

J had his own reasons to worry: he continued at intervals to feel "terribly depressed." Strangely, he wrote, "I have always felt that depression is a purely physical thing." He feared that the family curse might already be settling on him. The strain told: near the end of October he had to postpone a second trip to Washington, "as I smashed hell out of my car." He complained of being broke; he complained that he was in love; to Kay Boyle he lamented that he would lose money on *A Glad Day* because he had printed only five hundred copies. He asked Kay to forgive him royalties, and she answered generously, "For heaven's sake, don't worry about royalties."

J roused himself out of his depression to call on Cummings. "He is without any question the best man in the country," J wrote to Ezra. "I am going to commission him to do some Greek translations for me, as that will sell much better than his own work, and he needs the money." Ezra was pleased: "This tellink th KUMrad kz ter trans/ Catullus izza step in th right DIrecxshun. Mebbe you'll be worth yr/ salt yet." Cummings offered some poems instead, writing, "Our hero needs lucre." When J could not raise enough cash, Cummings and J concluded, both with reluctance, that they couldn't afford each other.

While he had been dancing amicably around Cummings, J and Henry Miller were at loggerheads. "I don't think I'll be sending you any script after all," wrote Miller. Their views were "diametrically opposite": "What I'd like to see published you either can't or won't take . . . You're thinking now about your public, your buyers, your family etcetera . . . And I think only of what I want done. Deadlock." Miller had a point, or several points. J *was* thinking about the reading public, the booksellers, and the courts. But he often claimed that the strongest voice came from the court of family opinion, chief magistrate, Aunt Leila. While J would sometimes maintain that he doubted whether she had read a single book he published, he trotted her out whenever badgered by a pesky author.

To Miller, worse than the rejections were J's attempts to understand him: J's "ill-advised criticism and preaching," his attempts to set him on the right "track." J had suggested that Henry was a "mystic." "If anybody is on the earth, it is me!" he exploded. "But I have a big wingspan. I can fly. I have polarity. What I am after essentially is 'reality,' which is beyond religiousness, beyond mysticism." As he typed, Miller cooled down, telling

J not to feel hurt. "Shit, it isn't only the 20 years difference between us," but the difference in what each had lived through. Miller then added some advice of his own, which J must eventually have come to appreciate: "The great problem in life is how to keep your integrity without rendering your efforts null and void." J's sense of mission and integrity did not allow him the comforting singleness of purpose that characterized Miller. Back in May 1937, Miller had written to J in some excitement about Lawrence Durrell's *The Black Book*, which he had just read in manuscript. While J now said he was "very much impressed" by the *Black Book* typescript and wanted selections from it for the next annual, he felt that his obligation was to American writers: "About an Englishman I don't care so much." Obligation or not, J was considering publishing *Tropic of Cancer*, but he held back. "The obscenity in *Ulysses* was much better integrated than it is with you," he told Miller. "With you it sticks out like hell."

As Europe rolled toward war, J strove to maintain his detachment and skepticism, but the alarums kept causing consternation among his growing assortment of authors. No one was more apolitical or anarchic than Henry Miller, yet no one reacted with greater rabbity panic when war seemed imminent: Neville Chamberlain, the British prime minister, appeared to be prepared to stand firm against Hitler's proposal to annex the Sudetenland. Henry bolted from Paris to Marseilles, hoping to take ship for America, all the while cabling everyone he could think of for funds. J wired $200, to be an advance against future royalties. Then Chamberlain capitulated to Hitler at Munich, and the storm subsided. "I am very glad that it should be *you* who takes me on as American publisher," Henry wrote in confirmation.

In November 1938, J scored a tremendous publicity coup when he and New Directions were written up in *Time* magazine. J wasn't sure, but he thought that the appearance of the two journalists at his door had everything to do with the fact that Frank Norris, the managing editor of *Time*, was in love with J's former girlfriend Elizabeth Duval, who was still very friendly toward him. Family disapproval or not, J now told *Time* that he *would* publish *Tropic of Cancer*. It hardly mattered that half the article was devoted not to ND but to *Cancer* and to Durrell's *Black Book*: anything under the *Time* magazine headline "Dithyrambic Sex" was good publicity for "experimental writing."

By the end of the year, J had initiated his career as Pound's main

American publisher with a 519-copy run of *Culture*, republished later as *Guide to Kulchur*. J reproduced Gaudier-Brzeska's profile portrait of Ezra on the jacket, but the printer used a soiled plate, and Ezra shot back, "Why does Nude Erect/ represent me with a wart or spot on my NOSE , which aint in the iriginal Gaudier ?? DEtail, son DETAIL." A week later Ezra, mollified, sent a postcard acknowledging an advance copy of a New Directions Pamphlet, his translation of the *Ta Hio: The Great Learning of Confucius*: "vurry neat and handsome/ Than Q." Pound would remain loyal to J and ND for the rest of his life; reciprocally, J would never waver in his support of Ezra.

After nearly three years in business, New Directions had much to recommend itself to authors. J's publication in December of Schwartz's *In Dreams Begin Responsibilities*, a collection including the title short story, poems, and a play, shows his developing grasp of the essentials of publishing. His first concern was to time the publication for the fall list. He planned an advertising campaign that would cost $1,000 in notices alone in such organs as the *New York Herald Tribune*, *The New York Times*, *The Nation*, *The Saturday Review of Literature*, *The Southern Review*, *Partisan Review*, and *The New Republic*. In addition, he would send out nearly a hundred copies to reviewers. J designed the book himself, specifying Bodoni type on cream-toned paper and a binding of black cloth. When Schwartz asked for the white linen that J had used for Williams's *White Mule*, J replied that he considered the white covers Williams's signature "property"; besides, J added, white gets dirty on bookstore shelves. If white was suitable for the Whitmanesque bard of Rutherford, surely black was the color for Schwartz, a writer with the somber tones of Dostoevsky.

•

Suddenly J's love life took a dramatic turn. "You were right about Theodora," J admitted to his mother. He had found out that he was not really in love with her by crashing into love with someone else. "I just had developed the idea of being good and respectable and being in love with a good person," he said. All that was now over: "I shall never contemplate being good or respectable again . . . I am by nature a wild one and anything else is just fooling myself." He had met Diana Reeve through common friends and had casually invited her over, but after an argument with her at dinner he had caught her looking at him; then, "like a sledgehammer," "like an avalanche," they were smitten simultaneously. "It just hit me all of a sudden without any warning at all and I never knew anything like it." Unlike Theodora, Diana was "not at all pretty," but she had style, carriage, and "a pale, sensitive face." She wore her hair wound in a "double crown" atop her head, and her whole bearing reminded J of her classical namesake. Although it had nothing to do with his loving her, J reported that "this girl is a Lowell and a Roosevelt (Theodore's branch)," and "they are rich as pigs." Diana was a grand-niece of Harvard's former president Abbott Lawrence Lowell, and she took J to Lowell's mansion in Boston. J was on his best behavior, but it slipped out that he was a writer. "Diana, why are you always attracted to worthless men?" the patriarch demanded. (She would later write considerable poetry under the pen name Diana Lowell Roosevelt.)

As a publisher, J received an unexpected gift from FDR when he cut the postage rate for books from eight cents a pound to a penny and a half. After all his fulminations against the president, J should have been nonplussed to receive an invitation from Eleanor Roosevelt for a "Small Dance" at the White House on December 27. J evidently accepted the summons, yet he did not think the event itself worthy of comment. Love was far more important.

The World at War

... talk about the road to war, it makes me sick.
                                        —James Laughlin to Ezra Pound

With New Directions taking up more and more of his time, J felt that he should graduate from Harvard, three years after most of his classmates. He passed his term examinations, and on February 8 he "rolled out of bed" to read on the editorial page of *The Boston Herald* a letter from Ezra proposing his old friend the Massachusetts representative "Uncle George" Tinkham for president. Tinkham had opposed nearly every measure FDR proposed, except for the repeal of Prohibition. It promised to be an exciting year.

Back at Harvard for the spring term, J applied himself to his course work, ingeniously melding his New Directions authors with classical figures. For the formidable classicist E. K. Rand he proposed "Coriolanus Old and New," a comparison of versions of the Coriolanus story by ancient authors such as Livy, Florus, Dio Cassius, Plutarch, and Dionysius of Halicarnassus with those of Shakespeare and Delmore Schwartz, whose "Coriolanus and His Mother" poem "really stands up excellent well" in a line-by-line parallel reading with the play by "Old Bill," J told Delmore. After J's graduation, Rand would write fondly to his "once pupil," concluding, "Believe me, my dear friend, with the constant hope that you will live to be old enough to love Horace."

J received plenty of conflicting advice on what to do with his publishing business. Bill Williams needled him about past lapses, and J replied with some humility that *White Mule* had been "pretty still-born" owing to his lack at the outset of promotional expertise. Schwartz told him that it had been a mistake to publish Patchen: J should have gone with Berryman, Bishop, Barnard, almost anyone else. So what if "the old doctor" had compared Patchen to Donne: "You know that Williams will praise anyone unless he writes blank verse and his name is Schwartz." Complicating his cash flow problem was that J could not get at the principal of the trust that his father had set up for him, he told Delmore, "until my mother dies and she is healthy as a horse."

In mid-1939, J had written to Patchen accepting, "with glowing words," Kenneth's second volume of poetry, *First Will and Testament.* The poet's back, injured two years before while he was attempting to repair a friend's car, had given out after a failed operation, and he was bedridden, unable to continue at the WPA's Federal Writers' Project in Hollywood. The Patchens were about to retreat to his parents' home in Acton, Massachusetts. J offered them employment and Aunt Leila's cottage in Norfolk—pending her approval. They called on J in Cambridge, and Miriam Patchen was appalled at the half-finished meals left on dishes, the piles of clothes on the floor. "These Harvard apartments, where lived great minds being trained," she would recall, "looked like a surreal set for a Renaissance engraving!"

The Patchens were to keep accounts and make large shipments. As J's stock of unsold copies grew, Norfolk became increasingly the center from which large shipments were made, which required the presence of a reliable and strong-backed accomplice. Higgins would make smaller shipments from the stock in Boston but mainly deal with printers, designers, artists, and authors. J would rush over from Cambridge, work on a book design, write letters, chat, then swing an ax to cut firewood—to keep *his* back loosened up. Kenneth was greatly moved to discover his photograph to be the only one in J's room when he went there to retrieve a book J needed.

J had another motive besides their literary judgment for hiring the likes of Schwartz and Patchen. "It was a definite part of the program to try to provide employment for writers I knew who didn't have a job," J said years later. He knew that such wages as he could pay were not generous, but he figured that at least the relatively light duties that he assigned would leave them time for creation. Soon, however, Kenneth was complaining that press work was taking too much time away from his writing and that his back hurt. The Patchens left in December, giving Kenneth's health and his creative demon as the reasons. According to J, their departure was accelerated by Aunt Leila.

And J had other troubles requiring diplomacy. One particular point of contention between Williams and J was the mounting reputation of Eliot. When J commended to Williams *The Family Reunion*, he must have known he was in for trouble: "If you want to see poetry as is poetry—hard as a rock and beautiful as the queen's tit—look at the choruses in Eliot's new play." "I'm glad you like his verse," Williams fired back by return mail, "but I'm warning you, the only reason it doesn't smell is that it's synthetic . . . Birdseye Foods, suddenly frozen at 50 degrees below zero." J explained that he himself sought to "get an effect of tension from the war between the strictly artificial visual pattern and the strictly natural spoken rhythms." This was not what Williams, Pound, or Eliot were doing, but J could trace elements of his own prosodic practice to all three of his elders: Williams for simplicity of statement and commonplace imagery; Pound for linguistic inventiveness and European allusions; the Eliot of the plays for the natural rhythms of conversation. J aimed, he said, to "also try to write concretely, using everyday objects for your symbols and allegories, and to avoid poeticisms." J published examples of his current style in *Furioso*, the poetry magazine just started at Yale by James Jesus Angleton, who had visited Pound the summer before in Rapallo. During the war, Angleton would rise meteorically in the Office of Strategic Services, emerging as the increasingly paranoid director of counterintelligence at the CIA, destroying many careers—and ultimately his own.

Along with his focus on graduating and on practicing his own poetry, J lined up thirteen titles for the year's New Directions list, including the Joyce symposium *Our Exagmination Round His Factification for Incamination of Work in Progress*, an import from Sylvia Beach's Shakespeare and Company. J's life was dominated, however, by his return to school, where he faced five Divisionals, "a terrible catastrophe that comes once in a Harvard lifetime," standing between him and his AB: one each on Dante, Lucretius, Roman literature, and Italian literature, and one on the continuity between the Roman and the Italian periods. He was too busy even to ski.

J was writing well, however. His short story "What the Butler Heard" appeared in *Fantasy* magazine. By deftly entering the minds of the butler and of Harriet Whitten, second daughter of the household, J had composed

a story that might have been by D. H. Lawrence parodying Henry James—
or the other way around. He had based it on the Woolsey household, with
his old love Sara as Harriet. The butler lacks the subservient instinct of a
servant and becomes fascinated by Harriet because she is "different."
With the utmost subtlety, J builds suspense and an air of threat. He
catches the counterpoint of dinner-table conversation between Harriet
and her teenage lover, on the one hand, and the jealous butler's thoughts,
on the other. The butler, seized between the opposed jaws of his passion
and his station, cannot declare himself.

And then J stopped writing short stories. Many years later he would
say that he had "abandoned fiction" because he "couldn't think up plots."
True, most of his stories had *donnés* that came from his own experience
and observation, and perhaps he thought that his fiction was becoming
too self-revelatory. Another reason, more likely, was that J was unwilling
to put out the *continuity of effort* that fiction, even short fiction, required.
Poems, he would invariably say, *came to him*: a more or less complete treatment of a situation or an emotion would enter his mind, and he would
write it down. Fiction required disciplined persistence.

Aunt Leila had liked the idea that her Jamesie take up publishing until she saw the actual books. J for his part felt that he had to tread delicately, both for obvious financial reasons and because of his affection for
his aunt, genuine "in spite of her prejudices." When J proposed that Delmore and Gertrude move to Norfolk as his assistants, Aunt Leila replied
"in the nixative": she remembered the Patchens, and she had read part of
In Dreams Begin Responsibilities and decided that Schwartz, who had used
the word "fuck" twice in his book, was "a mixture of sex-fiend and Communist" against whom her nephew had to be protected. And she stood
strong against Henry Miller still. In this she had an ally in J's mother, who
scolded him in such forthright terms for publishing Miller that J replied
in kind: "Dearest Mums: I was very mad at you for your letter of a week
ago and swore to high heaven I would never have another thing to do with
you as long as I lived, but that has passed along now and I am fond of you
as usual . . . You are wrong about Henry Miller because the people who
buy my books like that sort of thing. I get no support at all from your class
of people so I don't need to bother with what they think."

Miller cautioned J that if he held to his plan to bring out *Tropic of
Cancer*, he could face prison and the loss of his publishing venture. Gen-

erously, Henry said that he would not "reproach" him if he canceled their agreement for family or other reasons. J reaffirmed his intention, only he was "waiting for some cash to turn up," as he wanted to set aside $5,000 against possible legal fees and certain promotional expenses. Then something occurred that he should have anticipated: Aunt Leila read the article in *Time*. With Uncle Dicky supporting her, she laid down the law: if J persisted in his plan to publish those horrid books by Miller, they would not, *could not*, continue to support his publishing—and, by implication, J either. The Carlisles measured literary value by the social and moral code in Galsworthy: honorable behavior in all matters, devotion to justice, respect for women. It was a world that Lawrence, Joyce, Miller, and J himself scoffed at as being hopelessly lacking in verisimilitude. J backed down.

Meanwhile, J was gradually developing a binary view of European Fascism: inasmuch as it appeared to be improving the standard of living of the Germans and Italians, it might have virtue, but it did not export well by force of arms. He thought, agreeing with Bill Williams, that Ezra should grow up. "I urgently counsel your eminence not to sign letters to America with arriba españa, as you did to Wms the other day," J wrote to Ez. "He nearly had apoplexy. There is such a thing as not hanging oneself by the neck . . . Please be cautious Erudite Sir." Williams took the fall of Republican Spain very hard, and here J was firmly on Bill's side. "He's off you," J said evenly to Ezra. J himself was "all for" the Pound/Major Douglas monetary theories, he told Delmore, but not for the Fascism of Franco, Hitler, and Mussolini. Il Duce might understand Social Credit, but then why would he try to "bag *useless* colonies"? J would remain, lifelong, a convert to Ezra's economic theories, not at all to his politics.

Still, J was prepared to make a public assertion of his own position on the coming conflict and was one of the signatories of Dwight Macdonald's June 1939 war manifesto, a plea for American neutrality, under the sponsorship of the League for Cultural Freedom and Socialism and published in the fall issue of *Partisan Review*. Kay Boyle, Katherine Anne Porter, Rexroth, and Williams were among the signatories. Three years ago the young were generally pacifist, J wrote to Ezra in April, but now they had been inoculated with war fever. "Latest development I noticed last night at the moving pictures. For the first time in this country that I've seen they had the Star Sprinkled Spanner at the end . . . Yes sir, we are being whipped up, toyed with, massily and crassly incited to go over and fight another moral, idealistic war in order to move heavy goods by the old method."

Wystan Hugh Auden and Christopher Isherwood had disembarked at New York in January 1939, and Auden soon turned up in Cambridge. He expressed admiration for Schwartz's *In Dreams Begin Responsibilities* and predicted a meteoric career, but J on meeting him could not bring himself to ask the English poet for an advertising statement. "Auden I just don't like, but please keep that to yourself," J told Delmore. "I have decided he is the Ovid of the day," J added by way of explanation, as if Auden too merited banishment to the island of Tomi. J maintained a selective double standard: he was certainly not overtly homophobic, but *certain* homosexuals made him feel uncomfortable. Auden was one of these, and J disliked both him and his poetry. Part of J's unease owed its existence to the openness of Auden's sexuality, and his assumption that he *belonged* in the literary-homosexual community that existed sub rosa in Eliot House, a community that had been at Harvard in the time of Kirstein and much further back still.

More unsettling was the threatened arrival in America of Ezra Pound. "Not megalomania, but a sense of responsibility carried to the extreme" motivated him, as his daughter would remark. He wanted to prevent the war and to refocus the country on its original ideals through a good dose of the early presidents. To accomplish this, Ez volunteered his services to J to "SELECT the works of the Founders of the U.S." for the dollar library that J had proposed. This was to inform the public in general and Bill Williams in particular. "The reds or pinks are fading," Ezra announced somewhat prematurely, and "as a dago immigrant Bill ought to learn a little American history."

J responded with a short note of admonition: "IF you come you have got to decide whether you want to be disliked./ If you come as a Poet and keep absolutely mum about money/ jews/ fascism you will be liked/ If you mention any of them subjects you will have one hell of a time." Ezra ignored all the caveats and set sail on short notice.

J tried not to be distracted by the arrival of Ezra Pound in New York Harbor on April 20. "Welcome, Deified Sir," J wrote, but he would *not* meet the ship, commenting that he did not want to be "underfoot," in view of Ezra's doubtless "superior intentions." Munson also tried to warn Pound in a cable to the ship: "GIVE ECONOMIC BUT NOT POLITICAL VIEWS TO THE

PRESS WHEN INTERVIEWED." Ezra ignored his advice as he would J's. While still aboard the *Rex*, Ezra unburdened himself to a reporter and proclaimed Mussolini a great man. Ezra had been corresponding with Senators Robert Taft and William Borah, Representative George Tinkham, and others in Washington, most of them Republican, but had some expectation of an audience with the president, hoping to persuade him not to intervene in the coming war. Delmore defended Ezra to J: "I think you underestimate all the good he did when he was still in his right mind." Williams was more negative than Delmore had been, telling J, "The man is sunk . . . unless he can shake the fog of Fascism out of his brain." Ezra traveled to Washington, where he was courteously received by at least four senators and the future vice president Henry A. Wallace, but FDR ignored him. J kept his distance too. "Wot price yr comin to this beeutiful seat of the nat. govt. fer a spell?" Ezra queried J—who stayed put in Cambridge.

Schwartz and Miller might get J into trouble through their use of the sexual *f*-word, but he was equally aware of the danger of being associated with the political *F*-word. "My connection with Pound always lays me open to attacks of being a Fascist and that is not very pleasant," he told Delmore. While he wanted the New Directions annuals to be "strictly non-political," J aspired to fly his own colors, writing a verse "Letter to Hitler," apparently intended as an antiwar poem. The result was enigmatic to a fault. Had he read the "Letter," Hitler would doubtless have been nonplussed, but *Partisan Review* printed the poem in the summer issue, and J placed it in *NDPP 1939*. J's antiwar and isolationist sentiments were shared by many of his generation: the slaughter of millions on the Western Front was too recent a memory.

Ezra turned up in Cambridge on May 13 to visit his star pupil. J arranged for Ezra to stay with Ted Spencer. Untactfully, Pound trounced his host at tennis—Spencer was quite vain about his game. J escorted Ezra to Sever Hall, where he gave a reading to a capacity audience, his voice ranging from inaudible softness to yelled emphases. Ezra was recorded on May 18 for the Harvard Vocarium series declaiming his translation of "The Seafarer" while accompanying himself on a pair of kettledrums. The next day J drove Ezra to Yale for a reunion with James Angleton. To Kay Boyle, J presented a rosy picture of Ezra's visit. "They all expected an ogre and found a very delightful raconteur instead . . . he is mellowing more and more and not exploding at people." How little Ezra had mellowed became apparent a few days later when he was at his old college, Hamilton, to receive an honorary doctor of letters. At the alumni luncheon following the ceremony, he interrupted the main speaker, the journalist H. V. Kaltenborn; a loud wrangle ensued, and the college president intervened to restore order.

To most of his friends, it was painfully apparent that Pound was out of his element in America. In Italy he might be *il signor poeta*, someone to whom even Mussolini would give a respectful audience. In New York, Washington, or Cambridge, he passed for just another crank. A few days after the Hamilton affair, Slocum put Pound on the ship for Genoa. It was a disappointed man who sailed away.

Around this time J drafted "A Portrait of Ezra Pound," which would be published in *The University Review* at the end of the year. In the nine-page article, J skimmed over Pound's reputation as the "father of modern poetry" to focus on a basic dichotomy: that Ezra was both "a baffling complexity of activities and ideas" and "underneath a singleness and simplicity of motive." The single core motif at Ezra's heart was his self-appointed mission as reformer and liberator. Clear out the deadwood, he said. "Be against all sorts of mortmain." Then "make it new." Principal among the causes of rot was the "financial oligarchy" that, through usury, perpetuated the poverty of the common man by strangling initiative. War was simply another stratagem of the banking/armament partnership. His experience of London during World War I had turned Ezra, J wrote, from the "delicate verse forms" of lyrical poetry to the "mordant, colloquial epigrams" of the mature poet. In nationalizing much of the financial sector, Mussolini appeared to Pound to be moving toward the Social Credit monetary system, but Ezra did not see Fascism as a prerequisite for bringing about Major Douglas's reforms. Recognizing Ezra's faults, lacunae, and contradictions, J nonetheless concluded that for his gifts to American literature, as well as for his high aims, "he deserves American honor and love."

•

On June 5, 1939, seven years after entering Harvard, J completed his honors paper on Lucretius and Dante—neatly blending his Latin and Italian majors—and fulfilled the other requirements for his degree. "Well Harvard is all over and now I can answer a few letters and feel human again,"

J wrote with obvious relief to Kay Boyle. "I cleaned up the exams all right and will get a diploma and all that in due course and Christamighty what a lot of onions that was to peel." He did not mention that he would graduate cum laude. Then J sent Kay a postcard saying that he would not, after all, publish Carnevali's free-associational *Autobiography* that she had over the course of years cajoled and bullied the author into completing. She responded in a long letter that "your refusal to print it alters every feeling I had about you," a letter that ended with a direct command: "I want you to do the Carnevali book." To please Kay, he told Delmore, he was willing to publish it, "if I could be convinced that it would not be bad for the press." He was not to be convinced. While Carnevali would be featured twice in the anthology, no book of his would appear from ND. Kay was bitterly disappointed, and for a year she did not write to J.

J launched his New Classics series in 1939, to be sold at a dollar each. Intended as a run of the best modern books, it began with Williams's *In the American Grain* and was followed the same year by Rimbaud's *Season in Hell*. Two years later Stein's *Three Lives* would appear in the series, until eventually more than twenty-five titles would constitute a very significant collection. In conjunction with these New Classics would be the Makers of Modern Literature series, initiated by Harry Levin's *James Joyce*. Both series were to be part of J's "attack on Academic reaction and senility." Levin's monograph and many other titles in the ND Makers series would become classics in their own right.

With his little affair of a Harvard degree settled and an ambitious publishing program of a dozen books for 1939 well under way, J set out on a cross-country bookselling tour late in the summer. He had already discovered a distinct lack of enthusiasm for advance-guard literature in the Midwest and the West, where he would come away after a couple of hours at a bookstore with orders for a handful of books, one or two for some titles, none for most. In contrast, he had been shocked the first time he pulled up in front of the Gotham Book Mart and opened the trunk of the car for Frances Steloff. "I'll take twenty-five of those, a hundred of these, and fifty of the Williams," she said. The woman who had started her business life as a hungry waif selling flowers from a tray in Saratoga Springs had blossomed into a major benefactress for the scion of Pittsburgh steel. By late September, J had arrived in Los Angeles, peddling books as his great-great-uncle had peddled crockery. Most of the buying agents were women, and J made full use of his striking presence in the cause of selling literature. He would stride in wearing his Austrian loden jacket, instinctively assuming the guise of a "shy, nice boy" that somewhat softened the impact of his intimidating height and his handsome face. "I was good looking in those days," J would recall with his asymmetric smile, readily admitting the erotic appeal in his sales approach—modern troubadour poets sold by a troubadour publisher.

•

Germany invaded Poland on September 1, and the declaration of war against Germany by Britain and France two days later was a call to action on the part of a number of ND authors. Henry Miller was visiting Durrell in Greece, and in December he again cabled frantically for passage money. Steloff set about collecting his fare, promising to refund J's contribution if it was not needed. J was willing to send the $100 requested, but he had not forgotten that Henry had kept an earlier bailout sum as an "advance." Stein and Toklas rushed from Bilignin to Paris to spend two days collecting winter clothing and battening down the hatches: they took only two paintings back to Bilignin, a Cézanne and Picasso's portrait of Gertrude, leaving the rest on the walls of their apartment. The American consul in Lyon urged them to return to America, and they spent a night packing for their escape, but next morning Gertrude told Alice, "Well, I don't know—it would be awfully uncomfortable and I am fussy about my food. Let's not leave." They stayed on in Bilignin, and Gertrude continued to write, including a fragment of *Mrs. Reynolds*, an autobiographical novel in which a sinister figure named Angel Harper, a version of Adolf Hitler, appears. Kay Boyle flew on a clipper from Lisbon with her children, Laurence Vail, and Peggy Guggenheim. Only Ezra seemed to be taking it all calmly. "You and Geo Tinkham are more set on having a yourapeeing war than are the inhabitants of that continent," he groused to J. On the burgeoning war, J and Ezra were in full agreement, although "grampaw" took more personal responsibility: "And as fer wot Ez Sez/ Yourope wd/ rather spend a billyum on war than listen to Ez. soon enough."

As individuals J knew scurried to survive, to escape, or to join up, it quickly became apparent that the writing marketplace had gone on a war footing. In England there was a mass die-off of literary magazines, including *The Criterion, The London Mercury, New Verse,* and *Twentieth*

Century Verse, while in the craving for culture among civilians and combatants alike a new crop sprang up like a sowing of dragons' teeth: Cyril Connolly's *Horizon*; Tambimuttu's *Poetry London*; *Personal Landscape*, founded by Durrell and others in Cairo; and, just over a year later, *The Penguin New Writing*, edited by John Lehmann in London. Virtually nothing new appeared in the United States—all the more reason for J to struggle to keep his anthology afloat. The demise of *The Criterion* especially was a body blow to him; in his letter of condolence to Eliot, J wrote, "The remaining English magazines are pretty much hop-toads by comparison."

In his preface to the 1939 annual, composed when "the New & Improved World War has been in progress for almost a month," J addressed the question, why concentrate on fine literature just as the world was mobilizing for war? J had an answer ready: "Let us oppose the principle of destruction with the principle of creation." He also took the opportunity to accuse the major publishers of abrogating their responsibility to the public and providing profitable "journalese" rather than books composed with "essential technique." These miscreants abdicate "their responsibility as arbiters of taste," cheapening literature to give easy pleasure without the "chewing" required to derive nourishment from the likes of Williams and Cummings. In order for the "*art* of writing" to continue to be practiced, "cloisters and catacombs" will have to be created in which the artists can survive the coming "dark age." J envisioned New Directions as becoming just such a protective space.

J's thoughtful and daring preface was followed by outstanding contents: more poetry by Berryman, Bishop, Patchen, Rexroth, Dylan Thomas, among others, and by J both as himself and as Tasilo Ribischka; prose by Kay Boyle, Patchen, Thomas, and Williams; the entire text of *Blood Wedding* by García Lorca; three chapters from *Tropic of Capricorn*; Harry Levin's "On First Looking Into *Finnegans Wake*," marking the first critical essay by a major scholar in the anthology; and New Directions' first foldout illustration, showing a mural by Juan O'Gorman, a Mexican artist and architect influenced by Diego Rivera and Le Corbusier. It was the longest annual thus far, with 390 pages of text. Lorca would turn out to be ND's most significant acquisition in 1939. Murdered by Franco's minions more than two years before, he was virtually unread in America. The inclusion of a long excerpt from Lawrence Durrell's *The Black Book*, introduced by a passage quoted from Eliot's statement to the effect that it was "the first piece of work by a new English writer to give me any hope for the future of prose fiction," seemed to be a step toward Durrell's becoming a New Directions author. Appearance in the annual was a frequent precursor to book publication by New Directions.

In October, J sent *New Directions in Prose and Poetry 1939* to press. When the anthology with its selection from *Capricorn* hit the bookstores, J's mother sent her chauffeur around Pittsburgh buying up copies of the annual so that she could burn them. "This was excellent for trade," J recalled years later. Also good for trade was a generally positive review in *Time* magazine. The annual was bracketed with Dorothy Norman's *Twice a Year* as having "proved vitality," with Lorca's drama and the excerpt from Durrell's *Black Book*—as in the previous *Time* article on ND—singled out for praise. New Directions had also published "three redeeming books" in the past fortnight, the *Time* review continued: the "druidical Welshness" of Dylan Thomas's *The World I Breathe*, the reprint of Williams's *In the American Grain* ("solider stuff"), and Schwartz's translation of Rimbaud's *A Season in Hell* ("fully competent, lucid"). This notice, plus a laudatory review in *The New York Times*, helped push the 780-copy first edition of the Rimbaud to a rapid depletion—all copies hand printed, boxed, and signed by the translator, thirty on expensive Worthy Signature paper. In a letter to J, Eliot judged Schwartz's book "fairly good," and one critic found it "close to the original." Then came trouble. A scathing review by Justin O'Brien in *The Kenyon Review* used words like "sacrilege," Philip Rice in *Poetry* urged that the book be removed from circulation, and Mary Colum in *The Forum* pointed out that Schwartz had rendered Rimbaud's key verb *je rêvais*—I dream, muse—as "I review." J had accepted Delmore's assurance that he had had the French vetted by "an expert," whereas he had done nothing of the sort. Delmore himself had referred realistically to his French as "high school." Ironically, the physical beauty of the edition called extra attention to it. Soon J decided that a second, revised, edition would be necessary, and an agonized Schwartz suggested that he pay out of his own pocket for copies of the new edition to exchange for any of the flawed first editions mailed in by outraged customers.

The first book of Henry Miller's to be published in America, *The Cosmological Eye*, came in for an equally sound drubbing. J had been involved in more aspects of the book than in any other for the year: he edited the text, designed the jacket and the layout of the book itself, and wrote a preface. For the cover, J superimposed his good right eye, photographically transposed to the left side, on a cloud bank. The dust jacket copy named Henry "Lawrence's heir in the struggle to re-assert the natural in man." J's preface addressed the paradox that "one of the really important and permanent writers of his generation" should never before have had a book appear in his native country, while four of his titles had been published to acclaim in France. J called on "Time" to be the adjudicator, time that had bestowed classic status on Aristophanes and Catullus, on Rabelais and "Shakspere." Among moderns, Miller towered over "the neurotic mice writing their slick-surfaced piffle, like a mountain over sandhills." On November 21, Ralph Thompson devoted his entire *New York Times* column, Books of the Times, to Miller's often "noisome," sometimes "extremely fancy" language, his self-absorption, his anarchic attitudes. Nor did J himself escape stricture. True, he had gone out of his way to offend the literary establishment. Thompson wrote of J's publishing acumen: "My impression is that Mr. Laughlin is, as has happened before, somewhere between 50 and 75 per cent off. Henry Miller is a freak." Ezra thought well of the annual but cautioned J, in bold emphasis, "**Miller too much on the hole. after all, others have shat.**" Still, by mid-1940 the anthology had sold out.

With Higgins gone to pursue his own writing, J resolved late in 1939 to move the center of New Directions operations to Cambridge. Both Schwartzes would work for him, and they were to find an apartment with extra space for ND.

All told, it had been a good year for New Directions: J had followed up on the appearance of Lorca in the annual with a pamphlet edition of *Blood Wedding*, the author's first American book publication, and the New Classics series promised well. J now planned to drive his second new Buick, a graduation present from his mother, to New Orleans for the 1939 meeting of the Modern Language Association, held between Christmas and New Year's and already the major annual display of new scholarly books and student texts. Delmore, thanks to the initial critical triumph of *In Dreams Begin Responsibilities*, was given star billing by the MLA. He was presenting a paper titled "The Isolation of Modern Poetry" at the convention, and J invited Gertrude and Delmore to travel with him. But then, after taking

the Schwartzes to see the Allen Tates in Princeton and then on to Pittsburgh for a friendly lunch with "the whole Laughlin tribe" on December 24,
he sent them off to drive his car to Louisiana, while he continued on
alone. The main draw for him at the convention was to meet John Crowe
Ransom, editor of *The Kenyon Review* and the leading voice in New Criticism. And J was especially eager to have contact with Robert Penn Warren and the southern "Fugitives"—those who, like Tate and Ransom, had
published early work in the journal *The Fugitive*—as a balance to the
"eastern seaboard liberals," the New England literati.

In New Orleans, J saw Albert Erskine, business manager of *The Southern Review* and an editor for the Louisiana State University Press, and
asked him to take over as manager of New Directions. Erskine was non-
committal. He was the fourth husband of Katherine Anne Porter, nearly
twice his age, and he invited J's party to visit them in Baton Rouge on the
return journey. For two evenings they were entertained at Erskine's cottage; he cooked for the guests, who included Cleanth Brooks and Ransom,
and Porter retired to her room and hammered her typewriter after dinner
each evening. Directly after the New Year's dinner, J departed for Florida
with one of the Brooks sisters after arranging for the Schwartzes to drive
north with Arthur Mizener, future biographer of F. Scott Fitzgerald.

J had an undisclosed reason for his detour to Florida. He drove to Key
West to persuade Elizabeth Bishop to become a New Directions poet.
They appear to have gotten on famously. She walked J around the quiet
town, an architectural transplant from the West Indies: wooden frame
houses with verandas, bougainvillea hanging over the walls, the air
sweet with frangipani. Bishop and J photographed each other sitting on
the steps of the Square Roof, which had been a well-known mulatto
brothel, and she agreed to appear in J's Five Young American Poets
series.

While this was going on, J became embroiled with Ezra. J reported to
him from Kansas City that he was in "great disfavour" with his "compatriots." "Now reverend Sir," J counseled, "I hope that you will soft pedal that
German Propaganda stuff." Most stores were refusing to carry Ezra's books
either because they saw him as a Fascist or because they thought the youth
were no longer interested in him. J ended by saying that he hoped Ezra
would not be "downcast" by his "gloomy forebodings," adding, "but I feel
that an even iller day than usual is upon us." J stated baldly, "Now I imagine you will be wrothful with your servant and consider that I am traiter-

ous [sic] to you and next thing to a Jew. But no. I am merely trying to hit the efficient balance—to do as much as I possibly can for your honour's books without getting in a jam by going the whole hog for your honour's programs. Do you see what I mean? I want to push you hard as poet and writer, but not get tangled up in the political end."

In his next letter, J repeated that the coming years would be "bleak" for Ezra on account of his views, "but I believe in you and will stick with the ship and see it through to better times." The Cantos would come to be "recognized as an epic of money, of the greatest world importance," and "prophetic" of what was to come. Even in publishing The Cantos, however, J warned Ezra that he would not print "anything that can be fairly construed as an outright attack on the Jews and I want that in the contract in the libel clause." J continued, "I think anti-semitism is contemptible and despicable and I will not put my hand to it. I cannot tell you how it grieves me to see you taking up with it." Also, while Jews might have some part in "the unjust money systems . . . it is just as much, and more, the work of Anglo-Saxons and celts and goths and what have you." He added, "I just think that it stinks to hell to persecute the poor bastards, who, for the most part, are just as decent as anybody else, and I imagine there are probably more skunks among the British than the Yids." J went further to comment on some of his own past pronouncements: "I have at various times let myself slip into anti-semitic utterances but I'm ashamed of it and renounce them. It was a childish weakness."

While J did not apologize for his disagreements with Ezra, he tried to sound a reassuring note: "I think I can assure you that you will not suffer by having me as your publisher." New Directions was growing, "beginning to cut some ice in this land." As for the political news that Ezra wanted to disseminate, J said that he would be willing to run off and mail a fortnightly broadside on the mimeograph machine that he intended to acquire for ND, only there must be nothing in this newsletter to connect it either with Pound or New Directions. The anonymity was necessary because "if anybody smelt you in it . . . they would simply discount the whole thing as lies," and because J would not let ND become associated with anything resembling propaganda. Give facts and name names, fine, but "absolutely no reference to the Jewish question." Ezra gave no indication of being offended or enraged but continued to advise J on publishing matters.

Pound did defend himself to J by pointing out that he had absolved the Jews from certain charges and that he neither attacked *nor refrained from attacking* on Semitic grounds. "All right/ d'accord/ not 'solely as jews,'" he wrote, adding with boldface emphasis, "But no immunity **SOLELY as jews; solely because jews**." While he thought that *some* Jews were part of the problem of economic injustice, as early as 1919 Pound had written, "Inasmuch as the Jew has conducted no holy war for nearly two millennia, he is preferable to the Christian and the Mohammedans."

It showed the open give-and-take of their relationship that J could make it clear that he would not buy into either Pound's support of Fascism or his vocal anti-Semitism, while Ezra could maintain his stand on principle. At a time when Charles Lindbergh was publicly advising the United States not to oppose Hitler, and the Harriman Bank was the main Wall Street connection for German companies, to oppose Fascism was not so much a given as it would be in the half century following the war. J was for neither the war nor for any totalitarian order. Nor was Rexroth, as an anarchist and pacifist; nor was Henry Miller—the war was disrupting his writer's life; nor was Delmore Schwartz, who was afraid of the draft.

Anti-Semitism remained the real sticking point between poet and publisher. Pound persisted in denying that he was an anti-Semite, insisting instead that he was only against *certain* Jews and behavior that he associated with those specific Jews. In another letter to J, Ezra returned to the theme of anti-Semitism, offering for publication over his signature "I do NOT consider it antisemite to WARN the millions of working jews that THEY and NOT the big usurers and monopolists are endangered by the activities of high finance and monopoly." "How about giving me some tangible armor athwart the rage of all my hebe friends and customers," J countered, and proposed a contract along the following lines: "The author further affirms that the book contains no material that could properly be called 'anti-semitic,' that is, which treats of the Jews in a propagandistic, as opposed to an artistic, manner." This didn't get past Ezra: "I shall NOT accept the specific word anti-semitic in the contract. there will have to be a general formula, covering Me[nn]onites, mohamedans, lutherans, calvinists . . . ALL ideas coming from the near east are probably shit/ if they turn out to be typhus in the laboratory, so is it. So is Taoism/ so is probably ALL chinese philos; and religion except Kung [Confucius] // I am not yet sure/."

Ezra and J finally agreed on unspecific language that would afford some libel protection for ND without offending Pound's principles. "All right, m'dear Caesar Andromache NIBBLES," Ezra wrote without clarification, to which J replied, equally cryptically, "I am satisfied about the Jewish situation." For Ezra, language was not a weapon for attacking ethnic minorities: words were simply missiles ready at hand to bounce off an enemy's skull. If "Jew banker" evoked the specter of usury, of the tyrannical grip of compound interest, he felt free to apply it, whether the target was Jew or gentile. Frances Steloff had been far more prescient when she had warned a younger James Laughlin to moderate *his* language: "Names have a way of bouncing off books and sonofabitch is a rubberball."

•

In December, J confessed to being the translator of *The Fourth Eclogue of Virgil*, "Printed for the friends of New Directions and James Laughlin at Christmas." He could afford to be extravagant: J and his brother had been attempting in the Pittsburgh Orphans' Court to acquire a sum that they believed was due them under the terms of Uncle Jim's estate, and on December 26 the Pennsylvania State Supreme Court had found in their favor. Acting on the court's instructions, the trustees paid out the accrued income. The money came most opportunely: J had written earlier to Mary Barnard that ND had been losing heavily. Because of this windfall, he now allowed himself a full schedule. The greater war might be raging in Europe, but J had won a very significant battle. He now had funds for a year or two of publishing—or for some new venture.

12

Worlds Apart:
Books at Cambridge, Ski Lifts at Alta

No tears come to my eyes when I hear of the set-backs of your libido.
I read of it with great interest, as I would read of Asia.
　　　　　　　　　　　　　　　—Delmore Schwartz to James Laughlin

Soon after mid-January 1940, J was back north from his rambles in the South, and Delmore's hurt feelings had healed for the nonce. Kenneth and Miriam Patchen had decamped from Norfolk for the tolerant anonymity of Bleecker Street in Greenwich Village. There was a chance of a part-time teaching position at Harvard for Delmore, and Gertrude would become the full-time manager for New Directions, with her husband as an editorial reader at $10 a month. On February 6, the Schwartzes rented an unfurnished apartment at 41 Bowdoin Street in Cambridge. One large room was designated as the New Directions office. J realized that his rather haphazard distribution of books through a Cambridge apartment and a sequence of mad dashes to Norfolk would no longer suffice, so he negotiated an arrangement with the American Booksellers Service in lower Manhattan to take over shipping.

As American involvement in the war increased, Delmore raved, "That son of a bitch Roosevelt, if he gets the Embargo Act repealed, will have us all in the trenches by spring . . . As my grandmother would say, let him drop dead." The teaching of German was removed from many American secondary schools, yet J began deliberately to push German literature to highlight the artistic achievements of major writers in German and as a counterbalance to war hysteria. It was a courageous move given the national climate. New Directions' first book originally written in German would be the Czech Franz Kafka's *Amerika* in Edwin and Willa Muir's translation. In his annual for the same year, J included "A Note on Kafka" by Aldous Huxley and a letter from Thomas Mann thanking him "for daring to publish this strange book." He printed the letter in German as well as English. J was not about to turn against a language and a literature on account of a war. For the following year J planned as a major publication a bilingual edition of Goethe's *Faust* (*Part I*) in Carlyle MacIntyre's rendering, with illustrations by Rockwell Kent. The book had grown out of the artist's challenge to MacIntyre to produce "a modern *American* translation." "If you will, I'll illustrate it," he had promised.

Henry Miller had left Greece three days after Christmas 1939 on a ship bound for New York. By early March he was living near the Gotham Book Mart. His destitute father was dying of prostate cancer in Brooklyn across the East River, and Henry appealed to J for an advance on his next book, because J had said that he could request money "any time you need funds badly." Now was the time, Henry said. He was in *desperate* need of funds; Henry owed "about $25,000" collectively to hundreds of people, since he had never actually earned a living after leaving the employ of Western Union in 1924. "People are expecting great things of you," Henry continued, even though "every day" someone told him that J was a "dilettante." "Maybe you are," said Henry, "but you won't be with me because I am too earnest and sincere to let you be if you wanted to be." It was an unusual letter for a publisher to receive from a suppliant author, but Miller was an old hand at combining badgering with begging. He was making a collection of essays and stories for *The Wisdom of the Heart*, which ND would publish the following year, and he was finishing the manuscript of his Greek trip, eventually to be called *The Colossus of Maroussi*. Miller was angry over J's editorial changes in *The Cosmological Eye*, more furious yet at the contract he received. "One would think you were dealing with a thug or a maniac instead of a sensitive, intelligent author," he told J. By mid-April their relationship had deteriorated further. "Better drop the idea of doing a new book," Henry now said. "We see things too differently, I'm afraid, to ever come to any real agreement." Then, on July 3, J wrote a terse letter rejecting *Colossus* as not "suitable for publication under my imprint"—thus missing the timely publication of the book many would come to consider Miller's best (ND would eventually publish it). J reminded Henry that under "my rights" ND retained first options on his other books. Given Miller's famously independent nature, the future of J's publishing relationship with him seemed tenuous at best, and Henry would sign a contract with Doubleday, Doran, not ND, for *The Air-Conditioned Nightmare*.

•

By mid-March 1940, J had arrived in the Rockies, drawn in part by a pair of skiing events: the Harriman Cup races in Sun Valley, Idaho, and the first Fédération Internationale de Ski downhill and slalom competition at Alta, a pristine new ski area up Little Cottonwood Canyon near Salt Lake City. The beauty of both Sun Valley and Alta drew J powerfully, and exhilarated by a reconnection with Dick Durrance and the world of high-country skiing, by mid-April J had bought "a little piece of cottonwood land along Trail Creek on the old Brass Ranch property" near Hailey, Pound's birthplace. In June, Durrance married Margaret "Miggs" Jennings, who had been named as an alternate U.S. Ski Team member for the aborted 1940 Olympics. Dick had been working as a cinematographer, producing a pair of films to publicize Averell Harriman's Sun Valley, and Dick had inquired about Alta. The site was much less developed than Sun Valley, but as a ski area it was even more promising. Suitable terrain extended up to the summits of Sugarloaf and Mount Baldy, both more than eleven thousand feet, for runs of prodigious length.

To the young Durrances, the idea of developing their own ski area seemed a glorious adventure. Alta had a romantic past as a silver-mining town back in the 1880s, with twenty-six saloons, dancing ladies, and stores offering all the necessities of civilization, especially liquor and dynamite, but "as a ski resort," Durrance realized, "Alta was floundering." The old town had been destroyed by fire and avalanches, and the new ski lodge was "a skeleton with a roof on it," the single backless Collins chairlift a primitive contraption. It had only become operational in January 1939, with lift tickets at twenty-five cents. In the summer of 1940, Durrance proposed to Joe Quinney, a prominent Salt Lake City lawyer and member of the local Winter Sports Association, that he and his bride take over the development of Alta. The place needed someone with directing vision living on-site to complete the lodge and manage the entire operation. And it needed money. Dick picked up the telephone and called J, by then back in Norfolk.

J might have been reluctant to begin another complicated and expensive undertaking just as New Directions had begun to establish momentum, but Dick was adamant that this was an unparalleled opportunity: a promising business in its infancy, prime skiing in unspoiled terrain. Dick had thought out a plan that did not require J's full-time commitment. He and Miggs presented themselves to J as a team: Dick would establish and manage the Dick Durrance Ski School, and together he and Miggs would stock and run the ski shop and the lift. J realized that the land up for lease had a north-facing slope that would hold snow longer and that would retard the solar degradation of powder snow, great advantages in the days before snowmaking equipment. More than that, he had simply fallen in love with Alta. With the settlement of the claim in the Orphan's Court in Pennsylvania, he had funds at his disposal that he would not have to steal from his publishing. In his verse the beauty of the Wasatch Mountains became juxtaposed against the horror of "another useless hope- / less war":

```
Afterglow goldens the
peak its rock beak glows

like raw blood and red
red is the snowfield.
```

He and Durrance agreed on a partnership, with J providing most of the cash, Miggs and Dick most of the management and all of the ski instruction, and Joe Quinney as a third partner. J immediately liked Jessie and Joe Quinney, and their son, Dave, five years J's junior, was one of the best local skiers. Jessie's family was prominent in banking: her brother Marriner Eccles was the chairman of the Federal Reserve Board, and a fiscal opponent of Ezra Pound's bête noire Henry Morgenthau, FDR's Secretary of the Treasury. From the first, Quinney and J operated on interconnected principles: *no borrowing*; and any profits were to be reinvested in improving the Alta infrastructure. "I have acquired without doubt the most beautiful small ski resort in USA and will fool around with same for awhile," J announced to Ezra. "I don't think it will interfere much with immortal publication. I got plenty time during blizzards to read immortal manuscripts."

In 1935 there had been no ski lodges in Utah, but during the winter of

1935–36 the U.S. Forest Service had hired Alf Engen, the Norwegian-born world ski-jumping champion, to search for sites that might be developed for recreational skiing. Engen told the Forest Service that the Alta slopes were promising but that the terrain would not hold snow because the miners had denuded the slopes to obtain shoring timber. He persuaded the Forest Service to have the Civilian Conservation Corps plant hundreds of trees. Thus from its very beginnings, Alta became associated with conservation, whereas many other skiing venues were criticized for *causing* erosion and for the degradation of the environment. Construction of a lodge and other facilities began at Alta in April 1936. When the Denver and Rio Grande Western Railroad contributed $25,000 toward the construction of the Alta Lodge and the Collins chairlift in 1939, it was in conscious competition with the Union Pacific and its Sun Valley development. The promise of the place was stupendous: an amphitheater framed by the imposing Flagstaff, Superior, and Baldy mountains of the Wasatch Range, with the slopes of the Collins, Rustler, and Peruvian Ridge gulches rising thousands of feet. So J agreed to put up $25,000 for the lease of the Alta slopes from the Forest Service, conditional on his completing the Alta Lodge at the head of Little Cottonwood Canyon. The lodge would open on November 29, 1940, and it would eventually have accommodations for fifty guests in plain but comfortable rooms and in dormitories.

•

Before Alta became a serious distraction from his publishing and as the skiing season was shutting down in April 1940, J turned full-time to preparing the New Directions list for the year. "There is joy in our camp," he told Eliot, because of Delmore's Guggenheim; his letter crossed one from Eliot congratulating ND on a "most interesting list" for the previous year. The first American edition of Pound's *Polite Essays* appeared in a joint publication with Faber. Even fussy Ezra had to admit that "the olde Eliotic serpent has done a damn clever job in selectin the Perlite": it was "much better readin" than *Make It New*—Eliot having returned the favor Pound had done years before in editing *The Waste Land*. This was to be a major Pound year, despite J's forebodings of the troubles that lay in the Boss's future, and sales were good: the *Ta Hio* was "selling merrily," *Culture* had sold out, and stocks of *Polite Essays* and *ABC of Economics* were down to a few hundred copies each. J scheduled no fewer than five of

Ezra's books for 1940, nearly half of the eleven volumes planned and more by a single author than he would ever again attempt in one year. Four books would bring all the completed cantos under the ND roof, thereby establishing J's claim to be Ezra's principal American publisher, and *Cantos LII–LXXI* would be an American first for ND. Early in 1940, when J saw the latest cantos, the "Chinese" followed by the John Adams sections, he had suggested that their author add an explanatory preface. This Ezra refused categorically: "Nobody can SUMMARIZE what is already condensed to the absolute limit . . . SHIT for the attitude of the pooplik. The POINT IS that with Cantos 52/71. a NEW thing IS. narrative with chronological sequence. Read 'em before you go off half cocked," he demanded. Besides, Ez always insisted that the intelligent reader didn't *need* notes; if interested, he or she should dig for the knowledge. New Directions published these cantos on September 17, 1940, but with a small booklet, *Notes on Ezra Pound's Cantos: Structure and Metric*, in a slipcase pasted inside the back cover. Ezra approved, so long as it was not printed as a preface. The pamphlet was credited to S.D. and H.H.—Schwartz, Delmore, and J using his father's initials in memorial, he said. The pamphlet did not reach Pound, perhaps stopped by Italian censors "as it contained a good deal of my candid explications of current history," J surmised years later to Ezra.

•

J might feel that he was losing Miller, but he was becoming midwife to Williams's *Paterson* as well as to Pound's *Cantos*. Williams had been musing over a long poem to be set in the polluted Passaic River valley at least since his publication of the short poem "Paterson" in *The Dial* in 1926. The Rutherford poet had been stung into a high level of discontent by ND's reissuing of successive volumes of Ezra's signature work. The old sense of rivalry surged in Bill, and he felt that he must answer Ezra with a "personal epic," only one that was non-allusive, that was American in idiom and subject, rather than European and, he thought, artificial. Thus, *Paterson*.

J continued his encouragement of new talent as well. He initiated the *Five Young American Poets* anthologies, devoted to those under thirty who had not yet published a book of poetry. J hoped that these "group books," at $2.50 for a hardbound volume, would sell better than slim volumes each devoted to a new poet. He allotted about forty pages for each author.

These anthologies would contain an introduction by each poet, a facsimile of a poem in holograph, and a photograph. J planned in the first example to include John Berryman, Elizabeth Bishop, Randall Jarrell, W. R. Moses, and George Marion O'Donnell. Meanwhile, he continued with his plans, formed in 1939, for initiating in 1941 his Poet of the Month pamphlets, to sell at thirty-five or fifty cents in paper covers, $1 hardbound, $4 for a year's subscription. Each would be printed by a different distinguished typographer, on fine paper and, if feasible, hand set. This added to the administrative and editing work but also to the appeal of the series. J kept at the Makers of Modern Literature series, which he outlined to Eliot in April 1940: "Blackmur is doing James. Tate will do Flaubert. Schwartz thinks he can do your excellence. Howard Baker will do Hardy. Phil Horton, Rilke; Philip Rahv, Trotsky. That is just the start"—none of these would appear, but there would be many others in the series. The Makers titles were intended to reach the "earnest young people" who were being cheated out of an education and being led to the "wrong things." They were intended to be solid in scholarship, "yet not pedantic, readable, fairly imaginative, not weighted down with footnotes or learned apparatus." Such was J's strategy for an assault on academe.

The 1939 annual sold out by February 1940, and J had laid the foundation for some good long-term sales: Dylan Thomas's comical *Portrait of the Artist as a Young Dog* would rank among the score of bestselling ND books. Dylan wrote to J that he had another quasi-autobiographical collection in the works, this one "a proper city book, and far free-er in style than the slight, 'artful' other stories." But Dylan left the title story, which he called "a novel-in-progress," unfinished at his death. New Directions would publish a larger collection in 1955, pieced together from many sources, as *Adventures in the Skin Trade*.

J's lack of tact forced a reconstitution of the *Five Young American Poets* volume. When J suggested to Elizabeth Bishop that her presence as the only woman in the collection would give it "sex appeal," she withdrew from the project. "I somehow feel one should refuse to act as Sex Appeal," she wrote, with some asperity, to Marianne Moore; J had not divined the depth of her reserve or her fear of being known as a lesbian. J often seemed incapable of holding his tongue. He told Eudora Welty of his negative opinion of the poet David Schubert, and this got back to Katherine Anne Porter—who had recommended Schubert to J in the first place. Porter confided to the dramatist Harvey Breit, "As to Jay . . . the most astonishing row of gangster epithets rises to my thoughts, you know, like jerk, punk, heel."

In the case of Bishop, J also overreached by pushing too hard. After Random House had rejected her poems in early 1939, she agreed tentatively to J's earlier proposal for a first book of her poems, but then he tried to get her to sign a five-book contract. A slow, careful writer, she refused, reluctant to commit what would turn out to be her lifetime output in number of volumes.

J, still wanting a woman poet, replaced Bishop with Mary Barnard, chosen through a balloting of his friends. He wrote to Barnard on August 10, stating that she would be "raised to glory" and signing himself "Jack Rip." He managed to offend her too, by requesting four copies of twelve of her best poems so that he could get the four men in the volume to pass on her: he could not risk "a dog-fight in a shoebox," J explained to her. She resented having "got in on the quota," but she had long wanted to have a book published by ND, and being in a collection of five poets came close. There was truth to Barnard's remark about a quota: there would be just one woman in each of the three volumes in the series.

J was determined that New Directions should continue regardless of the war in Europe, and in August 1940, expecting to be drafted, he renewed his request to Albert Erskine to fill in for him. Erskine moved to Cambridge, and Gertrude Schwartz acted as his secretary until his departure for New York in late 1942. The chance of being killed in the war was on many minds, but it seemed arbitrary and irrational when John Wheelwright died, struck by a drunken driver while crossing a street. J was deeply shocked, one of his cherished friends snuffed out.

J had come to depend on Delmore as arbiter. When he had serious doubts about an essay submitted by Howard Nemerov, poet and J's schoolmate at Harvard, he turned it over to Schwartz. Delmore pronounced it "just no good at all." J was relieved to agree with him: "It struck me as the most obvious, pompous bilge." J was considering Randall Jarrell for the Poet of the Month series, but Delmore dismissed him: Jarrell "bores me stiff." Rexroth should have stuck to writing "the most obscure poems ever written," since "now that he has become clear, even barbarians can see what commonplace thoughts were concealed in his obscurity." Nor did Delmore spare Ezra, writing a hyperbolic but cogent assessment to J: "The man is the biggest jackass in the world and working hard at getting even bigger, but he has the best ear for versification since Milton . . . Poets will be learning their metres from Pound for the next two hundred years." J had been worried that the charge of anti-Semitism would be leveled against Pound for *Cantos LII–LXXI*, but Delmore assured him: "Your concern about attacks on the Jews can be dismissed." Pound had merely quoted a remark, probably apocryphal, attributed to Benjamin Franklin. Apart from that, there was nothing in these cantos "about us poor bastards."

On the basis of reading F. O. Matthiessen's *American Renaissance*, Schwartz recommended him to edit Melville, and J got "Matty" to make a selection of Melville's poems for a Poets of the Year volume in 1944. When a submission passed muster with Delmore, it was usually good. However, signs of friction in J's relationship with him continued. Timing seemed always an issue: when J wanted Delmore to get the revised Rimbaud translations to him quickly, Schwartz replied, "What about not rushing me on anything? . . . [T]he rush is shortening my life and you're always in a rush." More serious were his complaints about money: in October 1940, he demanded an advance of $300, which he said J had promised him verbally. Delmore anticipated J's objections: "As for your advice against it on the grounds that I will spend it, this is correct: What do you think I want the money for except to spend it?" Perhaps it was a clever move to mollify Delmore, or perhaps it was his genuine sense of being responsible for him, but J made Schwartz the beneficiary of his life insurance policy at around this time.

Ezra, despairing about Europe, revised his campaign to keep America out of the war: he would go on the air. Also, the money question had become critical for him: after Italy and Britain had declared war on each other in June 1940, Dorothy could no longer be sent funds, nor could Ezra receive royalties from England. When a German officer he met on the tennis court told him that there was "good money" to be made in radio, Pound applied to the Ministry of Popular Culture (Minculpop). By the end of the year, he had begun to draft speeches to be read by English-speaking announcers in the employ of Rome Radio for *The American Hour*, a program of news, commentary, and music. Soon he agreed to broadcast weekly himself for Rome Radio, "on distinct understanding that he was not to be asked anything contrary to his conscience or his duties as an American citizen." Minculpop agreed to pay him 350 lire, about $17, per broadcast.

"Ezra Pound speaking," he began his broadcasts, "Johnnie Adams, the first, the real father of his country, the man who picked General Washington, George, to lead the Colonial armies against a damned, stinking and cheating British Government," and he was off and running in "Aristotle and Adams." The crooked money system was behind the present war, and a recurrent theme was upholding the U.S. Constitution. There were stridently anti-Communist diatribes, virulent attacks on Roosevelt, and tirades about the "Jewish conspiracy." The talks were not notably intelligible: some officials were afraid that he was a spy sending out encoded information, especially when he read out entire cantos over the airwaves. The image of Italian cryptographers puzzling over the Ezratic texts provides almost the only note of humor in the situation. J told Ezra that "yr. politics have cooked yr revered goose to a point you wd. not believe."

•

In February and March 1941, J was at Alta, discussing with the Durrances the layout of ski runs, improvements to the ski lift, and the completion of the lodge. They agreed that the ski school should avoid the autocratic discipline of the Austrian schools, and soon Alta informality would become a byword in the skiing fraternity. For J, Alta meant a return to the fine camaraderie of his antipodean trip, and he was made welcome in the Durrance family circle. Miggs was warmhearted, pretty, and fun-loving. J certainly enjoyed her company, as well as that of Dick's younger sister Elizabeth, also a competitive skier. J preferred to call her by her Austrian nickname, Lisl, and before long he was engaged to her. In a note penned some fifty years later in a shaky hand and dropped into a folder of material for his projected *Byways* autobiography, J wrote, "Lisl as transfer of my love for Lisl [sic]. I cannot adulerate [sic] my best friend's wife but I can love Lisl Durrance. Harbour adulterous thoughts." From the context, J's second "Lisl" was almost certainly a slip for Miggs.

J's friendship with Rexroth was also developing rapidly, and this was compounded by their shared love of the wilds. Kenneth was passionately serious about his poetry, his translations, his essays on the San Francisco scene, while cultivating the image of a rugged outdoorsman and an iconoclast. Nor was it mere show in Rexroth's case, fortunately for J, who spent Easter 1941 rock climbing with him in the Sierras. Kenneth taught him the rudiments of using climbing ropes, pitons, carabiners. They were

descending a vertical chimney when J slipped and, in his words, "my extremities became completely dissociated from the petrine substance."
Rexroth, descending above him, managed to hold the considerable weight
of J in suspension, dangling like a spider from a silken thread, until he
could regain his footing. Although J did not say it in so many words, Kenneth had saved him from almost certain death. After this adventure,
Rexroth's letters went at once from formality to "Dear Jim." J's habit became to alternate work at the lodge with quick trips to San Francisco. He
would stay with Rexroth and Marie Kass, who had married Kenneth the
year before, formalizing a fairly long relationship.

In an aside that would have infuriated the San Francisco poet, J confided to Schwartz, "Rexroth's poetry may be mediocre but as a person he
is delicious. Haven't been so diverted by anyone in years." J changed his
opinion of the poetry later, and Rexroth would become one of ND's most
published authors, with twenty-eight books all told, written, translated, or
edited. Kenneth in turn had a low opinion of Delmore's poetry, asking
J sarcastically, "Is it really true that you plan to publish nothing but the
Complete Delmore Schwartz from here on?" Rexroth delighted in the
abrupt dismissal: of Bill Williams's dictum "No ideas but in things," Kenneth snapped, "Infantile."

To the outsider, theirs appeared a curious relationship. Kenneth and J
called each other "Honey"—Rexroth favored Honey Bear for J, Kenneth's
wife was Marie Bear, and the dog was Rex Bear—and insulted each other
outrageously. Kenneth had to make noise, as if to force the acknowledgment of his anarchy, his sexual mores, his rightness on any topic. "Honey
Bear," he would bellow, "you don't know shit from shinola!" They hiked
the Sierras in summer with a pack donkey and skied in the winter, living on
Kenneth's tomato-and-pasta concoctions, fresh-caught golden trout, and
desserts made from dried fruit. Marie was almost as much at home on
the trail as Kenneth and did not hesitate to leave her responsible nursing
position for weeks of backpacking with him. She impressed J as being
delightfully different from the Bennington girls he flirted with and from
the heiresses he pursued. She was a liberal Socialist in politics, widely
read, gifted with a "sense of humor both ironic and frisky," tall and with
spectacular red-orange hair.

By 1941, J had a struggling publishing company, a vast north slope of
deep snow looming over him and threatening an avalanche of debts—and

sundry women in love with him. He felt himself tormented by love and wrote several poems in which lovers visited him in his dreams or failed to answer his passionate letters: "love love huntress re- / lentless I know you'll / be after me as long as / I live but why not take / a lesson from our dog / who only hunts for fun!"

•

In May, J found lodgings in Westwood in northwest Los Angeles. Soon he became part of a circle that included Man Ray and his future wife, Juliet Browner, and a circus bareback equestrian friend of Juliet's, *and* Ariane LeVaillant, a teenage Swiss ice-skating prodigy watched over by a protective mother. The Man Rays were most hospitable, and the great artist-photographer made a portrait of J looking dreamy and languorous, "soul dripping out of my eyes," J said. He and the bareback rider "drifted together" while he longed for Ariane, but the mother kept her girl in sight. J was still "wisting and twisting" when he left for New York at the end of the summer.

Much more important than the Man Ray group for J was his encounter with a graphic designer named Alvin Lustig, a year J's junior, who had studied briefly with Frank Lloyd Wright at Taliesin East, the architect's studio in Wisconsin, but hated the place. J described Lustig as "a very sweet, gentle person, Jewish, couldn't have been nicer," and praised his "steadfastness of purpose." Lustig was then experimenting with print forms in a small shop in Brentwood in the San Francisco Bay Area. J commissioned four book designs from him for 1941, beginning with Henry Miller's *Wisdom of the Heart*. Other book cover artists tended to seek out eye-catching colors, forms, and representational scenes with little more than a nod to the author's writing. Lustig wanted instead to capture in image and symbol some divine essence of the book. First he read it, J said, to "get the feel of the author's creative drive." For Miller, Lustig drew a mirror-image geometric shape, blue on a yellow ground. A red arrow cut across the center of the book, as if aiming at the heart of the matter. Other designs followed in rapid order: for Carl Rakosi's *Selected Poems*, Nabokov's *The Real Life of Sebastian Knight*, and Harry Levin's *James Joyce*. For Levin's critical monograph, Lustig created a generic design that would serve to identify the Makers series. Each of the subsequent six monographs would feature the same design, a stylized hand writing with a steel-nibbed pen, differing only in color from the other volumes. Early in the new year, 1942, Lustig designed J's first *Ski Alta* brochure, with a startling photograph of Dick Durrance skiing through a giant snowflake. From 1941 through 1955 he would produce covers for New Directions, images that became the public face of ND and would revolutionize cover design.

By August 1941, J was back at the ski lodge. His engagement to Lisl Durrance ended, and J took up with Margaret Ellen Keyser, a friend of the Durrances' and the daughter of Paul Keyser, president of the Utah Consolidated Coal Company and one of the stalwarts of the Winter Sports Association. She was a petite brunette, a competent skier, with a lively, outgoing personality. She had attended the top private school for girls in Salt Lake City, where she was considered bright and a bit bookish. She was smitten by the tall young easterner, and by the beginning of 1942 they had become lovers. Alta seemed made for romance—a skiing dream in winter, a blaze of flowers around a mountain lake in the late spring.

The Durrance/Laughlin partnership soon discovered that running Alta was not going to be all fun. An unreliable lodge manager had to be dismissed; a cook chased Miggs with a cleaver and had to be evicted by the sheriff. The first winter a terrific avalanche on the other side of the Rustler slope—not part of their Alta operation but very close by—killed a young skier, and they realized that avalanche control would be mandatory. Alf Engen's brother Sverre was appointed a U.S. Forest Service snow ranger, and he experimented using a 105 mm military mortar to trigger avalanches before they could build up enough mass to be catastrophic.

Despite the recurring crises, J thrived at Alta. He "really loved the place," Durrance recalled. J's feeling for Alta bordered on the religious. "You've got to keep some places like God made them," J would say years later. "If you overdo it, you'll destroy Alta." This realization came to him early, and the deliberately slow development that he mandated kept Alta from entering the race toward glittering resort hotels and condominiums as at Aspen, Vail, and Sun Valley. His partnership with the Durrances worked well, romantic tensions aside. J lived simply in a single room at the lodge. Dick said that J "was very quiet, never complained, didn't interfere, but he made good decisions." The great skier evaluated the capable one: "He loved powder skiing and was good at it, but most of all he loved ski touring. That was the joy of his life. He'd go ski, and then shut himself up in his room and work on New Directions and his writing." Durrance was aware that "with the help of a typewriter and a Dictaphone," J was running a publishing company "out of his room in the lodge." From the first, J strove to keep skiing relatively affordable for the locals and for all others who shared his love of it. Only reluctantly did he allow a day lift ticket to be increased from $1.50 to $2.00, and the tuition for six days at the ski school came to only $15.00.

Soon a pair of wings identical in size to the original building completed the lodge, but it remained spartan. One upstairs wing was a dormitory, and on each of the two floors there was a communal bathroom. An open stairway led four flights down steeply from the parking lot to the lodge entrance; there was a chute beside the steps so that guests could slide their gear down. Skiers put up with the primitive conditions because Alta provided unexcelled skiing. Early guests, some of whom stayed most of the winter, included a clutch of magnates, acquaintances of J's or Durrance's—the Champion spark plug family from Toledo, a pet-food manufacturer from Connecticut, and a Delaware Du Pont. The commentator Lowell Thomas became a regular guest, and such Hollywood stars as Errol Flynn and Claudette Colbert appeared, as did the ballerina Moira Shearer. The lodge barely met expenses; most of the profit derived from the ski shop, the school, and the lift. When J incorporated, his venture would be legally split into two entities, Alta Lodge and the Alta Ski Lift Company.

For evening entertainment, skiers could sing songs in the lodge or walk out to visit the mayor, George H. Watson, entrepreneur and visionary, in his rough miner's cabin. Sole survivor of the old mining days, Watson had clung on, buying up abandoned mining stakes and running tours to Alta. In the 1930s he claimed to be the only permanent resident. Doc Watson loved Alta and he loved people. He gave out signed membership cards for a completely bogus outfit of his invention, The Great American Prospectors Association, and his stories made up an oral history of the canyon. He served one of two equally lethal highballs to friends, according to the season, a "Pinetree" in warm weather, a "Ski Ball" in winter. His recipe was basic: a tall straight bourbon with either a sprig of pine or a snowball plunged in it. He was a "sweet guy," J thought, and a marvelous PR person for Alta.

For the rest of the war years J would struggle to get new J-bar lifts built up the Rustler and Peruvian ridges and then convert them to proper chairlifts, with backs to the seats. J's talents did not lie in engineering or mechanics, and he was glad to let others design and construct the lifts— although in his later years he liked to give the impression that he had picked up tools and pitched in. This his Alta subordinates dismissed with tolerant grins, speaking in the easy parlance of the West: "No, J was the boss. No doubt about that. He stood around and watched. But he was a good guy." What J really enjoyed was the utter democracy, the complete lack of formality. "Yessir they're all named / either Ken or Stan or Don," he would write, "you shake hands / with anybody you run into / . . . and by / god it makes a country / that is fit to live in."

With all the excitement, both in skiing and in romance, the wonder is that J found time for New Directions. In fact, J remained engaged in every element of publishing, from seeking out new authors to wrapper design: he designed the jackets for nineteen of the first forty-three ND volumes. But it was editing that took most of his time. Looking back over the years, J would say that his 1939 annual was his finest, but as a tour de force in scope and depth, *New Directions in Prose and Poetry 1940* surpassed it at 620 pages, including a photo essay on sharecroppers by Walker Evans, from his book *Let Us Now Praise Famous Men*. J divided this ambitious volume into seven sections, "Young Americans," "The American Scene," "Of Writing and Writers" (which contained George Orwell's "Inside the Whale"), "New Directions in Design," "A Little Anthology of Contemporary Poetry," "Chainpoems," and "Values in Surrealism," with Wayne Andrews, Charles Henri Ford, and J among the dozen translators. Many of the earlier stars were missing: no Pound, Williams, or Thomas. And in a distinct break from his early stridently antiwar stance, J dedicated the anthology to "The Men of the Royal Air Force," in recognition that, in his own words, "the future of free culture and of the kind of writing that New Directions stands for depends in great measure upon the outcome of their courageous battle."

J made a further implied acknowledgment of the increasingly warlike stance of America. In his preface to the annual, he issued a "recantation": he had come to the conclusion that he had been far too indulgent toward breaches in "formal discipline." Now he maintained that "a sense of form is an essential ingredient of the best writing, especially of writing which seeks to go in new directions." J seemed to have dropped the exhortative voice of his previous prefaces, except when he mounted his political-economic hobbyhorse: "There will be no reality in democracy until there is economic democracy." Therefore, he concluded, "instead of building planes and guns, let us build homes and schools and good farms."

At Delmore's insistence, J considered *Der Dreigroschenroman* by Bertolt Brecht for the New Classics series but rejected the novel because he thought that it "bogs down awfully in the middle." Instead, he decided to publish H. R. Hays's translation of Brecht's *Mother Courage* in the annual for 1941. Brecht had written the play at tearing speed following the German invasion of Poland, and it had just premiered in Zurich in April 1941. Brecht intended the play to be staged using techniques that would come to be known as Epic Theatre and the *Verfremdungseffekt*—the deliberate estrangement of the actors from the conventional expectations of realistic theater, achieved partly through speeches and behavior inappropriate to situations: Mother Courage's daughter is killed by soldiers, whereupon, deadpan, she strips the corpse so as to sell the girl's clothes. Profoundly leftist and anti-Fascist, Brecht was unpublished and virtually unknown in America before ND's *Mother Courage*. Some critics would eventually pronounce it the greatest play of the century. Schwartz next urged that J reprint *Miss Lonelyhearts*, the 1933 novel by William Carlos Williams's old co-editor Nathanael West. J had had his eye on West at least since 1935 and was willing to take a chance "if the plates would fit our size." He was still not to be rushed, however, and ND would not issue *Miss Lonelyhearts* until 1946.

When it came to New Directions, J still placed the greatest confidence in Schwartz, telling him that he wanted Erskine to stick to being a business manager and leave the literary advice to Delmore, "to tell me what's what." J wanted to print some Marguerite Young poems in the 1941 anthology and would "if you approve of them"—Schwartz did. Erskine could hardly do right in J's eyes: "Just no zip to him." In June, J asked Emily Sweetser to join the staff as Erskine's assistant, with the understanding that she would take over from him eventually—at half his salary.

The nagging problem of Ezra continued. Various friends during the past few years had urged Ezra to return to America, and to this J had added his voice. "Waaal, as to my recoming to U.S.," Ezra replied, "what do I DO when I get there/ go on board of Chase Bank or teach tennis in Noo putt ? or clean latrines in the MacLeishery ?" (Roosevelt had appointed MacLeish

Librarian of Congress in 1939.) Then, at least twice during 1940 and again in the summer of 1941, Ezra announced that he would soon leave for America, but complications arose over his passport. Eventually, he was told that his passport would be renewed for a period only long enough for him to be repatriated, and at first Ezra refused to accept this condition. The official went out of his way to be abusive, and Ezra responded with like language.

Not fully aware of Ezra's predicament, J had continued to communicate in the usual jocular tone of their exchanges. He was wavering on the marriage front, and despite his venture at Alta he felt as if he were treading water. In a final attempt to get Ez out of the likely war zone, J tried to persuade him to come "HOME, where a man can get a conversation with you . . . The course of world affiars [sic] does not inspire me to thought if you see what I mean," J added guardedly. "Will keep the press running for face and front and to do any good when any can be done, but in general my world outlook might be said at this time to be nego-passive." Ezra refused to budge. "Wot do you suggest I come home ON?" he replied on September 17, "and then: WHY? If you can't find anything up to yr mental level; how shd/ I find anything up to mine?" In Rapallo he had the companionship of "one first rate writer," Enrico Pea; several journals were printing Ezra's essays; Mary was doing a fine job translating Hardy into Italian; and a performance of Vivaldi's *Juditha triumphans* had been "bloody good." "As you know," Ezra capped his argument, "I like a little kulcher and don't see how as I shd/ git more in goonville/ . . . Wot you need is a li'l trip to Yourup as a refresher," Ezra added, seemingly oblivious to the war raging on several fronts. J would not hear again from Ezra until 1946.

Everything changed on December 7. Japanophile that Pound was, he was dismayed by the Japanese attack on Pearl Harbor and by the U.S. entry into the war. He realized that as an American citizen he would have to tread most carefully. He applied for permission for Dorothy and himself to remain in Italy, which was granted, although he continued attempting to leave. Since J could now no longer send royalties accrued by his books published in America, the Pounds were faced with the real prospect of starvation without Ezra's stipend from his broadcasting. He drafted a statement to be used beginning January 29, 1942, to introduce him, with lines to the effect that "Dr. Ezra Pound . . . will not be asked to say anything whatsoever that goes against his conscience, or anything incompatible with his duties as a citizen of the United States of America." When the last diplomatic train left Rome on May 13, 1942, carrying consular staff and journalists, Pound, waiting on the platform, was apparently denied permission to board. Before Ezra was able to resolve the situation of his extended family, old Homer Pound broke his hip and was bedridden with a chest infection, unable to travel.

Ezra would never waver from his contention that he was acting as a loyal American, and there is no evidence that the Italian government made any effort to influence the content of his broadcasts. His radio audience would apparently remain small, but from at least October 2, 1942, the American Foreign Broadcast Intelligence Service was listening to—and recording—his speeches. So too, soon, was the FBI. Evidently very few in America, apart from the security agencies, tuned in to Pound. J mentioned only that he was unable to locate Ezra on the shortwave dial. Ezra's friends reacted to the broadcasts with dismay or outrage or both.

•

J had spent the few years since his graduation from Harvard veering from writing poetry to publishing that of others, grappling with Delmore Schwartz and Henry Miller and Kenneth Rexroth, and he had quite suddenly found himself running a range of ski slopes. His early fear that Alta would be closed down because it was not essential to the warlike preoccupations of many in the nation's leadership was about to be rendered moot. On November 28, 1941, J was in Milwaukee as a representative to the annual National Ski Association convention. The army had belatedly awakened to the need to train soldiers in ski warfare: no longer seen as being merely recreational, skiing suddenly became part of "our nation's defense." When the United States entered the war, there was no longer room on the sidelines for J or for any American, and J became actively involved in the Allied war effort. Dick Durrance was asked by the War Department if he could train paratroopers for war on skis at Alta. He collected ten of his racing colleagues and formed at Alta what the army called the Experimental Winter Survival Training Center. In mid-January 1942 the first troops arrived, 150 men, the 503rd Airborne Infantry Battalion from Fort Benning, Georgia. They were billeted near the Salt Lake City Airport and came up by truck for daily ski instruction, with J helping on logistics. Most of them were southerners who had seen little if any snow, and the unit had been deliberately selected by the army to see whether it was possible to train non-skiers to become ski-borne troops in short order. Parachute training had conditioned the soldiers to roll forward when they hit the ground. In skiing you fall backward. "They broke a lot of legs," said Durrance, before they learned to fall correctly. About a third became proficient skiers, Dick estimated, while another third learned to ski passably. The training experiment was deemed a success, and the army built a specialized winter training center to be called Camp Hale, just north of Leadville, Colorado. This became the home of the famous Tenth Mountain Division. Soon after the 503rd left Alta, the Durrances themselves departed: Miggs was expecting their first child, and they felt that conditions in Little Cottonwood Canyon were too primitive for a baby. J's direct involvement with troop training ended, but not his commitment to Alta.

13

Real Butterflies and
Metaphorical Chess: Vladimir Nabokov

The author seemed to him a terrible snob, intellectually, at least . . . He added
that Knight seemed to him to be constantly playing some game of his own invention, without telling his partners its rules.   —Vladimir Nabokov

In his draft preface to *New Directions in Prose and Poetry 1941*, J had
again come out against the war, promoting his own literature-come-what-
may agenda. After Pearl Harbor, with the issue on the point of going to
press, he cut the entire preface. This would be the first anthology to appear minus an editorial statement. For similar reasons, Henry Miller
withdrew his *Air-Conditioned Nightmare*—the vision of America that it
presented was too bleak—and Rexroth pulled pacifistic poems already
accepted by *Partisan Review*.

Acting on the suggestions of both Edmund Wilson and Harry Levin, J
had solicited a manuscript from Vladimir Nabokov in January 1941.
Nabokov offered two novels, *Despair*, already published in England, and
the typescript of *The Real Life of Sebastian Knight*, unpublished—the first
novel that he had written in English. Within days J asked Nabokov for
advice on a small collection of Russian poetry that he was contemplating,
naming Boris Pasternak as a special interest. Yes, the Russian replied, "by
far the best" recent poets were Pasternak and Khodasevich. Pasternak,
especially, was "a real permanent poet." With what J soon discovered
was a typical Nabokovian absolute judgment, his new correspondent
added, "The best poetry produced in Europe (and the worst fiction) has
been in the Russian language." Nabokov was a veteran author who had
written a number of books under the pseudonym Vladimir Sirin beginning

in the 1920s, but, as he cautioned J, he was a "novator" in Russian literature whose works were banned in his homeland, read only by a handful of intellectual Russian expatriates. Only "one of my worst" novels, *Laughter in the Dark* in his own translation into English, had been published in the United States. Nabokov, when he did not hear soon from J, began to fear that he had been rejected. Meanwhile, Delmore Schwartz read *Sebastian Knight* and recommended its publication. "Very elegant and subtile," J pronounced the Russian's writing. J wrote to Nabokov in June expressing interest in *Sebastian Knight* and mentioning an earlier letter that Nabokov never received. Within days after his June letter, J cabled an offer of a straight 10 percent royalty and requested options on Nabokov's next three books. "PLEASE WIRE ANSWER AND RUSH PUBLICITY MATERIALS AIR MAIL," J concluded, suddenly in a great hurry. Nabokov was not a chess master for nothing, and he refused to jump. While he was delighted to be published by ND, he said, because he had only recently landed as an impoverished refugee in America, he would like an advance on royalties: "The financial question is still very acute with me." J came up with $150, which Nabokov felt obliged to accept, since *Sebastian Knight* had suffered three years of rejections. The two men met at Palo Alto in early July, and almost immediately J had to apologize for a typo in the jacket proof for *Sebastian Knight*—and in his letter about the mistake he misspelled the Russian's name as "Nabokoff." Without comment, Nabokov addressed his reply to J as "Mr. Laughton."

J's allergic reaction to all advances beyond very nominal ones had multiple grounds. Yes, he was constitutionally tightfisted, but that was by no means the whole reason. The capital that he was willing to risk in publishing was limited, and an advance took away working cash for operating expenses. And a lot of money at one time was bad for some authors, he was sure. The worst effect of large advances, in J's eyes, was that they enabled well-endowed mainstream houses to monopolize promising writers. From the author's perspective, there was an important trade-off to accepting a low advance from New Directions: a virtual guarantee that titles would be kept in print until the public caught on to them, and almost from the first the firm had a reputation that drew buyers and bookstores toward the titles on the backlist. In the long run, the author stood to earn more money than she or he would have through a single large advance from a mainstream publisher: eventually, royalties from the backlist, like compound interest, would work actuarial magic. Understandably, J often found it hard to make this argument convincing to needy writers.

J's most original venture of 1941 was finally to launch the Poet of the Month series on January 2 with William Carlos Williams's *The Broken Span*. The idea was to celebrate a different poet each month. J would have liked to emulate the English fine-press volumes or the French *livres d'artistes*, but he seldom had enough working capital left over after budgeting his ambitious annual lists. So he decided on a series of thirty-two-page booklets, intended to appear monthly. J wanted to encourage the art of fine printing and to feed his own love of beautiful books, and in the previous year he had published *Koheleth: The Book of Ecclesiastes*, illustrated by the American painter Emlen Etting, designed and printed by Peter Beilenson at the Walpole Printing Office in Mount Vernon, New York. This slender and elegant boxed volume was New Directions' first example of hand-set printing and a forerunner to the Poet of the Month series.

In this first year of the series, through heroic effort J actually succeeded in bringing out thirteen "of the Month" booklets. Enter the leviathan Book-of-the-Month Club lawyers, threatening New Directions with a copyright infringement suit over the phrase "of the Month." In an out-of-court settlement, J agreed to change his series title to "of the Year," beginning in 1943, in return for a cash payment of $500, and from then on he would refer in correspondence to the series as "Poets of the Month/Year," or POMY. J considered himself fortunate both to have escaped a legal battle and to have wrung some money out of the book club. The POMY figures would drop to seven in 1943 and eight in 1944, with a single (and final) volume in 1945. There were never more than a few hundred subscribers at any given time, and J was forced reluctantly to conclude that selling poetry at bargain prices was not economically sound. Most bookstores refused to stock the little volumes: too easily overlooked on the shelves, too cheap to allow for a decent profit, too easy to shoplift. Still, there were publishing triumphs in the series: Williams's *Broken Span*, Brecht's *The Trial of Lucullus*, Berryman's *Poems*, Merton's *Thirty Poems*, Rilke's *Poems from "The Book of Hours,"* and Dylan Thomas's *New Poems*. J offended Edmund Wilson by rejecting his poems for the series, and soon Wilson would be advising his friend Nabokov to drop ND.

In quality if not in sales, 1941 was outstanding. Nabokov's *The Real*

Life of Sebastian Knight received generally good reviews, with the *New York Herald Tribune* calling it "a little masterpiece of cerebration and execution." From a publishing point of view, the timing could hardly have been worse: the book appeared on December 18, when the appeal of cerebration was lost in the patriotic fervor called up by the Japanese attack. Only after ND's 1959 post-*Lolita* reissue of *Sebastian Knight* did the novel sell well in America. Miller's *Wisdom of the Heart* became a reliable seller, and Harry Levin's *James Joyce: A Critical Introduction* accorded Joyce respectful treatment as a modernist innovator. By giving students clear guidance toward understanding what Joyce was about, Levin helped establish the author in university curricula, and the book, as of this writing, has remained continuously in print. Not part of the series yet also aimed at the colleges, John Crowe Ransom's *The New Criticism* had such an impact that the book's title became the name of a long-reigning critical method. Ransom advocated close analysis of the text itself, especially of poetry, to the virtual exclusion of such traditional professorial modes as the historical and linguistic approaches. New Criticism would hold sway in academia until the 1970s, when Deconstruction took hold.

Amid the sparring with Schwartz, Miller, and Nabokov, amid the skiing, and despite J's own writing, during the year he put together what would prove to be the largest of the entire fifty-five-edition run of New Directions anthologies. *New Directions in Prose and Poetry 1941* contained 729 pages of text. In it he published some very important translations: Brecht's *Mother Courage*; Breton's surrealist poem *Fata Morgana*; a previously untranslated fable by Kafka; a section devoted to Soviet Russian poetry, including translations by Nabokov. Delmore was represented by a verse drama and an essay on poetry. One of the other features was "A Little Anthology of Contemporary Poetry," more than a hundred pages devoted to twenty-one mainly American poets ranging from Berryman to Marguerite Young. J pushed the anthology into yet another field with "New Directions in Phonograph Records," poetry recordings reviewed by Harry T. Moore, who would emerge after the war as the author of the first major biography of D. H. Lawrence.

Randall Jarrell, omitted from J's anthology, wrote a scathing review of *NDPP 1941* for *Partisan Review*, calling it "a reviewer's nightmare . . . a queer mediocre hodge-podge in which a few nice and a good many awful things are smothered." Jarrell found almost nothing to like in the anthology, beginning with the "Notes on Contributors," written, he said, "by an anonymous Goody Two-Shoes who rattles like Mr. Laughlin—nobody else errs with the same aura of optimistic benevolence." J of course had written the notes himself.

In the New Classics series, J brought out a "corrected edition" of Rimbaud's *Season in Hell*, with the flaws in the original Schwartz translation addressed. The third New Classic was a reprint of Stein's 1909 *Three Lives* from the Random House plates, with a new introduction by Carl Van Vechten.

Bill Williams mentioned again to J that "there's also the poem *Paterson* I want to bring finally to a focus." The story of Williams and New Directions could be summarized as the saga of the evolution and publishing of his many-volumed verse epic. And *Paterson* was indeed Williams. "That is why I started to write *Paterson*: a man is indeed a city," he acknowledged. What he needed to include were things, details, that he knew intimately, "an image large enough to embody the whole knowable world about me." Pound for sound, Williams for image: these elements J learned from them. Williams was in the ascendant: he was invited to read at Harvard. "He was funny as a crutch and had the audience completely with him," J reported to Patchen.

J was still writing poetry, although he was coming to wonder just why: no one seemed to notice, except Rexroth when J told him he was going to give it up. Keep at it, Rexroth urged. "Any art is most like sex in that it presupposes a response," replied J, adding, "In my case that response has for a long time been prodigiously lacking . . . This doesn't mean, though, that I'm going to hurl my typewriter out into the cruel night."

•

For some time J had been considering moving the operational center of ND to Manhattan; he was reluctantly becoming convinced that the great city was where an American publisher should be. However, this move was conditional on several factors: if Gertrude's job remained essential to the Schwartzes' well-being, J would not make the change. He told Delmore that he considered him "our most valuable asset" and would not act without his acquiescence. By May 1941, J was hoping for a 4-F status from his draft board: if this came through, he planned to fire Erskine "in a nice way." When it came, the parting with Erskine led to hurt feelings, with the departing business manager blaming Schwartz for J's complaints about him. Erskine's marriage with Porter had broken up the year before, and he would join Random House in 1947, where he would have a brilliant career as editor for the likes of Faulkner, Robert Penn Warren, and Eudora Welty.

J's business arrangements might have appeared haphazard, too dependent on friendships and the whims of those friends, yet he was evolving a reasonable organization. He realized that he could no longer be the sole salesman for ND, and he had engaged agents to sell on commission in the West and the South. He defined Delmore's role to be to "set the high literary tone," greeting his friend as "Melancholy, Fate-destined Bard," and signing himself with an Ezratic "Uncle Remus."

Ultimately, J abandoned his resolve to move New Directions to Manhattan and encouraged Gertrude and Delmore to lease a yellow six-room mansard-roofed house at 908 Memorial Drive in Cambridge, facing the Charles and owned by Harvard. The Schwartzes moved into the upstairs apartment September 6, 1941. "There certainly has not been so much disorder since the Jews left Egypt" was Schwartz's despairing comment. J paid the rent but eliminated Delmore's $10-per-month reader's stipend. Schwartz countered by demanding a dollar-a-month honorarium, stating, "It is a symbol and I am a symbolist." Delmore kept up a steady fire of advice, much of it prescient: print Pound's collected essays "as soon as possible," publish Pasternak, publish Nabokov, reprint Dylan Thomas.

The yellow house became the new home of New Directions. Harry and Elena Levin lived next door, and for the first year and a half they and the Schwartzes were friendly, inviting each other for dinners and chatting into the night on the front steps. Schwartz declaimed in what Alfred Kazin called "gulps of argument," his enunciation slightly blurred in his excitement. J listened happily to Delmore and Harry "talking pessimistic," as Elena called it. Delmore wrote a ditty in quatrains, to be sung to the tune of "Frankie and Johnnie," on the supposed Manichaean duality of the Levins' infant daughter, called by the Russian Elena "Goodka" or "Badka," depending on her behavior. Delmore inserted himself in a stanza all too near the truth: "Next door there lived a poet. / His name was Mr. Black. / He sent his verse to the editors, / The editors sent it back." Then, for no reason the Levins could figure out, Delmore cut them off. Such behavior became more pronounced over the years as his paranoia deepened. Early in their relationship, most of the banter exchanged by J and

Delmore was friendly. "Look, Buffalo Bill, you didn't catch on about the proofs," J admonished Delmore, echoing Cummings's poem "Buffalo Bill 's / defunct," when he asked for a delay in attending to them. "Paolo," Delmore taunted J, naming him after one of the lovers in Dante. "Satanic Throne," J addressed one letter, alluding to his friend's Mephistophelean side, black Schwartz. Increasingly, Delmore chided J for spending so much time "with the ski hotel." Emily Sweetser handled much of the publishing business—until Delmore's ill temper and weeklong silences drove her to quit in October 1941.

There was a rumor in the autumn that Bill Williams wanted to find another publisher, and Schwartz urged J to "bend every effort" to retain him, "since he is a very great author and you have only one other one"— Pound, or perhaps Delmore's wry nomination of himself. Williams conceded that he did not expect to live entirely from his writing, then told J, "But if I am well paid then it would really help me to move ahead in my craft." He admitted that J had helped him greatly, and he was willing "in the present and as long as we know what we're about" to help J: "You're established as a publisher and I've cleaned up my portfolio." However, Bill now wanted "more freedom to go as and where I please." In his own mind, he had already "thrown Laughlin," as Williams told Zukofsky. "He has done fine by me," Williams admitted, "but he's also been helped by me so I owe him nothing at all." Then, in September 1941, he stated bluntly to J, "You're too busy writing and living to look after a publishing business so I have made up my mind to go out after another publisher." He had come to think of J as his publisher of last resort.

Despite Williams's threatened departure, J's morale seemed high, and he boasted of publishing "about twenty books of 'Advance guard' writing a year." One volume that was hardly avant-garde was *A Satire Against Mankind* by John Wilmot, Earl of Rochester, which J brought out in his POMY series. Harry Levin edited and introduced the volume; it was designed by Victor Hammer, the Vienna-born artist, and hand-set and printed by his son, Jacob, together running the Wells College Press in Aurora, New York. J wrote years later that it was "one of the most elegant little books New Directions ever published," and it led to a long-standing friendship between J and Victor, a "compulsive perfectionist." The Hammers printed on dampened sheets, and a print run could be a mere thirty copies.

J followed up on his inclusion of Berryman in *Five Young American*

Poets 1940 by inviting him to be a Poet of the Month in 1942. After championing Berryman, Delmore continued to prod J: he should publish the poems of Lawrence Durrell because he was "bound to go far as a novelist," and especially Bertolt Brecht, who was *"wunderbar."* Brecht, J would later concede, *was* "rather wonderful," so long as he was not "preaching a Marxist lesson." J wrote from the West telling Delmore to send "any Brecht" to him at Sun Valley, yet J dallied, missing later Brecht titles. In 1940, Durrell had sent a collection of his poems and then became angry with J for not publishing them. "I shall have nothing more to do with New Directions," he fumed to Henry Miller. "I'm not going to have it from that cream cheese intelligence which edits half a million pages of pretentious balls a year and can't even acknowledge a book of verse." Henry, however, while he would continue to remind J that "I harbor a deep grudge against you," appeared to be ready to make peace. J was discovering that authors required a great deal of coddling.

When J asked Mark Van Doren for a small collection of poems for the POMY series, he gained an author whose ego did not require constant stroking. The manuscript J received became *Our Lady Peace and Other War Poems*. In publishing Van Doren, J was mixing good poetic judgment, useful networking, and friendship in approximately equal quantities. Van Doren was useful to J because he attracted and fostered creative people— Zukofsky, Berryman, Lionel Trilling, Thomas Merton, Lawrence Ferlinghetti, Jack Kerouac, Allen Ginsberg, Donald Keene, and Clifton Fadiman had all been his students at Columbia—and he was ready to steer them to New Directions. He was also a neighbor: he had a farm near Cornwall, just over the mountain from Norfolk, and often when J had a good day on the Hollenbeck River, he would share his trout with Van Doren in exchange for a drink and conversation about literature.

Delmore, on the other hand, remained invariably vehement in both his approval and his antipathies. He said it would be "pointless" to publish *The Crack-Up*, already rejected by Scribner's: F. Scott Fitzgerald was the forgotten "laureate of the Twenties." It was a terrible mistake to engage Charles Henri Ford to translate Baudelaire: Ford was an incompetent versifier, ignorant of the "spiritual conflicts" in the Frenchman's poetry. And Delmore seldom missed a chance to deride Kenneth Patchen, "one of the world's most painful vulgar banal and incredible human beings." J went serenely on with his plan to publish Kenneth's *The Teeth of the Lion* in the 1942 Poet of the Month series, despite Delmore's opinion. Delmore's relationship with J was also strained because of his own work. In December 1941, Schwartz sent J the first two hundred pages of *Genesis*, the autobiographical epic that Delmore had been talking about for a decade. He asked J to publish this separately as "Part I"—and it would be the only section ND would bring out.

J's periodic preoccupation with Alta continued to enrage Delmore. The tone of his letters shifted from teasing to downright accusation as the weight of his paranoia bore down upon him. In a long letter written on January 7, 1942, and addressed to "Dear Mr. Laughlin," he accused J of having called him a drunkard, traitor, and schemer. There was the matter of a "putative campaign" against him, which Delmore in the same letter called an "imaginary campaign" that "never was . . . only resentment." The fact that J did not spend more to advertise his books rankled, and Delmore claimed that he had gotten better offers on his novel in progress from other publishers. It was a bitter, invective-filled letter, with Delmore's growing persecution mania twisting the import of any of J's remarks that could be construed as insulting. Part of the difficulty stemmed from Delmore's repeated assertion that his own writing had to come first, and so he did not want to be tied to a specific schedule or a formal job designation. And while J wanted his advice, he knew intuitively that Delmore would not produce reliably as a salaried employee. During the present contretemps the sole copy of the revised first part of *Genesis*, sent to J, went missing.

Faced with the prospect of having to reconstruct his changes from incomplete early drafts, Delmore pleaded with J to "make one more effort" to locate it and to fulfill an earlier promise to him to hire a manager capable, "at least within reason," of attending to the publishing—"since you have obviously decided to spend your life skiing and falling off roofs, or whatever it is you find so engaging in romantic Alta." When J suggested that Delmore might be suffering from a neurosis, Schwartz replied, "I suggest that you just call me ill-tempered." Four months after vanishing, the typescript turned up under the floorboards of the Alta mail truck, or so J claimed. Then he lost the page proofs, *after* Delmore had gone through the ordeal of correcting them. Nonetheless, Delmore's sense of humor and his genuine devotion to J, plus J's own forgiving nature, could still permit their relationship to recover from many blows. Soon after the crisis of the lost material, Delmore nominated J's poem "What the Pencil Writes" and his short story "The River" for anthologizing, commenting, "What a fine writer you could be, if you did not feel so devoted to your pleasures, such as running second-rate hotels."

J's love life out west had become so active that he solicited the advice of Bill Williams: he was seeing, at the very least, Margaret Keyser in Utah, as well as the ice skater and the acrobat in Los Angeles. "Oh well, Jim . . glad you keep your prod busy," replied the poet-doctor, carefully spacing periods. "One of them is going to get you someday or maybe not, I love 'em all. I don't know a fruitfuller field to poke around in." Williams's letter turned out to be prophetic: on March 24, 1942, J and Margaret were married with some suddenness. J had begun to get cold feet as the date approached, but his family told him that he must go through with it. His mother and brother came to Salt Lake City for the small family wedding, as did Aunt Leila and Uncle Dicky. "Christ and a bear!" exclaimed the father of the bride, raising several Presbyterian eyebrows, but J liked the expression well enough to adopt it for his own. "I congratulate you most cordially," wrote Nabokov on hearing a rumor of the marriage, "it is a very pleasant state as far as my own experience goes."

By early April, J and his bride were in Norfolk, and it became apparent that Margaret was pregnant. J single could camp quite comfortably on the third floor of Robin Hill, but with a family he required an establishment of his own. Aunt Leila as usual had an answer: Jamesie must live near her, so she had an old farmhouse of hers, known as Meadow House, across Mountain Road fixed up and restored. This meant moving out the Deloy family, but Leon Deloy was a loyal groundsman to Aunt Leila, and he did not object, at least not to her. A rolling meadow was the defining feature of the property, a field of some eight acres behind the house: long grass and clumps of hemlock, and studded with large granite boulders. A meadow needed sheep. Again, Aunt Leila chose: Scottish West Highlands sheep, small, tough, black-faced, with long, matted brownish-blond wool. The sheep had slender legs and in their periodic panics ran nimbly across the meadow, changing direction in unison like a school of herring. J christened them the Gabriel Heatters, after the radio commentator who began each of his wartime broadcasts by calling out in his fruity voice, "Ah, my friends, there's ba-a-ad news tonight"—or "good," to suit the case. J became inordinately proud of his sheep and on rare occasions would serve guests small homegrown chops. The picture window of the living room, the large windows of the eventual formal dining room, the sunny small dining room off the kitchen—all these faced the meadow. The front of the house, facing west, was a place where visitors parked cars and admired the tall, dark oaks and maples. The view toward the east, the meadow, was light, open. The property reflected two sides of J's character: brooding, dark, hidden as the woods hid the front of the house from the road; and open, bright, uplifting, expansive like the meadow vista.

For a cook Aunt Leila introduced Wonza Hunt, daughter of her own beloved cook, Hattie Williams. Wonza and her husband lived just outside Norfolk. She was an excellent cook, but more than that, she was able to balance service with self-respect. J saw it as perfectly natural that he should be looked after by someone who had shared his experience of Zellwood, and to Wonza the Laughlins and Carlisles were family.

J had not after all been declared 4-F, marriage was not enough to save him from the draft, and he seemed resigned to service. "I go in the army end of next week," he wrote in April 1942 to Eliot, adding, "But have fixed everything up so New Directions will keep rolling." He reported to the Norfolk Board on May 2 but was "rejected for training and service" with the unelaborated and somewhat ambiguous comment "Does not meet the physical and/or mental requirements of MR 109." There is no definite evidence that any strings were pulled, but there were family members of sufficient political standing to nudge the outcome with a single telephone call. J must have been grimly amused that some mental defect could have been a factor in his rejection. More than fifty years later he would state in verse, "I'd managed with / Some effort to avoid the war." His skepticism about political motives, his hatred of jingoism, even a latent class snobbery kept him aloof, and he agreed with Ezra that American participation in the European conflict would be a mistake. For the profit margin of J&L, the war was a godsend: after sustaining a loss in 1938, the company had posted a profit of $3.2 million in 1939 and $10.3 million in 1940; its peak wartime steel production in 1944 exceeded by twelve times the tonnage of 1938.

New Directions was doing relatively well also; while so much was being rationed, books were not. And by the spring of 1942, J had conclusively decided that a New York presence was essential. On April 20 he rented space at 67 West Forty-Fourth Street in Manhattan, in the office suite of George W. Stewart, a skiing friend and mountaineer. Stewart had been the New York area book distributor for ND during the previous year. J's idea was to keep most of the editorial work at Norfolk and handle production and sales from New York. The decision was momentous for J. For the rest of his life there would be a geographic separation between his publishing base and his home life. Except for periodic forays into the cultural world of New York, he detested the city, of which he said, "Babylon is too pleasant a name." Norfolk was a retreat, a refuge, increasingly his hermitage. Daily commuting was not feasible; it was at least a three-hour drive to New York, and there were no convenient railway connections.

In mid-May 1942, J met with Nabokov and commissioned two books: a monograph on Nikolai Gogol and a small volume of verse translations of Pushkin and Fyodor Tyutchev; this latter would appear, with the addition of poems by Mikhail Lermontov, in 1944. It soon became apparent that Nabokov was having trouble completing his Gogol monograph, destined to be the first textual study of Gogol in English. "I am plodding furiously at and through Gogol," he wrote in a deliberate oxymoron. The meticulous Russian had decided that most of the already translated critical writings on Gogol, and even the few translations of the writer's primary work, were "so abominably botched" that he was forced to translate everything that he wanted to quote. He found that the need to work on Gogol eight or ten hours a day was "rather devastating," and he told J, "both as a publisher and as a friend," that the remuneration that J had suggested was inadequate. Nabokov was at once unflinching in his judgments and forthright in expressing them, as befitted a man descended from a fourteenth-century Tartar prince. He approved marginally of Bernard Guerney as a translator but said that neither Isabel Hapgood nor Constance Garnett nor anyone else was acceptable. Among reviewers he detested most Clifton Fadiman of the Book-of-the-Month Club, and J cautioned Nabokov, "I wouldn't attack Fadiman if I were you. He is a very influential critic and also the type who would never forget a slight and be nasty to all your novels for ever after." Then J fired a shot of his own: "Everyone knows he is not very bright and not worth attacking."

Finally, in May 1943, Nabokov would post his "Gogol through the Looking-Glass" to J, telling him that the strain of having to translate Gogol into English and then to translate his "Russian ideas" about the writer had exhausted him: "I am very weak, smiling a weak smile, as I lie in my private maternity ward, and expect roses." Fearing that Nabokov's monograph would lose money, J kept the copyright in his own name so that it would not be charged against ND.

•

In early October 1942, J was at Alta, while Margaret, nearing her term, languished in Norfolk, watched over most solicitously by Aunt Leila. On the eighteenth she was rushed to the Hartford Hospital, an hour away from Norfolk, where she produced her firstborn, Paul, eight months after the wedding. J barely arrived in time for the event. He still appeared to feel that he had been trapped into the marriage. He did not visit his wife in the hospital as often as she would have liked, yet he found his infant son "most engaging." Leaving Margaret in Norfolk, J soon returned to Utah, but by late November he was on his way back east, pausing in Milwaukee to attend the annual convention of the National Ski Association of America.

On December 6, J went to a cocktail party at Lincoln Kirstein's uptown apartment in Manhattan, where he spotted a small shy figure in a corner and joined him, a "little fellow with baggy pants sitting all by himself and looking very nervous." In his later accounts, J made this appear a chance encounter, but it was not. Kirstein had given J typescript copies of a number of poems by a virtually unknown young playwright named Thomas Lanier Williams III. The small man with a sharp nose and curly dark hair was not yet known as Tennessee—although he had so named himself to the Group Theatre in New York in 1938. He had gone to Kirstein's on that evening expecting to meet J, and vice versa, and he was tense about the encounter, writing to his parents, "I hope we get along amiably at this first meeting." He very much wanted to be published by New Directions simply because he liked what the company stood for, adding, "I could not be printed under better auspices." J's soft-spoken manner soon put Williams at ease, and when they discovered that they shared a love of Hart Crane, J recalled, "we became almost instant friends." Their family histories contained many points of contact: Tennessee's father, Cornelius Coffin Williams, was related to Henry Coffin, grandfather of J's Uncle Dicky; and Tennessee too numbered among his ancestors Revolutionary War heroes, Presbyterian divines, and distinguished statesmen and educators. J at once committed himself to publishing his poems in *Five Young*

American Poets, and Tennessee plunged into the task of polishing. At thirty-one he was over the age limit that J had set, but if J realized this, he did not let on. J's timing was lucky: *Battle of Angels* had failed in both Boston (too sexy) and New York (too obscure), so Tennessee had decided to concentrate on publishing poetry and short stories.

Vastly dissimilar in various ways, the two men discovered that they shared traits, both physical and emotional. Tennessee also had impaired vision. His left eye had developed a cataract that had been removed through a painful "needling" operation only the year before, and he would continue to suffer from eye trouble for the rest of his life. And even more significant to the men's makeup was their troubled relationship to their parents. Tennessee's mother had certainly set her two sons against their father, and this had exacerbated the young Tom's insecurity. Just as J worried about insanity, Tennessee feared that like his adored sister, Rose, he might descend into mental illness. He also found himself blocked when it came to giving in love. "For love I make characters in plays," he would write almost twenty years later. "But after my morning's work, I have little to give but indifference to people." While it was not true that only work mattered to either man, J was certainly also driven by work to the extent that he seemed to feel that personal attachments could be placed on hold while he pursued goals in writing, publishing, or skiing.

About a week later Williams sent J a typescript of his short play *The Purification*, which J would include in his next anthology as *Dos Ranchos*. Tennessee was less confident about his poems, saying that he would accept J's opinion with equanimity, "even if you advised me to devote myself exclusively to the theatre for the rest of my life." J responded quickly, "I am very excited with the poems you sent. It seems to me you ARE a poet . . . You have some of that wonderful quality of Éluard—strange insights that reduce to highly poetic images." They met to discuss over lunch what Tennessee referred to as "my lyrical triviata."

Tennessee's first important appearance as a poet came in *Five Young American Poets*. Tennessee's love life would always be fraught with wild fluctuations, betrayals, reconciliations; his writing for the theater would veer from blazing success to dismal failure and back, repeatedly. He would eventually turn against and fire even his faithful and long-suffering agent, Audrey Wood. However, his relationship with his publisher would remain one of the few steady beacons of his life. This relationship was grounded from the earliest times on their mutual appreciation and understanding, on "a genuine rapport." Tennessee's open homosexuality did not stand in the way of the affection J clearly felt for him, although after the success of *The Glass Menagerie* in 1945, J would tend to avoid seeing him in the evening. "You had to see Tennessee by lunch," he maintained. "Then these unpleasant hangers on would come in," a "scroungy bunch." J did not add that it was during the convivial afternoons and evenings that Tennessee often drank to excess.

Tennessee knew that J appreciated him as an *experimental* playwright, and he wanted the substantive criticism that he could count on from J. "The kid has it," J wrote to Bill Williams, "that beautiful lyric excitement that was in Lorca." Tennessee admired J for his policy of encouraging new poets, and the fact that each felt that the other was underappreciated as a poet constituted a further bond. Tennessee suggested to J that he become his exclusive publisher. "As my first real publisher," he wrote to J, he would like a photograph of him, "preferably on skis," for his gallery of "persons of importance in my life, such as Crane and Chekhov." Tennessee was pleased to have a skiing publisher, and the sun-adoring playwright was even discovering a fondness for snow, the "snow-covered desert of Taos," where he and Frieda Lawrence were working on a play based on the story "You Touched Me" by her late husband. Months later Tennessee asked J to become his literary executor, explaining to him, "It would be dreadful if all my papers fell into the family's possession as they would burn the best because of impropriety." Both men not only tended to trust or distrust others on instinct but shared an ability to inspire friendship and loyalty.

•

J's gift for friendship did not appear to permeate his feelings for Margaret. Nonetheless, at this early stage he was trying to make the marriage work, and he gave Margaret a cut gem, musing about the meaning of the stone in a short poem, "On the Gift of a Sapphire to My Wife": "A blue stone seems a / hard cold thing to say / love," but he concluded with the thought that like the stone his love should "most endlessly endure!" He seemed to be trying hard to convince himself of his love, even as he made ironic note of man's "little thought" and of the eternal sapphire. But he liked the poem, and he would recycle it in his 1994 *Collected Poems*, adding to the title the name of a later wife.

By the close of 1942, J seemed to be giving more thought to his two businesses. He went to Manhattan for lunch with the Russian-American Philip Rahv—"My GAWWWWD what a tank!"—to discuss a possible monograph on Dostoevsky for the Makers of Modern Literature series, and met José García Villa: "Marvelous little guy. Like an affectionate squirrel." Villa, a Filipino, wanted to be in POMY. "OK by me," J wrote to Delmore. "He worships Cummings, which puts him in good with me." ND might make a profit of a "few dollars" on receipts of $15,000, and Alta was "booked solid for months ahead," promising future riches. With the Durrances gone, Alta desperately needed more on-the-spot leadership than J's publishing obligations permitted, as he realized. Shortly before Christmas, Fred Speyer, after twice refusing to take over running Alta, came up to ski with his wife, Coke, despite knowing that the lift was down. The sight of the silent lift was too much for him, and the next day the burly ex-wrestler agreed to become general manager, a position he would hold for sixteen years.

Nineteen forty-two at New Directions was short on full-length books; of the fifteen titles for the year, twelve were POMY pamphlets. However, J brought out two major collections: an extensive *New Directions in Prose and Poetry* and *An Anthology of Contemporary Latin-American Poetry*, edited by Dudley Fitts and Dudley Poore, a bilingual edition subsidized by Nelson Rockefeller, coordinator of inter-American affairs in Washington. The timing and the funding of this anthology by the government were not gratuitous coincidences: many in the Spanish- and Portuguese-speaking nations to the south were sympathetic to the Axis powers, and someone in authority realized that a focus on Latin American poets might help generate warm feelings for the colossus of the North. It was the first comprehensive survey of the field to appear in the United States.

In February, Margaret and J headed for Utah. He needed to see how Speyer was working out, and the Keysers wanted to see their grandson. J deposited wife and baby with the grandparents down in the thick fog of Salt Lake City and then drove in palpable relief up Little Cottonwood Canyon "into glorious sunlight, with the sky a perfect blue." "You can imagine how that raised my rather exhausted spirits," he wrote to the family back east. "It was like a promise of a new and better life." Mayor Watson welcomed J "with such rhetoric as has not been heard since the days of the Byzantine courts." Soon he was skiing in his shirtsleeves. The lodge was booked through the first of April, so he was sleeping in a small room with the manager's baby. The lift was running well, staffed by Japanese-Americans who must have been glad to be on furlough from the internment camp at Topaz. Even the cook and the ski shop and wait staff were Japanese, J said, "mostly college graduates and very nice." The nisei were supposed to maintain a curfew at Alta, but there were no guards, and they were not segregated from other employees.

In January, the ski lift and lodge grossed more than $6,000, and after the immediate bills were paid, there was $2,500 to put in the bank. J predicted "a nice little profit" for the winter *if* all went well. It was easy to comprehend why J so loved Alta. He had a product—snow and slopes—that many people wanted, and his employees seemed to him to be fine uncomplicated people good at their basic tasks: solving the mechanical problems of the ski lift, providing plain solid food and drink for hungry skiers, making up warm beds for those with luxuriously tired limbs. How different from publishing! Books that few wanted, authors and editors seething with neuroses—while the publisher himself lay in worried insomnia. And whenever J could ski, he slept well.

Margaret soon joined J at Alta, camping about in various parts of the crowded, noisy lodge: the storeroom, the ski room, and finally the ski shop. She had left Paul in Salt Lake City in the care of her family and a nursemaid. J was eager to move away from the lodge and into the caretaker's apartment then being renovated up the road, because Margaret was playing bridge day and night, a "tendency" that J "utterly deplored"—although whether it was because he viewed the game as a waste of time or because she had won $30 from his customers he did not say. A significant amount of drinking went with the card sessions too.

East or west, the fact of his marriage nagged at J. School friends thought of Margaret as bright and lively, and she was lovely as well, but although she fit in at Alta, she could not travel comfortably in J's literary world. Alfred Kazin's *On Native Grounds* monograph had appeared earlier in the year, to be dismissed by J in words that disparaged Margaret's understanding. "My wife is eating up Kazin like ice cream," J wrote to Delmore, "so now I KNOW he is no good."

Wartime restrictions were complicating J's publishing schedule and his relationships with his authors. Bill Williams proposed a volume of his uncollected poems, but J held back. As he explained to Bill, "There is a

W[ar] P[roduction] B[oard] order limiting publishers' paper to 90% of their 1942 use. This is hitting me hard because four of my 1942 books were postponed because of manuscript delays." Unconvinced, Williams complained to Mary Barnard that "Jimmy (who never saw it [the typescript])" had rejected his book, "because of an ostensible lack of paper." The whole truth was that J was not happy with the amorphous gathering of early and recent work, prose and verse, that Bill had proposed. Soon Williams was sounding out Duell, Sloan & Pearce as a possible publisher, and then Random House and Harper & Brothers, but to no avail. He appeared to be stuck with ND and J.

J himself was developing good editorial judgment, independent of the importunities of his mentors. He subscribed to a great many small journals and magazines, scanning their pages for new authors who might be candidates for his anthologies and eventual book publication. Urged on by Delmore, J had certainly not given up on Brecht, and he accepted *The Trial of Lucullus* for the POMY series. The next year New Directions would publish *The Private Life of the Master Race* in Eric Bentley's translation and with his incisive introduction. It was the right time to publish Brecht. Although German, he was well-known as a refugee from Hitler's Germany, and his Communism was not yet a drawback: the Soviets were America's allies. J envisioned a run of Brecht volumes and a collaboration on them with his champion, Bentley.

J's major discovery in 1943 was Thomas Merton. Van Doren had been Merton's favorite professor at Columbia, prior to his becoming a Trappist monk in 1941. J saw literature as a vast enterprise dependent on individual effort plus a symbiotic relationship between artist and mentor, between an artist and various predecessors. Van Doren was an important link in this chain, and he took it upon himself to send J a "small sheaf" of Merton's poems. Although they did not strike J as typical advance-guard New Directions fare and were overtly religious—J admitted to a prejudice against religious verse—he was impressed by the "vividness of language and freshness of imagination" and decided at once to publish them in the POMY series. In fact, Merton had sent a few poems several years earlier to J, who had passed over them, but with Van Doren jogging his elbow, J looked again. In his revised opinion of Merton, J showed the span of his judgment: what recommended Merton's early verse to his intuition was its accessibility. What J saw was that the poems were "verbally colorful," that they were "full of rich imagery and inventive fantasy." Given the soaring drive of his imagination, J thought Merton had the potential to develop into a major poetic voice. His subsequent emergence as just such a poetic voice, in parallel to his role as inspirational prose essayist encouraged by various Catholic churchmen, was in large part due to the early and continuing publishing support given him by New Directions.

Nabokov had been awarded a Guggenheim Fellowship to begin June 1943 for work on a novel. He asked J if he knew of a place where he could board with wife and son for the summer. "Great rocks, a lake and plenty of wildflowers are essential desiderata," he specified. J offered Alta Lodge at a very reasonable $6 per day, room and board for Vladimir, Véra, and their nine-year-old son, Dmitri. The Nabokovs found the lodge more rustic than they had imagined, but the main attractions for Vladimir were the lepidoptera in the Wasatch Mountains. As soon as the snows melted, the Alta slopes bloomed with scores of species of flowers, "just a sea of bloom," J said: cream-white and blue columbine under the aspens, the feathery disks of cow parsnip and of yarrow, pink geraniums, mountain bluebells, baneberries, the twelve-pointed golden stars of arnica, and the blue columns of lupine in the meadows, and on the treeless higher elevations the red splashes of Indian paintbrush. Within weeks Nabokov had filled dozens of boxes with mounted butterflies.

Once, J guided his guest into the high meadows and slopes. As they walked, the lepidopterist called out the Latin names of the flowers, naming the butterfly that chose each as its preferred pabulum. They talked writing, "And Nabokov told me that / What came next in the story should / Never be what the reader expected," J would recall. Nabokov was particularly eager to obtain specimens of the little blue *melissa* and of the allied *annetta*, so he had his net and other collecting gear with him. They climbed higher and higher up thirteen-thousand-foot Lone Peak, and then, descending in the failing light of late afternoon, they found themselves on the icy crust of a steep snowfield. This would have presented no difficulty had they been wearing nailed boots instead of tennis shoes. Both fell and began sliding. Nabokov snagged a small outcropping of rock with his net, and J as he slid past grabbed the Russian's foot. Then, with his knife, Nabokov hacked toeholds until they could get off the slope. "If it hadn't been for that butterfly net," J would say dramatically, recounting the event, "I wouldn't be here."

Despite such a bonding experience, there was evidence of strain between J and Nabokov. On one occasion, when J left Vladimir exploring a meadow to scale the adjacent peak, he inscribed the Russian's name in the log of ascents. Nabokov was not amused. They argued over what was to go into the Gogol monograph, with J insisting on a biographical outline, plot summaries, and a list of suggested readings to match the other student-directed Makers of Modern Literature texts. J sought Nabokov's friendship, but this was to be a miss. "He didn't want any jejune ninkapoop to be his friend," J remarked much later. "He wanted bigbrains such as Wilson and Levin to be his friends." Nabokov remained unfailingly polite, but he maintained a distance: "He would force a smile for me sometimes but it was a long-ways-away smile." Still, Nabokov seemed to enjoy himself thoroughly at Alta, and under the stimulation of healthy exercise and successful entomological captures, his work on *Bend Sinister* progressed well. When he departed at the end of August, Nabokov gave J a display box of beautifully mounted lepidoptera.

•

On the night of July 9, 1943, Operation Husky was unleashed against Sicily, and by September 3 Allied troops had crossed to the mainland. Five days later Italy capitulated. It was not to be the end of conflict in Italy, for the Germans took military control of those areas still unoccupied, and bitter fighting lay ahead. On July 26, while J and Nabokov were pursuing the blue *melissa*, a federal grand jury in Washington indicted Ezra Pound for treason.

J was much aware of the danger Ezra would be in from American authorities as soon as they could lay hands on him. Seeing the need to marshal powerful allies, he wrote to Eliot in language calculated not to alert the censorship: "Naturally it is now the fashion to kick our red-maned friend pretty generally around . . . I don't see that you can always expect a man of genius to have common sense and you should be thankful for the one and indulgent of the other. Don't you agree?" Evidently, Eliot did. In November, even more alarmed for Ezra's safety and still choosing words to disguise identity, J wrote again to Eliot about "our old friend the rabbit": "Do you suppose there is any way of getting him moved up north [to Gais]? He might be all right there." J was afraid that, during the collapse of Fascist Italy, partisans might lynch him.

Unbeknownst to his American friends, on September 10, 1943, hours ahead of the seizure of control by German forces, Ezra had set out on foot for Gais, leaving his trademark malacca cane and wide-brimmed hat in the care of a hotel clerk in Rome and borrowing heavy boots and a military map from his friend Admiral Ubaldo degli Uberti. The admiral offered him shelter, but he refused it. Another friend provisioned him with one hard-boiled egg and some fruit and bread, and marked on his map the best way to leave the city on foot and without attracting attention. He headed for Gais. Ezra felt that he might not survive the chaotic times that he foresaw—he had told a Minculpop staffer that the Americans would probably shoot him—and he wanted to set the record straight for his daughter. He walked fifty miles northwest to Rieti, got on a train with a bunch of demobilized Italian soldiers, was kicked off the train by the Germans, walked into Bologna, got as far as Verona on another train, and so onward until, 450 miles later, he arrived at Gais with blistered feet and found Mary out on an errand. To the startled Frau Marcher he said merely, "Müde"—weary—and collapsed on Mary's bed. That night, after the Marchers had left them alone, Ezra, ordinarily the most voluble of men, cast about for the words to begin his confession. Finally, he said to Mary, "I don't know how much of this you already suspect, the doors at Sant'Ambrogio are not exactly soundproof." But no, Mary had never overheard a revealing conversation between her parents. She was not aware that her father had "another" wife, or of the existence of Omar Pound in England, whom Ezra had claimed was his son by Dorothy. It was three in the morning before he said, "Mi par d'aver detto ogni cosa"—that's all. He had not mentioned the indictment for treason, which he had heard broadcast over the BBC. Then Ezra headed back south, buoyed with the euphoria brought on by his adventure. Meanwhile, J did not even know whether the Boss was alive or dead.

14

Tennessee Williams Triumphs

I am crazy about Jay. He has become my little shiney god.
Why does he bother with me?

—Tennessee Williams

J's personal life seemed to be smoothing out. Any resentment that he might have felt over the inconveniently early appearance of his firstborn, Paul, appeared to have evaporated. In his letters to his family, he seldom missed an opportunity to say something nice about his son, whom he always wrote of as simply "baby." "He really is more and more charming," J wrote from Utah to Aunt Leila. "He's terribly good, but of course why shouldn't he be with all the care and admiration and attention he gets." J believed that Alta was now in "pretty good shape," but he was also looking forward to a vacation as soon as the new man he had hired to oversee the skiing program arrived. "It has been very interesting work running the place," he said, "but an awful nervous strain because of all the uncertainties and the difficulty of handling the Japs"—J had recast the nisei into a problem to excuse his wayward moods, a new "'combative' vein" that his aunt had complained about. Margaret was enjoying the house they had rented in the Cottonwood suburb of Salt Lake City, even though J did not get down to it very often, blaming the gas rationing. She was pregnant again, and both hoped that it would be a girl. J rationalized that his own "maladjustment" was owing to the five-year span between Hugh and himself, so that they were always fighting rather than cooperating. His children, if born close together, would have "friendly temperaments" and "the ability to get along easily with other people."

The relationship between J and Delmore Schwartz continued to gyrate wildly. Toward the end of 1943, Delmore issued three ultimatums: that he be given one-half share in New Directions; that he be paid an annual retainer of $2,000 as editor and author; that he be given a complete accounting of his royalties, along with a letter of apology from J. A list of charges and grievances followed. Further, Delmore said that half of the accomplishment of New Directions was due to sheer luck, the other half in equal parts to J's "money and energy and ambition" and to his, Delmore's, ideas and initial success. Instead of only two lamentable books by "Whiz Bang," as Delmore now called Patchen, J, left to himself, would have published *four*. J shrugged off the tirade.

J was paying more attention to publishing than Delmore would acknowledge: Harcourt, Brace let Djuna Barnes's *Nightwood* go out of print, allowing ND to bring out the novel as a New Classic. J wrote in some excitement to Eliot asking permission to reprint his preface, which pointed in the novel to "a quality of horror and doom very nearly related to that of Elizabethan tragedy." Also, six New Directions poets, each championed by J, had been featured in readings held at the New York Public Library: James Agee, Horace Gregory, Langston Hughes, Marianne Moore, Patchen, and Bill Williams.

Despite positive indications, J was finding it difficult to keep his several lives in balance: Alta, publishing, and being a father. For a change from managing Alta, he would go alone to the Westwood area of Los Angeles and stay near the Man Rays at a small hotel. Tennessee Williams visited J at his suite, where he met Man Ray and Henry Miller—which in turn set the stage for a reconciliation between J and Henry. "He made a profuse and profound apology to me in the presence of several people," Henry reported. "Now he can't do enough for me." This smoothed the way for the eventual publication by ND of some twenty Miller titles. J changed his mind about *The Colossus of Maroussi* and bought the rights from Colt Press, the original publisher.

On November 30, 1943, J was in Pasadena for the second performance at the Playbox of Tennessee's *You Touched Me!*, his dramatic adaptation of D. H. Lawrence's short story. J enjoyed the play but found it "a bit too earthy or theatrical." Not so the author, who thought that Margo Jones had done a "beautiful job" with the staging, and he told Audrey Wood, "This is the first time anything of mine has been done to my own satisfaction."

J decided not to publish *You Touched Me!*, but Tennessee had already written in his journal, "I am crazy about Jay. He has become my little shiney [sic] god. Why does he bother with me? It is so easy to ignore a squirt like me." Four years later, discussing his friendships, Tennessee said that he had "relatively few close friends" and named "such persons as" Audrey Wood, Margo Jones, and J. To his agent, Tennessee said that J had sent him an advance of $25 against the publication of forty pages of his verse in the Five Young American Poets series. "Laughlin is a rara avis, a very rich boy with a good heart and ready sympathy," he said. "He is a terribly sweet person underneath his austere skin."

Seven years into his career as a publisher and realizing the importance of his files, J sent the first installment of material to Harvard. Thereafter, ND would periodically deposit batches of manuscripts in the Houghton Library. Access was restricted to qualified scholars, J quipped, "provided that they wear white cotton gloves and do not chew gum."

Without warning, J's satisfaction was interrupted by a tremor on his personal Russian front. "I wonder whether you will think it very unethical of me if I cancelled our agreement," Nabokov wrote to J about *Three Russian Poets*, his booklet of translations about to appear in ND's POMY series. Another publisher had just offered ten times the ND advance, which Vladimir proposed to repay, plus a 10 percent increment. "I would like to oblige you," J replied, "but I don't see how I can. Your volume is part of the series and I have nothing to substitute." It was due at the press in two weeks, and it had been promised to the subscribers. "Terribly sorry!" he concluded. Nabokov replied emphatically by cable: "PLEASE DO NOT START PRINTING POEMS. I DON'T AGREE WITH YOUR STANDPOINT."

J halted the production process, but he hardly backed down: promising the poems and cashing the checks confirmed the acceptance of the contract. "It seems to me that if you are going to behave this way no one can dare to trust you with an advance," J said sternly. If Nabokov wished, he could return all J's advances, and they would then negotiate each book on an individual basis. "I have had several unhappy experiences where a friendship was wrecked because of money dealings and I don't want that to happen to us."

Nabokov made a counterproposal that included acquiescing to the ND publication of the poems, but with a reversion-of-rights clause added, and the return of the $250 advance on his next novel. Or, should J wish to "cancel our agreement altogether," he was prepared to return all advances.

What clearly offended the Russian most about J's letter was "one pretty odd passage"—probably the one that he took to be impugning his honor, not being able to trust him. "Soignez vos expressions, mon cher"—Mind your language, concluded Nabokov. J accepted Nabokov's first set of new terms and apologized twice, even though he seemed genuinely baffled at what he might have said that was so offensive: "Please just put it down to my too readily excitable temperament." He should feel free to place his novels elsewhere, J continued. Significantly, J revealed his view of publishing fiction at ND: "I have never felt that our press was at all suited to the handling of novels. They are a fish apart. I feel that we do very nicely on the poetry, criticism and translations, but, as poor *Sebastian* bears witness, not so very grandly on novels." Sounding more Russian than Nabokov in his syntax, J ended his letter: "Please to believe in my sincere regard and, if it isn't presumptuous to say so, friendly affection."

Nabokov had not told J the whole story: it was Doubleday that had offered the large advance, and the book was to have been not merely his translations of the poems but a set of essays by his friend Edmund Wilson introducing the three poets. J had won this round against both Nabokov and a major publisher. On other occasions he was willing to cooperate with the enemy. In 1943 he had reprinted two E. M. Forster titles, leased from Knopf, *The Longest Journey* and *A Room with a View*, and Henry James's *The Spoils of Poynton*, produced from the original Houghton Mifflin plates. These reprintings encouraged the revival of the American reputations of both authors and began a pattern that ND would repeat over the years: reprint a "forgotten classic" that had been allowed to go out of print, at which point the original copyright holder would awaken and reclaim the rights from ND—reaping the principal rewards.

J entrusted Alvin Lustig with many of the covers of the New Classics series, and soon his dust wrappers in bold primary colors laced with abstractions or swaths of solid blue and tan became the characteristic New Directions cover: a strong, uncluttered appearance that was credited with doing much to establish a new look in American jacket design. From 1944 until his death eleven years later, Alvin would move back and forth between New York and California, but wherever he was based, he designed for ND. He was very conscious of the opportunity that working with J offered. "Rarely is the graphic designer given the chance to act upon what he considers his highest level upon a problem of serious intentions,"

Lustig wrote. His concern was the *emotional* center of the book; it was *culture*, not "art" in isolation. A book cover was a public statement. In his covers he attempted to translate J's challenging authors into public language. In philosophical as in graphic terms, Lustig was ND's perfect designer, and his jackets accomplish this miracle of *correspondence*, the evocation of the text itself in graphic design.

Having designed so many jackets himself, J was especially appreciative of Lustig, and sales of the New Classics series increased threefold after his covers were issued. Bookstores began to devote window space to ND books that had once languished on back shelves. When J told Lustig that because of the rising cost of color printing, he could no longer afford two- and three-color covers, Lustig designed the basic black-and-white covers that became the recognizable facade of the later ND "paperbooks," J's own term. For one of these, Italo Svevo's *Confessions of Zeno*, Lustig would use a close-up of his own face, fragmented in the printing with a tracery of white: the personality in dissolution.

Margaret was expecting their second baby in March, but she was having cocktails with her parents at a friend's house on February 15, 1944, when the placenta broke without warning; J was at the movies and had to be paged. Paul Keyser started his car to drive Margaret to the hospital and promptly got stuck in the snow, "swearing a blue streak and shouting, 'Why do they have to have babies?'" Leila was born before midnight, about a month premature. J was much more attentive than he had been over Paul's birth and missed visiting his wife in the hospital only one day. Twice he brought flowers. Margaret told J's mother, "It's funny what a difference two years has made in him." Babies still alarmed him, but he was trying. When his daughter was a few months old, Margaret and her mother visited California, leaving J with the nursemaid. "I am to feed Leila Myrtle's night off!!!" he exclaimed as if it were a phenomenon.

J recommended Tennessee Williams to the American Academy and Institute of Arts and Letters for a $1,000 grant, calling him "the most talented and promising young writer whom we publish." He asked Tennessee for something he could print in *Pharos*, the magazine that he was planning to launch as a less expensive alternative to the big annual, with each issue to be devoted to a single work. Tennessee sent the play *Battle of Angels*, later to be revised as *Orpheus Descending*. The early version would appear in the spring 1945 double issue of *Pharos*, the first issue of the magazine, printed at the *Deseret News* printing plant in Murray, Utah. This was Williams's first book-length publication. J had a secondary purpose: he wanted to enlist Margaret as the editor of the *Pharos* series. The magazine was to be the centerpiece of his campaign to encourage her interest in publishing, to have her become his active assistant. He hoped that if he gave her a responsible task, it would cut down on her socializing. Probably he surmised, too, that her drinking was noticed and talked about by the staff at Alta. Margaret did not embrace the cause, and *Pharos* would run for only four issues: the double issue for Tennessee's play—two printers quit because of the "sinful text"—then two more volumes consisting, respectively, of Harry Levin's monograph on Stendhal and Pound's pair of Confucius translations, *The Great Digest* and *The Unwobbling Pivot*. When by 1946 an insufficient number of subscribers had signed up, J changed the title to *Direction*, which would continue to appear in different formats for a few years, and it would include such significant titles as Nabokov's *Nine Stories* and Boris Pasternak's *Selected Writings*. Whether he was managing Alta or editing books, J let it be known to Margaret that his work came well ahead of their social life. This was not turning out to be the kind of marriage that either had hoped for.

New Directions 8, the anthology under a truncated title, appeared in the autumn, and Delmore Schwartz in a review for *The Nation* attacked J's preface for its "inexpensive righteous sentiments" while praising J for printing Tennessee and William Carlos Williams. Pablo Neruda was one of the poets in the Latin American section, and in his "Editor's Notes" J wrote, "I am personally much impressed with Neruda . . . For me he is as good in his vein as Paul Éluard." By the time the Nobel Prize committee added its imprimatur in 1971, J had decided Neruda was "a really nasty man," "arrogant . . . I couldn't stand him," though he did not retract his opinion of the poetry.

Since his marriage, J had been spending much of his time in Utah. He admitted that the affairs of New Directions would be run more expeditiously if he were in Manhattan, "but I prefer to be here," he told Delmore. "For what is life but to enjoy it, and certainly in the scales of happiness a fine day in the bright sun and snow on one of our mountains here is of more worth than publishing a book by a dyspeptic author." The mix of hard physical activity at Alta, hedonistic release, and publishing books kept him sane, he was sure. And Alta continued to offer excitement. The snow mass was piled high on the peaks in March 1944, and one evening Sverre Engen, gazing up at the heavy snow buildup on the Superior slope, called the lift man Buck Sasaki over. "Bucko, what d'you think?" "Something's going to give," he replied. "I think we better shut it down." No sooner had they gotten all the skiers off Superior, grousing and complaining, than the whole side of the mountain seemed to come loose, taking trees in its path and "rolling right up to the Lodge terrace."

Under the influence of Alta and a routine, J returned to poetry, sending a few of his newer poems to Rexroth. "I cant [sic] tell you how pleased I am you are writing again," Kenneth responded. "And how impressive your poems are." He encouraged J to seclude himself for a year with wife and "little ones" and write for "the future." J's poetry was "so god damned much better than the current mumble." Coming from Kenneth, this was high praise. Nor was Kenneth, boasting to J of amatory conquests, a calming influence. J was living a freewheeling life himself during his furloughs from Alta to California, to the extent that he found himself threatened with blackmail by an irate husband. Nothing came of it.

During the summer of 1944, Tennessee had been dropping hints to J about his "new play," which he described as "a sentimental family portrait," later adding, "I doubt it is for the commercial theatre." "It" was *The Glass Menagerie*. Margo Jones—J described her as a "fireball"—helped Tennessee fight off the insistence of the actor and producer Eddie Dowling for a happy ending, but Dowling did risk casting the fragile-appearing Laurette Taylor as Amanda Wingfield. Once acknowledged to be among the greatest of American actresses, Taylor had been largely absent from the stage for sixteen years, battling alcoholism.

Despite the icy gale that was blowing across Lake Michigan, on December 26, 1944, J was at Chicago's Civic Theatre for the opening night of *Menagerie*. Jo Mielziner's shadowy scrim, back- and front-lit by fifty-seven lines of electrical equipment, allowed Tennessee's "dream play" to fade in and out of reality to Paul Bowles's haunting musical score. The night before the opening, Taylor had been discovered passed-out drunk behind the furnace in the theater basement. Tennessee nervously calculated that he had just enough savings to retreat to Mexico, after the inevitable flop, and write his next play.

He wouldn't need to. Taylor, J said, "was really something"; her "tremendous performance . . . put the play across in Chicago." Tennessee agreed, writing, "There was a radiance about her art . . . which gave me the same shock of revelation as if the air about us had been momentarily broken through by light from some clear space beyond us." J himself even made a cameo appearance in name. "There was young Champ Laughlin," says Amanda, naming one of the suitors of her youth. The Chicago critics were extravagant in their praise, and after two weeks of small audiences the public caught on, and the playwright's income jumped from a $10-per-day stipend doled out by Audrey Wood to $1,000 a week. Suddenly he was a man of means, a bestseller, no longer one of J's starveling authors.

J wanted to publish *Menagerie* as soon as possible. Tennessee was more than willing to give it to him, but there was a problem: a $100 advance Bennett Cerf had paid Tennessee back in 1940 against his "next work." He now asked Audrey Wood to "extricate" him from this earlier contract. To J he wrote, "I need not tell you again how happy that would make me for I would like all my shy intrusions on the world of letters to be thru N.D." Tennessee argued that Cerf and Random House had "not shown one spark of interest in my work or existence" and that in any case the advance would have applied to *Battle of Angels*, which J had already published in *Pharos*. J offered to pay Random back the advance, but Cerf cannily elected to postpone his decision until the play opened in New York. J began to fear that an author he considered his discovery might slip away, even though Tennessee protested his loyalty to New Directions. "JAY!" Tennessee wrote sternly. "How silly of you to think I was letting you down about the 'Menagerie' publication!"

When the play opened to generally good notices at the Playhouse Theatre in New York on March 31, 1945, Cerf decided that he *did* want it. *Menagerie* went on for nearly six hundred performances and won every major drama award except the Pulitzer. Cerf certainly did not win any kind feelings from J, who remained watchful on the sidelines, and when *Menagerie* was allowed to go out of print in 1949, he bought the rights from Random House for his New Classics series. By then, Tennessee would be recognized as the most important new voice in American theater, and J was well established as his publisher. Both instinct and luck had gone into the connection: J was not really a passionate theater person and did not see a great number of plays, and while he recognized the virtues of Tennessee's stage dramas, he preferred his poetry. J seemed to think that with Tennessee and Lorca, along with Brecht and a few plays by "the other Williams," Bill, he had done his part for modern theater.

Despite J's various distractions, despite the wartime shortages in staff, paper, and other supplies, ND brought out eighteen titles in 1944, including Thomas Merton's first book, *Thirty Poems*, in the POMY series; Brecht's *Private Life of the Master Race*, translated by Eric Bentley; and Joyce's *Stephen Hero*, edited by Ted Spencer. New Directions published the third and final *Five Young American Poets*, which included Tennessee. Tenn was delighted to be recognized as a *poet*, writing to J, "The check for the verse looks more impressive to me than an MGM pay-check and I feel like it ought to be framed." Jarrell, critical as usual about New Directions publications, saved the worst for Tennessee: he "must be one of those hoaxes people make up to embarrass *Poetry* or *Angry Penguins*." Jarrell made him the excuse for the only mention of J in the review: "If Tennessee Williams wrote more like W. C. Williams I should think him another of Laughlin's pseudonyms." Undaunted, J considered Tennessee a "wonderful romantic poet" and a "magnificent" writer of short stories, gifted with a "pure narrative drive, psychological penetration, and that lovely fantastic, light, self-mocking style."

Nineteen hundred forty-four had been a critical year for J. New Directions was doing well, and by the end of the year the gross amounted to more than $30,000. Praise and commendation had come in from various quarters. Still, J was discontented, his mood shifting. He had taken to seeing an analyst, who told him, so J claimed to Schwartz, that in "sublimating" his urge to write through his interest in other writers, he was not fulfilling his own "psychic need." "I feel more and more that my role is to write," he concluded, "and that can only be done from a still center of repose and meditation." He realized too that he was not the only one suffering: "This constant strain and pressure of overwork hasn't been at all fair to Margaret." He made no mention of his wandering eye, but implied in his letters to those closest to him was his feeling that his life was slipping rapidly away, unfulfilled. When he read Italo Svevo's characterization of a particular woman, "every word and every act of hers showed that she believed in eternal life," he recalled the two people in his life whom that statement fitted perfectly: Clara St. John at Choate and Aunt Leila. "That is the way I think of you," he wrote to his aunt, "and it is the reason that you mean to me what you do, and as no one else does." If he could not be sure of eternal life himself, at least he could take comfort in someone dear to him who could.

15

Norfolk:
The Eastern Seaboard Reclaims J

The track of the ermine
the track of the mouse

tracks of a deer in the
snow and my track that

wanders and hesitates.
—James Laughlin, "In the Snow,"
from *Some Natural Things*

As the war wound down in Europe in early 1945, a seller's market for books grew in America: people had money, and there were good marketing opportunities. Soon the colleges would be flooded with veterans taking advantage of the GI Bill. J was still making most editorial decisions for ND, and it was becoming increasingly awkward to manage an operation based in New York from the removes of Alta and San Francisco. J had to make up his mind whether Alta would be his primary focus, with San Francisco as his literary arena and publishing as a sideline, or whether he would put his main effort into New Directions, with Alta as a lucrative hobby that could underwrite his publishing.

Certain factors nudged him back toward the East. Aunt Leila embarked on a further renovation of Meadow House with the expectation that J and Margaret would make it their permanent abode. "So excited about the house," J wrote to his aunt. "It sounds wonderful." Aunt Leila had missed her nephew: now she was campaigning to win him back from Alta. J needed his aunt also. "Norfolk is the only place I can think of where I would want to settle down," he told her, "and that largely because you are there." So Norfolk became J's home and center of operations. It became his practice to keep his main files in Norfolk, and his card system was his memory bank, with his correspondence files as backup. Eventually, the ND files and boxes of unsold books overflowed the White Cottage to fill the attic at Meadow House as well as hundreds of shelf feet all over the house and, ultimately, a vault in the basement.

In September 1945, J hired the writer Hubert Creekmore, who became a dedicated editorial assistant. Related to Eudora Welty by marriage, he was a quiet man whom J described as "a southern cavalier," but he possessed a quirky sense of humor. From the sedate "Dear J" of his early letters, he had taken to addressing J differently for each succeeding letter: "Most Illustrious Out-sized California Easter Bunny," "Peregrine Prometheus," and "Dear Hibiscus of the Stygian Temples"—to which J replied with "Paidean Polyp." He was a talented translator from French, Latin, Provençal, and German and a good editor, and he was also writing a novel. In late 1945, J employed Robert Lowry, another novelist and a book designer, to handle production. Soon Lowry was functioning as office manager and designing jackets for Merton, Henry Miller, Tennessee, and others. When his novel *Casualty* was a New Directions success in 1946, he resigned to write full-time.

Over Delmore Schwartz's continuing objections, J published Fitzgerald's *The Crack-Up*, left unfinished at the time of the author's death, and the out-of-print *The Great Gatsby*. These novels helped ignite a Fitzgerald resurgence. *Gatsby* sold so well in the New Classics series that Scribner's quickly reclaimed rights to the novel, but *The Crack-Up* was securely a New Directions copyright. It sold sixteen thousand copies and would have done even better had not the still-extant paper restrictions prevented reprinting. "I had terrible fights with Edmund Wilson," who edited it, J recalled—he had restored some of Wilson's cuts. The older man was "utterly furious," called J "an insolent puppy," and would never again have anything to do with him.

Ezra Pound was about to reenter J's life. Ezra and Dorothy and Olga Rudge had struggled through the war, existing in a tense ménage à trois at Sant'Ambrogio after being ordered to leave the coast. During the final year of the conflict, food shortages rendered them almost skeletal. On

April 20, 1945, the first American jeep entered Rapallo. Ezra dressed with formal care and walked down from Sant'Ambrogio to place his knowledge of Italy at the service of the U.S. authorities, but no one seemed to comprehend him. On May 3 two partisans, "ex-Fascist convicts" with an unsavory reputation among the local peasantry, hammered on his door with the butt of a tommy gun. "Seguici, traditore"—Follow us, traitor— they said. Ezra slipped his volume of Confucius and a Chinese dictionary into his pocket and complied. The pair had heard that there was a reward out for his capture, but the *partigiani* leaders at Lavagna were searching for war profiteers and minor Fascist officials, and they had no warrant for Ezra's arrest: he was free to go. Ezra demanded to be taken to the nearest American command post so that he could turn himself in, and his long ordeal began: three weeks in Genoa, then on to the U.S. Army's infamous Detention Training Center outside Pisa, the DTC, where he was kept for another three weeks in a cage reinforced with heavy-gauge steel runway grids. Exposed to the blazing sun, the rain, the glare of acetylene flood- lights, with a cement floor to sleep on, Pound continued losing weight, until his mind and body broke. The DTC medical staff, concerned for his sanity and his life, had him placed in a tent with a cot. Ezra was then given a pencil and a lined pad by a Jewish chaplain. A black fellow pris- oner made him a small table. Eventually, he was allowed to use the infir- mary typewriter. Under these improved conditions his spirits began to revive, and by early October he had completed another decad of the *Can- tos*, typing the draft now in the Beinecke Library at Yale.

Only in late August was Dorothy officially notified of her husband's whereabouts, and it was not until September 4 that J was able, through Archibald MacLeish in Washington, to confirm that Pound was indeed under arrest and to obtain an address for him. J wrote at once, ensuring Ezra that although he had "many spiteful enemies," he also had a few friends who would try to help. Helping Ezra required a delicate balancing act: J. Edgar Hoover had been after MacLeish for hiring left-wingers, and stridently anti-Roosevelt Republican politicians had tried to block his appointment in 1939 as Librarian of Congress, charging him with being a Communist despite his record of writing and giving speeches warning against *both* Fascism and Communism. "No one would be more shocked to learn I am a Communist," exclaimed MacLeish, "than the Communists themselves."

J, acting independently as soon as it became evident that Ezra would be charged, asked his friend Julien Cornell if he would take the case. Cornell was a lawyer with a good record in arguing civil liberties and conscientious objection cases and was the author of a widely quoted book on civil liberties law. And as a Quaker, he sympathized with Ezra's pacifist stance. Knowing Br'er Rabbit better than anyone else, Eliot stipulated to J, "What I think is essential is that he should be persuaded to put himself entirely in the hands of a good lawyer and not attempt to talk much except under his lawyer's instructions." Ezra already had other ideas: he had told Olga that he wanted a lawyer merely to *advise* him on how to defend himself.

A story was going the rounds to the effect that Ezra would not be put on trial "owing to insufficiency of evidence," and J hoped that he might soon be freed. Under U.S. law, two witnesses are needed who could testify that they were present when the accused committed each specific alleged treasonous act. J tempered his guarded optimism with a realistic assessment of those lining up against Ezra. "There are so many venomous little people around here who want to get their slimey [sic] hooks into him," he wrote to Dorothy. Although Cornell had told J that it would be very difficult to convict Ezra of treason as the indictment was then worded, J feared the force of opinion: "Public sentiment . . . is very strong in favor of conviction."

J had been planning a campaign to restore Ezra's reputation from the moment he began his ill-judged broadcasts, and now, at this most uncertain and threatening juncture, J still intended "a revival campaign for the poetry," provided "I can get him to pry himself loose from those morticians who hold his copyrights." The campaign would include a "complete volume" of the cantos "as soon as things quiet down a little."

J had a reason for not supporting Ezra too publicly. "Inside a fortnight my books would be barred from the several hundred important stores . . . and I would be out of business," J explained to Dorothy. Cautiously, J hesitated to name names in his correspondence: "The person now deceased [Roosevelt] whom he attacked is a martyr and a God. His memory is enshrined in the hearts of millions of suckers." Nonetheless, by mid-December J would be writing to Eliot about his plan for a joint publication of new cantos. But this was in the future, when, without warning, on November 16, 1945, Pound was summoned to the DTC office and told that in an hour he would be boarding a plane for America. Always fastidious about his person, he was not given the opportunity to dress for the occasion. He still hoped that he would be permitted to argue his own case, and he did not know that a particular attorney had been designated to represent him. *That* particular fix was in, and J was the primary fixer. J would not see him until the end of the year.

Some of J's other friends were thriving. Gertrude Stein survived the war comfortably in Bilignin: Bernard Faÿ stood high with the Vichy regime in Paris, and he was able to prevent Stein and Toklas from being sent to a death camp. Safely in America, Henry Miller behaved as if the war had not happened, and he suddenly became a millionaire in inflated postwar francs. His Paris publisher, Maurice Girodias, sold the *Tropics* to countless GIs, but Henry could not be paid outside France owing to currency transfer restrictions. Then, in a devaluation, his francs lost most of their value. To Henry, it was just his usual bad luck.

•

J brought his family east by train in June 1945, and he was in New York for the opening of Brecht's *Private Life of the Master Race*. J was proud of having published the book and of having introduced Brecht to the American reading public.

That July, J moved his Manhattan office to 500 Fifth Avenue, across Forty-Second Street from the New York Public Library, where he shared space for a time with the ski wax developer Fritz Wiessner, "that charming Silesian who looks like an owl," J called him. Wiessner was a famous and controversial mountaineer, having led the disastrous 1939 attempt to be the first to conquer K2, the world's second-highest peak. J was in his office on July 28 when a twin-engine Mitchell bomber narrowly missed his sixty-story tower and crashed into the Empire State Building. Thirteen people died in New York's first catastrophic encounter between plane and skyscraper. J wrote a poem about it: "Flames poured from the windows / into the drifting clouds & sirens / screamed down in / the streets below."

Nabokov's French reputation far exceeded his American one, but he was still pleasantly surprised when a company in Paris offered $3,000 for the world film rights to *Laughter in the Dark*. Nabokov asked J if he would be satisfied with 10 percent of the amount, and J agreed. Such windfalls, as well as anthology, reprint, and foreign rights agreements—under the umbrella "subsidiary rights"—were already becoming important income sources for ND and its authors. As certain authors became canonical in academe and were increasingly anthologized, J would see 50 to 90 percent of the funds paid to these authors or their estates be derived from such rights, but this was not yet an argument he was in a position to make to Nabokov. By the next year, Nabokov was firmly declaring to J his "feeling . . . that movie rights should be kept entirely out of publisher's contracts." His logic was that before films existed, the "book industry" still prospered. Later Nabokov would invoke the same logic in reference to paperback rights. The book industry *had* changed, and by the mid-1950s it could be argued that only by sharing in secondary rights was it possible for publishers such as ND to bring out hardbound avant-garde fiction: the risk factor would otherwise have been too great.

Soon J's relationship with Nabokov was showing further signs of strain, this time because the Russian wanted to sign *all* foreign contracts, even those treating publications for which ND held world rights. J would always be glad to consult with Vladimir, he said, but the final decisions belonged with the copyright holder, ND. Nabokov would not budge. "It is a matter of principle with me that I am to sign my own engagements," he said. Then Nabokov announced peremptorily, "There will be no sharing of translation or movie rights." From this time on, Véra took over most of the correspondence with J, and either "My husband does not care to create a precedent . . ." or "Vladimir hopes you have not forgotten . . ." became a standard prefix for all manner of edicts.

Although it might not seem so to the bedeviled author attempting to make a living by writing, there *was* a set of loosely agreed-upon standards endorsed by the Authors League of America governing agreements between authors and those who would handle their works, whether by originally publishing them or in selling secondary rights. New Directions' standard royalty was 10 percent of the retail price on hardbound volumes (except for a few favored authors such as Merton, Pound, Tennessee Williams, and William Carlos Williams, who received 15 percent), paid after the book had earned back the original advance. Secondary rights included reprints, anthology and serialization usage, film, radio and television broadcasts, dramatization, and foreign rights. The publisher was also entitled to a percentage of the proceeds of such rights. Percentages were not strictly codified, and there was an understandable tendency for authors to resent fiercely money earned by their efforts that went to fattening the publishers' coffers. The wonder was not that J frequently found himself in tense standoffs with various authors but that so many of them remained his friends.

J's first real book of his own poems appeared from New Directions in 1945. He selected twenty-three poems, from the overtly autobiographical "Easter in Pittsburgh" and "On the Gift of a Sapphire to My Wife" to the philosophical and sardonic "Old Dr God." *Some Natural Things* was designed and printed at the Prairie City Press in Iowa and was chosen for an exhibition by the American Institute of Graphic Arts as one of the fifty best-designed books of the year. Critical reaction was nil: J had deliberately omitted sending out review copies because, as he explained, "I would get mostly insincere flattering reviews from people who want me to publish their books or spiteful reviews from people whose books I have turned down."

A few months later J sent Tennessee a copy of *Some Natural Things*, and the poet-playwright commented, "There is an almost terrifying candor here and there—more than I would dare." Tennessee singled out "The Avalanche" for praise. In this carefully veiled poem, J wrote, "If you can explain the / secret of the avalanche," why the snow mass can remain dormant for years before breaking loose, "then I can / tell you why it is that / I after so many years / of gradual petrifaction" must "suddenly without reason" break loose. J's identification with the fallen avalanche, "an icy mon- / ument to self-destruction!" is clear. His affective self is waking up from its "petrifaction," and he fears the outcome while he is powerless to avert it.

Dudley Fitts responded the day he received J's volume of poetry with a judicious evaluation that did not mention the internal struggle Tennessee had found, but concentrated on the technique. Fitts understood the parameters J had set for himself: "You have made that short two- or three-line stanza, with its subtle enjambments, definitely your own: you are about the least derivative voice I know." Fitts concluded that J's poetry "has the minor elegance of the Alexandrian gentry in the Palatine." Marianne Moore, Rexroth, Kay Boyle, Mark Van Doren, and even Berryman praised the poems highly. This was not enough to overcome J's diffidence. Instead of concentrating on poetry, he took golf lessons with the Norfolk pro. On one outing he saw seven balls in the pond and went in after them.

In the process, he caught a large frog and fed the legs to Aunt Leila for lunch.

On November 13, 1945, J was in Boston at a party that included Tennessee Williams, F. O. Matthiessen, and Ted Spencer. Tenn had read out loud from his work, "not out of vanity but out of self-distrust." He needed reassurance: "I'd hoped we'd have more time and less company last night," Tennessee wrote to J. "There was a lot I wanted to talk over with you, mainly my work." The presence of others, however, had made him shy. "You are my literary conscience—the only one outside myself—so I am over-awed by you and it isn't easy to talk to you." Always attuned to the moods of those he liked, he told J, "I am disturbed by your apparently real dissatisfaction with your own life," and he offered his careful attention, "if you think I am able to advise or help in any way." Tennessee was clearly drawn to J, and seemed to be hinting at a more intimate relationship than it was in J's nature to permit, but he was right in his assessment of J's discontent. However, J, unlike Tennessee, did not slide easily into confession. Although he shared the playwright's habit of introspection, J had given up on writing fiction, and the thrilling novelty of being a publisher had become dulled by the drudgery of correspondence, fiscal planning, editing, selling, and all the other mundane details of the book business. Equally distressing was his growing realization that his marriage had been a mistake. Margaret and J were grievously mismatched in their expectations of life and of each other.

There was something else. J was again ripe for the Muse, and for him she was invariably embodied in the real, often in some chance-met woman whom he at once idealized. This Muse, in real or abstract form, was Margaret's true competition, far more formidable a rival than any mere paramour.

16

The Prodigal Returns: Ezra in the Dock

> Ezry Pound speakin' . . . Whom God would destroy,
> he first sends to the bug house.
> —*Radio Speeches*, January 29, 1942

During the night of November 18, 1945, a man with a patchy beard, clad in a baggy coat, trousers, a soiled army sweatshirt, and handcuffs, stepped from a C-54 army transport onto the tarmac of the Washington airport and was taken by a squad of armed men to the D.C. jail. "The thought of what America would be like / If the Classics had a wide circulation / Troubles my sleep," Ezra Pound had written some thirty years earlier. Now he was about to sample a parody of life in his native land. Partly because his was the first indictment in the United States for treason following World War II, and because the Nuremberg trials had begun just two days after Pound landed, his case aroused great interest, and there was a surging movement for vengeance. Two days later Julien Cornell met with Ezra. J was not present, as he had wished to be: Margaret's father had died, and he had flown to Utah for three weeks.

Cornell was shocked when he first saw his client in the prison infirmary. He wrote to J, "I found the poor devil in a rather desperate condition. He is very wobbly in his mind and while his talk is entirely rational, he flits from one idea to another and is unable to concentrate . . . We spent most of the time talking about Confucius, Jefferson and the economic and political implications of their ideas." Cornell seems not to have realized that this erratic associational discourse might simply be Ezra. The lawyer apparently resolved on an insanity plea at once and brought up the possibility with Pound. "In fact he told me that the idea had already occurred to him," Cornell reported. At some point Ezra handed Cornell a small suitcase of manuscripts to be given to J. In the worn grip J found, in his words, "the pencilled notebooks of the 'Pisan Cantos'" and the revised copy typed by Ezra. "To my thinking," J wrote later, "this is about as important a literary manuscript as we have in our times." He immediately began referring to these as "The Pisan Cantos," and the name stuck.

On Friday, November 23, a federal grand jury session returned the indictment: Pound's case was to go to trial. Over the next few days Ezra alternated between urging the immediate publication of his Confucian translations because of their "world shaking" importance and of his *Pisan Cantos* and suffering severe attacks of claustrophobia when the jail was placed in lockdown after five prisoners escaped. When Cornell next saw Pound, four days later, the two men talked poetry for an hour, and then, abruptly, the lawyer told Ezra that he was to be arraigned that afternoon and would have to "plead to the indictment," to admit guilt or affirm innocence. He advised Ezra to "stand mute" before the court, which would then be obliged to enter a "not guilty" plea on his behalf, as one not competent to cooperate in his own defense. Ezra was struck dumb. "His mouth opened once or twice as if to speak, but no words came out," Cornell reported. "He looked up at the ceiling and his mouth began to twitch." Then he said he felt ill and wished to return to the infirmary. Ezra evidently still cherished the belief that he would be able to stand up in court and demolish the government's case through the force of his own testimony, legal arguments, and logic. It is not clear whether Cornell explained to him at the time that by standing mute, Ezra would be opening the way to an insanity plea.

During the court hearing the nineteen counts of the indictment were read, including charges that Pound had been a radio propagandist for the Italian government and that he had counseled the enemy in operations against the United States. When the time for his response came, Pound remained silent. Cornell declared that he was "not in condition to make a plea" and requested that the judge enter "not guilty" on his behalf. Judge Bolitha Laws ordered his transfer to the Gallinger Municipal Hospital for evaluation and "treatment, if found necessary."

By mid-December, J still had not seen Ezra, because his early attempts to secure a pass to visit the prisoner had been inexplicably blocked. "Perhaps I am in the bad books," J wrote to Eliot. However, J was soon allowed to visit Ezra and was relieved to find him able to discuss his writing cogently. Ezra told J that the manuscripts handed over to him by Cornell were the first installment of documents given in trust for his daughter.

Four psychiatrists, principal among them Winfred Overholser, superintendent of St. Elizabeths Hospital in Washington and future president of the American Psychiatric Association, examined Pound over a period of ten days and unanimously assured the court that he was "suffering from a paranoid state," "insane and mentally unfit for trial, and in need of care in a mental hospital." J reported that they saw Pound's "illness" as the "culmination of a tendency of many years' standing," worsened by his sufferings at the Pisan DTC. The psychiatrists diagnosed a "delusional (paranoid) disorder, grandiose type." Based on their testimony, Judge Laws pronounced Pound incompetent to stand trial. The prominence of the expert witnesses carried the day. The three army psychiatrists who had examined Pound at Pisa were never even contacted about their findings, which had been that he was suffering from "anxiety neurosis" but not from "a major mental disease." Some later commentators argued that the State Department *preferred* to have Pound locked up as insane rather than to risk a trial of uncertain outcome, while others at the time suspected that Ezra had tricked the experts to save his neck. J believed that, given the seething climate of public opinion, a death sentence would not have been an improbable outcome of a trial. In September, the Brooklyn-born William Joyce, a.k.a. Lord Haw-Haw, had been convicted of treason in Britain for his pro-German broadcasts and would be hanged the following January. J told Eliot that when the insanity decision was read, Ezra seemed pleased. He was remanded to St. Elizabeths, where he was placed in Howard Hall, a high-security section with barred windows, built in 1855 to hold the fiercest of the insane. This Ezra termed the "hell-hole."

J considered Ezra's present condition to be the result of a long progression of bizarre fantasies: he had said over Rome Radio in March 1941 that conflict with Japan could be settled if the United States would exchange Guam for "color and sound films of the 300 best Noh plays," a gesture that would show respect for Japanese culture; and even while he was being held at Gallinger Hospital, he had said to J, "I thought they were bringing me to Washington to send me to Tokyo to help MacArthur convert the Japs from Shintoism to Confucianism." J was sure that Ezra's condition

corresponded to the psychiatric term "confabulation," the inability to separate fantasy from reality.

Meanwhile, J continued his program for rehabilitating Ezra's reputation, through a line of publications and the encouragement of "the good
critics" to resume writing seriously about his work. J—and others, including Hemingway—took pains to draw a demarcation between the generous and decent Ezra they knew and the wartime demagogue lashing out
in frustration and desperation against perceived enemies. It made for
some fancy rhetorical footwork: Pound should not be judged for attacks
on the American conduct of the war and for anti-Semitic statements in
the broadcasts on the grounds of his delusions and intermittent manias,
yet he should be revered—and sprung from St. Elizabeths—for the sane
and grand achievement of his writing. J told Eliot that Ezra particularly
wanted his translation of *The Testament of Confucius*—J would publish
this in 1947 as *The Great Digest*, together with *The Unwobbling Pivot*—to
be printed as soon as possible, saying that it would answer Eliot's old question, "What does Pound believe?" J's own beliefs were clear. He might be
strongly anti-Fascist, yet the Allied victory celebrations left a bitter taste.
"Their great victory parade is trumpeting under my window and the streets
are mobbed with happy plebs," he wrote to Merton. "It seems to me that
the celebration of military 'glory' is about the greatest of sins."

While the Pound furor was going on, Williams fretted over *Paterson*,
demanding typesetting that included interspersed verse and prose, erratically occurring long and short lines—in other words, a visual effect of
words and lines liberated from the page. J objected that the cost would be
prohibitive. Then he found a solution: George W. Van Vechten, a hand-set
printer in Metuchen, New Jersey, who was willing to provide Williams with
innumerable proofs at various stages. Van Vechten and Williams took to
each other, and a beautiful text grew from their cooperation. After *Paterson* had gone through several page proofs, it could be published, Williams
asserted, "if they can ever find Laughlin to OK the procedures." J, although
away from Norfolk and Manhattan, had remained intimately connected
with the production. "Dear Bill," he wrote from Stowe, Vermont, "I'm sorry
to have been silent . . . getting moved up here for the winter. A real little
New England town with no more taint of civilization than a sawmill."

J was also caught in the middle of the Pounds' money troubles. Dorothy was unable to join Ezra because her American passport had lapsed in

1941 and her funds in England remained blocked owing to her stateless condition, while Ezra's American account was held by the custodian of alien property. Cummings—although himself living more or less hand to mouth—came to the rescue by handing Cornell a check for $1,000, which he had just received for the sale of a painting, and Hemingway contributed the same amount. J sent a check for $500, on top of the much greater sum that he had already spent on Ezra's behalf. The authorities spent far more money building a case and in an effort to provide the necessary witnesses had flown over six Rome Radio technicians for a couple of months of high living in Washington, but it transpired that none of the technicians knew enough English to testify as to what they had heard Ezra utter.

Eight staff psychiatrists at St. Elizabeths Hospital reexamined Pound over a period of seven weeks. Ezra appeared to view this like a debate, one in which he had to spar against many opponents. Only two of the psychiatrists thought that Pound might be even borderline delusional, and although most found neuroses and a "psychopathic personality," none judged him to be psychotic or "in a paranoid state." Dr. Overholser brought these staff reports in his briefcase to the new sanity hearing, confiding to Cornell that he disagreed with his subordinates and would not produce their reports unless so instructed. When a government lawyer asked if he had received opinions from his staff, he replied that he had them in his briefcase. Overholser was an intimidating witness, and he was not pressed to produce the staff opinions. On February 13, 1946, at a daylong hearing, Overholser and the three senior psychiatrists of the first sanity inquest again unanimously declared that Pound was insane. Ezra remained silent, but when the prosecutor questioned Overholser about Pound's "belief in Fascism," the prisoner leaped to his feet and cried out "in great anger," "I never did believe in fascism, God damn it, I am opposed to fascism." Judge Laws ignored the outburst. The jury took just five minutes to find Pound "mentally unfit to be tried."

Back went Ezra to St. Elizabeths. When J visited him the morning after the court hearing, Ezra was delighted when J presented him with freshly typed copies of *The Pisan Cantos*, fruit of his bitter six months at the DTC. Within hours Ezra had read them over and returned the typescript to J, who was sure that Ezra's ear for the "music of poetry" was unimpaired. However, J said, "his mind did wander frightfully." Ezra maintained that he "could not understand why the Jews wished to conspire to hang him since he had worked out a complete plan for rebuilding their old temple in Jerusalem."

Nineteen titles made 1945 a full year for New Directions. Among the more significant were Fitzgerald's *Crack-Up*, Henry Miller's *Air-Conditioned Nightmare*, and Tennessee's *27 Wagons Full of Cotton and Other One-Act Plays*. A volume of Gerard Manley Hopkins's poems marked the end of the Poet of the Month/Year series after a run of forty-one volumes. There were many reprints, necessary to keep the titles alive, but hardly new work: Fitzgerald's *Great Gatsby*, Isherwood's *Berlin Stories*, Joyce's *Exiles*, books by Henry James and Evelyn Waugh. J realized that he would have to concentrate more on ND.

17

San Francisco, Alta, and Ezra (Again)

GODDAMMMMMMMMMMMMMMMMMMMMN
it

—Ezra Pound to James Laughlin

Valentine Miller was born in Berkeley in November 1945, and J sent a silver spoon. "Dear Lorenzo," Henry wrote with a nod to the munificent de' Medici. "That silver spoon gave me the jitters." For the first time J admitted to Henry that he had two children: J had kept quiet about his family as if their existence were a guilty secret. He now wrote, "You sound very happy and I envy you. I wish you would keep your eye open for a little piece of land around there for me to buy. I'm crazy about that country and hope to get down again this year in May." J sounded a wistful note. For the "little piece of land" he pictured just such an escape cabin as Rexroth had in the Sierras—not the sort of place to which J would bring wife and family. Nor was his own behavior likely to contribute to tranquillity at home. At a Halloween dance party in 1945, J had met Gertrude Huston. Recently a war widow, she threw herself into life with a reckless gaiety fueled by loss, and to her best friend, Sylvia Abrams, she described "the *funniest* man," whom she had just met: "He was SO-O-O tall my hands could barely reach his shoulders, and he said he was a stove salesman"—understood as a joke. Born Freedman, Gertrude was a graduate of the Parsons School of Design in Manhattan. She had been employed at the Helena Rubinstein beauty salon and later at the Blaker Advertising Agency. Soon she began to take on freelance book design work for New Directions and J was teasing her in his courtly fashion. Her covers suggested the influence of Alvin Lustig but tended more toward the whimsical: for the second printing of Thomas's *Portrait of the Artist as a Young Dog* she made a line drawing of a show-clipped French poodle, anglicized with a pipe and derby, sitting at a typewriter. It was humorous, but it certainly was not Dylan. Gertrude was blond, undemanding, and great fun to be with—a relief from the stresses of J's marriage.

J spent part of the winter of 1945–46 in Alta, from which he typed in lowercase to Doc Williams: "dear bill/ another ski fall and another broken wrist." Alta now had three chairlifts, the Rustler, the Peruvian, and the refurbished Collins. New runs had been designed, many of them keeping the names of the slopes that went back to frontier days: Alf's High Rustler, Stone Crusher, Bear Paw, and Wildcat Face. A Salt Lake City man named Chic Morton left his used-car business for a job as lift employee and bartender at the Alta Lodge. He did everything with intensity, and his single-minded commitment to the needs of skiers became legendary. J responded to Chic's love of skiing, his devotion to fly-fishing, and his skills with men and machines. Chic became J's closest friend at Alta, and J would often stay at his home.

•

By mid-1946, J thought that the charges against Pound might be dismissed, but he kept mum about his thoughts to Ezra. "Speak to me not of politics," J warned Ezra. "The world is conducted by buffoons, ignoramy and nuts. I don't want to bother with it. Literchoor is my beat." He spent a good bit of the summer shepherding Poundian work through the press, enlivening his letters to the Boss with various greetings: "Yr Excellence," "Intangible Prince," and "Metrical Monarch." J relayed to Ezra Eliot's strongly urged change in the intended title, *The Unwobbling Axis*: "Possum says fer you to call it PIVOT not AXIS on account of the recent You Know What." Ezra concurred. *The Pisan Cantos* presented a more complicated set of problems. Even for a Pound manuscript, this one, with some emendations scrawled in pencil on toilet paper, was difficult to follow. Eliot wrote to J, "I really think that almost everything, including rhythm, should be sacrificed to protect Ezra from the scholars"—those who would zing him for a misspelled name. J asked Fitts to check on "furn" spellings, but he was unable to find anyone "who can draw chink characters." Encouraged by Fitts, J intended to bring authenticity and uniformity of style into the "chinkograms" in the entire *Cantos*. Over the years Pound had taken them from many sources, copying some in pencil or crayon, while Dorothy drew others for him. J opined that it was "all damn foolishness because nobody can read the characters but Ezra," to which Eliot agreed, yet both men felt that they owed accurate calligraphy to Ez: he set so much store by it.

J was less persistent in his unofficial guardianship of Ezra's daughter. When J wrote to Mary Rudge suggesting that she attend college in America, she felt herself academically unqualified, and besides, her father had never told her that she *should* get a university education. Neither Ezra nor J told her where the funds might come from: the existence of a trust was never mentioned to her. Proud, independent, yet always seeing herself as a dutiful daughter, Mary resolved instead to marry as soon as she came of age, that same year.

J did not encourage Mary one way or the other, being preoccupied with New Directions. George Leite, the founder of Circle Editions, had produced two spoofs of the annual by 1945, *New Rejections* and *No Directions*. The parody showed that ND was in some danger of becoming establishment, and more substantial evidence of this was a five-page write-up and interview in *Publishers Weekly*, "New Directions Completes Its First Decade." To the *PW* correspondent, J mentioned Dudley Fitts as the inspirer of his love for books, judiciously passing over Ezra. J repeated his sole criterion for publication—artistic merit, "divorced from political, racial or geographical boundaries."

New Directions was far removed from the seemingly youthful folly of 1936. Informality might still reign in the office, but the staff of six, counting J but not some temporaries hired for the fall and winter publishing seasons, still included Hubert Creekmore and Robert Lowry as J's principal editorial assistants, with Alvin Lustig's lovely sister, Susan, as business manager. Alvin did most of the designing, but there was not enough work for him to be a full-time employee; he produced book covers for Knopf and Noonday as well and had until recently been director of visual research for *Look* magazine. ND had thus far published some 145 books, a considerable number for a small staff.

In July 1946, Dorothy Pound arrived, having finally been issued an American passport and allowed access to her funds in England. Dorothy moved into a small apartment a short walk from St. Elizabeths and settled down to a routine of long hours of secretarial service to Ezra and daily visits for the fifteen minutes permitted to relatives of inmates. Visitors remarked on his inability to remain focused on a subject even for the length of a sentence and blamed the noises, stenches, and other distractions of Howard Hall. J surmised to Eliot that Overholser was wary of those among his subordinates who maintained that Ezra "was not so mentally ill he could not be tried." Superintendent Overholser definitely did not want their views aired.

As if on cue, a midsummer squall blew up when Ezra finally saw the 1940 publication of *Cantos LII–LXXI*, which had not reached him earlier because of the war. "My Deeah Jas," Ezra's scrawl exploded across several pages, "do you realize that if a man weren't already in bug house, to read J. Quincy Adams on cover when it shd. be John Adams père not fils is enough to putt a man there . . . **BALLS**. John not J.Q. . . . Oh hell you went to Haavud." Then, more calmly, "Blurb not bad but Harrold Hairbrain is ignorant as a sow's cunt of American history. Has never read the Constitution . . . Quincy / oh eternal fahrts." Harrold Hairbrain was Ezra's play on Hiram Handspring, and the essay enclosed with the *Cantos* was signed H.H.

Bill Williams's *Paterson* (Book I) finally appeared, and it became clear that critical opinion was shifting in his favor. The first review, by Isaac Rosenfeld in *The Nation*, praised the poem, and Randall Jarrell in *Partisan Review*, finally approving of an ND book, wrote that if Williams could maintain this level for the next three books of *Paterson*, it would be "the best long poem any American has written." Auden and the American anthologist Oscar Williams also praised the book, and Robert Lowell would echo Jarrell's words in *The Sewanee Review*. On the strength of Jarrell's review J would ask him to introduce Williams's *Selected Poems* in 1949.

During this time, J struggled to take the measure of postwar publishing. He correctly anticipated a growth market in the universities, but with the exception of such titles as Goethe's *Faust*, Kafka's *Amerika*, and Faulkner's *Light in August* (1947), few of the ND books from the years immediately following the war were likely to appear on many course reading lists. J planned a new series to begin with *The Selected Writings of Dylan Thomas* in 1946. The idea was to bring out a representative selection of writers whose works were either difficult to obtain or unavailable in English. J intended collections of Cocteau, Henry Miller, and Pasternak, but only the Pasternak would appear in the series, in 1949. The idea was slightly ahead of the times, with Rinehart energetically entering the college text market later in 1948 with its fifty-cent paperback reprints of the classics. J, however, was not yet ready to embrace paperback publishing: he still preferred the substantial heft of hardcovers. A couple of other ND series moved along well: by 1952 the New Classics series would reach thirty-five titles, the Direction series twenty-three. The Makers of Modern Literature series of critical monographs would eventually reach sixteen volumes. One reason for the proliferation of series on the ND list was to focus publicity: teachers and students would find the Makers series conveniently grouped, the general educated public would find the Modern Readers list inspiring, and so on. Or so J hoped. Also, J found that an invitation to join a major series could help to recruit significant authors.

On September 21, 1946, J left for London, taking with him the key for the men's toilet at ND—"What can he do next?" asked Creekmore with a shrug. The trip was undertaken partly in the hope of cementing Dylan Thomas more firmly to ND. Allen Tate had recently become an editor with Henry Holt, and now he was encouraging a campaign that included promising an advance of $750 and fare to America for the improvident Welshman. In J's eyes, this amounted to a cardinal sin: author rustling. Still complaining about "that mean Laughlin," Dylan was willing to see J, and over drinks he signed a new contract that included a proviso that he not negotiate with another American publisher. Dylan also wanted to discuss "my America-ward plans" but found J unsatisfactory on this, beyond acceding to Dylan's request that he look for a quiet place for the poet and Caitlin in the "Adirondacks"—but near New York, Dylan stipulated, in defiance of geography. J tried to discourage Dylan from visiting the United States, fearing his bent for drinking up financial windfalls. Also, J surmised correctly that Dylan was deeply rooted in Wales. At least Dylan now stopped referring to J as "little."

J was in Paris during October, and Henry Miller urged him to visit the Egyptian expatriate Albert Cossery, who wrote in French of the very poor, the "Men God Forgot," and Raymond Queneau, an old friend who had become a senior editor for Gallimard. Both men would become New Directions authors. J asked Albert Camus for permission to publish his *Caligula* and *Cross Purpose*, and he received an affirmative: "Je vois que vous n'êtes pas épicier." With this acknowledgment that he was neither a vulgarian nor a greengrocer, J was able to add Camus to his list. Then J picked up a Swiss route map and a second-class railway pass in Lausanne and climbed the Matterhorn with an excellent mountaineer as his guide.

From Lausanne, J traveled to Rapallo, where he stayed in the Pounds' apartment. Although he tried to keep nostalgia out of his letter to Ezra, J found Rapallo more attractive than ever: "a place fit for a human soul to enjoy its mortal carnality." Besides, Ezra's bust by Gaudier-Brzeska stood on the terrace, where "the inhabitants of the West flat have made a shrine of it, surrounding it with flowering plants. Quite made me bawl to see it so." He was received affectionately by Lola Avena, and he visited Olga Rudge up at Sant'Ambrogio, leaving her with a "small cache of dollars against any emergency," and he assigned her a translation job for ND. J visited Ezra's mother in the hospital and reported on Mary, who was "acting like an Army mule," J said. She had just married Boris Baratti—Prince de Rachewiltz, after he claimed a title once in the family—and would give birth to their son, Siegfried Walter, in April 1947.

Aside from behaving like a dutiful son to Ezra, J was searching for cheap Italian printers with the ability to typeset English with tolerable accuracy: "The inflation here is rising faster than whatever figure you desire to figurate," J wrote to Ezra, speaking of conditions in America, "and I got to be looking for sources of production in low cost of living countries." On this quest, he traveled to Verona to see Giovanni Mardersteig about a pair of hand-set volumes: Gide's *Theseus* and the poetry volume that he had promised Dylan Thomas. The major Italian publisher Mondadori agreed to print Herbert Read's *The Green Child* for ND in 1948. In every respect, it had been a productive trip.

In 1946, New Directions produced the largest annual tally of books thus far, twenty-four, including Neruda's poems under the title *Residence on Earth*, *The Selected Writings of Dylan Thomas*, and a reprint of Nathanael West's *Miss Lonelyhearts*, which helped bring about a revival of interest in the author. Unexpectedly, James T. Farrell's pamphlet *The Fate of Writing in America* had considerable critical impact. Farrell, author of the bestselling *Studs Lonigan*, sounded not unlike J, arguing that in advancing the commercialization of culture, mainstream publishers placed a premium on the promotion of established authors.

One of the stars of the New Classics series, Djuna Barnes, joined the ranks of J's more troublesome authors. Though J doubled his first offer of an advance of $150 and Lustig designed the cover, Barnes was not pleased with *Nightwood*. She finally condescended to meet J, stiffly, in 1948 when she was in a Manhattan restaurant with T. S. Eliot. "I want an edition of *Nightwood* that will last a thousand years," she had told J in imperious tones. J's first postwar annual was notable for two discoveries who would become Nobel laureates: Octavio Paz and Pasternak, both virtually unknown in America.

Although ND had grossed a fairly impressive $118,000 in 1946, with the inflated postwar production costs, this did not mean a profit. In fact, J claimed that he had been forced to make up a deficit of $27,000 out of his own funds. The end of most wartime restrictions in the United States was followed immediately by a dramatic jump in prices of supplies and services. These soaring costs hit publishing hard, and as a result, in an effort to achieve profitability, ND print runs now ran as high as eight thousand copies, at least five times what they had been in the 1930s.

J had become reconnected with a friend of his boyhood: Jack Heinz. Jack had skied casually back east and was now crisscrossing the country pro bono as the national chairman of Community Chest. J invited him to Alta. Like J, he had lost his father early, in 1941, and then had immediately taken over as CEO of the vast Heinz enterprises. In a reversal of their early friendship, on the slopes J assumed the role of leader. Heinz quickly became an avid skier, and the two men would try to meet each winter at Alta, Sun Valley, Alberta, Stowe, Klosters, Zermatt, or Davos, and skiing turned them into the best of friends. In later years, Jack would ring J up and say, "In three hours my plane will meet you at Bradley [Hartford's airport]. We're off for Stowe." Or Mont Tremblant or Alta. J was still skiing competitively, and in the annual intermountain cross-country ski championships in January 1947 near Alta he finished fifth in a field that included such professionals as Corey Engen, future captain of the U.S. Olympic Nordic team, who came in first.

J's travels and his competition skiing had been a welcome relief from a publishing venture that with success had become bewilderingly complex—hundreds of authors, international tax obligations and copyrights, translation negotiations. But what really threatened to drive J around the bend were the complaints of his authors. In his submission to Harvard for the *Tenth Report of the Class of 1936* he lashed out: "Writers are the most difficult people in the world to get on with . . . Yes, there is a lot of <u>good</u> in a lot of people, but in only about one in three can you get it at the precise moment when you need it most." Then he added in a somewhat less truculent tone, "Which may or may not be a personal deficiency."

J spent the spring of 1947 with Rexroth; it was an especially exciting time to be in San Francisco, still J's favorite American city. "Hills are a fine thing," J told Tennessee, "and it gets even better when to these you can add water and fogs. Also Chinese food. And Rexroth, one of the unique minds alive today." The poet Madeline Gleason organized the first Festival of Modern Poetry, in 1947, at which a dozen poets, including Kenneth and the young Robert Duncan, read their experimental verse. The event was significant for according the first public recognition to the avant-garde poetry being produced in San Francisco. Eventually, literary historians would come to consider Rexroth and Gleason the creators of the San Francisco Renaissance, not only a movement in poetry but also a cultural reaching out to Asia. From this time on, J's scope would span two cultural poles: New York and San Francisco, to which an important but more narrowly focused nexus, at Black Mountain College near Asheville, North Carolina, would soon be added.

With Pound still in the news, J was able to arrange for magazine publication of individual cantos, to precede the appearance of *The Pisan Cantos*. This complicated J's life: Ezra, he complained to T. S. Eliot, "keeps inserting Chinese characters in the margins like mad." J made a last-ditch attempt to get characters printed in New York's Chinatown: "Got a wonderful dinner but no help on karkters. Visited every Chinese paper and printer in the area. They have all the characters there but wouldn't set them for me." J threw up his hands and flew to Europe, leaving Creekmore in charge at ND and admonishing him to ride herd on the "chinkeries" in Ezra's texts, to be shared with Faber. Eliot emphasized the need to produce a standard text for American and English editions. "I too would have liked to eliminate references to Jews and Kikes," J agreed with Eliot, "but Ezra would have none of it." Ezra, meanwhile, "rants and raves at my delays."

In February, Pound was moved from Howard Hall to the more relaxed Cedar Ward at St. Elizabeths, due apparently to Overholser's testimony that it might benefit him and to the pressure applied by Cornell's (unsuccessful) application for bail so that he could be moved to a private institution. Dorothy now seemed "very frightened" at the prospect of taking over Ezra's care herself. A year later Ezra would be moved for the final time during his incarceration, to Chestnut Ward for the senile in the same building. Poignantly, from his small, high-set window, Ezra could glimpse, through the hemlocks, the Capitol, where he had once hoped to change the course of American history as a trusted adviser.

Ezra's demeanor gradually reflected a more settled mind and even a certain contentment, and his living arrangements had improved with his move to the Center Building. For one thing, he could now have visitors for three hours each afternoon and also on Sunday mornings. Ezra tried to put his affairs in order—he had made a will before the war, but it had not been properly registered in Italy—and with Dorothy's full acquiescence directed J to send all funds accrued at ND to Olga. "Tell Olga to for godsake take the cash so as not to worry EP any further," Dorothy instructed J. Olga by this time had been given an official secretarial position by Count Chigi at the Accademia Musicale Chigiana in Siena. J now referred to her as "the Lady of Siena" in his diplomatic balancing act; his code name for Dorothy became simply "the Lady." J described Ezra as the "king of the ward," summoning other inmates, the "zombies," to fetch extra chairs for visitors and even having one designated by him, like a Renaissance potentate, as his official "taster"—because, he claimed, Bernard Baruch, who had been FDR's economics adviser, was plotting to poison him. Incomprehensibly, throughout his years at St. Elizabeths, Pound was given no treatment or therapy whatsoever.

And thus J's triangular life continued, yet he seemed no closer to balancing in a satisfying manner the demands of his marriage, his skiing, and his publishing. There were elements of each that he enjoyed, although nowadays he tended to mention only his children, not his wife. His life threatened to become a string of escapes—to Gertrude, to the slopes with Jack Heinz, to Europe on publishing business. It did not add up to a prescription for happiness.

18

Guide to the Godhead: Tom Merton

A great many times my mind has suddenly emptied of whatever I was doing or
thinking and a sort of glow has entered . . . which is identified with the Idea of God.
                                            —James Laughlin to Thomas Merton

J had no sooner returned from his 1946 European jaunt than he headed
west, skiing and discussing plans at Alta in December, then moving on to
San Francisco, where he stayed with Rexroth. During much of this sojourn Gertrude Huston was with him, ostensibly to handle New Directions business while he attended to his ski lift operations. He visited
Henry Miller at Big Sur in May and paused briefly in Los Angeles, and
then he and Gertrude drove north. They "hit the crap tables" in "wonderful Nevada towns like Winnemucca and Tonapah" to wager silver dollars
instead of chips. J's uncharacteristic gambling owed a lot to the relentless
gaiety of Gertrude's personality. They paused in Alta before proceeding to
Taos, where they stayed in early June.

"I am not good with people," J would tell Thomas Merton. "I mean
them well, but the ready and empty word does not come easily to me." In
fact, J was usually *very* good with people: good with his authors; good
with publishers and lady booksellers; good with his subordinates, whether
at ND or at Alta. Paradoxically, however, the closer the kin, the less good
he sometimes was: he would never have a truly close relationship with his
firstborn, and his marriage to Margaret was seldom on track these days.

Being good with people as a publisher meant juggling relationships
with many authors who simply could not get along. William Carlos Williams had been dead set against Eliot since the appearance of *The Waste*

Land, Pound and Stein could not abide each other, Williams had mortally offended Stein and vice versa, and so on. Rexroth came with his own set of violent antipathies. George Oppen was "crazy"—because he had accused Rexroth, successively, of being "a 'passed' Jew & a communist," not to mention "a Pro-Nazi Trotskyite." Oppen was independently wealthy, and the chronically broke Rexroth did not like those with money. "If you care to," he told J, "you can put on your tombstone 'The only rich man Rexroth ever liked.'"

A shift was occurring in J's attitudes. To an extent, Rexroth had become the new Pound in J's life. Both of J's chosen literary gurus were outspokenly pacifist, but Ezra came to his pacifism from the Right, with a monetary emphasis, while Kenneth's was adamantly the anarchist Left, political and social rather than economics-based. J and Kenneth complemented each other. J had the gift of recognizing artistic value over an enormous range. Rexroth played the devil's advocate to J's appreciations, jabbing ruthlessly wherever he suspected cant, false values, weak art. While he was capable of making fine distinctions, he tended toward the violent antipathy, the hammering judgment: Lawrence Ferlinghetti was a "meretricious fraud," Tennessee was "the queen of Leland's Harry's Bar set," Henry Miller, "like all reformed panhandlers," was an "insufferable snob," and his work would not survive, Hubert Creekmore was a "nincompoop." Rexroth hated the poetry of E. A. Robinson and of Robinson Jeffers and said that Schwartz's "wilted watch metrical system" in his *Genesis* was "awful soporific." On the other hand, Patchen, William Carlos Williams, and D. H. Lawrence could indite no wrong. J would argue with Kenneth—and remain independent.

Usually, J ignored Rexroth's more dogmatic pronouncements, but he often trusted his advice. When Viking authorized ND to bring out a *Selected Poems* of D. H. Lawrence, it was to Rexroth that J went for advice on which poems to include, and he goaded Kenneth into writing an introduction. Kenneth was not always successful in getting action out of J, however: for years Rexroth urged Ford Madox Ford's and Wyndham Lewis's novels on J, as well as Pound's *Classic Noh Theatre of Japan,* but was successful in moving J toward the Pound only. Sometimes when J did publish what Rexroth wanted, the two would bicker like schoolboys over who had recognized the work's importance first: Rexroth wanted credit for Herbert Read's *The Green Child;* J countered that he had met Read at a cocktail party and learned about the book from the author himself. In the main, J took Rexroth's diatribes with all the bland equanimity that he could muster, but when Kenneth accused J, wrongly, of having shown his introduction to Lawrence's *Selected Poems* to Diana Trilling for criticism, J lashed out. "If you tell people I am ashamed of your Lawrence preface you are a liar . . . You are as neurotic as hell," he scolded Kenneth. But Rexroth's most frequent refrain was that J was not picking up the coming poets. Soon, said Rexroth wildly, "they will put you in the Smithsonian Institution along with Fulton's paddle wheel."

J always tried to divorce considerations of politics, sexual morality, and personality conflicts from his friendships and his publishing alike. But he had his limits. He had felt that he was stretching matters far enough when he published the anarchist Rexroth's *The Phoenix and the Tortoise*, with its sensual lines telling of "The dark juice rising between the thighs / Of the laughing, falling girl." The title poem was really a philosophical treatise, but Rexroth's marketing advice was to "drop the philosophy and push the pussy." J said that one of Kenneth's poems "about fucking in the beeloud glade" was embarrassing. Not that he was against the subject matter in principle: "There are ways and ways of talking about fucking in poetry and that, in my opinion, does not get away with it."

•

On March 1, 1946, Merton had written to J that his abbot, Dom Frederic Dunne, had approved a new project for him, a confessional book "autobiographical in its essence, but not pure autobiography . . . a cross between Dante's Purgatory and Kafka and a Medieval Miracle play." Merton hoped to start on it soon and finish it "fairly fast." J expressed interest. Then, on August 17, Tom announced that the manuscript had turned into straight autobiography, and at great length—he projected at least 650 typed pages. It might not be "your dish," he added, "but I will certainly let you have the first look at it." In his response, J neither reaffirmed nor denied his wish to consider the manuscript. So on October 21, bypassing J, who was in Rapallo on Pound business, Tom posted the *Seven Storey Mountain* typescript to his agent, Naomi Burton, telling her that Robert Giroux at Harcourt, Brace might be interested. In December, Giroux cabled his acceptance, and the next April, Tom wrote apologetically to J, "I am sorry we got crossed up on the autobiography, but it was definitely not a book for you and I explained that in a letter. So when you made no special reference to it in replying I took it for granted that you agreed with me." Contrary to J's later version of the story, that he had been off skiing when the manuscript arrived, it was never sent to him. Evidently, J did not want to accuse Tom of having broken his word, and "blame it on my skiing" had become one of his standard excuses.

The Seven Storey Mountain became the year's nonfiction bestseller. While J would admit that this was one of the "big fish" that had gotten away, he claimed that it was his "honest opinion," given ND's reputation for avant-garde books and the small amount of publicity that he could afford, that had he published it, "Seven Storey could have gone almost unnoticed." Whether this was special pleading on J's part, and whatever chagrin he might have felt at missing out on the 600,000 hardcover sales of The Seven Storey Mountain, there had been no contractual agreement. In Tom's mind there evolved a tacit understanding that Giroux would publish his prose, New Directions his verse, but Burton was quite willing to steer even prose to J, such as Seeds of Contemplation (1949) and Merton's translations from Latin of the "Desert Fathers," published as The Wisdom of the Desert (1961).

Certainly J never seemed to blame Merton for losing a crack at The Seven Storey Mountain. J had been invited through Merton's abbot to Our Lady of Gethsemani monastery near Bardstown, Kentucky, as far back as 1945. Now, after driving from California, J finally made it to Gethsemani, arriving on June 12, 1947. The countryside around Bardstown seemed bleak, parched, and the monastery itself more like a prison than the European monasteries that J loved. However, instead of the long-faced aesthetic, surrounded by "Grouchy old monks ponderous / In penitence" that J expected, he was greeted in the guesthouse by the ebullient, sturdy figure of Tom Merton, eager to talk about New York jazz and a hundred other subjects—the monks, not allowed newspapers, were starved for news. Trappists were supposed to be mumchance, and even to speak privately with a brother monk, Merton had to obtain permission from the abbot; given license to communicate with an informed visitor, he burst forth in voluble speech. "He had a wonderful gaiety," J would write, "about his vocation and about life." As Merton described their meeting, "There was a man sitting in a low rocking chair. When I entered he stood up and became as tall as a tree." They felt an immediate rapport. Merton thought J naturally religious, "a simple person . . . I like him very much. He is the kind of person I can understand." They discussed producing a parallel-text translation of *The Dark Night of the Soul* by Saint John of the Cross and then walked outside the monastery, where a woman J introduced as his wife was painting a watercolor of the gatehouse. She did not loiter, Merton remembered, "but, seized with panic, went back to her painting at a safe distance from the monastery." It was Gertrude Huston. On subsequent visits, J was lodged in a suite designated for visiting church dignitaries— "vast, dank chambers decorated with the most atrocious religious art."

Within a few years the new abbot, Dom James Fox, relaxed the rules so that Brother Louis, Merton's name at Gethsemani, was allowed to drive out for the day with J, "because I was a publisher who brought the monastery money." Merton's substantial royalties were tax-free, being in the name of the Abbey of Gethsemani. Merton would borrow a formal clerical habit out of the storeroom—to impress the brother manning the gate— and would sally forth clutching an ecclesiastical briefcase. Once well out of sight of Gethsemani, he would step into the woods to change into blue jeans and an old sweater, with a beret to conceal his tonsure, to metamorphose from Brother Louis into genial Tom, suitably incognito for a round of country bars—his favorite bourbon was Heaven Hill—chats with farmers, and feasts of Kentucky ham in redeye gravy. Often they drove to Lexington for lunch with their common friend Victor Hammer, reveling in his wife Carolyn's excellent cooking, the fine Pommard or Nuits-Saint-Georges, and the Courvoisier. What with the wine and the wide-ranging discourse, sometimes they missed the seven o'clock gate closing. J would have Tom stand on his back so that he could reach the top of the wall, and J would shove him the rest of the way up. Then J tossed the end of his belt to Tom, who braced himself while J held the other end and walked up the wall, just as Rexroth had taught him to scale rock faces. "I'm *alive!*" Tom had exclaimed. The two laughed hysterically, like schoolboys on an escapade. "We have done the Devil's / Work today," J said, but the monk replied, "No . . . we've been working for / The angels; they are friends of mine."

Dom James Fox was the product of a varied education that included a stint at the Harvard Business School, but he thought that Merton's ideas ranged too widely, and he would decree in 1950 that the journals of the soon-to-be-ordained Merton could not be published during his lifetime.

However, Dom James was also aware that Merton's *Seven Storey Mountain* was an unsurpassed recruitment text for the order and that Merton, despite his chronic difficulty in following the vow of obedience, was a person of profound integrity and religious feeling. After he was ordained as Father Louis, Dom James made him his personal confessor—a tactically astute move as well as an expression of confidence, since it placed any discourse between them under the seal of the confessional.

J was struck by the dichotomy in Tom's nature: he spoke about wanting to become a Carthusian or a hermit living in the solitude of contemplation, yet no one seemed to love good company and conversation more. J himself was subject to similar contradictory impulses. When he asked Tom later why he remained at Gethsemani, despite all the restrictive rules and petty tyrannies, when he could make a living writing *and* still do good works outside the abbey, he replied, "This is where God wants me to be." "Tom had this overwhelming need to make a sacrifice for God—something I have no conception of," J said. A doubter, J spoke about wanting to believe, but Tom wore his religion inconspicuously, like an old sweater. Whatever his internal struggles, his belief appeared to merge seamlessly into his being. J and Tom would meet only once or twice a year, but years after Tom's death J would say that he had had only two *really* good friends—Robert Fitzgerald and Tom Merton. (His choice of names would vary with time.)

Merton's monastic vows, rather than considerations of money, artistry, or personal idiosyncrasy, constituted the main complication in publishing him. J and Tom had to contend with not only the diocesan censor but also a whole array of superiors, including the Trappist Abbot General, hemming Merton in on matters of dogma. Conscious that periodical publication of his verse would build readership and increase sales of books, J offered to send around individual poems to magazines. Soon he was acting as Merton's unpaid agent, and J told Tom that he used the rewards from publishing him to indulge his own messianic bent: "The profits which we make from your books here at New Directions are all turned back into the business and used to publish the books of young unknowns who need help to get started." Here, J ran afoul of Tom's scrupulous morality. Half in exasperation, the monk accused J, "You are in no sense preoccupied with the moral implications of what you publish: and neither am I—until you somehow make me partly responsible!" Provoked in turn, J replied, "I would never want myself to publish anything which would lead anybody into sin." "I pray for you and the children and N Directions—and I liked a lot your letter about the problem of moral tone," Tom responded, mollified. "I know we see things very much alike."

J, moreover, was dependent on Merton in a way that he probably never admitted even to himself. Unable to swallow the whole cloth of Presbyterian Christianity, J must have hoped at some level of his being to be hoisted into heaven by the monk's shoelace. For J was a spiritual hypochondriac. He had spoken about his chronic doubts to Tom, who replied sympathetically, "You are not at all made for the misery of the cannibal world you have to live in." Tom suggested prayer "in a simple way." J asked for book titles that would help advance "my desire to increase the spiritual component of my life."

Tom evidently sensed that a part of J's unease had to do with the state of his marriage. J had spoken approvingly to him about D. H. Lawrence's belief in "the sacramental character of human love." In the abstract this was fine, according to Tom, but while Lawrence rooted his concept of love in the individual's "physical being," the achievement of marriage *as a sacrament* depended on the relationship being "absolutely purified of all *selfishness*." J had felt constrained to call off a trip into the Sierras with Rexroth, "as the children are always sick or the nurse is sick or there is some reason to stay home and fuss . . . The symbol of my life is shutting endless doors so that there won't be a draft . . . I am trying real hard to be a good husband and father." For J to leave the demands of self out of his marriage to Margaret—ah, that was a tall order.

19

Troubles in Europe, Public and Private

Jammed standing in the
corridor of a limping
German train I share

at least their hunger's
dirty smell and rub my
aching guilt on theirs.
—James Laughlin, *Report on a*
Visit to Germany

J's 1947 *Spearhead* anthology was intended to highlight the better side of publishing. Not part of the run of New Directions annuals, it had both a pleasant and a serious purpose, J wrote in his "Editorial Notes." The former was to celebrate the tenth anniversary of ND through the reprinting of some of the best of the first ten years of *New Directions in Prose and Poetry*. While he recognized the excellence of many recent American critical essays, J said that lack of space had led to his decision to omit writing in this category, and to print the work of American citizens only. The serious charge was to present an "impartial" survey of "significant *experimental* and *advance guard* writing in the United States during the past decade," no matter who the publisher. These writers J defined as individuals trying to work outside the "technical limits" then current, to distinguish them from other writers, perhaps equally gifted, who had chosen to write within established traditions and forms. Thus, he had not included Katherine Anne Porter—although "no one alive today produces *better* writing"—or

Wallace Stevens while featuring Cummings and Bill Williams, "who have driven all their lives toward new idioms and new metrics." Although J made the final decisions, his choices were informed by "an extensive poll of competent critics and editors" whose names J kept strictly anonymous. Of all the authors J wished to include, only Eudora Welty was omitted, to his "great regret": her agent had demanded double the cash payment accepted by all the other writers. Many of those in the very first ND anthology were given space in *Spearhead*, including a selection of J's own poems, and to that nucleus were added, among others, Agee, Djuna Barnes, Berryman, Charles Henri Ford, Jarrell, Maude Hutchins, Anaïs Nin, Patchen, Rexroth, Rukeyser, Saroyan, Schwartz, Karl Shapiro, Robert Penn Warren, and Tennessee Williams. Each of these had already appeared in some ND publication.

J continued his assault in *Spearhead* on what he castigated as "the commercial publishing of books" in America. With couched lance, he charged at a host of American giants: "As the book club memberships grow, swollen by the diseased response to pressure advertising, the reaction of the offended minority of readers who take pride in individual taste and judgment becomes more violent and more vocal." Hence J's holy war, the third-person voice held before him like a shield: "Ten years ago the editor of New Directions smelt the corruption beginning to fester in American publishing and founded the New Directions movement to combat it—a David so microscopic Goliath could not even see him, a vox clamantis in deserto as Clifton Fadiman once expressed it." He concluded with a sentiment so internationalist, coming at the moment of American pride in victory, of American hegemony, that it appears to have passed unnoticed: "Who better than these writers know that words like 'country' (except when it is used to mean the opposite of 'city') must be eliminated from the vocabulary of all languages?"

J thus chose to eschew nationalism, to embrace internationalism even as he launched an anthology of American writers. It was an extraordinary insight for a politically cautious American to voice at the end of a hot war and the beginning of a cold one. As if to underscore his internationalism, J dedicated the volume to that uncompromising friend to all serious writers everywhere, Frances Steloff, "because no one has done more than she to further the cause of good books by non-dead writers." Frances wrote to J that while many had said nice things about her and the Gotham, no one else had spoken "quite like this": "All I can say is that more than ever I shall try to deserve it, meanwhile love and gratitude from the heart as always." She closed with three lines that J surely hoped could apply to himself as well:

To live is to love
To love is to work
To work is to see God.

Time magazine gave *Spearhead* a condescending review: Berryman, Schwartz, and Jarrell were writing well by turning *away* from experimental forms, but most of the others "now seem to be acquiring literary paunches."

J's *Spearhead* preface might have continued his attacks on mainstream publishers, but he had long moved beyond his disparagement of academe to embrace the scholars. He had eagerly published Joyce's *Stephen Hero*, the urtext for *A Portrait of the Artist as a Young Man*, after Ted Spencer had brought to his attention the acquisition of the manuscript by Harvard. On the West Coast the opinionated and irascible Yvor Winters was firmly an ND author with five books written or edited. J considered him his man at Stanford—before they parted ways over J's refusal to publish his disciples. In his campaign to resurrect Pound, J argued strongly for an inexpensive selected poems aimed at the college market, against Ezra's worry that such would cut into the sales of *Personae*. "The main thing is to have a selection which will appeal to the not too bright blokes who run poetry courses in the colleges," J told Dorothy, relying on her, as he often did these days, to persuade Ezra. This she was able to do.

Throughout the spring, J had remained preoccupied with *The Pisan Cantos* and the growing impatience of its author, who accused J of spending "3/4th yr time slidin' down a ice cream cone on a tin tea tray." After one particularly "irate plaint" from Ezra, J remarked, "It is at least cheering to note from the vehemence of your expression that health seems to be returning as aformerly [sic]."

With Eliot's prior approval, J met with Auden, Cornell, Cummings, Eliot, Fitts, Robert Fitzgerald, and Allen Tate to discuss a scheme for obtaining Ezra's release. J planned to publish *The Pisan Cantos* during the following summer, and he was confident that this volume of the cantos stood high among Ezra's masterpieces. J was careful to keep his name out of circulation on the Pound issue, but his network of literary associates was in operation. In 1943, MacLeish, then Librarian of Congress, had appointed Tate to be Consultant in Poetry in English. Tate had immediately proposed to MacLeish the appointment of a body of Fellows in American Letters to advise him on the annual consultancy and on "the advancement of literature." Under this spacious umbrella, Tate wanted to establish an award for poetry. He persuaded the Bollingen Foundation, established in 1945 by Paul Mellon, son of the Uncle Andy of J's boyhood, to fund an annual award of $1,000 for the best book of American verse for the year just ended. The winning selection would be decided by the library fellows. J and Eliot hoped that if Pound were given the Bollingen Prize, the Department of Justice would be embarrassed into freeing him.

Ezra might be securely located at St. Elizabeths, but J never knew where Tennessee's next missive might be fired from—New Mexico, New Orleans, New York, Nantucket: wherever he was, the playwright seemed to be in the throes of a crisis. While he was in Provincetown, a stroke of excellent fortune turned up in the form of a young actor, Marlon Brando. Tennessee thought his reading of the part of Stanley Kowalski in *Streetcar* the best he had ever heard and took immediate steps to get him signed up. Now Tennessee's loyalties included Wood as his agent, Margo Jones as his producer, Brando as his favorite male lead, J as his publisher. "Whenever it is possible I want to have my professional connections with persons I know, understand and am fond of, reciprocally," he told Wood. Tennessee's homosexual pickups and J's marital infidelity did not override the embedded gentleman's code to which both tried to adhere: they were loyal to each other and kept faith.

Of course, there were inconsistencies. Gentlemen did not talk about money: J did so constantly and usually with a purpose. "Book business going very badly to hell," he lamented to Bill Williams to excuse small royalties. "Sales just half what they were last year."

J and Margaret squabbled about money too, but there was more than one serpent in their Norfolk Eden, as Aunt Leila insinuated herself into J's spiritual life. Through Clara Sage, an adept in the Unity spiritualist group—"a dear old lady . . . certainly not a charlatan," J said—in Pleasantville, New York, Aunt Leila communicated, as she had long done, with an angel named Lester, who began to transmit messages from J's dead father. These messages of encouragement J found "very vaguely expressed, and not in his characteristic medium." In this intercourse aunt and nephew shut the skeptical young wife out entirely.

During the autumn of 1947, J prepared for an extended stay in Europe. His reasons were multiple: his short trip the year before had made him hunger for a real reconnection with France, Italy, and the Alpine regions; rising production costs in America showed the wisdom of scouting out cheap printers overseas; and he had procured a few commissions to report on the coming Winter Olympics for American ski magazines. Probably he thought also that the change might help his tottering marriage. While he might have preferred to escape for some months of bachelor freedom, he knew that both Aunt Leila and his mother would certainly not approve of his traipsing off for an extended sojourn without wife and children. So the family must come along: Margaret was delighted—her experience of Europe was very limited. She imagined having her husband to herself for a long romantic interlude in a mountain chalet.

On November 8, J, Margaret, the children, and a nanny—paid for by Aunt Leila—set sail on the Cunard White Star liner *Mauretania*. By midmonth J and Margaret were established at the Chalet Pardenn in Klosters, Switzerland, with the intention of wintering there. Klosters was "very quiet and sober," J wrote to Dorothy Pound. "It is a good place to work, and I am getting caught up with a lot of reading." With Paul and Leila in kindergarten and a "wonderful maid" who shopped, cooked, cleaned, and ironed for $25 a month, Margaret was free for daily hikes in the mountains with J, outings that left her "almost dead" trying to keep up. Still, Margaret sounded happy. J arranged for an exposition of New Directions books in Paris in December, to be followed by a party for French writers. All this cost a good deal, and J was prepared to leave his wife in Klosters as an economy measure. She was not to be denied Paris. "We have reached a compromise about trips," Margaret said. "I can go on any if I pay for them."

Before leaving for Paris, at St. Moritz J rescued a little girl, lost and freezing on the mountain, but heaven, to be sure, was not watching carefully over J himself, and a skiing fall left him with a badly sprained left foot. And his back was affected as well.

Back at ND, *A Streetcar Named Desire* appeared at the end of the year in a startlingly bright jacket by Lustig. Tennessee wrote that the design was "original and striking," but he objected to the "sort of shocking pink which reminds me of a violet scented lozenge." Susan Lustig, who had watched the printer mix the ink, averred that the color was lavender, not pink, and she called Tennessee "a pudgy pill." Pink or lavender, the value of the *Streetcar* first edition would rise with the playwright's fame, until sixty years in the future, when a signed copy would be offered at $25,000. Getting a final text from Tennessee was a triumph in itself: he was harder to pin down than the god Proteus when it came to the printed word. He could not see his plays without wanting to revise them, even throughout rehearsals. J would try to snatch the prompt copy and set from that. Thus, ND would publish Tennessee *as produced,* unless the author objected strenuously. *Streetcar* went on to win a Drama Critics' Circle Award and a Pulitzer Prize.

New Directions at year-end seemed to be thriving in J's absence. Some dozen volumes had come out to "terrific reviews," and there were many large orders. "Jay is in Europe being absolutely repulsive," Susan Lustig wrote to her brother. "He hurt his back skiing, of course, so has time to bombard us with hundreds of little toilet paper notes telling us to do things, diabolical things," all the time reminding his harried staff that they were in the "January slump." "Once that man gets an idea in his head he refuses to change it," she concluded grimly.

Margaret wrote to J's mother, "J. & I are getting along better than we ever believed possible . . . Now we are so companionable—it's a marvelous relationship." And J had bought her a Christian Dior dress. J told a different story to his mother: "I must regretfully report that things are going extremely badly. The more I try to do things for M. taking her with me on all my trips and spending money on her which I just don't have to spend, the more she drinks and is dissatisfied and unable to divert herself." His mother had been planning to join them in Europe. Don't, J advised her: "I think it is going to be a pretty messy winter." Perhaps it was his fault that matters had reached this point, J added: "I should never have married someone who was not sufficiently interested in my work to provide amusement for herself by participating in it." He could not *both* carry on his New Directions projects and amuse his wife. "I am behind with my work," he told his mother, "and have neither the time or the inclination to waste amusing her." Now he had reached a "calm detachment," he said somewhat ominously, and did not want advice or help: "Just leave it to me."

Not that J really managed a detached calm. The emotional gale that

Margaret and he were caught up in continued in full force. Her mood seemed to J to shift so wildly that he doubted her sanity. "I really think she is crazy," he wrote twice in the same letter to his mother. With all his unhappiness, J was unreserved in his praise for his little daughter. "Simply adorable, the most delicious child I have ever seen," he wrote to his mother, and he tried hard to evoke similar feelings for his five-year-old son. "Paul is much more reserved and harder to get close to," he thought, "but he is very sweet when you get through to him." To his mother, J accused Margaret of infidelity but added, "It's all my fault for not providing enough amusement for her." Although J said that he remained fond of her, the time had come to make a clean break, while Margaret was young enough to find "another good husband." By February 22, J had concluded, "We simply loathe each other and have nothing in common but the children," and said that he wanted his mother's backing in "getting rid of her." This was to head off Aunt Leila, who would predictably push for a reconciliation. She continued to plan the future for J and Margaret: while they were in Europe, she was extending Meadow House by almost fifty feet to the south in a two-story addition that would spread thirty-eight feet to the east from an impressive front door. The new section would add to the home a formal dining room and a large living room with a stone fireplace, as well as five more bedrooms.

•

Nineteen forty-seven had been busy and productive at New Directions, and the thirty-three titles meant a very full year. The list was especially strong in translations from the French. J launched a short-lived Modern Readers series with Louis-Ferdinand Céline's *Death on the Installment Plan* and Svevo's *Confessions of Zeno*. And he had finally cajoled an important collection of shorter works, *The World Is a Wedding*, out of Delmore. For the first time, the firm showed a confirmed though small profit.

J traveled the last week of January 1948 to Milan, where he spent considerable time with Elio Vittorini, autodidact and son of a railroad worker, whose anti-Fascist novel *In Sicily* was influenced in style by Hemingway, who contributed an introduction, his only appearance in a New Directions book. *In Sicily* became the first ND book to be featured on the first page of *The New York Times Book Review*.

Ostensibly, J's reason for settling in the Alps was to cover the Olympic

Winter Games at St. Moritz for *The Saturday Review of Literature, Town and Country, The Ski Annual*, and *Ski News*, reportages that he turned out in due course. Jack Heinz and his second wife, Jane Ewing, joined J and Margaret for a week at St. Moritz in early February. Jack and J skied over the Theodul Pass below the Matterhorn and on to Breuil-Cervinia in Italy. From there they took the cable car—"one of Musso's good works," J said—back up to the pass, skied diagonally across the glacier and then down to Zermatt. Pointedly, J told his mother that Jane Heinz "works at pleasing Jack & keeping him amused." When the party left Zermatt, Margaret refused to go with them.

Ten years before, when J was casting his marriage net in Boston waters, he had stressed his need for a partner who would firm up his seriousness of purpose, who would stimulate him in knowledge and discussion, who would curb his wandering eye through her own goodness and quality. In other words, who would be a gentle sea anchor to his drifting tendencies. Instead, J reflected bitterly, he found himself married to someone *he* must perforce direct, guide, and entertain, like a child. He leafed through his Choate *Principles of Geometry* to find in the hollow "parallelograms & squares" a metaphor for his state of mind: running on empty.

When he was neither skiing nor watching others ski, J had been visiting printers and publishers in Verona and Geneva. Mondadori quoted print and bind rates to J that were half those he was incurring in the United States; even with freight and customs duty, he would achieve substantial savings. He had also arranged for a distributor in Italy for New Directions books. His Italian trip turned into something of a triumphal progress, and he was invited for meals at the homes of the three largest publishers, Bompiani, Einaudi, and Mondadori. Each publisher told him that the ND list was the best in America, "the one which had the most appeal for literate Europeans." J spent a day with the Weimar-born Giovanni Mardersteig, founder of the Stamperia Valdonega in Verona. "Elegant simplicity," J would characterize his work, "nothing gets in the way of the text." He loved especially the Dante typeface Mardersteig had designed. "My printing heroes are Didot, Baskerville, and Mardersteig," J said.

A Pound publication problem surfaced, which J and Creekmore tried to sort out by mail. Ezra was conscious that in Cantos 72 and 73 he had written intemperately, and he wanted them excluded from the new collected edition, which was to include everything else through *The Pisan*

Cantos. "Now as I recall you don't want now to print the two cantos of Cavalcanti written in scuryoulose wop," J reminded him, and suggested the insertion of a note explaining the gap in numbering. Ezra didn't want this either. "Say nothing about any <u>lacuna</u>," he commanded. "I bet we get over a hundred letters about those two damn Cantos" from librarians demanding to return the books as defective, J remarked to Eliot. Creekmore asked Dorothy if they could simply include a note stating that these cantos would be published "at some later date." Ezra scrawled in large letters in the margin of Creekmore's letter a note aimed at J: "**I have told that dam fool NO 6 <u>times</u> Curious that a man ass enough to confuse J.A wt J.Q, A shd expect animals of equal faculty to notice mere numerals**." Years after the fact, the Adams slip still rankled. J acceded reluctantly to his wishes, and having had enough of publishing, Creekmore left soon to join the English faculty at the University of Iowa. One of J's decisions while he was in Europe was to replace Creekmore with David McDowell, who had been representing ND in Europe. McDowell came across as a very polished southerner and something of an intellectual. J was won over and moved him to the New York office as sales and promotion manager. It soon became apparent, however, that McDowell was acting more for himself than for ND.

Julien Cornell now thought that there was a good chance of obtaining Ezra's release through the formal filing in the Washington District Court of a writ of habeas corpus to the effect that Pound must be either brought to trial or released. The district court turned down the writ, and Cornell appealed, but to his astonishment Dorothy intervened in March 1948. "Please withdraw the appeal at once," she wrote, without giving any reason beyond her claim that Ezra must be "kept as quiet as possible" and should be spared further court appearances.

J also believed with reason that Dorothy's own motives for not allowing Cornell to act were complicated by her desire to keep Ezra and Olga apart: so long as he was in St. Elizabeths and declared incompetent, Dorothy had him under her control. Free, he might return to Olga. Ultimately, it turned out that the decision to withdraw Cornell's writ of habeas corpus had come at least as much from Ezra as from Dorothy. Later Ezra said, "Jas, I will only come out of here with flying colors . . . and a letter of apology from the President . . . and a statement that I was right all along."

Twenty-six years later, when J read the omitted cantos for the first time, he would be at once impressed and shocked. J's vow to Pound had prevented his reading the manuscript so long locked in the office safe. "Except for the beauty of the Italian, which amazed me, in its effective parody of Dantescan style, though without the rhyme, they gave me the shakes," J confessed to Hugh Kenner. These cantos must have been composed, J judged, "when Ez was at the height of his paranoia." They were "utter and abject Fascist propaganda." Not until 1986 would the Italian cantos finally be incorporated to make a complete edition of *The Cantos*.

A chance to see Germany in the throes of reconstruction appeared, J said, when "my / Old friend Herbert Blechsteiner / In Cologne" invited him on a tour of Germany. Blechsteiner was the name that J gave in *Byways* to Edouard Roditi, and the "tour" was a highly suspect business trip in a staff car wangled through army connections—Roditi was working as a translator for the U.S. Army in Berlin—to buy up stolen artwork from GIs and sundry others. Roditi spoke seven languages fluently and translated from more than ten, ranging from Danish to Turkish. He passed J off as a "bigshot in the OSS" to the sergeant assigned as their driver, who saluted J on every conceivable occasion. J's travels with Roditi were unforgettable. "I was terribly distressed by all that ruination and starvation," J said. "Hard on the heart," he wrote to Mary de Rachewiltz. "The Austrians get only 1500 calories of food a day and are all terribly thin and wrinkled. We get 5000 as tourists . . . but it makes us feel like pigs."

In Frankfurt too he registered the human suffering and traveled several miles to the south to Darmstadt, where he saw "grey hungry men" clearing debris from bombed houses, men who picked up and then discarded as useless a twisted spoon, which he then slipped into his own pocket: "I want / their spoon I'll take it home / back to the other world I'll / need it there to learn to eat." Munich affected J even more deeply, since he compared his youthful memories of the regal city with the smashed and empty spaces lining the Maximilianstrasse, the Ludwigstrasse, and the Marienplatz. The factories that were the targets of the Allied airmen lay outside the city center, but, as J commented wryly, "the aim of those who / Released the bombs was not / Good."

In early June, J reached Rapallo, which he found "hardly like old times." Following Ezra's instructions, J made a selection of the correspondence that he deemed most valuable to add to the material held in trust for Mary. With Dorothy dancing attendance upon Ezra at St. Elizabeths and Isabel Pound recently dead, only Olga Rudge remained nearby, at Sant'Ambrogio. J once more followed the *salita* up the hill to see her.

J's eight months in Europe had been a time of the wildest swings in mood and accomplishment. He had done good work in renewing contacts sundered by the war and in establishing new connections with authors, publishers, printers, and distributors. He felt that he was making progress toward resolving Ezra's status and helping the Pound family as well. His Alpine trip with Jack Heinz had brought him even closer to a man he liked and admired, and together they had shared some of the finest skiing of J's long experience. On the other hand, he had attended only fitfully to his publishing, and his relationship with Margaret had deteriorated to the point that he wanted an exit more than anything. Ligaments torn in a ski mishap and repeated sinus infections were manifestations of the strain that he had been under. Worse was awaiting him in America.

20

Bollingen Affair
Rocks Library of Congress

If the hoar frost grip thy tent
Thou wilt give thanks when night is spent.
—Ezra Pound, final lines of *The Pisan Cantos*

J's European sabbatical with Margaret had produced valuable contacts, but it had not been emotionally relaxing. He returned to Norfolk in mid-July 1948 and soon was embroiled with Rexroth when Kenneth Patchen printed in *Partisan Review* and without permission J's casual comment placing Patchen with the acknowledged best American poets. J felt that he had to respond in print, and the next thing he knew he was chided by the other Kenneth for being "intimidated" by *Partisan Review*. Rexroth saw J's letter demanding a retraction, duly printed in the July *PR*, as disloyal to Patchen, while publishing him was "one of your justifications for having existed." "Stop *badgering* me! My nerves won't stand it," J replied in real annoyance. "I'll quit the whole business in a day or two at this rate." In fact, J *was* ambivalent about Patchen's verse, which he thought "terribly uneven": some dozen "extremely beautiful" poems, many others flawed.

Following up on the clash over Patchen, Rexroth asked for a large advance to fund a projected trip to the Orient. New Directions was in financial trouble, J said: *Streetcar* had saved ND last year with sales of 14,000 copies, but this year's Williams play, *Summer and Smoke*, J felt was "not good." Consequently, he was pinning his hopes on Giuseppe Berto's *The Sky Is Red*. He was right on both counts. Tennessee's play sold only 3,075 the first year, 615 the next, but Berto's novel was picked up by the Book Find Club. These outcomes were still in the future when J answered

Rexroth querulously: "I don't have the strength or the funds to keep up with you." J might have blamed the financial picture at ND for his mood, but the main cause of his unhappiness was personal: "I am dead tired. I've burned myself out with the thing and just don't give much of a damn any more . . . I just want to go way the hell off somewhere with you know which and never be heard of again." "You know which" meant Gertrude Huston. Her position as J's regular companion was acknowledged around the office, and in a very real sense theirs was a partnership. Gertrude shared many of J's artistic tastes, and she was an important designer for ND. Certainly she would have married J if he had made an explicit proposal, and almost certainly he implied that he would *like* to marry her, excusing himself that he was unable to divorce Margaret until he could convince aunt and mother that it would be the best course "for the children." Perforce, Gertrude bided her time.

J's discontent was widely distributed, both at work and at home. The expansion of Meadow House was still ongoing, and books were stacked in closets while the carpenters finished bookshelves. Sales were down, and his disputes with the two Kenneths had further soured his mood. He used an interview with a journalist for the *Waterbury Republican* to restate his commitment to writing of high quality, but he admitted that he now felt that "experimental writing in America has run dry." Among young writers only Carson McCullers and Jean Stafford, neither of them ND authors, showed real promise. He was more impressed with the writers he had found in Europe, such as Cossery and Berto. It fit his mood that he was supervising the laying of a cesspool at Meadow House.

Despite his many laments during his stay at Klosters, within months after his return to the United States J was writing to Kay Boyle, "Europe was wonderful and I miss it dreadfully." A major burden was the pileup of publishing business. "I seem to be so awfully jammed up these days with an enormous accumulation of work," J complained to Ezra. "I've finally taken to dictating on the machine, which saves a certain amount of time, but it also means that I answer all the letters that come in, instead of answering only a third of them, as I used to do before."

Tennessee Williams, in town for the October 6, 1948, opening at the Music Box Theatre of *Summer and Smoke*, handed J the typescript of Paul Bowles's first novel, *The Sheltering Sky*. The novel had been rejected by Doubleday, Random House, and other publishers. J accepted it at once.

Tennessee's play was accompanied by music composed by Bowles, who also attended the premiere. With one of his top authors plus another he had just signed thus represented, J steeled himself to attend the first-night party, held in Tennessee's apartment. Among those present were the director Margo Jones, Gore Vidal, Truman Capote, and the agent Audrey Wood. It was J's first meeting with Maria Britneva, the irrepressible hazel-eyed Russian-English ballerina turned actress, Tennessee's confidant and protective demon since their meeting at a party at John Gielgud's London lodgings the previous June.

The night of Britneva's arrival in New York in September, Tennessee had taken her to see *A Streetcar Named Desire* and had introduced her to Marlon Brando, who raced around the city with her behind him on his motorcycle and helped put up curtains in her apartment. Maria entertained Tennessee by skewering his friends with unflattering comments: his companion Frank Merlo was "the Little Horse" because his teeth were so large; Capote had a voice "so high that only a dog can hear it." Vidal countered this by naming her "Miss Pig" after watching the petite lady demolish an enormous ice cream sundae. Her very unpredictability fascinated J. While it might seem that her flightiness would remind J of precisely that aspect of his wife's behavior that he greatly detested, Maria was entertaining *in herself*, whereas Margaret *needed to be* entertained. Or so it seemed to him. Tennessee's frequent visits to New York provided occasions for the three of them to meet for dinner. J and Maria were at a restaurant alone late one evening, Tennessee having already left to board a midnight Pullman for Chicago, when she decided that she had forgotten to say "something important" to him. J knew that there were trains to the city boarding passengers at both Pennsylvania Station and Grand Central Terminal, so they dashed by taxi to Penn and ran through the train shouting "Tennessee!" No response. On to the other station, same procedure. In the last car a surprised Tennessee poked his head and bare torso through the curtains. "I forgot to say goodbye," said Maria. Soon it was evident that Gertrude Huston had serious competition for J and that J himself had rivals for *la Ruskaya* in the persons of Brando and George Plimpton, editor of *The Paris Review*, while Maria herself cherished the dream that she could win Tennessee away from homosexuality. By the time J flew to Alta for a couple of weeks in mid-December, he was glad to be out of New York—partly because Maria was hovering about New Directions, angling in vain for a job.

"I depend so much on your critical opinion," Tennessee wrote in some alarm to J when his verdict on a couple of poems was slow in coming, "as there are times when my own seems to fail me." J found himself in something of a quandary regarding Tennessee: he knew that virtually *anything* Tenn wrote these days would sell, so J felt that in advising Tenn he had to "lean over backward lest I should have to accuse myself of a commercial motivation." So J preferred to wait, he told Tennessee, "until you yourself are ready." It made for a delicate minuet, in which neither partner was confident enough to take the lead.

Knowing that Tennessee often typed out only a single copy of his newest work, J took it upon himself to have copies made for his safe at Norfolk and for the ND office files. When Tennessee sent J a draft of *The Rose Tattoo*, J responded with a long letter about the "terrific fires" in Serafina and a prediction that "your work is going ultimately to develop along another line" from *Menagerie* and also from "the Elizabethan plays of violence." "I was a sounding board for him," J realized. "He wanted to talk to somebody. I think he knew that he couldn't trust these sycophants who were around him and didn't know anything about anything." In the early years Tenn had sought advice from Audrey Wood, but gradually his paranoia led him to distrust her.

J knew that Tennessee needed reasoned reassurance, but he preferred a reciprocal joshing relationship with his friends. Having congratulated Alvin Lustig on reaching an agreement with Knopf, J added proprietorially, "Now, please be sure that you invent for them a style that is totally different from mine. Otherwise, my feelings will be very hurt." When Lustig announced his marriage to Elaine Firstenberg, J admonished him, "Get the upper hand immediately, and you will never lose it! That is the key to happiness." Then came J's last word on marriage: "This is, after all, a very historic occasion, like the scalping of the last white man by the Indians in the State of Arizona." Alvin was quite capable of holding his own, and after J had carped at three previous attempts at a design, he replied, "I was not kidding on the Pound. Frankly I feel that Pound is a rather sinister character and the cover probably projects that too much for your taste."

J pressed Elaine and Alvin to visit him at Meadow House, but he spent the entire evening hunched over his stamps, meticulously applying hinges to them. He barely addressed his guests. It was inexplicable. His affect was momentarily blocked.

•

In October 1948, Eliot began a two-month residence at the Princeton Institute for Advanced Study, where J met him for a strategy session about Pound on November 15. J followed this up with a second lunch with Eliot, this time including Robert Lowell. "It was swell to see you," J wrote as Eliot set off for Stockholm to accept the Nobel Prize. "You spread a good peaceful glow in a horrid world." While J's careful planning with Eliot was going on, Ted Spencer nominated *The Pisan Cantos* for the first Bollingen Prize, to be awarded in February 1949 under the jurisdiction of the Library of Congress. Charles Norman's *The Case of Ezra Pound* appeared from the Bodley Press, and it helped to keep Ezra's name current. "Not as bad as I had feared," J conceded. "But he's a squeak who gives me the pip." The Library of Congress fellows assumed that *The Pisan Cantos* would be the majority choice, but there was by no means harmony among them. The poet Katherine Garrison Chapin, whose husband, Francis Biddle, had been the attorney general who indicted Pound for treason back in 1943, was urged by him *not* to award the prize to Ezra. Karl Shapiro voted for Pound, then changed his vote to Bill Williams. Spencer died of a heart attack before the final decision, but since he had voted for Pound in the initial balloting, the fellows decided to count his vote for the *Cantos*. In the official tally, it was seven votes for *The Pisan Cantos*, four for *Paterson* (Book II). Both books had been published by New Directions, a mere six weeks apart.

Luther H. Evans had succeeded MacLeish as the Librarian of Congress, and he had told the Bollingen Committee to follow its mandate: literary quality was the sole criterion for judgment. When the winner was announced on February 19, 1949, J was in Europe to write several commissioned ski articles. *The New York Times* ran a front-page headline: "Pound, in Mental Clinic, Wins Prize for Poetry Penned in Treason Cell." Paul Engle, director of the Iowa Writers' Workshop, said that Ezra's poetry intended the destruction of America. The Bollingen award was still provoking an "enormous press reaction" when J returned on March 20, but he was not at first alarmed: the editorials were mixed, and some, such as that in the *New York Herald Tribune*, argued for the "purity of poetry, and its isolation from politics." J immediately committed the relatively large sum for ND of $600 for newspaper advertisements celebrating the award and listing all Ezra's titles in print. However, there was certainly no impetus toward springing Ez, and J continued his campaign to restore and build Pound's reputation.

J was now in the uneasy position of having to mediate between Ezra and the classicist Rolfe Humphries, whom J had asked to write an introduction to the *Selected Poems*. Then, when Ez saw Humphries's remarks about his alleged "violations of the peace and dignity of the human race," Ezra offered a "compromise" emendation to Humphries: "I believe E.P. to be a complete skunk when not writing poetry." In the end, neither antagonist would budge, and the *Selected Poems* appeared without an introduction.

Whether or not J's campaign was responsible, Pound's reputation seemed to be improving. In September even *Life* magazine was "pestering" J (to no avail) for permission to photograph Ezra at St. Elizabeths. J operated as a gatekeeper against scholars and would-be biographers as well, dutifully consulting with Ezra: "Nothing since 1939 to be shown to <u>anyone</u>" was the Boss's typical response. In fact, he was willing to talk to almost anyone who came to St. Liz—except reporters. This prohibition Dr. Overholser enforced without J's involvement.

Conditions in publishing remained bad as spring progressed, and J found himself "overwhelmed with work," forced to devote much of his time to production and promotion while the manuscripts piled up mostly unread. One manuscript that he did read was John Hawkes's novel *The Cannibal*. Hawkes had been recommended to J in 1947 by the major Conrad scholar Albert J. Guerard, and he would become a prolific ND author. Tennessee, however, continued to account for a goodly share of ND's bottom line, as *Streetcar* would pass the 15,000 mark for 1949; new editions of *Menagerie* and *27 Wagons Full of Cotton* were heading for the bookstores at the beginning of April, and Tennessee thought these reprints "stunningly well-done." Tennessee's books at ND had earned him $7,500 for 1948; although the major part of his income came from stage royalties, this was still a figure that most ND authors would have been very glad to earn. Tenn was storming ahead, with rough drafts in hand of at least two works, *The Roman Spring of Mrs. Stone* and *The Rose Tattoo*, while J lamented that in months he himself had written only "a strange little poem . . . comparing Paul Bowles to an airplane engine." This he sent to Bowles in Tangier, who replied, "It is nice to be flattered when one is so far from everything."

•

On Ascension Day, May 26, 1949, J was at the Abbey of Gethsemani to witness Tom Merton becoming Father Louis over three days of ceremonies. Several of Tom's closest friends had been invited, including Merton's Harcourt, Brace editor, Robert Giroux, and, J said, "the infidel Laughlin." It was the infidel who pronounced the entire ordination "a drama, something never to be forgotten," and who wept through most of the High Mass. The next morning J took Communion from Father Louis's hands. If there were any sins particularly on J's conscience, one of them might well have been envy: Giroux had brought for Tom the 100,000th copy of *The Seven Storey Mountain*, bound in morocco leather.

In June the Bollingen controversy flared up with renewed violence. Robert Hillyer was asked by *The Saturday Review of Literature* to write a pair of articles on the award of the Bollingen, which he willingly did, attacking not only Pound but Eliot, the Bollingen Prize Committee, the New Critics, and New Directions. Pound's poetry in general was a "vehicle of contempt for America," an endorsement of Fascism and anti-Semitism, a "ruthless mockery of our Christian war dead." There was a far-reaching conspiracy, he said, that ran from Paul Mellon to the Fellows in American Letters at the Library of Congress. Hillyer had been awarded the Pulitzer Prize for poetry in 1934 and now had used the Bollingen award to continue his campaign against Auden and Eliot, whom he saw as his chief rivals. Appointed young to the prestigious Boylston Professorship at Harvard, "he drank himself out of it," according to J, and at the time of the Bollingen flap was a mere visiting professor of English at Kenyon College, largely forgotten as a poet.

Hayden Carruth, editor of *Poetry* (Chicago), described the first stage of the discussion circulating in print as "lively but intelligent," before Hillyer's articles changed the tone for the worse. Carruth counterattacked: the assault, he wrote, was not merely on Pound but on poetry. So Carruth set out to defend poetry itself, more important than ever at a time when "monstrous systems and sterile philosophies" had deprived so many "of the inherent privilege of aesthetic performance." This was a tragedy because "only in poetry is man knowable to himself." This conclusion resonated within J's own efforts at writing. After reading Hayden's "fine editorial on the Pound question," J initiated a correspondence that would lead to a lifelong friendship. As a matter of principle, Carruth felt obliged to resign from *Poetry*. Only the man at the epicenter seemed unmoved: Ezra prepared a statement for the press—"No comment from the Bug House"—but decided not to issue it. He referred to the Bollingen as the "Bubble Gum Award."

While Luther Evans stood by the decision of the fellows, Congressman Jacob Javits of New York demanded an investigation, and a resolution passed on August 19, 1948, by the Joint Committee on the Library ruled that the Library of Congress should abstain from giving awards. The Bollingen Prize was taken away from the library, its administration transferred to Yale. The library also gave up awards in chamber music and printmaking. "Of course we just printed the Hillyer articles and the editorial to start a controversy," Harrison Smith, editor of the *SRL*, admitted. "It was a great success."

Publication in October 1949 of Paul Bowles's first novel, *The Sheltering Sky*, was the major fall event for New Directions, and it put Bowles on the literary map. J claimed discovery, although he credited Tennessee with bringing them together. The English reviews were generally excellent, and J wagered nearly $1,000 on prepublication advertising. The pack of American reviewers was split, howling either rage or approval. Tennessee wrote an extravagantly laudatory piece for *The New York Times*, and William Carlos Williams, in the same issue, placed *The Sheltering Sky* at the top of his list of the year's best books. Nelson Algren contributed a "real stinker" for *The Saturday Review of Literature*, but favorable reviews soon appeared in *Time* magazine and *The New Republic*, the latter by J's friend Jimmy Stern. David McDowell used his contacts at the *Saturday Review* to secure favorable notice—one of McDowell's last services for ND, before his departure late in the year for Random House. One result of all the notice was that the first print run of 3,500 copies sold out almost immediately, so a second printing of 45,000 copies, a record for ND, had to be rushed through in January.

Early in the new year the book hovered between eighth and tenth places on the *New York Times* bestseller list, the first ND book to make the list at all. J thought it a "very good book" and credited McDowell with having done a "magnificent job" in building up advance interest. J worried to Bowles that "other publishers" would "try to steal you away," and he pledged to keep up the advertising and sales pressure. Bowles in turn promised J his next book. But Bowles was far from happy: he blamed J's merely average first printing for the book's not having sold many more copies. This next book, a collection of short stories, was to be part of the Direction series; then, when the good reviews of *The Sheltering Sky* started to come in, J envisioned it as a companion volume to the novel. J saw Bowles as someone worth pushing, and he spent what was for ND a considerable amount in advertising, about $7,000, "to try to make a big thing" out of *The Sheltering Sky*.

J was quarreling again, by mail this time, with his "best friend" Rexroth over *The New British Poets*, which Kenneth had edited but which J now wanted shortened. Rexroth didn't mind a small, compact book, because anthologies "are read on hikes with the head nestled in a coppice of pubic hair," but when J sent the manuscript off to the printer without informing him what had been cut, he was outraged. "You turned it over . . . to an empty headed NYC cocktail fairy," he said accusingly, adding that J was not willing to admit that he was "no longer an 'advance guard' publisher" but the purveyor of the work of a no-longer-young lot, "yourself included," that featured Miller, Bill Williams, Pound, and Rexroth. Apart from them, there was "junk by people like Kay Boyle & Djuna Barnes who are about as modern as bathtub gin." *Spearhead* was "depressing." "Do you realize that you are rapidly becoming an antique like HL Mencken?"

J was hurt by the letter, although he admitted to having been "highhanded" over the anthology and offered to restore most of the cut material. More than a year before, he had lent Rexroth $750 toward buying a house—the poet had had to move out of his Potrero Hill rental after ten years—and J was upset at the thought that his loan was "sitting doing nothing" when he was short on cash himself. "Will you get it through your head that I am broke?" J wrote in a tone of real bitterness. He had intended to honor Rexroth through his collection *A Small Book of Poems*, but now he was withdrawing the dedication: "I don't want to embarrass you."

New Directions urgently needed more office space, and in March 1949 J moved to a Sullivan-baroque flatiron building at 333 Sixth Avenue, where ND shared the eleventh floor with another publisher, Pantheon Books. Kurt Wolff's Pantheon, publisher of contemporary European authors, occupied the bright front rooms in the narrow northern point of the building, while ND crouched in the relative gloom of the back rooms. ND would take over the entire floor when Wolff moved uptown, giving

Alvin Lustig the office in the salient prow of the suite: the natural lighting was best there, and his eyes were already beginning to fail because of his diabetes.

The move was significant on both economic and symbolic levels. Not only had ND gained more space at a lower cost, but fittingly it had moved out of the geographic domain of the mainstream publishers: Random House, Simon & Schuster, and Scribner's all had offices uptown. Now ND was firmly in the Village, a block west of Washington Square Park, within an easy walk of the old Chelsea, where Dylan Thomas soon came to drink and quarrel, and of 4 Patchin Place, where J could drop in for tea with Cummings, warily eyeing Djuna Barnes's firmly closed door opposite. Cummings was one of the very few people Barnes liked, and she did not mind when he leaned out his door and yelled up at her window, "Are ya still alive, Djuna?"

That summer, in an unusual move for the publicity-averse J, he appeared as one of the troika of directors of the Goethe Bicentennial Convocation and Music Festival, 1749–1949. The event was held from June 27 to July 16 in Aspen, Colorado, and J set up the festival bookshop. The whole event was organized in conjunction with Robert Maynard Hutchins, chancellor of the University of Chicago, and included presentations by the Spanish philosopher José Ortega y Gasset, Albert Schweitzer on his only visit to the United States, Stephen Spender, and Thornton Wilder. J was particularly impressed by Wilder, "the most extraordinary man." J found him "something of an old maid and rather affected in that sense, but a real humanist." Hutchins, it would transpire, was much impressed by J.

The year ended with the appearance of Jorge Luis Borges's "The Circular Ruins" in the anthology for 1949, an important first. Borges, with a considerable following in his native Argentina, was then virtually unknown in North America, but as soon as J saw his disjunct prose and soaring imagination, he knew that it was for such a writer that ND existed. Early in the next year, fourteen years into publishing, J authorized "An Analysis of the Business of New Directions," six pages dense with cost figures and commentary, covering the past decade. The gross sales figures had climbed from $6,702 in 1940 to $232,831 in 1949, much the best year thus far. Even so, ND had lost $20,193 over the course of the same year.

•

Using a combination of acuity, intuition, and plain luck, J had been doing commendably from the outset through an entirely unconventional approach to publishing: in selecting books, he ignored popular sales appeal in favor of innovation and merit; he planted the editorial offices in a rural cottage, not in one of America's great publishing centers; he hired needy authors rather than publishing professionals; he took chances on translations from other languages and "forgotten classics"; he patiently kept in print authors and titles that lost money, waiting for the public to catch on. From 1936 to 1949 only a million books had been sold—not even small potatoes by commercial standards—but the ND catalog was staggering in quality and scope. In poetry especially, J's list read like a syllabus for majors in modernism. From an avant-garde enthusiasm, New Directions had grown to become a formidable though still small publishing house.

Despite his accomplishments, J was in the doldrums, discontented on all fronts. He must turn some significant corner, or he would lose interest in publishing and a lot else besides. The question was, which corner?

21

Crises at New Directions

If you of all people don't understand what New Directions is about and don't want to back me up, then what is the use of my going on with it? I might as well quit and enjoy life.   —James Laughlin to William Carlos Williams

Nineteen fifty began for J with an invitation from Carson McCullers for the January 5 opening night on Broadway of the novella that she, mentored by Tennessee, had adapted for the stage: *The Member of the Wedding.* The play would ultimately win the Drama Critics' Circle awards for best play for 1950 and for best first play—her only one in fact. On the twenty-first J was back in the theater, this time for the American premiere of Eliot's *Cocktail Party,* which he found "absolutely delicious." J could hardly have missed the parallels with his own situation: an unloved wife, a husband who can love nobody, the husband's headstrong mistress, and an Unidentified Guest who turns out to be a psychiatrist. He said that Eliot showed "professional showmanship which I had never thought him capable of," and he urged Tennessee to see the play before it closed, "which probably won't be very long." It would run for 409 performances.

Meanwhile, William Carlos Williams's stock was high and still rising. Each successive section of *Paterson,* from the appearance of Book I in 1946, had received great critical acclaim; and honorary degrees would follow from SUNY Buffalo, Bard College, and Rutgers. The president of Rutgers declared him to be the poet laureate of New Jersey, "the significance of which must largely have escaped him," commented Williams. He had turned sixty-five in September 1948, and by hospital regulations he could no longer practice obstetrics there: a large portion of his income had disappeared. For years Williams had longed to concentrate on his writing. Now that retirement was being forced upon him, he had no pension and very little saved. At the end of 1949, J had put *Paterson* (Book III) and *Selected Poems* up for Pulitzers, which neither work received, but in 1950 Williams received the National Book Award for his poetry. He had become, after Frost, probably the most admired poet of his generation.

Wasting no time on gratitude to New Directions, Williams wrote J what amounted to an ultimatum: he wanted to retire from medicine completely within a year, and to take advantage of the publicity generated by his several honors, he wanted between three and six books out in the next year—most of them still to be completed—including a volume of short stories; the *Autobiography*, to be published "simultaneously" with *Paterson* (Book IV); a *Collected Poems*; and, finally, *The Build-Up*, the third novel in the *White Mule* sequence. "The demand is there, the works are there," Williams wrote disingenuously, adding with a note of threat, "All I need is a publisher." He was tired, Bill said, and he had suffered a heart attack back in 1948. J twitted him about his sudden burst of energy and proposed that ND bring out a uniform edition of his works, beginning with a *Complete Poems* in two volumes. Given Williams's mood, it did not help that J closed by announcing that he was off to Aspen for some skiing, adding, "But don't let that dampen your ardor." Two days later Williams wrote stating that he would talk to McDowell, now at Random House, about taking over his prose—the poetry would stay with ND. "Have a good time," Doc Williams signed off. What J did not yet know was that the ambitious McDowell had criticized ND's sales management to both Williams and Bowles, while telling Bennett Cerf, before he was hired, that he could bring a few ND authors with him.

"What a magnificent kick in the teeth that is," J responded. "Yes, a lovely reward for a decade of work and faith and sacrifice." It was a bitter letter, unfocused and repetitive, mixing recriminations with grudging affection: "But go your way—with my blessing. You are a loveable cuss, and I'll be sore for a few weeks, but it will pass." J pointed out that only two of Bill's books had recouped publishing costs. Worst of all was that Bill was threatening to go to J's most hated rival publisher. "Make a nice chunk of money, if you can," said J sarcastically, "for Bennett Cerf so that he can have lunch every day in 21 [the pricey haunt of celebrities] and get a few more jokes for his column!" Despite his anger, J was collected enough to ask Bill to stipulate in his contract that his new publisher must consult with New Directions on format, so that the eventual "definitive edition" could be more economically produced.

Williams replied with a brief, calm letter: "That clears the situation quite a bit; I just don't think you're much interested in sales." He volunteered that "if I go anywhere it won't be to Bennett Cerf whom I detest as much as you do." Less than three weeks later Williams wrote J to say that Random House was exactly where he *was* going. "Laughlin cannot give me a living," he excused himself to Zukofsky. Williams ended up accepting an advance from Cerf of $5,000 for three prose works. ND would publish his poetry, Bill told J, Random House his prose. Over the next five years Williams published five books with Cerf, including, despite his promise to J, two volumes of poetry, *The Desert Music* and *Journey to Love.*

While the Williams crisis was at its peak, J had to report on the first Fédération Internationale de Ski World Championships at Aspen. The trip turned into a reunion with old friends, for Dick Durrance had been largely responsible for the selection of the site, and as master of the course he had laid out the giant slalom. Miggs Durrance took photographs to illustrate J's article. "As one might expect from Dick," J said, "it was a deeply thought out and challenging course . . . I tried to ski down it myself after the race and found myself continually in hot water." The course was a real "bitcheroo." "Try it on your piccolo!" he challenged the skiing community. J pronounced this "the finest ski meet ever held in America"— although no Americans won medals. J took Margaret with him, carrying in his pocket an admonition from Aunt Leila to be patient with her. Margaret was nursing a sore rib from a fall, but she enjoyed the social life. Once he came upon her patting the governor of Colorado on the head and calling him "cutey-pie," but J had to admit that she was controlling her drinking fairly well, and when she had a good grip on herself, she made "a fine impression."

While J was in Aspen, Dylan Thomas landed, alone, in New York, and, hungover and despite bouts of vomiting earlier in the day, gave a stunning performance at the 92nd Street Y Unterberg Poetry Center in Manhattan, for which he received $500. Then he plunged into a cross-country saloon tour, reveling in the role of Welsh bard with money in his pocket. J warned John Malcolm Brinnin, acting as Dylan's agent for his American tours, "I don't see how he can survive long at the present pace."

In March and April 1951, J was in Switzerland and Italy, traveling at Easter to Dorf Tirol and the Schloss Brunnenburg for an overnight visit with Mary—ecstatic over the birth of her second child, Patrizia—and the handsome and talented Boris de Rachewiltz, whom J called "her zombie husband" and disparaged to Rexroth: "He will make you a knight or margrave in his order—the Knights of Canossa—for a million lire." Henceforth for many years J would address his letters to *Principessa* Mary de Rachewiltz, to the annoyance of the very democratic Mary, *castellana* of her own castle yet clinging to her peasant upbringing.

•

The Sheltering Sky was selling well, but Bowles, urged on by McDowell, had come to believe that it would be doing much better had J given it a better advertising thrust. The original contract between Bowles and ND had said nothing about subsequent books, but Bowles had made a spoken commitment to J to give him his next manuscript. However, when Cerf made a sizable offer for *The Delicate Prey*, Bowles chose not to honor his promise.

So Bowles departed for Random House, lured by an advance of $5,000 for the volume of short stories. It was a "sad story," J said, "that wretched William Morris agent [Helen Strauss]—she was a real tough bitch—went for a big advance with Bennett Cerf." (She had actually negotiated the contract with McDowell.) In J's opinion, Bowles was "a sort of vague type" who would have continued happily with New Directions had he not been led into temptation. J had misread Bowles's nature: he might appear vague, yet he was really cold, clearheaded, detached. He would say later that "all I needed from the States was money," money that would permit him to live anywhere else.

In J's private version of the *Inferno*, there was a special place for raiding literary agents, even below that reserved for unscrupulous rival publishers and for authors who betrayed him. J clung stubbornly to his own resolve *never* to lure away an author contracted to another publisher. "I am too Pure Hearted," J remarked with a certain irony, after he had turned down a novel by Randall Jarrell. "He was then under contract to Harcourt Brace . . . I will never get ahead in this incarnation. Next time Bennett Cerf is going to be born as a pig and I will be pure Objectless Consciousness." Early in the same year J would reject William Burroughs's *Junky*. Burroughs had killed his wife in Mexico City, in a drunken attempt to reenact William Tell's marksmanship, and such goings-on filled J with horror. In 1955 he would reject Kerouac's *Dr. Sax* as well. J never expressed regret over missing these chances to help launch the Beats: their lifestyle as much as some of their writing offended his sensibilities.

In late spring J called upon an ailing Carson McCullers in Nyack, New York, and had lunch with her. McCullers had brought up the question of giving some of her books to New Directions, but J, much as he admired her work and liked her personally, told her that he could not do this without a clearance from Houghton Mifflin. "You know how strongly I feel about the stealing of authors," J wrote to the agent Audrey Wood. His "primary obligation" was to the "young and unknown writers," whom he could publish "if our 'big time' authors like Tennessee and Tom Merton stick with me."

Publishing McCullers called for some adroit maneuvering on J's part. J wrote to his cousin Henry, flattering him that McCullers might be the "brightest jewel" in Houghton Mifflin's corona of authors and mentioning casually his, J's, new membership at the Century Association, bastion of East Coast intellectuals and political heavyweights. The last time they were together, in the bar of the Commander Hotel in Cambridge, J had paid for the old-fashioneds, and Henry had had a very good time, "charmed as I was by your wife," he added. J had learned when to take out his wallet. Now Henry gave his blessing to publishing *The Member of the Wedding*, provided the author consented. McCullers approved, and the next year ND published her play.

While J scorned networking for its own sake, he was delighted when friendship could be combined with mutual profit. Jacques Barzun had sponsored J at the Century, and increasingly their association fed J's collection of little magazines: Barzun would sort through his shelves for duplicate periodicals or ones to be discarded. These he would turn over to J, who either bought or offered swaps for them. The transactions were conducted with quaint courtliness on Barzun's side, and J's collection of periodicals grew to huge dimensions. In such waters J maintained his quiet trolling for new talent.

And so while 1950 was taking shape as a major crisis year by J's lights, by most other measures the year was turning out well for New Directions. Tennessee, Dylan Thomas, and Merton remained committed to ND, despite efforts to entice them away. Books that other publishers had allowed to lapse were now reprinted as classics on the ND list. J would bring out titles during the early 1950s by Conrad, Ronald Firbank, Henry James, McCullers, and Robert Penn Warren. Stendhal's *The Green Huntsman*, never before published in English, appeared from ND. Bowles's *Sheltering Sky* was still "rolling merrily along," with Merton's *Seeds of Contemplation* doing well too: "So virtue and vice contend for the upper hand," J wrote. There was other evidence of the impact that New Directions was having: an article in *Publishers Weekly* stated that one category of customers, students, tended to ask for the location of shelves stocked with ND books rather than for specific titles. Across the country there was a growing nucleus of readers who bought anything with the ND imprint.

Robert Giroux's assault on New Directions for the exclusive rights to all of Merton came in mid-1951 when he proposed to Naomi Burton that "henceforth Harcourt, Brace act as exclusive American publisher of Thomas Merton"—which would effectively cut ND out, even from publishing Merton in the poetry pamphlets. It was a matter of "sound business judgment," Giroux argued, that his firm be given "exclusivity" in handling "all his work in whatever form, non-fiction, fiction, or poetry." Burton had stressed to Merton that J was not a very orderly businessman, to which Tom replied that he himself was "even worse." "Look, Naomi, to put the thing on a concrete and human plane," Merton wrote, "Jay is a good guy. He likes to come down here. It does him good to come down here. He has a soul and a destiny to work out for himself which is more important than books." Tom and J agreed between themselves that the poetry and certain prose works would be ND's province, while some major projects would be Harcourt, Brace's. J might still proclaim Giroux a friend, but his move to preempt all of Merton was evidence that for some, printer's ink outweighed the blood of friendship.

Partly in reaction to criticism from his authors and attempted raids like Giroux's, J considered a formal linkage with a major firm that would take over from New Directions the problems of advertising, sales, warehousing, shipping, and accounting, leaving him only the editorial and production functions. His friend Charles "Cap" Pearce of the publishing house Duell, Sloan and Pearce suggested that he discuss the matter with Robert Mercer MacGregor, who had just spent three years restoring the viability of his Theatre Arts Books after severing just such a hookup. MacGregor was a slight, intense man, six feet tall, with a long Celtic upper lip and a cum laude Harvard AB, who dressed impeccably and favored a sheer-sided haircut that made his ears seem even more prominent than they were. He argued forcefully that J would be playing with potential disaster. The larger firm would inevitably slight the smaller, and the commission men would ignore J's non-mainstream writers while they peddled bestsellers.

MacGregor followed up their meeting with a tightly reasoned three-page letter. A larger publisher had to be primarily concerned with "covering his overhead" through the relentless pursuit of bestsellers, "textbook lists," and fads, while small outfits such as ND and Theatre Arts Books operated through a backlist that required careful "nurturing" through "assiduous circularization" and correspondence with bookstores and salesmen. Big firms had to fire off broadsides; a specialized small firm had to operate with the discrimination of a surgeon. "It was probably lucky advice," MacGregor commented years later, since the era of corporate mergers was about to hit publishing, and ND would have been diminished in any reshuffling of alliances. When the Paragon Mailing Service of Brooklyn, which warehoused and shipped ND books, offered to take over the accounting as well, J again asked MacGregor's advice. MacGregor approved of the Paragon plan, but he suggested taking over "the nettling load of billing and shipping" himself, having already solved these issues for his own company. J countered with a proposal that MacGregor work for ND as a supervisor: he could continue his Theatre Arts business, and J would sweeten the bargain by giving MacGregor an exclusive selling option for all ND books within the New York area. MacGregor would not have to worry about *what* to publish for several years; J admitted that he had saddled ND with a production backlog that would last two or three years, even if nothing new turned up. J cannily implied that the future of ND was in doubt and that MacGregor would be doing him a signal favor. MacGregor accepted. He would apply himself to shoring up the company and soon move Theatre Arts into the suite of offices occupied by ND.

Bob MacGregor started at ND on June 14, 1950. Hiring him would turn out to be the most momentous personnel decision of J's publishing career.

MacGregor's varied experience suggested an adventurous nature: Moscow correspondent for *The New Republic* in 1935, with the United Press in Peking for several years, a Bronze Star Medal with five battle stars from his World War II service. He had been married to the American sculptor Emma Lou Davis, whom he had met in Moscow, where she was working on the mosaics in the subway system, but he was now living with George Zournas, his associate at Theatre Arts Books. It was MacGregor who changed the nature of the publishing house, bringing it a mature professionalism. Instead of the erratic brilliance of Delmore Schwartz, the edgy truculence of Kenneth Patchen, the hesitancies of Hubert Creekmore, or the personal ambition of McDowell, not to mention the many distractions of J's life, with MacGregor, New Directions finally acquired consistent management. Meticulously correct in spellings of names and proper forms of address, MacGregor answered letters promptly (on the whole) and kept accounts in an orderly manner. Most important, the presence of a competent manager reliably on-site led to the development of a professional staff dedicated to publishing. Specialists in production and publicity were hired or were developed from existing staff. Despite his sternness and his fussiness, MacGregor was respected and even loved by his underlings. Junior members called him *Mister* Mac-Gregor even as they smiled at his foibles. If he expected a good deal from people, he was also extremely conscientious and diligent himself, and he was genuinely kindhearted. He had enough self-esteem not to be intimidated by his new boss, and he had a witty humor. A few months into their relationship, J apologized for not writing. "Dear J—As for the silences," MacGregor replied in a note, "I shall be greatly disappointed if we don't have weeks of them, while we communicate through vituperative memos. Bob."

While J continued to complain of the constant pressure of work, that he had no life of his own, that he lived an "awful rat-race," to Kay Boyle he let slip that, nonetheless, "life goes along very rapidly and pleasantly." As he came to realize that MacGregor was at once highly competent and completely trustworthy, a lot of the tenseness disappeared from J's mien. It was fortunate for New Directions: J had been so distressed by the defection of Doc Williams, so worried over the downturn in the book market, so harassed by the business details of publishing, that he felt he had no time left over to do what he really enjoyed about publishing—read journals and manuscripts in the hope of discovering the next Tennessee or John Hawkes. With MacGregor on hand, the sustaining power seemed to be coming back into the very air J breathed.

22

Crisis at Home

Let's step on daddy's head shout the
children my dear children as we walk
down a road on a sunny summer Sunday.
—James Laughlin, "Step on His Head"

J was finding more joy in his offspring these days, and in so doing, he had rekindled his relationship with his muse. "Let's step on daddy's head," he wrote about Paul and Leila trying to jump on his shadow. "I duck with my head so they'll / miss," he continued, and the children "screech / with delight and I moan oh you're / hurting you're hurting me." But there is a dark thought in this otherwise idyllic poem, as J realizes that there will come a time when his children will really hurt him, "(as I stepped on my own / father's head)." He hopes that he will have "love enough" to bear the pain when it comes.

J's resolve of two years before to separate from Margaret had wavered, yet he was still hardly reconciled to his marriage. The "comfort and spiritual support" that he derived from Aunt Leila should, he knew, come from his wife, yet their relationship had become "a fruitless battle of wills." "Probably much of Margaret's discontent and nervousness is the reflection of my own instability," he realized, of his inability to connect with her. "I do not have the gift of the human touch, and have not known how to draw her out and nurture her good qualities." It was not that simple. There was always his aunt: she anchored him. "You are the Word that I can read," he cried out to Aunt Leila. "I was given many great gifts, many of which I know I have not properly utilized, but the capacity for firm decision was just not one of them . . . I am stubborn but wavering, too." Margaret had little chance against the unremitting power of Aunt Leila's support and love.

J, Margaret, and the children were now trying life in a Manhattan apartment—with Aunt Leila, who had suggested the change, paying part of the expense. J had also decided that he needed to spend more time at the ND offices, and Margaret felt trapped at Norfolk, where Aunt Leila and Uncle Dicky were apt to pop out of the shrubbery at any hour, "just to see how you are getting on." It was an infuriating comic-opera turn that Margaret knew better than to complain to J about. She at least was enjoying the city and was paying the substantial wage of $200 a month to a maid good enough to double as a nanny. Performing his editorial work in Manhattan was difficult because J depended on his library and files in Norfolk. Before Aunt Leila's visits, he would send her detailed instructions on which proofs and books to bring.

At New Directions, MacGregor and the staff were working at full capacity, so J could not shift to any of them what he referred to as his overload. He felt that Margaret's resentment of his work stemmed from her inability to foresee "any future outcome" that would free him from some of the demands on his time and also provide them with a reasonable income. "With the inflation pushing costs up all the time I can't say that I see any myself," he admitted. J had talked out his worries with Thornton Wilder, who told him to stick with ND. J knew that he was expected to muddle through yet also that he was unsuited to muddling through: "I am most aware of my own lack of patience and forbearance."

Wilder might be encouraging, but J was attacked along the usual lines by Rexroth and Pound. Kenneth chastised J for achieving a "social success" with New Directions. "Why don't you wake up to the fact that you are not what you think you are," Rexroth stated rather than asked. J had "become the publisher of the post Djuna Barnes and NeoCapote schools." His criticisms of J did not deter Kenneth from demanding bigger advances. "I am sick of arguing money with you," J finally replied. "I am bankrupting myself for writers like you—spending money that I have no right to spend since it should be handed on to my children, as mine was to me." Ezra also excoriated J for sins of omission and commission. What had ND done, he asked rhetorically, but publish a "few books that feed the mind, and a mass of crap, lollypops, cocacola, heroin and worse . . . 80% rubbish"?

Meanwhile, the Chinese-American Achilles Fang at Harvard was diligently composing his "Note on the Stone Editions" for the revised *Confucius: The Great Digest & Unwobbling Pivot*, and D. D. Paige had done a fine job editing *The Selected Letters of Ezra Pound, 1907–1941*. Somewhat mollified, and grudgingly accepting the slow progress, Ezra wrote to J, "MO-lasses, wot IZ MO-lasses," adding cryptically, "Gawd bless Jas/ fer havin more feet than the resTUvum." Dorothy wrote to J, "Achilles the greatest possible comfort! Has been such a relief to EP." Some of his "chink" calligraphy had been printed upside down in the proofs of the *Cantos* volume, and in exasperation Ez had taken to writing "top" and "bottom" for each character. Now *finally* someone was helping him who not only knew Chinese perfectly but understood *The Cantos*. Fang sent Pound a version of the Chinese national anthem—under the First Republic—for him to sing "if only to break the monotony of St. Elizabeths." With his bilingual expertise, Fang was a valuable and generous recruit to J's circle of Poundians. Even more important to J was Hugh Kenner, whom J had encouraged to write on Pound, Lewis, and Bill Williams. J would work with Eliot and Kenner on various Pound publications, including Kenner's monograph *The Poetry of Ezra Pound*.

Delmore Schwartz's paranoia increased, including his accusations that J was cheating him over money, until by the late 1950s, during the periodic crescendos of his screaming vituperation, J said, "You could hear him across Sixth Avenue." Then one day he strode into J's Manhattan office carrying a battered stray feline, which he tied by the leg with a length of twine to J's typewriter. He followed this gambit with the accusation that J and Nelson Rockefeller had seduced his second wife, Elizabeth Pollet. "That's how crazy he was," J sighed. "I got used to it." Once a person had entered J's good books, he would put up with almost anything. "I *loved* Delmore," he explained years later. However, if anyone got into J's bad books, he cut no slack. "Did you see that ASS [Oliver] Gogarty's yap at James Jesus Joyce in the SRL?" J commented to Ezra. "Some body shd get the roach powder after that one."

When Tennessee sent the latest draft of *The Rose Tattoo*, J read it and responded quickly, analyzing the way the dramatist had "telescoped and condensed" both character development and narrative "in deference to the needs of the stage." He noted further, "This work must be judged in the proper historical perspective." J thought that the lines in Italian were "effectively used" and that "with a few exceptions" they were "right and idiomatic." To get "authentic intonation," he would make sure that Sicilian, not Tuscan or Venetian, idioms and orthography were employed. Of all ND authors, Tennessee was the most appreciative of his publisher's attention to such details.

Both of J's Williamses were doing well, and J was beginning to get over his feeling of betrayal by William Carlos. Rexroth concurred with J's championing of this particular author: "I think Wms the equal of Eliot and Pound & superior to anyone else in contemporary US poetry." Frost and Carl Sandburg might have been in the running, but there is "too much fake in them," whereas Williams is both real and adult, Rexroth continued, "in spite of, or because of, his suburban innocence and chronic hot nuts." Rexroth found it "touching" that Bill had dedicated his *Collected Poems* to J, "after the way you have kicked him around in favor of his namesake and the Harry's Bar fairies."

Bill Williams was proceeding well on *Paterson* (Book IV), and J kept reminding him that ND was planning on an eventual *Collected Poems*. The relationship between J and Rexroth was complicated by what amounted to a fraternal bond. Each saw in the other his own weaknesses. With Guggenheim money (both J and Bill Williams had been among his references), Kenneth had spent 1949 in Europe, not telling J that his new lover and future wife, Marthe, was meeting him there—because J, a "neurotic troublemaker," would try to persuade him not to divorce Marie. In *The Dragon and the Unicorn*, Rexroth exalted sexuality as "one of / The most perfect forms of / Contemplation." Such sentiments showed him to be a provocative mentor for J.

Maude Hutchins's second novel, *A Diary of Love*, appeared in November, and almost immediately there were calls for it to be banned in Chicago. "Novel Shocks Chicago Cops," ran a screamer in *The New York Times*. The members of the police censor board asked a judge to see whether he agreed with them that it was "vulgar, purple and in spots filthy." He did. Mayor Martin Kennelly then delegated his public relations director to read the novel and report to him. The mayor had said that he "would not ban any book on an ignorant policeman's say-so" and that several professors and a clergyman had assured him that the book was "OK." This was Chicago, after all! Aunt Leila read a one-sided press account and jumped to conclusions. Margaret telephoned J to taunt him with his aunt's negative reactions. The local Hearst papers drummed up the ban, probably to attack by association the author's ex-husband, Robert Hutchins.

Maude was herself almost as much an outsize character as her famous ex. She had won the Charles Warren Prize for a sculpture in 1925, and then she had turned to painting, poetry, and finally fiction. A dark-haired, strikingly handsome woman, she dressed in trademark black and white and at one time flew her own plane. After she became a New Directions author, J came to dread taking her out to lunch—it was not that she behaved badly; it was just that she would not let him order food until after *she* had passed an aperitif stage numbering many martinis. Steeling himself, J flew with Maude to Chicago, and with his support she gave a highly successful "Anti-Censorship Luncheon" at Normandy House on December 29, 1950. The Chicago branch of the ACLU published a six-page brochure defending her book. (In December, *Diary* brought in $4,867 in New York sales alone, a very high figure for ND.) The evening of the anti-censorship luncheon, J was at the Erlanger Theatre for the world premiere of *The Rose Tattoo*, which would be awarded a Tony as the best play of 1951.

Muriel Rukeyser was "raising bloody hell" over Alvin's jacket for her *Selected Poems*, and J told her that she could not be in the New Classics series unless she accepted a Lustig design. "She is a bloody nuisance," he grumbled. Even Tom Merton, usually the most undemanding of men, was disputing Alvin's judgment about the illustrations to the text of *Bread in the Wilderness*. "What I want from you is a very clean and handsome job of design," J wrote to Alvin. "Nothing fancy or expensive." Lustig was now widely recognized in the art world: because of him, a young Andy Warhol appeared, to produce four jackets for ND beginning in 1951; and Ivan Chermayeff, before founding the brand-designing firm bearing his name, would work as one of Lustig's assistants.

For J, December had been hell, a fitting culmination to a bad year. The month had started out fairly well, Margaret being "sweet with me," J said, and he, trying to be fatherly, took Paul for an afternoon outing to the beautiful Cloisters museum along the Hudson. The boy ran wild, to the alarm of the guards. Somehow, J assumed that his cowboy-mad eight-year-old would be as interested as he in the Unicorn Tapestries. Christmas at Norfolk was a disaster. Margaret had attacked J for every conceivable shortcoming. "She would not leave me alone and was constantly deviling and tormenting me until my selfcontrol was completely shattered," he said. To his aunt, he wrote a letter ringing with notes of unparalleled desperation: "It has come to this: it is a question of my saving my own sanity. I am a nervous and sensitive person and I just cannot stand up any longer under this torment of goading and intriguing. Perhaps if I can get away to the mountains soon and get a decent rest and get my mind cleared up it will be all right . . . But right now I am just emotional mincemeat, and I can't take any more for a while."

J's marriage had at last openly imploded: he and Margaret were not living together in the new year, and J sought the advice of an experienced doctor, confiding to him as a medical man "things about Margaret's peculiarities, which I would not know how to tell you," J rather tantalizingly wrote to Aunt Leila. J banked on his aunt's Victorian sensibilities to prevent her from demanding specifics in what was certainly his ex parte account. J knew the recipient so well that in his letter he struck all the right chords, embellished with grace notes and punctuated with arpeggios, six pages in his flowing longhand, with nary a blot or cross-out.

Aunt Leila stepped in and, with J's approval, in a letter of warm love and humane understanding, unseasoned by reproaches, convinced Margaret to go to the Silver Hill Hospital near New Canaan, Connecticut, which specialized in psychiatric illnesses and substance abuse. She responded very well after a short stay and soon was writing from Murray, Utah, to Aunt Leila, "I can't imagine ever wanting to take a cocktail." This did not presage a repair of the marriage, however. By June 1951, Margaret had finally engaged a lawyer to handle the divorce. She had delayed, hoping for yet another reconciliation, but J wanted a formal separation. J agreed with Margaret to cooperate on sharing the children and arranged to buy a modest house for her as part of the divorce settlement.

•

In October 1951, J published Hermann Hesse's *Siddhartha*, largely to silence Henry Miller's clamor. J had resisted Henry's urgings for several years. "Seems like a find to me," Henry had told him in 1947. But it would not be until August 1949 that J got around to reading the French text and agreed to publish it if a satisfactory English translation could be obtained. J thought that the book was "Buddhism with a sugar-coating . . . all prettied up." *Siddhartha* was precisely the sort of book that Miller could be counted upon to adore: ostensibly the life of the Buddha, it struck J as a bit of soft-core quasi-mystical Orientalism. The book languished for a time, selling just above a thousand copies the first year, but when it was reissued as a paperback in 1957, it would be adopted as a canonical text by the hippie generation, becoming ND's all-time bestseller, moving 317,603 copies, at its 1970 peak, in a single year.

Around this time, Miller finally completed his long screed about the books that had influenced him and suggested "The Plains of Abraham" as a title. This J found incomprehensible and suggested "something really 'corny' like 'The Books in My Life.'" Miller agreed, and the volume became a steady seller under J's title. J had never thought of Miller as a "highbrow" writer: "To my mind, you belong in the great popular tradition of Cervantes, Rabelais and Balzac." This, of course, was exactly what Henry wanted to hear. "These fellows with the new criticism," J continued, warming to his subject, "in their high-powered little cult around New York and the university towns are only a thing of the moment. The masses will be reading you when they are all forgotten."

From March 1951 through mid-May, J was at Alta. One reason he now wanted the divorce to be accomplished quickly was that after Alta he was to be joined in San Francisco by Gertrude Huston—acting as his secretary—and he knew that this could lead to further complications that he did *not* wish to have to explain to his aunt. For the second year in a row, J was entertaining an offer from his ski lift partner Joe Quinney to buy Alta Lodge. J was "sorely tempted." He said that he wanted to simplify his life. Uncle Dicky advised him to hold out for more money, so J was dithering.

The long-term outlook at New Directions was promising. The fact that nearly all of the New Classics series had appeared, or soon would, on college reading lists demonstrated the acuteness of J's judgment. German literature remained under a chauvinistic cloud in the anglophone world, but J had published an eclectic assortment: Goethe, Hölderlin, Rilke, and Brecht. Conspicuously absent were any of the classic Russian or Spanish writers, but J was perforce opportunistic in his choices: the Russians were already well represented on the lists of the large commercial houses, and who else from Spain but Cervantes would be purchased in quantity by students in the 1950s?

J saw Ezra and then headed for London and Paris to collect accounts and visit friends. J folded himself into "a tiny little car" and made various excursions, including to see the poet and "dear fellow" Vernon Watkins in Wales. J had settled into the Phyllis Court club at Henley-on-Thames and met several times with Eliot. He showed Eliot a sheaf of Merton's poetry, and the sage of Faber remarked soberly, "I'm afraid Father Merton does not take enough pains with some of his lines"—Faber wasn't buying. On August 23, Eliot took J and Tennessee Williams to the Garrick Club. Tennessee was on his best behavior with "the greatest living poet," and he had brought a first edition of *The Cocktail Party* for him to sign. "The conversation between the two of them was simply wonderful," J recalled, "they really hit it off." En route to Geneva and Milan, J detoured to the Dordogne to see Heinz Henghes. The sculptor and creator of the New Directions colophon had aged well: striking face of a wise clown with asymmetrical eyes, tufts of hair protruding from his weathered face. Henghes had become a cherished friend.

While J was away, Aunt Leila and his mother helped Margaret pack up her belongings in Norfolk, an event J was glad to miss. "Since the children have moved out to Utah I feel so cut adrift," he said. Margaret found J's request for specific time to be spent with Paul and Leila "most upsetting," said that she would not have the children used for "bargaining," and worried that he might marry someone she disliked. For himself, J maintained that his experience with her would make him *very* choosy about another mate, adding that the welfare of the children would be a guiding factor. J did not receive a word from Margaret about the children all summer.

In December 1951, Henry Miller admitted to J that he and his third wife, Janina Lepska, had separated and that he had custody of the children. "Glad you are able to keep the kids," J wrote to Henry. "They will be company for you and you can educate them." J added, "I miss mine a lot." He was again disillusioned with New Directions, dissatisfied at Alta, at loose ends. It had been a time of fracturing: his relationship with Bill Williams was in doubt, his marriage ending. J felt that his life was in crisis. Alta and his publishing were suffering from the general economic situation; he was too frantic, too depressed, and too busy to write poetry; his home life had evaporated.

23

Public Service: Intercultural Publications and Other Efforts

It does not seem excessive to say that Europe is too important to be ignored.
—Robert Maynard Hutchins, "Memorandum on a Trip to Italy"

In mid-1951 a not unwelcome distraction from J's various problems came his way in the form of a series of meetings in Pasadena with Robert Hutchins, an associate director of the Ford Foundation since his recent resignation from the University of Chicago. Party to their discussions was the foundation's president, Paul G. Hoffman, former administrator of the Marshall Plan. By 1950, Henry Ford II had instructed his philanthropic organization to enlarge its focus to impact the foreign arena: Soviet tanks had crushed an uprising in Prague, Mao's forces had pushed Chiang Kai-shek across the straits to Formosa, Russian influence was expanding in the Middle East, and Western European intellectuals were refugees, demoralized, or dead. Some Americans in positions of prestige and power at places as diverse as the liberal centers of learning and the CIA had awakened with a jolt to the realization that the United States might have won the hot war but that it was losing the cold one. European intellectuals in particular saw American culture at best as a compound of Mickey Mouse and cowboy films, at worst as unbridled materialism, imperialism, and racism. Hutchins hoped that "cultural exchange can do much to dispel these misconceptions."

Hutchins was a leading figure in American education and had been recognized as such almost from the moment of his appointment at age thirty as president of the University of Chicago. He had restructured the law school and had attempted to revise undergraduate curricula around the Great Books program that he and Mortimer Adler set up. Hutchins was outspoken in his opinions and had a reputation for being cold and reserved, yet not one blithely to suffer fools. Always controversial, he had nonetheless held sway at Chicago from 1929 through 1951. He and J shared many character traits, yet J was better able, from his long experience with the likes of Ezra, Delmore, and Nabokov, to control his impatience. In their initial discussions, J sketched to Hutchins what he thought was needed: a beautifully produced magazine that would present American culture not only in literature but in art and music, history and philosophy as well. J saw his role as idea man, a pro bono consultant. On September 18, Hutchins turned him loose: "We want to begin to work in a serious way on the proposal for a quarterly magazine for European distribution."

J discussed this specific project with Hutchins during the first two days of November 1951. As a title for their flagship publication Hutchins adopted J's suggestion, *Perspectives USA*. Its mission, J wrote in his formal proposal, would be "to publish abroad in translation in various foreign-language editions a quarterly magazine of selections from American literary and scholarly journals which would fairly represent the best American writing and thinking on the highest level in the sphere of the humanities." The rationale behind the journal was that there was nothing from America that was widely dispersed abroad beyond such "popularized media" as Hollywood films and *Life* and *Reader's Digest* magazines, all of which "arouse the derision and contempt of foreign intellectuals and students," and thus promote "the false concept of America as a commercial imperialist." While there were fine American magazines, postwar currency restrictions kept them by and large out of the hands of foreign readers. J hoped that a "climate of peace" would be fostered through the presentation of "America's non-materialistic achievements."

Each issue would be published in four languages, English, French, German, and Italian, with perhaps Spanish to be added later. The English issue would target Britain and the remainder of its tottering empire, as well as the educated classes of Scandinavia and the Orient. The rationale for both the German and the Italian issues was to promote democracy in the former Fascist countries and to link them culturally to the United States. J's aim was to publish a subsidized journal that would eschew advertising—"Not even for Fords!"—and any hint of propagandizing the

"American Way," which would only build resistance against what must be a subtly communicated message: that American culture and American democratic institutions deserved to be taken seriously on parity with the best the world had to offer. J advocated an informal panel of "rotating editors." He suggested Alvin Lustig for both cover design and interior layout, with the polylingual Edouard Roditi to be in charge of translations.

A few days later Hutchins asked J if he would like to have a crack at running the magazine. J announced himself thrilled. "I never expected anything for myself," he said, "but if you can sell me to your board, you can count on my giving this thing my full time—I'll even forget about skiing for a while—and my very best effort." For fifteen years New Directions had been trying to circulate the American and European avant-garde on a two-way path. Now J saw a chance to be paid for doing just that. There was also the inducement of working with Hutchins, whom J would call "the greatest man/mind I ever knew."

On his return to New York, J had a long discussion with MacGregor, who agreed to take over New Directions while J was running *Perspectives USA*. To compensate him for assuming the entire responsibility for ND, J would double his salary to $12,000 and promote him to managing director. There was still the question of the approximately $10,000, on the average, that J put into ND annually from his private income to make up publishing losses; these he could apply against his personal income tax, since his company was unincorporated. He had always kept the ND accounts himself, but if he were away, he would have to hire an accountant. To cover his operating costs at ND, he would need from Ford "pretty close to $24,000 a year." With that he could "break even." He would still have his "personal income," so the foundation would not have to pay him a salary as such.

Fine, replied Hutchins tersely, by return post: "We are all very pleased about everything." From this time on J would refer to Hutchins as his "master" in the art of succinctness. Once, after objecting to a few minor stylistic points in an otherwise flawless editorial by Hayden Carruth, Hutchins concluded, "But you know me—an adjectiveless, pronounless sourpuss." J would recall years later, "Some of his best letters read only— 'No. Sincerely.'" "I have never been a 9 to 5 boy," J told Hutchins, adding that he would "beat my ass into ploughshares to do you the best job I can." J now achieved a measure of financial security greater than he had heretofore enjoyed. Quickly, a strong friendship also developed between J and W. H. "Ping" Ferry, who worked closely with Hutchins on publicity. Ferry had been Henry Ford II's speechwriter despite being fiercely unconventional and outspokenly left-wing in politics. J called him a "strange mixture of toughness and sweetness" and "a great fixer-upper." The three men made a curious trio of foxes inside the Ford hen coop.

The foundation trustees approved a grant of half a million dollars in December 1951 to fund Intercultural Publications Inc. (IPI), under which *Perspectives USA* would function, for five years. J plunged into every aspect of the magazine business. After all his cracks about mass culture, he even visited "the Chintz Factory in Pleasantville"—the headquarters of *Reader's Digest*—and came away with the promise of a list of the best European distributors. Working at incredible speed, J told Hutchins on December 1 that he had lined up all the contents for the pilot issue except for articles on philosophy and music and that he would send the lot to the printer on December 12. J included articles by the art historian Meyer Schapiro and Thornton Wilder, poetry by MacLeish and Robert Lowell, fiction by William Faulkner. Ben Shahn—never a member of the Communist Party, but once a sympathizer—was featured in the art section; J made a point of stipulating that contributors would be selected on the basis of their work, not their politics. J snatched several copies from a protesting bookbinder before the glue was dry and airmailed them to Hutchins, who replied by telegram: "FRIGHTFULLY PLEASED WITH PILOT ISSUE MANY CONGRATULATIONS AND MUCH GRATITUDE."

The plan was that "to avoid any taint of cultism," each subsequent issue would be prepared by a guest editor selected from a galaxy of stars: Lionel Trilling would edit the second, Jacques Barzun the third, a staff consortium—with J himself as the most involved—would take over the fourth, Malcolm Cowley the fifth, and thereafter R. P. Blackmur and the Columbia philosopher Irwin Edman. With the reality of deadlines, the fine concept of employing a pool of rotating editors would prove too cumbersome, and from the eighth issue on J simply assumed the primary responsibility himself. J hired Hayden Carruth as his "project administrator."

J opposed loading the IPI board with men from large publishing outfits: too many were "inherently anti-intellectual, though they don't know it themselves." He ended up with only six board members, and two at least were clearly his choices: Alfred A. Knopf and Jack Heinz. The one troublemaker from J's point of view was William J. Casey, in his then guise as president of Business Reports Inc. After a wartime career in the OSS, Casey was conducting various publishing and other business ventures in New York. Not until 1981 would he return openly to intelligence work, to head the CIA. In retrospect, J asserted that he was there "to keep an eye on wicked me," adding, "I knew the awful Bill Casey only too well." The Ford Foundation would make India its first overseas project: India was the major Asian nation experimenting with democracy; and there was widespread poverty, which made the country a promising target for Communist agitation.

Toward the end of January 1952, J was in Salt Lake City for the unpleasant but necessary formalities of his divorce from Margaret. It all went smoothly. She was living with a man named Devereau Jennings whom she would later marry; J expressed only gratitude toward Jennings. J was again considering selling Alta, but instead he and Fred Speyer formed a partnership to own Alta Lodge, thus relieving himself of some oversight responsibilities.

In mid-May, J took time out in Rapallo to be with his *Ruskaya*, Maria Britneva. They decided to get married, but J insisted that their engagement be kept secret until he could free himself from "other obligations." Margaret was not about to contest his decision, but Gertrude Huston certainly would. Maria teased J about "the Jewess," whom she nicknamed "Dye-Pot" in reference to her determinedly blond hair. Tennessee was Maria's main confidant, and he responded, "I am bursting with joy, purely unselfish joy . . . J. is the grandest person I have known in my life, the finest and purest." That J should be joined to Maria, who held "a similar place in my heart," struck him as an "old-time happy ending." J needed Maria to "lighten and brighten his life." For a time, Gore Vidal, Maria, and J traveled about Italy together as part of Tennessee's entourage— Tennessee sitting quietly "behind his shades with that cat lips expression on his face," leaping into the conversation when something that he found amusing came up. J *was* serious in his intentions toward Maria, for he took pains to entice her to Brunnenburg to meet Mary de Rachewiltz. "She is a person who can be a wonderful friend," J told Mary, "and I'm terribly glad that I got you two together."

With the summer "the burthen of parenthood" returned, conducted mainly during the weekends at Aunt Leila and Uncle Dicky's homes on

Nantucket. "From 7 AM till 10 at night I am exposed to the unremitting, unrelenting attentions of two bestial little egos which clamorously insist that their every moment, gesture and passing thought be watched, commented upon, and applauded." On Sunday evenings he proclaimed himself happy to "stagger onto the plane" for New York City and a chance to rest. It was clear to outsiders that J's relationship with his son remained troubled. He thought that Paul set out deliberately to thwart all direction that he tried to give him, but there had always been sparring that went beyond a boy's natural antagonism toward an authority figure. "J had some kind of animus against Paul, a psychotic block," recalled Carruth, who would become virtually part of the family at Meadow House in the later 1950s. Carruth considered him a "smart kid," nice, cooperative, just not with his father.

Soon there was friction at Intercultural as well. By May 1952, Rexroth was delivering ultimatums: J had promised to print three hundred lines of *The Dragon and the Unicorn* in *Perspectives USA*, but some hitch appeared to be developing. "If you decide not to use it," threatened Rexroth, "I am breaking with you absolutely and permanently." But toward the end of June, J and Kenneth were in the mountains of Northern California, and their old camaraderie returned. "Slept out in a sleeping bag under a big old Sequoia maybe 1500 years old," J reported to Hutchins. "In consideration of which longevity the harassments of your colleague seem but SMALL THINGS."

With the concerns of IPI hard upon him, J was somewhat removed from his friends in New Jersey. Finally, at the end of October 1952, Floss wrote to him about Bill Williams's second stroke, which had occurred in mid-August, just after the press had announced his appointment as Consultant in Poetry to the Library of Congress. Quite debilitated, Williams was granted a three-month delay, until December 15, before he was to assume his duties. Shortly prior to his departure for Washington, an official acting for Luther Evans informed Williams that the FBI and the Civil Service Commission would have to make a complete investigation before he could take up the post. When no satisfactory explanation was forthcoming, Floss and Bill went to Washington, even though Williams was partially paralyzed on his right side. In an interview with the chairman of the Library of Congress Loyalty Board—this was at the height of anti-Communist hysteria—Williams was accused of having been in Germany and Austria in 1910 and 1924 (both times mainly for medical studies) and of having written allegedly subversive poems (one titled "The Pink Church"); Williams's appointment was canceled, then reinstated with conditions, but ultimately "all rights" to it were waived by Williams himself. Attempting to help him, the Bollingen Committee awarded its prize (shared with MacLeish) to Williams, who had gone into a profound depression under the twin blows of the questioning of his loyalty and the loss of the consultancy. On his doctor's advice and fearing for his sanity, Floss committed her husband to a private mental hospital in Queens. It was a savage irony that the two poets J described as the twin poles of New Directions stood condemned, in the tabloids at least, of Communist and Fascist proclivities, respectively, and that both were in mental institutions, their conditions exacerbated by their treatment at the hands of Washington authorities.

The first issue of *Perspectives USA* appeared in October in a print run of 32,586 for all five editions: approximately 3,000 for the United States, 11,000 in England, 7,000 in France, 8,000 in Germany, 3,500 in Italy. After three issues of *Perspectives USA*, demand justified a print run of 50,000. This would mark the numerical high point of the journal. To make *Perspectives USA* more affordable in the depressed economies of Europe, it was priced at thirty-five cents, far below the $1.50 cover price in the United States. It was distributed in fifty-two countries. Liberal American intellectuals such as Malcolm Cowley and the Trillings supported *Perspectives USA*; the conservative Irving Kristol called it "that miserable Ford Foundation journal."

With *Perspectives USA* out, J set off for Rome on his way to Pakistan and India; Gertrude Huston went along as his secretary, but he carefully avoided mentioning her in his correspondence. With them was the IPI board member Robert Weil. Indian publishers had sought Ford Foundation assistance in the large-scale publication of Western books, and the two men were to assess the situation. Weil soon shared J's love for India: "The Lord Krishna really got into him too. Along about the Malabar Coast he had forgotten all about the Cold War and was breathing fire and Return-to-the-Sanskrit for all he was worth."

The most memorable part of J's trip was a visit to Madras in the south. Alarmed by the gains that the Communists had made locally in the recent elections, those prominent in the business community were eager to enlist the aid of the Ford Foundation, and J's party was courted lavishly:

tours of ancient temples and colonial churches around Madras; riding through the surf on a balsa sailing raft, watched over by "lifeguards like bishops"; a flight to Cochin on the beautiful Malabar Coast; tea with the maharaja of Trivandrum.

Partly as a gesture of appreciation to his Indian hosts, in Trivandrum J arranged for a troupe of Kathakali actors to perform in a private courtyard under "ominous torchlight," the dancers in violent motion, wearing masks of heroes and grotesque visages of demons and tigers. "I don't think I have ever been so carried away by any dramatic performance," J wrote to his family. Of even more significance was a visit he and Bob Weil made to the renowned Vedantist scholar Sri Atmananda, who "looked like Oswald Spengler made of black bronze." During his formal discourse, J felt an "emanation" entering him from Sri Atmananda. In a later conversation with J, the sage in fine English asked, "In America, tell me, what do / They teach you is between two / Thoughts?" When J could not answer, the guru said, "In / Time you may be ready for such / A question." Even the skeptical Weil was impressed, and the haunting conundrum remained with J.

J visited many of India's great cultural monuments, but it was the coincidental appearance of Omar Pound that would be given space in J's spotty diary. After a year in Iran, Omar was making his way back to America via Pakistan and India. He arrived famished in Calcutta, where J treated him to a huge meal and together they went to see Shantiniketan, the famous ashram and school of the Nobel Prize–winning poet Rabindranath Tagore, whom Ezra Pound had met and admired in London in 1912. As the black earth of Calcutta gave way to red laterite and the ragged city to a countryside of bright green paddy fields and groves of date palms, with eucalyptus and sal trees lining the roads, J and Omar entered the India of centuries ago. Shantiniketan means "Abode of Peace," and Tagore had envisioned it as a place where East and West might come together as an admonitory example to promote world peace. The architecture reflected his vision, with diverse buildings evoking different parts of Asia. The most captivating structure was the Upasana Griha, with its delicate panels of cream-white and colored Belgian glass set in arched doorways rising to the ceiling, the doors open to the surrounding garden. In this setting, it was easy to see India as a land of culture, philosophy, art, and music.

J and Gertrude spent several days touring in Egypt—a romantic indulgence for his companion: by camel to Giza, a quick glimpse of cosmopolitan Alexandria, a dash to the ancient splendor of Luxor, and then across the Nile to the Valley of the Kings. By the end of November, J was skiing in the Tirol, and the realities of the West began to reclaim him. While in Europe he found time to "resignate" Roditi, who had been playing fast and loose with Ford funds. "In the process of firing him," J said, "he managed to get me so sorry for him that I promised I would do his next book of poems at New Directions."

•

J was wary of Senator Joseph McCarthy's ongoing witch hunt for Communists. According to Carruth, J was "scared to death" that he or Intercultural would be accused of Communist leanings. Someone wrote to Henry Ford II that the foundation was supporting subversive publications. A copy of the letter was sent to J, and he feared that he would be called before the House Un-American Activities Committee, which was playing to tunes similar to McCarthy's Senate committee. If J really wanted a tranquil tenure, Hutchins and Ferry were dangerous playfellows: they had been working since 1951 to design the Fund for the Republic, one of the Ford Foundation's units, as a counterpoise to the fulminations of McCarthy and the linked activities of HUAC. Privately, J was strongly anti-McCarthy and equally anti-Communist, yet he retained his insistence that IPI be apolitical and even culturally neutral: the mission of its books program should "be not to Westernize the Injuns," he wrote, "but to strengthen their own indigenous culture so that they can take Westernization without losing the good adjustment to life that they have and we don't."

In a report on his trip, J stressed the "threat of Communist domination in India." In Kerala especially, many Communist candidates had been elected to legislative positions soon after independence in 1947. In southern India there was already a thriving Soviet book distribution network, and J recommended that IPI institute a Books for India program. Eventually, Books for India evolved into Western Books for Eastern Libraries and involved many countries.

•

Back in America, J made a western swing: San Francisco, Salt Lake City to see Paul and Leila, some days at Alta. Both the lodge and the ski lifts were doing well, but there were bank loans to be paid off. J felt that he had to keep on working for the Ford Foundation, even though there was a move afoot to force out Hutchins, and he thought that the directors would like to get rid of him as well. "If I didn't need the money I would resign," J wrote to his mother.

Instead of resigning, J was taking IPI in another new direction. As a cultural ambassador, he had his own agenda: he did not feel that it would be fair merely to push American culture abroad if he did not make a comparable effort to bring foreign cultures to the United States. This process he called "reverse flow" and "true exchange." To accomplish this, he proposed a cooperative venture with *The Atlantic Monthly*, under the editorship of Edward Weeks, a friend from his Harvard days: periodically, the journal would give Intercultural around seventy pages in one of its issues. The first of these would be *Perspective of India*, and other special issues in the series would include volumes on Brazil, Greece, Indonesia, Italy, Japan, and a combined issue on Holland and Belgium.

The choice of subjects for this "reverse flow" probably owed little to chance. India worried the United States because of its policy of tolerant neutrality toward the U.S.S.R. And the mutual goodwill that existed between the United States and postwar Japan and West Germany offered openings for cementing relationships, and similar considerations informed most of the other targets. Since most of *The Atlantic Monthly*'s Perspective volumes were printed in more than a quarter million copies, the distribution was judged sufficient to influence opinion. By most measures, the *Atlantic* Perspective issues were more successful than the IPI flagship journal.

One result of J's new interests was that he shifted ever more New Directions responsibilities to MacGregor. Under the duumvirate New Directions ran more smoothly than before, although, according to some of J's critics, it became less *new*, less daring. "It is what happens when without expanding a publishing house gets older," commented MacGregor calmly. J tried hard to resist this entropic weight with new writing talent, but his own focus on the task was now necessarily diffused. Another casualty of J's preoccupation with the Ford Foundation was the anthology: in 1952, for the first time since 1947, there would be no annual.

Nonetheless, J's old interest in foreign literature gained stimulus from his travels, and he kept sending MacGregor books and manuscripts for consideration. Also, MacGregor had lived in China during the 1930s, and his enthusiasms included Japanese- and Spanish-language books. The charismatic author and actor Yukio Mishima was a personal friend, and Bob championed Osamu Dazai, also a brilliant writer. The various anthologies produced during MacGregor's reign would contain dozens of writers unknown at the time in America: just as *NDPP* had served initially to introduce many American authors, it now threw open the curtain for new overseas talent.

The book business might be in decline as J said, but one person who was not put off by the state of American publishing was Barnet L. Rosset, a young World War II veteran and recent graduate of New York's New School who in 1952 bought a failing company called Grove Press. Ignoring the paperback revolution then beginning, Barney Rosset began to publish in hardcover, deliberately designing his books to resemble New Directions productions. Grove soon became the main alternative to ND for avant-garde writers. Rosset's first major coup was to become Samuel Beckett's American publisher. Through the agency of Georges Borchardt, he was shown the manuscript of *Waiting for Godot* and immediately flew to Paris to see the expatriate Irishman. Years earlier, Jim Slocum had urged J to consider Beckett's novel *Watt*, but as J remarked later, "I just didn't recognize what now seems characteristic of Beckett's greatness." This error in appreciation really galled.

Although J and Rosset would never become personal friends, J admired his rival's willingness to tread where he preferred not to: into the toils of the law in support of freedom to publish. "Let Barney do it," J would tell his staff whenever a manuscript that seemed liable to prosecution crossed his desk. J and Rosset quite amicably shared many authors: Borges, Bowles, Brecht, Camus, Neruda, Paz, and, of course, Henry Miller. And even H.D., who sorted rather oddly with Rosset's more typical writers. The ND spirit was catching.

24

"Le Chevalier sans peur et sans reproche"

I like
that stone burned

hot from loving you
am sinking deep in-

to a cold vast no-
where ice land.
—James Laughlin, "The Sinking Stone"

Early in 1953, J was informed by the French government that he was to be decorated with the *Légion d'honneur* in the rank of chevalier, principally for his publishing in America of Apollinaire, Baudelaire, Camus, Labé, Queneau, Rimbaud, and many other French writers. He lost no time in informing his closest friends, including Tennessee and Maria Britneva, who kept up a lively exchange. Maria's mother immediately christened J "le Chevalier sans peur et sans reproche"—the knight without fear and beyond reproach: a pronouncement that J's subsequent behavior would call into question. Soon Tennessee had "BIG NEWS" for Maria: "The Chevalier and Dyepot have PFFFT! as Walter Winchell puts it." J appeared to be genuinely attempting to break with Gertrude Huston; at least, he had told Tennessee early in February that he had not seen her "in a month or two," adding, disingenuously, that she was no longer working at ND. In March, J received his *Légion d'honneur* at the consulate general in Manhattan. "They made a very nice thing of it, with champagne and pretty speeches," he reported. Each person raised a glass in a toast. Mac-Gregor, permanently on the wagon, only touched his lips to his glass, and Hayden Carruth emptied it as well.

Hayden was now the coordinator of all things at Intercultural. It was a simple description of a daunting job. A highly strung man with a haunted sensibility that sometimes rendered him awkward in public situations, he was responsible for everything from seeing *Perspectives USA* through the press to freeing copies of the journal from foreign customs sheds. Perhaps it was an empathic reaction to Carruth's psychology that recommended him to J; that, and J's realization that Hayden needed encouragement in his poetry and a way of earning a living. He threw himself into the tasks and practically lived at the IPI offices in the luxurious Pierre. Sometimes, working late at night, he would appropriate one of J's fine cigars. He was sure that J knew this, but neither man ever said anything. Their relations shifted imperceptibly from employer/employee to friendship. J developed great respect for Hayden's poetic acumen and would often hand over one of his own poems. With his developed editorial ear, Hayden soon found that he could perfectly imitate J's style, and J came to count on him to smooth over his verse.

Someone who sought a job at IPI was Henry Miller's former Paris lover Anaïs Nin, who walked into MacGregor's office hoping that he would influence J in her favor. Bob recoiled from what he described to Henry as her "undirected venom." Henry did not rush to her defense. J's instinct had long been to stay clear of Nin. In her famous diary, she wrote that "everyone felt he was the logical one to publish me, but he persistently refused."

The first crisis of the year to involve J came when Tennessee's *Camino Real* hit New York after the reviews of the New Haven tryout had called the play "a severe mental challenge to an audience." New York reviewers savaged the play, while J praised its poetic language and blamed its director, Elia "Gadg" Kazan, for having missed the play's "philosophical depth and tragic beauty." When Tennessee defended Kazan, J shot back, "Nobody who really had a 'natural love of poetry' could have behaved the way he did over his former Communist friends." Kazan had named names to HUAC. Buoyed by J's support, Tennessee rejected his earlier notion that he should take a rest from the theater.

J found himself unable to stand on the sidelines; he decided that the first two issues of *Perspectives USA* were "awfully 'esoteric,'" that Wallace Stevens was too highbrow. Dump him in favor of Robert Frost, J advised. What *Perspectives USA* should aim for, he said, was to "break down the barrier between the academic world and the real world." J was wary of his English contributors. He asked Hutchins, then on his way to London, to "get it across to them that we are not at all interested in one more dead learned quarterly where myopic dons can butter or peck at each other." A difficulty of another kind came from Henry Ford II, who was worried that J was "using communists" as translators. Paul Hoffman's resignation as president of the foundation in February contributed to the insecurity J felt.

With three issues of *Perspectives USA* out, Bob Hutchins evaluated the reception of the journal. He spent April and May in France, England, and Italy, and he wrote a cryptic report to J: "No 'Perspectives' in Rome. Few bookshops in Rome. Backward country." Nonetheless, *Prospetti* had been a "smash hit," according to a study conducted by the cultural attaché at the American embassy; in fact, it was "the best single thing that any American agency" had done to "promote understanding of the United States in Italy." Circulation had jumped from an initial 3,000 to 10,000. In Paris, Hutchins met Thornton Wilder, back from Germany, who said that *Perspektiven* was doing very well. The reluctance of booksellers to stock the French *Profils* issues was invoked to account for a relatively weak showing in France, although an element of chauvinism was perhaps equally to blame: the journal was certainly viewed in some quarters as an American attempt at cultural imperialism. The British voiced the same reservations. Still, Hutchins argued forcefully for a concerted "European program."

•

MacGregor, meanwhile, had the ND program well in hand. He was now the recipient of many communications in Pound's original orthography, and he was given a new name, for Ezra decided to address him as mcHoRRRse, suggested by the Chinese character *ma*, horse, the initial logogram in the phonetic rendering of MacGregor into Mandarin. Maria Britneva less flatteringly christened him "Twitching-Unbewitching"—because he flinched whenever she stormed in. All this MacGregor bore with good humor. New Directions continued to publish new Pound titles regularly: *The*

Translations of Ezra Pound in 1953, the *Rock-Drill* cantos in 1956, the *Women of Trachis* translation in 1957, and the *Thrones* cantos in 1959. Mary de Rachewiltz came over in the spring of 1953 to see her father, and J hoped that she might persuade him to go along with Cornell's latest gambit, to petition for release on the grounds of incurable yet harmless incompetency. Mary felt too much deference toward her father to advocate this course, and he rejected it.

Infinitely forbearing with Ezra, J abruptly and coldly broke with Delmore Schwartz. For seven years J's relationship with him had been marked by unusual civility on both sides, and when, in April 1953, Saul Bellow confided to Delmore that Princeton wanted to engage him as a permanent lecturer, he said in exultation to J, believing that he had initiated the idea, "You make all my dreams come true." But then, days later, Delmore said that J had *not* tried to help him. J pointed out the many times he had assisted Delmore, including by paying him "the largest advance ever given by New Directions," and concluded by saying that all decisions affecting him would henceforth be handled at ND by MacGregor, at Intercultural by Carruth. A letter from J formally releasing Delmore from "all options on future books" followed almost immediately. It was like an excommunication.

Soon J's son was needling him as well, but with an irony now missing from Delmore's communications to J. "Dear Forgetful Soul," Paul wrote, "I want you to get me a Monogram Speedo Built Sabre Jet. It is a stick model in an oblong box." Paul added a sketch, ending, "Sincerely & If you don't bring it back madly yours."

Dylan Thomas landed alone in New York on October 20, 1953, brought over once more by John Malcolm Brinnin of the 92nd Street Y Unterberg Poetry Center. J attended the first of the two dazzling performances of the revised *Under Milk Wood*, with Dylan himself as the First Voice, and sent a note to MacGregor: "That 'play' of Dylan's is pretty good." The readings might have been triumphant, but Dylan was in terrible shape, suffering from gout and gastritis, his days and nights given over to drinking bouts. Apparently, he had eaten only a few proper meals since his arrival, subsisting instead on beer, an occasional raw egg, whiskey, and injections of various substances, including a powerful steroid, adrenocorticotropic hormone, administered by Dr. Milton Feltenstein, who had set the poet's broken arm on his previous visit to America. The two people most responsible for Dylan's well-being in New York and for the *Under Milk Wood* program, Brinnin and his assistant director, Elizabeth Reitell— who had become Thomas's lover on his previous trip to America—were unwilling or unable to take measures that might have reversed his onrushing collapse.

J was hardly surprised when Dylan lapsed into a coma at the Hotel Chelsea and died four days later in St. Vincent's Hospital on November 9 of an edema of the brain, brought on not by alcoholism but by pneumonia. Caitlin, who had flown over after Dylan was hospitalized, smashed a crucifix at the hospital, attacked people, and was taken away in a straitjacket to a private clinic on Long Island. Someone had to go to the morgue to identify the body. J and MacGregor drew lots, and J lost. A rubber sheet was drawn back to expose Dylan's face, "all bloated" and purplish. Then J had to confirm the official register of deaths. A very young and very small girl-woman poised her pencil over a pad. "What was his occupation?" "He was a poet." The girl paused. "What's a poet?" "Well, he wrote poems." J watched her write down, "Poet. He wrote poems." On the form itself she typed merely "Writer."

Knowing that Dylan had little if anything saved to support his family, by next day J had a memorial fund set up and an appeal ready for mailing, over the names of the "Dylan Thomas Fund Committee": Auden, Cummings, Arthur Miller, Marianne Moore, Wallace Stevens, Wilder, Tennessee. J did not append his name, feeling both that he had not earned a place in this company of authors and that his own name might encourage others to think, let the rich man handle this one. He telephoned Drue Heinz, the third (and final) wife of his friend Jack, and said, "Will you help me? We've got to get Dylan's body back to Wales." She immediately sent the sum he named. By the end of December, J had collected $15,000. "The death of poor old Dylan Thomas was one ghastly mess," he told Merton. If half the people now talking about Dylan had bought his books, J said accusingly, "he would have been on easy street."

•

J visited Robert Fitzgerald in Italy, where he was now living with his family. Jason Epstein of Anchor Books/Doubleday had offered Fitzgerald a contract to translate the *Odyssey*, and he was granted a Guggenheim. At last Fitzgerald was doing the work he felt he was born for: combining his poetic talent with his love of the Greek and Latin classics. J had considered Fitzgerald an intellectual forerunner, both at Choate and at Harvard. But it was far more than that: Fitzgerald had made himself the Greek, Latin, and Italian scholar that J had once mused about becoming, and he had kept alive the poetic calling that J had allowed in his own case to become submerged under so many other ventures. J felt a vicarious accomplishment in Fitzgerald's powerful translations.

J spent the latter half of January hovering about Maria Britneva, who was in Verona and Vicenza helping Tennessee with revisions for the *Senso* screenplay, which included a collaboration on dialogue between Tennessee and Paul Bowles. J wrote a tentative-sounding letter to Maria's mother, Mme Mary Britneva, in London: "I have missed her so much that I would like not to be parted from her in the future. If she cares for me enough, and if you too can accept me, I hope that she will marry me." J continued, "I think that with her love and help I can grow as a person and be what she would want me to be." One day at lunch with Tennessee in Rome, J spoke at length about Maria, shyly, lovingly, anxiously, clearly wanting Tenn to confirm his hopes for their future.

At J's request, Aunt Leila wrote "so feelingly" to Maria, inviting her to Robin Hill. She won over Aunt Leila, who found her cultivated. "Love progresses with whacks and bangs," J confided to Ping Ferry. "She is a real annoying girl—we have about 19 rows a day . . . [she is] essentially uneducated . . . but full of curious lore." She was charming in society, and Count Chigi entertained them at his Palazzo Saracini. "Dunno. Give it a try, I guess," J concluded, sounding doubtful. He sought marriage counseling from Drue and Jack Heinz, who immediately sensed that J was hesitating. "You must come and meet her and her mother," J pleaded with Jack.

Soon rumors were fluttering about that J and Maria would marry. The ceremony was to be Russian Orthodox, and Tennessee agreed to be one of the twelve to "hold the crown" over the heads of the matrimonial couple. "If this comes off, I'll be willing to <u>wear</u> the crown or even sit on it!" remarked the skeptical Tennessee. Maria in the meantime asked John Gielgud to be a crown holder, which J resented because of the actor's recent scandal over "misconduct with a boy." To J's even more intense annoyance, Peter Grenfell, Lord St. Just, a childhood friend of Maria's, turned up to announce that Maria must marry *him* instead.

Tennessee began to believe that the marriage would actually take place when Gertrude Huston telephoned him, now in Key West, for confirmation about J's intentions and to say that she had that very day resigned her "positions" at ND and with the Ford Foundation; she had up to that point remained a contract employee at each. J assured Maria and her mother that he had broken with Gertrude, adding, falsely, that marriage had never come into question between them. (J had once arranged for Aunt Leila to interview Gertrude: it had not gone well, and J's aunt had found her unsuitable—allegedly because Gertrude had admitted to being Jewish.) Maria mentioned the engagement to the cast of *Senso* in Vicenza, and Luchino Visconti and Franco Zeffirelli gave a party for them. Then J headed off for the Dordogne to stay with Heinz Henghes.

J and Maria rendezvoused in London, where their engagement was announced in *The Times*. Messages of congratulation and wedding presents started to reach Maria in London, while letters of frantic disapproval pursued J from Pittsburgh. "Jamesie! A RUSSIAN!" wrote his mother. "Can't you find a nice American girl who knows our ways?" Marjory Laughlin suddenly decided that Gertrude looked pretty good after all.

J now brought about a meeting with Maria, her mother, and the Heinzes: Maria at her most entertaining, telling story after story about her friends in the theater and film worlds, Mme Mary Britneva on the sidelines eyeing the principals with the calculating air of a mantis. Jack confided to his wife that the match would be a disaster all around, and that Mme Britneva was "a typical Russian mother," but he was too tactful to say these things to J, knowing his man. "You'd be bad for *her*," he said instead. More bluntly, Drue told J, "You're not to marry that woman." While J might have agreed with the Heinzes, he simply could not bring himself to have a confrontation with Maria, and in mid-March he faded away to India and Japan on Intercultural business, leaving Maria to make whatever explanations she wished. Mixing regret and jealousy, J dedicated a poem to Maria, comparing himself to a sun-heated stone melting itself into a glacier: "I like / that stone burned / hot from loving you / am sinking deep in- / to a cold vast no- / where ice land of / your loving some-one / else instead of me!" For J, it had been a close call—and he attempted to excuse himself by invoking a rival.

His Ford Foundation duties were the immediate justification for his trip, but the personal reason for the manner of J's flight lay in his long history of making varied and often conflicting demands of the women in his

life: he wanted beauty, wit, gaiety, excitement, inspiration, sensual pleasure, and these Maria had shown she could provide. But he also knew that
he wanted from a wife steadiness, calm good sense, a family haven with a
good dose of maternal pampering, managerial skills to help him run his
many ventures, and the kind of sober respectability that would sit well
with Mother and Aunt Leila. He would desire these latter qualities even
after mother and aunt had died. J did not express it this way, and probably
did not fully understand himself, but he was caught in the trap of his own
bifurcated nature: he wanted both the dangerous excitement, like the
sparks from a Bessemer furnace, cast off by a vital and passionate woman,
and the *luxe et calme* of the patient Penelope, keeper of the domestic
hearth. His romantic side wanted to pirouette with the dancers. Then, exhausted, he needed a spell of restorative silence and tranquillity.

J's itinerary hardly suggested a restful trip: Kerala, Madras, Mahabalipuram with its wondrous seaside temples, then off to Tokyo, where he was
treated to some "most strange and beautiful" Noh plays. Then J hopped
about the Far East, often spending only a day in each place: Rangoon,
Bangkok, Djakarta, Singapore, Denpasar in Bali, Kuala Lumpur, Hong
Kong, Manila, and finally Tokyo again.

J was fascinated by Japan, partly for the very reason that he found it
"harder to grasp" than any other land he had visited. The Japanese were
very polite, of course, but it was clear to J that they all wanted the Americans to *please go home*. He enjoyed a visit at the home of Pound's friend
by correspondence, the poet Kitasono Katue, sitting on the floor of his
"tiny parlor" amid piles of books. Word of a "very, very sad" Maria reached
J from his Ford Foundation colleague Elisabeth Mann Borgese. "Poor Maria," he replied, "Men are monsters . . . But one keeps on footling about."
Through Santha Rama Rau, whose father was now the first Indian ambassador to Japan, J met Donald Keene, who was then working on his two
major anthologies of Japanese literature. Keene accompanied J to Kyoto,
where J enjoyed especially a walk to the Fenollosa tomb at Miidera, guarded
by simple geometrical stone figures amid trees.

From Tokyo, J wrote Aunt Leila a long account of his breakup with
Maria.

By May 1954, Maria herself had to admit that the engagement was
over. "It appears we have inherited Maria for the summer," commented
Tennessee wryly. To flee the humiliation, Maria departed on a Mediter-

ranean cruise, intending to spend the summer with Tennessee and the Bowles circle in Tangier. When J and Maria finally met again, J brought up a commedia dell'arte explanation for his flight: she had become tired of seeing him wearing the same rather stained Thai silk tie on every occasion, so one day she went to the via Condotti in Rome and returned with eight fine ties, purchased with her own small wages. J had been appalled: "What are you going to do with all *my* money?" "Why, have you *got* any?—I'll spend it, of course!" replied the lady with spirit. She would confirm the tie incident in her memoirs.

Much later, J, kneeling at the confessional of Aunt Leila, told a still different story. His feelings toward Maria had changed to the point that he no longer thought that a marriage with her would work, he said. It was an adage with J that nothing was harder than to analyze one's own feelings, so he tried instead "to envisage what life would be like with Maria, how she would fit into our family picture and be with the children." It was the lifemanship question that unseated his love: "What worried me chiefly was her excess of energy and vitality . . . that it would not be a restful and peaceful life." Years later he confirmed this basic version to his then vice president at New Directions: "She was great fun to be with, but after a few days I just couldn't take it anymore." J had also misjudged Maria's commitment to the theater, thinking of it as a passing fancy. It was not.

By the first week of June, J was briefly in San Francisco to see Rexroth, and on the eighth he landed in Pittsburgh for a reasonably comfortable reunion with his mother, now that Maria was, he thought, safely out of his future. Back in New York, J was soon seeing one "Deborah"—family name undisclosed—whom he considered an eligible candidate to become the next Mrs. Laughlin. He would realize "how really desperate I was to find help in a solution for the future." It was this "same urgency" that had "made me cultivate Deborah." With this resolve settled in his mind but without having explained it to his aunt, J took Deborah with him to Norfolk to meet an unsuspecting Aunt Leila.

She was indeed amazed, since J's letter written from Tokyo and telling of his break with Maria had never arrived. J must have realized that there was a bit of frost in his aunt's reception of his new lady friend and of himself, but he returned to New York without having had a chance for a private talk with her. The letter that pursued him to the city shook him badly. "You make girls fall in love with you," Aunt Leila charged, implying that he was a callous victimizer. He had treated Maria very shabbily. He had published "lousy" writings that had harmed him. And so on. "Really, Aunt, you are harsh," J accused her in turn while admitting that he had been "bad" in his behavior, wrong in publishing perhaps 10 percent of the New Directions titles. But he defended himself on the overall quality of his publishing and, without any admission of hypocrisy on his part, against the charge that he preyed on women. Aunt Leila forgave him, of course.

•

Delicate negotiations had been under way with Nabokov during 1953 for the reprinting of *Laughter in the Dark*. Nabokov was demanding that ND relinquish all film and radio rights. However, he was in a weaker position with ND than formerly, since by now he had published with three other U.S. firms as well. J no longer had much to gain by placating this difficult author. At this juncture, Nabokov offered J an unnamed manuscript that he termed a "timebomb": J must provide an address where it would reach him "personally," and he must promise that he alone would read it. The novel was *Lolita*. J finally received the typescript in October and rejected it almost at once: he and MacGregor judged it "too toasty" for ND. Although they felt it to be "of the highest order," they feared "repercussions both for the publisher and the author." Publish in Paris with Olympia Press, J advised. Reluctantly, that is what Nabokov did.

Why was J so cautious? Not only did he have the certain disapproval of his family to consider, but his new bosses at the Ford Foundation—Hutchins had been levered out as associate director—might well fire him if New Directions were named in a court case over a scandalous book. Barney Rosset had not yet wrestled Lawrence's *Lady Chatterley* through the American legal system, and while the language in *Lolita* was far less blue, the seduction of a minor was more volatile than adultery with a gamekeeper. Yet in 1958, when Putnam published the first American edition of *Lolita*, there would be few legal challenges. Millions of copies were sold. When asked in later years which books he regretted missing, J would usually mention *The Seven Storey Mountain* and all of Samuel Beckett's production. He maintained that he had "relinquished," not lost, *Lolita*. The tale of the nymphet had made him uncomfortable.

J's inclination was invariably to avoid trouble with the authorities, yet when Kay Boyle asked for an affidavit attesting to her loyalty as an American, he sent the document at once. Her husband, the war hero Joseph von Franckenstein, had been "suspended as a security risk because his wife was a member of the Communist Party from 1940 to 1944." This was untrue, but Kay had been one of hundreds so named by a former Communist and paid informer, Louis Budenz. Over the years that it took Kay to clear her name, she was blacklisted by radio, television, and magazine agencies. J helped out with a small advance here, a reader's fee there.

J had really grown tired of his Ford Foundation job. He hated having to be much of the time in New York, when what he really wanted to do was live in Norfolk, to read, and perhaps to write. Now he had to decide whether or not to sign up for several more years. One night in early September he awoke in a panic from a dream: he was short of breath, and he was convinced that his heart had stopped. He staggered to the telephone and called his Norfolk doctor, Richard Barstow, who listened carefully and then cut in: "If your heart had stopped, you could not have made it to the phone. Come around in the morning for a cardiogram if you want, but all you have is a bad nightmare."

Before long, the job decision was taken out of J's hands. In October the Ford Foundation trustees decided to terminate IPI, not, they said, because they were unhappy with J's management, but because the foundation had decided to get rid of "independent" organizations under its funding umbrella. There was a parachute of $500,000 to guarantee the continuation of *Perspectives USA* through number 16. The foundation felt that *Perspectives USA* had not made a sufficient mark abroad. The sixteenth and final issue of *Perspectives USA* would appear in 1957. J would include Carruth's major article "The Poetry of Ezra Pound," both for the sake of keeping Ezra's name before the intellectual public and because he knew that Pound was well thought of in Europe. However, European evaluations of *Perspectives USA* were hardly flattering. "Only the German edition could be considered a success, the French was a complete failure, while the English and Italian had only a mediocre diffusion," wrote Ludovic Tournès in a detailed analysis published in the history journal *Vingtième siècle.* The French were put off by a predisposition to anti-Americanism that led them to see *Perspectives/Profils* as propaganda.

For his part, J thought that his initial objective, to "fill the great gaps in knowledge of American culture that had developed abroad during the war years," had been met "fairly well." The priorities of the foundation had simply shifted. Only later, with its reorganization in 1967, would the Ford Foundation move back into the cultural arena. J now seemed more cheerful than he had been for years. Probably the resolution of the future of IPI and *Perspectives USA* had something to do with his improved state of mind. IPI had robbed him of the time to read little beyond manuscripts for foundation projects, had left him without the will to write any poetry, and had distracted him from New Directions, "which is, after all," he said, "my first love and real responsibility."

Still, ND had been doing well thanks in part to MacGregor's interest in good translations, which resulted in a "definitive" bilingual Baudelaire *Les fleurs du mal*, Flaubert's *Bouvard and Pécuchet* and *Dictionary of Accepted Ideas* (this last translated by Barzun), Céline's *Guignol's Band*, Lorca's *Selected Poems* and *Comedies*, and Rexroth's translations from the Japanese. Dylan Thomas's *Under Milk Wood* and *A Child's Christmas in Wales* sold well because of the public controversy surrounding his death. At Tennessee's insistence, there had been only a limited edition of *Hard Candy*, his volume of short stories. "This is something to which I would apply my phrase of 'clean dirt' . . . honest and clean," J had said earlier, when he had advised publication in Paris. It was not so much the courts that Tennessee feared as his mother. "He was really scared of his mother," said J—who remained a bit scared of his own.

25

Missing a Few Beats

The Beat Generation . . . beat, meaning down and out
but full of intense conviction.

—Jack Kerouac

With scant warning, Uncle Dicky died in December 1954, a devastating
loss for his formidable spouse. According to a favorite niece, she "changed
completely after she lost him and was very lonely." One result was that
Aunt Leila became even more possessive toward J, and his daily visits became more than ever the center of her life. There was also a shift in what
a grand-niece called her "God-based reality," a change from a life lived in
the acceptance of an indwelling God toward a direct pursuit of the oc-
cult. Propelled by her great sorrow and loneliness, she attempted to communicate with Uncle Dicky through her spiritualist, Clara Sage, who had
long been employing her otherworld contact, Lester, on Aunt Leila's behalf. He assured Aunt Leila that Uncle Dicky was happy and "content" in
his "new home." Lester advised Aunt Leila on various "problems," including "M."—Maria Britneva—and J himself, but he failed to give advance
warning when Maria suddenly arrived unheralded in New York. It would
be a mistake to write off Maria as a fortune hunter: she was proudly independent and resented her *need* at times to accept gifts. Tennessee said
that "the help she needs is artistic and emotional, not material, primarily."
She had wanted to become a dancer and, when her physique failed her,
an actress; however, she was too indelibly herself to assume any stage role
convincingly.

For his part, J was profoundly distressed by Maria's materialization.
"As you have gathered," J wrote to Tennessee, "all this business with

Maria is driving me half crazy." He paid anonymously for her to see a psychiatrist, but Maria was able to "worm it out of the doctor" where the funding for the sessions originated, and J in turn learned from the man that her motivation was solely to "alter her personality so that I would like her." Gertrude, meanwhile, fled to Key West during the Christmas holidays to visit Tennessee and Frank Merlo. The scenario was threatening to turn into a play by Tennessee.

In early January 1955, Audrey Wood sent J a typescript of Tennessee's new play, *Cat on a Hot Tin Roof*. "Frankly, I am still shaking all over," J wrote to the author after reading it, and no wonder: the Cat of the title was based on Maria. "It is really shattering, a small atom bomb, and in parts as strange and true as Dostoievski." "Brick is a terrific character," J said, whose relationship with Maggie the Cat is doomed by his homosexuality. Did Tenn see in J's inability to cope with Maria's stupendous vitality a model for the Brick/Maggie tensions? J was no homosexual, yet he had long realized that he was attractive to men as well as to women, and there was an uncanny reciprocal understanding between J and the gay dramatist, an empathy that sustained their friendship. J was fascinated by the doppelgänger, and despite their manifest dissimilarities Tennessee was in a sense his double.

A Broadway success, the play, J thought, would do equally well in book form, and by September it was in a third printing. During the summer Tennessee sold *Cat* to Metro Goldwyn Mayer for half a million dollars. In the meantime, J had been reading "the most applauded younger American poets," looking for material for the summer issue of *Perspectives USA*, and in his opinion they were, in general, "simply decorators." "They have a lot of technique and produce a beautiful surface, but they say absolutely nothing" and seem afraid "to touch real life or real human emotions and problems." This, J said, was exactly what made Tennessee's poetry so powerful, the "authentic emotion." He asked Tennessee to put together a small collection of his poetry, and Tennessee suggested to MacGregor that they enlist J's help in preparing the book of poems: "His sense of cadence, what I lack most, would be a great advantage, and why not use it." J agreed to help. *In the Winter of Cities* would appear from ND in 1956; the reception was what both J and Tennessee expected: few critics were willing to consider him a poet.

One New Directions poet whose technique was hardly impeccable

was Tom Merton. Despite frequent jousts with authority, Father Louis
was made master of novices in 1955. With the enormous success of *The
Seven Storey Mountain*, Merton had become world famous, the best
known of all Cistercians—if not of all living Catholic writers—a powerful recruiting magnet for Gethsemani. Young men drawn to the order by
the book clamored to study under Father Louis. This position of responsibility did not stop him from teasing the monastery in verse for whatever
he disliked about it, including the items sold at a good profit in the gift
shop. Tom had a taste for humor, parodying Joyce Kilmer's "Trees" in
"CHEE$E": "I think that we should never freeze / Such lively assets as
our cheese." J adopted a similar tone in many of his own poems. He supplied Tom with books, and after Camus and Faulkner were intercepted by
the abbot, Tom suggested using Dr. James Wygal, the consulting psychiatrist for Gethsemani, as a conduit. New Directions would send the books
to Wygal, and Father Louis would pick them up when he shepherded a
group of postulants to the psychiatrist's office. So Tom was able to read
Henry Miller, Djuna Barnes, and a number of others whose very names
would have set fire to the abbot's breviary.

J still adhered to the idea that ND books should be hardbound, but he
was gradually coming around, in part owing to the success of Rosset's Grove
paperback list—Beckett, Brecht, and Genet had become major sellers for
him. Paperbacks were hardly a new idea in 1955. They had been widely
produced in nineteenth-century France, and other countries had followed
suit. By the mid-1890s the paperback boom was over in the United States,
partly because the Copyright Act of 1891 had halted the pirating of English titles. During World War II the American paperback industry was
reborn: the small books saved paper and were easily portable by the troops.
When another publisher asked to lease the paperback rights to Lorca's
Three Tragedies, MacGregor urged instead that ND reprint it as a "paperbook," a semantic twist that J may have coined—and certainly adopted—to
indicate a higher-quality publication. He agreed to a trial, to begin with
an arbitrary number, NDP52. Elaine Lustig, in consultation with her
now-blind husband, produced a cover that was itself a masterpiece, a
montage of photo images: moon, wave, and cross to represent the three
plays, and "Lorca" written in the sand, which Elaine had scored with a
stick on the beach at Santa Monica. The Lustigs' cover had a major impact
on jacket design: seemingly disconnected photographic images, linked by

symbolism and coupled with spare typography, became commonplace on American book covers.

When the initial response to the Lorca was promising, MacGregor issued Dylan Thomas's *Portrait of the Artist as a Young Dog* the next year as NDP51, a retrograde numbering. Both *Three Tragedies* and *Portrait* were very successful. Annual hardcover sales for the Lorca had been around 450 copies, while the paperbook sold 10,000 in the first year. ND began in 1956 to reissue the backlist in paper and to publish some titles such as Bentley's revised *Bernard Shaw* (1957) and Ferlinghetti's *Coney Island of the Mind* (1958) in paper from the outset as "originals." Alvin Lustig's black-and-white cover designs for the discontinued Modern Readers series were adapted to these new paperbooks and became synonymous with New Directions for a generation of readers. J noticed that reviewers tended not to review paperbacks, short of brief notices, even if they were first editions. "Paperbacks sell by display," he came to realize, "people seeing them in the racks, rather than what the critics say."

Beginning paperback publication, albeit somewhat belatedly, was probably J's most important single publishing decision. Priced at between ninety-five cents and $1.25, far more than the twenty-five-cent Bantams, the ND paperbooks still garnered a considerable college market. Pound's long-view dictum was proving true: Doc Williams, Lorca, Dylan Thomas, and Ezra himself were now on reading lists across the nation.

It became ND's frequent practice to publish clothbound and paper editions simultaneously, beginning with Fitts's revised *Poems from the Greek Anthology*: hardcover for libraries and reviewers, paper for cost-conscious readers. The appearance of quality paperbacks, whether of the long-acknowledged classics or J's avant-garde authors, was significant for the publishing industry at large. With the exceptions of Doubleday/Anchor, Grove Press, and a few smaller outfits, softcover mass-market paperbacks were usually sold as time killers and marketed with lurid covers that promised sex, violence, and fantasy. Even venerable classics were produced in paper format between covers that promised titillation. Not so the ND paperbooks: chaste, even stark covers, symbolic art, larger in format, good paper, with "perfect" bindings that did not shed pages during a first reading. From now on there were "quality paperbacks" in America, as J was careful to point out, distinct from "mass market" and "pulp fiction" offerings.

In midwinter J and Jack Heinz took a western trip together, to San Francisco and Reno, but mainly for ski touring. Through all this activity, J kept working on New Directions matters. He always had manuscripts with him and would get up early each morning to read them. When he and Jack came off the slopes in late afternoon, Jack would pitch headlong into bed for a nap, but J would take his Dictaphone up to the Ship's Cabin, as he called his Spartan private room in the lift building, and, with a cup of tea or perhaps a highball at his elbow, would dictate letters for a couple of hours before dinner. He would write any names or words that he thought his typist might not know on a lined sheet; this he would wrap around the Dictaphone belt or, later, cassette tape and post it to New York for transcription, mailing, filing. The letters, signed with his name by a secretary, would go out bearing the date of the typing, not of J's dictation, and "flimsies," carbons made on tissue-thin paper, went into the files. There were two noticeable differences between his autograph letters or those he typed himself and those he spoke into the machine: there was a lot more slang, more original and pithy utterance, when the ear of a secretary did not come between him and his correspondent, and his dictated letters tended to be considerably *longer*.

J went in February to Paul's school for Eaglebrook's Winter Carnival. "They even had a race for the fathers," J wrote to his mother. "I came in second. Slow wax." His twelve-year-old son was at the top of his Latin class and average in English and math, but he seemed to ignore or dislike most of his schoolmates. He had set and printed a poem of his own, J added approvingly. In late March they were together again in Stowe, Vermont. The boy spent mornings at a ski school on Spruce Peak and in the afternoons skied with his father. He seemed already worried about making a living, telling his father, "What will I do when I grow up? I can't write like you." J's relationship with Paul might be improving, yet as Sherry Mangan said, J still seemed "a terribly lonely man."

•

J landed in Paris on April 20, 1955, on the first leg of an extended trip. Jack and Drue Heinz traveled with him to Istanbul, Tehran, and India. They stayed at the Darband Hotel in Tehran, the long ridge of thirteen-thousand-foot Mount Tochal in snow above them. They visited the archaeological museum, where a pair of broken bronze visages set *en face*

by a "sentimental curator" suggested to J a "powerful impact of hot ven-
ery amid all that cold stone." This, linked to the telephone voice—or
imagined voice—of a lover "now half way / around the world," inspired
him to write one of his best poems, "In the Museum at Teheran." The Gre-
cian bronze heads

> seem to be whispering something
> that the Gurgan lion & the wing-
>   ed dog of Azerbaijan

> must not hear but I have heard
> them as I hear you now half way
>   around the world

> so simply & so quietly more like
> a child than like a woman making
>   love say to me.

Filled with good feeling, J reported that "the Persians are *real* nice," and
they erect statues of poets in the town squares. Well-traveled Drue was
impressed, the more so because of J's reaction. "I always remember your
face as you came into the blue-domed square," she told him years later,
"and said, 'You will never see anything as good as this, even in India!'"

Soon J was back in New Delhi and using the Ford Foundation office
at 32 Feroz Shah Road as a base. "Many people called on me, thinking
they would get money from the Ford Foundation," J said, "but they didn't."
He ranged widely, spending time in Bombay and especially Madras, where
he encountered Donald Keene again. The two men swam in the ocean off
Madras, went to see an Indian play, and traveled back to Bombay, where
they stayed with Santha Rama Rau's father, Sir Benegal. It was indeed a
princely household, and the majordomo confided to J that the chef could
cook for six months without duplicating a menu.

J set his mark on the memos of the Ford Foundation, Indian extension:
He banned "Foundationese," crossing out those locutions that especially
grated. He forbade such phrases as "the benefit of your thinking," "a matter
of incontrovertible urgency," and "a residue of continuing practice in acquisition." "Humdinger," on the other hand, was pithy and fine. With his "caus-
tic blue pencil," he completely won over Jean Joyce, his executive associate.

When he departed, her letters on IPI business would follow him. "I miss you, too," she would conclude, "and often, often a mist of sadness settles over me that you have gone."

J's primary purpose in south India was to promote publishing that would become self-sustaining through the Southern Languages Book Trust that he would establish. The purpose was to print modern and classical literature, primarily Indian but also Western in translation, in low-cost editions in the four principal south Indian languages, Tamil, Telugu, Kannada, and Malayalam, a conscious attempt to "cross-fertilize the major Southern languages" and also to counter the influence of a publishing and distribution network already established by Soviet Russia. One reason he emphasized classical Indian texts was to "intensify the revitalization of traditional indigenous values"—a barrier against Communism.

The best part of this trip was the excuse to travel widely in south India, seeking advice from Indian literati on texts for translation. He traveled to the middle highlands around Mysore and Bangalore and then to the Malayalam-speaking region south along the coast toward Pondicherry, still French colonial in architecture and cuisine. J intuitively grasped Indian social manners. When a new friend, Govindarajulu Naidu, came to New York, J sent him to Hutchins. "Do not be put off by his extreme diffidence and modesty," J wrote. "This is an old and time-honored Indian wrestling hold. He is a real smart apple." Professional gatherings often began with an invocation: a priest would split open a coconut, place it on a silver tray before a censer of smoking camphor, and then an acolyte would hand the tray around to the participants. Afterward, J was expected to give a speech. It was nothing like a New York publishers' luncheon.

J flew on May 27 to Colombo in Ceylon, where Santha and Faubion Bowers took him to see Paul Bowles's Taprobane, a tiny island of black basalt. The writer was not in residence. Back on the mainland, J visited the intricate Chidambaram Hindu temple, inspiration for the 108 postures of the classical Bharata Natyam "celestial dancers," the *apsaras* that, rather like Valkyries, ideal in nature but unattainable by mortal men, keep company with the shades of heroes. He seized on the concept of the *apsara*, an idea dangerous to one of his romantic nature.

J became friends with a number of Indian writers, including Mulk Raj Anand and R. K. Narayan, but of all his many contacts in India none made a greater impression on him than Raja Rao, whom he visited at his estate near Trivandrum. J hoped to persuade Rao to give him the new novel that he was rumored to be writing. He wrote in English, so there would be no question of a distorting translation. For two days the patrician of Mysore and the patrician from Pittsburgh circled each other warily, riding bicycles around the Malabar Coast. Finally, Rao decided that J's "enthusiasm / For Indian life and culture" was genuine, and he placed in his guest's hands not a new manuscript but a copy of *Kanthapura*, published in London in 1938, but never in the United States. J saw that it was a "masterpiece" and accepted it at once.

This magical part of India won J's heart—"South India is just beautiful," he wrote. Everywhere villagers crowded around J and Rao, wanting to know where J came from and what he ate to grow so tall. Under Rao's tutelage J learned to eat curry with his fingers off a fold of palm leaf, "for no / Brahmin would ask for utensils." It was very hot, and Rao lent J a dhoti, which he found cooler than his European attire, but more than once he caught the folds of his garment in the bicycle chain and fell, to the cheerful amusement of the locals. Pedaling back with Rao through the dusk, J would recall "The loveliest natural perfume / I've encountered anywhere in / Any country": the night smell of Indian cooking fires, the pungent smoke from burning dried cow patties, mingled with the scent of curry, cardamom, cinnamon.

J returned in early August to America, reluctant to dive back into family problems. Margaret was drinking again, and Aunt Leila had made reform her mission. "I've never seen her so stirred up," J reported to his mother. He was resolved not to let Aunt Leila "push me around in everything" as formerly, but he was glad of her as his go-between with Margaret and for her intercession in the matter of his children. In the meantime, J was conversing over the telephone with Maria Britneva about Tennessee's coming volume of poetry, "and hope to be seeing her soon." She had not given up on marrying him but had evidently decided that her best chance lay, for the nonce, in a pose of friendly detachment.

Neither J nor Rexroth had been much interested at first in the Beat Generation literary movement that had begun in and around Columbia University in the mid-1940s with the confluence of Jack Kerouac, William Burroughs, and Allen Ginsberg. After Ginsberg turned up in San Francisco in 1954, the Beats would impinge on Rexroth's orbit and thence on J's. It was his bad luck to be on the East Coast on October 7, 1955, missing the poetry reading at San Francisco's Six Gallery, with Rexroth as the master of ceremonies. Philip Lamantia, Michael McClure, Philip

Whalen, Ginsberg, and Gary Snyder declaimed to more than a hundred people packed into a tiny room. Ferlinghetti was a quiet presence in the audience. Kerouac collected money for wine, passed around gallon jugs of burgundy, and led rounds of cheering. He would depict the event in *The Dharma Bums*, which featured Rexroth as Rheinhold Cacoethes—"bad manners"—or, as Kerouac would describe him in the novel, a "bow-tied, wild-haired old anarchist fud." (Rexroth was all of forty-nine.) McClure's "For the Death of 100 Whales" prefigured the emergence of the ecology movement as a motif in American poetry. The audience was boisterous and enthusiastic from the first, but then Ginsberg, the second-to-last poet to read, gave the world premiere performance of *Howl*, ending in tears. The audience exploded. The final reading, by Snyder of his "A Berry Feast," would inspire the Beat focus on Zen. The media hailed Rexroth as the father of the Beat Generation, a label he disliked. The reading brought the young participants national fame. Avant-garde poetry would never be the same.

City Lights Books would publish *Howl*, and Ferlinghetti would be arrested in 1957 for publishing and selling obscenity. J and Barney Rosset were among the many who testified for the successful defense. Young writers had already seen Rexroth as a possible conduit to publication by New Directions, and at various times he recommended each of the original Six Gallery readers to J. Gradually, J's perception of the Beats as drug-besotted hedonists, as disordered in their writing as in their bohemian existence, gave way to a selective respect. Perhaps J, like many others, had confused the Beats and the hipsters: both, in his view, led messy lives and experimented with narcotics. But as Snyder was to say decades later, "the Beat generation had a harder-edged politics" than the hippies of the 1960s. Some Beats, like Gregory Corso, managed to combine a disordered life with a productive commitment to poetry.

What grew up in San Francisco was a network of poets, with Rexroth at the center of the web. Over the previous decade he had become a catalytic figure in American literature, and not only on the West Coast. He urged J to publish Robert Duncan, Kerouac, Corso, Rukeyser, Charles Henri Ford, Carl Rakosi, Levertov, William Everson, David Antin, and Jerome Rothenberg. During 1949, Rexroth had met Ferlinghetti in Paris and suggested that he come to the West. Ferlinghetti had been invited to Kenneth's Friday evenings almost from the moment of his arrival in San Francisco in 1951. By 1955, Ferlinghetti had founded his own publishing company, City Lights Books. His first title was his own *Pictures of the*

Gone World, his second Rexroth's *Thirty Spanish Poems of Love and Exile*, his fourth Ginsberg's *Howl*, and he would soon collaborate on publications with New Directions.

Ferlinghetti made a distinct contrast with Rexroth. He was completely fluent in English, Italian, and French, his first language, and he held a doctorate from the Sorbonne, whereas Kenneth was a defiant autodidact. Highly gifted both as a poet and as a painter, Ferlinghetti avoided self-promotion with a modesty rare among Bay Area poets. Not that he lacked presence or fortitude: as a U.S. Navy lieutenant commander, he had commanded a subchaser during the D-day invasion and then had served in the Pacific, seeing Nagasaki two weeks after the A-bomb blast. In Ferlinghetti's mind, City Lights Books was not merely a bookstore and a publisher: it was a place, he said, where people could meet and "find out what was happening."

Rexroth and even Ferlinghetti were critical of J for not catching on early to the importance of the Beats, but in fact J had been giving them space as early as 1948, long before the term was coined, by including Robert Duncan in *NDPP*, then Charles Olson in 1950 and Ginsberg in 1953. True, he did not seem especially interested in any of them, until Ferlinghetti published *Howl* in 1956. "Allen suddenly got good," he wrote to Ferlinghetti, although J would never publish a book by Ginsberg: he viewed Allen as a City Lights discovery.

J might have missed the reading at the Six Gallery, yet the West Coast had become almost as much a part of his literary domain as New York. He was quite consciously out to extend the poetic and intellectual reach of New Directions—across the United States and also toward Europe.

It might seem surprising that J missed the Latin American "Boom" novelists, despite his ties to Paz and Neruda. For one thing, Carlos Fuentes, Mario Vargas Llosa, and Gabriel García Márquez were almost exclusively prose writers, and they tended to write *long* novels. Still, this Boom trio was profoundly experimental, carrying modernism into postmodernism, which would have made them a good fit for ND. J, however, was not comfortable in Spanish, and, except for Borges and a few poets, he was not much interested in Latin American writers, at least until after they became priced beyond his purse. Missing the Beats was less excusable.

James's father, Henry Hughart Laughlin, experimenting with a Lincolnesque beard, ca. 1935 (From *The Way It Wasn't* by James Laughlin, copyright © 2006 by the Estate of James Laughlin. Reprinted by permission of New Directions Publishing Corp.)

J's mother, Marjory Rea Laughlin, ca. 1938 (Collection of Leila Laughlin Javitch)

J's brother, Hughart Rea Laughlin, and J, ages ten and five, at Big Springs, Pennsylvania, 1919 (Collection of Leila Laughlin Javitch)

Leila Laughlin Carlisle, J's "ogre aunt," at Nantucket, ca. 1940 (From *The Way It Wasn't* by James Laughlin, copyright © 2006 by the Estate of James Laughlin. Reprinted by permission of New Directions Publishing Corp.)

J and Ezra Pound on the *salita* above Rapallo, Italy, ca. 1934 (From *The Way It Wasn't* by James Laughlin, copyright © 2006 by the Estate of James Laughlin. Reprinted by permission of New Directions Publishing Corp.)

William Carlos Williams at
Norfolk, Connecticut, ca. 1938
(Courtesy of New Directions
Publishing Corp.)

Gertrude Stein, with
J holding Basket, near
Bilignin, France, 1934
(From *The Way It Wasn't* by James
Laughlin, copyright © 2006 by the
Estate of James Laughlin. Reprinted
by permission of New Directions
Publishing Corp.)

Lola Avena at her secret
swimming grotto near Rapallo,
ca. 1935 (Photograph by James
Laughlin. Photos from the James Laughlin
Archive used by permission of the New
Directions Ownership Trust)

J described his skiing handicaps: "I always feel, muscularly, like a scarecrow, made in a dozen sections with loose hinges in between." Shown here on the slopes ca. 1941 (Photos from the James Laughlin Archive used by permission of the New Directions Ownership Trust)

The U.S. Expeditionary Alpine and Nordic Team—Dick Durrance, Stephen Bradley, J, and David Bradley—with their host, Duke Kahanamoku, in Hawaii, 1937 (From *The Way It Wasn't* by James Laughlin, copyright © 2006 by the Estate of James Laughlin. Reprinted by permission of New Directions Publishing Corp.)

Aunt Leila gave J her cherished "White Cottage" in Norfolk, Connecticut, to serve as his publishing base. (Photos from the James Laughlin Archive used by permission of the New Directions Ownership Trust)

J's office in the White Cottage, 1941 (Polly Forbes-Johnson)

The New Directions colophon, based on Heinz Henghes's sketch for a sculpture, redrawn here by J (Courtesy of New Directions Publishing Corp.)

The Cosmological Eye
by Henry Miller

J used his own right eye on the cover he designed for Henry Miller's book, published in 1939. (Book cover image for *The Cosmological Eye* by Henry Miller, copyright © 1939 by New Directions Publishing. Reprinted by permission of New Directions Publishing Corp.)

Henry Miller at Big Sur, ca. 1944 (From *The Way It Wasn't* by James Laughlin,
copyright © 2006 by the Estate of James Laughlin. Reprinted by permission of New Directions
Publishing Corp.)

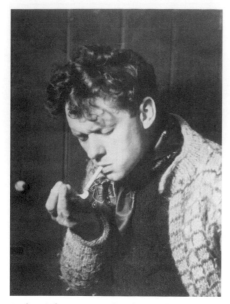

Dylan Thomas in the days when he referred to J as "the little tyke," ca. 1938
(Courtesy of New Directions Publishing Corp.)

Delmore Schwartz, who claimed sardonically that he had been told he looked like Marlene Dietrich, ca. 1940
(Courtesy of New Directions Publishing Corp.)

Kenneth Rexroth, poet, painter, anarchist, KPFA broadcaster, ca. 1950
(From *The Way It Wasn't* by James Laughlin, copyright © 2006 by the Estate of James Laughlin. Reprinted by permission of New Directions Publishing Corp.)

J and Margaret Keyser Laughlin at Alta Lodge, Alta, Utah, ca. 1946 (Photos from the James Laughlin Archive used by permission of the New Directions Ownership Trust)

J and his "best friend," H. J. "Jack" Heinz, ca. 1955 (From *The Way It Wasn't* by James Laughlin, copyright © 2006 by the Estate of James Laughlin. Reprinted by permission of New Directions Publishing Corp.)

J and Mary de Rachewiltz below the Capella San Pietro near Schloss Brunnenburg, ca. 1951 (Collection of Mary de Rachewiltz)

Gertrude Huston in Austria, ca. 1952 (Collection of Sylvia Abrams)

Maria Britneva and Tennessee Williams, who remarked, "It seems we have inherited Maria for the summer," ca. 1954 (From *The Way It Wasn't* by James Laughlin, copyright © 2006 by the Estate of James Laughlin. Reprinted by permission of New Directions Publishing Corp.)

The original cover by Elaine and Alvin Lustig for the 1947 hardcover edition of Federico García Lorca's *Three Tragedies*; it was revised for the first New Directions "paperbook" of 1955. (Book cover image for *Three Tragedies* by Federico García Lorca, copyright © 1947 by New Directions Publishing. Reprinted by permission of New Direction Publishing Corp.)

Thomas Merton, a.k.a. Father Louis, at the Abbey of Gethsemani in Kentucky, ca. 1960 (Photograph of Thomas Merton by Naomi Burton Stone. Used with permission of the Merton Legacy Trust and the Thomas Merton Center at Bellarmine University)

J in earnest conference with Robert MacGregor, circa 1955, of whom he said: "I repeat, Bob WAS ND, but so discreet few knew it. A great publisher in every way." (From *The Way It Wasn't* by James Laughlin, copyright © 2006 by the Estate of James Laughlin. Reprinted by permission of New Directions Publishing Corp.)

Denise Levertov with J at Tobey Pond, Norfolk, mid-1960s (Photograph by Ann R. Laughlin. Collection of Leila Laughlin Javitch.)

J and Gary Snyder with Snyder's wife, Masa Uehara Snyder, at Kitkitdizze, 1974
(Photograph by Ann R. Laughlin. Collection of Leila Laughlin Javitch)

Poet, painter, publisher, scholar—and U.S. Navy Lieutenant Commander in World War II—Lawrence Ferlinghetti in front of his own City Lights Bookstore, ca. 2003
(Photograph by Stacey Lewis)

J with Robert Fitzgerald, the classical scholar J once dreamed of becoming, 1978
(Photograph by Ann R. Laughlin. Collection of Leila Laughlin Javitch)

J at the Gotham Book Mart with Frances Steloff and Andreas Brown, ca. 1978
(From *The Way It Wasn't* by James Laughlin, copyright © 2006 by the Estate of James Laughlin. Reprinted by permission of New Directions Publishing Corp.)

Guy Davenport, the author and polymath whom J called "Master of those who know," ca. 1997 (Photograph by Douglas P. Haynes. Courtesy of New Directions Publishing Corp.)

Meadow House, Norfolk, Connecticut, with the new office wing at the left, and the original part of the house at the far right, 1998 (Photograph by Ian S. MacNiven)

Ann Laughlin beside the sheep meadow, Meadow House, 1979 (© Virginia Schendler)

J in the living room at Meadow House, 1979 (© Virginia Schendler)

26

Trumped in the Marriage Game

It is a woman's business to get married as soon as possible,
and a man's to keep unmarried as long as he can.

—George Bernard Shaw, *Man and Superman*

As Alvin Lustig's diabetes worsened, Bob MacGregor had suggested he try treatment from the controversial Dr. Max Jacobson, and soon Alvin joined Bob in the cocktail of "hormones and vitamins and enzymes" with which "Dr. Max" seemed to be treating half of New York and Washington, including then senator John F. Kennedy. MacGregor was sure that Dr. Max gave Alvin the "courage to make it possible for him to function in a miraculous way." Nothing more poignantly exemplifies the fortitude with which the half-blind artist confronted with humor the terror of sightlessness than his creation in 1953 of the sequence for the opening frames of the *Near-Sighted Mr. Magoo* cartoon series. On December 5, 1955, Lustig succumbed to diabetes. J recalled to Merton the "pains and love" Alvin had devoted two years previously toward making *Bread in the Wilderness* such a beautiful book: "His going was a great loss to me, both because he was a pillar of the work at New Directions, and also a fine and loyal friend." J read a poem by Catullus in Robert Fitzgerald's translation at his funeral.

After Lustig's death, J turned back to Pound's involuntary restraint: Archibald MacLeish had talked to a brother of the president about Ezra's situation, but Milton Eisenhower elected to do nothing. J now told Mary that only "a purely legalistic approach" stood much chance of success. "You must somehow put the squeeze on Dorothy to bring in an appeal to the court that it is illegal to keep a man who will never be well enough to stand trial in custody for the rest of his life." If Dorothy was unwilling to risk an appeal, Julien Cornell seemed equally unwilling to pursue aggressive legal avenues that might have led to dropping the charges against Pound or at least to bringing his case to trial.

Ezra seemed to be healthy and "in fine spirits." He willingly corrected and marked up the proofs supplied by New Directions, "but he never remembered what or how he had marked," and he kept no records. This meant that when the proofs for the Faber *Cantos* came along, he would mark these without reference to his earlier emendations, thus creating a minefield for future scholars trying to ascertain the author's final intention. By May 1956, J's Capitol contacts implied that if Eisenhower were reelected, he would no longer fear antagonizing the Jewish vote and so might request the Justice Department to drop the indictment.

•

Aside from the twin triumphs of the Lorca and Dylan Thomas paperbooks, 1955 had been ND's slimmest year since 1937, with only nine titles published. True, J had proclaimed his determination to trim the list, but fewer titles inevitably meant fewer sales. J would have to face a loss of $24,000 for the following year, exactly his IPI salary. He would have to decide between gambling on greater paperback production or cutting back severely on staff and restricting output to special limited editions. His preoccupation with the Ford Foundation had taken its toll. J had not found new poets who "really excite me very much" and in 1956 published only such old hands as Merton, Patchen, Pound, Rexroth, and the two Williamses.

At this point, J had a quarrel with Gertrude, whom he was again seeing regularly, over the number of dinner invitations he was accepting to be the "extra man," which meant that she was not invited; and he had been seated at dinner next to Greta Garbo, "lovely and very fascinating." He and Gertrude had argued before, but this time, only days into what promised to be merely the customary hiatus, he met a woman at Santha Rama Rau's Manhattan apartment whom he at once described to his mother as "A-1," well connected, educated at Foxcroft (where most of the girls rode to foxhounds), Radcliffe, and Oxford, read a book a day, liked skiing and modern painting, and knew India from experience. In summary, J said,

"This one I'm sure the Aunt would like." It was Ann Clark Resor, whose parents, Stanley Burnet Resor and Helen Lansdowne, had built their J. Walter Thompson Company into the largest advertising agency in the country. What J did not know was that Ann had resolved to marry him the moment she had seen him stepping out of the elevator at a Ford Foundation function, a decision she confided to Griselda Ohannessian, who had earlier shared an apartment with her. J was not as decisive as Ms. Resor, but he allowed Santha to play the matchmaker and invited Ann to Meadow House for a weekend of Wonza's cooking, with Santha and Faubion Bowers as chaperones. Tantalizing his mother, J did not mention to her his guest's name.

Aunt Leila, who had long tried to keep J married to Margaret, immediately accepted Ann. Her family, her intellectual interests, and her poise recommended her to J's arbitrary aunt. Ann had been brought up in a cultured and intellectual environment. Mrs. Resor had been an early benefactor of the Museum of Modern Art, and she had given Ann on her seventh birthday a small Klee painting, a pattern repeated often during her young years with original works by Miró, Rouault, and Lautrec. The artists Peter Hurd and Peter Blume had been guests of the Resors at their Wyoming ranch, and when Ann was seventeen Pavel Tchelitchew painted her portrait: a solemn, tall girl, attractive rather than beautiful but with lovely red-auburn hair. From adolescence on, Ann had spent her summers at the Resors' large spread, across the Snake River from the town of Jackson Hole, where her parents entertained the famous—the novelist J. P. Marquand, the film actor Wallace Beery, Gloria Morgan Vanderbilt. In between day rides and weeklong pack trips into the mountains, Ann and her two siblings, Stan and Helen, had done the chores of ranch hands: wrangling, debarking pine logs, painting buildings. As a very young woman, Ann had been in love with Chuck Pillsbury, a pilot who was killed in World War II. Then she was engaged to a navy pilot but had decided that she did not want to lead an itinerant—or lonely—life married to a military man. Now she was thirty-one and still unmarried.

The weekend at Meadow House was a great success. Ann Resor and the Bowers conversed easily, and Ann kept pace with J skiing through the woods and outmatched him talking about Protestant theologians. She had read Tillich, Barth, and Niebuhr, "which is more than can be said for yours truly," J admitted to his mother and aunt. She was witty, bright, amusing. "I do have very bad guilt feelings about abandoning poor little Gertrude," J continued, "but there is no question that a girl like Ann would be better for the children, and would fit right into the picture at Norfolk." Little things recommended her to J: when she opened her purse to find her coat check ticket, "you will never believe how *absolutely* tidy her handbag was."

Within days of meeting J, Ann had invited him several times for meals with her parents in New York. The Resors were a formidable couple. Ann's father had become head of the Thompson agency in 1908, when he was only twenty-nine, and eight years later, on the retirement of the founder, had bought the firm for $500,000. He managed the company and handled client services; his wife was in charge of the preparation of advertisements, the first woman to achieve prominence in American advertising. Stanley Resor had asked his future wife to become a copywriter for him nine years before their marriage, and a profound reciprocal respect underlay their relationship. Ann expected that she would be entering into a similar partnership with J.

It was often said about J that he never attempted to force his attentions on a woman: he was simply *there*, and many women found him extremely attractive. Ann had made her choice, and J gave no sign of wanting to escape. In mid-March he drove with his son on a ski trip to Mont Tremblant northwest of Montreal—an outing Paul had suggested to his father back in January. J now invited Ann to join them after a few days. Father and son paused en route for skiing at Cannon Mountain in New Hampshire, and to make profitable use of their time together, J spoke French to his son during breakfast and dinner and helped him to work up a report on Quebec as a school assignment.

Pretending naïveté, J said he was "much relieved" that his mother implied it was all right to drop Gertrude. Mother, to be sure, was much relieved by his assertion that he *had* dropped Gertrude. J suggested that his mother come to New York to meet Ann: "If you don't, it might be too late to prevent it." He did not spell out the "its." Meanwhile, Ann was passing muster with J's friends: Jo Ferry, Ping's wife, advised him to marry Ann, but J said, "The question arises whether I am up to her"; and the Hutchinses liked her.

The only problem, J thought, was their disparity in wealth. Ann was rich in her own right through a trust settled on her by her parents, while J saw himself as being practically on the breadline. "But I guess if Uncle

Dicky managed it I can too," he told his mother, bringing up his uncle's relative poverty compared with Aunt Leila's wealth. Ann did not seem to spend money on herself, and he thought that she would be content to "live simply" at Norfolk and help him with his "literary labors." In fact, Ann was already on the governing boards of several nonprofit cultural ventures, including the Museum of Modern Art, and would soon be on the board of directors of the Asia Society. She appeared to be in search of a cause such as J's cultural mission. "She seems very keen to have something like that on which to focus her energies," J wrote to his mother.

Ann would arrive at Mont Tremblant by March 21, and by the twenty-fourth J was writing to his mother that they were engaged: "It was fairly painless as we are both sort of crazy about each other." "I have not told The Aunt yet," J cautioned his mother. "A very suitable connection," he inserted into a description of Ann's many virtues to Elisabeth Borgese. He and Ann at once planned to go to Germany that summer on a *Perspective of Germany* project for *The Atlantic Monthly*—a funded honeymoon! J kept at his correspondence most mornings, and by the thirtieth, still skiing, he had gotten his mother's approval on the telephone, and the Resors had scheduled the wedding for May 19 at their home in Greenwich, Connecticut.

Ann Resor told Griselda Ohannessian that J was "a teddy bear." Her eyes undazzled by love, Griselda saw him as "precious, an artist-type, an intellectual snob," and probably a "pain in the butt." That this evaluation contained elements of truth did not prevent Griselda from accepting a job at New Directions that same year. With the wedding almost upon him, J bought Ann a ruby ring and himself a charcoal-gray Brooks Brothers suit. J caught himself hoping that Ann would not want to change "a lot of things . . . but, of course, if she wants to, I'll let her." To have their own place in the city, Ann found a new apartment at 124 East Seventy-Ninth Street. J was grateful that she had taken it upon herself to have his shoes repaired but was embarrassed when she actually shined them herself.

In the days before the wedding what J would refer to as "the 'problem'" surfaced. Gertrude Huston had engaged a lawyer and threatened what J's own lawyer thought was a "blackmail bluff": that she was in fact J's common-law wife. J was assured that the case would never come to court because there was no viable charge against him under New York law. Common-law marriages no longer existed in the surrounding states either, so Gertrude's claim would have to be based on the time she had spent with J in Europe and in the period following J's divorce from Margaret in 1952. Ann was being "understanding," but the affair cast a shadow of worry over J's own happiness. He had *not* mentioned his coming nuptials to that other claimant to his hand, Maria Britneva.

Both families turned out in force for the wedding. The reception was held in the Resors' shaded garden. Ann appeared stiff and a bit tense— perhaps it was the unflattering satin gown that she was corseted into— but the groom looked relaxed and pleased. "Everything is just as nice as could be," J wrote to his mother from the train on the day after the wedding. Ann was "such wonderful company . . . warm and affectionate."

J and Ann went to a secluded beach house at Hobe Sound, Florida, lent to them by the St. Johns of Choate, for a short honeymoon. J was not to be separated from his correspondence, however, and he used his Dictaphone to compose letters on ND business. Ann's work ethic in both intellectual and physical labor matched his own. In her view, a wife was an equal partner in a marriage: she was quite willing to concede to J his areas of expertise and responsibility, but she expected to run her own financial affairs and to create a comfortable order in her home. This meant bringing J himself to heel in those matters of personal tidiness and hygiene that he so admired in her. "All I have to give up is my libido," he told Drue Heinz.

Before J's marriage, Maria Britneva had declared that she thought that J would in time come back to her. Now that he was out of contention, in the first week of August Maria married Peter Grenfell, Lord St. Just, who had inherited £500,000 from his banker father back in 1941.

By early July, Ann and J were in Europe. J found the new German writers "not very exciting," he told Merton, "but the painters are." Soliciting contributions for the *Atlantic Monthly Perspective* issue was only one purpose of the trip. J was also searching for a designer-printer combination to produce a fine-press edition of Merton's *Tower of Babel* drama. This meant paying court to Gerhard Marcks, the typographer and sculptor of *Passage over the Styx*, a memorial to the victims of the Hamburg firebombing. J hoped to persuade Marcks to produce Merton's book in collaboration with Richard von Sichowsky, printer and professor of graphics. Marcks pleaded that his workload was too great, but he did invite the couple to tea at his studio. J talked up Merton, arousing Marcks's interest. The magnificent Marcks/Sichowsky *Tower of Babel* would appear the following year.

J and Ann continued on to the Schloss Brunnenburg to be entertained by Mary de Rachewiltz, who overheard Ann tell J, "I am putty in your hands!" Then, on a wonderful sunny day, the trio hiked to Vanni Schei-willer's mountain hideout at Vellau. Vanni regarded J and Ezra as his mentors, and he referred to Pound as the "Allevatore di giovani editori," breeder of young publishers. It had become a habit with Ezra: first J, then Vicari in Italy, Schifferli in Switzerland, Cavefors in Sweden, de Roux in France. J was continuing the tradition by encouraging Jonathan Williams, Ferlinghetti, and, at Copper Canyon, Sam Hamill and Tree Swenson.

Ann set herself, consciously, to comprehend everything that she could discover about J and his circle, and she made an excellent impression wherever she went. One fact was made abundantly clear to J by this trip with Ann: his new wife was no merely adoring yet capricious consort. Ann certainly loved him, she was eager to engage him intellectually, she expected to share in his ventures, and she asserted herself with the confidence born of her wealth and of the realization of her own intelligence. Here was a woman who would not allow herself to be shoved to the margins of a marriage, whether inadvertently or by deliberate intent.

•

Unhappy with the responses that he was getting from MacGregor, Delmore Schwartz wrote to J in July 1956, "I'm in the doldrums deep." In probably his last communication to J, Delmore sent a telegram that suggested "SMOKING THE PEACE PIPE." J appears not to have answered, the sad ending of a friendship that had meant a lot to both men.

Tennessee had drastically rewritten his superb one-act play *27 Wagons Full of Cotton* into the film scenario *Baby Doll*. It was released on December 18, 1956, and before long J had taken his wife to see it. "Ann and I enjoyed 'Baby Doll' very much," J reported to Tennessee, "though we felt it was uneven." *Baby Doll* caused a furor: the Catholic Legion of Decency got it prohibited in most American movie houses; Francis Cardinal Spellman announced from his New York pulpit that his flock should avoid the film "under pain of sin"; and it was banned in Sweden. The *Time* magazine review called *Baby Doll* "just possibly the dirtiest American-made motion picture that has ever been legally exhibited." Had J been in any doubt, Ann's response showed that she was no prudish Aunt Leila.

•

By December 1956, J had the feeling that Intercultural was really "slip-ping away," he confided to Carruth. "We really died when we were hardly born," he continued, "that evening when Hutchins was being sadistic and made Mrs. H. F[ord] cry at the Hoffmans' party." "Henry never liked Bob," J recalled much later, "but I think I was in at the kill . . . The little Catho-lic wife told Bob there was this great priest who was saving wrecked homes over the radio, whom the Foundation should support. Bob bit her to pieces and she ran weeping from the room. Exit Hutchins." "For me, I don't care much," J said. "I've been enjoying getting back into the ND rhythm—somehow more real, and I feel more like myself." Part of the rhythm was landing new authors through the network of friends: Hugh Kenner recommended to him Charles Tomlinson's first verse pamphlet, *The Necklace,* and so ND would eventually publish the poet Kenner judged "among the best in the English language this century." Then an-other author was added to J's front list when the Ohio-born writer James Purdy, courted by other publishers, decided that ND was the right fit for his work. "I am very excited about his possibilities," J told Tennessee, who had encouraged him to sign up Purdy.

J was trying hard to wind up IPI, and Ann was helping put together the ND annual, number 16. "A regular little factory up here in the coun-try," J reported from Norfolk. She also took over most of the driving, which now bored J, and ran Meadow House smoothly.

27

Fade-Out in Burma,
New Directions Revisited

> It is a land that Buddha came upon
> > from a different direction
> It is a wild white nest
> > in the true mad north
> > > of introspection.
> —Lawrence Ferlinghetti, *A Coney Island of the Mind*

On January 20, 1957, J and Ann departed for Klosters, Switzerland, for a week of skiing, although Ann was in the early months of pregnancy. Then they headed for India and Burma on Intercultural business. "I can't begin to tell you how wonderful it seemed to be back in India again," J would write from Rangoon. In spite of "great forward progress," much of the "colorful past" remained. "I was able to visit Somnathpur, Belur and Hallebid—a thrilling experience—and one evening in Madras we were lucky enough to have Bala Saraswati dance for us": she was the reigning dancer of the Bharata Natyam tradition.

J realized that he needed the advice of a publisher with mass-market experience, so he had persuaded Martin P. Levin of Grosset and Dunlap to join them. Levin and his wife, Marcia, traveled with J and Ann to make arrangements for the printing and distribution of Southern Languages Book Trust volumes. Together they solved the problem of financing: Indian banks had been reluctant to lend money to printers for their major expense, the purchase of paper, until J persuaded the Ford Foundation to guarantee such loans. The problem of distribution was handled ingeniously. Postcards were sent out soliciting book vendors, the postmen read the mailings—of course!—and many of them volunteered to become booksellers, carrying books as they pedaled through the villages on their routes. The Book Trust also resorted to that universal Indian vehicle, the moto-rickshaw; the three-wheeled scooters were converted into book-mobiles, painted on all sides with proclamations in English and the local language: "**Buy a Book *Today*.**" The Book Trust did not end when IPI shut down, but would continue as a thriving local publishing industry, with millions of copies sold.

For the present, J was simply glad to be in the Orient. They visited twelfth-century temples, J wrote to Hutchins, "where all the little stone gods were doing just exactly what they are supposed to do and some other little people were doing things that you wouldn't think they would want people to know they were doing if they really did them. But it was art, Dr., art supreme, and like you will never see in New Haven."

After ten days in south India, J and Ann flew to the golden land, Burma: the Ford Foundation asked him to produce one final *Perspective* collection for *The Atlantic Monthly*.

J found the people "extremely affable, very witty, and most proud," dis-interested in "western 'progress.'" Burma was J's first exclusively *Buddhist* country, and he wrote enviously that the Burmese had "figured out how to enjoy life"—because they were smart, had not overpopulated the country, and practiced Theravada Buddhism. However, "nothing gets done today that could possibly get done next week and everybody has a fine time about it." Ann, now some six months pregnant, flew back to America, and J wrote to her, playfully, as "Dear ChoppleChop." He had already decided that his *Perspective of Burma* would be undistinguished with regard to contempo-rary art and writing, but he too seemed to be affected by the relaxed liv-ing in the equatorial heat, remarking casually, "I guess I'll manage to get enough that is printable to make a fairly decent anthology." He could not hold himself back from heavily rewriting the submissions: "The vice of an editor who should be a writer himself if he weren't so lacking in gut to set about it," J lamented to Elisabeth Borgese. J met U Thant, subsequently secretary-general of the United Nations, who would share editing respon-sibilities with J and whose name would appear as editor on the *Atlantic Monthly* collection.

In April 1957, J flew to New York "to assist at and celebrate the arrival of Ann's firstborn, an eager little mollusc named Robert," who arrived on

May 6. To Merton, J claimed that his son had been named for three Roberts—Giroux, Hutchins, and Fitzgerald: "With three such Bobs to model himself on he really ought to turn into something!" Within a month J was back in Rangoon, where he had his son's horoscope cast: he would be "respected by the rulers, well versed in science, become famous and popular from the age of 18, highly passionate." The double-edged final point would prove true.

While he was in Burma, J's collection *The Wild Anemone and Other Poems* appeared from ND. For several years, J had labored over these poems, revelatory of his innermost longings. Sherry Mangan wrote that he was "deeply impressed," pleased that J had shed the dryness and "over-epigrammatic" quality of his early poetry. "Persist in virtue," Sherry admonished him, "and you'll yet go down to history as a poet rather than an impresario." The small volume was hardly an epithalamium on his recent marriage; rather, it celebrated loves gone by, and two of the poems he would eventually identify with Maria. In one of these, the poet imagines himself on an Alpine cable car, "& my love / rides up to you on / such a thin thread / of hope trembling in / empty space." The other poem concludes, "I think now I will just / stop running and / take it warm and / easy under your thumb." Living under one thumb or another seemed to be a mode that J was comfortable with.

J was finding it difficult to call up any focus on his New Directions work, even when it came to writing a foreword to *Fifteen by Three*, a substantial collection that would feature Verlin Cassill, Herbert Gold, and James Hall: most of J's text consisted of discussing American writing in general terms, followed by a jab at "the *New Yorker* rule book" for having stylized the American short story. For J, it was a poor performance. In his absorption with matters Burmese, J missed a chance to publish the American edition of *Justine* by a writer he had long wanted, Lawrence Durrell. It was a serious blunder: *Justine* and the three subsequent volumes of *The Alexandria Quartet* would each spend months at the top of the bestseller lists, and the *Quartet* would receive widespread critical acclaim as a tour de force in experimental fiction. It was high time for J to repatriate.

Finally, J got all the material for *Perspective of Burma* assembled and, although "awfully sad to leave Burma," boarded a Pan American Clipper flight for Rome. Burma, he told Merton, had been "just terrific. I liked it so much better than India, and . . . took a great shine to Buddhism."

Expressions of sadness at leaving Burma were far more prominent in his correspondence than references to his pleasure at rejoining wife and family. Apart from his *Perspective* collection, J's larger Burmese mission had not been successful. The foundation had seen that Burma was in danger of succumbing to "some brand of internal totalitarianism" and had hoped to foster democratic ideas. Five years after J's departure, a military junta would topple the civilian government.

Immediately on arrival in America, J picked up Ann and his new son in Norfolk, and they headed west for a family reunion that would include Paul and Leila. This was J's first experience of the Snake River Ranch. Ann's father had bought the first tract of land along the Snake in 1929, and by 1957 the ranch was about 5,900 acres, somewhat cushioned against encroachment by a Rockefeller ranch just to the north. "Yes, this Jackson Hole country is physically superb," J wrote. "The Grand Teton looks like the Dolomites, and the Snake River Valley is broad and lush." Contrasting with the majesty of the signature triple peaks was the rolling gentleness of the hay meadows, the moors of gray-green sage. J fished for cutthroat trout in the narrow Fish and Lake Creeks that laced through the pastures, and for really large cutthroat and occasional browns he assayed the roaring main stream of the Snake. And while J might deplore a culture centered on the cow and the tourist, the ranch itself was an unalloyed pleasure for Ann. She was an excellent horsewoman and rode steep mountain trails with perfect confidence. A family photograph with nineteen people on horseback was taken soon after J's arrival. "Leila rides beautifully, but Paul and I bounce," J complained. Still, he and Ann rode together often.

To his mother, J described Robert only as a "very cute little baby" who "does not seem to fuss much at all," sleeping through the nights. Ann had his care "very efficiently organized." "Ann seems to be enjoying him very much," J added, without saying whether he did or not. Robert slept in his parents' room, but the boy, he implied, was entirely her business.

J seemed to be enjoying reconnecting with his family, yet Paul exasperated him. "It is painful for me to have a son who wants to look at the rubbish on television all evening rather than read a good book," J said, but he had long since recognized that it was impossible to force the boy to do anything he was set against. A four-day trip with packhorses into the Gros Ventre range excited Paul. J himself did not enjoy one important aspect of the trip. "I hate horses. Horses hate me," he said. "When I try to put the bridle on they bite me." For J the adventure was redeemed by the presence of Kenneth Rexroth, who rode along with his seven-year-old daughter, Mary, and "kept us in stitches the whole time."

J was aware that he had been neglecting ND while he had spent five years concentrating on Intercultural and Asia, but he asserted that it had not been "a blind alley." His tastes in literature, art, music, and dance now included strong Indian and Japanese elements. He had emerged far more cosmopolitan, and his American and Euro-centered horizons opened out to add a distinctly Asian dimension. Back in the United States, through Intercultural in 1956, he sponsored the first American appearance of the great Bengali musician and composer Ravi Shankar, who obliged J with a private raga recital at the Resor seniors' Manhattan apartment.

With his return from Burma, the influence of his travels continued to appear in the New Directions front list. Previously, there had been a number of anthologies and books on Eastern writers and on Oriental themes by Westerners, books by Hesse, Merton, Henri Michaux, Pound, Rexroth. To these were added now or in the years soon to come Ilangô Adigal's *Shilappadikaram*; *The Dhammapada* by the Buddha; Bankim-Chandra Chatterjee's *Krishnakanta's Will*; an anthology of Bengali authors, *Green and Gold*; P. Lal's *Great Sanskrit Plays*; Raja Rao's *Kanthapura*. Robert MacGregor's interest in Japan was largely responsible, with J's concurrence, for the adoption of Yukio Mishima and of two novels by Osamu Dazai.

While J had been distracted by Intercultural, American poetry had achieved a major florescence. In 1956, Richard Eberhart had noted, "The West Coast is the liveliest spot in the country today." From his megaphone at KPFA, Rexroth had concentrated the focus on the Bay Area, where there were invariably several poetry readings each week. Postcards flew about with announcements of poetry nights: "Allen Ginsberg blowing hot; Gary Snyder blowing cool; Philip Whalen puffing the laconic tuba; Mike McClure his hip highnotes; Rexroth on the big bass drum." Eberhart stated that J's poetry had influenced Ferlinghetti's *Pictures of the Gone World*. An article in *The New York Times* the following year listed James Laughlin with Cummings and Patchen among a handful of "thoroughbreds in the poets' stable"; J was finally receiving wider recognition as a poet, thanks in part to his *Wild Anemone* collection.

•

Having turned somewhat tardily to paperbacks, New Directions was charging into the paperback market. Of the thirty titles for 1957, fourteen were paperbooks, including Kay Boyle's *Thirty Stories*, Hesse's *Siddhartha*, Pound's *Selected Poems*, Rimbaud's *Illuminations*, Dylan Thomas's *Under Milk Wood*, and, for the first time in paper, three of J's *NDPP* anthologies. Also, J's renewed involvement in ND was becoming apparent. In 1955 the English-born Denise Levertov, whom J had met in Paris in 1947, had sent him a collection of her poems. Rexroth had included her in his *New British Poets* anthology and had been urging J to publish a volume of her poetry, but his reply to Levertov was hardly enthusiastic. "As I wrote Kenneth, I like them," J responded, "but cannot seem to make up my mind whether I like them enough to go through the ordeal of publishing—for it is an ordeal these days when one has to battle so terrifically to get a poet across." In other words, J was not sure her poems merited the battle. Now, however, he selected several of her poems for *NDPP 1957*, and in 1958 he offered her a contract for a book of poems, sight unseen. He had made up his mind.

One project that ran on into 1959 was the publication of *The Henry Miller Reader*, which brought Lawrence Durrell to the ND list as an editor. Learning that a Henry Miller omnibus volume had been proposed for the Viking Portable Library series, J was reluctant to have Viking nab the profit from works by Miller that ND had kept in print for decades. After pledging to give the editor free choice on the contents, Henry could not resist jumping in with advice and demanded cutting the "Mona" passages from the *Tropics*. Durrell was aghast, saying that it would be like bringing out an anthology of Dante with "no mention of Beatrice!" Henry held firm. Knowing the difficulties under which he had labored, MacGregor conceded that "Durrell has obviously done an incredible job." Others thought so too: Barzun and Trilling asked for *The Henry Miller Reader* for their Mid-Century Book Club, and both the Readers' Subscription and the Marboro Book Clubs made bids for more than $8,000.

•

The resolution of Ezra's incarceration evolved more like a melting glacier than the rush of an avalanche. When Dag Hammarskjöld, secretary-general of the United Nations, read *The Cantos* for inspiration on ways to *find* world peace and stated publicly in 1954, "We must be seers and explorers like Ezra Pound," it was evident that his continuation in St. Elizabeths had become a source of embarrassment internationally for the United States. Vatican Radio broadcast an appeal for his release, and Italy said he would be welcome. Then, when the mobster and convicted felon Lucky Luciano was repatriated to his homeland, one Italian deputy asked, "If the U.S. can send us back such characters as Luciano without our asking for them, can't the U.S. also send us Ezra Pound on our request?"

As the campaign for Pound's release was building, the *New York Herald Tribune* published a three-part article on Pound's relationship with John Kasper, a notorious American racist who had been received by Ezra at St. Elizabeths. J doubted that there could be any favorable outcome while the Kasper flap resonated, but one day, while having breakfast with his brother-in-law, Gabriel Hauge, J related "Ez's sad story." "That poor man, that's awful, maybe we can do something about that," Hauge volunteered. Since he was the special assistant to President Eisenhower for economic affairs, with access to Attorney General William Rogers and to White House chief of staff Sherman Adams, he could move quietly behind the scenes. MacLeish had already enlisted the aid of Robert Frost, probably the most beloved poet in America at the time and one who, forty years earlier, had owed his first success as a poet to Pound's support in England. A letter "organized" by MacLeish and promoted by J was signed by Eliot, Frost, Hemingway, and many other figures of world standing. The trick was to ensure that this letter would actually reach Eisenhower or at least someone whose word he would take. In February 1958, it was routed to Rogers through Hauge. That same month Frost was Eisenhower's guest at an informal White House supper and discussed Pound with him. The president initialed a note implying that twelve years in St. Liz was enough. Sherman Adams took this note to the Justice Department, and on April 18, 1958, the chief judge, Bolitha Laws, who had committed Pound to St. Elizabeths in the first place, formally dismissed the charges and ordered his release. That afternoon Ezra went without official escort to Washington. J thought Ezra "terribly shaken by his release," lost outside the protective shell of St. Elizabeths.

A flurry of activity ensued. J suggested that Pound make a series of readings on tape, to be sold later to record companies. In mid-June, J went to Washington for the recording session at the Library of Congress. At first Ezra was hesitant, but then he got a grip on himself and read "Moeurs Contemporaines," "Cantico del Sole," and parts of the "Hugh Selwyn Mauberley" sequence in his rolling, bardic voice. J arranged for Richard Avedon to photograph Pound at Rutherford while Ezra was staying with Bill Williams: it was a hot day, and Avedon shot the two old poets out of doors, Ezra with his shirt unbuttoned to the waist. J summed up their often turbulent relationship: "I think the attraction for Ezra was that Bill would put up with him and listen, when most of the other people just thought he was an oddball."

When Pound left the United States on June 30 aboard the Italian ship *Cristoforo Colombo*, MacGregor brought champagne. J was on his way to the Snake River Ranch, unable to see him off. When the ship docked in Naples and the reporters asked him what twelve years in an American asylum had been like, he snapped, "All America is an insane asylum!" He followed this up with a stiff-armed Fascist salute. J grinned and groaned, thinking of incorrigible Ez, and he had his own take on the gesture: in the famous photograph Pound is smiling, he noticed, "probably laughing at his own joke."

•

While Ezra's years at St. Elizabeths were still dragging on, poetry had been going public. Dylan Thomas's wildly popular readings of 1951 and 1952 had brought poetry to the public, and the memory of these readings lingered in San Francisco, where in February 1955 the poet-pianist Weldon Kees assembled a small jazz group to which several poets read. In this vaudevillian atmosphere Ferlinghetti read his translations of Prévert, and in 1957 Rexroth invited him to take part in the innovative jazz-poetry evenings at the Cellar. J applauded the revitalization of poetry as a performance art. Philip Lamantia and Patchen, independently of each other, took the performance concept to Greenwich Village; *Time* magazine wrote about the performances, and *Life* photographed the Beats. Poetry had arrived in mainstream America, and San Francisco was where it was most happening.

Rexroth had come to recognize Ferlinghetti's genuine poetic voice, "completely independent of any other poet writing in English." Then, inspired by an unconditionally laudatory review by Rexroth of his *Pictures of the Gone World* and driven by his social and political passions, Ferlinghetti wrote out at blazing speed a series of twenty-nine interrelated poems and sent the lot to New Directions, almost without revision. Before leaving for Burma in early 1957, J had written enthusiastically to Ferlinghetti about his "'Coney Island of the Mind' collection," the title borrowed from Henry Miller's *Into the Night Life*. J told Ferlinghetti that he was "certainly getting to be a very good writer of poems." J had ordered a large printing because, as he wrote in the cover copy, "it seems clear that Lawrence Ferlinghetti is that rare phenomenon nowadays: a poet of real stature who will be admired by a wide audience." J's decision to publish *Coney Island* as a *paperbook* first edition, a breakthrough for ND, owed a lot to the example of Rosset. "I understand that Grove Press has had pretty good success doing new poetry in paperback form," J said, "and I think we ought to experiment with this, and . . . you are just the man to begin with, because you are so lucid, not to mention your wonderful wit and verbal color." J's enthusiasm for *Coney Island* was borne out by sales of more than 10,000 copies in twelve months, setting a record for a single ND poetry volume. Sales eventually surpassed a million copies.

New Directions had continued to publish Bill Williams's poetry while J was with the Ford Foundation, and seven titles, some of them reprints, had come out between 1950 and 1957. Their communications became less frequent but had continued friendly except in September 1953, when Williams, going back on his promise to J, gave Random House a volume of poetry, *The Desert Music*. "How can you be so brutal?" J had exclaimed; "Quite apart from sentiment and honor, it messes things up so to have poems which we will want to add to the *Collected* eventually under another imprint." Then, in 1955, Williams decided that the long "Asphodel" poem, which he had intended as part of *Paterson* (Book V)—and which he had also promised to J—did not fit there; it would go to Random to be the final poem in *Journey to Love*. Now, however, J was editing this latest section of *Paterson* for September publication. "J. has been occupied with a very careful study of the text for corrections I might have missed," wrote Williams to Zukofsky. It was a sign of his gratitude; reconciliation was in the air.

On September 17, 1958, Ann and J gave a party at her parents' Manhattan apartment at 66 East Seventy-Ninth Street to celebrate William Carlos Williams's seventy-fifth birthday and the publication of the fifth volume of *Paterson*. The event marked the full reconciliation between poet and publisher. Some seventy distinguished literati accepted J's invitation. It was a tribute to the respect and affection that the New York cultural scene had for Williams. In deference to Bill, J invited David McDowell; he did not accept. J found the guest of honor "very gay and bright and full of life and ideas." In his thank-you letter Williams said that if there were to be a sixth *Paterson* section, he would ask ND to publish it. This was not to be: a massive stroke felled him nearly a month later, and he would never again be able to make the required effort.

28

New Directions Twenty-Five Years On

He is the John the Baptist of American publishing.
—Clifton Fadiman on James Laughlin

J's life appeared to be going well at the beginning of 1959: several volumes of his own poetry were in print; Alta was thriving, with more than 40,000 paying visitors in the best years; and three children bore the Laughlin name. J was recognized worldwide as a major avant-garde publisher, and his personal friendships included an international assortment of intriguing characters, both obscure and famous. It would be bad joss to express contentment, however. "I am very disillusioned about the society in which we live," J wrote to "Dr." Bob Hutchins:

I also brood about the life on other planets, though impersonally, as I do not wish or expect to travel to them. But it is like I used to say to Uncle Tom Merton down there in Kentucky, I would say to him, Well, what about all those Indians and Chinese, what about them, there are MORE of them. You see what a low mind I have, Dr., it can hardly rise above statistics . . .

My low mind figures out that pretty soon it will just come to where they will say they will find a chemical to inject into people so that they will all have the bonvivery of Uncle Thornton [Wilder].

Low thoughts like this are the result of acting, as L. Kirstein once pointed out, as if one were interested in becoming Ambassador to Patagonia . . . This is not frivolity, it is simply the moment of facing up. Not having your character, Dr., I do not simply get up an hour earlier every morning and stare at my typewriter; the pill has to be chocolate.

Aside from his everlasting guilt over not writing, a part of J's discontent stemmed from a fracas with Nabokov over *The Real Life of Sebastian Knight* and his monograph *Nikolai Gogol*. New Directions wanted to reissue both in the paperbook series to boost college sales, but the author demanded that the former be reprinted in cloth only; he was willing to permit the binding of existing sheets of *Gogol* in paper but would not allow a new paper edition when the current stock sold out. On March 11, J spent "a very pleasant hour" with Véra and Vladimir, finding them "as agreeable and diverting as ever," yet he could make "absolutely no headway" on the points at issue between them. And Vladimir's intransigence was blocking ND's attempts to get his books issued in paper in England. It was also a principle with the Nabokovs not to use literary agents, even though J tried to point out to them that a *good* agent would negotiate sound contracts and probably increase revenue for them. J could awaken no logic in his Russian friends. No wonder Nabokov got into some "terrible messes" and kept changing American publishers, MacGregor noted. It might sound strange, J arguing on behalf of literary agents, since it was an article of faith with him that they tended to treat an author "like a commodity to be bartered in the marketplace," yet he also recognized the value of a focused sales approach such as an agent would promote. Over the years J had established understandings with agents whom he trusted absolutely: Agence Hoffman in Paris, Laurence Pollinger in the United Kingdom, and Erich Linder of the Agenzia Letteraria Internazionale in Italy.

The "chess game," as J came to call it, with Nabokov went on and on. In 1962, Nabokov would argue cleverly that ND could hardly have been envisioning paperback rights back in 1941, when such books were "practically non-existent." Check! "Just stand firm in a friendly way, I guess," J advised MacGregor, who in a two-page memo reaffirmed the joint rights of the co-proprietors, pointing out that the author had agreed to the terms in each case. Terming MacGregor's reply "disappointing," Nabokov went from suggesting that their lawyers settle the matter to demanding "arbitration." Knight's gambit! "I would say, politely, that we feel there is nothing to arbitrate and must maintain our position," J counseled Bob. "If they really want to sue us, we could back down <u>then</u>." Feint! MacGregor remarked ruefully that whereas Nabokov at one time described his "chief indoor hobby" as "thinking up chess problems for experts," he must have changed that to "problems for publishers." There were compensations for the match with Vladimir: during the twelve months ending June 30, 1962, the paperback reprint of *Laughter in the Dark* sold approximately 84,000 copies, and that year ND collected an agent's fee of $1,800 for film rights. Not until the year of Nabokov's death, 1977, would a paperbook edition of *Sebastian Knight* be published.

•

Alta had become so popular that J considered adding a fourth ski lift and enlarging the lodge. J did not really like the idea of expanding Alta, but new lifts and groomed slopes were what people expected, and there was a lot of money to be made in giving the public what it wanted. "It does them no harm," he rationalized, "and they are better doing that than helling around Salt Lake City. The Mormon Church thinks well of me. They say I raise the moral tone of Mormon youth." Ann did not share J's qualms about the burgeoning popularity of skiing, and she pushed Alta as being suitable for all ages.

The Alta Ski Lift Company and Alta Lodge continued to be operated as separate institutions, the one requiring technical and operational decisions, the other needing day-to-day oversight. One night there was a square dance and the floor broke. "I said, that's it," J would recall, and he decided to sell the lodge. Some days later he went hiking with William H. Levitt, a New York filmmaker who had come to Alta in 1954 to learn skiing and had, in effect, never left. Now, in 1959, J stood on a ridge of the Wasatch range, his gaze amorously tracing the familiar shapes. "By the way, would you like to buy the lodge?" he asked Levitt, speaking as casually as if he were offering his old station wagon. There was no mention of a price, until J said to Levitt, "I've been looking through my papers, and I think it will have to cost . . . ," and he named a figure. "That's fine," Levitt replied. A few days later J phoned, sounding agitated. "Bill, it will cost you a bit less than I told you. I just turned up . . . ," and he named a credit. More days passed, and it was J on the horn again, sounding almost speechless with embarrassment: "Bill, it's still *less*, but not as *much* less." Finally, the two men signed a contract that left the final figure blank, to be determined later.

J retained the Alta Ski Lift Company, which ran the skiing operation; Levitt owned the lodge. "We swapped some stock," Levitt recalled, "so we would each have a stake in the other's venture, but later we swapped it back." J wanted Alta to endure as the purist's ski range of his original conception, and Levitt subscribed to this vision. Keeping the prices down remained a primary objective for J. At one meeting of the ski lift staff, he asked, "What should we charge? . . . We have an obligation to the people in the valley." They settled on $16 for a day lift ticket, well below the cost at nearby ski venues.

Even the workaholic MacGregor described J as "enormously busy" in the spring of 1959. Alta, New Directions, family—everything seemed to require his attention. In early February, J went to Sarasota to help Aunt Leila with the maintenance of her properties, taking with him five of Purusottama Lal's translations of Sanskrit plays for a careful reading, "since this is a project close to his heart," as MacGregor told Lal. J had met P. Lal—he always used merely the initial—in Calcutta in 1954. He had chanced upon Lal's "transcreation" of Kalidasa's *Shakuntala* in an obscure magazine and, impressed with the idiomatic vigor of Lal's writing, offered what seemed to the young Punjabi a "princely advance" for translating six plays from the Sanskrit. Lal called his work transcreation because he saw his challenge not merely to render an actable text in English but to create a bridge for the non-Indian audience to cross to the various levels of Sanskrit culture. J in turn saw *Shakuntala* as the *clou* to the volume, a key work little read in the West, although praised by many from Goethe to Tagore. The volume, begun at J's urging in 1954, would include Lal's scholarly introduction, making it both an introduction to Sanskrit drama and an excellent teaching text. Lal came to Meadow House, and J teased Professor Lal about living in Soviet-leaning West Bengal and christened him "Profsky." The name stuck, as Lal's friends adopted it. J got Lal on skis and tried to teach him the basics. "I was a hopeless student," Lal admitted. "I just couldn't take a single step without falling flat." Lal let his instructor off lightly: "I suppose he realized that's all a Hindoo c'n do."

•

Lodged in the Italian Alps but hardly reveling in his freedom, Ezra was finding life at the Schloss Brunnenburg a torment: cold stone walls and creaking wooden floors, high ceilings, ill-fitting windows, inadequate

heating system. J sold for a "fairly decent" price the rights to the tape recordings that Ezra had made at the Library of Congress, trying to produce as much income as he could to meet the varied financial needs of
Dorothy and Omar, Olga, Mary, and of course Ezra himself. J was also
trying to find paying guests for Schloss Brunnenburg, necessary if Mary
was going to meet her bills and make desperately needed repairs and improvements. Brunnenburg was a folly, according to J, "a money pit," four
stories of crumbling nightmare. If there was money in the Pound estate,
Mary reasoned, why could not J simply give her the funds she needed
without turning her into a cook and maidservant to guests? Pound's intention, expressed in his holograph will of 1940, was that his literary remains
and royalties would be entirely hers. Because it was written years before
he had been ruled incompetent, its validity had nothing to do with his
sanity: the problem was that the will had not been notarized, which would
have made it valid under Italian law; and for the will to be recognized in
America or Britain, it would have to be valid *in the country in which it was
written.* The idea that this will might not stand up in court was inconceiv-
able to Mary. For his part, Omar, a small, resolute man with a twinkle of
quiet humor about him, thought that he had already made a generous con-
cession in allowing all the present royalties to go toward Olga's upkeep. In
his view, this counted against Mary's claim to an eventual full inheritance.
Nor was Dorothy, while willing to see her rival supported, also willing to
see her son excluded from any final settlement. Great irony, that the man
who had tried in his *ABC of Economics* to set straight world economy
should now be caught in such a money trap! All this landed on J's tall
shoulders.

And he still wanted to write. His Pittsburgh novel might be long abandoned, yet he kept attempting short stories, admitting to Mary de
Rachewiltz, "I have started quite a number in recent years." Then he
would lose the thread of inspiration. Poetry was more congenial, but he
remained diffident. Then Mary translated some of his verse into Italian,
and it came as a "lovely surprise" to the author when her translation of "my
poem about the café in Rome" appeared in a magazine. "I think it reads
much better in Italian," he commented. If Mary wanted to translate enough
to make up a small book, J said that he would be glad to help out financially. Gaberbocchus had just published a small volume of his poems in
London, and Alain Bosquet was translating a selection into French for

Seghers in Paris. J was on his way to acquiring a small but significant European readership. Eva Hesse—not related to Hermann Hesse—living in Munich and translating Pound into German, soon undertook to render some of J's poetry into that language.

J was happiest in his conscience when he could combine publishing business with pleasure. Early in June he broke loose for a long-anticipated visit to Gethsemani to discuss the publication of Merton's translations of the desert fathers, to be titled *The Wisdom of the Desert*. J was able to persuade Giovanni Mardersteig in Italy to design the volume for printing in America at Halliday Litho in Massachusetts—a delicate matter, since the meticulous owner of Stamperia Valdonega usually printed himself whatever he designed. J felt that this division of tasks was necessary both to ensure U.S. copyright and to make possible speedy reprints.

After saying repeatedly that he intended to print Miller's *Tropics*, J was now challenged by Barney Rosset, who in March 1959 had risked publishing the first unexpurgated *Lady Chatterley's Lover* in the English-speaking world and had followed this up with a telegram to Miller offering a $10,000 advance against the American publication of both *Tropics*. Rosset was prepared to share the publication with ND, if J preferred it that way. Miller replied to Rosset that he thought such a venture would be premature, since *Chatterley* would surely be challenged in the courts, and in any case that ND held the first option on all of his, Henry's, works in America. J appreciated Rosset, "a good, and an aggressive, publisher," but he was "very pleased" that Miller had mentioned ND's rights, and approved of his instinct to hold off. J said he had never found a "first class literary lawyer" who thought that the *Tropics* stood a chance in an American court, although *if* he could be convinced that the climate had changed sufficiently, ND would consider attempting publication or else entering into a cooperative venture with Grove.

Rosset was not to be so easily fobbed off, however, and following the July 21 legal finding to the effect that *Chatterley* was not obscene, he raised the ante to a guaranteed $50,000. J told Henry that "Rosset's offer is so stupendous for you that we should not take anything but a favorable attitude toward it." Perhaps still hoping that he would refuse Rosset, J warned Henry that the clearing of *Chatterley* would not necessarily mean the vindication in the courts of the *Tropics*. "After all," J wrote, "*Lady Chatterley*, except for the four-letter words, is a rather 'sweet,' even a conventional book. Whereas the *Tropics* are anarchic," because they attack "the bourgeois order"—to which any judge would likely belong. Henry would have to weigh the risks. That worthy fired letter after letter to J and MacGregor in turn, agonizing over the chances of prison for Rosset and maybe himself, all with the tantalizing thousands so nearly in his grasp. J commented wryly that he admired Rosset for charging in "like the Light Brigade"—which J knew had been a major military blunder. Henry ran to his astrologers, "always reliable and accurate," who promised that this would be "the biggest year" for him. "Well, fuck a duck, eh!" concluded Henry. He said yes to Rosset.

Grove spent more than $250,000 on legal fees but sold some three million copies of *Tropic of Cancer* during the next few years, coming out slightly ahead on the venture. J expressed no regrets that ND had not after all published *Cancer*, but he now rushed to reissue out-of-print Miller titles. J was quite willing to surf, risk-free, in another publisher's wake.

•

In the summer of 1959, J and Paul worked on a ski hut in Colorado, and then J took his family to Europe, leaving only Robert behind with a nanny. J discussed Ernesto Cardenal, another of Mark Van Doren's former students, with Octavio Paz in Paris; Paz spoke "very highly" of Cardenal. The Laughlins had a fine sojourn in Mary's castle, and then they deposited Paul at his school at Schloss Stein east of Munich. J drove Ann and Leila south for a day with Mardersteig and his family in Verona and saw Ezra in Rapallo.

Ezra looked very well, and he was eating "with the usual gusto," "like a youngster." However, they were distressed to find him "at the bottom of the pit of melancholy." He complained of a periodic "inability to think." His conversation ran on dying, and he showed J the ending that he had drafted for *The Cantos*, to the effect that the "central truth" hinged on who actually *issued* money. The Boss himself called his condition "aboulaya," and J thought that it might be largely "psychological, a sense of frustration because he can't get anything done to save the world, get his ideas across, get people to do things." The messianic desire was still there: only the will was failing. A more likely explanation for his depression was that because Ezra was no longer in the restricted and structured yet protective environment of St. Elizabeths, the breakdown foreshadowed in the

Rorschach tests administered to him nearly fourteen years before was occurring. If he had been adjudged sane by a majority of the psychiatrists at the asylum, it was hardly surprising: stress-free environment, no psychosis. Time, also, was wearing him down. Dr. Overholser had told J that depression was a common sequel to paranoia as sexual drive declined.

Perhaps the most important part of the trip, in J's mind, was his attempt to reconcile Mary to the fact of her father's illness. Over the years, she had persisted in seeing him as the sane victim of individuals and a system that had conspired to lock him away because they disagreed with his ideas. "You are miserable because you think you may have let him down in some way. But you haven't," J told her. What she had witnessed since her father's return to Italy—"deviousness, hostilities, inability to recognize obvious facts"—was the "reality": it was the culmination of "twenty years of progressive illness, with all the deterioration that involves."

J must have been remembering his own father as he tried to impress this grim diagnosis upon Mary. Above all, she should feel no guilt: she had done everything "which a loyal and loving daughter could do." In the meantime, the best thing she could do was to show her father "detached, non-interfering affection" and wait until he himself realized his need for expert medical/psychological intervention. J was locked in his multiple roles as agent, publisher, financial adviser, friend, family counselor, surrogate son.

J was no sooner back in Norfolk than Mary wrote to him of her father's arrival in Dorf Tirol, now determined not to die but to live. When Domenico de' Paoli arrived to discuss musical projects with him, Ezra sang most of his *Testament de Villon* for his guest. Ezra had picked up from Mary's writing table a copy of J's recent poetry volume and read it through, saying "Yes, yes" all the while, before passing it on to Dorothy. "I hope this will convince you that I am not translating you out of flattery or friendship," Mary told J. MacLeish obtained a grant of $500 from the Emergency Fund of the American Academy, J reported to Mary, to be used for any expenses incurred in Ezra's upkeep. Pound was clearly rallying: he ate turkey at Christmas and capon at New Year's. He got out of bed at midnight to see 1960 arrive and to enjoy champagne with family and friends.

It ended as a good year for New Directions, too: twenty-two titles, with eight paperbooks among them, including Tennessee's *Sweet Bird of Youth*; Denise Levertov's first major publication, *With Eyes at the Back of Our Heads*; and volumes by Pound, Sartre, Céline, Raymond Queneau, and Merton. *The Henry Miller Reader*, edited by Durrell, sold well, pairing as it did two writers near the peak of their popularity. Kerouac's *Visions of Cody*, with illustrations by the author, was an indulgence in fine printing. J's one acknowledged regret was that he had not succeeded in obtaining a book by Salvatore Quasimodo, who was just awarded the Nobel. "We're disappointed," J excused himself, "old Mondadori was holding out for a vast sum of money."

The paperbook program had become the mainstay of trade sales and now represented 40 percent of total receipts, despite more than three hundred hardbound books in print against only forty-seven titles in paper. Still, some authors, notably Tennessee, asked that most of their titles be kept in hardcover. Another 15 percent of ND's income now came from "secondary rights"—television and book club rights, foreign editions, rights for mass-market paperbacks, and the occasional film windfall.

For a couple of years Denise Levertov and her husband, the novelist Mitch Goodman, had been occasional guests at Meadow House. J and Denise had worked together with the ND designer Stefan Salter on the jacket of *With Eyes at the Back of Our Heads*. "I feel great pride, J., in our joint effort," she wrote. Others liked the volume too, and before long Levertov was getting multiple offers for readings at colleges and was publishing in such journals as *The Nation, Poetry*, and the *Quarterly Review of Literature*. The only sour note struck was in a review of *With Eyes* by the ND author Jean Garrigue—"a little on the catty side," Levertov remarked to J, "as you said it might be." J replied, consolingly, that he thought the reviewer was piqued by professional jealousy. "You are on the right track," he told Denise. "Just follow your nose and plug your ears to the offstage noises." J soon discovered that his association with Denise was not to be routinely tranquil, and any comment of his that could be interpreted as criticism brought on a certain defensiveness: when J pointed out as a matter of information that she had given the poet and anthologist Donald Hall a special rate for the use of poems, cutting out ND's share, she took this as a slight on her honesty. His exchanges with her are studded with her retractions and apologies, which she invariably signed "Love."

•

On February 13, 1960, Ann gave birth in Manhattan to her second child, christened Henry. J seemed pleased, calling him "a cute little button." "Ann takes these things most easily, and is in excellent spirits," he told Mary de Rachewiltz. J wrote to Henry Miller a month later that "little Henry . . . has already distinguished himself by letting fly a good stream on a copy of Pound's *Cantos* that happened to be near the table where he was being changed the other day." This J found "auspicious." In contrast, young Robert, Henry's sibling, was showing signs of future trouble, although to call him at nearly three sensitive and high-strung was not to mark him as different from millions of other boys his age. He was also bright and observant, remarking of his tiny brother, "He can't do much, can he?" But soon J was wondering to Robert Fitzgerald if the child might benefit from "moral instruction from his namesake."

J tried hard to be an attentive father, but he was stretched thin. He had planned to fly to Europe to ski with Paul during the boy's Easter vacation, but it was accounts time at ND and "the usual chaos" obtained; consequently, J canceled. He realized how disappointed Paul must be, so he asked Elisabeth Borgese if she and her two daughters would like an expense-paid trip to go skiing with Paul. Then, before Elisabeth had time to write an acceptance, J wrote a similar proposition to Mary de Rachewiltz, who had offered to have Paul visit at Brunnenburg. J suggested, since she had often talked about taking Siegfried Walter to Egypt to see Boris at his archaeological projects, "If it weren't too expensive, and if you and Walter could get away, I'd be glad to stake you all to the trip. I feel very badly about letting Paul down on his skiing vacation, and would like to arrange something quite interesting for him." It was all arranged in a flurry of cables and air letters. All that remained was for J to cable an embarrassed retraction to the Borgeses: "TERRIBLY SORRY PAUL'S PLANS APPARENTLY CHANGING GOING EGYPT WITH RACHEWILTZES"—J concealing his full involvement behind that "apparently."

Boris volunteered that it would be nice for Walter to have Paul along, but the only person not much pleased with the trip turned out to be Walter, who resented the extent to which his mother catered to this tall, older American boy. For his part, Paul flourished under the attention, and it was hard to recognize J's withdrawn son in Mary's description of him:

"great fun and often a help, an ideal travel companion." Immediately on arriving back at the Schloss, Paul had read a number of J's special editions "with great enthusiasm," saying that he "wished you would give him copies too!" J, trapped in the tensions between them, had not thought that his son would be interested. Just as J's mother had worried about his aloofness during his early teens, J had been concerned about his son for the same reason, and he rejoiced when Paul indicated that he was "truly fond" of the de Rachewiltzes, since "he has never been one to make any friends at all before." The seeds of Paul's future concentration on Arabic were planted on this trip.

Merton and the Zen philosopher Daisetz T. Suzuki had been corresponding since 1959, and J wanted to publish a collection of their letters and other writings. Enter Dom Gabriel Sortais, the abbot general, who forbade publication of the exchange as an "inappropriate" linkage with a nonbeliever. J felt "quite badly" about the abbot general's decision, believing that dialogue between faiths was precisely what was needed. So J dodged, publishing the dialogue between Merton and Suzuki as "Wisdom in Emptiness" in *NDPP 1961*. J declared that he was "so very happy" to have something "so exciting" in the annual. He had gotten out only four anthologies between 1951 and 1960, for which he gave various excuses. Now, J said, with Tom's contributions, "I'm getting my enthusiasm back again."

Tennessee Williams's enthusiasm needed restoration as well. He came to MacGregor with lamentations about not being able to accomplish "my little day's sting of work," and he was depressed: "I am tired of writing and writing is tired of me." MacGregor took him to Dr. Max Jacobson, who merely stared at him and then injected into his veins a concoction that he made up. Tennessee came to depend on this alchemy—"Of course, the primary element was speed," amphetamines, he realized—but he certainly perked up. He claimed that in the years of the treatments he had done some of his best writing.

J was still working with Ezra; his daughter, Mary; Eva Hesse; and other scholars to produce reasonably authoritative Poundian texts in several languages. Sometimes there were useful crossovers, as when Eva Hesse in Munich, rendering *Thrones* into German, spotted errors in the English text that J himself had missed. Hesse had turned out to be far more than a sensitive translator, with her "absolutely remarkable eye for mistakes in all languages." Realizing the importance of a uniform body of work available from a single imprint, she strove to keep all of Pound in German together. Mary and Eva had become close friends, and Mary tried to emulate in Italy Eva's handling of German-language Pound publications. In America, Norman Holmes Pearson at Yale functioned as a collection point for Ezratic errata, while Achilles Fang at Harvard was meticulously polishing the calligraphy in the cantos.

At this time a small bilingual volume of J's poetry appeared, selected and translated into Italian by Mary. She had started with her favorite poem of J's, "The Wild Anemone," and used the local name for the flower, *Pulsatilla*, as the title of the book. J received Mary's translations with "great excitement." When Ernesto Cardenal translated some of J's poems into Spanish for an anthology that he was compiling, J was "much flattered," pleased to be appearing in yet another language.

J went out to Rutherford to see Bill Williams and found that despite the strokes that had left his speech impaired and one hand virtually useless, "the old vim and humor are all there." J was helping him improve the consistency of the "styling and stage directions" of his plays for publication in the projected *Many Loves and Other Plays*. Henry Miller, Nabokov, and Pound were among the authors that J as editor "never fussed about"—or where fussing did no good—but Bill welcomed his involvement. It was a chore that J felt he simply had to take upon himself, "to be sure it was done right," he said. But it was more by way of penance for the animus that he had once harbored against "old Bill." Also, J had mellowed, had gained in self-knowledge. Not only had he forgiven Williams for his decade-long defection from ND, but he had come to blame it on his own attitude, once communicated with such brutal frankness to the older man.

Back home, J wrote a short story titled "A Visit," in which the publisher MacDonald goes to the home of the lawyer-poet Evans to apologize for "bitter letters" written after a rupture in their publishing relationship many years before. MacDonald was the name that J had used for the narrator in the autobiographical short story "This Is My Blood," about his own father's death. Looking back at the self-righteous younger man that he then was, J wrote of his protagonist, "MacDonald was a great believer in his own virtue and fully expected his just rewards for it." To the poet Evans, half-crippled by strokes, MacDonald says that he is sorry for the things he had said. "I knew you didn't mean all that stuff you wrote me," says Evans. But MacDonald will not allow himself to be let off so lightly: "I guess I did mean it then. But I shouldn't have. And I don't now." It was a handsome apology, and Floss Williams would recall the actual visit years later. The story would not be published until 1978, and there is no evidence that Williams ever saw it in manuscript.

The visit also made J think over where Bill Williams stood in American poetry. J recorded his real or imagined conversation about language with Williams, having the old poet say: "They've figured it out. It's taken thirty years but they've caught on. It's American now. It really sounds the way we sound . . . But Pound never looked for it . . . all that Greek and Italian . . . and his crazy Chinese, singing Chinese to himself down there in the bughouse . . . And Eliot just going backwards as fast as he could pedal." BillYUMS had always measured himself against Br'er Rabbit, wanting his approval while criticizing the allusive nature of his poetry, whereas he had hated the entire direction of Eliot's verse. Now J credited Williams with having told him about the new voice and meter of American poetry: "I don't know if I ever really made it a metric . . . It has to be speech and something else, too. It's nothing to do with scansion or tum-tee-tum but there has to be a base under the way the lines fall." J saw this as also a fair description of his own search for a metric and of the predominant voice of ND poets.

Williams might be firmly back on the New Directions roster, but by 1960 it was clear that Giroux was again attempting subtly to insert distance between Merton and ND. "A problem has arisen," Tom wrote to J in May about the volume he had prepared. "Bob Giroux thinks that *Problems and Pardons* as a title comes too close to *Disputed Questions* which is the title of the book he now has in galleys." To J, Tom remarked with dry irony, "I am not overpowered by the resemblance personally." At first Giroux had demanded the postponement of the ND book indefinitely, and when Tom would not agree to this, he ultimately accepted *The Behavior of Titans* as the new title for the ND book. Giroux had left Harcourt, Brace for Farrar, Straus and Cudahy in 1955, ultimately taking with him Merton, Eliot, and Flannery O'Connor among some twenty authors in all.

Next, Giroux offered to handle for Merton the foreign rights on all of his books published by ND, eliciting a sarcastic response from J and a snide one from Tom. "It is very kind of Bob Giroux to volunteer that he might help out on the foreign rights of the books we do for you," J wrote to Tom, "but there is certainly no reason for this at all, as we are quite capable of handling it." "I'm a little suspicious of Giroux in this," Tom inserted at the foot of a letter to Bob MacGregor. "Be careful he doesn't try to interfere in any of the New Directions."

J could be stubborn, and so was Merton, besides being frequently impatient; Giroux possessed those qualities too and added to them a sharp temper when his wishes were crossed. By the end of 1961, Merton and Giroux were at loggerheads over *A Thomas Merton Reader*, which collected writings originally brought out by several publishers. J was prepared to be generous about permission to use anything of Tom's that ND had published, but Giroux's demands had a peremptory ring. "A friend of ours is trying to push me around," J wrote guardedly of Giroux to Tom, who came in squarely on J's side. "I am very sorry about the people at FS," he apologized to J; "you simply have to stand for your rights." Merton now threatened to leave Farrar, Straus. "I have let them know that we are no longer friends and I have indicated I am thinking of quitting them," he told J. If this was a hint to him, J did not attack with an offer.

•

Speaking at the 92nd Street Y in Manhattan in April 1960, Rexroth said that Denise Levertov was the best poet of her generation, with Creeley as second best. J thought that both poets had profited from Williams's voice. "Your idiom, Bill, is so unique that no one following you can approach it without danger," J wrote, "it's high tension wire. Creeley and Levertov . . . have taken your direct simplicity of statement and they use your ellipses and they write 'American' . . . but they are imposing their own sound pattern on the framework." Denise agreed with J that she was "on the right track," which for her meant "what is determined and shaped by inner necessities." J was conscious that he also had risked echoing Bill too closely, telling him, "You were always the one I felt the most drawn to as an innovator in verse (far more than Ezra, whose style is really very old-fashioned when you analyze it in terms of what you have done in 'American'). But I knew I had somehow to 'fight' you—as well as draw from you." J's resistance had taken two forms: "First, there was the entirely artificial visual pattern." Because he was so immersed in Williams's "cadences," J said, poems would come to him in these cadences. "The metric is intended to give a totally arbitrary visual pattern which 'works' against the colloquial cadence of the enjambed lines, which is the way I read them," he would explain years later. In tinkering with the lines to sculpt them into the tight form of his typewriter metric, J would inevitably alter the sound patterns so that his lines would no longer resonate like Bill's poems. The other sound patterns that had echoed in J's head from childhood on were snatches of song and rhythm from Presbyterian hymns. "Lilting the lines to myself," he said, "as I work over the visual pattern helped, I think, to overcome the tendency I naturally have to sound like you."

Aunt Leila was an increasing worry for her nephew. She took up a good deal of Ann and J's time during May 1960; at eighty-six, she was in the hospital in Hartford, with an operation scheduled for early June. J found himself caught up in a round of visits to her bedside, talking to doctors, and "all that sort of very distressing experience." She came through the operation "in fine style" and was brought to her home to recuperate. J resumed his daily visits, although she was confined to wheelchair and chaise longue. Throughout the year she battled on, gradually lapsing into silence. In October, Elisabeth Borgese came to Norfolk for several visits, clearing J's woods with chain saw and hand tools—"nobody works as hard as you did"—and cheering the family with her vitality. His Norfolk neighbor Brendan Gill tried to cajole J into a smile. "Sexuality is a scourge," he teased. "Three times a day is plenty."

July 1960 became a month of crisis on the Pound front, when Ezra returned to the Schloss Brunnenburg very pleased with himself, spent an evening in "great exuberance," and then promptly went on a hunger strike. It took Boris's tact and power of persuasion to prevent him from destroying his files. For most of the month they went through "pretty near hell." Ezra's family should have appreciated the irony of the situation: he had behaved with perfect sanity for most of his years at St. Elizabeths, but now, at home, he was acting like a madman. By the end of September he was physically well but "just depressed, depressed, depressed," Mary reported. "All he says: 'I've made too many mistakes.'" By January, Ezra's mood had improved "immensely," thanks in part to a "very charming" Chinese lady Mary invited to the Schloss: now the old poet was back to studying Fenollosa. But the upturn was short-lived. Off went Ezra alone in the spring to stay in Rome with his old friend Ugo Dadone, who soon

had to summon Mary. More visits to the doctor followed, then a clinic in
Rome; Ezra now had heart trouble and high blood pressure in addition to
his depression.

Since he did not seem to be improving, Mary moved Ezra to the Martinsbrunn Clinic, half a mile south of Brunnenburg. He was growing committed to Olga exclusively, just as Dorothy had feared would happen; the
legal wife now depended on J to keep her informed about her husband's
condition. In mid-August 1961, Mary wrote to J that she was sure he
was dying. That July, H.D., in her early life courted by Williams and
engaged to Ezra, had had a severe stroke. The linked trio of ND poets appeared to be racing one another toward eternity.

After a bad year for publishing in which J had to put $31,000 of his
own and his mother's money into ND to make up losses, his scruples
against paperbacks were falling before the onslaught of economics. J still
far preferred the aesthetic appeal of hardbound books, but he was successful in persuading Denise Levertov to go directly into paper on *The
Jacob's Ladder*. He estimated that he could sell five to ten times as many
copies of her books in paper at $1.35 than hardcover volumes at $3.00. A
modest revolution was occurring in American publishing: reviewers who
used not to look at paperbacks were now willing to review them, especially poetry first editions from quality presses. Also, librarians were increasingly willing to buy paperbacks, both to stock branch libraries and to
have them rebound in hardback.

One of the most significant ND books of 1960 was Gottfried Benn's
Primal Vision, the first anthology in English of the leading German literary expressionist, a writer concerned with nihilism and the "revaluation of
all values," who proclaimed his "doctrine of the world of expression as the
conqueror of nationalism, of racism, of history." Contemporaneous with
Eliot and Pound and like them an innovator in poetry, he had influenced
two generations of German writers, and before his death in 1956 there
had been much speculation over his chances for a Nobel Prize. He was
another of J's controversial choices: eminent German writers who had fled
the fatherland during Hitler's rise condemned him for staying. Benn was
attacked by both left and right, the former because he had served as an
army surgeon in World Wars I and II and had written in 1933, "I personally declare for the new state," yet he had also been subjected to vicious
attacks by the Nazis, his writings banned, his medical practice restricted.

He was a leader in the revolt against the tyranny of form, and this was enough for J.

By the beginning of 1961 it was clear that Aunt Leila was dying. She had periods of confusion and "inanition," when she could hardly speak, times when her nephew thought he could see "the soul fighting / For life in her eyes." When the pale spring sunlight began to melt the snow, two of her groundsmen, Leon Deloy and Theodore Sylvernayle, placed her in a wicker chaise longue and carried her outside so that she could gaze on her garden. Even though Aunt Leila had slipped into an inward-directed silence and immobility during her last months, her death on May 13 at age eighty-seven shocked J into a depression. Ann and J were soon caught up with dealing with the Carlisle estate, and amid all the necessary legal maneuvering his depressed mood eased. It couldn't have hurt that he was Aunt Leila's principal heir, and there were considerable properties, not only in Norfolk, but in Nantucket and Florida as well.

There was also a problem owing to "collateral probate" law: because Aunt Leila had owned houses in Nantucket, Massachusetts tried to collect death taxes on her entire estate. J fought this ruling in tax court and won, but the experience unnerved him. Whatever financial insecurity he might have felt was now either gone or baseless, yet Aunt Leila's death weighed heavily upon him, and even six weeks later he could refer to it only obliquely as an excuse for his silence. J and Ann did not move into Robin Hill as Aunt Leila had wished, and J claimed that it was because *Ann* believed the house to be inhabited by ghosts. Nothing could be less likely in the steadfastly rational Ann; if there was a ghost, it existed through J's inability to enter the house without seeing his aunt in every room. They put the house up for rent.

•

As the twenty-fifth year of ND came around, J had talked about a *New Directions Reader*, to include a preface or an appendix that would provide a brief history of the firm. The volume was conceived of as a Christmas gift for friends and publishers, and the history text would be cut from the book for general sales. J felt that he should make the selections and write the history but lacked, he said, strength and time. Actually, he shrank from deciding which of his authors to include. He was also "discouraged about" having an office party: at the previous one, J said, the eccentric and often derelict writer Joe Gould had systematically stolen liquor, and "somebody threw one of the typewriters out the window."

Ultimately, J ducked the task of writing a history and nominated Carruth: "I feel that you understand New Directions and its erratic navigator as few others do, and that you could present us in a sympathetic way." Hayden's personal life had been rather in crisis, and J thought that the work would provide occupation and welcome distraction for his friend. So Hayden set out to compile the anthology and compose a history of New Directions, and J suggested that he live in the White Cottage to be close to the ND files.

As soon as school graduations were over, J was off on some "tripping about" that he had promised himself: Alta, Salinas, Big Sur, and San Francisco. Ann stayed home with the four children. Carruth maintained his easy liaison with the family. He took Paul in his MGA to the sports car races at Lime Rock, Paul bought an MGB, and the poet showed him how to maintain and tune it. Ann kept busy, but she was patently lonesome for her husband. Hayden found Ann attractive, but neither seemed to think of the other qua man or woman. He wrote to J, telling him bluntly that if he had a wife like Ann, he would come home and pay her some attention. "She was the best friend I ever had," Hayden recalled years later. Months after he moved to Norfolk, Hayden met and would later marry Rose Marie Dorn, a German immigrant who cared for the children of Ann's sister, Helen Hauge. J would not return to Norfolk until the end of August.

Although she apparently did not complain to her family or, very likely, to anyone else, Ann was discontented. She certainly loved J, but he was often away, and she had too fine a mind, too strong a managerial drive, to be content to be stuck in small-town Connecticut with the children. In marrying Ann, J had acquired the eminently competent and stable manager that appeared to be his main expectation in a wife; however, she *wanted* to be a part of J's working life and had a personal fund that she set aside for projects as varied as underwriting a specific publication or paying for a maid to help Mary at the Schloss Brunnenburg. Such involvement J welcomed, yet he could not bring himself to see her as his *apsara*, his muse.

J attempted to sum up his life: "Too much of too many different things—no one of them well done enough to be really satisfying—though all of them interesting . . . BUT—too much scurrying around—not enough time for reading, thinking, enjoying the family, writing those novels I always meant to write, and just plain sitting-under-the-Bo-tree trying to figure out what life is really about." Seen from the outside, his publishing venture was rich in statistics: hundreds of titles published and even the occasional modest profit, but he could not bring himself to see true accomplishment in mere statistics.

A *New Directions Reader* is a fair summary of the first twenty-five— actually, twenty-seven—years of ND. The table of contents was predictable: Apollinaire, Barnes, Benn, Borchert, Borges, Bowles, Boyle, Brecht, Breton, and so on. Carruth slipped in one, only one, poem by J himself: the sensual narrative poem "The Trout." The titles alone were sufficient to document ND's signal role in establishing literary modernism, with a great many major American, British, and European authors in poetry and prose represented. Drama, with the notable exception of Tennessee Williams, was largely absent. Women were somewhat underrepresented, and writers in the non-European languages were decidedly so, partly a consequence of the difficulty in finding good translators. A few of the women J had wanted to publish—Elizabeth Bishop, Marianne Moore—had been recognized early and had gone to other publishers. J's interest in Asia generally and MacGregor's in Japan had brought in a number of Oriental writers, but there were no Africans (unless one counts the Egyptian-French Albert Cossery) or African-Americans. Perhaps J was simply tone-deaf to the African-American voice, added to the fact that writers on the order of Langston Hughes, Gwendolyn Brooks, and James Baldwin had been taken on early by mainstream publishers. Black writers were not apt to think of ND as a likely publisher: with no African-Americans in the early catalogs, and with the firm's reputation for paying low advances, ambitious and talented black writers tended to look everywhere else.

Still, the ND list was very impressive, with many of the magisterial voices of modernism not merely represented but established in the literary canon thanks to J's efforts. Pound and William Carlos Williams had been virtually unread when J first published them. Ezra had written, "Make it new," and over the years J had recognized and published important new voices writing in English and had published early translations into English of countless other writers. Poetry presented a different look on the printed page thanks to ND, and Tennessee Williams had thrown out the "well-made play" in favor of the psychologically focused drama, expressed in the language of poetry. Modernist fiction had grown out of the iconoclastic prose of Joyce and Stein and had flowered at ND, and Henry Miller's example had shown succeeding novelists how far they could go in treating the human condition. At the center of the twentieth century, New Directions stood like a literary polestar.

29

Tennessee, Henry, and Tom

You are a very disciplined writer . . . Now I wish that one time you would try being undisciplined . . . it might be more like a long prose poem, not a narrative, just a sequence of reflections, moods, attacks, jabs, punches, cries of rage.
— James Laughlin to Tennessee Williams, 1962

If ND had percolated along smoothly in recent years, so, evidently, had J's children's lives. Paul was on the waiting list at Harvard but was accepted at Dartmouth, where he decided to go. Leila was accepted by every college she applied to and elected Harvard-connected Radcliffe—"So I shall have a child at Harvard, as it were, anyway, and that is nice." Whatever his complaints about his alma mater, J was a loyalist. And he was clearly delighted when Harvard reconsidered, and Paul decided to matriculate at his father's old school.

Parochial in his worries, J was inclined to shrug off the big picture these days. The country was in a nuke-induced panic, and even Norfolk people were building fallout shelters—but not J. He thought the whole shelter movement was a "great swindle." He preferred to focus on New Directions, which was benefiting from the revolution in paperback poetry publishing: Ferlinghetti's *Coney Island of the Mind* was selling more than 15,000 copies a year, and a cheap reprinting of Gregory Corso's *Happy Birthday of Death* had sold 5,000 copies in 1960. In contrast, Levertov's *With Eyes at the Back of Our Heads*, published at her adamant insistence in hardcover, had sold only 300—and her book had been well reviewed, while Corso's had gone unnoticed.

Djuna Barnes was an author even more stubborn than Levertov. After she had accused J of shortchanging her on royalties, he lost patience and told her that she was straining the respect for women that he had learned "at my mother's knee." Thereafter she would confront him on the street to demand, waving her cane under his nose, "And how are your mother's knees, Mr. Laughlin? Have you published any more rubbish lately?" J jested that Djuna was the only person he had ever been frightened of, and MacGregor referred to her as Madame Legree. But to help Barnes financially, J readily consented when Robert Giroux asked for permission to reprint *Nightwood* in a *Selected Works* edition of her writing. When J planned a deluxe edition for 1961, she stalked into his office, tall, thin, and erect, her shoes beautifully polished, wearing a leopard-skin coat and leaning lightly on a silver-headed ebony cane to favor her left side. She was very concerned over the quality of paper to be used; it must last a thousand years, she stipulated.

Tennessee felt that he needed to chart new territory after *The Night of the Iguana*, not attempt to repeat the modes and manners and preoccupations of *Menagerie*, *Streetcar*, or *Cat*, and wrote a pair of "long-short or short-long plays" under the collective title *Slapstick Tragedy*. "I think they have a new quality for me," he confided to J, "perhaps they're my answer to the school of Ionesco, but they're not just funny, they're also supposed to be sad: I mean 'touching.'" Typically, publishers encourage their authors to continue in an established vein. Not J. "I would love to see you really tear into this un-life (as dear old Cummings would have called it) situation with a tremendous, give-em-hell satire," he wrote to Tennessee. "Maybe that's what you're getting toward in the 'Slapstick Tragedies' . . . There are passages in many of the earlier plays which indicate to me that you could move right into Swift, and be terrific at it." The gist of J's long letter was that Tennessee should let himself go, "be wilder, perhaps savager . . . regardless of whether it fits into the conventions of formal drama, the well-made play."

For the rest of his life, Tennessee's critics would pan each new play and lament that after *Iguana* his career had irrevocably faltered. J considered *Iguana* "crackerjack," but he always encouraged Tenn to innovate, not repeat. Many years later, a few years before his death, Tennessee sat in the front corner office of the then-relocated New Directions, facing south toward the Statue of Liberty, and discussed the publication of his plays with J and some of his staff. Someone remarked on the experimental quality of many of his plays. Tennessee exclaimed plaintively, "But I *am* an *experimental* playwright. I've *always* been an experimental playwright. I don't *want* to write the same plays over and over again." Seeing that he had interpreted the comment as a criticism, J murmured in soothing tones, "Tenn, we *know!*"

In early August 1961, Pound went into a "bad slump" in Merano, and by the twelfth Mary had "little hope" for his recovery, the doctors even less. Abruptly, he swore off medicine, asking only for Brunnenburg water to drink, and he ate some ginger that his grandson brought. Then, within three days, he was talking volubly, and his head seemed to be clearing, although he was immersed in self-recriminations: he felt guilty at having "raised such hopes," he had "double-crossed everybody," he worried that his grandchildren "won't get anything." When he was weak but lucid, he spoke with love and consideration, "but as soon as he has any strength," Mary told J, "he seems to want to use it to destroy." His apocalyptic personality was short-circuiting: sparks, cutouts, occasional thunder.

On Easter 1962, Ezra would experience a resurrection of sorts, emerging from the Martinsbrunn clinic to spend the holiday with Dorothy and the de Rachewiltz family, after which the whole group proceeded to Rapallo, where Dorothy lodged in the Albergo Italia while Ezra trooped up the hill to Olga in Sant'Ambrogio—a reprise of ancient days. Mindful of the expenses faced by the Pounds, J gave Ezra a 75/25 percent split on anthology rights from ND instead of the usual 50/50. When Sherry Mangan died on June 24, 1961, his passing seemed to signal a rush of illnesses and departures. H.D. died on September 27, and then Bill Williams suffered another severe stroke but survived with diminished capacity. Cummings died just a year after H.D., and J wrote to Mary, "He was a dandy. I hope it doesn't upset EP too badly."

J brought about a curious introduction—Henry Miller to Tom Merton—in their public personae, at least, the sinner and the saint. Before long, Henry was writing, "I feel closer to him, his way of thinking, than any other American writer I know of." Tom responded to J, "Well, that is a testimonial. I am really warmed by it. To me that is an indication that I am perhaps after all a Christian." J was delighted and told Henry, "You and Tom have so much in common and your wonderful spirit of understanding humanity, that I hope that some time the two of you can get together." Soon Miller and Merton were corresponding regularly.

The growing Merton/Miller friendship fed J's fascination with doubles—the Austrian painter of portrait doubles Egon Schiele, himself/Handspring. J's own relationship with Tom went far beyond his yearning for a religious mentor. Might not Tom be another alter ego, J thought, his soul-saving spiritual element? Tom had a Zen side, could ease himself into that contemplative calm that J hoped to achieve, thus far in vain. All his life J had been haunted by bipolarity. He and Tom could be seen as the two halves of a double being. Tom was the inward-focused man, the hermit, seeking to know himself. J was the outward-focused man, self-fleeing through his obsessive pursuit of external goals: publishing, skiing, women. Tom spent many hours keeping solitary vigils in his fire tower or walking alone in the woods. Most of his journeys were internal, yet out of them he filled many books. In J's excessively busy life there had been too little introspection but many travels, places, doings, people. When he tried to write about the events of his life, apart from a few fine early stories, something blocked his inspiration. There was never enough time for thought, realization, self-awareness. Even when he was alone in the woods or the mountains, he was most often skiing or climbing, pursuits requiring constant alertness and split-second decisions. Only in poetry could he approach his inner self. He had recognized various other mentors, but he needed Tom Merton to complete his personality. J drafted a poem, "It Does Me Good," in which a lowly gardener, forbidden to look upon the face of the Oriental emperor, realizes that the "emperor rules by my humility." Probably J saw himself as partaking of both plodding gardener and lonely emperor.

J's life was threatened by complexity, while blessed simplicity escaped him. By the end of 1961 it had become clear to him that without adding several new employees, his firm could no longer keep pace with rising sales and the growing size and complexity of the backlist. So J signed a contract with the publisher and book distributor J. B. Lippincott of Philadelphia to sell ND books on a commission basis, eliminating all direct selling. Lippincott's permanent sales staff dwarfed the handful of "commission men" currently responsible for selling ND books. "Our new sales and distribution agreement with Lippincott is working out beautifully—they are increasing our sales everywhere greatly," J soon reported to Mary de Rachewiltz, "but to keep up with them, and they run absolutely on schedule like a good railroad . . . is quite a task for us." For instance, it meant a "terrible sweat" for ND to rush out copies of Pound's *Love Poems of Ancient Egypt* in time for the salesmen to show it around in June.

On February 21, 1962, Judge Samuel B. Epstein of Chicago issued his momentous decision on *Tropic of Cancer*: he ruled the book not obscene. J revealed nothing but delight in the decision, no regrets that ND had not published it. "There is one judge that has some sense," he wrote to Henry. Rejoicing was premature, however, for the novel would be on trial some sixty times across the United States through 1964, when the Supreme Court ruled in Miller's favor.

One of New Directions' achievements in 1962 was the publication in May of a major collection of Jorge Luis Borges's writings in English, an honor ND shared with Grove Press, whose edition of Borges's *Ficciones* appeared the same year. *Labyrinths & Other Writings* caught the attention of many reviewers. From being renowned only in Spanish- and French-speaking circles, Borges quickly gained an international reputation. Within ten years other American publishers would recognize that Borges had become a hot property.

•

Notwithstanding his roguish grin, no one had become more serious about the major issues of the day than Tom Merton. The arrival at Gethsemani of the Nicaraguan poet Ernesto Cardenal as Brother Lawrence, one of his novices, had opened his eyes to Hispano-American civil unrest—in August 1957, Father Louis had read a poem of Cardenal's attacking the United Fruit Company, arbiter of life and death in Central America. In September the Van Dorens visited Gethsemani and told Tom about racial violence at the Little Rock Central High School. Neruda's work Tom already knew; now Cardenal connected him through Mexican magazines with Octavio Paz; then J would bring Nicanor Parra to Gethsemani in 1966, and the two men would become friends. Parra's antiwar poetry spurred Merton on. Most powerfully of all, Tom was stunned to read by chance some magazine articles detailing the atomic bombing of Japan. He had been effectively cut off from the world for sixteen years. Now he decided that he must know all, and for him, to know meant to speak out.

Merton took the title of his next book from the name the Japanese used for the Hiroshima bomb: they had recognized it as the first of its genus, an "original child." In forty-one brief paragraphs, Merton in cool deadpan traced the political decisions that led up to dropping Little Boy. He paraphrased Truman: "We found the bomb . . . and we used it." Merton's irony seemed obvious, so J may be pardoned for thinking it "absolutely amazing" that booksellers should have shelved Merton's *Original Child Bomb* in the children's section. The illustrations by Emil Antonucci were hardly aimed at children either but evoke the towering horror of the mushroom cloud. The author took the mistake more calmly than his publisher. "Sorry *Original Child* got in with Peter Rabbit in the stores," he wrote to J. "You never know how you will be understood." The book had already caused trouble in France with the abbot general, Dom Gabriel, who, after "being beastly about the whole thing" with a "serene authoritarian righteousness," had unexpectedly reversed course and allowed publication.

Peace and disarmament did not sit well with the Cistercian hierarchy in America either. It was Merton's articles attacking the Pentagon, the military-industrial complex, and President Kennedy's policies that led Dom James to ban political articles. Father Louis got around this by circulating his "Cold War Letters," mimeographed by his loyal novices, to his extensive mailing list, and J and Ping Ferry became key conduits in the distribution of Merton's samizdat publications. Once J spotted the tall, gaunt figure of Dom James, his white robes billowing in the wind as he strode across a field, and accosted him: "Father Abbot, I am only a Presbyterian, but it strikes me that God would want Father Louis to write about the bad things in the world." "'James,' Dom James replied, 'God wants us to pray . . . and *He* will make the world better.'" "I didn't agree," J wrote later, "but I loved Dom James." Then he crossed out "loved" and typed "liked."

Hutchins had moved back west, and he kept urging J to come to Santa Barbara: "I must tell you, Doctor, that this is the place for you. All fine, clean, upstanding Republican types interested in their chip shots." J visited Hutchins, Ping Ferry, and the Center for the Study of Democratic Institutions in Santa Barbara, which Hutchins had founded and headed in 1959 as an offshoot of the Fund for the Republic. J aligned himself with Ferry, the most radical—J preferred to say "advanced"—of the group: the two of them advocated unilateral disarmament, on the ground that with unfettered development of nuclear weapons, "something is bound to go boom by accident." J brought Tom into the Santa Barbara antiwar circle. He and Tom were united in being appalled that most people were passive in the face of "normalcy," and they were determined to storm a few military-industrial barricades, which in Tom's case had meant writing *Original Child Bomb*, "The Machine Gun in the Fallout Shelter," and his Auschwitz poem, "Chant to Be Used in Processions Around a Site with Furnaces." In a letter written to J on the last day of 1961, Tom concluded, "It is curious to face a New Year with the expectation that there might be nothing left standing at the end of it." To both men, this seemed a reasonable fear. In 1962 the discovery of Soviet nuclear-armed missiles in Cuba, "fifteen minutes' flight from Chicago," brought the world closer, probably, than it had ever been to all-out nuclear war.

J despaired of the American public, now made up, Tennessee suggested, of "emotional astronauts" divorced from reality. "Your phrase," J agreed, "really hits the button . . . there is this unbelievable apathy about the nuclear arms race while people sublimate what's left of their 'souls' playing Walter Mitty–John Glenn on trips to the moon." J had lost confidence in the president. "I must say I am disgusted with Kennedy," he continued. "I had great hopes that he would turn into somebody with a touch of greatness, but as far as I can see he's just a politician," one capable of "some crazy stunt" merely to get reelected. Many of J's friends had already taken the path of open protest. Kay Boyle, Ferlinghetti, Rexroth, and every other artist and writer J knew in San Francisco seemed to be a peace activist. In New York, Denise Levertov and her husband, Mitch Goodman, and George and Mary Oppen were among those involved in demonstrations. In all this J, although no marcher, reconfirmed his adherence to his adage of a quarter century before, that "the word-worker" must assume the lead in thought and direction.

30

Publishing and Writing: They Never Get Easier

No artist needs criticism, he only needs appreciation.
If he needs criticism he is no artist.

—Gertrude Stein

The year 1962 was a good one for ND authors, with John Hawkes receiving a Guggenheim Fellowship and a National Institute of Arts and Letters grant, Levertov also a Guggenheim, Carruth a Bollingen, Ezra Pound the Harriet Monroe Award. Both Levertov and H.D. had books nominated for the National Book Award in Poetry, although neither won. Among the new publications were major works by the two Williamses, *The Night of the Iguana* by Tennessee and *Pictures from Brueghel and Other Poems* (which would be awarded Bill Williams's only Pulitzer, posthumously); also Hawkes's *The Cannibal* and Corso's *Long Live Man*.

It turned out to be a record year for New Directions' earnings as well: according to MacGregor's meticulous tabulation, $241,515.09 in receipts from book sales, $58,961.45 from permission rights, and various other sources for a total of $423,071.50. To arrive at this sales figure, ND kept 264 titles in print, an astounding number considering the small size of the firm. Only three volumes sold more than 10,000: Hesse's *Siddhartha* accounted for 24,654 copies; Ferlinghetti's *Coney Island of the Mind*, 15,155; and Sartre's *Nausea*, 13,404. Eighty-eight titles sold fewer than a hundred copies each. These figures certainly justified J's early decision to go for major European writers and eventually to publish them in paperback. In theory, a book was dropped from the list if a minimum feasible reprint order of 1,500 copies could not be expected to sell in five years. However, both J and MacGregor were extremely reluctant to enforce this rule. The books were their children.

Of all New Directions authors, J came to dislike Edward Dahlberg even more strongly than he had Berryman, but he was so sure that *Because I Was Flesh* was a "masterpiece" that he decided to publish it and became intricately involved in editing the "mass of bits and pieces" into a coherent whole. In this he was aided by Dahlberg's wife, Rlene, and by MacGregor—while the genius himself was basking on Mallorca. For various reasons, Dahlberg made J's flesh crawl. He discovered that Dahlberg was hypersensitive to perceived insults, suspicious, bizarrely obtuse. Once Dahlberg stormed through the ND offices, tearing book jackets off the walls because none of his own were displayed. J tried very hard not to upset Dahlberg over the editing, telling him, "Again and again I was caught in wonderment by some wonderful phrase or perception," but explaining that there were a great many "little details" in the text sure to annoy or distract readers. "Now I do hope you will understand, my dear Edward, that I am not being critical," J assured him. "It is a great book." Dahlberg's letters alternated between truculent demands and servile unctuousness, yet before he consigned J conclusively to Erebus, Dahlberg said that his relationship with J was one of the warmest he had ever experienced.

Dahlberg would never become a big moneymaker for ND or for himself. He survived, meagerly, teaching here and there, writing book after book as well as essays, criticism, short stories, reviews, all the while claiming, "I've never written a line for lucre," then quickly adding, "But even a pensive maggot expects his supper." Once J made the mistake of telling Dahlberg, "Edward, money is my cross." "Couldn't I carry it a while for you?" Dahlberg replied.

J sent Dudley Fitts an advance copy of Dahlberg's *Because I Was Flesh*, and his old mentor replied to "Dr." Hiram Handspring that after years of making it a rule not to think of Dahlberg at all, "I like the damn book." J worked hard to promote *Because I Was Flesh*. He paid for a series of advertisements with blurbs from well-known critics; the book was coming out with Methuen in England and in translation in Germany, and he gave Dahlberg contacts with agents for Czechoslovakia, France, Israel, Italy, Holland, Scandinavia, and Spain. The book was well reviewed in the

United States and became a runner-up for the National Book Award in 1965—but sales remained meager.

J suffered acutely over Bill Williams's latest stroke, which had cut into his mind. "He hasn't come back very well," J lamented, "but that beautiful radiant smile still breaks through now and then." Mostly, Williams seemed miserable and discontent. When he heard that his old friend Cummings had died, his only comment was "Lucky guy!" Williams wept when Kay Boyle visited him at the end of the year, both of them profoundly moved. "His tears are still on my face" was her poignant recollection a quarter century later.

On November 11, 1962, Williams wrote his last letter to "Jim," one of his last to anyone, a heroic effort of erratic phrases and misstrikes, the best typing that his many strokes now permitted him. He commented on the "lively interest" that the English critics were finally showing in his books. Edited into coherence, his last lines read, "You have been very faithful, it is deeply appreciated. I wish I could write as I could formerly. Affectionately, Bill." Then, on March 4, 1963, as the winter was showing signs of ending, Williams died. "It was what he himself really wanted," J said, "since he was utterly miserable and frustrated when he could no longer write."

J went to see Bill off, so to speak, driving to Rutherford with Ann, MacGregor, Denise Levertov, and her husband, Mitch. It rained during their crossing over the Jersey marshland, but they emerged from the funeral parlor to sunshine, blue sky, and a crackling wind: just the sort of spring weather that Bill had loved. "It was a very good turnout," J reported. Ezra had roused himself to send a telegram to Floss: "A magnificent fight he made of it for you. He bore with me sixty years, and I shall never find another poet friend like him." "This is the one that means most to me," Floss told Denise, her voice breaking for perhaps the first time that day. "I hope you can say a few prayers for dear old Bill Williams who went to heaven, or so I assume," J wrote to Merton. J's ambiguity about Christianity still left him uneasy on both sides of belief, desiring the comfort of religion, yet never sure: "They didn't have any religion at the funeral at all, but just read from his poems and had a eulogy, which sort of upset me."

J was once more working regularly on publishing affairs. A new edition of *The Cantos* was due, and J told Hugh Kenner that it was "beyond my powers" to handle this "terrifying problem." Kenner agreed to step in and take over the process. Eva Hesse had started with the Faber pages, collating her corrections with photocopies from Achilles Fang, Reno Odlin, William Vasse, and others, and especially from Mary de Rachewiltz, working in English and consulting the partially corrected Lerici Italian edition. In October 1963, Hesse wrote to J that there would be some eight hundred corrections. Even Mary was having trouble getting answers from her father, and when she *did* manage to get him to help with her translation of *The Cantos* into Italian, he would often go back and revise or "correct" the English text as well. Thus, there were now at least three versions with claims to authorial authority: ND's, Faber's, and the "Brunnenburg" text.

Ezra sent a list of corrections in December via Olga Rudge, to be followed by another list in January routed through Dorothy Pound. The startling notation "The idiot!" in Canto 23, included with the second list, should have led to the addition of an exclamation point, which would have changed the reference of the vituperative comment from the immediately following "Odysseus" to the preceding "'Derivation uncertain.'" Surely, Pound was heaping scorn on the lexicographer who had failed to arrive at the true derivation, not on the hero: "ἤλιος, ἄλιος, ἄλιος=μάταιος [the sun, fruitless, fruitless=vain, empty, idle] / ('Derivation uncertain.' The idiot! / Odysseus furrowed the sand)." Inexplicably, the editors ignored this authorial correction.

Kenner became concerned that they might be spoiling Pound's puns. For instance, the canceled word near the beginning of Canto 52, "Stinkschuld"—"stink[ing] debt," in unidiomatic German—was a bilingual play on the German pronunciation of the banker Rothschild's name, *rot-schild*, literally "red shield." This the editors restored.

Yet another vexing problem remained: the "missing" cantos, 72 and 73, which Ezra himself had withheld since the 1940s. J did not have these cantos in manuscript and, on account of his promise to Ezra, had not even read them, but now he asked Mary if ND could examine the text so as to make an accurate estimate of the number of printed pages that the two cantos would require. Then, if Ezra still refused to allow publication, the new edition would be printed with a skip in the numbering, to allow space in some future edition. Although Ezra did not want them to go into this edition, he now definitely expected these "Italian Cantos" to be printed in the eventual "FINAL" edition. J decided to print a small run of the "old, bad" edition to silence the "many howls" from customers. In early June 1963, Ezra would undergo a radical prostatectomy, which solved his urinary problems while it "made me into a cunt," as he remarked with mordant humor to J. The operation also marked the onset of Ezra's silence.

In mid-February 1963, J came into a new obligation when Tennessee named him and Bob MacGregor "the new custodians and arbiters of my posthumous Mss.," to be part of a consortium that would include the executive secretaries of the Dramatists Guild and the head of the English Department of the University of the South, the latter institution already designated as the main beneficiary of his estate, after his own and his sister Rose's deaths. Frank Merlo was dying of cancer, and Tennessee himself had been feeling ill for months—so it was not mere "morbidity," he explained to MacGregor. "I don't want my work to fall into the hands of Hollywood and Broadway hucksters, and I think that you all would keep me from turning in my grave so violently that I would plough up the graveyard." A month later Tennessee wrote to MacGregor, "Today I said to myself, Face it, baby, you're dying. Can you do it decently or will you make a mess of it like most thing[s] in your life?" Dying or not, Tennessee had rewritten *Summer and Smoke* as *The Eccentricities of a Nightingale* for a New Directions collected volume and was rewriting *The Milk Train Doesn't Stop Here Anymore.*

J's two older children had evidently inherited his impatient genes when it came to education. After two years at Harvard, Paul took a leave of absence and departed for Beirut to continue studying Arabic. He had let it be known that he did not want to undertake a language that his father had anything to do with. Leila stuck it out at Radcliffe for an equal span, achieving high grades but making no secret of her boredom: in 1963 she set off for India, planning to march with Vinoba Bhave, who, influenced by Gandhi, had launched the nonviolent Gift of the Land movement. She stayed for a time with P. Lal in Calcutta and took walking trips. Mixing pride with exasperation, J wrote to Kay Boyle, "The latest from my nutty but wonderful daughter in India is that she has gone off with a Sikh poet who doesn't speak any English to visit with his family for a Punjabi wedding."

Frank Merlo died in the autumn of 1963, and Tennessee's depression intensified. Soon, however, his grief was subsumed in the wave of public anguish brought on by the assassination of President Kennedy on November 22. "I am very sorry for him and his family," said Tom Merton to J, "but more sorry for the national dance of death . . . such a symptom of our whole condition." "The whole business about poor Kennedy is so dreadful that I will say nothing about it, it has given us all a terrible jolt," J wrote to Mary de Rachewiltz. Ezra broke his silence to send a telegram to Jacqueline Kennedy: "GREAT GRIEF TO ALL MEN OF GOOD WILL / HEARTFELT CONDOLENCES / GREAT MAN AND PRESIDENT."

•

Despite thirty-three titles, 1963 was hardly distinguished in terms of publications by ND: many of the books were reissues. However, the year marked the initiation of the World Poets series, beginning with the future Nobelist Octavio Paz's *Sun Stone*. The year had also featured the publication of the large volume *The Letters of Wyndham Lewis*, Tommaso Landolfi's *Gogol's Wife and Other Stories*, Ihara Saikaku's *Life of an Amorous Woman*, Vernon Watkins's *Affinities*, and Raja Rao's *Kanthapura*—fruit of J's Indian sojourn.

When Ann's mother died in early January 1964, Ann decided to sell her own Seventy-Ninth Street apartment and look for one closer to 333 Sixth Avenue. J and Ann rented a modest apartment that took up the second floor of a small brick building at 9 Bank Street: a living room facing the street, a kitchen, then two bedrooms at the back. It was a few blocks south of the intersection of Fourteenth Street and Eighth Avenue and a brisk walk of seven minutes from the New Directions offices. The building itself was unpretentious, four stories tall and three windows wide, with brownstone lintels and a small dormer under the roof. A carved wooden entry door was the only really attractive feature. Bank Street would remain J's Manhattan refuge until his final decade.

Ann inherited many of her mother's paintings—oils by de Chirico, Gris, Lautrec, Magritte, Marin, Miró, Rouault—and decorated the walls of Meadow House with them. "A small museum," J commented drily, while acknowledging that his favorite painters were Klee (they had four) and Magritte. To be sure, J collected on his own. "I have about 70 early Cocteaus," he would later tell a friend, "of which 15 came from a dealer in LA, who had them from a stranded French sailor." J's most controversial painting was by Balthasar Klossowski de Rola, whose *nom de peinture* was Balthus. *Virginity and Desire* hung in J's office at ND: a nude adolescent girl, legs apart, upon a couch, with an indolent expression that implied masturbation. This Lolita figure disturbed some visitors so much that, J said, they would move their chairs so as to avoid gazing at it. Finally, he sold the painting and replaced it with a *"nice* painting," a landscape by his cousin Marjorie Phillips. "I miss her," J said of the Balthus. "I had gotten very fond of her and she didn't upset me at all."

Now that Ann had come into a major inheritance, she and J decided that it would be prudent to define New Directions as a financial enterprise separate from his own capital and investments. On June 22, 1964, a certificate of incorporation was filed in New York State, and on July 1 the board of directors held its first meeting: J as president and treasurer, MacGregor as vice president and secretary, and Ann as a third director without title. J lent the new corporation $25,000 at the outset and retained nearly all the stock. MacGregor bought heavy green minute books, soon to fatten with the details of corporation management and evolution.

With the formal incorporation of New Directions, the name of the contracting agency on all contracts had to be changed from simply "James Laughlin" to either "New Directions Publishing Corporation" or "James Laughlin Proprietorship." J scanned the list of publications going back to the beginning and, so as not to impose a burden on ND, transferred to his own proprietorship list any titles that he wanted to keep in print, despite their questionable commercial viability. And he took financial responsibility for all future ND anthologies. Two ND authors, Djuna Barnes and Vladimir Nabokov, would not agree to have their contracts transferred to the corporation—Barnes, because she suspiciously resisted any and all change, Nabokov, apparently, because he thought it would be easier to impose his wishes on J as an individual than on a faceless corporation. Eventually, J came to favor keeping the Nabokov titles in his own name both from "sentimental feeling" and precisely *because* they were "good earners for the Proprietorship"; this enabled him to compensate himself for the losses he incurred on most proprietorship titles.

J now joked that he had "made it on the literary scene" because two of his poems had just appeared in Eva Hesse's hometown, Munich, in the excellent poetry magazine *Akzente*. Ferlinghetti had offered to publish a large volume of J's poetry, but J, though pleased, vacillated: did he really want to come out before the greater public as a poet? His few earlier volumes had been mainly given to friends. Then, in 1964, Charles Tomlinson wrote a letter in appreciation of J's verse: "One seldom has such a feeling of undiluted pleasure: they are really marvels of grace, poise, fineness of mind and ear. They urge their matter with such modesty and bring one so simply and irresistibly into the presence of the deepest things . . . (Lowell surely owes a debt to 'Easter in Pittsburgh' in his 'Life Studies'?)." J was astounded and delighted and immediately typed out a reply:

> Your letter about my poems is quite the most astonishing thing that has happened to me in many years, and I hardly know what to do about it, except to tell you right out how much pleasure and renewal of confidence it has given me.
>
> When I was in my twenties I felt very strongly about writing poems and hoped to become a poet in a serious way. But then I became involved in the publishing, and other things, and also came to feel that my personal need to write rather differently from others my age, which had led me to my eccentric visual structure, which can hardly be justified in terms of the traditions of poetry, was really just perversity and eccentricity . . . Having them printed now and then has been a kind of little personal amusement, or vanity, which seemed pretty harmless . . .
>
> Recently, however, Lawrence Ferlinghetti . . . asked if he could bring out a collected volume. This raised quite an issue in my mind, because to accept his kind offer would mean changing my stance, so to speak: coming out of the little private world and accepting responsibility in a public way . . . but your wonderful letter, coming out of the blue, has a strong effect to persuade me that I should do it.

J's major *Selected Poems* would not appear from City Lights for another twenty-two years, but Tomlinson's praise led J to resurrect his old ambition.

The *New Directions Reader* of 1964, like the *Spearhead* anthology that had preceded it by seventeen years, provided a comprehensive summation of ND's achievement. Writing about the volume in *Partisan Review*, Richard Kostelanetz cited J for "importing the latest in European writing," for publishing the first or at least very early books of American writers who brought prestige rather than profit, for reviving neglected American writers, and for pioneering critical monographs with his Masters of Modern Literature series. He credited ND with publishing the first books in America by Borges, Éluard, Lorca, Pasternak, Dylan Thomas, and others, and for reviving interest in Nathanael West, Pound, Gertrude Stein, and Rexroth. Kostelanetz concluded, "The *Reader* makes us wonder what the current literary scene would be like if ND had never existed."

The thirty-nine titles published during 1964 were the second-highest count in the history of ND, among them books by Dahlberg, Robert Duncan, Hawkes, Stevie Smith, Levertov, and two by Tennessee, and it was also a big year for translations: two from India and an anthology of contemporary German poetry; new editions of Borges, Cocteau, Hesse, Rilke, Sartre, and Valéry. The firm would average nearly twenty-eight books per year throughout the 1960s, a reflection of the time and energy J was again putting into publishing.

•

After months of delays, J suddenly broke loose for a rapid three weeks in Europe, taking Ann along for visits with Eva Hesse in Munich; three days with Ezra and Olga at Rapallo; a rendezvous with Leila, just back from India, at Elisabeth Borgese's place in Forte dei Marmi; a trip up to Schloss Brunnenburg, where Paul was waiting for them; by train to the Dordogne to see Heinz Henghes. They spent two "very expensive" days in Paris, and J had lunch with the author and publisher Dominique de Roux, who got J to agree to write for his *L'Herne*. De Roux was a natural ally for J. He too showed a preference for writers undervalued or under one cloud or another: Borges, Pound, Henri Michaux, Ginsberg.

J charged Mary with obtaining her father's views on the disposition of his papers. When she asked Ezra where he would prefer his papers to go, Yale or Texas, he replied simply, "Whichever you can get more out of." "With my mother it is a hopeless case," Mary commented. "Too emotional—and as I've already said, I fear her irrationality more than Dorothy's legality." Then there was the question of Omar: J and the lawyer Herbert P.

Gleason were convinced that Omar's reservations over the sale of the archive to Yale were personal in origin, not monetary. Mary had lived all her life with the stigma of illegitimacy as the daughter of Ezra's mistress, and recently, in a fine twist of irony, it was bruited about and would later be widely accepted that Pound was not after all Omar's father. Apparently, Dorothy, piqued over Mary's birth to Olga, had decided that the thing for her to do was produce a child as well. She traveled alone to Cairo, met Hassan El Rifai, a handsome Egyptian officer, and voilà, Omar. (Dorothy corresponded with her Egyptian lover for years, until the war intervened.) Like Olga, she could not see herself actually raising a child, so Omar was shipped off to his maternal grandparents in England. Ezra, though knowing the truth, willingly acknowledged paternity. Gleason's suggestion was that in the event of the sale of the archive to Yale, certain personal papers could be "legally sealed" for a stipulated time, thus concealing the ill-kept secret of Omar's paternity. To Mary, J fleshed out his argument:

> I can well understand that it might go against the grain with you to make such a "deal." But I do recommend it as a practical matter. You may say, why should Omar be "protected" when I wasn't? The answer to this, I think, is very simple. What you are really protecting is one aspect of your father's honor. He, as the perfect gentleman he has always been, did, at that time, what he thought was the "honorable thing," and he has stuck by it ever since . . . You can say that he did wrong—and maybe he did—but he did it, and I think you should stick with it, hard as it is to bear. It is totally unfair, but so are a lot of things in life. And if concession on that point should lead to a happy solution on the financial front, I would do it, if I were you.

J knew that this course might well be unpalatable to Mary. "At least I have given you the best advice I am capable of," he concluded. "I realize, too, that you put more stress on principles than I do. I respect you for that, but I would rather see you have decent living conditions than sacrifice yourself for 100% abstract verity."

When J saw Pound in Venice the following January, 1965, Ezra told him to push Omar toward accepting the Yale offer. A good shuttle diplomat, J went quickly to Rapallo to present the case to Dorothy, and next he flew to London to consult Omar's lawyer. Then Dorothy weighed in with a somewhat different proposal: a "literary trust" to support Mary, her children, and her mother; and a "money trust," the income from which would be split between Mary and her heirs and Omar and his. Neither resembled what Ezra's holographic will had called for, but J counseled Mary on the expediency of a compromise, avoiding a court fight. He thought that Ezra, meanwhile, "seems to live mostly in an interior nightmare of guilt and remorse." Reluctantly, Mary acceded to J's advice.

The truth was that a most complicated and delicate situation obtained: Omar quite reasonably, recognized as the legitimate son, wanted whatever was coming to him; Dorothy was protective of Omar's claims and certainly resented Olga's hold over Ezra; Olga felt "real hostility" toward Mary and had told J repeatedly how she herself had walked a twelve-mile round-trip during the war to give English lessons at a dollar an hour. "So why should Mary expect any money?" Olga would conclude. And since Pound had never put anything about the trusteeship in writing, it all hinged on J's word. Mary tended to see the matter in simpler terms: her father intended her to have his manuscripts and letter files as a support for herself and her children, should they be in need. She had two children to educate and a castle to make habitable. So why could not her father's intentions be carried out?

It was a relief for J to leave the Poundian wrangles behind and fly to the Yucatán for a writers' conference in November 1964. J especially liked the Chilean Nicanor Parra, and the two diverted themselves by translating a poem of Parra's. Nicanor, J decided, was "a wonderful guy, besides, I think, a good poet." Adding Parra to his roster of friends certainly enhanced J's interest in Latin American poets, and on the spot he proposed that ND publish a small collection of his verse. J sent Merton several of Parra's books, and Tom praised his "good tough and sensitive delivery." Soon Tom was proposing that he translate a selection of the poems of Parra and of Fernando Pessoa and call it "Two Antipoets."

Tom Merton appeared to be in reasonably good health, but in 1964, on the twenty-third anniversary of his entering Gethsemani, he asked J to become his literary and artistic executor jointly with Naomi Burton. He was almost fifty, he said, "and besides that," he told J, "I am in a real corner-turning mood." He was being allowed to spend greater amounts of time alone in his personal hermitage, and he expected to be able to eliminate most of his contacts with the external world—exactly what he had envisioned when he first entered the monastery. He also asked J about making a will, and J nominated Julien Cornell. The Trappist might be at soul a hermit, happiest when meditating in his woodland cabin, or so he thought, but he *did* care about what would happen to his work on his death, and he did not trust his brother monks to make publishing decisions or even to preserve his manuscripts.

•

In January 1965, J visited "sad old Ezra" and Olga Rudge in Venice. Sunk in gloom, Pound remained eerily silent. J pleaded, had he added *anything* to the cantos? At this, the old man turned his hawk's visage toward him: "Jas, I can't get it down, it won't cohere." Olga suggested to J that he take Ezra out to lunch at a favorite trattoria. He spoke not a word as J talked on and on, hoping to strike the merest spark. Finally, after at least an hour's monologue, J ventured, "What was Djuna Barnes like in the Paris days?" "Waal," Ezra said deliberately, "she warn't eggzackly cuddly." Ezra's longtime doctor, Giuseppe Bacigalupo, son of his previous doctor, maintained that Pound's silence "was a real psychological or possibly neurological block," that even at dinner among company he liked, he *could not* ask for what he wanted. Perhaps Ezra was being clinically accurate when he said, "I did not enter into silence; silence captured me." A day or two later J saw Dorothy, completely abandoned and ignored by Ezra, in Rapallo, where none of her old friends remained. *The Cantos* hung like an ill omen over both Dorothy and Ezra, pressing them down: she, unable to reach or help her husband of fifty years; he, unable to bring about the ending that he had in his luminous past spoken of to J. Following Dante but with a focus on earth, not heaven, he had wanted to write a final section that would describe the *paradiso terrestre* that his economic reforms would lead to.

In January 1965, T. S. Eliot, long recognized as the arbiter of poetic standards in his time, died, and a silent and ethereal Ezra Pound made the trip to Westminster Abbey for his memorial service. Eliot had found considerable happiness in his second marriage and confidence in his poetic achievement. He had also achieved a balance in his work: "For me it's been useful to exercise other activities, such as working in a bank, or publishing even." Such variety was good for J as well, however much he might have resented, at times, the diffusion of his energy.

After at first seeming to acquiesce in cooperating on a new *Selected Cantos*, Ezra, now seventy-nine, pronounced *The Cantos* a "botch." "DEAR JAS," he wrote, "I hope you/ will find some way/ to print something/ that will remedy past/ errors. if you do that/ I will sign it 200 times./ yours/ E.P."

J believed that a good deal could be "straightened out" on the issue of Pound's estate if Ezra would only "make some effort to be pleasant to Dorothy." She was staying at Brunnenburg, and on September 11, 1965, what Mary described as "the final break" between Ezra and Dorothy occurred: she made the four-hour car trip to Vicenza with Vanni Scheiwiller to see the Tokyo Theater perform a Noh play. She had waited for fifty years to see one and was determined not to miss this opportunity. Ezra was in attendance with Olga, and he neither sat with Dorothy nor said goodbye to her when he left. "So I fear all she has left now is a strong desire for vendetta and the power of the law," Mary concluded.

•

At a party early in 1966, Don Allen of Grey Fox Press recommended Gary Snyder to J, who replied, "Those Beat Generation guys never answer their mail." Nevertheless, J eventually wrote to Snyder in Kyoto, asking for some poems. In his reaching toward Asia, J had become receptive to Snyder, considered the first American poet to "gaze almost exclusively . . . toward the East," and he had studied Japanese, Chinese, Pali, and Sanskrit, mastering the languages enough to translate poetry from Chinese and Japanese into English. He had just sent the manuscript of *The Back Country* poems to his English publisher, Fulcrum Press, which forwarded the printed book to J for him to offset from. Soon J was receiving letters in Snyder's meticulous calligraphy. Snyder was a poet to whom the Beat label no more applied to his writing than to his habits, and he was an exacting verse craftsman. Discipline spoke in his every act, whether in his brushstrokes, his home building, or his person. Snyder defied categorization: he was an iconoclastic poet, an environmentalist, and in terms of personal possessions a minimalist—at one point he claimed as his "life motto," "Don't own anything you wouldn't leave out in the rain." He was at home in forests, whereas most West Coast poets other than Rexroth were urban. Fiercely independent, he passed over most grants and university opportunities, preferring instead arduous and often dangerous manual labor: he had labored as a fire lookout and a "chokersetter," handling logging cables. In 1948 he had worked as a licensed seaman and was proud of having served on a ship for nine months without anyone realizing that he had been to college. If there was a key word to describe Snyder, it was the place he assigned to *work*: whether in squaring a roof beam with an adze or mastering a koan, for him the exercise of work had itself a holy purpose. Perhaps this was where he and J found the most common ground. J might strike only glancing blows at Buddhism, and he would never become a skilled craftsman with his hands, but he and Snyder shared a belief that a worthwhile life and a profound work ethic were inseparable.

J also made contact at this time with a friend of Snyder's, the strikingly photogenic poet, dramatist, musician, and actor Michael McClure. Like Gary he was a veteran of the climactic Six Gallery reading. McClure gave J a copy of his recent privately published volume, *Poisoned Wheat*; J responded, "I always enjoy your poetry, or almost all of it," and he told Ferlinghetti that he would like to see McClure's new play, *The Beard*, also privately printed. This McClure sent at once. The play features a meeting between Billy the Kid and Jean Harlow, one reviewer wrote, and the "climax—a real one"—involves "a sexual act that is usually described in Latin." Two of the productions were raided by the police; Andy Warhol proposed to film it; the ACLU packed one audience with a hundred "expert witnesses," in order to get the charges of obscenity dropped. It was enough to scare J off, at least for several years, but not Grove Press, which leaped on *The Beard*.

In July 1966, Delmore Schwartz was struck down by a heart attack in the hallway of the Columbia Hotel, a dismal establishment off Times Square, and died on the way to the hospital. J read about his death five days later in *The New York Times*. During his final decade Delmore's manic depression had accelerated into severe paranoia, and he had spent time in a mental hospital. Those attractive qualities that had made J so long tolerant of his abusive letters and wild behavior had won Delmore other supporters, and he had been unanimously recommended at the end of 1965 for tenure by the English faculty at Syracuse. In January 1966, without warning, Delmore had left Syracuse for Manhattan, frequenting the Reading Room of the New York Public Library and several bars, living in cheap hotels, where he spent much of each night typing furiously. In his last verse notebook he had written, "The poisonous world flows into my mouth / Like water into a drowning man's." It was a miserable end for a friend on whose judgment J had once depended and for whom he had held such great hopes.

31

Confessor to a Monk

Follow the ecstasy.   —Nicanor Parra to Thomas Merton

J never then nor later thought of Tom Merton as a sinful man, but in mid-1966 he found himself in the role of confessor to Father Louis, for Tom had fallen powerfully in love with a student nurse less than half his age. After enduring chronic back pain and spinal deterioration so severe that his hands, he told J, "go dead a lot of the time," he had undergone a cervical fusion operation in St. Joseph's Hospital in Louisville. A week after the operation, at the end of March, a lovely young woman had entered his room, saying that she was "his nurse" and was going to give him a sponge bath. And she had questions about his *Sign of Jonas*. Soon they were laughing over *Mad* magazine and the *Peanuts* comic strip. Admitting that "we were getting perhaps too friendly" by the time she left on her Easter vacation, Merton wrote in his journal that "her affection—undisguised and frank—was an *enormous* help in bringing me back to life fast."

When J arrived with Nicanor Parra at Gethsemani on May 5, they took Tom out for a picnic and a drive, giving him change when he asked to use a pay phone. He said that he just intended to speak to his hospital friend, Margie Smith, but within twenty minutes the girl was in the car with them heading to dinner at the airport restaurant. It was Kentucky Derby weekend, and the sometime-Communist Parra was intrigued by the chance to observe the American rich descending from their private jets: "Ah, so this is capitalism," he said in high good humor. J divined the whole situation and was alarmed for Tom, while Parra was charmed in his romantic soul by the beautiful girl and the agitated priest, remarking that they should "follow the ecstasy"—by which, Father Louis grasped, "he meant evidently right out of the monastery and over the hill." "This of course I cannot do," Tom wrote in his journal. "I have vows and I must be faithful to them." J was trying to be protective of the reputations of the two principals and sat doggedly on, until Nicanor kicked him under the table and J finally realized that Tom should be left alone with Margie to sort things out. Margie and Tom walked out over the cool grass, and that evening Tom wrote, uniting God to his newfound earthly love, "This is God's own love He makes in us / As all the foolish rich fly down / Onto this paradise of grass / Where the world first began." Perhaps more than the others, J sensed Margie's shock at the situation she found herself in: she did indeed very much love Tom, but she was also a deeply sincere Catholic who would not merely throw herself into an affair. J respected both her intelligence and her steadfast character, and Margie realized that of all Merton's friends J was someone she could trust. For his part, J felt some guilt: a guest of the monastery, he was helping a Trappist break the rules, possibly to the endangerment of his soul.

The romance continued, and Tom would eventually write eighteen poems to Margie, the secret Heloise to this intact but chaste Abelard. Tom took J entirely into his confidence, and periodically he sent his "S" poems, letters, and journal entries to J for safekeeping. "I always obey my nurse," Merton wrote in his poem of that title. "Because I am always broken I obey my nurse / Who in her grey eyes and her mortal breast / Holds an immortal love the wise have fractured."

Merton was deeply shaken: never in his storm-tossed days before entering the monastery had he experienced such love. "I realize that the deepest capacities for human love in me have never even been tapped," he wrote, "and that I too can love with an awful completeness." He indulged in a fantasy about leaving the order and marrying. Then the brother at the switchboard, perhaps inadvertently, overheard one of Tom's conversations with Margie and, duty-bound, reported it to the abbot. Father Louis went unbidden to see Dom James. Rather to his surprise, the abbot was "kind and tried to be understanding to some extent—his only solution was of course 'a complete break.'" Dom James was not only Tom's friend, but he wanted to keep this most valuable asset in the order and specifically in *his* monastery, and he responded to Tom's crisis with considerable sensitivity and sympathy. At the height of Tom's emotional turmoil, a woman he had corresponded with visited, and she and Tom drank and swam in one of the lakes on the monastery grounds. By his own admission, Tom became so drunk that he nearly drowned. Before Tom and Margie met alone for the last time, in mid-July, a number of people, including J, Victor Hammer, Ping Ferry, Dr. Wygal, and the abbot, had each according to his bent and opportunity reasoned, pleaded, scolded.

The lovers apparently held their final conversation in the summer of 1968. "We are two half people wandering / In two lost worlds," Tom wrote in heartbroken realization. As confidant to Tom, J was sure that nothing beyond a few kisses had transpired. "A tremendous psychomachia was taking place within him," J opined, afraid for his mental balance. At Tom's request, J initiated inquiries toward setting up the Merton Legacy Trust, charged with control of Merton's literary affairs should anything incapacitate him. By November 1967 the trust was in place, with two women who were close to Merton, Naomi Burton and Tommie O'Callaghan, and J as the members.

Certainly the strain that Merton was under was enormous, his anguish genuine—as was Margie's. Tom said to J in a considerable understatement, "To fall in love again after twenty-five years of isolation was, to me at least, an event." For his part, J felt under greater stress than he had been even during Ezra's worst crises: such was the depth of his *emotional* empathy with Tom and his situation. After informing J that there was "nothing more going on now" between himself and Margie, Tom added, "If I die or something, I wish you would let her know." Then he brought up his will again.

•

While this crisis was going on, J was working at the anthology for 1966, which would include a complete volume of the poems of the Spanish Rafael Alberti; fifteen poems by Tomas Transtromer, who would be awarded the Nobel Prize in 2011; and "The Cassia Tree," a collection of earlier "re-creations" from the Chinese by William Carlos Williams in collaboration with the T'ang-descended poet David Rafael Wang. J also included translations from other Chinese poets ranging from the eighth-century Li Po to that dedicated versifier Mao Tse-tung—who seems not to have been paid royalties. This emphasis on foreign poets occurred because the best of the young American poets were securing publishers' advances far beyond anything New Directions could pay, whereas fine poets from abroad could be printed in English translation at moderate rates.

For J, the second half of the 1960s decade was turning into a period of consolidation. At present, ND appeared to have a stable roster of reliable sellers. One of these, Jack Hawkes, remarked, "When I think of 'reader,' I think of Albert [Guerard], Sophie [Hawkes], and James Laughlin. I have three people who are, in effect, 'reader.'" J told *Newsweek* that he was "enthusiastic" about Hawkes and that he was "respectful of" Ginsberg, Corso, and Ferlinghetti. J could no longer identify with the anti-establishment avant-garde. He was still looking for good young writers, but, he said, "I just haven't seen any recently . . . Some of these kids who come around to see me seem to think that all you have to do is take a pill and set back and whatever comes out is literature. Well, it ain't."

•

J seemed to take calmly the death of his mother at the close of 1966, and he now spoke warmly of her. "From all you have told me of her I can see she must have been a really wonderful person," Tom Merton remarked. Soon J was distancing himself from her death through humor, his way of disguising his pain over the loss of a parent whom he had come, finally, to appreciate and to love. "My saintly mother, now in Heaven, <u>loved</u> hospitals," he told Tennessee, "and kept thinking up useless parts of her stomach which could be excised, so she could get back into the West Penn." J seemed more affected by Pound's condition: a recording of Ezra reading his poetry at Spoleto in 1966 was so sad and monotone that it "almost made me cry," he confided to Hugh Kenner. Paradoxically, with the death of his parent J expressed an increased interest in his family. "I find that as I get older I enjoy children more," he said, adding with pride that nine-year-old Robert now signed his verse attempts "Robert Carlos Roberts."

The Nabokovs, meanwhile, surfaced to smile upon J. "Mrs. N in New York for just today," MacGregor wrote to him. "Very friendly. Asks if we will sell back the rights to one or more of the three titles." This J annotated, "Glad she keeps cordial. No interest in selling by me." A year later Nabokov would be in the news because he was leaving Putnam and had accepted an advance of $250,000 from McGraw-Hill for a novel and two nonfiction works. This was followed by his deification in a cover story of six pages in *Time* magazine. In 1970, Vladimir would actually employ the salutation "Dear Jay" and allow a further hint of warmth: "I have been hunting butterflies in Sicily this Spring, but always remember with a nos-

talgic thrill the lupines and aspens of the Rockies." Before long, J was
sending his limericks to "Dear V":

There once was a man of the net
Both tennis and pale blue Annette
Whose love of the dollar
Made publishers holler
"Have done, Sir, you'll ruin us yet!"

In 1973, J would nominate Nabokov for the Nobel via the New York PEN
chapter.

More startling than Nabokov's rapprochement with J were Allen Gins-
berg's few days with Ezra Pound in October 1967. Ezra admitted to Allen:
"But the worst mistake I made was that stupid suburban prejudice of anti-
Semitism. All along, that spoiled everything." Allen had told Ezra, "You
manifest the process of thoughts, make a model of the consciousness, and
anti-Semitism is your fuck-up, but it's part of the model as it proceeds."
There was clearly a rapport established between the "Buddhist Jew," as
Allen identified himself to Ezra, and the author of *The Cantos*. Allen
offered, "Do you folks need any money?" Ezra said nothing, but Olga
responded, "What we really need is time."

Nineteen sixty-eight turned into a blood-drenched year in the Ameri-
cas and in Europe: Martin Luther King was assassinated in April, Robert
Kennedy in June. On October 2, Mexican soldiers and paramilitary forces
opened fire on a peaceful student demonstration in the Plaza des las Tres
Culturas in Mexico City, killing about one thousand. It was ten days before
the scheduled opening of the Mexico Olympics, and Octavio Paz resigned
his ambassadorship (to India) in protest. Campuses erupted throughout
Latin America, and in France and Italy as well, over government actions
and conditions at their schools. It was too much for J: he condemned the
students. His liberal leanings and his anti–Vietnam War stance notwithstanding, his ingrained distrust of popular agitation blinded him to the
barriers faced by the poor at the gates of the universities. J never quite
realized how the other 99 percent lived.

Throughout 1968, J was much concerned with protecting those Pound
titles that had gone out of copyright. For years he had respected Ezra's
wish not to publish drafts of the late "in progress" cantos, but Ez himself

had given out manuscripts to various enthusiasts. Two months later Ezra gave his approval for a "Drafts and Fragments" volume, and by June he had sent New Directions a new foreword to *The Spirit of Romance*, written on J's urging so that the copyright page would sport a valid new date in Pound's name.

J wrote in April to "Dr. / O Autaukthon," a.k.a. Dudley Fitts, a letter in the form of a poem in free verse: "How fare you on the heaving bosom of the troubled winedark?" J was glad to be able to declare to Fitts, the man who had introduced him to Pound in the first place, that Ezra had retracted his anti-Semitism. Three months later Fitts would be dead at sixty-five.

•

Leila Laughlin and Daniel Javitch were married on August 3, 1968, before the justice of the peace in Norfolk, and J pronounced himself "very pleased to have such a congenial son-in-law." Born in Montreal, son of a distinguished expert on reforestation of Russian Jewish descent, Daniel was at Harvard working toward a doctorate in comparative literature with a specialty in the European Renaissance and was a protégé of Harry Levin's. He was fluent in Italian and several other European languages, but even more important, he radiated warmth, and a quizzical humor would help him deal with his idiosyncratic father-in-law. Leila and Daniel had met at Harvard three years before, and in 1967 they had toured India for two months, after which Leila had stayed on for another four months in Calcutta, studying Bengali with the intention of becoming a translator. After the wedding the young couple left for a year of advanced study in London, Daniel at the Warburg Institute and Leila at the School of Oriental and African Studies.

Early in 1968, Dom James retired and followed Father Louis's example by moving to a hermitage on the Gethsemani grounds. With the election of Flavian Burns as abbot, Tom's horizons expanded immeasurably. Father Flavian had been influenced in his decision to become a monk by *The Seven Storey Mountain*, he favored the liberal reforms discussed in the Vatican II sessions, and like Tom he had lived as a hermit. Adamantly against standing for election to leadership himself, Father Louis had campaigned vigorously for Father Flavian, who had been a novice under him and much later his pastoral confessor while he was seeing Margie. In

May, Dom Flavian gave Tom permission to fly to California to conduct a workshop for a party of nuns. Tom had a wonderful meeting with Ferlinghetti and slept on a mattress on the floor of City Lights.

Soon Tom was planning to attend a conference in Darjeeling, organized by J's friend Amiya Chakravarty, that would involve Buddhists, Hindus, and Jains as well as Catholics—precisely the sort of ecumenical gathering Tom had long envisioned. Then he would go on to a congress of Asian Catholic abbots in Bangkok. In great excitement, Tom wrote to J for help with the details of traveling: for instance, how did one go about obtaining an American Express card? Gethsemani probably had a credit rating, J replied somewhat doubtfully, but otherwise "I suppose I must," since he had possessed an American Express card for many years, and would be happy to vouch for Tom—"as long as you don't leave it in some opium den."

In a very real sense, just as Merton was drawn to the East, his religious life was coming full circle: it had been a Hindu monk, Mahanambrata Brahmachari, who had told Tom during the restless casting about of his Columbia days that he "ought to turn to the Christian tradition, to St. Augustine." Now Tom was planning on keeping "a spontaneous notebook type of thing," which would grow into the skeleton of *The Asian Journal*. By September 5, Tom was in contact with the Dalai Lama. "This seems to be turning into a fabulous project," he told J.

With a sense of tidying his affairs, Tom sent J two poetry manuscripts, one of them *The Geography of Lograire*, influenced by Parra's "doctrine of anti-poetry," to which he intended to add sections for the rest of his life. He made up a list of things J was to take care of should he die during his travels: finish the notes for *Lograire*, complete his *Asian Journal*, watch over Margie's welfare. Brother Patrick Hart, entrusted with Tom's correspondence during his absence, warned him not to drink tap water but to "be content with wine or beer with his meals." "If I just die of amebic dysentery on the banks of the Ganges, that in itself would be superb," Tom wrote gaily to J, adding as an afterthought, "Though doubtless unpleasant." In October, Tom was off for Asia. Protesting all the while that he should be in humble lodgings as befitted a poor Trappist, Father Louis clearly enjoyed the Oberoi Grand in Calcutta and the Hotel Connemara in Madras, as well as the respect and adulation he received from Catholic prelates, Tibetan lamas, and Hindu holy men alike.

Before Merton left for the Orient, J flew to Europe, taking along Ann and Robert, now eleven, and Henry, eight. J enjoyed the boys' pleasure in Mary's fairy-tale Brunnenburg and in a splendid Munich toy store. After the toy shop, they seemed to enjoy most climbing Notre Dame, the Eiffel Tower, and up to the dome of St. Paul's—climbing being in their blood. Europe, however, had gotten "horribly American," especially France, with "millions of little automobiles and terrible traffic snarls, neon signs, too much advertising everywhere, and frightful prices." Far more depressing, however, was Ezra's condition: he was still physically vigorous but "sunk deep again in his melancholy, hardly speaking, and then only monosyllables and completely negative about himself and his work when he did speak." In three days, J did not see him smile once. When he could be coaxed into speaking, Ezra was ferociously disparaging of himself and his work. Ezra's was a grim old age, so diminished was he from the vital man of prewar Rapallo and Venice, the defiant Ez of St. Elizabeths. J hoped that he himself would never suffer such a collapse in spirit.

Back in New York, J lamented to Tomlinson, "Things continue much too busy around the office. I seem to spend most of my time answering business letters that don't interest me." His discontent bit into his sleep and health alike, and he appeared to himself to be moving toward some sort of crisis.

•

When J was running New Directions on his trust fund plus what he could cadge from aunt and mother, he had an excuse for the pittance he paid to his often part-time employees such as the Patchens and the Schwartzes. "You could buy a lot with a dollar back then," J liked to say in excusing his low wages. The problem was that a dollar no longer bought much, and ND salaries had not kept pace with inflation. J had by 1966 inherited from both Aunt Leila and his mother and was by the measure of the times a wealthy man. This had little effect on his personal frugality, and if anything, it made him even less aware of how the rest of the world got by. He had by and large kept a good staff by hiring a disproportionate number of women, who would work for less than men, and, as some of the ND staff realized, by seducing his employees to the holy cause of Literature. This did not mean physical seduction—J with one significant exception kept his amatory side largely clear of the office—but he was able to an amazing degree to win his employees over to his messianic sense of artistic mission, of doing good for *Kulchur.* So J was somewhat taken aback when Else Lorch, for some years his personal assistant, said that she was considering moving on. She was a divorcée, she was putting three children through college—aided by the "graciousness" of Ann Laughlin, who would later help Griselda Ohannessian in like manner—and she had to think of her retirement. J promised better compensation, and she stayed at ND. The episode awakened in J an awareness of the need for financial security on the part of his employees, and in 1971 he would have his accountant present a list of raises, as well as pension and profit-sharing plans. This still did not bring ND salaries up to those paid by large publishers, but at least it meant that one did not *have* to be independently wealthy to work for J.

In his escape from routine, Gethsemani, and America, Tom Merton was having a superb time on the subcontinent. He had three long conversations with the Dalai Lama in his exile at Dharamsala about the techniques of meditation in Buddhism and Christianity. In Darjeeling Tom discovered a special kinship with Tibetan Buddhist monks. His openness and eager, accepting curiosity made one Tibetan pronounce him a "rangjung Sanjay," a natural Buddha. Of his visit to south India, Merton wrote, "Surely with Mahabalipuram and Polonnaruwa my Asian pilgrimage has come clear and purified itself. I mean, I know and have seen what I was obscurely looking for." It was in Ceylon that the immense tranquil statues at Polonnaruwa of the Buddha, standing, sitting, and reclining, especially spoke to Tom. "Looking at these figures," he said, "I was suddenly, almost forcibly, jerked clean out of the habitual, half-tied vision of things, and an inner clearness, clarity, as if exploding from the rocks themselves, became evident and obvious." He wrote with the consciousness of having achieved the mystical experience that he long felt had eluded him.

Then, suddenly, it was all over: J received news that his friend had died on December 10 in a freak accident. After giving a talk titled "Marxism and Monastic Perspectives" at an ecumenical conference of religious persons outside Bangkok, Tom concluded his remarks with "So I will disappear" and retired for an afternoon nap. Some sharing his cottage thought they heard a shout but, after a casual check, decided everything was all right. He was found about an hour later lying on his back naked, a switched-on electric fan across his chest, a deep burn and some cuts on his torso. He had apparently taken a shower to cool off and touched a shorted fan, and 240 volts of direct current had gone through him. A nun who was a doctor examined him and pronounced him dead. His body was flown back to America in the bay of an air force plane carrying the bodies of U.S. service personnel killed in Vietnam. With the body came a small brown traveling case addressed to J: the drafts and notes for Tom's *Asian Journal*. "It seems he was electrocuted," J wrote to Ernesto Cardenal, "but at least it was quick."

32

This Obdurate World: The Sword Falls

I wish you some of the tremendous things there are in Easter and which the new-hat people will never find out about until they get cleaned out inside—and I wish you some of the things that the merely pious people will never find out about until they get rebuilt inside by the process that they secretly fear. In fact I wish you the things that I wish for myself and which I will have to get turned inside out before I will really get.   —Thomas Merton to James Laughlin

J was overwhelmed by Tom Merton's death, so much so that he found himself unable to face the memorial service at Gethsemani. It had not been without drama. At Tom's burial, a nun tried to jump into the grave with his body. The abbot had Merton's monastic robes burned because he was afraid that relic hunters would break into Gethsemani. For J, the most bizarre happening was the appearance at New Directions of a wild-eyed woman who announced that Merton had been reborn as a *tulku* and that J must lead an expedition at once to Tibet to find the baby and bring him to America.

Later, J went privately to Tom's grave to leave a potted plant and to "hold my own little service for him alone in the pine forest near the lake." "His death really knocked me for a loop," J wrote to Margie as, a year and a half later, he sat hunched over the tangled labyrinth of holograph scrawls that Tom had entrusted to him, struggling to shape them into what eventually became the coherent text of *The Asian Journal*. Without much conviction, J fell back on the old Christian formula: "I suppose we have to accept it as 'God's will,' but I just can't get reconciled to it yet, he was so full of life and his writing, I thought, especially his poetry, was getting

better and better all the time." Setting aside his own grief, J tried to reassure Margie that Tom had sensed fully the depth of her devotion to
him: "It seems clear to me that he did understand, and that you were as
close to him as any mortal person could be." "Looking back," J wrote years
later, "I'd say that Merton was the best combination of lovableness and
brilliance I ever knew."

Family and friends had died, and over the past decade there had been
heavy losses, but in many cases the vital, creative fires of the deceased
had flickered and dimmed before the end. Such was manifestly not the
case with Merton. But it was more than that: J had depended *spiritually*
on Tom. He felt intuitively that Tom—able to believe wholly in a personal
God in a way that eluded him, James Laughlin—might be the means to
his own salvation. J had depended on Tom far more than their infrequent
meetings suggested, and editing his *Asian Journal* became a way of continuing that linkage. When Edward Rice, one of Merton's oldest friends,
wrote that Tom had died a Buddhist, J responded angrily that it was a
"complete fabrication" and "totally mendacious," that the *Journal* made it
clear that he was merely interested *as a Christian* in learning from the
rinpoches. "I'm a Buddhist," J might say, but he admitted that he was what
Rexroth called a "phony Buddhist": he liked the *idea* of Buddhism, especially the metempsychosis. Ann might be an avowed atheist, but J said he
couldn't go that far. He might fight shy of formal religion, but he was
sure he felt *something*. Presbyterianism, Roman Catholicism, Buddhism,
mere names: J yearned toward faith itself, yet he could not countenance a
defection from Christianity by his spiritual guru.

It bothered J greatly that Tom, to judge from passages in his sealed
journals, which J as a Merton trustee was privileged to read, seemed not
to have had "a major mystical experience." "It is ironical that Tom, who
tried so hard, may never have had such an experience," J wrote, "while I,
who never tried at all, was given it." In his younger years he was climbing
Mont Blanc on skis and had left a ski hut at two in the morning for the
final assault. "About four, before the dawn, the whole sky above the peak
was suffused with a golden radiance," J continued. "I heard angelic music
and my beloved father's voice spoke to me from nowhere, telling me of his
love. I did not see him, but it was his voice. The whole event lasted perhaps five minutes." In denying Merton such an epiphany, J chose to overlook Tom's revelation at Polonnaruwa, perhaps because the spiritual
agency was *Buddhist*, without a hint of Christian "angelic music."

In the traumatic weeks that followed Tom's death, J paid little attention to a publication that, months earlier, would have caused him considerable satisfaction: he was included in the company of Snyder, Levertov,
Parra, Pound, and others in *Stony Brook*, a new journal of experimental
poetry, and he was identified *only* as a poet.

J pulled himself together and set out to complete the notes for *The
Geography of Lograire*. This did not prove to be too difficult, since he had
Tom's introduction to guide him, and in form this "personal epic" was in-
debted to Pound's *Cantos* and to Williams's *Paterson*. "The 'geography' of
the poem," J would write much later, "simply is that of Merton's mind,"
and this opening fragment, J thought, was his poetry "most liberated from
convention." Soon J was deep in early Mesoamerican history, reading *The
Book of Chilam Balam*, Bernardino de Sahagún, Bishop Diego de Landa,
and Miguel Covarrubias on the Maya and Aztecs; perusing Ibn Battuta's
Travels in Asia and Africa, 1325–1354; studying the Ranters of seventeenth-
century England, the Ghost Dances of the Dakota Indians, and the cargo
cults of Melanesia; and a lot else. However, when it came to certain passages that sounded like material from India, J said, "I was stumped." Then
a letter arrived from a prisoner on death row who had been reading Merton and Oriental philosophy, and he identified the mystery passages as
from the Ashtavakra Gita. "The originality of *Lograire*," J would write,
"lies in Merton's use of parody and reconstructed myth." In his opinion,
Lograire was "far and away the best thing he ever did in poetry."

The main task that Merton had bequeathed to J was more formidable.
For one thing, Tom had not attempted a coherent manuscript for *The
Asian Journal* but had left three notebooks and a couple of address books,
along with postcards and notes on loose scraps of paper. One black-bound
ledger turned out to be a "private" journal, partly duplicated in a spiral-
bound notebook. The third notebook, a small pocket one, was filled with
hastily scrawled words and phrases, many in Pali, Sanskrit, and Tibetan
spelled phonetically, all clearly intended to guide Tom's memory in the
book he planned to write. It was a case not merely of checking Merton's
quotations from Indian and Tibetan writings for accuracy but also of deciphering the reported conversations. This would involve the editors in
delicate, nuanced decisions; for instance, the Dalai Lama had spoken to
Tom "off the record" on the Tantra, and these remarks, if not sensitively
edited, could easily become dogma. J developed an editorial group—himself,
Naomi Burton, and Brother Patrick Hart, with Amiya Chakravarty as

consulting editor. Employing his familiarity with Tom's "rather difficult handwriting," rendered especially problematic by the jerks and jolts of Indian conveyances, Brother Patrick typed a rough copy from the journals and notes. Burton's special province was to ensure the literary flow of the text. Soon J was in correspondence with many of the Buddhists Tom had met. Despite the hard work, "it was a happy time because I felt that Tom was at my side urging me on and lending a helping hand." Toward the end of 1969, J estimated that completing the editing of the *Journal* "looks like a three or four months' job." He was off by almost three years.

Unexpectedly, in June of that year Ezra and Olga flew to the United States for a fortnight. The first J knew of their visit was a telephone call to New Directions. It was Olga, who said that they were in a midtown hotel and that she had not written ahead because of the Italian postal strike. That afternoon J escorted them to the New York Public Library's Berg Collection for the opening of an exhibit of the manuscript of *The Waste Land*, presided over by Valerie Eliot. Ezra wept when he saw the typescript with his annotations of so long ago. J described his old master, "now gaunt, but so beautiful, a lordly man in your frail dignity." Ezra said nothing but shook hands with admirers. Then Siegfried Walter de Rachewiltz drove him to Norfolk to stay at Meadow House. Pound in his dark suit walked in the woods and sat on the dock at Tobey Pond, not complaining when several children, finding the silent bearded man amusing, pelted him with buns. When young Henry Laughlin, hearing Walter so address him, asked Pound if he too could call him Nonno—Grandpapa—Ezra turned his hieratic face toward the boy, and his lips moved. "Honored," he said quietly.

By sheer coincidence, J was to receive an honorary doctor of letters at Pound's Hamilton College in Clinton, New York, and Ezra in academic robes sat on the stage next to his now-famous pupil. But it was Pound who was given a spontaneous standing ovation by the Hamilton students. In the presence of his old master, J was commended as publisher and poet: "Perhaps because he is himself a poet of warmth and delicacy, he has shunned the values of the marketplace . . . Most important to this audience, he has long been the principal publisher of Ezra Pound, who received an identical honor here thirty years ago this Wednesday." On the way back to Norfolk, they paused at a fast-food restaurant, and when it came time to leave, Ezra had vanished. J found him wandering among the trees near the parking lot. "Why don't you discard me here," said Ezra hoarsely, "so that I won't be any more trouble to anyone?" J would recall it as "the saddest night . . . I can ever remember."

The next day J and Ann installed Ezra and Olga at Bank Street and entertained them until their departure. Pound met with Mary Hemingway, Marianne Moore, and Robert Lowell and his second wife, the writer Elizabeth Hardwick. Ezra and Olga walked to New Directions to greet the staff that had published so many of his books. "He . . . was very courtly, though silent, with our young ladies," J recalled. Mary and George Oppen appeared, and Ezra sat half an hour with them, pleased but in almost total silence. At the airport J asked Ezra when he might return to America, but the old man only said cryptically, "I'll be lucky if I get past Paris tonight." J never saw him again.

•

Toward the end of March 1970, J was in Alta for two weeks. A new lift, the sixth, was planned, the Neversweat, eventually to be renamed Sunnyside. Soon an article would appear in *Holiday* magazine identifying "the little known resort" as offering "probably the world's best skiing." "Alta's popularity," the article continued, "has been limited by its relatively restricted accommodations and the absence of the sort of frantic ski life that draws winter vacationers to the Alps and some of the more social western resorts." Many skiers appreciated Alta precisely because of its limitations: the absence of boutiques, the cozy, informal atmosphere of Alta Lodge. To conform with Utah liquor laws, only beer was sold in the bar.

J was again writing poetry. In mid-1970 he sent Carruth a copy of *The Pig*, beautifully printed by Walter Hamady at his Perishable Press. Carruth noted "how your humor and pathos play so naturally into each other's hands." Keep it up, Hayden continued, "this shows that you *are* at work. In the end you are going to have a group of poems with no waste, very solid; a small group but a fine one." Nicanor Parra, asking advice on a prospective translator, struck the right keys: "Well, James, you know better than anybody what must be done. You are both poet and publisher (and friend!). Love/ Nicanor." Then Parra was among a bevy of poets touring the White House when without warning the First Lady appeared to be photographed with them. In consequence, Fidel Castro canceled Nicanor's invitation to Havana. "I was sorry to hear that your little romance with Patricia Nixon has ruined your political love life with Cuba," J ribbed the poet.

J was planning on Wyoming by mid-August, when he started to feel vaguely unwell. Always a bit of a hypochondriac, but this time urged on by Ann, he bestirred himself to see Dr. David Luchs, attached to the Torrington hospital. Luchs ran a variety of tests, found nothing definitely wrong, and prescribed some mild palliatives. "These past weeks I've been rather under the weather," J confessed to Carruth, "some mysterious distemper which the doctor's prescriptions don't seem to do much for." By late September he was still feeling "rather shaky." "I am still conserving my health," he reported in mid-October. J now felt well enough to work outdoors nearly every day, and his verse flowed on. Still, he continued out of sorts; there was a malaise, a lethargy, a vague feeling that something was off, in body and spirit.

Ann had been insisting that J seek help more aggressively, both medical and psychiatric; in the latter she had to overcome his skepticism and deep-seated wariness. Psychoanalysis might be intellectually interesting to him for the insights offered on human behavior, but as he had maintained for many years, "I have always shied away from it": the bones rattled too suggestively in his psychological closet. Then Luchs recommended Dr. Benjamin Wiesel, the longtime director of psychiatry at the Hartford Hospital. J was by now desperate enough to try almost anything—and since Luchs had recommended Wiesel, it was not as if he had given in to Ann. With interests in both neurology and psychiatry, and an embracing love of literature and music, Wiesel was an excellent choice for J. His wide experience included having been one of the first Allied doctors through the gates of liberated Buchenwald. J decided that Wiesel was brilliant, and the two men were soon exchanging letters as "Dear Ben" and "Dear JL." Wiesel was a pragmatist who believed in a minimal reliance on drugs but who was not averse to prescribing them when he thought a case would not respond adequately to the methods of psychoanalysis alone. Probably he realized that J lacked the patience for analysis.

J himself was convinced that he was in bad shape, that his valetudinarian period had begun in earnest. His depression had become so deep that he was subject to frequent bouts of nausea. He said he suffered from abulia and anhedonia, and to these symptoms he added another mark of the bipolar personality, the extravagance of his correspondence, "a blather of words, a lot of logodaedaly." In his overactive imagination he relived the specter of his father strapped into a tub of chilled water. Wiesel listened carefully as J poured out the narrative of family mental illness and his own fears. J even told Wiesel a great deal about his love life. Wiesel decreed that he could keep one lover, "Little Lolypop"—that is, Gertrude—whom J claimed to love "in a totally non spiritual way." Perhaps Wiesel divined that *this* relationship would pose the least threat to J's home life yet was necessary to his physical and emotional well-being.

J claimed now to be "investing" $25,000 annually in stamps, mainly of the British colonies. Wiesel told him that his stamp collecting was anal compulsive, a compensation for not having gone into Jones & Laughlin Steel. Instead of spending his evenings playing with stamp hinges, he should be reading manuscripts or the classics. J decided to "let the collecting slide" and gave his twenty valuable albums to Paul. In the years to come, J would categorically date the onset of his bipolar illness from this, his fifty-sixth year.

33

One Troubadour Revives,
Another Departs

"If you capsize, don't fight the current. Pull your knees up to your stomach, keep
your nose above water and wait till the current washes you ashore." I guess that's
the sum of my wisdom.

—James Laughlin, reporting the advice of Abe Yokum, Snake River boatman

Once he was sure that J's problem was a bipolar disorder, early in 1971
Dr. Wiesel put him on lithium, which had only been approved by the
FDA the year before as an addition to the limited pharmacopoeia for treating the acute mania of manic depression. J was later prescribed Elavil and
Etrafon to counter the insomnia that the depression induced. The improvement was dramatic, although as Wiesel had warned his patient from
the outset, he could expect not a permanent cure but rather a series of
defenses and counterstrokes.

Although Wiesel's diagnosis was the verdict J had been dreading since
his young manhood, it came almost as a relief. He was suffering from a
hereditary disease, not a character disorder or a purely physiological pathology that would kill him in short order, the psychiatrist assured him.
It seemed to explain a great deal, notably his alternating moods of ego-
driven assurance and abysmally low self-esteem. His insomnia, which
came in the small hours of the night, was a common symptom of the manic
state. J's shying away from emotional closeness, with either his wives, his
children, or his inamorata, was also typical of manic-depressive personalities. Even the many suicides in the family now made sense: one in six
diagnosed seriously manic-depressive persons committed suicide. Most
reassuring was Wiesel's confidence that J's condition could be treated.

Soon he was stabilized at a daily dosage of 300 milligrams of lithium carbonate, about half that required for treating more intense cases, but enough to maintain the lithium level in his bloodstream at a safe 0.51 millimoles per liter. In this J was lucky, since fully a third of those diagnosed as manic depressives did not respond to the medication. And he was most fortunate that in Ann he possessed a wife willing to put up with his mood swings that could include regression to adolescent behavior. Once he stood behind Ann, seated at the dinner table among guests, charging his pipe and deliberately dropping stray shreds of tobacco in her hair. She reacted with cold anger, and J resumed his seat with a smile: he had gotten a rise out of Mummy.

With Wiesel's prognosis as a justification, J edged toward becoming a hermit, as if in imitation of Tom Merton. It was perhaps no mere coincidence that the onset of bipolar illness followed hard upon the sudden death of J's religio-psychic double and worsened as he neared the end of his engagement in the monumental editing task that Tom had bequeathed to him. Putting *The Asian Journal* into publishable form was J's way of maintaining his connection with and of grieving for Tom.

Toward the end of the year J felt much better; the nausea had gone away, although there was still occasional dizziness. With Ann's encouragement, he worked most of the time at Norfolk these days, whenever possible inviting people to Meadow House rather than going to his New York office. Merton's *Journal* still needed much polishing, and in January 1971 Naomi Burton and Brother Patrick Hart arrived for four days of line-by-line discussion. Merton had described the sky above Kanchenjunga peak as having "a few discreet showings of whorehouse pink": Naomi wanted to change this but was overruled by the others. On one particular passage, recalled Brother Patrick, "We were having a devil of a time." "Any brandy in the house?" Naomi asked J. He found a dusty bottle in the kitchen and poured her a glass. This she downed, returned to the journal, turned it upside down, and immediately read out the passage that had stumped them all. J enjoyed their company, with Ann catering to every need of the guests. Each person had two bottles of beer at dinner—never fewer nor more—and Brother Patrick would play tunes from *Fiddler on the Roof* on the piano.

J was still a diligent editor, but the faculty that appeared to have suffered most was his memory: he no longer trusted himself to recall details of contracts, mailings, names. Many letters now contained lines such as "my files are in New York so I can't be sure." In April he experienced bouts of something like "'morning sickness' as if pregnant," he admitted to Mac-Gregor. "I have the same complaint," Tennessee then told J, missing the point. "I'm afraid we have entered into a time of life when we must engage in various delaying actions and strategic withdrawals from the front lines of our early years." When his manic phase reigned, J worked feverishly in the woods, clearing ski trails, building an embankment, constructing a dam and fish ponds, planting water lilies.

Now that he had a recognized ailment and had been told by his doctor to take it easy, J could with a fair conscience indulge himself a bit. Part of this meant watching more television. He installed a set in a small room upstairs in the original part of Meadow House, where he could sprawl, Ezra-like, in a dilapidated overstuffed chair with his feet on a hassock. Soon *Hawaii Five-O* and *Kojak* were added to the theater and music programs that he had always permitted himself. Someone introduced J to paddle tennis, and it became "the new rage here."

Perhaps the fact that he was feeling fragile made J agree to an interview at the end of April with the freelance writer Linda Kuehl. He began on the safe ground of the founding myth, with Pound telling him to forget poetry, and he defended Ezra as he had always done, but the main focus of the interview was on the history of New Directions. Given his allegiance to the classicist Pound, Kuehl asked, where did J's interest in the surrealists emanate from? Surrealism was "lively and often fun," J replied, although he was never sold on it. J tried to characterize various ND authors. Hawkes's latest novel, *The Blood Oranges*, employed his "stylistic voice" to ring new changes on comedy and parody. "I think that's the real test of the 'great' writers, that they don't just repeat themselves but keep pushing on in new directions to greater subtlety." J singled out as other examples on the ND list of "pure 'genius'" James Purdy and Edward Dahlberg. J pronounced himself "very conventional and traditional" in his leisure reading; he stoked his pipe and picked up Proust, Tolstoy, or Ford's *Parade's End.*

Back in 1945, J had estimated that the ND "audience" consisted of only twenty-five thousand committed book buyers. Over the past couple of decades there had been a radical change, he suggested to Kuehl: "A great many people are now interested in the interior-directed writer." The universities themselves had changed, in a positive way, and he named

Pound, Lorca, Sartre, Dylan Thomas, and his two best-known William-ses among those who had become "standard fare." The barrier between the constantly shifting "high-brow" avant-garde and "mass culture" had fallen, J continued in his best evangelical—and optimistic—mode. At the outset worried about exposing himself to his interviewer, soon J was wor-rying about her being able to place the article well, about her being paid an adequate sum—just as if she were a New Directions author whose career he had nurtured. Two years later the interview would be published in *The New York Times*.

•

Rexroth might have lambasted J often enough, but when Kenneth's mono-graph, *American Poetry in the Twentieth Century*, came out that year, his considered appreciation of J came through—and his affection: "For over a generation modern literature has owed more to James Laughlin . . . than to any other single person . . . Laughlin worked day after day, often till far into the night, himself, and hard, to publish writers who often were far less good than himself, year after year, for little thanks." Then the old anarchist lashed out: "If he lived in a civilized country his chest would be covered with medals and his wall with honorary doctorates."

Tennessee, unlike Rexroth, had never wavered in his loyalty to J and to ND, loyalty that J reciprocated. It was partly the instincts the two men shared: when the playwright announced that his "credo" held that "ro-manticism is absolutely essential . . . the ability to feel tenderness toward another human being," it certainly struck a chord in J's lifelong search for an ideal love. Then there was the intense work ethic that both men felt: neither could be idle for even a day without the torment of conscience. And there was the matter of a moral core, strong, despite what others might see as their moral lapses. "I'm a moralist, yes," Tenn insisted to the Chicago radio personality Studs Terkel. The publication by ND of Tennessee's col-lected plays was a major effort, with work on the series beginning in 1971. *The Theatre of Tennessee Williams*, a project initiated by MacGregor and continued under Peter Glassgold's and Peggy Fox's supervision, would run to eight volumes by 1992, and as lost or forgotten plays were discovered, ND would continue to publish Tennessee's dramatic work outside this series, as well as collected editions of stories, screenplays, essays, and poems.

J's association with Dr. Benjamin Wiesel was turning out to be a de-termining factor in his life, just as his encounter with Pound had been early on. When Alvin Rosenfeld, editing Wheelwright's *Collected Poems* for ND, invited J to talk about his authors at Indiana University in Bloomington, "I was rather frightened," J said, "as I had never tried anything of this kind." He took his worries to Wiesel, who had long realized that J needed to believe in himself again, to be convinced that he was doing something eminently worthwhile in order to function, even to survive. You have so much to tell, to teach the coming generations, *give of yourself,* he commanded his patient. Nervously, J set down conditions: a question-and-answer format, no set speeches. He fortified himself at the outset with two Inderal tablets, yet still was "a-tremble." Pulling himself together, he focused his eyes on "a pretty coed," and soon he was enjoying himself: "I found that I liked preaching to the students about contemporary literature." This new departure came conveniently at a time when J was bored with publishing. He had long kept silent: now was the time to speak, in obedience to Ecclesiastes's command to speak out.

A fortnight later J spoke on publishing in an informal setting at a conference on bibliography at the University of Toledo. He did what he called his "comic turn" on the history of New Directions, leaving it to such "eminences" as the Beinecke curator at Yale Donald Gallup and the D. H. Lawrence scholar Warren Roberts to do the heavy work. Especially now that he was more than ever disinclined to leave Norfolk except when he could justify it to himself, these university gatherings became welcome for their social and intellectual camaraderie. The old rebel was finding unexpected pleasure in academe.

That autumn J had not been much in New York, and he was losing track of the flow of regular New Directions business, even turning over the royalty payments to Else Lorch and Frederick Martin, who had been brought in as managing editor a few years earlier. It still took about eight months for ND to go from final manuscript to publication, but J now let others write most of the letters of excuse. "Without my blackboard to look at," he said, he was finding it hard to keep the publication schedule in mind. This large surface, undeniable as Moses's tablets and scored into a grid of white lines, hung on the wall of his office at 333 Sixth Avenue, with two years of publications chalked up in vertical columns. At last he was finishing up the footnotes and the glossary of *The Asian Journal.* In the final editing, he was greatly helped by Peter Glassgold, hired the year before, following editorships at *The New-York Historical Society Quarterly* and *The New Leader.*

MacGregor described Glassgold as being "quite remarkable" in the unobtrusive cutting and pasting of text so that it would read flawlessly. J still felt that he and his co-editors should not presume to make excisions from the *Journal* draft except where absolutely required for clarity. The result was what may be the most all-inclusive of Merton's books: metaphysics and esoteric philosophy jostle against phrases from comic strips and newspaper stories, and even Tom's chagrin about airline overweight charges appears.

When *The Asian Journal* was published in 1973, the reviews were largely laudatory. The *New York Times* reviewer, Tom's biographer Edward Rice, complimented the editors on having done "a remarkable job in deciphering the manuscript" and claimed that the book demonstrated Merton's "very real attraction to Buddhism . . . without denying his Christianity." Debates about Merton's intentions would increase rather than abate, with some holding that he had intended to sever ties with Gethsemani. Conspiracy theorists maintained that Merton had been assassinated by Opus Dei so that he would *not* leave the Church.

The year 1971 closed on a triumphant note for ND when the Nobel Prize was awarded to Pablo Neruda.

•

Nineteen seventy-two began with the deaths of two ND poets. When Kenneth Patchen died on January 8, J wrote to the other Kenneth that he was feeling "very sad" despite the terrible suffering that Patchen had endured for so many years. "His death marks the end of a chapter for me," J continued, remembering both their many "scraps" but also "his devotion when he was living down in the cottage here on the place, doing all the work of getting the books mailed out, while I went skiing or roamed around the country." Patchen's final communication with J had been a cryptic command: "When you find out which came first, the chicken or the egg, you write and tell me." J had been unable to conjure up similar charitable emotions over John Berryman's suicide the day before Kenneth's death, however. Despite the obligation to speak well of the dead, J passed final judgment: Berryman drank, and J had "always found him absolutely impossible to get along with." He was "so preposterous and sly and arrogant." Berryman's behavior had overbalanced his gifts, so J's tolerance slept.

Another death had reverberated through the ND circle. Yukio Mishima's dramatic seppuku shocked the world, and J remembered him as "a shining face and beautiful manners." He did not presume to judge Mishima for his act, but only wondered why so "Westernized" a man would choose such a death. Tennessee had first encountered Mishima in New York, neither of them knowing the other's professional identity, and they had become friends. They had met for dinner in Yokohama only weeks before the suicide, and Mishima had given Tennessee a "touchingly grave" lecture on sobriety. Tennessee had felt that "something was deeply wrong with him and in retrospect I think he had already decided upon the ritual suicide and was telling me goodbye." Henry Miller found MacGregor's letter to him about Mishima's suicide exciting and stimulating, and Henry's "Reflections on the Death of Mishima" resulted.

Late in March 1972, J visited Hugh Kenner in Santa Barbara. Kenner had just published *The Pound Era*, which brought together Eliot, Joyce, Wyndham Lewis, and many other notables in Ezra's circle of friendships, and J called it, with justice, "the most remarkable book about Ezra Pound ever written." Amid the excitement of discussion with his erudite colleague, J pulled out a chair partially obscured by "the geometry of the dining room" and sat down firmly on Jasper, the Kenners' cat. The event had a famous precedent, since it transpired that the architect and futurist Buckminster Fuller had previously sat on the same cat in the same chair. J turned the episode into a poem of sixteen lines, embellished with eight footnotes: "The Kenners' Cat / on whom I sat went by the / name of Jasper and Bucky / Fuller also sat upon said / cat." Such a stalwart cat, J continued, who "holds his place against a / man" must in another life have been Genghis Khan, Attila, Hannibal, or El Bertrans—or "was he just another cat?"

J had been listed as the sole editor of the New Directions anthologies from the beginning, but in 1972 he consulted MacGregor about adding Peter Glassgold's name to the title page as co-editor. MacGregor, watchful of office dynamics, suggested a campaign of quiet praise that included adding the insecure Fred Martin's name to the masthead. So beginning with volume 25, the anthologies would be credited to a triumvirate, with Glassgold continuing to do most of the work. Beginning in 1972, the anthologies would appear biannually, with half the usual number of pages to cut costs. The change did not help financially: *NDPP* would come out twice yearly through 1982, losing money each time.

J was glad to continue MacGregor's campaign of praise. He had always been ready to laud good work by his staff, but his preoccupation with *The Asian Journal* and the onset of his bipolar swings had distanced him somewhat from ND. And while he did not entirely stop driving, he refused to undertake the 130-odd miles into New York City behind the wheel, waiting instead until Ann could chauffeur him, but he continued to "personally read and pass on" every title published. Now the periodic fluttering of missives from Norfolk became a steady shower, notes saying, "Good letter to Henry" or "You certainly held the fort well on the Nabokov situation." Written on oddly shaped scraps of paper that he snipped with a huge pair of tailor's scissors, these notes became known affectionately in the office as "Norfolk confetti."

A sign of J's improving sense of well-being was his present assessment of New Directions. The growing row of "sturdy volumes" of Tennessee's plays contributed to his feeling "that I have been part of something very important in the course of American drama and literature," he told the author. To have published Tenn and *The Cantos* and the *Paterson* volumes and Merton: perhaps he had not wasted his life, after all. He even showed tolerance toward what he considered crass commercialism, when Hallmark Cards proposed to bring out an edition of Henry Miller's *Smile at the Foot of the Ladder* under license from ND. Although MacGregor found the edition "somehow offensive," he too had to admit to Henry that, with more than 28,000 copies sold by August, "the text is getting around in a big way," and through bookstores other than those that usually dealt with ND.

J's relationship with Gertrude Huston continued quietly. She was not on salary but was paid per book. When the Lippincott salespeople pleaded that a jacket for Queneau's *Flight of Icarus* that reflected the book's comic nature would make it easier to sell, J suggested diplomatically to Gertrude that she "inject into the design some element" that would indicate "a howlingly funny book." She pretended to take him literally, amending the cover to include a winged putto in a small cloud, crying out to a falling Icarus, "A HOWLINGLY FUNNY NOVEL." It was precisely this sort of tease that J enjoyed about Gertrude.

By mid-1972 it was clear that ND was once again in financial trouble: the payroll was large in proportion to income. Economic doldrums had hit, and after reaching a high point of $1,270,244 in 1970, ND's gross sales dropped below a million dollars in fiscal 1972. Griselda Ohannessian, who had not worked for the company since 1962, was surprised by a telephone call late one evening. "I just happened to be in the neighborhood," said MacGregor disingenuously, "and I wondered if I could talk to you for a few minutes." Then he told her that he was worried about Fred Martin's competence: Martin had some talent as an editor, but he was timid and indecisive. In a way, this had been all right by J, who could never forget the disaster of the ambitious David McDowell luring away Paul Bowles and Bill Williams. MacGregor rehired Griselda on the spot to be publicity director, and her responsibilities soon grew. With Bob's encouragement, she started attrition at ND, usually by the expedient of not replacing resignations, rarely through firing, until the number of employees dropped from fourteen to the seven-to-nine range that would continue for the next thirty years.

Concurrently, as the economy worsened, production costs soared: President Nixon had instituted a price freeze, yet this the printers and binders easily circumvented by tacking on "special handling charges" for tasks once performed as a matter of course. So as not to have to price books beyond college students, MacGregor turned to the relatively new method of photo-offset printing—"composition that is done by some sort of photo machine which I don't understand," said J distrustfully, unsure that he could call the result a book.

Throughout the recession, J remained true to the *concept* of Social Credit, even as he astutely played the stock market—conservatively, to be sure. He saw the United States heading toward cultural and economic disaster: the young were uneducated, the junk bond system was bad, the capitalist system itself was "awful." Tennessee had absolute confidence in J as co-trustee for Rose Williams, and almost a decade later J could report to him, "By moving around in money market instruments, all safe ones of course, I think I have nearly doubled the value in ten years." Another friend, the Pound scholar Richard Taylor, was the inadvertent auditor of one of J's business conversations. The phone rang, and Taylor started to leave but was peremptorily motioned back to his seat. J listened a few moments, then broke in: "No, NO!!!! I DON'T want to have anything to do with THAT! No. NO! I don't want to be mixed up with anything like that. No, NO—certainly NOT." J hung up, cast his eyes "extravagantly heavenward," and sighed, "My stockbroker."

With Pound in his eighty-sixth year, failing in health and remaining largely silent, he suddenly landed at the center of yet another award gone bitter. The literary committee of the American Academy of Arts and Sciences in Massachusetts nominated Pound to receive the annual Emerson-Thoreau Medal for the highest level of total literary achievement. The committee, headed by the Henry James biographer Leon Edel, included Harry Levin and J. The council of the academy, mainly biologists, physicists, and social scientists, after hours of "strident debate," voted narrowly to deny Pound the medal. Ezra said only, "It matters." The president of the academy, Harvey Brooks of Harvard, wrote that Pound's "anti-Semitism and Fascism" could not be ignored.

What had clearly been intended as a rebuke to Pound and his partisans backfired on the committee. Three members of the academy resigned immediately, among them Hugh Kenner, who remarked on the inconsistency of his having been honored by the academy for *The Pound Era* while the subject of his book was rejected. Then Katherine Anne Porter returned her medal as a protest, and, J pointed out, "the 'bad' Academy in Boston" had become an embarrassment to its sponsors. Questions of awards for Ezra became moot when he died quietly, with Olga at his side, on November 1 in Venice. The day before, the doctor had told him that he must go to the hospital, and the personnel with the water ambulance wanted to carry the old poet to the boat on a stretcher. No, Pound had insisted, and had walked, erect, over the cobbles to the canal, "your own man to the end," as J said in remembrance. "The Academy now has to face the moral superiority of death," pronounced Harry Levin.

Although he said that it was "a great blow," Ezra's death did not prostrate J with grief, partly because it had been so long expected. J did not fly over for the funeral, excusing himself to Mary de Rachewiltz somewhat lamely that he had let his passport expire. A service was performed by Benedictine monks on the island of San Giorgio, and then Ezra's body was placed in one of his beloved gondolas for the trip to the cemetery island of San Michele for burial in the Protestant section. "But your Jerusalem," J commented, referring to Canto 74, "was your city of Dioce / whose terraces are the color of stars, your Paradiso terrestre." Later he wrote for his *Byways* file,

Quandocumquigitur nostros mors claudet ocellos
when when [*sic*] and whenever death closeth my eyelids
still shall I behold you as I saw you that first day in Rapallo
you were striding down the passeggio with such determination
that I said to myself, though I didn't yet know you well,
that man is going to save the world if he can

that benevolent man, that learned man
ANAXIFORMINGES, one of the lords of the lyre.

J took part in a commemoration on November 20 at Yale. Four of the
biggest names in American academe and literature shared the stage with
J: Louis Martz, Cleanth Brooks, J. Hillis Miller, and Robert Penn Warren, who all read from Pound's poetry. J spoke about his personal relationship with Ezra, naming him a "great teacher" in the days of the Ezuversity.
Then he swung into an oblique attack on the anti-Pound lobby, questioning why he had not been awarded the Nobel Peace Prize, let alone the
prize for literature, on the ground that Pound had striven all his life to
"expose the economic causes of war." Noting that Ezra had written it in
1933, J quoted a paragraph from the *ABC of Economics*, "which perfectly
expressed everything that is wrong here now, the Vietnam war and Nixon's policy of economic concealment." "This made a big hit with the students," J reported. He closed by reading the "Usura" Canto: "With usura
the line grows thick / with usura is no clear demarcation / and no man can
find site for his dwelling."

What would have been greeted with incredulous derision thirty years
earlier was now widely accepted: that the two great lines of descent in
American poetry are Pound/Eliot leading in one direction, Williams in
the other: diverging currents emanating from three old friends. "A Quiet
Requiem for E.P." was held on January 4 by the Academy of American
Poets at the Donnell Library Center in Manhattan. The round of anecdotes, witticisms, and a summation of Ezra's achievements was moder-
ated by Leon Edel, and the panelists were J and three distinguished
Roberts: Fitzgerald, Lowell, and MacGregor. Mary de Rachewiltz and
Olga Rudge were in the audience. A voice in the hall rang out demanding
that the panel take up the issue of anti-Semitism, but the interruption
was ignored. Robert Lowell read the Canto 115 fragment containing the
lines "A blown husk that is finished / but the light sings eternal."

34

Dropping the Pilot

Turtle Island swims
in the ocean-sky swirl-void
biting its tail while the worlds go
on-and-off
winking

—Gary Snyder

In 1973, J's troubles settling the Pound estate resumed: "You can imagine the sweat and swivet I have been in trying to help all the various Pound family members with their difficult problems and keep them separated, and keep from having to give any advice, not wishing to take sides." J remained embroiled in Ezra's final folly for all of February and on into March.

One thing was clear from J's activities: he was facing up to his responsibilities again. A call came in from Ernesto Cardenal, and J exclaimed, "What the devil are you doing in New York?" The anti-Somoza revolution was raging in Nicaragua, but an earthquake had demolished most of Managua, and the poet-priest was on a rare visit north to raise relief funds. They met at Bank Street, the "door-high man . . . / brimming with love," Ernesto called J, who in turn found the stocky poet "very lovable and engaging; he was sort of like a shaggy Teddy bear . . . emanating a feeling of love, in spite of being such a Marxist." They raised glasses of Portuguese wine that Nicanor Parra had left. "To Tom, I'm sure he'll be enjoying this party / wherever he is!" said J. "He's here," responded Cardenal, who signed a contract on the spot for *In Cuba*.

J and his family flew to Wyoming for their annual month amid the "natural solitude" of the Snake River Ranch. It remained a working ranch with plenty of livestock, but as J added parenthetically, "Cows, of course, I count as solitude, as they don't make much fuss." Then, while hastening to a hole in the stream where he had seen "a simply enormous cutthroat trout," J attempted to vault a stock fence—"instead of crawling under it as I should at my age"—but slipped and landed with his full weight on one of the posts. He crawled to one of the ranch roads and was soon picked up, and X-rays revealed three broken ribs and a slightly punctured lung. For nearly a week in the Jackson hospital he admired the "nymphet Florence Nightingales" and played with the electric controls on the hospital bed, seeking in vain a comfortable position. J suddenly found poems "floating around in my head." He began to write them down, and soon he had the core of his *In Another Country* volume, "a good by-product of the hospital," the story of his early romance in Rapallo with Lola Avena, a fish that did not get away:

> *Giacomino!*
> she called vieni qua splashing her
> arms on the clear green water vieni
> subito and so I followed her swim-
> ming around a point of rock.

On October 1, 1973, Pound's Merano archive was opened in the basement of the Beinecke Library, a bevy of lawyers hovering to protect the interests of the varied clients, but J, though back in Norfolk, was absent; his ribs hurt too much for the drive to New Haven. In December, Dorothy Pound died, and J regretted the end of her weekly letters to him. Turning to Henry James for a phrase to describe her, J said that she was the "real thing."

•

Although J was more than ever willing to speak on his favorite authors, after his accident he was again pulling away from direct involvement with New Directions. "We get down to the city about every other week for a day or so," he told Jerome Rothenberg, "but I can't confess that it fills me with euphoria." J still tried to keep his eye out for new writing: "I do like to take a partial look at anything at all promising which comes through the screening process to me." Anything that the staff thought could possibly be an ND book was sent to Norfolk. J called Snyder's *Turtle Island* "really wonderful" and singled out "The Bath" as a poem "likely to be anthologized as a classic." The book was awarded the Pulitzer Prize for poetry in 1975. *Turtle Island* was perhaps the most ecologically polemical of Gary's books: save the planet, save *all* life. McClure and Rothenberg might be promoting a similar message, but Gary had become the most widely recognized eco-aware poet of his generation, his public readings enormously popular.

J's hospitality to writers and scholars had already become legendary. He enjoyed listening to people who had compiled bibliographies or were writing biographies of his authors, and he enjoyed calling forth his memories for them. If he and Ann had to go out before his guests arrived, even people he had not yet met were likely to find a small note pinned to the screen door of the main entrance to Meadow House: "Come in and make yourself at home. I'll be back at 11." They were free to wander the house, to admire the library, the Mirós, the Henghes sculpture.

Commendably, Kenner was pressing J for a listing of the changes made in various cantos during the long course of their publication by New Directions. J was sure that the answers to Kenner's questions existed somewhere in the files, at the ND offices, at Norfolk, or even abroad in the files of Mardersteig or Vanni Scheiwiller. J even recalled seeing a "fat folder" labeled "Cantos corrections" in the White Cottage. Don't worry, he told Kenner, "nothing is ever thrown away, and it is certainly around somewhere." In some desperation J made what turned out to be his final and lasting decision on the cantos: yes, "we" could go on and on, revising and "correcting," but what we have done—and by "we" he meant that loose phalanx that included all who had worked on the cantos, both ND staff and outside scholars—will have to stand so long as our copyright lasts. By then he would have left the scene, J noted with an element of satisfaction, and then *everybody* can edit *The Cantos* to his or her heart's delight.

Summer 1974 witnessed a major eruption on the part of Henry Miller. MacGregor traced Miller's discontent to visits from his old friend Durrell, teaching for a term at Caltech in Pasadena, who told him of a $50,000 advance on his latest book. Henry began with a mild enough letter to MacGregor complaining that his royalties from ND seemed to remain between $5,000 and $6,000 a year. When MacGregor, who had just lost part of a lung to cancer and was in no mood to coddle Henry, tried to point out that the figures were not bad, Henry blew up. "I regard the publisher . . . as the natural enemy of the author," he raged.

Averting his mind from Henry's tantrum, J courted some less irascible writers. He and Ann visited Diane and Jerry Rothenberg in San Diego in 1974, both scholars of northeast Indian lore. Rexroth strongly endorsed Jerry: "He is a true autochthone. Only here and now could have produced him—a swinging orgy of Martin Buber, Marcel Duchamp, Gertrude Stein and Sitting Bull." "He knows so much in every field," J said. The Rothenbergs' friend the writer David Antin evaluated the relationship of their guests: J and Ann "shared a cultural space," he recalled, there was a camaraderie, "they were good friends."

In mid-November, J and Ann visited Gary Snyder and his Japanese wife, Masa Uehara, at Kitkitdizze, his self-built and self-sustaining complex in the Sierra Nevada. This Gary was developing "as a sister-center of Nagaoka," a Zen retreat near Kyoto. Snyder guarded his privacy, but a few years earlier he had sent J beautifully drawn directions annotated, "If captured eat this map." Gary together with Allen Ginsberg and Richard Baker had purchased a hundred acres amid tall pines on a fire trail, miles from the nearest pavement. Snyder had constructed a solar-powered home, and Ginsberg erected Bedrock Mortar nearby, his meditation cabin. Gary and J discussed their love of the woods, and J put his host into a poem, "My Old Gray Sweater": "Gary jokes that / he wants to re-enter the food / chain he wants to be eaten by / a bear." For himself, J proposed a Christian/Druid symbolism: "I'd like my sweater just / to rot away in the woodlands let / the birds peck at it and build / their nests with the gray wool / please nail me to the big oak." Gary lived his Buddhism, the way Tom Merton had lived monastic Christianity. Gary was careful to distinguish between the dour Calvinistic attitude toward work and the joyous Buddhist one: "The goal of living is not to consider work work, but to consider it your life and your play." Work and ritual melded. Gary spoke to J in phrases resonant with wholeness: "Finding the ceremonial, the almost sacramental quality of the moves of daily life is taught in Buddhism. That's what the Japanese tea ceremony is all about." "Gary is one of the few people who really seems to have a soul," J said.

On November 22, 1974, Robert MacGregor died. He had not wanted to spoil J's western trip by letting him know just how rapidly his condition was deteriorating. "It was a terrible blow to me," J wrote to Kay Boyle. "He was my right hand at New Directions for 20 years, and he took all of the dirty work off my back, such a kind and generous and understanding man, we will not see his like again." MacGregor, he said with justice, "had brought a professionalism to the firm." Underneath the clichés and the practicalities, it was clear that J *was* stricken, and it was not just that he had lost his publishing partner. Back in September, when he had seemed to be "making good progress," J had written to MacGregor's sister to the effect that "Bob's emergency" was also his, because "over the years he has looked after me, a devotion and fidelity such as I have never found in any other friend." J and Ann cut short their trip.

An agnostic, MacGregor had been introduced to Zen Buddhism by George Zournas, and the funeral was celebrated at the Zen temple in lower Manhattan, a "beautiful service," J thought, with a eulogy by the *roshi*. Before the statue of the Buddha were displayed photographs of MacGregor and of Mishima—appropriate because the service was held on the anniversary of Mishima's death. "I'm sure he has been reborn, or will be," J proclaimed of MacGregor. "Well on the way to Bodhisatvahood, I would say he is." J followed this up with a memorial at the Friends Meetinghouse, as if to give Bob the option of a Christian afterlife. Appropriate for the somber occasion, it was a particularly cold, wet evening.

35

On the Road: Performer and Poet

Oh hell, I could go on and on, and that's why I say
that we live in a palace with endless rooms and corridors.

—James Laughlin to Anne Janowitz

Robert MacGregor's death was a major blow to J and to New Directions as well. He had made it possible for J to take months and years away to travel, work for the Ford Foundation, write poetry when the inspiration could be coaxed along, and develop Alta, all without seriously weakening ND. In fact, MacGregor's economies and financial astuteness gradually resulted in years of fairly steady profit, due in part to such authors as Purdy, Lorca, Mishima, Daisetz T. Suzuki, and Osamu Dazai, who had been developed by MacGregor or had joined the list on his urging. He even managed his dying well. "I have never seen anyone meet a hard fate so courageously and so serenely," J wrote to Henry Miller.

When it had become probable that MacGregor would not recover, he and J had decided upon Fred Martin to succeed him; New Directions tended to promote from within rather than hire new senior people. Mac-Gregor had not been in the habit of going to J with complaints about personnel, knowing that he did not want to hear them. Bob made decisions about hiring and firing, and J accepted them with a nod or at most a comment such as "Well, that's too bad, but I suppose there was no other way." And although the senior staff had shared MacGregor's doubts about Martin, they did not see it as their place to intercede either. Griselda Ohannessian might have seemed an obvious candidate instead of Martin—she was steady and experienced, and had the confidence of J and, especially, of Ann—but J was evidently not ready to accept a woman as his vice president. At the board meeting the day after the memorial service for MacGregor, Martin was designated vice president, while Ohannessian was promoted to marketing director and Peter Glassgold to senior editor.

MacGregor's death marked the onset of a time of crisis for New Directions, coinciding as it did with a severe slump in American publishing and in the general economy. J was forced to jump back into correspondence and editing responsibilities that for years he had gladly left to Bob. With the stern and steady hand of MacGregor guiding him, Fred Martin had performed reasonably well, but when he was faced with the responsibilities of vice president, his judgment appeared to become paralyzed, and he found it difficult to make either editorial or financial decisions. The size and quality of the front list suffered, and that is what the salesmen sell from. Sometimes when a discovery was made, the staff did not follow up on it. J picked up Nathaniel Tarn's *Lyrics for the Bride of God*, even though he judged it "hard digging, he's so bloody cerebral." However, Ohannessian hated his work, and Martin failed to push for further titles. Tarn went elsewhere, and only after J's death would he return to ND.

Martin tried consciously to pattern himself on J; however, while he too liked being around authors, Fred seemed to favor those with homes in the Sierra Nevada or Priory Gardens, London, rather than unknowns in garrets. Peter Glassgold was a fine and meticulous editor, a scholar in Hebrew, Greek, and Aramaic, and he was able to spot quality writing, but his personal tastes ran to work that was arcane and esoteric beyond even the most adventurous ND standards. Griselda Ohannessian was notoriously blunt and outspoken, and she got along reasonably well with Henry Miller and Corso, who seemed not to mind when she called their bluffs, yet she was likely to turn down a book because a few phrases or erotic scenes disgusted her, whereupon she would dig in her (sensibly low) heels and no amount of argument could budge her. She made no secret of her dislike of the writing of certain current or prospective ND authors, such as Ferlinghetti and Guy Davenport, and made few concessions to diplomacy in her dealings with them. The fact that the eccentricities of ND's governing troika frequently brought them into internecine conflict did not help. Griselda's dislike of Freud was well-known in the office, and once, when she was holding forth at length about God, Glassgold leaped to his feet: "I can't stand it! You talk on and on about God, who doesn't exist, and I can't mention Freud, who did!"

A glance at the five years of New Directions offerings following the death of MacGregor shows that the course of the firm could increasingly be charted along three lines: new titles or reprints from the backlist of important writers with good sales records; writers that ND believed should be pushed even though they did not yet sell well; and an assortment of authors such as Philippe Jaccottet and Paul van Ostaijen, who, however valuable and interesting they might be, could scarcely be expected to find a wide audience. Merton's successful *Wisdom of the Desert* led to the Wisdom series; *The Wisdom of the Sufis* was followed by volumes dealing with the Upanishads, the Zen masters, the Spanish mystics, Saint Francis, the English mystics; but there were also missed opportunities. All in all, New Directions seemed to be sailing with a lashed-down tiller, unwilling or unable to strike new bearings. At this point, J found his supposed failings portrayed in fiction: Saul Bellow published *Humboldt's Gift*, and J recognized Delmore Schwartz as the model for Von Humboldt Fleisher, a paranoiac poet who believes that men of importance are taking his wife to bed. Then there is Humboldt's friend "Hildebrand the playboy publisher of avant-garde poets, himself a poet," hired for thirty thousand a year by "Wilmoore Longstaff . . . archduke of the higher learning in America." Longstaff was Robert Hutchins to the life. Humboldt does the editorial work for Hildebrand while he is off skiing.

·

In 1975, New Directions produced one of the most expensive—and beautiful—books it had ever offered: Henry Miller's *Nightmare Notebook*. Henry was furious: "Christ, I never thought N.D. would put out a book costing $150.00!! Never, never!" "He's a complicator," J said, his harshest criticism these days about any author who made life difficult.

Fred Martin's response to financial losses and to any criticism was to publish fewer books and to avoid spending money on new projects. Then, in one of those casual introductions that had characterized ND hiring from the very beginning, the foreign rights director, Elizabeth Marraffino, suggested in June 1975 that a young college teacher who had been laid off during one of New York's budget crises apply as a summer fill-in. Peggy Fox was assured that there was no future for her at ND, that this would be a temporary position only. Within months, two resignations opened positions, and Fox was put in charge of copyrights and foreign rights. A highly organized worker, she was assigned editorial responsibilities in the area of her graduate studies. Soon she had become Tennessee's editor, beginning with *Androgyne, Mon Amour*, as well as a voice in decision making. Some years later, Ohannessian and Fox together persuaded J to publish Borges's *Seven Nights*. It sold well, justifying other gambles in the future.

J continued to speak of the "flood" of correspondence and typescripts that poured in "without abatement." "I've decided on the appropriate inscription for my tombstone: 'He drowned in paper.'" J continued to be sought after as a speaker, which further complicated his life. "I have been invited to break wind at a conference on poetry publishing sponsored by the Library of Congress," he told an old friend, "and since they are prepared to PAY, I am prepared to make a fool of myself." Despite comments like these, he was enjoying his college lectures and welcomed questions from students, but he became testy—"a grouchy old man"—when pressed on Derrida, Bakhtin, or deconstruction, which he referred to as "the latest nonsense": "The pedants of deconstruction / are lathering each other's backs / with their own shit," a glancing reference to Dante's *Inferno*, he drafted in verse.

In May 1977, J was invited to the Academy of Arts and Letters to receive the Award for Distinguished Service to the Arts. Robert Lowell was granted the National Medal for Literature, Saul Bellow was given the academy's Gold Medal for the novel, and two important ND writers were inducted into membership, Tennessee and Eugenio Montale, along with one writer J had hoped to acquire, Elizabeth Bishop. When J complained of feeling inferior, Dr. Wiesel teased him: "If you opened your golden mouth you would have had them in the palm of your hand."

Dan Allman, hired as production manager, was put in charge of book design in 1977 and took his responsibilities very seriously. Soon to be named art director as well, he saw his role as including being an agent of change. "Time to try new things," he told J. Inevitably, there was conflict with Gertrude. "A little Jewish girl from Brooklyn," Dan called her, "who pretended to southern airs and graces." She was also highly independent, tended to pass over instructions of which she did not approve, and sometimes threatened to "call *James*" when she was crossed. Then, at the end of 1978, a "major flap" ensued over H.D.'s *End to Torment: A Memoir of Ezra Pound* when Gertrude, ignoring Allman's instructions, gave Ezra equal weight with H.D. on the cover. Gertrude refused to alter her design, and Dan asserted his overall authority. He had already proved of considerable value to ND, and J did not intercede on Gertrude's behalf. This ended her regular work for ND, although J would still ask Gertrude to design an occasional "Proprietor's List" book for him and their personal relationship continued. Hermann Strohbach became ND's regular designer through the 1980s and would continue, with others, until 1997. J was fascinated by H.D.'s novel *HERmione* because the character George was clearly based on Pound, and the central situation depicted George/Ezra's return to America in 1910 in a vain attempt to persuade H.D. to marry him. In 1986, J would place H.D.'s massive *Collected Poems* on his proprietorship list to shield ND from losses, but by then her books were greatly contributing to pushing his personal front list earnings over the $40,000 mark.

In 1978, Gertrude designed the layout and cover for J's latest book of poems, *In Another Country*, using a romantic profile photograph Ann took of him and Gary Snyder at Kitkitdizze. To sharpen the dramatic impact of Ann's photograph, Gertrude inked out Snyder. Compounding the pattern of relationships, Robert Fitzgerald contributed a foreword, and Ferlinghetti published the volume at his City Lights press, although J had actually designed and paid for the volume himself: "I thought the elegance of Palatino [type] responded to one of my tricks, which is to work in a 'classical sounding' phrase, for contrast, among my colloquial phrases." The title poem celebrates J's Italian lover, Lola Avena, her voice caressing him "as if she / were holding something as precious / as the golden testicle of a god."

One of the pleasures that J now permitted himself was to use copies of his volumes of poetry to reconnect with a few select amours of his youth. He sent *In Another Country* to Sara "Papagena" Woolsey, and her reply to "Dear dear P" showed her still more than a bit enamored of him. Thirteen years later she would write to him about another poem, "The dreams, the sounds, the loves are still with me. They always have been." J replied in kind, still linking her, too, with *The Magic Flute*: "It helps in old age to have such good things to remember about a very wonderful person." J sent a copy of *In Another Country* to Tennessee, then staying at Wilbury Park near Salisbury with Lady Maria St. Just. He wrote to J, "This distillation of your poetry has been a great joy to me and to Maria. You've never shown an adequate confidence in the unique quality and beauty of your work." For himself, Tennessee added a familiar valedictory note, "There's little time or strength left," closing the letter with a tribute: "Very briefly and truly, I want to say this. You're the greatest friend that I have had in my life, and the most trusted."

Honors poured in. They left J "grateful for the attention" but rather indifferent: a LittD from Colgate; the Carey-Thomas Award for publishing excellence; a PEN Publishers Citation, with an encomium delivered by Denise Levertov. In accepting the PEN award, J said that it might with more justice have gone to Alfred A. Knopf, whom he called "the greatest thing in publishing that ever was." Knopf would be recognized by PEN two years later.

The ND lease on the offices at 333 Sixth Avenue had expired at the end of May 1977, but since the landlord seemed content to continue the arrangement, no sense of urgency existed. Then, at the beginning of October 1978, after an occupancy of nearly twenty-nine years, New Directions was given a "notice to vacate" within a month. A frantic search ensued, and a suite of eleven rooms plus two washrooms and a few closets, occupying the entire nineteenth floor, was located in a handsome twenty-story art deco structure at 80 Eighth Avenue. The building narrowed in square footage from the tenth floor on up. It was, J said, a much better suite of rooms, although somewhat less in total area than at 333, and it was only a four-minute walk from his Bank Street apartment. The former tenant had been a Teamsters Union local, and there was a small barred *guichet* through which members had paid their dues. This artifact was scrupulously preserved, to the delight of the more proletarian among ND authors. There was even a small balcony, which the future publicity director, Laurie Callahan, would eventually convert into a garden of flowers, herbs, and miniature fruit trees. In time the cherry tree would produce enough fruit for one pie, which Callahan would bake and serve to the ND family in a fitting annual ritual. J chose for himself not the large corner office with windows to the south and west, a view that included the Statue of Liberty, but a smaller and much darker west-facing office. He retained his battered wooden desk, with a stash of Oreo cookies in the bottom right drawer. A long oak table in the corner office accommodated the entire staff for meetings; at one end stood J's ruinous straight-backed leather armchair with dislocated springing, an instrument of torture in which no one else willingly sat, with the exception of Fred Martin: it gave him a sense of authority.

The book world was changing too. Lippincott was swallowed by

Harper & Row in 1978, but the larger organization continued to handle distribution for ND. Then, at a Harper sales conference on Long Island, J heard books referred to as "products"—semantic anathema to him. George Brockway, president and chairman of the board at W. W. Norton, suggested a link between the firms. Brockway's rather old-fashioned courtliness matched J's; publishing, J hoped, could remain for him a gentleman's occupation. On January 9, 1979, he signed an agreement whereby Norton would take over the handling of accounting and royalties as well as distribution for ND. These changes relieved ND staff of much clerical work; however, New Directions would remain completely independent in decision making and management.

"Something good has happened, well two things really," J wrote in March to the guardian of his sanity. "After not writing a poem since I went on lithium, I wrote three the other day, all in a burst. I'll send you one of them as it may amuse you to see that my unconscious is still decapitating females." J had in fact written a few poems in the years since 1970 and had been sending his poems to Dr. Wiesel, who maintained that he could take J's "mental temperature" by them better than by hearing his "hypochondriacal complaints." The other good thing was that J's love of music had returned. Now he listened to a long-playing disc each night while he smoked his postprandial cigar. He liked Scarlatti best these days, and his longtime standbys were Vivaldi, Hummel, and Mozart, and masses by Bach, Brahms, Haydn, and Verdi. Another indication of his state of mind was the improvement in his penmanship. Although J was not about to admit it, he was feeling better than he had in years.

J's creativity was indeed increasing. While his days continued more or less as before, under the influence of his various medications he would awaken between 2:00 and 4:00 a.m. with the lines of an embryonic poem swirling in his head and shuffle downstairs to his old office behind the kitchen. Sitting at his typewriter, he would tap out the poem: "Everything is oneiric dictation, except for a little line polishing." Then he would send copies to various mentors—Martin Bax, Carruth, Davenport, Donald Faulkner (a poet and professor of creative writing at Yale), Daniel Javitch, Tomlinson.

Despite his resurgence as a poet, he could not let go of New Directions, and the old compulsion to be in on everything remained. He arose at 10:30 and made a daily trip to the Norfolk post office, standing by his box to sort through his mail, often returning for the afternoon delivery.

J kept his hand in, but running parallel to his reluctance to relinquish the decision making at ND was a genuine relief that his staff could and would run the firm quite competently in his absence. In addition, he handwrote, typed, or dictated about fifteen letters a day. He worked on his investments and presorted his papers for the town clerk, who came in once a week to file. After lunch he read manuscripts, spent a couple of hours at golf or fishing, and returned to submissions until it was time for his 5:30 vodka and tonic. After dinner he read *The New York Times* and then put in an hour on Greek classics (in translation), Latin classics (in the original), or Italian and perhaps watched a program on television. Then it was back to correspondence and manuscripts, often until 1:30 a.m.

Yes, New Directions was being run competently but not with much newness of *direction*. One of the loudest critics among the authors was Henry Miller, who at age eighty-seven and in the midst of a romance, passionate on his side, with the starlet Brenda Venus, fumed that Ohannessian was "the unique live wire in N.D." and that the firm had "a very poor reputation both among book buyers and book stores—too slow, too rigid, too conservative." Secure in his belief that he was about to become a Nobel laureate—he had gotten everyone he could think of to write letters of support to Stockholm—Henry ordered ND to give the film rights for *The Smile at the Foot of the Ladder* to Venus for nothing.

By the early 1980s a new J had emerged: he relied almost entirely on his ND staff to run the publishing house. He had long wanted a history of New Directions but had shot down Carruth's 1961 effort. He still labored under the delusion that a chronicle of ND could be written that would relegate him to a mere shadowy figure somewhere in the wings. He considered a prose autobiography, but then it struck him: Why not write his autobiography in verse, a loose collection of poems, each treating an event or person important to him? He had a second personal verse form that he called "busted trimeter" and that he had evolved from Rexroth's *The Dragon and the Unicorn*. J would write after Kenneth's death that this simple rhythm had been "Tossed to me from wherever / He is by the Cranky Old Bear." At first glance it might look like J's "typewriter metric," except that there were greater variations in line length and no hyphenated-word enjambments, and the lines began with capital letters. Thus the *Byways* sequence was born. He had "more or less" given up the typewriter metric, he said, because some saw it as an "affectation." What emerged he called "voice-cadenced free verse": "It's really / Just a prose cadence, broken / As I breathe while putting / My thoughts into words."

He began to sort letters, clippings, photographs, pamphlets into files: Ambit, Ancestors, Andrus, Angelica, Ann, Auden-Aubrey, Aunt Leila, Austria, Bacigalupo . . . Eventually, J had almost two hundred *Byways* folders in an open-topped wooden box at navel height on a special stand. The folders functioned as repositories of mnemonic aids rather than complete records of an event, his travels in a country, or the file of a specific correspondence.

As J turned more and more to sifting through his past, his life began to take the shape of some great postmodernist work in progress in which the membranes separating reality and fiction, and past, present, and future, become increasingly osmotic. He was moving ever further into the avant-garde, living a life of experimental fictions. In the wakeful hours of darkness he gave birth to poem after poem, mining the lodes of memory and fantasy. Usually, he sent a copy to the main subject, but it was useless for that person to write back in alarm, "That's not the way it was!" "That," J would be apt to reply, "is the way I like to remember it." Then he would add, "Don't worry, I'll change your name before it's published." When Ginsberg denied J's "myth" that he, Allen, had tried to attract Doc Williams's notice by leaving copies of his poems under the milk bottles at 9 Ridge Road, J declared, "I'll continue to tell that one because I know it is TRUE. I'm positive. It is what *should* have happened." Even his current correspondence tended to merge into the *Byways* wake: he would type a letter, decide that it was grist for the autobiography, and pop the original into his files, sending a carbon to the intended recipient.

J might have turned publishing and even skiing into vocations, making rational decisions and keeping a wary eye on the bottom line, but in his writing he tried to preserve the joy of avocation, the sense of play. As he sifted ancient files for *Byways* material, he typed or scribbled tiny notes, which he stapled to drafts. "There is some color here which will do just as well in English, though the nutty German tickles me," he told himself. J had learned French and Latin grammar well enough at Choate to receive top honors, but he lacked the patience and the true linguist's mania for perfection in minutiae. Languages were games one picked up like paddle tennis or golf, to be played for entertainment. For him, German evoked skiing, Italian young love, Latin erotic Catullus, French the culture of

Paris, Provençal Ezra Pound and the troubadours. J's mind rippled across languages like a jazz musician riffing.

Miller wrote his last letter to ND in October 1979 and died less than eight months later, on June 7. "Henry Miller gone," wrote J to Fred Martin. "That's the end of an era." In fact, while Henry had been one of ND's major authors from the first, he was of the second rank in J's esteem, and Henry on his side had not counted J among his really close friends. The letters reveal this: pedestrian on both sides, Henry's complaining or demanding, J's somewhat stilted, correct, a bit perfunctory. "Glad to know that dear old Hennery did not die in penury," rhymed J after receiving a statement on his finances.

Nor was ND doing badly throughout 1980. J gave the Norton sales staff major credit for the profit of nearly $24,000 at the end of the fiscal year in June 30, reversing the string of losses (with the exception of a tiny profit in 1976) of the previous five years.

J saluted Tennessee on March 26, 1981, his seventieth birthday, recalling "how much pleasure you have given me in those years: the opening night in Chicago of Glass Menagerie; and then of so many other wonderful plays; visits in Key West and encounters in various parts of Europe; your beautiful poems; and above all your loyalty to New Directions which has made possible the publication of so many young and unknown authors. Long may you flourish!" Tennessee lamented J's "semi-retirement," but J commented, "I just wish that were true. I seem to be working as hard as ever."

J drafted an introduction for Pound's translations and enjoyed the research. It was excellent therapy: "I had more excitement, more sense of being alive again, digging into the old books for the quotes and stringing them together than anything in years." More therapy was J's teaching at Brown University—and he was being paid $5,000 for seven lectures. His presentations were not written down: "I just talk them out of my head as I go along." His disarming appearance of rambling belied the fact that he always had a firm structure in mind and got through the material that he intended to cover. J warned the students at Brown that he would not turn in their grades until each had recited four lines of Latin for him—Catullus, Propertius, it did not matter what. He wanted them to feel "how the words move in the line, 'rubbing themselves' on each other." Wiesel prodded J toward autobiography. "At last the autobiographical work," he said soberly. "You can put life into otherwise dull literary history because you were there."

The autumn of 1981 found J back in England and France, this time as consultant for Lawrence Pitkethly's Voices and Visions film about Ezra Pound. It partook of the elements of a sentimental journey: Paris, Rapallo, Venice, Provence. The production crew retraced Ezra's early route around the Albigensian sites and filmed J on the ancient battlements of Hautefort. J interviewed Basil Bunting for the film in Hexham, Northumberland, priming the poet with a bottle of single-malt scotch. Eighty-one years old and still writing, as a young man Bunting had earned the praise of Pound, Yeats, Bill Williams, and Zukofsky. He astounded J by deriving Pound's musical phrasing in the *Homage to Sextus Propertius* from Whitman's "Out of the Cradle Endlessly Rocking," quoting from Whitman and Pound to support his point.

J could not have embarked on the project without feeling deeply moved, and his emotional agitation was redoubled when he fell in love with Cristine Moszynski, the French aristocrat who was Pitkethly's film editor. "Variety" was her nickname, and under the heady influence of her sensual charm and sophistication, "that thrilling, thrilling French voice," J felt his "interest in French" reviving. She read Proust "all the time," wore red slippers, and was "so surréaliste." Their conversation was entirely in French, and J strove to resuscitate and improve upon his vocabulary and even to make love in the language. "She has gotten me to writing in French again," J said. "I speak it to her as I hear it and then she fixes up the grammar." "Elle jette mes paroles dans l'air / comme un jongleur," he said in verse— She throws my words into the air like a juggler. As they coursed about troubadour-haunted Provence, J imagined himself as an aging but still passionate Bertran de Born celebrating a highborn lady. He wrote about the Provençal troubadour Marcabru, who once claimed, "Non amet neguna, ni d'autra non fo amet," that he was one who "never loved anyone and never was loved by anyone." J was aware that as an elderly lover he cut a somewhat ridiculous figure: "Les Vieillards / s'amourachent trop facile- / ment," he wrote—Old men fall in love too easily. But he could not help himself.

His emotions blended with his thoughts of mortality. "Will there be time coming after?" he asked. "The old poets converse with me / my past is an echo of their earlier pasts / is memory only a parody of what really happened?" J's love for Variety opened a new wave of passion in his life.

Sensuality and poetry, linked, had haunted him all his life but never with such intensity. It was as if Variety had shattered the dam holding in check both his emotions and his logodaedaly. The words simply cascaded forth.

For a time J imagined that his love was truly requited. Then Variety informed him in a "distant little voice" that she thought she loved someone else, softening the blow with a gesture at once intimate and devoid of sexual meaning: "of agape / of caritas," J thought. "It helped if only some- / what to diminish my despair," he wrote. "Je veux me grimer"—I want to play an old man's role—he titled another poem. His competitor was a "jeune poète qui res- / semble plus à Rimbaud / qu'à Byron." Faced with this rival more Rimbaud than Byron, whom Variety entertained in the expensive hotel rooms J booked for her, he now saw himself as "le vieux bouffon qui pour / quelques mois te faisait / rire et puis t'assomait"—he who had made her laugh now bored her. He felt so betrayed that he put aside for some years the poems that he had written under "horrid Variety's" inspiration.

J's emotional and creative life would never be tranquil again.

36

Lured by the *Apsaras*

> He
> will be forever earthbound
> if he dares to touch the
> long hair of an apsaras.
> —James Laughlin, "Apsarases,"
> dedicated to Vanessa Jackson

Occupied as J was by New Directions manuscript reading and correspondence as well as by love poetry, he claimed not to be clear in his own mind as to why he continued also to act as a lecturer and "literary entertainer." J could say no, but he chose not to. Underneath his diffidence, "J thought very highly of himself," his friend and portraitist Virginia "Gigi" Schendler said, and he welcomed the recognition. Again, "I don't know exactly why I do this," he excused himself to Tennessee, "except that it rejuvenates me to get out in the college world and meet the young students, who are so wonderful." "Rejuvenates" was the key word.

J and Ann went to Santa Barbara late in 1981 to see Rexroth, who had suffered a serious heart attack the past December, followed by two strokes. He was only seventy-six, but it was clear that he could no longer call back his once-formidable constitution through sheer will, and he was too impatient to work at the voice therapy that might fully restore his power of speech. On his return east J was featured at a party at the Gotham Book Mart to celebrate the inaugural issue of Brad Morrow's *Conjunctions*, for which Rexroth had served as consulting editor. Morrow had suggested making the first issue a Festschrift in honor of J. "Let me call Jim and get his take on this," Kenneth replied. He reported with Rexrothian hyperbole: "I spoke with Jim last night and he sounded like a blushing bride being carried upstairs on her wedding night." Within a month Kenneth's heart attack would occur. It was fitting that Rexroth's last significant effort was a salute to J, and he could not resist a few jabs. "I wouldn't have had a career without Laughlin, and I look on Laughlin as, I suppose, my best friend, and always a good comrade," Kenneth said. "I just write him abusive letters about literature, saying why does he publish such shit in New Directions." At this, Rexroth had laughed.

Acclaim continued to arrive: a profile in *The New York Times Book Review,* a ceremony months later at the B. Dalton bookstore in Greenwich Village, an invitation to speak on Bill Williams at Manhattan's Donnell Library Center. "I think it's a sign of old age," commented J. New Directions authors were doing well also. When Walter Abish's *How German Is It* received the PEN/Faulkner Award for Fiction, the book quickly sold six thousand copies, but J's pessimism did not allow him to gloat. "With us it's sometimes like the story about the woman at a cocktail party," he said, "who came up to the British publisher Jonathan Cape and asked, 'Do you keep a copy of every book you print?' He replied, 'Madam, I keep thousands.'"

On the night of Sunday, June 6, Kenneth Rexroth suffered a second massive heart attack. Carol Tinker summoned the paramedics, who hooked him up to a monitor: the EKG machine overloaded, blew a fuse, and he was gone. Kenneth had been adamant that he wanted to be buried with his face looking out over his feet at the Pacific. As the coffin was lowered into the grave, Brad Morrow, the head pallbearer, noticed to his horror that it was pointed in the opposite direction. He decided against making a scene: the old anarchist could take up the matter himself with the Almighty.

J and Ann headed for Europe in June for a stint of filming with Pitkethly. "Happy Hollywood days," wrote Dr. Wiesel in valediction. "I know you will p o u n d it out for the camera men." They went to Pisa, looking for some sign of Ezra's fateful DTC, but all they found were a pair of garbage tins marked "U.S. Army." (They had been even less successful in Northern Ireland: a quick side trip to Portaferry turned up no sign of the ancestral Laughlins.) In Venice they visited the beautiful church of Santa Maria dei Miracoli, site of Ezra's favorite stone cherub and mermaids. J was quite enjoying being the continuity figure, tying together Pound, books, people.

It had become his own memorial to Ezra. J hardly seemed to mind that the film was costing more than expected, and he lent Pitkethly $30,000.

•

Early in July 1982, J and Ann spent a week at the Centrum writers' conference outside Port Townsend, Washington. J did his "yatters," as he called them, and after his last talk he was mobbed by attendees clamoring for more of his "funnies." A crowd followed him to the campus house where they were staying; Ann turned in, but J held court until very late. Scott Walker of Graywolf Press urged J to write his memoirs, and Carol Jane Bangs, the conference director, encouraged him as well. By the end of the evening there was a tacit understanding that she would handle such library research as would be required. As the group dispersed, J insisted on walking Bangs to the parking area. Gallant in the moonlight, he took her keys, unlocked the car, and held the door for her. Although J would later claim that he had willed it, a single casual kiss from Carol, spontaneously given in the moonglow, gave him leave for romantic fantasies and frequent letters, sometimes twice in a day, to "Dearest Carol." He had spent only three minutes alone with her, J wrote, yet "I want to be alone with you in the rainforest, or by the water which stretches out to Japan, or in Provence, the place of my dreams."

Inspired, J returned to a prose memoir, which he referred to as his "Ought-to-bugg-offery," envisioned anew as a collaboration. Added incentive came when Alfred Knopf said he would publish these "meeeemoirs." This became "our book" in J's letters to Carol, and within a month Knopf had offered an advance of $7,500. Soon Little, Brown came in with a matching offer, and Knopf raised the stakes to $10,000. All proceeds were to go to Carol, J said. He was sure that she would collaborate "out of the kindness of your heart," but he didn't want to "exploit" her "or anybody else." He made new alphabetical lists that repeated and expanded his earlier list for *Byways*. Memory dwelled everywhere around J, but he found out almost at once that his memories refused to stay neatly compartmented. An affectionate remembrance of Dr. Wiesel drifted into a description of the bipolar states of his grandfather and father and then became a presentation of the personae speaking through his writing. J explained,

The great modern Portuguese poet Pessoa had four personae, writing differently for each one. I too, though not aspiring to imitate Pessoa, am four writers. 1) I am myself, trying to describe the life around me in very simple concrete stories; 2) I copy the poets of the Greek Anthology, Catullus, the Troubadours and other ancients in whom Pound instructed me; I write macaronics and centos, and imitations of Herrick and Rochester; 3) I am a mischievous fellow named Hiram Handspring, who does funny-papers in free verse; and 4) I write American-French sentimental poems in French, remembering the basic French that I learned in my year in Switzerland, because I became for a while "amouraché" as the French put it (that is, an inflammation of the senses) with a girl named V., who deserves her own chapter in this circumambulating book.

He wrote in whatever voice struck him as appropriate for the inspiration of the moment. Ann let it be known that she was unconcerned by what might be revealed in J's autobiographical drafts. "Oh, that's just J," she said with deft ambiguity.

One of J's doubles was redoubled when he invented as a doppelgänger for Hiram Handspring an academic critic, "a learned idiot," Professor J. Roger Dane, who cast a doubtful eye on Hiram's amatory versicles, writing in *A Structural View of Contemporary Verse*, "By my count, 81% of Handspring's published poems are about women. Yet, on the available evidence, he does not appear to have been very successful in this field— far more misses than hits." J was recasting his life in postmodern terms, with fictions annotating fictions annotating autobiographical fact. The name Dane glanced back toward the ancestry of the Laughlins. All this explains in part J's fascination with double personalities, Romain Gary (who wrote also as Émile Ajar), and the self-portrait doubles by the painter Egon Schiele. In J's analysis Gary had shot himself (in 1980) over the tension of *wanting* to be two people, whereas Schiele had accepted his double nature to the point of realizing that two men needed two women, so he had courted the Harms sisters, marrying Edith and making Adele his "affectionate model." J saw in the *acceptance* of his own multiple natures a hedge against suicide. It was, he said, an "obsessive need." Dane was a "fraud," a professor of dental surgery masquerading as a literary pundit, a role J had assumed with self-conscious irony.

J had also placed Carol: she was My Lady Maeut of Montaignac in the troubadour poems, and before that she was a girl in Catullus. By his fifth letter to Carol, J was writing conspiratorially about "our project": he had told no one, he said. She could move to New York and work in his office at New Directions, but it would be "sticky" if she came to Norfolk to use his archives. "I must explain that for twenty years I have been a prisoner, guarded by a benevolent but strong minded gaoler," he wrote. Were he to admit the collaboration to "the Major Domo," Ann would bring forward her own candidate, probably the local librarian who needed to pay off her mortgage. "Despite all the surface activity I have felt pretty moribund for a long time. I need to feel alive _inside_," he wrote to Carol. "You do that for me."

J's friendship with Robert Fitzgerald remained a constant in his life: J had entrusted the selection of his poems for _In Another Country_ to Fitzgerald. Pointedly, he told Carol about Robert's recent marriage to "his lovely young wife Penny." The fact that the Fitzgeralds seemed happy and compatible despite the wide difference in their ages fueled J's own dream of a new union, whether or not it was solemnized by marriage vows, although J did not suggest that Carol leave her "esteemed husband" for him. J set out to impress Carol with his wealth, implying that she would not lose from her association with him: "While ND runs only slightly in the black, my income from investments and trust funds runs about $1,000 a day, and my ski lift business in Utah netted $830,000 after taxes last winter."

For all of his complaints, J was where he liked to be. He now felt like a Provençal court poet in love: he could compose endless poems to the object of his adoration, secure in the knowledge that he was very unlikely to find his comfortable existence threatened by demands for rescue. He reveled in the role of hopeless aspirant, although he would have seized the chance of a tryst with Carol if offered. He joked to her that he was a "goofy truffador," "a troubadour who likes to gorge on paté truffé."

Then—"Hosannah & Eureka!"—after dithering over the project for ten years, on the evening of August 12, 1982, J typed out the first few pages of a _prose_ autobiography. He picked his friendship with Merton as a starting point, and he enjoyed the writing of it. Meanwhile, Ann had connected a change in J's attitude to their visit to Port Townsend. One day at dinner she told him, "You were so funny when we were in Italy and now ever since we were at Centrum the house is frosty as the frigidaire." J parried with a quip about the thermostat, but in truth he was mooning like a teenager over Carol. Inspired by his new collaborator, J wrote many long letters to her about his autobiography, suggesting sources and library collections for material, recalling incidents to include. "Ubi sunt qui ante nos in hoc mundo fuere?" he queried—Where are those who came before us into this world? The truth of his feelings lay mainly in his adjectives: it was "my dear father," Maria Britneva St. Just was a "nice girl but too domineering," Henry Miller was "that sweet but dirty old man." Soon J was proposing ways that he and Carol could "conjoin" and, if she found life with him fulfilling, marry. She could even become an editor at ND.

•

Hilda Doolittle was now a major presence on the ND backlist, and J, as agent for her daughter, Perdita, followed closely the fortunes of what was rapidly becoming a scholarly industry. Barbara Guest sent her biography in manuscript, and J found it "marvelous . . . a real story," so different from "that awful [Janice] Robinson book," another biography of H.D. When Susan Friedman sent him an expanded proposal for her edition of the H.D./Bryher letters, J urged *her* on, hoping that the appearance of this rare exchange would go far to deflect the "wild surmise" of the earlier biographer that Perdita was really D. H. Lawrence's daughter.

On September 30, there was a conference for the salespeople responsible for the national promotion of ND books. J's presentation seemed to go well, but at the luncheon for the group at the New York Yacht Club Fred Martin "got a bit pickled" and nearly fell into the trophy case. Although J characterized Fred as "this pompous little man with his pompous little beard"—J had *never* liked beards—he valued him for his business sense and his "almost filial devotion to me." J did not know the whole story: for several years the staff had been covering for Fred's incompetence. Then, suddenly, Gary Snyder announced that he wanted to give his next book to the North Point Press—just to help an old friend, Jack Shoemaker, the publisher. J had thought of Gary as his "best friend," he said, and he was at a loss over what to tell him. However, J had let slip that ND might cease publication a certain number of years after his death, and Gary did not wish to be left without a committed publisher. The final shove had come from Martin's visit to Kitkitdizze, when Snyder had been appalled by his behavior. Gary went to North Point but remained on cordial terms with J, who did not blame Gary. "There were special pressures in that wigwam," J said, and ND made it clear to Snyder that he would always be welcome back.

There were enough pressures in J's wigwam as well, largely because of his long-distance and unrequited courtship of Carol Bangs. J's distress over the defection of Snyder was minor in comparison with a letter he received from Carol, a letter that left "all my grandiloquent fantasies blasted away." She had told him, in effect, that her husband's relationship with their two children should not, could not, be shattered. "I am not a home-wrecker," J answered. He had allowed his imagination to outstrip reality. "Tonight I am deeply sad but alive."

J still wanted Carol to continue as his literary collaborator and suggested that she come to Norfolk with her children during the months when it was warm enough to live in the unheated Grey Barn. He brought up to Ann having Carol stay in the barn as a matter of scheduling, to make sure that it had not been promised to someone else. Ann's response, "hysterical and vitriolic, full of deepseated hate," was directed at J and took him by surprise. He was told that Carol could *not* live in the barn, *nor* work in the Meadow House archives, *nor* live in Norfolk. If J and Carol wanted to work in a rented house in New Haven, that would be acceptable. Ann departed for Manhattan. Furious, J at once called his lawyer, who told him that he could probably get a court order enjoining Ann from forbidding his friends access to houses that he owned or co-owned. It was sad evidence of the change on both sides from their early years together. For J to consider legal action missed the point when the real issue, whatever his rationale, was the proposed introduction into their circle of a younger woman. "ATRA DIES, one of the blackest days," J said. "I have had ENOUGH."

Regardless, J encouraged Carol to find lecturing engagements for him on the West Coast and looked forward to being near her, even though the "ground rules" that she had laid down stipulated that he was not to make an amorous nuisance of himself. And he continued to plan on having Carol spend months working on his Norfolk archives. Soon this began to appear possible. Back from New York, Ann chose not to refer to her outburst and was clearly trying not to provoke J. At the end of November she wrote a cordial letter to Carol offering the use of the Grey Barn in May and of one of her cars after Henry brought it back from Harvard. "The archives will furnish plots and color that no writer could think up!" she concluded. "I know you will be a big help to J." He posted a large file of Pound material for Carol to start in on.

Nineteen eighty-two continued to be a portentous year for J's vulnerable heart, for by early October he was in London, where he met Vanessa Jackson at Dr. Martin Bax's home. She was the editorial assistant for *Ambit* magazine. Under five feet four, Vanessa had a mane of reddish-roan hair and a rapid delivery—words tumbled from her as if she were afraid she would run out of time to express herself. She was a lecturer at Winchester Art School, created large bright abstractions in her Clerkenwell studio, and wore jeans in preference to gowns. She was also a voracious reader, and a good part of their first conversation consisted of Vanessa's naming American writers and J's responding, "Why, I published him." He returned to America days later and wrote a first letter, at once self-pitying, yearning, and revealing: "Probably by now you will have forgotten meeting me at Martin's that evening, but I cannot forget you. If you will indulge an old and rapidly decaying man, you were so lovely and so bright." J was sending her "one of my atrocities," a painting from his flower series. Then he used a line that echoed his teenage stories of insecurity: "If you think that there is any hope, please guide me what to do next." J's real hope was not for his art but in his heart: "I have seen our film"—he was referring to the Pitkethly production on Pound—"on the big screen and I think I am lovable. But I just can't love myself. In a remote way, will you? I have this need, like wanting to be President." *Variety* had wounded the old poet-lover in the locus of his romantic illusions, and Carol had pushed him gently aside. J looked now to Vanessa to stanch his heart's bleeding.

Before long, J was writing Vanessa several letters a week and poems in English, French, and transliterated Greek. Although Vanessa never claimed more than the educated European's smattering of traveler's Italian, French, and German, J imagined her fluent in all languages. "I tell the birds you can stop now," he wrote, since he now hears "a more lovely music," her voice in his dreams. In "La Luciole" he imagines her escaping like a firefly from his hand: "Je te vois voltigeante dans la / nuit et je te poursuis . . . mais / quand j'ouvre la main tu n'es / pas là." She became his reigning *apsara*: consoling, desirable, but, for the present at least, untouchable.

As inspired as J might have been by his infidelities, they surely damaged his marriage. Ann was hurt, although her devotion to him continued and evidently also her love for him. But an ironic tone came into her discourse: when a letter from Vanessa arrived, Ann would say, "Here's one from your Little Ray of Sunshine." It was not Ann's style to complain or J's to indulge in demonstrations of affection around the house. "I baked fresh bread for him every day and he never noticed," Ann told the Pound and Williams scholar Emily Wallace. Just what was J thinking? A clue might lie in an enigmatic but tender poem that he dedicated "for Ann." "You Were Asleep / when I came to bed," he wrote, "you stirred but / didn't really wake and / stretched out a hand to / cup my face as if you were / holding a bowl or a ball." Had J finally recognized the depth of her love and devotion and his own failure to reciprocate?

During the week before Christmas, J was in New York with Pitkethly recording voice-overs for the Pound film. Pitkethly scolded J: "James, you are being too professorial, for God's sake loosen up!" "It was Variety," J commented, "the fetching cutting girl from Argentina, who finally did get me loosened up. She started tickling me and I began laughing and got relaxed and talked colloquially." J had not yet assigned to Variety the adjective "horrid"—and he was writing to Carol Bangs, so his French lover was morphed, condescendingly, into the innocent-sounding "cutting girl." Also "QV"—Queen Victoria—had announced that she would "'try to become a sophisticated European wife' and not meddle in my private emotions. God, I hope she means it." He might not be a good poet, J said, "but I have the nature and needs of a poet."

J had been feeling "pretty uncomfortable" during the autumn, but he had not gone running to Dr. Wiesel, because he knew that he had brought on the "s[ui].g[eneris]. symptoms" by "writing extravagant letters to innocent young girls," in direct contravention of the psychiatrist's counsel. "Two reasons for the heautontimorumenic obstinacy," he continued. "First, I enjoy writing these letters so much and they are so extraordinary. I bet I am one of the better logodaedalists since S. J. Perelman." This was part of the charm of writing to Wiesel: J could pretend to assume the mantle of genius without seeming hubristic. J had another reason for courting discomfort: "In the slightly hypermanic state I write many more poems, which also makes me feel good."

Maybe J did after all realize that something had cracked in Ann's love for him. Her *devotion* to his needs seemed unchanged, but she was finding his infatuations wearing, however long on fantasy and short on consummation they might be. She had certainly known about Gertrude Huston and had tolerated his fascination with a long line of *apsaras* over the years, but she was finding it hard to accept some of the late arrivals,

Carol, Vanessa, and Variety especially. Perhaps she had hoped that by his late sixties he would finally have outlived his search for some indescribable and elusive ideal. For his part, J closed his heart against Ann.

•

J was teaching a seminar at Brown that would continue throughout the spring of 1983. "The faculty people liked it, but I'm afraid I diachronated the students into the ground with my nekuyas, and periploi, and polymetises, and Latin from St. Ambrose," he reported. "I put them out of it and they didn't know when to laugh at my polylingual jokes. I'll descend from the ladder for the future ones and just tell stories." J ran the Brown seminar like a ringmaster. He was supposed to be team teaching with Anthony Oldcorn and Keith Waldrop, but he also brought in a string of guest lecturers: the Pound scholars Hugh Kenner and Louis Martz, and, once, Mary de Rachewiltz. There was great hilarity when J read a poem that contained three quotations from *Don Giovanni*, and Waldrop and Margot Schevill, a well-known singer and anthropologist married to a member of the Brown faculty, sang relevant passages from the opera, a cappella, with Waldrop as Leporello and Schevill as Donna Anna. Not every session was a triumph. One friend of Pound's, who had learned Chinese at Ezra's instigation, gave a lecture of unremitting dullness. Waldrop glanced around at the students: many were asleep. Then he looked at J: he too had dozed off. Nonetheless, J derived real pleasure from his teaching at Brown, and he would eventually bequeath to its John Hay Library much of his collection of the great moderns.

On February 25, 1983, J was scheduled to be awarded the Medal of Honor at the National Arts Club on Gramercy Park. Dr. William Eric Williams, the poet's son, spoke, as did Jack Hawkes, Fred Busch, and Lawrence Pitkethly. Tennessee Williams promised to come, but then he remembered that he was scheduled to head for Sicily, and so on Peggy Fox's urging he sent a statement to be read. Unexpectedly back in New York, yet still a master of stage timing, Tennessee died the night before the ceremony as the result of an apparent overdose of Seconal. That afternoon J closed the door to his office at New Directions and tried to capture his feelings in verse, in words that suggested that he was beginning to come to terms with his own death. Brad Morrow, the emcee, read Tennessee's final message to J from the podium: "It was James Laughlin in the beginning and it remains James Laughlin now, with never a disruption or moment of misunderstanding in a friendship and professional relationship that has lasted for forty years or more." After typing that he had been "meant for the quieter and purer world of poetry than for the theatre," Tennessee canceled the next sentence and wrote in by hand the prophetic words "And now as a time for reckoning seems near, I know that it is the poetry that distinguishes the writing when it is distinguished, that of the plays and of the stories, yes, that is what I had primarily to offer you." This salute, J remarked, "touched me more than I can say," and then he read the poem he had just written: "Tennessee / called death the sudden subway and now he has taken that train," but he had left behind "so many fine things to remember / that I can live again in my mind / until it is my turn to join him on the sudden subway."

37

"Il Catullo americano"

Catullus is my master and I mix
a little acid and a bit of honey
in his bowl   love

is my subject & the lack of love.
—James Laughlin, "Technical Notes"

Even a decade later J would weep when he read his valedictory poem for Tennessee. "I loved him—he was my friend," he said. Not many people saw J let down his guard. "How easily J cried, at least at the movies!" in the anonymity conferred by darkness, remembered another friend, Deborah Pease. "We saw Louis Malle's *Au revoir les enfants* and at one point I glanced at J and saw tears running down his otherwise impassive face." The man who habitually deflected his emotions with wit, irony, or silence in face-to-face situations could still be ambushed into tears: here, by a film treatment of friendship and anti-Semitism. A lifetime of public reticence had not so much blighted his affective life—*that* was revealed in his poetry—as posed a powerful bar against achieving closeness with those he loved.

Tennessee's death brought Lady Maria St. Just back to America, and she let it be known that she was not going to be a mere figurehead executor. A *Collected Stories* was planned, and there was discussion about a candidate to write an introduction. "I'll call GORE"—in Rome at the time—announced Her Ladyship peremptorily, picking up the phone in Peggy Fox's office: "Hello GORE, this is Maria . . . You *will* write an introduction!" "Yes, Maria!" Vidal replied without demur, and in due time one of the finest of all statements about Tennessee appeared in the mails. "I cannot write any sort of story, unless there is at least one character in it for whom I have physical desire," Vidal quoted the playwright. "Tennessee's stories need no explication," Vidal concluded his essay. "So what are they *about*? Well, there used to be two streetcars in New Orleans. One was named *Desire* and the other was called *Cemeteries*. To get where you were going, you changed from the first to the second. In these stories and in those plays, Tennessee validated with his genius our common ticket of transfer."

Now that he was in demand on the college circuit, J was overcoming his lifelong aversion to textual analysis. But when some students wanted to apply semiotics to Pound, J handed out a paper applying semiotics to the "Usura" canto and challenged them to explain in simple language what it all meant. They could not. "That hushed them up a bit," he said happily. But when Richard Sieburth, a young Harvard scholar, lectured by invitation to J's class at Brown, J reported it as a "stupendous" presentation on Pound's structure. And when Anne Janowitz wrote to J for permission to reprint in her dissertation on Canto 74 some of his verse about Pound, not only was he flattered to be cited, but he himself typed out notes on sources, implying that *she* was doing him a favor by allowing him to carry on so. "I know you know all that I see in it, but let me pleasure myself by running through a few lines," he wrote, allowing his mind to leap from the "city of Dioce" to Frobenius and Wagadu to Italian postage stamps showing a circular city as the headdress of a goddess, warning Janowitz that "EP thought of himself as foxy"—in other words, *caveat lector*—and then himself spilling over into reminiscences of his own travels in troubadour country. For J, literature had to come alive, and there was no impermeable boundary between the worlds created by Catullus or Hawkes and his own life, between his present and his favorite authors of every epoch.

In May 1983, Carol Jane Bangs was able to take a month away from Centrum to work with J on his prose autobiography. After she spent a few days lodging at the Chelsea so that she could go through some of J's New Directions files, J and Ann installed her for three weeks in the Grey Barn. J quickly established a routine with his collaborator: she would come to his office late in the morning, they would discuss her work, and J would give instructions, after which he would leave for golf or to read ND manuscripts. Sometimes they had lunch together. Ann seemed to have decided that Carol was not—or no longer—a romantic interest for J. Although J would maintain for the rest of his life that "he was still working on our book," he became increasingly distracted by the verse of *Byways* and by a continuing succession of newer *apsaras*.

Vanessa arrived from London in mid-August, and she was invited to the Bank Street apartment for dinner with Ann and J. The young woman found her meeting with J, almost ten months after their encounter at Martin Bax's party, highly disconcerting. He stared, or rather glared, in her direction, finally wondering out loud if she were not an "impostor": he had remembered her hair as black. She was not the same person, he said, leaving it to Ann to entertain her. Finally, toward the end of the evening, he thawed out, and the tension eased: this *was* the woman he had met in London. "Could the blackness of the dress you wore at Martin's have distorted my memory of your chevelure?" he asked her. "You Came as a Thought," J titled the poem that he enclosed with his letter of the following day, "when I was past such thinking / you came as a song when I had / finished singing you came when / the sun had just begun its set- / ting you were my evening star."

J showed Vanessa around his favorite Village spots, and they dined at the Gauloise. He called her Strawberry, and sometimes they spent days together at the Hotel Chelsea on Twenty-Third Street, when J would work at the office while she painted in a friend's studio. He wrote "Una Ricordanza Tenera" about their Chelsea days, a tender poem about a quarrel made up when "I knelt at the / bedside to present my contrition," a pot of African violets. J adopted a new code name for Ann in his letters to Vanessa: PR, short for public relations. She had become his public consort: "Ann's Social Steamshovel Weekends" the family called those times when all the beds in the three houses on the property were full.

•

During the spring of 1983, Fred Martin spent a month at a clinic for alcoholism after yet another intoxicated display. He returned to New Directions, but when his erratic behavior at the annual meeting in May of the American Academy of Arts and Letters was reported to J, Ann convinced him that Fred must be let go. J relied heavily on Ann's advice in personnel matters: "HOW would I meet such penible situations without Ann to bolster me up?" Reluctantly, he telephoned Fred and asked for and received his resignation. J was up to four lithium tablets a day but was still "very jumpy" in the mornings.

Griselda Ohannessian was named to succeed Martin as vice president. This in itself represented an evolution in J's thinking, almost certainly urged on by Ann: he had actually chosen a woman to run New Directions. By this time Ohannessian had a strong record of responsible management and effective dealing with some of the less tractable authors, and she was utterly devoted to ND. The trio of Ohannessian, Peter Glassgold, and Peggy Fox had launched important collected editions of William Carlos Williams and Tennessee Williams. In the reorganization, Glassgold remained editor in chief. Fox continued as senior editor, handling foreign rights, copyrights, and contracts as well, and she was given responsibility for the Pound, W. C. Williams, and Merton estates.

Increasingly, Ohannessian and Fox ran New Directions. Peggy had been advising Fred Martin on financial management, and she continued in that function with Ohannessian. Griselda initiated the Revived Modern Classics series, but she kept stubbornly to the old ND mantra, that books should be "priced down where the students could buy," with the result that ND books were often priced below the competition. Dan Allman finally, with W. W. Norton's and Peggy's encouragement, prevailed upon Griselda to authorize raising prices across the board, and ND's profit picture improved dramatically.

In the autumn of 1983, Lee Bartlett and Hugh Witemeyer at the University of New Mexico organized a series of lectures for J at several universities from Missouri to California. J listed topics on which he was prepared to speak, ranging from a history of New Directions to "Pound and the Troubadours." He liked to complain about how nervous these lectures made him, but he was offered jobs at three of the institutions. J often sat in on classes during the tour, enjoying the students because they did not know enough about him to be awed into silence.

Ann did all the driving. Although she knew Wyoming and the adjacent states well, she had never been to the Southwest, and J wanted especially to show her Mesa Verde and the Canyon de Chelly. It was on this trip that J met the Albuquerque poet Jimmy Santiago Baca, a protégé of Levertov's while she was poetry editor of *Mother Jones*. Like Corso, he had blossomed into a writer while in prison. Soon ND would publish several volumes of his poetry. Witemeyer himself was a figure who invited epic comparisons: nearly as tall as J, he, like a younger Laughlin, could range all day on mountain trails and hold an audience transfixed with his stories. He had an intuitive understanding of J and insisted on plenty of time in the speaking schedule for sightseeing and golf. J scored a hole in one "on the great course at Tucson." Two years later J would ask Witemeyer to edit a selection of the Laughlin–William Carlos Williams correspondence for Norton, the first of a correspondence series featuring J and his author friends.

It would have been an entirely satisfying trip but for what J called "this miserable affair of Robert." Like his father, Robert had been on lithium for years, but now had stopped taking his medication and was in a Los Angeles clinic. The news of Robert's crisis caught up with Ann and J as they drove north to Salt Lake City, and she talked without letup about him, until within a few hours J suffered "a bad recurrence of the old shortness of breath." Far back, Robert had been expelled from Choate and then the progressive Putney before being sent to the Institute of Living in Hartford, Connecticut. He wanted no part of college. He had been treated by many psychiatrists, and he had been in and out of mental institutions. The trouble for J was that Ann wanted to involve him constantly with Robert, and she was making the most of their car-bound togetherness to persist in what J termed "proing and conning." Back in Norfolk, J asked Wiesel to intercede for him: "I wish there were some way you could get her not to take it out on me, before I react in hot temper."

One outcome of this trip was a commitment from Sandra and Harry Reese of the Turkey Press at Isla Vista to print a hand-set *Stolen & Contaminated Poems.* Harry persuaded J to write "Not-Notes" to follow his poems. The "stolen" poems were *imitatio,* "outright thievery" from classical poets, "where, say, Ariosto is retelling a scene from Ovid"; *contaminatio* was a rhetorical term that described, as J explained, "the juxtaposition of incongruities," with a mixing of sources and sometimes of the languages involved, in a deliberate *sullying* of the originals, "making fun of our debased culture." Harry taught printing and book design at UC Santa Barbara, and his wife did much of the actual printing and multicolor plates for their press. Sandra Reese came for a few days to Meadow House to design the volume. J was formal in manner, rather courtly. Once in the small hours she heard shuffling footsteps, and his form appeared in

the open doorway of her room. "Oh, I see you're still asleep," he murmured. "It must have been the angel who kissed my cheek." He turned
and walked slowly away.

J resolved to stop accepting most invitations to lecture because he
found plane travel more and more tiring, the partially obstructed arteries
in the muscles of his long legs complaining in the cramped seats. He also
wanted to husband his time and energy for his memoirs. J ended 1983 in,
he thought, reasonably good health: some shortness of breath, but no depression. He was only seeing Dr. Wiesel around once a month, and even
then "chiefly because I love him so much, he is so funny. He tells the best
Jewish stories I've ever heard." With a certain pride J added, "He says I
am the most complicated and eccentric customer he's ever had." J now
only took half a valium when insomnia struck or when he had to fly: "This
is not fear of flying but 'airport terror.' Ben [Wiesel] says I can't handle any
situation I can't control, such as missing a plane or a connection." During
1983 he addressed himself to arranging the aftermath of his own mortality. He mentioned to Donald Lamm, president of Norton, that he had a
plan for keeping ND going after his death, and he implied that he would
make some provision to cover losses, provided the larger company would
guarantee to keep ND afloat. He felt dual responsibility: to his authors
and to his core employees. He drafted the first of several revisions of his
will, to provide funding for the continuing operation of the firm.

"I keep too busy to be gloomy," J wrote to Vanessa. He desperately
wanted her to be a part of that world that death could not touch, invent-
ing a vicarious life with her. When the temperature dropped to minus
twenty at Norfolk, he wrote, "Today we (that's you and me) went skiing
but it was so cold we had to turn back after about 15 minutes . . . I was
afraid you might freeze your nose. Without a nose you would be a Picasso
woman. I'd still love you, of course."

J was awarded the Signet Society Medal for Achievement in the Arts
at Harvard. His son was now a Harvard senior, and J lay on Henry's bed
before the presentation dinner, trying to calm his jittery stomach. It would
be "an interminable evening," and he would have to give a comedic speech.
"Maybe I could be brought in on a wheelchair?" he wondered. "That would
be dramatic and appropriate to this venerable organization." The main
speaker was Brendan Gill, who embarrassed J by naming him the best publisher in America. "Bob Giroux is much better, and everybody knows
that," J commented. The citation proclaimed that this *"servant of the ser-*

vants of the muse" had remained steadfast to his calling, even if it meant sometimes "*to scandalize one's uncles.*" Some of these uncles, at Harvard at any rate, would not cease to be scandalized and would veto various proposals over the years that J be given a Doctorae Honoris Causa at his alma mater. Such was the price for publishing Ezra Pound.

Whenever he could, J worked on the "Not-Notes" for the Reeses. "I lost a day because of my failing memory," he wrote in seeming lamentation. "I thought 'Felix qui potuit rerum cognoscere causas'"—Happy is he who is able to understand the causes of things—"was Lucretius himself, and went through the whole text of 'De Rerum Natura.'" Finally, J recalled that it was from *Virgil's* tribute to Lucretius. As the Reeses struggled to reproduce his poems in hand-set type that approximated his typewriter metric, J had to admit that he was making their lives difficult. "Where this system collapses is when you get thin 'i's, 'l's, 't's in type and the matching visual lengths are lost," he told Harry. "I suppose I should compose on a type-stick, but then it wouldn't be typewriter." J trusted neither the quality of his own typing nor the accuracy of his proofreading eye. Finding that Harry's editorial acumen was as meticulous as his printing, J simply turned most decisions over to him, telling him "you are the greatest since Gutenberg." J was delighted when, early the following year, Harry suggested printing another volume of J's poetry, and *Heart Island and Other Epigrams* would eventually appear in 1995.

J acquired a new toy, a Canon desktop photocopier. He soon discovered a use for it as a designer's printing press on which he created whimsical letterheads to suit subject, recipient, and his own mood, often copying etchings and cartoons from the *Dictionnaire infernal* and from an 1855 Paris magazine that he had found in a Manhattan bookshop, or creating abstractions with paper clips and rubber bands. J was finished at Brown for the semester, and he attacked his projects, beginning work on a William Carlos Williams film for the Voices and Visions series, lamenting to Vanessa, "Dearest Dora Bubble," that since Williams had spent so little time in England, he had no excuse for coming to see her. "Your letters gladden me," he told her, "I do <u>need</u> them, and I need the thought that you love me"—the *thought* of her love he believed was enough to sustain him. Spring came late. "The sheep are scraggling in irritation in the meadow," J told Vanessa, "no new grass yet." He would lean over the fence to commiserate with them.

In June 1984, Jones & Laughlin Steel merged with LTV Steel and the family name vanished from Pittsburgh business rosters. J "felt a sense of tragedy about it," his friend Don Faulkner said, "but he had so distanced himself that he did not feel personal guilt"—and he had long since dumped his J&L stock.

•

Increasingly, J found himself saying final goodbyes. Robert Fitzgerald lay dying in the autumn of 1984, and J phoned nearly every day. After Robert's death, J wrote "A Leave-Taking," surmising that he had gone "not, I think, to dark Erebus, but to a happier place / Reserved for the good & the great, for our friends the Greek & Latin poets. / And I believe that such a land exists though I am uncertain of its location."

This death hit J especially hard and made him yearn to escape. He and Ann decided on a winter trip to the Alps, and when Henry announced on short notice that he and his longtime companion, Carlene Carrasco, were getting married in December, they decided to make it a foursome. They traveled to Zell am See, not far from the Grossglockner in the Kitzbühel Alps, one of J's favorite places half a century earlier but not now. "Lotsa Great Art but the girls have big feet and look constipated," he wrote. He sent Ann and his son off to ski the magnificent slopes, while he walked or sat talking quietly to Carlene. Here at the site of so many youthful adventures and dreams of literary accomplishment, J wondered to her whether he had done the right thing in his schooling. He said that he felt intimidated by the academic world because of his own lack of an earned advanced degree. "I don't know if I could ever have done anything like that," he mused. The old bipolarity still haunted him: he knew that he knew a great deal, but in a haphazard way. He still doubted his ability to plow a straight furrow, and it nagged at him.

J pondered the inadvisability of returning to places of happiness, the inn at Zermatt, the Due Torri restaurant in Verona. By any measure but his own he had accomplished a lot; he had so much to find joy in. But had his ventures and travels brought him real knowledge? Had his marriages or his liaisons given him lasting happiness? He wondered whether perhaps his discontent was simply an expression of the human condition. On the back endpaper of his Flaubert he copied out the master's pessimistic words: "Without the Concept of Happiness existence would be more bearable."

His son Robert was twenty-seven and at last seemed to have found in film erotica a consuming interest; at least he talked expansively about directing. In late February 1985 he was staying at the Bank Street apartment, and he asked his mother to come over in the evening to see a video production. Ann excused herself just before nine from the supper she was having with her sister, Helen, uptown. J was dining elsewhere with Lady Maria St. Just and some other friends. The door at 9 Bank Street was bolted from within. Ann could hear her son walking about, and they even spoke through the door, which he refused to open. Fearful but unwilling to summon the police, she telephoned J and waited for him to come. Finally he arrived and they both spoke to Robert, but he would not allow them in. It was a neighbor who finally persuaded them to call the police. The door of the now-silent apartment was forced, and they ascended the stairs. Sensing what they would find, J attempted to hold Ann back. Robert lay in the bathtub, the still water red about his lifeless form. "The floor / was a carpet of blood," J wrote in "Experience of Blood," a coolly dispassionate poem. "I never knew there was so much blood / in a man until my son killed himself." With a kitchen knife, he had stabbed himself and cut his wrists, before, J said, "expiring, classically, in the bath." J's actions at the time seemed as dispassionate as his poem, but they were his way of working out the sorrow and guilt he felt for not having been able to help his tormented son. He worked for four hours to wipe and scrub every trace of blood from the apartment: "I couldn't have asked anyone else / because after all it was my blood too." In fact, J had altered the story for dramatic impact: Daniel Javitch had assisted him.

Robert's death brought a further ordeal: J had to identify the body at the Bellevue morgue. There was a fairly lengthy wait, during which J worked out an inscription on the wall "in somewhat cockeyed Latin," listening to Muzak renditions of Schubert's "Ave Maria" and of "Jesu, Joy of Man's Desiring." Dropping her decorous poise for a moment, the young woman manager barked into an intercom, "Damn it, Harry, what are you doing with Number 29 down there?" and Robert materialized in the Viewing Room. "He had now the long, thin face of his ancestors because there was no blood left in him," J noted. To himself and to Robert, J "spoke silently": "I pray you will have a good crossing."

38

Revision of Things Past

When he was young he read many books,
he devoured them. Later he tried to be a
writer. But he discovered that words
have a life of their own, often not
saying what he wanted them to say.
　　—James Laughlin, "The Life of Words"

"Ann is holding up well," J wrote a few days later to Harry Reese, "and I just don't let myself think about it." J's evasion was characteristic, and Ann had always coped with trouble by taking charge: of her own emotions and by busying herself with needful activity. But for all her brave front, she was deeply saddened by her son's death. J's own feelings were mixed. He wrote a witty letter to Guy Davenport, headed "O Maestro di los che sanno"—Master of those who know. He summed up, very briefly, Robert's psychoanalytic treatment and death, concluding, "In his situation, I think I would have done the same, though perhaps with a less symbolic procedure. Very disturbing—but no condolence is expected. Those roisterers on Olympus deal with us at their pleasure." His son's death had brought a certain element of relief to J: a disturbing problem that he had been unable to resolve was over. He had been more profoundly affected by the loss a month earlier of the man for whom his son had been named, Robert Fitzgerald.

From this time on, Davenport entered the sanctum of J's regular correspondents, of those who helped J live his inner life. With Davenport, J could indulge his logomania and his puns without appearing to be showing off: Guy was easily his match, and he had been weaving in and out of J's ken since 1973. Guy had visited Pound at St. Elizabeths and had written a dissertation at Harvard under Harry Levin's direction on the early cantos, which became a book; he had known Doc Williams; he lived in Lexington, where he taught at the University of Kentucky, and was welcome in the circle of Merton's friends, the Victor Hammers and the photographer Eugene Meatyard. He was proud of his Danish ancestry, yet with his intense dark eyes, helmet of black hair, and heavy eyebrows he did not look Scandinavian. He lived a quasi–bachelor life in a good-size urban house, and his best friend was Bonnie Jean Cox, head of women's studies at the University of Kentucky.

It had always been a part of J's nature not to be threatened by those who possessed talents or pools of knowledge outside his own. As the two men explored each other in their letters, J developed absolute confidence in Guy as a sage. To send Guy his Brown lecture notes describing Ezra reclining with his head below the level of his feet so that the sperm would flow to his brain was to provoke a disquisition on the folklore of sperm. "Sperm is from brain *to* testicles in classical mythology," Guy wrote. "The brain was a reservoir of oily gunk which lubricated the joints and made a solution for the seed." And so on at length. And Guy was an artist in paint as well. His portrait of Ezra was *"remarkable,"* J said, even though "it makes me so sad because you've caught the misery of those last years. His body so thin, the look of hostility and confusion in his eyes." J requested a contribution for the fiftieth annual, and when "Wild Clover" arrived, he burst out, "ZOWIE!! Your botanical *pastourelle* of tumescence is so beautiful." Self-deprecation was another trait the two men shared. Guy referred to his meticulously crafted writings as "my ravings," and he was dismissive of his paintings: "I'm essentially a comic-strip artist—everything obvious and boldly colored, with ZAP! And GRR-R! for dramatic *pouf.*"

Carlene and Henry, having resumed their honeymoon with a trip to Brazil, had cut their visit short to attend Robert's funeral. Now they planned to go on to Chile. "Why don't you come with us?" Carlene asked J and Ann. "We could see Nicanor," said J, brightening. "Let's call him," Henry interjected before his father could change his mind. They toured the Santiago regions of Conchalí and La Reina, and J attended Parra's class at the University of Chile in Santiago; a student demonstration brought out the troops, and a tear-gas grenade came through the window for a whiff of Chile under the Pinochet dictatorship. J and Nicanor took refuge in the men's room. "Thank you especially for arranging with the authorities for the exciting events at the university," J wrote later to Parra. They made a pilgrimage to Bellavista to see La Chascona, home of the late Pablo Neruda. They drove south through San Vicente, Curicó, and Talca. Together they "perambulat[ed]" the shady streets of Talca, talking, Parra in his "Anti-Poet" mode, J as Hiram Handspring:

AP: Is it true that when the horse looks back the landscape changes?

HH: Who would prefer teargas to buying five kisses?

"I don't know what came over me that I began to sing like crazy," Nicanor remembered. "You gave me so much new energy." They experienced a minor earthquake: "Unheimlich"—weird—J thought. The countryside around Valdivia was lovely, "like northern Italy." For J, Chile was a wonderful escape; Ann carried her grief along, silently.

His contacts with his author friends still stimulated him, but J was finding it increasingly hard to retain much interest in the old New Directions standbys. From 1972 through 1983 there had been two *NDPP* anthologies per year; then only one appeared in 1984, and J was having serious doubts about the anthology planned for 1985. "There may be some good backed up stuff that I have forgotten about," J confided to Ohannessian and Glassgold, "but this new batch of stuff for ND49 is very discouraging." He proposed a new policy: that they abandon any pretense of a regular schedule and publish only when enough good material had come in. As an alternative, he suggested that they switch to the "Pushcart system"—that is, reprint the best from various little magazines rather than insist on finding unpublished material. As a drastic alternative, he considered abolishing the annual. He did nothing. The fact that he no longer made an effort to impose any decision showed that he really was relinquishing control.

J's *Stolen & Contaminated Poems* finally arrived from the Turkey Press, beautifully bound by the Reeses themselves. "What a book!" J exclaimed to Harry. "Or perhaps a series of paintings with type." J appeared to have succeeded fairly well in laying the ghost of Robert through evasion, whereas Ann proposed making a film on bipolar disorders, with the practical aim of informing sufferers who might not have recognized what was wrong or how to cope with the disease. From the first, J disapproved. To him, it smacked of obsession, of Ann's tendency to mull over difficulties. Ann was not to be denied. The film was her way "to make up to him," to pay her own debt to Robert, J decided. Soon she was in consultation with several biological psychiatrists, and the project that would lead to *Four Lives: A Portrait of Manic Depression* was born. The completed hour-long film presented case histories, informational rather than research-driven. It would be widely shown on public television, with Ann listed as the executive producer.

Nineteen eighty-five was Pound's centennial year, and J was in demand at conferences across the nation. Since many scholars attended every meeting, J assumed that he must compose a new talk for each, and he planned carefully: "Humor at Maine. Pedagogy at Yale. Economics at Alabama," and "maybe I'll do his love life at San José." J no longer felt that he had to crusade for the mere acceptance of Ezra as a major poet: that battle was won; now he could focus on the approach to Pound. "I am about the last one alive who knew him as he was in his prime," he told Parra, "and I try to dispel the nonsense put out by the post-structuralist critics." The Alabama Pound conference went all right, J said, with one quibble: "My talk on economics was a failure as no students asked me for plastic explosives to blow up banks."

The anniversary of Ezra Pound's birth was celebrated by a gala program on October 29 at the Library of Congress and by a lecture series at Yale. In November, J's "Solving the Ezragrams: Pound at 100" appeared on the first page of *The New York Times Book Review.* The article lauded Pound for his accomplishments in translation, essays, criticism, and especially *The Cantos,* and J described his wartime predicament and the course that sent him to St. Elizabeths. But to call Ezra's wartime broadcasts "controversial" was unwise on J's part, at least without explaining himself: the *controversy,* to those familiar with the facts, lay not in the content of the broadcasts but in Ezra's *intent. The New York Times* printed a sprinkling of letters attacking Pound.

When Humphrey Carpenter sent J the typescript of his Pound biography, J replied with a seven-page letter of specialized knowledge, critiques, and anecdotes. J cautioned Carpenter against losing readers in expositions of theory and then gave his own explication of Pound's method of contrasts: "I think here that most Poundians would say that the Luminous Detail and the Ideogramic Method were a bit different . . . The 'ideo' comes from Ez looking at the characters in Cathay, and seeing that meaning words rub on each other without small syntactical connectives. So he could put things or phrases together paratactically . . . He wants to have the disjuncts combat each other and stir up the reader's mind to form judgments." J also warned against imputing symbolic intent to Ezra in instances where he probably intended literal meaning: one scholar had debated at length "what the half-full glass of water stood for," but Mary de Rachewiltz had told J emphatically, "I remember that day he was writing that canto and he was sipping from a glass of water." Another mistake, J said, was to think that Pound assumed roles as a sort of tease. "I wouldn't call the impish Ez a persona," he said. "That was just Ez." He was what he seemed.

•

In September 1985, Vanessa Jackson arrived from London for a fellowship at Yaddo. J proposed that they collaborate on a fine-press limited edition: she would provide a dozen woodcuts in color, and his poems would appear on alternate pages. *The House of Light* became perhaps the most beautiful of all J's volumes of poetry: Monotype Poliphilus impressed on cream Rives paper, deckle edges, with Vanessa's woodcuts silk-screened on facing pages. Under Vanessa's influence J was overcoming his reluctance to use the telephone. There was now an answering machine in the south office, and J would watch for the blinking light—"the lighthouse of love," Ann called it—and listen to the voice before answering. By November, Vanessa had moved in with her friend Jill Levine in New York. J had been watching a film on Perseus and Andromeda, he told Vanessa, and had concluded, "I don't think we can rely on the gods to look after us." Therefore, he had worked out plans A, B, and C. The first two involved ways of subsidizing Vanessa—studio, apartment—in a way that would preserve her independence. He knew that she had a serious relationship of seven years' standing in England, and in any case he had never proposed to her a permanent separation from Ann. Plan C he termed a "stopgap": a trip together to Sicily. To his astonishment, J now discovered that he had a critical if intermittent sexual dysfunction. "What can this be?" he wrote to Wiesel. "Guilt, anxiety, over-excitement?" To Vanessa he said,

"I've been rather down ever since the French girl put me through her wringer. It was a deflating experience." He told Vanessa that merely being close to her was "like a seal" on their very real mutual affection. Reading Flaubert's correspondence in Francis Steegmuller's translation, J underlined the key word: "Finally I'm beginning to have an erection . . . But how hard it's been to get it up! Will it stay?" (Viagra was still thirteen years in the future.) As usual, J tried to work out his feelings in verse, with a nod in title and first line to Delmore Schwartz. "Under His Microscope," J wrote, "the scientist of love / is observing a most / fascinating little crea- / ture she is delicate . . . but his lens / cannot interpret her signs."

Early in May, J took part in a joint reading by American and Indian poets at the garden cafeteria of the Metropolitan Museum of Modern Art. Gregory Corso led J around the tables, introducing him to people neither of them knew: "This is my *son*, James. Gary says he is a good poet." J read seven of his own poems, deliberately ending with "My Muse," who, like Gregory himself, usually called in the night "at the most inconvenient hours." He hoped that Corso would make a scene when he heard the line "The last time Gregory called it was to ask me if I would leave him my teeth in my will." But Gregory didn't rise to the bait, and J worried that he might have hurt his feelings.

Ann was well aware of the intensity of J's correspondence with Vanessa. They shared a love of books and of abstract art—not *too* abstract on J's side—by such people as Stuart Davis, Charles Demuth, John Marin, and Charles Sheeler. But there was much more to it than that, and if he did not divulge the details to Ann, she must have guessed that there were some extended meetings. In May, J flew first-class to Europe for a fortnight. In Paris he and Vanessa had a long weekend of Picasso (whom J still disliked) and Brancusi and Le Palais Royal–Musée du Louvre, an elegant dinner at Le Grand Véfour under branched candelabra, where they sat on the Jean Cocteau banquette, drinks at La Coupole and Le Dôme. Vanessa discoursed on painting and deduced from the brushstrokes which painters were left-handed. J walked her about the haunts of his early sojourns: 7 rue Edmond Valentin, where he had been received by Joyce; 70 bis rue Notre-Dame-des-Champs, where the Pounds had served tea to the Hemingways, and so on. Many of the places and episodes would appear in J's romantic fantasy, *Angelica*. It was a glorious sentimental journey: old memories, new sentiment.

Back home, J complained of daily sinus headaches that he swore were caused by pollen, and he considered a trip to Norway, "which is said not to have such plagues." Then, instead of Norway, he bolted to London on July 21 to see Vanessa again. After a few days they flew to Milan and on to Sirmione, then by boat to the Grotto of Catullus. They saw the amazing Mantegna frescoes in Mantua, made a brief pilgrimage to Rapallo, and took the train to Salzburg, the city more than any other evocative of J's youthful adventures. The most fanciful Mozart opera set the tone for their visit to Vienna: *Die Zauberflöte*, emblem of J's Papageno fantasies. A feast of Brueghels, Vermeers, and Titians followed at the great Kunsthistorisches Museum, and at the Albertina J got special permission for them to see the erotic paintings by Egon Schiele. Their cultural tour ended in Vienna, where Vanessa fell in the bathroom of their hotel and cracked two ribs. J escorted her back to London and departed in a couple of days.

A parcel arrived at Vanessa's London apartment: it was a dress that J had ordered made to her measurements in Salzburg. But the true celebration of their times together was *Tabellae*, in an edition of one hundred copies, their "secret book," which they designed together, with the letters *V* and *J* locked together in the frontispiece design. J had a copy bound in blue vellum for her. In a poem titled "Last Words," J quoted those of Goethe and of Gertrude Stein and then predicted his own: "My last / word as the car began to skid was / 'Strawberry' will history know I was / sending my ultimate breath to you?"

•

In late summer J was increasingly troubled with what he termed "frequencia micturatoria," and after X-rays and a cystoscopy in late September he submitted to a prostatectomy under a spinal anesthesia at the Charlotte Hungerford Hospital in Torrington, Connecticut. "He was on his best behavior at all times," J wrote of himself, "and, curious as he was, asked no personal questions about the nurses' lives. All those stories lost." Soon he discovered that the operation had rendered him conclusively impotent. Only in this physical aspect did it affect his lovemaking: he remained ardent and, when making love, seemed happy, in a boyish way, confident that he could give and receive pleasure without the final act of copulation. He seemed to feel liberated to love in the spirit and the intellect, an idealized poet-lover now removed from the need to demonstrate sexual athleticism.

As he drew closer to the Reeses, he came to realize that Sandra and

Harry were that two-headed creature that he himself had never achieved: a marriage of equals, even an establishment of equals. For a few years he had directed nearly all his letters to Harry, but now he discovered that while Harry might be the artist in paint and collage, the professor of de- sign and printing, Sandra was an expert editor, as well as printmaker, typesetter, and printer. J began to address most of his Turkey Press letters to her. On the island of Antigua with three generations of Laughlins over Christmas, J was bored after two days, so he drafted sixty autobiographi- cal pages. "That bores me too," he wrote to Sandra Reese, "but I'm told I owe it to literary history. When young I was such an arrogant idiot. Bad influence of Ezra?" At the Publishers' Lunch Club in New York soon af- ter, J gave an address on "Henry Miller's non-sex life. They liked that." Given J's condition, *that* was rather appropriate.

•

J's *Selected Poems, 1935–1985* appeared in the spring of 1986 from City Lights, with a jacket designed by Gertrude Huston and supporting blurbs by Marjorie Perloff, Davenport, and Robert Fitzgerald, each making refer- ence to the uniqueness of J's gifts. Perloff was the most apt in describing him as "our poet of Chekhovian longing, a poet for whom love always holds a measure of delight even as does the language that embodies it." Many of the poems had appeared in a wide range of magazines, both well- known and obscure: *Harper's, Horizon,* and *The Nation; Almanacco dello specchio* (Milan), *Exquisite Corpse, Oink!,* and *Poetry Australia.* J *did* still care about seeing himself in print.

The volume received a very negative review in *The New York Times.* His "linguistic philosophy rests on unadorned simple speech," wrote the reviewer, who objected that the poems were "all too often prosaic," devoid of "the enrichment of poetic image." He found J's poems about lost love "badly overstated" and suffering from "an excess of sentimentality" and said his borrowings were "awkward." A "capacity for wit" surfaced only in some of the Hiram Handspring poems. J did not respond, but Hayden Carruth came to J's defense. "To criticize a book one must understand it," he said, continuing that the reviewer "clearly doesn't understand what Mr. Laughlin has done in his poems, doesn't see the layering voices of wit, irony and fantasy, or the breadth of literary sources, or the range of learning; doesn't understand the poems as literature, in short."

With a historian's consciousness of anniversaries, J set about preparing volume 50 of *New Directions in Prose and Poetry*. In this issue he reprinted much of the original 1936 issue, appending a long part 2: "New Directions— the Years That Follow." In his introduction J included a mea culpa: "Each of the early numbers of the anthologies began with my vehement and quite preposterous introductions—remarkable combinations of arrogance, ignorance, and Poundian propaganda." But those anthologies would not have been the legitimate children of a young Turk, of a would-be revolutionary, without attacks on the old order.

J usually avoided such events these days, but he accepted an invitation to a luncheon in Manhattan to honor the late Christoph Schlotterer of the Carl Hanser Verlag. J arrived, looking pleasingly scruffy in an old blazer set off by a rumpled silk tie from his Burmese days, and was seated at one end of a wide rectangular table. A bit late as was his habit, Roger Straus then made a grand entrance, resplendent in a perfectly tailored white suit accented by a paisley ascot, having clearly cast himself in the role of the great American publisher, and sat at the opposite end of the table. Course followed course, accompanied by appropriate wines. Those seated in the middle of the table found themselves turning their heads like spectators near the net at Wimbledon as J and Straus told anecdotes. At first imperceptibly, the attention shifted to J, telling fabulous stories in his quiet way, until by the end of the meal the audience was his alone. Straus sat on in angry silence. He knew—everyone in publishing knew— that J was called "the last of the gentleman publishers."

Ezra was once again occupying J, as he prepared his *Pound as Wuz: Essays and Lectures on Ezra Pound* for the Graywolf Press. J wrote one passage as a poem dedicated to Vanessa, partly quoted from Canto 74, to place Ezra at the DTC: "We know the scene; / The scene is a flat field north of Pisa / Where a small road runs west down to the sea / A flat field under Carrara snow on the marble . . . / 'In the death cells in sight of Mount Taishan.'"

If Pound refused to remain quietly dead, it was in no small part because of J's instigations. When Carey Perloff, artistic director of the Off-Broadway Classic Stage Company and daughter of Marjorie, was visiting at Meadow House, J casually handed her a battered typescript saying, "I have this thing by Pound in my drawer. I don't know if it is complete. Would you look at it?" The "thing" turned out to be the poet's translation of *Elektra*, laced with American slang and 1940s film lingo and including his annotations. J had harbored the manuscript for more than forty years, waiting for a suitable moment to spring it on the right person. Carey Perloff immediately thought of Pamela Reed for the title role, and on November 1, 1987, Reed would star in the world premiere in New York. J pronounced Reed's rendering of Elektra as "the best thing I've seen, as acting, since Gérard Philipe as the Prince of Homburg 100 years ago in Paris." He had helped to "lubricate" the production, J's term for a modest bit of financial underwriting. ND would publish the text in 1990.

On February 23, 1987, Jack Heinz expired at his home in Florida. He had known for months that he was dying of stomach cancer and had come with Drue the previous autumn to Norfolk to tell J, but it was still a deeply grieving man who attended the funeral in Pittsburgh—J's last strong tie with his birthplace gone. "I looked down from the lectern and saw four ex-Presidents and three mayors of Pittsburgh and even that S.O.B. Henry Kissinger and I got so nervous that I dropped my notes," said J in an embellished version of the event. He was left, he said, with "57 memories of happy times we shared that will never be forgotten." J discovered that Jack had willed back to him the Alta stock bought so many years before.

By the beginning of 1987, Ann had decided that J's depression and anxiety had become almost as bad as they were before his lithium treatment began in 1971, and his tremor had increased. On her urging, J finally agreed to consult Dr. Noble Endicott, a New York specialist in bipolar illness. J found himself unable to tell Dr. Wiesel that he was seeing another psychiatrist. Finally, Ann wrote to Wiesel: "J's gratitude to you is boundless. He said to me yesterday, 'It was Ben who got me to start lecturing. He urged me and urged me.' In his Byzantine way, now J feels embarrassed to consult anyone else." When Ann showed J a copy of her letter, he wrote in distress to Wiesel. "I feel so disloyal," he cried, "like knifing a dear friend . . . But you know how she is. A bulldog. Nothing can resist her." Through Ann, Wiesel tried to reassure J that he was not hurt by J's changing psychiatrists, and to the patient he wrote, "I assure you that I do not feel knifed by Mac the Laughlin."

Still rattled by Jack Heinz's funeral, J was convinced that he too would not be around much longer, assaying some long lines of free verse under the title "After I'm Gone." "You can remodel the breakfast room," he began, "you can clean my mess of books and papers out of the living room . . .

you can cook things that have anchovy or coconut or parsley in them / you can have all the broccoli or eggplant or zucchini you want for dinner." He hoped that he would be missed: "Wherever it is I'm going, up or down, I'll certainly miss you." Sentimentality, humor, and a dash of the maudlin—it matched his mood.

J cast about for some plausible explanation for his recurrent tremor, nausea, and dizziness. Ann might have coerced him into seeing another shrink, yet he cleaved to Wiesel. "I don't think it's the little London bird," he told Wiesel. "She is no threat or guilt." In fact, J decided, "the process of 'adoration' has become burdensome—letters, calls, trips." The idea that his sexual drive might have been drastically reduced by the prostatectomy was too disturbing to contemplate. Suddenly he hit upon a plausible cause: "It is that damned prospect of the autobiography which is hanging over me. I really hate everything about it." He dreaded the research needed, the effort required "to write it decently," the years, given his slow pace, "even the vanity aspect." "People are always expecting me to go back and check for accuracy," he told Peggy Fox, adding truculently, "but I'm not about to."

In May, J was back to see Dr. Wiesel in "extreme distress from old and new symptoms." When a sequence of medical tests proclaimed him in remarkably good health, J was forced to conclude that most of his symptoms stemmed from his head. His short-term memory remained "terrible," his dyslexia persisted when he typed yet did not appear in his longhand—it did not occur to J that, his coordination faulty, he had merely become a poor typist. His allergist said that he was allergic only to cats. "But I am not ailurophilic and we have none," the patient objected. His hot flashes— meticulously, he clocked them at 99.3 degrees—were relieved by Valium. They flared when Ann talked about her *Four Lives* film and when he couldn't find a book that he needed for a quotation. His responses to Ann were the more intense because she told him that the film depicted electroshock therapy in action. This was enough to bring back J's memories of seeing his father in duress. He refused a screening categorically, accused Ann of being "so manic about the film," and taunted her about it at the family dinner table.

Late in August 1987, Wayne Andrews died, "the last, I think, of those who were in ND number 1," wrote J in simple remembrance. Except himself, he did not add, nor was he correct: Mary Barnard, Kay Boyle, and

Olga Rudge were still alive. J even neglected his correspondence, announcing in late October, "I have been these several months in a burrow of abuleia (Ezra's term), a phase in the cyclothymic rhythm." With all the health worries, mental and otherwise, J had stopped working on the prose autobiography. Finally, he had to admit to himself that the Sylvia Beach model would not work for him: she had been gifted with a selective memory that allowed her to focus on the essentials of a person or event; J's memory was disordered, overcrowded. Instead, he returned to poetry. "Yes," he told the Reeses, "after a long drought I've been dishing up a lot of dubious verse lately, dubious because it's 'synthetic' rather than the old spontaneous." Many of these poems were partial translations or reorderings from his favorite classical authors. On September 1, *Pound as Wuz* appeared to generally favorable reviews: "Mr. Laughlin's clear love of Pound helps humanize the formidable master whom T. S. Eliot acknowledged as 'the better craftsman.'"

J was gradually facing up to the eventuality of his own demise—after a lifetime of alternately evading and toying with the idea. Acknowledging the Reeses' offer to hold a copy of their latest hand-set treasure for him, he responded, "I've reached the stage where I'm busy getting rid of books rather than adding more. Sad thing is that none of the children are interested in non-utilitarian books." J was concentrating on placing his rare volumes where *he* wanted them to go.

39

Witness to Mortality

You are our uncorrupted and incorruptible witness to an age.
—Guy Davenport to James Laughlin on receiving *Random Essays*

In response to Davenport's "extollatory" letter about *Pound as Wuz*, J teased that, thus encouraged, he might next write on "your secret favorite, Ella Wheeler Wilcox," a turn-of-the-century sentimentalist. "Please don't," pleaded Guy. Always generous in sending free New Directions books to his friends, J scolded Guy for laying out "good Kentucky money" for a batch. J's mood seemed to have improved: he was seeing an inamorata of a few years' standing, patrician, Bostonian, who could quote his poems to him, making them sound "so lovely in her soft, deep, slow voice." J described Deborah Pease as "a dreamy girl but a little odd." They had many friends in common, including George Plimpton, with whom she worked on *The Paris Review*. "You're as incurably susceptible to a well-turned ankle as my protégé . . . the lifeguard at the Y," remarked Guy. "Middle age is a second adolescence." At least J was no longer complaining about his mental state or physical ailments.

Late in February 1988, J and Ann flew to California for a pair of university appearances that he felt he could not refuse because "I like both of these people very much": Marjorie Perloff wanted him at Stanford and then Gary Snyder at the University of California, Davis. J read his own poetry to a class of young poets, and Snyder responded extemporaneously. Profoundly moved, J asked him to set down his points, and Snyder wrote a series of impressionistic phrases, a note that J carefully filed: "James Laughlin's poems in an ancient, honorable, & classical niche of personal-historical open-emotion-natural-cultivated wild & free ancient & trained poetic lyric." This would turn out to be J's final appearance before a class.

J was still interested in everything that went on at Alta, but he had to admit to himself that downhill skiing was beyond him, that only gliding along the cross-country trails that he had made on the old fire tracks near Meadow House was still possible without risking serious injury. In 1988 the last major personnel change at Alta occurred when Onno Wieringa stepped in as general manager to replace Chic Morton, who had resigned the position the preceding year.

•

For years the main focus on health in the family had been directed toward Robert and then J, but in midsummer 1988, Ann, "who never was anything but very healthy," began to experience abdominal and back pains. She ignored these symptoms. When she finally submitted to a thorough examination, the diagnosis was shattering: she had myeloma, which had spread from the bone marrow throughout her body. After an operation, largely futile owing to the extent of the cancer, a powerful drug regimen was prescribed. "Ann is getting some of her strength back and, happily, the chemotherapy pills have not made her nauseated," J told Sandra Reese. Sometimes Ann felt strong enough to go out to brunch, "but it hurts to see her having to walk with her head and shoulders bent over from the osteoporosis." By early 1989, J was writing optimistically to Ferlinghetti that Ann "is making great progress in getting the myeloma under control with chemotherapy." Friends noticed that he had become markedly more solicitous of Ann, shocked into realizing how important she was to him.

For some months J had written no poetry, but he had a number of books coming out: *The Bird of Endless Time*, a collection of fairly recent verse with Copper Canyon, and the rest prose, much of it going back to his young manhood—*Random Essays* from Moyer Bell and *This Is My Blood* in a limited edition from Yolla Bolly, to be followed in 1990 by the Moyer Bell *Random Stories*. "All at once, in my old age," commented the author without noticeable pleasure. J's vision was worsening, and he had been told that he had cataracts. Finally, his left eye, the weaker one, was operated on, and he ended up with better vision in it than he had ever experienced.

A New Directions author had returned to the list in April 1988, when

Life Being the Best & Other Stories appeared in the Revived Modern Classics series, a small collection of Kay Boyle's work, dating mainly from the 1920s. This was the first ND paperbook with a full-color cover. It was J's tribute to Kay as "one of the great beauties and figures in expatriate Paris" and a "remarkable poet," however, printed in the fiftieth anniversary issue of *NDPP*, that led her to write a letter of reconciliation: "Again my thanks, dear Jay, and my gratitude that we are publisher and author again as well as friends." J sent her a copy of his just-published *Bird of Endless Time*, and she responded warmly, singling out a number of poems for comment: "In the best of your poetry it is your emotions that surface, without classical notes or references." She suggested that, like Ezra, J was often afraid in his verse to seem unintellectual, uneducated, and thus he overcompensated.

Late Sunday morning, February 26, 1989, J dozed off sitting in his favorite old overstuffed armchair in the main living room. Suddenly flames awoke him. Perhaps a match or the still-hot dottle from his pipe had ignited the chair he was sitting in. He couldn't find a fire extinguisher—they had all been taken away to be recharged. He called Heidi, who was cooking lunch in the kitchen, and together they tried to drag the burning chair out into the yard. The chair stuck in the door, and then they attempted to beat the flames out with blankets. Quickly the fire began licking at the walls, which were hollow and provided a channel up which the flames would inevitably race for the roof. The Norfolk and Canaan volunteer fire departments responded and arrived in minutes, but by then the entire living room was ablaze. They were able to extinguish the fire before it spread further, but the damage was extensive. J and Heidi were treated for smoke inhalation and minor burns at Winsted Memorial Hospital.

When a friend called to commiserate, "We lost the Magritte" was J's laconic rejoinder—it had been the important oil *Mental Calculus* that Ann had inherited from her mother, and it took up the entire sum for which the house contents had been insured. J particularly regretted his *Maine Islands*, one of a series by John Marin. The Klees and some of the other modernist paintings were damaged but restorable. Whole shelves of books had also burned, including the Pound volumes in which J had written endless marginalia during the various revisions, his rhyming dictionary, his Sanskrit dictionary, and much of his collection of classical authors. His OED went, and years later J had still not replaced it. Many of the medieval and Renaissance books as well as Buddhist and Hindu texts that J had mined for his own poetry were gone. This loss would hit him especially hard when he came to proof his *Collected Poems* three years later. Papers in metal files were brown and brittle on the top edges but remained legible. Most of his correspondence and manuscript files were safe in the new wing and in the underground vault.

Almost worse than the fire itself was the depressing and tiresome aftermath. "Dearest Strawberry," J wrote to Vanessa, who retained her place in J's heart despite his growing fondness for Deborah Pease. "The days sludge along. That is about the right word—'sludge.' All the ashes in the central part of the house were wet down by the firemen's hoses and have literally to be dug out . . . The Henghes torso of a lady with large boobs and no head survived but the fire blackened most of her . . . And my little bronze dancing Ganesha, the Indian elephant god of good luck, was broken." A Brazilian cleaning crew singing in Portuguese crowded into the house, followed by local painters. Carpenters restored the more severely damaged floors, bookcases, and moldings. Temporarily, J rented Aunt Leila's mansion from the new owner.

Understandably, J was not paying much attention to ND, but when the young dissident poet Bei Dao's *The August Sleepwalker* was recommended to J by Peggy Fox, he replied, "If you all like the Bei Dao fire away," adding a caveat, "Success would depend on publicizing him as the 'new China.'" J had picked the right phrase for the moment; months later the Tiananmen Square pro-democracy demonstrations demanded a new China. ND would publish three more of Bei Dao's books in rapid succession.

•

"The doctors think Ann is holding her own . . . but she gets very tired," J wrote at midyear to Ferlinghetti. "Her spirit is excellent." They were now back in Meadow House, living in the kitchen wing, which included J's original office and a small dining room, with, upstairs, a large bedroom, the TV room, and two other rooms, but the "midriff," as J called it, of the rambling place still sounded with the tramp of workmen and the scream of drills and saws. J was coming to terms with the fire. "I've weathered it, emotionally, pretty well," he said, "but it's been mighty hard for Ann, coming on top of her illness."

J and Ann had from the first made no secret of her cancer. He might have appeared to be trying to ignore her condition, but in fact he was intensely aware of it. More than once a friend saw J in the Norfolk grocery quietly filling his shopping basket, tears running down his face. Suddenly Ann developed further alarming symptoms, and at the hospital they discovered that calcium had leached out of her bones and invaded her liver. "Nothing much I can do," J wrote to Vanessa. "I'm saying my mantras for her." His handwriting had deteriorated further. "I feel very numb," he said. "Only three weeks ago she seemed to be getting better. The pattern is clouded." Ann suggested to J that he get Gertrude to look after him.

The repairs to Meadow House dragged on and on; the floors had been stained mahogany, and the painters had to wait until they could be walked on. J's *Random Essays*, with an introduction by Robert Giroux, appeared in August, but J had no heart for rejoicing over it, even though Giroux's gracious comments sounded like a genuine peace offering. During Ann's periods of hospitalization, J could never bring himself to visit her. She didn't want visitors, he assured Santha Rama Rau, but Ann would hardly have sent him away: it was J's abhorrence of hospitals, his lifelong fear of death, and his dislike of being betrayed by his emotions.

With death waiting in the front bedroom, J drafted "Expectations," a mea culpa poem that brushed past his amatory adventures to focus on his aspiration to "word the world" (he was quoting Emerson). Had it been "too much / to expect that each girl / would be an Aphrodite"?

Ann was again hospitalized over a crisis but demanded of her doctors that she be allowed to return home, where her son Henry sat with her by the hour. "Beautiful love goes back and forth between them," J wrote. "She is happy with a kind of happiness I have never, and I feel my inadequacy, been able to give her . . . And this is a great contentment for me, to see them so close together. It brings me a sense of forgiveness." In the morning of the twenty-eighth, at home as she had wanted, Ann said that she was tired of the pain and the "bed-ridden life," that she was "ready to go." Eight hours later, without any apparent struggle, her heart stopped. "A 'good death' as they used to say," J concluded in his letter to Mary de Rachewiltz. A simple memorial service was held at the Norfolk Library; Ann had not wanted a church funeral or a monument. Leila spoke movingly of her admiration of Ann's steadfast nature, of Ann's equal concern for both her stepchildren and her own children. J started to deliver a valediction, broke down, and couldn't continue. A reception for family and New Directions employees was held at Meadow House. Ann's ashes were scattered in the sheep meadow.

J seldom went back to the New Directions offices after Ann's death, and only twice for the annual shareholders and board of directors meetings, toward the end of 1990 and 1991, respectively.

He "sort of fell apart for a while," friends thought. "Ann's death, though we saw it coming, was a blow, nearly a knock-out, certainly a knock down," J wrote to Davenport. "A great thing about Ann," he said to Vanessa, "was that no matter how ill she became she never lost her good disposition." He felt himself the victim of "glooms." For years his feelings for Ann had been ambivalent at best: he had seen himself trapped by his dependence on her, trapped also because he knew that he could not bring himself to divorce her and follow the wayward dictates of his heart. Now he was consumed by the realization of his loss, and he felt only admiration and gratitude toward Ann. He reproached himself for not having brought her happiness, but he could not bring himself to refer specifically to his infidelities or to his inattention to her. Shocked back to poetry, in his nighttime wakefulness he typed out, in the impersonal third person, a poem about his loss, touched with self-pity:

As he passes the open door
he can see there is no long-

er anyone in the room no one
is lying in the bed and no

one is attending the recum-
bent figure the water glass

with its bent drinking straw
is gone . . .

. . . in its neatness
and emptiness it is for

him a scene of terror
what can he do with

what is left of his life?

40

The Somnambulist

Often now as an old man
Who sleeps only four hours a night,
I wake before dawn, dress and go down
To my study to start typing.

—James Laughlin, *Byways*

It was dawning upon J that a cataclysmic change had occurred. All his life he had been kept headed into the wind by the sea anchor of one or another strong woman. Rebellion against that woman had defined his strivings. When he had thought, as a boy, that he was escaping Pittsburgh, it was more his mother whom he had been fleeing. In Aunt Leila he had found a surrogate mother, an even sterner one, one whose values, morally and religiously and in her relationship to others, were at root similar to Marjory Rea Laughlin's, only more pronounced. Aunt and mother had demarcated the limits of his publishing, had smiled upon his skiing venture—big boys need big toys—had tolerated his amatory adventures. Then Ann had come into his life, and by the time aunt and mother were both dead, ten years later, she was firmly established as his great maternal figure. It had not been the role Ann wanted: she had married him to be his wife—and to be a mother, yes, but to J's children, not to J himself. When J would not allow her to be fully his wife, she had hardened into the one role open to her, one for which her temperament, in a way, suited her. When J had mischievously dropped his tobacco trimmings into her hair, he became the teasing bad boy, and her reaction had been humorless anger. She reacted not as a loving mother but as a disciplining mother.

J realized now that he was absolutely free, and it frightened him. Suddenly he could do *anything*. He could marry Carol Jane Bangs or Vanessa Jackson or Deborah Pease or any other *apsara* he could woo and win. But these recent loves had made other choices themselves, and J lacked the stamina, the sexual drive and potency, the will, to find new ones. True, he was perhaps more than ever conscious of his charm, of his persuasive powers, and of a benign gentleness. He weighed these against his age, his disabilities. He had to admit that he was damaged goods, damaged by living, by psychic tics, by time. There was a further quandary. He could no longer win a lover and then fade away behind Ann when his own panic and doubt set in. What if the new lover became wife? Would he awaken to the realization that he had merely acquired a new jailer, as he had accused Ann of being? Freedom had come too late into his life—and he had no clue how to handle it.

Without the disciplined order imposed on the household by Ann, J's presence in the sprawling house shrank to four rooms: the kitchen, his old study with a large window overlooking the meadow, the small television room, and the large upstairs bedroom with the Miró paintings.

More than ever, he sought refuge in his typewriter, his trembling pen, his Canon photocopier. With these tools he returned to reconstructing his past. Ezra with age had lapsed into silence. J became increasingly loquacious, his inborn word love enhanced by the logorrhea of the bipolar, the pleasures of logodaedaly. To Davenport's praise of his *Random Stories*, J replied, "I think you are heautontimorumenonic if you can wade through those juvenile stories." J complemented his Greek- and Latin-derived vocabulary with deliberate sophomorisms: a poem might be a "daisy," a girl "toasty," a performance "wham bang." "I love words, I eat words," J wrote, "But I don't chase them / Like the poet Carruth, / Who when he was young / Studied a page of the / Big Webster every morning." No, words had to pop into J's ken serendipitously. "Today's new word was / Haecceity," he continued in his poem; he had chanced upon the Latin *haecceitas* in the work of "a very learned Irishman," he was reserving it "for / The pleasure of a word pal," and in due course he sent it to Guy. J toyed with old words and images: he made up a letterhead featuring a nineteenth-century engraving of a shaggy camel with the words "Semiotics is science envy" issuing from its mouth. To this, Sandra Reese responded:

Q. What do you get when you cross a Professor of Semiotics with
the Godfather?
A. An offer you can't understand.

"My dear old shrink," J reported to Vanessa, had advised him that a
change of scene might help—he hadn't left Norfolk for fourteen months.
His children made plans to get him away: Leila and Daniel Javitch departed for Italy early in January, with the understanding that J would join
them later in Rome. Before that, Carlene and Henry would escort him
around Egypt, Jordan, and Israel. J flew with Carlene and Henry to Egypt.
Since his previous visit in 1952, Cairo had sprawled into an appalling
megalopolis, a jumble of ugly cement block tenements, but they enjoyed
the magnificent collection of the Museum of Egyptian Antiquities. Only, J
noted, he saw just one statue of a woman, Nefertiti; the rest were of men.
Viewing the Sphinx and Alexandria followed. Then came a short flight
south to Karnak and Luxor—ancient Thebes—where literary tourists
are shown the bold "Rimbaud" scratched into the limestone by the poet.
    Three days later it was "a relief to be in tidy, well-organized Jordan,"
where they traversed another span of desert to see the towering rock-cut
city of Petra, preserved since Roman days by its isolation. J presented an
awkward figure riding down the steep cleft of al-Siq, the "shaft" leading
to the site, on a donkey—as though Quixote had in confusion swapped
mounts with Sancho Panza. Petra matched in grandeur the Egyptian antiquities. "If you put together the natural wonders of Canyon de Chelly in
Arizona with the temples of Angkor Wat in Cambodia you would have
something like Petra, but not all," J wrote. The intense biblical tones of
their visit to Israel left J unmoved: Jerusalem's Temple Mount, the Wail-
ing Wall, the Sea of Galilee. The rest of the trip covered old ground: a
quick sojourn with Mary at Brunnenburg; a visit to the Vatican after they
were joined by Leila and Daniel. Spain came last. "J was a good traveler,"
said his daughter-in-law, "he kept a pace."
    But as a ploy to raise J's spirits, the trip had been a failure, except per-
haps in his discovery that his Italian had not deserted him. "A moment of
happy vanity came to me in Urbino," he wrote in a short poem. "I was
dickering for a book and the seller / told me, 'Lei si difende bene in Ital-
iano'"—You defend yourself well in Italian.
    J returned to the open verse of *Byways*, small nibbles of remembrance

that he could handle in verse. And he kept an eye on New Directions. J said reflectively, "Before I die I'd like to discover another real rip-snorter—you know, like Ferlinghetti!" Not that he was actively looking, yet it was never in doubt at ND that although another hand might be on the tiller, the old captain was still in the master's cabin. J *was* concerned, moreover, that ND should endure for some years after his death, not for the enshrining of his name, but for the welfare and continued employment of his senior staff. In 1990, Ohannessian was sixty-three, Glassgold fifty-one, and Fox forty-four. In twenty-one years the youngest of these would be likely to retire. J made a new will that included setting up three trusts and naming as trustees Daniel Javitch, Donald Lamm, Griselda Ohannessian, and Peggy Fox. In addition to stipulating the publication of a *Collected Poems*, this will provided for the continuation of New Directions after J's death at the discretion of the trustees, but for a minimum of twenty-one years.

Critical to J's thinking in fixing this finite term to ND was that a number of the firm's copyrights on the works that formed the profitable armature of the backlist would be expiring in the decade following the year 2000, and that in consequence ND might cease to be economically viable after these copyrights ran out, under the "seventy-five years from publication" ruling then in effect. Among those due to expire were Pound's *Personae* in 2001, and some of Bill Williams's and Dylan Thomas's poetry in 2014, until a ruling that J could not have foreseen extended copyrights dramatically. After negotiations within the European Union extended copyright in 1993 to seventy years *post mortem auctoris*, in 1998 the so-called Mickey Mouse Protection Act would be pushed through to extend the Disney Corporation's claim to exclusive evocations of the mighty mouse by an additional twenty years. Publishers and authors' estates became the unintended beneficiaries of this extension of copyright to ninety-five years from publication for works published prior to January 1, 1978.

•

J garnered another award. "The Poetry Society of America wants to give me their Frost Medal . . . it's not for poems but just for being nice to poets," he commented in tones of disappointment. As the date approached, he found himself dreading the event and bolstered his confidence with a phalanx of supporters: Deborah Pease, George Plimpton, and Carlene and

Henry. Plimpton spoke at length from the podium, not on J, but about *The Paris Review*. Nonetheless, J got up in a sudden burst of energy and held forth, whimsically and amusingly, on Ezra, Social Credit, his own life with poets and poetry. Suddenly he began to shake all over, his papers rattling in his hand. He excused himself to the audience that it was "very emotional" for him, and he was rewarded with a standing ovation.

"I was sorry to hear about your difficulty at the Poetry Society presentation," Dr. Wiesel consoled him, "but I have confidence that your capacity for blabbing is still there and you should start in a small way with the New Yorker lady," Cynthia Zarin. Wiesel had taken over Ann's role of harassing J to come in for periodic checkups, telling him, "You should plan to live at least forever." So Zarin came to Meadow House over a period of several days to interview J for the *New Yorker* profile that she was writing. It did not hurt that Zarin was young and very attractive, and soon J found that he was enjoying himself. Freed from the shadow of the autobiography, J spoke at length on nearly every aspect of his life: the books he read and published, his friendships with writers, his travels, the sense of urgency that the bipolar threat had brought to his life, even the downhill skiing that was now beyond him. "I take great pride in Alta," he told her, "because it is the one place that's left that's a little bit like the old skiing." He enjoyed the blabbing immensely.

Throughout 1990, J cast about for a new mate. Gertrude Huston arrived with a suitcase of clothes and established herself in one of the guest bedrooms; she knew J needed looking after. He seemed pleased to have her company and solicitude, but he avoided making a commitment to her. Gertrude took a fall, and J had to look after *her* for a few days. Then he brought Vanessa Jackson over from London in mid-July. J hinted at marriage but could not bring himself actually to use the *m*-word; in fact, Vanessa had long since committed herself to the English artist John Dougill, whom she would later marry. Converting his disappointment into heartbreak, J drafted a poem, "The Parting," too distressing to him to send out for publication, about his despair at losing her. Elisabeth Borgese was then staying at Meadow House, filling the air with her vitality. J drove Elisabeth and Vanessa in his old Chevy station wagon to Tobey Pond, bouncing over the ruts and fallen branches, unable to turn his head because of the arthritis. Elisabeth, her boyish haircut sleek on her round head, churned back and forth across Tobey Pond as if she were training for the

English Channel. The indomitable Wonza returned temporarily to cook for them. "What a woman!" said the English girl. Gertrude, who had tactfully absented herself for a few days, reappeared on the last day of Vanessa's visit, "to take a look at me—I don't blame her," Vanessa said. She liked Gertrude, "somebody who loves you very much," Vanessa said to J in a minatory tone, and Gertrude decided that she was not a real threat after all. After Vanessa left, J wrote a poem titled "Longing & Guilt," in which he asked, "How much of / The distance that is now / Between them came about / Because he never learned / To love her in the way she / Needed to be loved?" His ancient inability to connect still haunted him.

He also hinted at marriage, again without ever saying the word itself, to Deborah Pease. She judged his need, his often childish dependency, even his occasional lasciviousness, his prurient flights, and drew back from taking on the responsibility. She deflected him, gently, without using the *m*-word either. "She can't cook," J said, in justifying his not having pressed her. J even threw caution to the whirlwind and asked the now-widowed Lady Maria St. Just to come and look after him but was rebuffed. "I'm not about to rush over to nurse an ailing old man!" she announced brusquely.

Gertrude, meanwhile, simply stayed on, taking care of J on the assumption that the role was hers by right. Finally, Leila told her father sternly, "Either you're going to have to marry her, or else send her away. The present situation is unfair to Gertrude." J did as he had done periodically throughout his life: he accepted the advice of a strong woman. He and Gertrude were married at Meadow House on December 5, 1990, with Gigi and Sylvan Schendler, the local justice of the peace, and a friend of Gertrude's present. J wore his "typical, slightly sardonic look," and Gertrude seemed happy. A quiet, relaxed evening followed. She telephoned Peggy Fox, telling her, "I want you to be among the first to know," confiding that she was now where she should have been decades ago, married to J and mistress of Meadow House.

Instead of feeling relief, J experienced deeper malaise. "I've been hoping things would get better, especially after Gertrude and I got married, but they haven't," he told Dr. Wiesel. "She's a comfort and good company, but the steady slide into abulia and anhedonia continues." That J should be afflicted with "insensitivity to pleasure" was a judgment, sure. "Mornings are a total loss of indolence, things pick up a little after lunch but in all I hardly do three hours work an evening," said the former workaholic. "Some mornings are very nervous, too. And there was one wretched day of paranoia when I imagined a New York bank was cheating me."

J remained, however, interested in publishing. When North Point, Davenport's publisher, was rumored to be going out of business, J offered to take on Guy as an author. Guy was delighted, but Griselda strongly advised against it. Her underlying reason, apparently, was Guy's fascination with pubescent boys, which her *pudeur* could not tolerate. Embarrassed by her opposition, J backed off and left it to her to write to Davenport. "This is typical Griselda," J would say of her on another occasion. "Prudent, cautious, no imagination." "I've always considered him perhaps the last of the great experimental writers," he told his top people at the office, making clear his preference without directly countermanding his VP's edict.

J continued to seek a compromise between tranquillity and creativity. He was disenchanted with Prozac. "It might as well be marshmallows for all the good it does me," he complained. "When we have guests logorrhea is almost unbearable. In the vein of a Brendan Gill monologue." "To reason, or to make my mind / Proceed logically through the steps / Of an equation, are things I have / Never mastered," J wrote. While it might *appear* like the random Brownian movement of molecular particles in a cloud chamber, J's mind invariably skipped and jumped with appropriate logic: now he addressed the ultimate conundrum of God's creation of human beings, his failure "to fashion separate and / Discrete mechanisms for evacuation / And reproduction." This had been due entirely to divine haste. "On the sixth day of creation / God saw that he was behind schedule, / He was not going to get finished / With the job on time." Behold the result: "These functions were combined"—to dubious effect.

Gertrude certainly understood J. She realized that in the reclusive life that he had chosen, that he had already been living for the better part of a decade, he was living in a continuous present, in which the gods of the *Greek Anthology*, Krishna and his milkmaids, Deborah and Vanessa and Papagena, Gertrude herself, and even the "latest nonsense" of scholarly criticism swirled in his head and issued forth like the spheres from a bingo cage. All this Gertrude knew, intuitively; she did not need an image from gaming to describe it, but she tolerated, perforce, J's dalliances and infatuations. And J was grateful. Proposing a reunion with Sara "Papagena" Woolsey, J said, "Cinderella is not difficult. A friendly type and a dear girl. She coddles me." But to Carruth, Gertrude confessed that being mistress of Meadow House was not all she had hoped for.

J's flow of wildly associative letters continued. His life, he explained to Papagena Woolsey, had become "a sort of drifting, not in a void, but in a dreamlike state, where what is real is whatever I'm writing—lots of poems and pages for my auto-bug-offery . . . or what I'm reading." His mind had become like an Indian godown, he lamented, one without an inventory: random images floated into his night-waking thoughts. He would lever himself out of bed in a gingerly fashion, descend the stairs to his office, find pipe and matches, and tap out phrases, lines, and episodes from his vast repository: *Byways* steadily taking shape and growing.

As he attempted to evaluate and sum up his life in verse, J became increasingly introspective. He wrote, "His Problem / Was an excessive interest / In the life of language. / There was no place for the / Emotions in his existence." Had he mistaken pursuit, excitement, danger, and conquest for deep feeling? "The words built a wall around him," he continued in the third person, "Shutting him off from those / He should have loved." After shying away from the personal for most of his life, J began to flirt with honest confession. Always wary of death, watchfully, like a connoisseur, J eyed it approaching. Time became the enemy. "How can we make it run backwards," he asked in "The Kitchen Clock." "Let it run / Gently backwards, pausing to / Greet happy times again: the / Day when the schoolboy wrote / His first poem." This was the pleasant use of time, taking him back to his youth and the vast future he had once foreseen. Likening his life to the mainspring, he would cajole his muse "until the spring / Breaks and it doesn't matter / What you do any more." J copied out a sentence from his Flaubert, "I make myself drunk with ink as others do with wine." As his body slowed, J's mind raced faster than ever, conscious of diminishing time.

It was a relief to give himself over to verse. His *Byways* typescript was evolving into his *Cantos*, and there was substance to the comparison. Pound's epic might be an attempt to sum up the course of civilization, a distillation of his erudition and his leaps of intuition, his friends and his lovers. Ezra's will and creative drive had given out before he could complete his great poem. J would see what he could do, employing different verse forms and putting in far more of the personal, but using similar free associational methods—*parataxis* in the ancient Greek sense, phrases, events, characters rubbing up against each other—and every language in his mental armory. J continued reading his *Greek Anthology*, especially the passages from Lucian, "looking for classical recollectives." One problem, however, was that his poetic gift was more lyrical than narrative, and the axles of his stories and longer poems creaked.

"Es ist die kraenkliche Geist den sich dem Koerper vergiftet," J wrote to Wiesel—It is the ailing spirit that itself poisons the body. When Wiesel was operated on for lung cancer, J said to the psychiatrist's receptionist in half-feigned remorse, "All those cigarettes he smoked to get through hours of nuts like me complaining." In spite of his aversion to hospitals, J arrived to inquire about Wiesel, who called him to his bedside. "As you saw, I'm all shook up," J wrote after the visit. "You're more than a friend, you saved the end of my life." J had also finally come to realize what a comfort Wiesel had been to Ann after Robert's death. "I was mighty hard on her," J now admitted. "If I'd gotten home early we might have saved him . . . Guilt, guilt!"

J told Drue Heinz, "I've been doing some pages for my MMMEEEmoirs." He figured that he was now sleeping only four hours a night, and ideas pressed painfully upon his waking brain. It eased him to set them down on paper, and verse freed him more than prose from any obligation to factual accuracy. The events and relationships that he reconstructed were genuine, yes, but whether they were strictly factual or simply true to his emotions and wishful thinking concerned him less and less. Ancient carnal loves might be graced with idealism, those unconsummated endowed with sensual life. With the first faint light, he could begin to make out the white forms of the sheep, black-faced, in the meadow, "Making the pattern of the stars / In Canis Major." Resting his eyes from his machine, he watched for the dawn to come up "circumspectly," signal for his ritual invocation to "Apollo, god of the lyre," "Asking he keep an eye on me / That I commit no great stupidity." A powerful confessional force gripped him. Some of the *Byways* poems celebrate idyllic and innocent early loves, but others describe quite sordid adventures, ones that even as they occurred had made him feel guilty and unclean. Why memorialize these? An image materialized of the lonely, wakeful old man reliving sensuality—"she was good inside, / Like honey"—but male boasting seems to have little part in these unburdenings.

One story, *Angelica*, he wrote out at length in prose, subtitling it *Fragment from an Autobiography* when he had it privately published in an edition of two hundred copies. To the young woman whom he likened to Botticelli's Venus, he gave the name Angelica Bowditch—suggesting both the nature and the Boston Brahmin bloodlines of Deborah Pease, one of the two *apsaras* (the other was Vanessa) whose interactions with J formed the core structure of the book. J took Angelica from the name of the heroine in Thackeray's *The Rose and the Ring*. To Peggy Fox he called the *Angelica* book a novella, claiming that it "really is 80% fiction," and he wrote on the front free endpaper, "For Peggy / this fabrication / from J"— fabrication, perhaps, but Pease was shocked at how accurately he had portrayed her character. J wanted neither Gertrude nor the family nor his office staff to read it "for now." "What you do with it when I'm gone is up to you," he continued to Peggy, deftly shifting responsibility.

The *Angelica* story is a framework that J built up carefully to contain his memories of Pound and his impressions of Italy, as well as a setting for a handful of his own poems. He was not in the least concerned that the events described often bore no resemblance to reality. "Imaginary events become more and more important, at least to me, as I age," he told Davenport. "You'll see that when you read *Angelica* . . . The whole biz of the love pilgrimage to the Tempio in Rimini is completely imaginary." As in his poetry, J was writing both what actually took place and what he *wished* had happened, without distinguishing the factual from the fictive. Deborah had worked closely with him on the book, and at her request he sent Angelica to a nunnery at the end, a resolution amusing to them both.

One old love who refused to become simply a subject for *Byways* was Lady Maria St. Just, who through her control of the Tennessee Williams copyrights continued to affect New Directions. It was all very well for J to write to Peggy Fox, "I don't want to have any dealings with Maria—I'm tired of her antics." Yet only days after stating this, J found himself constrained to write to her in support of Margot Peters's proposed biography of Tennessee. Peters had traveled widely researching Williams's life and had spent two days interviewing J about him, believing that she had Lady St. Just's backing. To J's mind, she was right for the task, "a dignified person and won't try to sensationalize." Then Maria decided that Peters was too independent and a "total snake." J was well aware that Maria could and probably would take Tennessee's books away from ND if she was opposed on the biography issue. Maria refused Peters the necessary permissions, and she abandoned the biography. Maria had already blocked Lyle Leverich's ongoing biography of Tennessee, for similar reasons, and it would be published only after her death.

For all of his complaints about Maria, when she landed in New York, J was quite willing to accompany her for an evening rendezvous with Sonny Mehta of Knopf, which kept him out so late that Gertrude called Peggy Fox at home in a vain attempt to discover where her wandering husband was. J still felt the need to assert his habitual independence, yet he was not oblivious to the suffering he was causing. "I fear I make her unhappy a lot," he confessed. "I can't talk to Little Mitten, except to tease her . . . I'm going to go off for lunch and afternoon [in NYC] without any explanation. If she asks questions I'll make up some Gargantuan fantasy— and see what happens." All of his complaints and resentments about Ann seemed to have vanished: she was now "dear Ann" when he had occasion to mention her. "It Is So Easy / to stay in love with someone / who is dead," J wrote, setting his ruthlessly graphic poem in the Valley of the Kings at Thebes: "nothing remains / of her imperfections   the em- / balmers removed her heart and / it gives me no more trouble." Ann, even dead, still stood between him and Gertrude.

As 1991 drew to a close, he named among his "present anxieties . . . how to handle my eroticism which continues though I am now impotent. Fantasy poems, I guess."

•

In July 1992, J revisited his ancestral Ireland. He invited Vanessa Jackson and John Dougill to travel with him and Gertrude. They spent three days in Dublin, then they hired a car, and Dougill drove. They toured Counties Kerry, Clare, Galway, and beyond, around the coast, through Killarney, traveling for about ten days in a leisurely fashion. John was almost as tall as J, and the two men, shoulders nearly touching, filled the front seats, so Vanessa and the even shorter Gertrude saw the country through the side windows. When it rained, J read Yeats and wrote "Yeatsy" poems. "I loved it," J said, "and I went into a big Yeatsian swoon." Part of his purpose in the trip was to persuade Vanessa to write his biography, ignoring her protest that she was a painter, not an author. Vanessa thought that J was nervous about Portaferry: they never saw it.

Back in Norfolk, J's life remained simple. Breakfast he made himself, cold except for tea, since he had never cooked and was convinced that he could not. Donna came from Norfolk village to prepare a noon meal for him and Gertrude, and dinner was often soup and a salad. He still loved his childhood favorite, junket. Each meal was followed by a single good cigar, making up his three-a-day limit. Dr. Luchs had warned him years back that the smoking would kill him. "But I'm still here today," he wrote with a hint of smugness. And he insisted upon large, powerful cigars: "A Bolivar is both / Stimulation and consolation." His moods varied, but most of the time the lithium circumscribed the bipolar swings. "When I'm depressed I don't find much funny about life," he told Papagena Woolsey, "but when I'm up, I find life pleasant."

Most of J's urgings to excess he poured now into his verse, writing "picture poems" and "epigrams"; he proposed to the Reeses that they print a book of these. Soon he was rewriting the old story of Apollo, love-stricken for the incomparable Daphne, whose divine father changed her into a laurel just as the pursuing god overtook her. J saw himself in the god, striving for an ideal beauty, an ideal love, eternally to fall short of his goal. "Since thou can'st not be my bride, / Thou shalt at least be my tree," he wrote, looking out his windows at the stands of chaste white birch, the solitary shadblow, the tangles of bittersweet like the uncombed hair of maenads.

Meanwhile, J was up to page 300 of the proofs of the 560 pages of his *Collected Poems*. Whenever the arthritis, which had moved up to his neck, did not bother him too much, he sat at his typewriter, scrolling out poems in his various metrics. Typing, however, was indeed painful, and he was still burdened with considerable correspondence. He engaged Kathy Basetta, a local woman with young children, to come in two mornings a week to take dictation and type letters. Soon he felt comfortable enough with Kathy to reminisce to her about Aunt Leila and about Robert's suicide, knowing that she would not be critical of him.

In December, J was still engaged in "pencil to pencil combat with the idiotic printers of the CP in Alabama. The only thing they can set right is a poem with no visual complications, no notes, no epigraphs, no insertions . . . I'll dominate those Alabamians if it kills me, which it is doing." It was even worse when J came to his picture poems, most of which, pursued by his perfectionist demon, he had to "reposition, slash and chop" for the photo-offset reproduction. What with his tremor and his eyesight, he had to make two or three attempts, sticky with rubber cement, on each page. He drafted a short poem, "The Departure":

They say I have to go away soon
On the long trip to nowhere.
Put things in order, they say.
But I've always been disorderly
So why start that now?
Not much time, they say.
What to do with it?
Not much different, I think,
Than what I've been doing.
My best friends have always been
The ones in books.
Read a few pages here, a few there.
No complaints, few regrets,
Thanks to everybody.

Race Toward Self-Knowledge

I fear death because I can't recall that Dante mentions any book in Hell.

—James Laughlin to Guy Davenport

The Irish trip had been good for J. On his return he gave a reading of his poetry at the Norfolk Country Club, and on October 25, 1992, he and Charles Tomlinson marched and intoned for the unveiling of Bill Williams's plaque in the American Poets' Corner of the Cathedral of St. John the Divine in Manhattan. The designated readers had to wear robes and carry candles—J said because the deacon could not afford to light the cavernous nave—and it all seemed "spooky." There was a "goodly crowd," and J imagined that he heard "Bill's goat-like laugh floating across the Hudson." Then, on November 10, J was featured in a program commemorating New Directions at New York's Cooper Union, reading poems that he had "written to" Ezra, Bill Williams, Rexroth, and "Dotty [that is, Dylan] Thomas." Walter Abish, Carruth, George Plimpton, Ginsberg, Robert Giroux, and Eliot Weinberger shared the stage with him.

Davenport sent J the typescript of *A Table of Green Fields*, and J wrote to his ND staff of the ten stories, "What ravishing invention and fantasy." Griselda's opposition had faded. "Don't worry about it," she snapped to Declan Spring when he called Guy's eroticism to her attention. Guy received an acceptance and a contract. "A dream come true," J said. "I've always wanted to have a Guy Davenport on the ND list." J's eagerness to sign him on as an ND author was hardly justified by likely sales, Guy warned him. "If you would like to know what a quixotic idealist you are, O Publisher," his royalty statement showed that seven of his titles had earned "a grand total" of $2 over the past six months. J went meticulously over the *Green Fields* manuscript, and Guy expressed astonishment that a publisher was actually *reading* his work, instead of merely handing it to some sub-editor. Not that J was finding much to do. "I have never seen such a perfect manuscript," he wrote to Glassgold. In the end, ND would also publish 7 *Greeks*, a collection of Guy's translations; *The Cardiff Team*; a reissue of *Da Vinci's Bicycle* as a paperbook; and, in a signal departure from the usual ND book, a generous selection in color of Guy's paintings and drawings.

Guy's letters were a "solace." With Pound and Rexroth long gone, "my hunger gnaws." J craved a constant supply of ready wit and esoteric trivia. "It is important for me to know that the Noble Romans had their togas washed in pee and rinsed in lavender," he exclaimed to Guy. "I'm sure you're aware that with Ezra, Rexroth and Fitzgerald gone you are fast becoming a literary dad (though perhaps the ages aren't quite right)."

The Houghton Library sent J a large box of Tennessee's unproduced and unpublished drama manuscripts, inquiring about their disposition, and while J did not spot any masterpieces, he decided that, like Ezra, Tenn should have a volume of his drafts and fragments. This would result, over the years, in various productions of rediscovered plays and their publication by ND. Alarmed by what he saw as the Houghton Library's dilatory handling of Tennessee's manuscripts, J was determined to ensure that *his* archive would not be allowed to languish uncataloged. So he stipulated that certain of his books could be sold by the university, up to the sum of $80,000, to finance the sorting and cataloging of his archive, and he wrote into the final deed of gift to Harvard the proviso that if the work were not accomplished within two and a half years of his death, the material would revert to his estate. J let it be known to his four trustees that in his opinion the entire archive should in that event be offered to Yale.

•

The palimpsestic stories in Davenport's *Green Fields* and the associative range of his letters spurred J on to ever more revelations. More even than wishing to revise and perfect his past, he still wished to understand himself. He was perplexed by the intense sexual preoccupation that had driven him to seek intimate relations with many women throughout his life. It was not enough for him to reason that most men young and not so young have a lively interest in sex. Stories by Guy that unflinchingly treat adolescent masturbation spawned the memory of J's own earliest sensual epiphany: "This is an important subject which I have not seen anatomized with such specificity in any other work . . . Think of what I might have accomplished in a lifetime had I not been in thrall to the Demon of Lubricity." Not only did the energy and drive wasted on sexual adventuring prey upon J, but so did the misuse of time that might better have gone into his publishing ambitions. In his poem "Grumpus at 78," J asked, "What happened to the energetic / (and sometimes radiant) young man / who was going to do such wonders / to raise the level of literature / in our land"?

Still, J had not ceased fishing for new poets, and when he read Anne Carson's poems in *The American Poetry Review*, he wrote to her that he was "fascinated" by them. "If you have more poems in the vein of 'The Truth about God' I'd be glad to consider them for a book." When he discovered that she was a professor of Greek at McGill and a painter of volcanoes, he was hooked. She was, he decided, "a master of the intellectual glimpse," up there with his declared favorite in the genre, Charles Simic. "Esteemed Volcanist," he addressed her, and sent her a poem allegedly by "Sardonicus of Tyre": Carson replied that if she were his analyst, she would approve of his dealing with his "anger" in his poetry. "Fortunately," she added, "I'm just your Greek advisor." While J enjoyed corresponding with her, his intentions were not amorous. "She not toasty," he had to admit reluctantly.

On Election Day 1992, J went dutifully to the Norfolk town hall to vote, "always an ordeal" because he hated *all* dealings with authority. When "the two Bubbas" won, J opined that "George Slime can slink off to Kennybunkport." J liked Clinton—"I call him 'Smiley,' not 'Bill,' because he is always smiling." J's one reservation was on fiscal policy: "My worry about 'Smiley' is that I think he could be blandished by the bankers." J had sent Clinton a modest campaign contribution and was rewarded with a copy of *Clinton: Portrait of Victory*, inscribed "For Jim/ With my heartfelt thanks/ Bill." J commented, "My library is now complete."

J knew that some called him the Duke of Norfolk behind his back, and he deliberately courted eccentricity. "I've developed a tone of self-deprecation which is blatantly arrogant," he said. It was a pose he knew others saw through: "It doesn't fool anybody." Once he overheard one of the Norfolk postal clerks say, "He's pretty stuck on himself, isn't he?" Not that they were down on J: "They've always liked me since the day I was coming in with my arms loaded with packages so I couldn't reach out my hands, and I hadn't tightened my belt properly, so my pants fell all the way down to my ankles. I'm the village comic character."

Honors kept rolling in, which J accepted even while complaining about the disruptions they involved. "Nobody unnnerstans me," he said to Davenport. "All I want is to watch the sheep eat and piddle out my little verses of lost loves. New Babylon gives me the poop." In truth, he both was pleased and felt under obligation to those who had, after all, shown him appreciation. He was awarded the National Book Foundation's Medal for Distinguished Contribution to American Letters at the Plaza Hotel on November 18, an honor, he said, that came to him "for being lifelong a friend of lost literary souls."

J survived his public ordeal and returned to seeing Davenport's *Green Fields* through the press. He mandated that Gertrude design the cover, work she had largely given up after a botched operation to relieve the pressure on her optic nerve caused by a web of blood vessels. "I have spaghetti on the brain," Gertrude would joke to Peggy Fox; in fact, she had gone nearly blind after the procedure. She was still painting, however, "wonderful watercolors of floating flowers: roses floating in the sky over St. Mark's Square." J had a particular reason for wanting to "raise her spirits": at a showing of her work in the Norfolk library only J's relatives had bought paintings. Consequently, Gertrude "fears she isn't good and has stopped painting." J had usually been considerate of the feelings of his employees, but tender concern for a wife's had been all too rare; Gertrude, in a way, now filled both subordinate and spouse roles.

"Nummusquanamuckqunmanit"—God is angry with me—J now intoned in the Narragansett language, for he had new fodder to "logotate" with. Rosmarie Waldrop, Keith's wife, had lent him Roger Williams's seventeenth-century *A Key into the Language of America*, which she was using as a stalking horse for a long poem of her own. In J's case, it was like giving matches to a pyromaniac: "Tunna-awwa commitchichunck kitinckquean?" he brought out next—Whither goes your soul when you die?

J was still mulling over the problems posed by the several women in his life, and again he turned his musings into verse, writing "The Two of Them": "One kept his stomach full. / The other nourished his imagination. / It was a perfect arrangement / Until some confusion arose / As to which one should do which." On the advice of Alice Quinn, poetry editor at *The New Yorker*, J had once more given up the visual couplet pattern of his typewriter metric. "It was a kind of obsession," he admitted, "a snobbery to be different." His verse was becoming more relaxed. There were indications that J was more approving of Gertrude as well. She had "requisitioned" *Green Fields* one evening to look it over before working out a design for the book, and then, instead of joining J in the TV room for her three favorite sitcoms, she had read Davenport until midnight, when she announced to J, "He's wonderful, I never read any book like that."

Throughout 1993, J would be concerned with the publication of his shorter poems, titled *Heart Island and Other Epigrams* after the Reeses suggested using a title derived from one of the individual poems. J worried over the illustrations, but he did not want them slavishly reflective of the verse. He made no demands on the arrangement of the poems: "I never pay much heed to the order of poems in a book . . . I am so grateful for this project. It helps with the pain." He followed every detail and corrected the galleys; they were nearly perfect, he told Sandra. "It's going to be a dandy book."

All January, J was tortured by what he liked to think was simply arthritis: "On bad days it goes up into my head and even down into my jaw." He appeared for a talk at the New York Public Library, got through it on pills, and vowed to retire for good. His performance went well, "langwidge flowed like the foam," and he counted seventy-three laughs. As often happened, someone asked J at the end who his favorite contemporary poets were, and he produced his current stock answer: he himself was his "third favorite, but the first two are matters of national security which cannot be divulged." Gertrude spotted "Angelica" in the audience and maintained a "glacial and menacing silence" during the subsequent dinner at La Caravelle. "Why can't some girls understand that it is Nature's wish that men scatter their seed a bit," J confided to Guy. "Ann . . . understood that truth perfectly and there was never any fuss." A lapse of memory, or another wishful reconstruction on his part? J really did seem to be worried about the survival of his literary leavings and entrusted to Peggy Fox the carbons of his poem drafts. He named her and Daniel Javitch his literary executors.

Vanessa wrote to J that she and John Dougill were going to marry on her fortieth birthday and hoped that J would not be too upset. He wasn't. Then for two pages he "eulogized . . . the happiness, the apogeiticy (surely no such word) of our years of contiguity." His *Collected Poems* appeared from Moyer Bell in April, and six months later he had found only one newspaper review: that upset him.

Not that J had become exactly a tame cat: to one of his *apsaras* he wrote a poem, "The Mistress of Improbability," in which he laid bare his nature, comparing his emotions to those so powerfully expressed by Yeats, in which J concluded:

> But is it possible, given my nature
> And my amorous history, to erase
> So many years in which love meant
> Passion, meant assault, meant conquest?
> Yeats wrote: "You think it horrible
> That lust and rage should dance
> Attendance upon my old age."
> You do scoff at Yeats as a frustrated
> Old man, but I'm deep shrouded in his
> Bitterness.

There were three constants in J's life these days: "The three P's: Pain, People and the Post." Some of the visitors were welcome, but others were tolerated because of J's sense of obligation: a Pound scholar—"species musculus barbatus"—who invited himself for a day to consult the archives, then stayed for three; a scriptwriter for a film on Tennessee; a dealer in rare books who paid J $6,000 for some of his duplicates. "If I had foreseen to save 10 copies of first editions of the early ND books, I'd be rich," J commented. And he still patiently searched his library for the answers to queries from his staff and wrote soothing letters to disgruntled authors. "Perhaps you think of me as a soothsayer," he wrote to Guy, "but I'm really just a soother."

New Directions had good news for J: Barbara Epler, hired as an assistant editor in 1984, had soon distinguished herself by signing on Camilo José Cela, Susan Howe, Clarice Lispector, and Muriel Spark, and now initiated the Bibelot series, paperbooks of under a hundred pages in a format that would fit into a shirt pocket, each intended as a reintroduction to an established author, including Ronald Firbank, Henry Miller, Dylan Thomas, and Tennessee Williams. Some Bibelots sold well, and the series would eventually reach twenty-two volumes.

•

With Ohannessian cutting down her working hours and projecting full retirement, a decision had to be made on her successor. Glassgold as editor in chief expected to become vice president, but he wanted to write a novel of his own, and in any case the position required someone with broad managerial experience. Peggy Fox had worked in almost every area of publishing, and away from the office J said that "her middle names are memory, precision and efficiency," adding with a typical flourish, "God created a jewel in Peggy." J left it to Griselda to make a recommendation. The situation was debated with considerable heat on the nineteenth floor of 80 Eighth Avenue, and Peggy emerged as the clear choice. Griselda informed J of the staff consensus, and J wrote on a small scrap of paper, "Peggy—I hope you are as happy with G's 'plan' as I am. With you at the helm I'll not be afraid of shipwreck." Then he quoted a line from Leopardi's *L'infinito*: "E il naufragar m'è dolce in questo mare"—And shipwreck is sweet to me in such a sea.

The board of directors' meeting of November 1, 1993, confirmed that, effective January 1, 1994, Ohannessian would become managing director at a reduced workload and Fox would take over as vice president. Glassgold's resignation as editor in chief became effective immediately, with the understanding that he would continue as a freelance consulting editor.

•

July was exceptionally hot. "The heat is combusting me," J complained, which reminded him to tell Gertrude, who urged eventual cremation, that he wanted to go to the worms instead, because Elisabeth Borgese had assured him that poets feel the heat of the fire. "For my obsequies: only one lonely *myosotis sylvatica*," the wood forget-me-not, he stipulated. J's irritated state showed in his attitude toward Gertrude. He remained grateful for her care of him, yet was critical when she ventured into Norfolk society on her own. "G. has been taken up by the fast social set here and is running about with them and seems happy," he told Gigi Schendler. "The little fool does not realize she is their comic doll and will be dropped when another amusement turns up."

Finally, in the summer of 1993, the long-projected reunion in Cornwall, Connecticut, of Papagena and Papageno was arranged, and J wrote in "Remembrance": "Now two quite / different people will be meeting / again for the first time in many / years." J was eager in anticipation, nervous; Sara Woolsey was slim, graceful, still lovely. The conversation ran to children and grandchildren, but Sara's smile was as he had remembered it: special, enigmatic. Sara stunned him by asking what he had meant by tearing the wings off the moths and throwing them on her pillow, nearly sixty years earlier, an event that had vanished entirely from his mind. J suggested his sexual frustration, a diagnosis of psychic castration. He hinted at a missed lifetime together, had she only taken the initiative—he pleaded his shyness—or had she later acquiesced when he had asked her to come to a friend's apartment in New York. J wrote Papagena and this startling denouement into *Byways*, leaving Sara's question about the moths unanswered.

That summer Dr. Wiesel died, and J remembered him fondly: "He preserved for my old age the work that I've loved best to do: publishing books that will be around after Robert Ludlum and Judie Krantz are forgotten, writing verses that are about the great past and the present, teaching kids who love literature in the colleges." The path that Ezra had started J on, Ben Wiesel had enabled him to follow into old age.

J felt worse and worse as the summer progressed—arthritis pains, headaches, dizziness, and at times he walked with two canes. In early August he collapsed and was taken by ambulance to the hospital. His condition was diagnosed as a minor stroke, and he feared that he was losing his mind. Further tests were inconclusive, so perhaps he had not had a stroke after all. He seemed disappointed, and Gertrude tried to tease him out of his depression: "You see, J, people will still love you even if you haven't had a stroke." "Oh, I's *so* thirsty," he said, changing the subject. "I'm sorry, J," she replied firmly. "It's against the rules to have water." At this he flared up: "I rescind the rule!"

By mid-August, J was clearly recovering, although he complained that he was "still dizzy and shaking," that he could not type, and that his eyes were "bleary." His handwriting had deteriorated so much that the post office began to return his letters marked "Address illegible." The worst result of his breakdown was that it had stopped his progress on *Byways*. A month after the episode the symptoms continued, and he was having trouble reading, yet he again rose in the small hours to draft poems. J acknowledged his approaching eightieth birthday: "Hard to believe. It has all gone so fast." He drafted "In the Nursery," on the regression to childhood of old age: "I'm nearly 80 but my wife and / The servants look after me as / If I were a child of about 4." Bowing to the importunities of Davenport, he sent it to Alice Quinn of "the <u>New Yawper.</u>" To his surprise and delight she accepted it, saying, "I think the world of you. This poem is so beautiful you must be faring fairly well." He wondered suspiciously whether she might have been saying nice things out of pity.

With his stroke as an advance warning of mortality, J set himself to wrestle to its conclusion his verse memoir of Bill Williams. He anticipated that it would take him ten pages. He intended an honest portrayal of his relationship with Bill from their first meeting at 9 Ridge Road. He would deal with Williams's driven poetic avocation and not shirk giving an account of his searching out of the eternal sexual mystery—"Not satyriasis. He simply / Liked women, drew material / For his work from them." "To look about is only human," J pronounced, "to write such poems divine." Once fully engaged, J found that he had more and more to say, unburdening himself of cherished memories, rancor, confessions. On January 5, 1994, he was able to exclaim, "Hallelujah, last night I finished the WCW piece." He had sixty-three typed pages. J knew that it was a rough draft, but he told Guy that he did not plan "to imperil your mental health by submitting you to this noble work." However, within two weeks a fat envelope containing the unedited text was in Guy's hands.

J was back to claiming that he had had a "small stroke," and he felt that he had come to terms with his condition. It explained and excused his memory loss and dizziness: he was not at fault for smoking his pipe and cigars; he was not a hypochondriac. Then he saw the head neurologist at Massachusetts General and his comfortable sense of certainty vanished. The "kind and learned old man (*benignus quam doctus*)" questioned him for an hour, studied his records, watched him walk in the hospital corridor. No, he said finally, no stroke, no "cerebral accident." J was dismayed. "I am not a psychiatrist," continued the doctor, but J's symptoms suggested a state of anxiety. "Could it / Be the unforgivable sins of the / Fathers," he wondered to himself, "sins from which there / Is no escape?" J became clear in his own mind "that the cause of my distemper is accumulated sinfulness, incrementum delicti—the spawn of wickedness—coating the lobes with the slime of nefasity [*sic*]."

Nunc dimittis servum tuum

I Float Between the Spheres

and the gutter I dream of
dzogchen and the blessed

nothingness of sunyata but
yet I swim in the vanity of

frivolous poetry & torment
myself with imaginings of

profane and forbidden love.
          —James Laughlin, *Stolen & Contaminated Poems*

"Carruth has done a superb job," J said, of his work on the Bill Williams section of *Byways*, "cutting, polishing, general *oop-befestiging*. He's a whiz. He wrote a new ending, making himself sound like me, which is a great improvement." Many poets fiercely resent others tinkering with their lines and show their work in progress to friends mainly for encouragement and praise. Not J: his gratitude to Hayden was genuine and heartfelt.

A *Table of Green Fields* appeared near the end of October 1993, and the reviews vindicated J's insistence on publishing the collection. "Unique Stories Break All the Rules," ran one screamer, while Davenport's old friend Clarence Brown at Princeton commented that "many readers have difficulty adjusting to the utter absence of evil in the prelapsarian paradise of his imagination." The *New York Times Book Re-*

view notice singled out for praise "Belinda's World Tour," based on an episode in a biography of Franz Kafka in which the Czech author had tried to console a girl for the loss of her doll by writing her letters in the doll's name: Guy supplied these "lost" letters. Belinda was the name of one of Guy's cats.

Lady Maria St. Just died on February 15 from heart failure brought on by rheumatoid arthritis. "Beloved friend," J wrote, "you are no longer here. / They telephoned last week to say that / Without my permission, without any / Warning, you had bought a one-way ticket." J deliberately echoed the "sudden subway" metaphor for dying that he had employed earlier in his poem on Tennessee's death. He was not about to let Maria leave his life: "Please fax me your / Confirmation that I am still there / With you, wherever there may be." Less sentimentally, J summed her up in prose: "She was a lively little Russian bunny."

Almost immediately, the dismemberment of the corpse began. John Lahr wrote an extensive piece for *The New Yorker* that told half the story: Lady St. Just was a ruthless autocrat who had exercised a stranglehold on Tennessee's literary legacy. "I wish you had taken on the biography. What extraordinary research," J commented to Lahr in a slyly ambiguous letter. "As I read, I felt like a fly on the wall of the Tower watching a bad Jacobean lady being tortured to death." Then he clarified his own feelings about her: "Maria was difficult but she certainly wasn't all bad. She imagined she was doing right by Tennessee's reputation. And time and again, earlier on, I watched her keeping him calm and cheered up when he was having severe nerves during rehearsal periods. She could always make him laugh. She kept me laughing." He would "try to bring out that quality she had" in the section on her in his *Byways*. (J's intended account of Maria would never be drafted.) Lahr had stated that Lady Maria aborted a fetus in 1951 and in the same paragraph detailed her affair with J, suggesting—without actually saying so—that J had impregnated her. She had also "wounded" Tennessee's art, Lahr said, and he advocated "reasonable use" of Williams's texts, published and unpublished, by "accredited writers, academics, and theatre artists," implying that she had blocked ND from publishing "standard editions of his great plays." J closed his letter by pointing out this error in Lahr's piece: "But New Directions does have a standard clothbound edition of the plays. The texts follow those of his final rehearsal scripts. I won't have some academic fussing with his work." The letter was at once a rebuke and a warning.

Privately, J had another explanation for the "vindictive" tone of Lahr's article: Maria, as Tennessee's "estatrix," had "stomped on his desire to write the biography." J made no attempt to defend stands taken by Maria that arose from the many anomalies of her character: those who knew her well recognized a mile-wide homophobic streak in her, a prejudice that did not prevent her from idolizing Tennessee and considering Gielgud and Vidal among her best friends. By the same token, an anti-Semitism rooted in her Russian petit bourgeois heritage was no bar, to her mind, from liking and admiring many Jews in her theater circle.

In May 1994, J finally held in his hand the Moyer Bell *Collected Poems of James Laughlin*. He felt that the book was far too long, calling it "the monstrous megalomaniad." After completing the proofing of the typescript, he had pronounced himself "exhausted—and dispirited." "So many indifferent, formulaic, repetitive poems. Love anatomized to the point of the ridiculous. Why didn't I throw most of them into the fire?" He consoled himself with his range of subject matter: he had counted "427 poems on different topics. Can Ashbery . . . tie that?" He proposed an appropriate title for his book: The Homeowners' Guide to Poetical Topics.

In 1995 the Academy of American Poets established the James Laughlin Award—formerly the Lamont Poetry Selection—$5,000 to be awarded annually for a *second* published volume of poetry. Drue Heinz endowed the renamed award with a grant of $500,000. Meanwhile, J was distracted by a succession of visitors, the most welcome being a long-absent Hayden, introducing his new wife, the poet Joe-Anne McLaughlin. "Carruth was gloomy as usual," J thought, "though he controls it better than I do."

J's new volume of poetry, *The Country Road*, appeared from Zoland Books, a small press run by Deborah's brother, Roland F. Pease Jr. For the cover J chose a painting by his cousin Marjorie Phillips of a country road near his parents' Big Springs farm. J saw the road as a metaphor for the path to Erebus, a journey to the underworld. The tone is set by "The Revenant," an unusually long poem for him, in which an unnamed dead companion—perhaps Maria St. Just—reappears. Initially, the poet meets his revenant around his home, but soon they talk about a trip to India: "I had been there but you / Never had." In India, "Will it even be / Granted to us that I may / Touch you and perhaps make / Love to you again?" J strove to achieve in his verse a sense of human closeness. In "The Music of Ideas," he assessed himself as one of "We smaller poets": "Our little /

Minds are incapable of the great / Organ fugues. Better to be silent?" His output answered his question: a total of six volumes of his poetry would be published in 1995.

His susceptible heart found inspiration in the daughters of his friends. He would swim along Tobey Pond to flirt with Brendan Gill's daughters and granddaughters—"Old men fall in love / With young girls readily":

They have dear memories they'd like
To relive while still they can.
Be kind to them, maidens.
The day may come when
You'll understand what it is
To need to recapture
The raptures of the past.

J's ailments were more than ever making him miserable. "I can only stand up for five minutes and then my back is aching till I can sit down," he wrote. J saw a neurologist in a futile attempt "to find out why I walk leftwards when I want to go straightwards and can't hit the right keys on the typewriter." "Ie wie nit was zula bedoota"—I don't know what this means—J wrote in the vernacular of the Swiss canton Graubünden, "for the last week my frail frame has been shaking like a leaf . . . I knocked to the floor a bottle of my favorite Gewurztraminer and fell backward down the stairs to the TV room, landing on my bumpus. Is this the last chapter?"

A major honor came to him on March 26, 1995, when J was given the Curtis Benjamin Award by the Association of American Publishers. The first recipient of the annual award, in 1975, had been Charles Scribner Jr., and it had gone to the leading lights of Doubleday, Harper & Row, McGraw-Hill, and Random House and to the heads of such university presses as Harvard, Princeton, and Yale. Then, on April 5, came an honor that J really cherished: he was inducted into the American Academy of Arts and Letters as a poet. Awarded membership at the same time were Charles Simic and Brendan Gill. Lincoln Kirstein was named American honorary member. J's recognition as a poet, "my recent beatification," had come too late for him to savor the moment, and he blamed Gertrude for persuading him to attend. The occasion was "all penible," beginning with the three-hour car ride that had set off his arthritic aches—this was his first trip to Manhattan in more than a year. He did admit to "a curious interest" in the ceremony, but he was humiliated to discover that he could not name people present whom he had long known. Sensing his discomfort, Simic and his beautiful wife took J to the bar. Then, so he would claim, he fell off the platform as the citation was being read. "But I got a bigger hand for that than the perpendiculars," he said, turning mishap to virtue, "a comic incident for 'Byways.'" This was one of J's inventions: he might have wavered, but no witness reported a fall. Worst of all, J said, was the post-ceremony dinner, which he left early. Over and above his personal discomfort was anguish at the "silence and curiosity" of his tablemates as he left: "I hope they all thought I'd had a heart attack and wasn't just drunk."

As so often in times of personal crisis throughout his life, J immersed himself in work, shoving along the publication of *A Balance of Quinces: The Paintings and Drawings of Guy Davenport*, which featured twenty-four of Guy's works in color. J had been after him to compile a book of his paintings, although he had seen little besides some drawings. Finally, Guy sent a portfolio, and J responded, "Dear Mike Angular—/ Wham! Bam! Bulandro! The paintings are TERRIFIC." Despite the cost, J opted for twenty-four color plates. *A Balance of Quinces* would appear in 1996. Guy's art ranged from chaste geometric abstractions to detailed sketches of nude male figures that would have made Aunt Leila blanch. "Some of them can be shown only in Denmark," commented the artist.

J had estimated 64 pages, but then he received 94 pages of text, a superb introduction by Guy's former student Erik Anderson Reece. So the book jumped to 128 pages, to make even forms and permit including all the paintings Reece discussed. "I think there is enough green in the till to handle this bigger book," he told Guy. J was quite prepared to stand the expense. Griselda objected, invoking ND's loose policy of not publishing more than one book a year by any given author: the rights for *Da Vinci's Bicycle* had reverted to Guy, and ND was planning to issue it in paperback, and *The Cardiff Team* was scheduled for 1996. J overruled Griselda. Guy offered to subsidize the publication out of his recent MacArthur "Genius" Award. No, J said, send me a bill. "The MacArthur loot should be reserved for riotous living and balloon trips to Denmark."

Toward the end of September 1996, J and Guy received advance copies of *A Balance of Quinces*: J was delighted with the beauty of the book, "page after page of handsomely laid out art." It projected "a feeling of simplicity, serenity and spaciousness." Perhaps J felt some regret that except for a very few art-and-text books done out of love and friendship, he had left this field of publishing so much alone. Gertrude, her eyes too weak to read the type, went over the illustrations with a magnifying glass and was "enthralled" by them. Guy credited J with having conceived of the volume in the first place and pronounced himself pleased, the color plates "little miracles of fidelity." He did not even seem upset that one black-and-white abstraction was printed upside down: "They look pretty much the same as sideways or right-side-up."

•

J's colleagues at New Directions realized that a new tone had entered into the Norfolk confetti: a kind of personal sweetness not there before. "Thank you," J now took pains to say, "for all that you have done for me." He had always taken the time to praise a good letter, a fine editing job, a perceptive decision. Now he seemed gentle and reached out with affection to his staff.

J was prescribed Relafen for his arthritis pains. Gertrude took the measure of her James. "His complaining is magnificent," she wrote to Davenport. "'My back hurts' 'My little finger on my left hand is paralyzed' 'I'm sleepy' . . . 'I'm not working hard enough' 'Do you think I'm fading?' 'I don't think it will be long now' 'Why do people say I look good? Do you think they see my sad state and are trying to be nice to me?'" But he was working, and she spurred him on: "When he talks about *leaving* I tell him he'd better finish *Byways* before he goes and that usually gets him started." J described himself as "very shaky" in health, and he decided that he had to give up golf: "My legs are now made of taffy." He wandered in his woods, picking up brush: his old compulsion for order. When he signed two hundred title pages of *Heart Island and Other Epigrams*, his signature was "so wiggly" that he apologized to the Reeses.

In November 1995, Peggy Fox, who had undertaken to edit a volume of J's correspondence with Tennessee, came to Meadow House to interview J about the playwright. Toward the end of the interview, Fox asked him to read "Tennessee," his poem on the death of the playwright, into the recorder. By the time he came to the last line, "until it is my turn to join him on the sudden subway," his face was streaming with tears. In explanation J merely said, "He was my *friend*." How much of his emotion was for dead Tenn and how much for himself?

•

In April, J was cheered by the first daffodils and green shoots, "because they cut the waiting time of my being able to swim in the lake." Finally, the heavy snows melted and the waterlogged land fed magnificent lilac, azalea, and laurel bushes. Doggedly, J attempted a return to golf but, even using a cart, could only manage three holes. However, he had mastered the fax machine, and in the first week of June he was busily sending messages to Glassgold, who was working on contract from his home to ready J's *The Secret Room* for ND to publish.

That August, J fell down the Meadow House stairs again, and this time he lay helpless for three hours before anyone came to his aid. Nothing was broken, but he had to endure a round of medical tests after the accident. He continued his daily walks about the nearby trails and lanes but consented to the silent company of "Draculus" Sandor, as he called his taciturn Hungarian handyman. His eighty-second year bearing down on him, J complained of "creaky legs" and slipping memory. He fell three more times in one week, but he returned to *Byways* and roughed out twenty pages. "The same old crap," he said.

On November 1, 1996, Peggy Fox drove Mary de Rachewiltz to Norfolk for a luncheon with J. Peggy left the two sitting alone on the couch, holding hands, the sheep meadow behind them, each sensing that this would be their final meeting. In 1997, New Directions published *The Love Poems of James Laughlin*, a slim and chaste volume. He sent a copy to Bési Starkey, an old friend and neighbor. Later she met J along Mountain Road, unshaven, rumpled, his mouth slack. "I didn't know where to look," she teased him, both of them knowing that she did not feature in any of the poems. He brightened, pleased to be called upon to act the roué, to have a woman flirting once more with him.

Gertrude came down with bacterial pneumonia in March 1997 but survived, while the deaths of others continued to haunt J. Allen Ginsberg died on April 5, but not before telephoning many friends from his deathbed. "I wanted to tell you," he said to each. A stricken Ferlinghetti sent J a copy of his free verse "Allen Ginsberg Dying."

J sensed that he too was slipping away, which spurred him to keep producing at racing speed. Out of his insomnia came a burgeoning interest in an old form. By January 1996 he had begun to write five-line poems, or "fivers," as he called them, and Davenport pointed out that pentastichs went back at least to Palladius in the *Greek Anthology*. J engaged Leslie Miller of Grenfell to design and publish *A Commonplace Book of Pentastichs*, which he thought would be the first such "anthology" ever published—an innovator still. Certainly five-line stanzas are common, but modern examples of tight five-line poems, apart from limericks, are very few. His volume could be a bedside book for those having trouble sleeping, he said, or "a waiting book for someone who is sitting in the library waiting for Gertrude or myself to come down." At the core of each pentastich might be a borrowing from Kay Boyle, a translation from Artaud or Plato, a rendering of seventeenth-century Thomas Browne, or a matching of his own life against the seasons. In "Spring Comes Again," J wrote,

> The spaces in time seem to be narrowing.
> Days rush along as if they were running a
> race. But the marching order of daffodils,
> hyacinths, and white clouds of shadblow
> are as military as when I was a child.

He was mastering concision: the shadblow tree outside his window, the lead soldiers he had bought as a child in London's Burlington Arcade, all sheathed in the poignancy of time and age.

Throughout 1997, J concentrated on readying his *Pentastichs* volume for the printer. Peter Glassgold agreed to take on the editing of this "hobby project," as J called it. As a mark of his lasting regard for Margie, J used a portrait she had made of him on the dust wrapper: Tom Merton would have been pleased. "I hooe this is a day when I can type properly," J pecked out, supplying most of the missed letters in jagged black ballpoint. "A wire is busted between my brain and my fingers." "Nunc dimittis"—Now you have dismissed [your servant]—J titled a short poem:

> Little time now
> and so much hasn't
> been put down as I
> should have done it.

But does it matter?
It's all been written
so well by my betters,
and what they wrote
has been my joy.

Chic Morton lay in a hospice in Salt Lake City, clearly on his way out. Buck Sasaki and Red Altum drove down from Alta each day at lunchtime so that Chic would not be without his game of hearts. On July 14 he died, J's last close tie to the original Alta crew. Then, late in August, Gertrude was diagnosed with an "indolent growth," a tumor the size of a grape on her lung. "Gertrude's illness gives a terrible jolt to me as well as much pain and confusion to her," J wrote. But it was small, he said, so "let's hope for the best." Her chemo injections caused nausea. "She's very brave about it," J told Davenport, "but it hurts me to watch her suffering."

In his need to knot up a lingering, nagging obligation, J returned to the subject of a history of New Directions. Sounding anxious, even frantic, he "beseeched" Hayden Carruth to take over writing the history once more—the story of ND that J had first commissioned from him back in 1961 and then rejected. Unable even now to hand J a flat refusal and wishing to relieve his obvious suffering over this particular loose end, Hayden agreed, knowing in his heart that he could not write the book.

J continued to be interested in the New Directions publishing schedule, but he was trying to conserve his energy. In the summer of 1997, Robert Creeley sent in the manuscript of *Life and Death*, and J wrote to the office, "Peggy—I don't need to see the Creeley ms. He's always reliable." His final memo to his vice president and literary executor was written on October 22 in answer to a series of her memos. He had clearly typed it himself, and there were numerous typos and strikeovers, reminiscent of the last letters of his dear friend Bill Williams:

Peggy—I'm glad you hd½ such ahinterestint ftnbroad.
I'give up on Leverich. Not my responsibiliityl.
Good for Rick [Taylor].
I give up on Waldrop. Not my dish.
I Don't understand what McCowan wants. Ho you can andle.
That's doog fews about WWN makinḃ good on anthology arreaer royalties. please thank them .

I8m tOO ill to tavel to Brown. Thak them .
I'm sinking raprodly. J

Then a postscript, still typed and with holograph corrections: "Gertrude
is   is holding up well*I* consider-ing the rigoros of her treatnments/ Love
to all."

A couple of years earlier, J had imagined his death—"No exact moment is recorded for / When I left time and entered / Space; nothing precise that I / Could put down in my diary. The / Journalists were vague
about it"—but as it approached, he gave no indication of being resigned to
extinction. In late October there was an emergency trip by ambulance to
the Sharon Hospital, twenty-four miles from Norfolk, but he rallied and
demanded to be taken home. In early November he was back in the hospital, his breathing labored; but awake, J could not abide not working. He
asked his nurse to take down some notes. His mind was on John Brooks
Wheelwright, destined for the "Wheels" segment in *Byways*. Methodi-
cally, J outlined eight points that he wanted to make, vignettes from the
life of his friend: some ancestors killed by Indians, Wheelwright crawling
the length of a carpet *under the weaving* for a party stunt, his Socialist
speeches, his crazed mother, his death crossing the street near his home.
J sensed that he was dying, knowing as he dictated these lines that he
would not live to complete the *Byways* saga or even, most likely, this segment. Was it denial, was it desperation, was it his inability to admit his
own death? Very likely it was none of these, but instead determination,
his work ethic, creative habit, courage; these qualities had carried him
throughout his life. Now they must serve him unto death. He insisted on
returning to Meadow House, where his condition steadily worsened.

November 12 was a Wednesday, one of Kathy Basetta's regular mornings, and she arrived in the faint hope that J would be well enough to
work with her. No family members were present, and she heard the "terrible sound" of his breathing as a male nurse tried to help him. Soon an
ambulance was called, and J died en route to the hospital. The cause of
death was given as a stroke, but that was apparently not the case: the
underlying cause appears to have been progressive supranuclear palsy,
leading finally to a neurogenic atrophy of the muscles of the chest. He
had suffocated. The man who had long spoken so eloquently could not
draw breath.

Thirty years before, J had told Hugh Kenner that the beautiful phrase "mors claudet ocellos" was "one of my favorites." Now, finally, his eyes were closed in death. "Write on My Tomb," J had titled a four-line poem more than a decade previously,

```
that all I learned in books
and from the muses I've ta-

ken with me but my rich pos-
sessions I have left behind.
```

His wishes were not followed. His tombstone in the Norfolk cemetery states simply, "James Laughlin / 1914–1997 / Poet / Publisher."

Epilogue

Because Gertrude wanted it, there was a funeral service for James Laughlin in the white wooden Congregational church in Norfolk. A lot of local people filled the pews, which would have pleased J, and Leila Javitch read some of her father's poems. He was buried in the Center Cemetery, on the edge of a forest preserve above the village of Norfolk, not far from the graves of Uncle Dicky and Aunt Leila—so that she could still keep a loving eye on him. Gertrude would die on August 26, 1998, after telling "Draculus" Sandor to burn J's letters to her.

A month after J's death his staff placed a notice in *The New York Times* with a simple identification, "Founder & Publisher of / New Directions / Poet," followed by several of J's favorite lines from William Carlos Williams:

> I have learned much in my life
>   from books
>   and out of them
> about love.
>   Death
>   is not the end of it.

Below that came the Henghes colophon and the words "WE CARRY ON / NEW DIRECTIONS." A memorial program was arranged in January 1998 by New Directions at the American Academy of Arts and Letters in Manhattan.

Despite his long and uneasy dalliance with thoughts of dying, J had not shrunk from planning carefully: the New Directions files still at

Meadow House went to Harvard's Houghton Library to bring the total up to 1,422 boxes of material, and some five thousand volumes of his library were willed to Brown University. He left ND his life insurance policy of $300,000, together with the stipulation that a *Complete Poems* be published. There was an additional $200,000 for a continuation trust, "to help ND carry on for as long as the trustees think it is worth doing so," as well as substantial additional funds. And Alta, still in Laughlin hands, continues to thrive as a prime skiing destination.

Nor did J himself fall silent with his death. *Poems, New and Selected* would appear the following year, and Hayden Carruth wrote that "his unflagging intellectual sensitivity is the most encouraging thing I know about old age." His *Byways* poetry—like Pound's *Cantos*, incomplete—was collected by Peter Glassgold into a definitive edition. Barbara Epler and Daniel Javitch delved into J's myriad boxes of notes and memorabilia to compile and edit *The Way It Wasn't: From the Files of James Laughlin*, a lavishly illustrated alphabetical compendium. And others would take up J's favorite cudgel. "American corporate monoculture is homogenizing the world," Ferlinghetti would warn, "but the poet and artist will be here trying to fathom man's fate . . . dancing on the rim of the world."

Griselda Ohannessian, who had relinquished the day-to-day operation of ND to Peggy Fox in 1993, was succeeded in 2004 as president and publisher by Fox, who continued to develop editions of what she referred to as the "Deceased Giants." Fox retired in 2011; Barbara Epler, who had added such important writers as Roberto Bolaño and W. G. Sebald to the list and has continued discovering new authors writing in many languages, assumed her positions, with Laurie Callahan and Declan Spring in senior management. New employees conversant with the electronic revolution in publishing are bringing ND into the world of print-on-demand books, e-books, online advertising, social media, Facebook, Twitter, and blogs.

New Directions would publish some 250 volumes in the decade following J's death. From the very first, most ND books had included the printed notice "New Directions Books are published for James Laughlin"; after his death, the staff decided to keep on using this exact notation. His spirit continues to inspire ND, "the lengthened shadow of a very tall man."

Appendix: Authors Published by New Directions

Kader Abdolah • Walter Abish • Valentine Ackland • Martín Adán • Prince Ilango Adigal • Conrad Aiken • César Aira • Ah Cheng • Henri Alain-Fourier • Rafael Alberti • Will Alexander • Ahmed Ali • Émile Allais • John Allman • Germano Almeida • Osama Alomar • Corrado Alvaro • Van Meter Ames • Alfred Andersch • Sherwood Anderson • Eugénio de Andrade • Wayne Andrews • Wang An-shi • David Antin • Chairil Anwar • Guillaume Apollinaire • Homero Aridjis • Paul Auster • Gennady Aygi • Jimmy Santiago Baca • Howard Baker • Honoré de Balzac • Carol Jane Bangs • Eric Barker • George Barker • Djuna Barnes • Willis Barnstone • Lee Bartlett • Jacques Barzun • Christophe Bataille • H. E. Bates • Charles Baudelaire • Martin Bax • Bei Dao • Gottfried Benn • Eric Bentley • Nina Berberova • Rafael Bernal • John Berryman • Mei-Mei Berssenbrugge • Giuseppe Berto • Adolfo Bioy Casares • Carmel Bird • R. P. Blackmur • Max Blecher • Johannes Bobrowski • Ádám Bodor • Roberto Bolaño • Wolfgang Borchert • Johan Borgen • Jorge Luis Borges • Jean-François Bory • Alain Bosquet • Paul Bowles • Kay Boyle • Coral Bracho • Kamau Brathwaite • Bertolt Brecht • John Malcolm Brinnin • Edwin Brock • William Bronk • Christine Brooke-Rose • Chandler Brossard • Harry Brown • Sir Thomas Browne • Buddha • Mikhail Bulgakov • Basil Bunting • Frederick Busch • Albert Camus • Can Xue • Diego Cañedo • Elias Canetti • Veza Canetti • Ernesto Cardenal • Patrick Carnegy • Edmund Carpenter • Warren Carrier • Hayden Carruth • Anne Carson • John Carswell • Mircea Cărtărescu • Joyce Cary • Horacio Castellanos Moya • Camilo José Cela • Louis-Ferdinand Céline • Blaise Cendrars • René Char • Bankim-Chandra Chatterjee • Rafael Chirbes • Inger Christensen • Chuang Hua • Tom Clark • Douglas Cleverdon • Stephen Clissold • Jean Cocteau • Marvin Cohen • Peter Cole • Elliot Coleman • Maurice Collis • Confucius • Cyril Connolly • Joseph Conrad • Benjamin Constant • Cid Corman • Julien Cornell • Gregory Corso • Julio Cortázar • Baron Corvo • Albert Cossery • Malcolm Cowley • Hubert Creekmore • Robert Creeley • Edward Dahlberg • David Daiches • Alain Daniélou • René Daumal • Guy Davenport • Lydia Davis • Margaret Dawe • Osamu Dazai • August Derleth • Tibor Déry • Helen DeWitt • Debra Di Blasi • Emily Dickinson • John Donne • Hilda Doolittle • Coleman Dowell • Édouard Dujardin • Robert Duncan • Richard Eberhart • José Maria Eça de Queirós • Ecclesiastes • Edward Edinger • Russell Edson • Paul

Éluard • William Empson • Shūsaku Endō • Sverre Engen • D. J. Enright • Jenny Erpenbeck • Caradoc Evans • William Everson • Gavin Ewart • James T. Farrell • William Faulkner • Hans Faverey • Robin Fedden • Francis Fergusson • Lawrence Ferlinghetti • Thalia Field • Ronald Firbank • Dudley Fitts • F. Scott Fitzgerald • Robert Fitzgerald • Hildegarde Flanner • Gustave Flaubert • Charles Henri Ford • E. M. Forster • Wallace Fowlie • Rudoph Friedmann • Christine Froula • Judy Gahagan • Rivka Galchen • Forrest Gander • Federico García Lorca • John Gardner • Jean Garrigue • Romain Gary • Wilhelm Genazino • William Gerhardie • André Gide • Oliverio Girondo • Peter Glassgold • Johann Wolfgang von Goethe • Nikolai Gogol • Yvan Goll • Paul Goodman • Christian Dietrich Grabbe • Julien Gracq • Henry Green • Samuel Bernard Greenberg • Allen Grossman • Martin Grzimek • Gu Cheng • Albert Guerard • Henri Guigonnat • Eugène Guillevic • Ferreira Gullar • Lars Gustafsson • Sakutarō Hagiwara • Russell Haley • James B. Hall • Sam Hamill • Knut Hamsun • Peter Handke • Henry Hatfield • John Hawkes • Samuel Hazo • Robert E. Heibling • Heinrich Heine • Rayner Heppenstall • Gustaw Herling • Felisberto Hernández • Robert Herrick • William Herrick • Hermann Hesse • Hilaire Hiler • David Hinton • Takashi Hiraide • Friedrich Hölderlin • Yoel Hoffmann • Gert Hofmann • Edwin Honig • Paul Hoover • Susan Howe • Gerard Manley Hopkins • Bohumil Hrabal • Hsieh Ling-Yün • Vicente Huidobro • Maude Hutchins • Ann Hutchinson • Qurratulain Hyder • Sonallah Ibrahim • Christopher Isherwood • Lêdo Ivo • Rabee Jaber • Philippe Jaccottet • Fleur Jaeggy • Henry James • Gustav Janouch • Randall Jarrell • Alfred Jarry • Robinson Jeffers • B. S. Johnson • Gabriel Josipovici • James Joyce • Ernst Jünger • Franz Kafka • Bilge Karasu • Mary Karr • Robert Kaufman • John Keene • Hugh Kenner • Jack Kerouac • Abdelfattah Kilito • Danilo Kiš • A. M. Klein • Heinrich von Kleist • Alexander Kluge • Vivienne Kock • Kōno Taeko • Dezső Kosztolányi • Elaine Kraf • László Krasznahorkai • Rüdiger Kremer • Miroslav Krleža • Shimpei Kusano • Rachel Kushner • Louise Labé • Choderlos de Laclos • Christopher La Farge • Madame de Lafayette • Jules Laforgue • Davide Lajolo • Carlton Lake • P. Lal • Giuseppe Tomasi di Lampedusa • Tommaso Landolfi • Deborah Larsen • James Laughlin • Comte de Lautréamont • D. H. Lawrence • Robert Lax • Irving Layton • Linda Lê • G. A. Legman • Sylvia Legris • Christine Lehner • Herbert Leibowitz • Sister Thérèse Lentfoehr • Siegfried Lenz • Giacomo Leopardi • Denise Levertov • Alvin Levin • Harry Levin • Wyndham Lewis • Li Ching-Chao • Li Po • Li Shangyin • Enrique Lihn • Clarice Lispector • Luljeta Lleshanaku • Robert Lowry • Donald MacAulay • Hugh MacDiarmid • Nathaniel Mackey • Xavier de Maistre • Stéphane Mallarmé • Oscar Mandel • Osip Mandelstam • Norman Manea • Abby Mann • Javier Marías • Carole Maso • Bernadette Mayer • Robert McAlmon • Michael McClure • Carson McCullers • Herman Melville • Thomas Merton • Douglas Messerli • Jeffery Meyers • Henri Michaux • Wilson Micks • Dunya Mikhail • Josephine Miles • Henry Miller • Yukio Mishima • Frédéric Mistral • Teru Miyamoto • Eugenio Montale • Merrill Moore • Paul Morand • Jean Mouzat • Herbert J. Muller • Mu Xin • James Munves • Vladimir Nabokov • Alan Neame • Pablo Neruda • Robert Nichols • John Frederick Nims • Amélie Nothomb • Joyce Carol Oates • Griselda Ohannessian • Charles Olson • Toby Olson • George Oppen • István Örkény • Montague O'Reilly • Wilfred Owen • José Emilio Pacheco • Michael

Palmer • Nicanor Parra • Geoffrey Parrinder • Boris Pasternak • Kenneth
Patchen • Ota Pavel • Octavio Paz • Victor Pelevin • Marjorie Perloff • Saint-John
Perse • René Philoctète • Pindar • Alejandra Pizarnik • Po Chu-I • Elizabeth
Pollet • Joe Ashby Porter • Ezra Pound • John Cowper Powys • Caradog Prichard •
F. T. Prince • James Purdy • Qian Zhongshu • Raymond Queneau • Gregory
Rabassa • Mary de Rachewiltz • Philip Rahv • Carl Rakosi • Margaret Randall •
John Crowe Ransom • Raja Rao • Herbert Read • Erik Anderson Reece • Pierre
Reverdy • Kenneth Rexroth • Rodrigo Rey Rosa • Charles Reznikoff • Keith
Ridgway • Rainer Maria Rilke • Arthur Rimbaud • Édouard Roditi • Selden
Rodman • J. Alexander Rolph • Guillermo Rosales • Evelio Rosero • Amelia
Rosselli • Joseph Roth • Jerome Rothenberg • Ralf Rothmann • Muriel Rukeyser •
Nayantara Sahgal • Saigyō • Ihara Saikaku • William Saroyan • Albertine Sarrazin •
Jean-Paul Sartre • Irmgard Schloegl • Delmore Schwartz • G. C. Schwebell • John
Scott • Peter Dale Scott • Winfield Townley Scott • W. G. Sebald • Aharon
Shabtai • Hasan Shah • Merchant-Prince Shattan • Kazuko Shiraishi • Andrew
Sinclair • C. H. Sisson • D. Howard Smith • Patti Smith • Stevie Smith • Gary
Snyder • Gustaf Sobin • Sophocles • Gilbert Sorrentino • Muriel Spark • Theodore
Spencer • Enid Starkie • Gertrude Stein • George Steiner • Robert Steiner •
Stendhal • Jules Supervielle • Walter Sutton • Italo Svevo • Emma Swan • Richard
Swartz • Antonio Tabucchi • Nathaniel Tarn • Yōko Tawada • Emma Tennant •
Dylan Thomas • Merlin Thomas • Norman Thomas • Tian Wen • Uwe Timm •
Charles Tomlinson • Federigo Tozzi • Tomas Tranströmer • Lionel Trilling • Yūko
Tsushima • Leonid Tsypkin • Tu Fu • Niccolò Tucci • Martin Turnell • Frederic
Tuten • Dubravka Ugrešić • Regina Ullmann • Giuseppe Ungaretti • Jane Unrue •
Paul Valéry • Mark Van Doren • Paul Van Ostaijen • Luís Fernando Veríssimo •
Enrique Vila-Matas • José Garcia Villa • Virgil • Elio Vittorini • Rosmarie Waldrop •
Martin Walser • Robert Walser • Wang Anyi • Wang Wei • Robert Penn Warren •
Vernon Watkins • Evelyn Waugh • Robert Way • Eliot Weinberger • Nathanael
West • Paul West • John Wheelwright • John Willett • Jonathan Williams •
Tennessee Williams • William Carlos Williams • William Eric Williams • John
Wilmot, Second Earl of Rochester • Yvor Winters • Xi Chuan • Curtis Zahn • Zinovy
Zinik • Louis Zukofsky

Notes

ABBREVIATIONS USED IN THE NOTES

ARL	Ann Resor Laughlin
B	Beinecke Library, Yale University
Bellarmine	Merton Collection, Bellarmine University
Berg	Berg Collection, New York Public Library
Byways	JL, *Byways: A Memoir by James Laughlin*, ed. Peter Glassgold (ND, 2005)
CJB	Carol Jane Bangs
CJB/C	Carol Jane Bangs Collection
CP	*The Collected Poems of James Laughlin 1935–1997*, ed. Peter Glassgold (ND, 2014)
DP	Dorothy Pound
DS	Delmore Schwartz
DS/JL	*Delmore Schwartz and James Laughlin: Selected Letters*, ed. Robert Phillips (Norton, 1993)
ELC/C	Elaine Lustig Cohen Collection
EP	Ezra Pound
EP/JL	*Ezra Pound and James Laughlin: Selected Letters*, ed. David M. Gordon (Norton, 1994)
GD	Guy Davenport
GD/JL	*Guy Davenport and James Laughlin: Selected Letters*, ed. W. C. Bamberger (Norton, 2007)
H	Houghton Library, Harvard
HC	Hayden Carruth
HHL	Henry Hughart Laughlin
HM	Henry Miller
HM/JL	*Henry Miller and James Laughlin: Selected Letters*, ed. George Wickes (Norton, 1996)
HRHRC	Harry Ransom Humanities Research Center, University of Texas, Austin
JL	James Laughlin
KB	Kay Boyle
KR	Kenneth Rexroth
KR/JL	*Kenneth Rexroth and James Laughlin: Selected Letters*, ed. Lee Bartlett (Norton, 1991)

Lilly	Lilly Library, Indiana University Bloomington
LLC	Leila Laughlin Carlisle
MdR	Mary de Rachewiltz
MdR/C	Mary de Rachewiltz Collection
MH	Meadow House Collection, Norfolk, Conn.
MP/C	Marjorie Perloff Collection
MRL	Marjory Rea Laughlin
ND	New Directions
ND/C	New Directions Office Collection and Files
NDPP	*New Directions in Prose and Poetry* anthology (year follows)
NYTBR	*New York Times Book Review*
PLF	Peggy Lee Fox
RMM	Robert M. MacGregor
S/HR/C	Sandra and Harry Reese Collection
TM	Thomas Merton
TM/JL	*Thomas Merton and James Laughlin: Selected Letters*, ed. David D. Cooper (Norton, 1997)
TSE	T. S. Eliot
TW	Tennessee Williams
VS	Virginia Schendler
WCW	William Carlos Williams
WCW/JL	*William Carlos Williams and James Laughlin: Selected Letters*, ed. Hugh Witemeyer (Norton, 1989)
WIW	JL, *The Way It Wasn't: From the Files of James Laughlin*, ed. Barbara Epler and Daniel Javitch (ND, 2006)

PREFACE

3 *"Getting around"*: James Laughlin to Thomas Merton, Jan. 26, 1959, Bellarmine.

4 *"The first person"*: Robert White Creeley, *Beat Writers at Work: The Paris Review*, ed. George Plimpton (Modern Library, 1999), 72.

7 *"Laughlin traces"*: Marjorie Perloff, jacket copy for James Laughlin, *Selected Poems, 1935–1985* (City Lights Books, 1986).

7 *"1997 was a year"*: John E. Lane, "The Year in Poetry," *Dictionary of Literary Biography Yearbook: 1997* (Gale Research, 1998), 43.

I. THE ANCESTORS

10 *his younger son*: This James Laughlin was the co-founder of what became the Jones & Laughlin Steel Corporation; of him, James Laughlin IV wrote in "The Ancestors" draft, *Byways* file, MH, that "his father was a James / and before him another James."

10 *"Dividetus pariter"*: JL, "The Emigration," *The Lost Fragments* (Dedalus Press, 1997), 8.

10 *Around 1819, Alexander*: JL to Erl C. B. Gould, JL Genealogy file, H.

11 *"largely interested"*: John W. Jordan, *Encyclopedia of Pennsylvania Biography* (Lewis Historical Publishing, 1918), 202.

11 *The family legend*: JL to Robert Maynard Hutchins, Feb. 23, 1952, H.
11 *"Where wide lawns"*: JL, *Byways*, 136.
12 *"The butler passed"*: JL, "Pittsburgh," *WIW*, 222.
12 *"Each of the contracting"*: *New York Times*, June 16, 1908, 9.
12 *the umbilical cord*: JL, "The Record of a Growth," unpublished typescript, Oct. 10, 1931, MH.
13 *As a small child*: Marie Edgerton to author, July 11, 2007.
13 *"that I heaped"*: JL, "Eventually Number 143," unpublished typescript, MH.
13 *"Wow! wow! wow!"*: JL, "Record of a Growth."
13 *"There was an enormous"*: JL to TM, July 12, 1947, *TM/JL*, 22.
13 *Marjory, however, was a Presbyterian*: JL, "Appendix: Thomas Merton—A Portrait by James Laughlin," *TM/JL*, 375.
14 *"shouting / sin sin sin"*: JL, "Easter in Pittsburgh," *CP*, 52.
14 *"A big cloud"*: JL, "This Is My Blood," *Random Stories* (Moyer Bell, 1990), 182.
14 *"As my eyes walk"*: JL, "The Country Road," *The Country Road* (Zoland Books, 1995), 15.
15 *"When I had done"*: JL to GD, Dec. 24, 1994, MH.
15 *Nantucket*: Details from various sources: Marie Edgerton, interview by author, Jan. 2, 2002; Laughlin file, Rollins College; JL, "Dr. Benjamin Wiesel," unpublished typescript, MH.
15 *"When can we go"*: JL, "Marjorie Phillips," unpublished typescript, MH.
16 *moved the entire town*: Marie Edgerton to author, July 11, 2007; "Pittsburger Buys a Town," *New York Times*, Aug. 12, 1907.
16 *kidnapping rumor*: JL to Hugh Kenner, Aug. 21, 1973, MH.
16 *"All were acts"*: JL, "Danny Chinese Saddle," unpublished typescript, MH.
16 *problem of Grandfather*: JL to Dr. Daniel Romanos, Dec. 25, 1991, MH, posits a bipolar disorder.
16 *Everyone called her Danny*: Marie Edgerton, interview by author, Jan. 2, 2002.
16 *"she'd said all"*: JL, "My Paternal Grandmother," *Byways*, 20.
17 *"little clucks"*: JL to GD, June 12, 1994, MH.
17 *She took James*: Marie Edgerton to author, Feb. 7, 2002.
17 *"The Big Dog"*: JL to Vanessa Jackson, Nov. 15, 1983, private collection.
17 *"Little Dog Peppermint"*: JL, "Prologue," *Byways*, 1.
17 *And he often read*: Marie Edgerton to author, Jan. 14, 2002.
17 *"Mother, James is"*: JL to GD, Dec. 7, 1992, *GD/JL*, 105.
17 *"Hugh was not"*: Marie Edgerton to author, May 2005.
17 *H. J. "Jack" Heinz invented*: JL to GD, Dec. 6, 1993, MH.
18 *"socializing"*: JL to CJB, Aug. 16, 1982, CJB/C.
18 *"for good behavior"*: JL, "The Iceman Cometh," *Byways*, 13.
18 *"project method"*: *Arnold School Catalogue*, 1936–37.
18 *"spent money like water"*: JL to Romanos, Dec. 25, 1991, MH.
19 *There was an excellent*: Marie Edgerton to author, Jan. 14, 2002, and March 3, 2007.
19 *His older cousin*: Marie Edgerton, "James Laughlin IV," unpublished manuscript, collection of the author.
19 *James spent hours*: JL, "My Paternal Grandmother," 19–21.
19 *he could claim*: Mary Catharine McAllister, *Descendants of Archibald McAllister of*

West Pennsboro Township, Cumberland County, Pa., 1730–1898 (Scheffer's Printing and Bookbinding House, 1898), 8.

19 *Edwards taught him*: JL, "My Paternal Grandmother," 22.

19 *"to show her"*: Ledlie Irwin Laughlin, unpublished genealogy, ca. 1925, MH.

19 *"suffered early Depression"*: Marie Edgerton to author, Feb. 7, 2002.

20 *James was taken*: "Danny Chinese Saddle" and "Eventually Number 143."

20 *"the poverty of childhood"*: JL, "For H.J.H.," address at memorial service, *Byways* file, MH.

20 *Of his funds*: JL, "Danny Chinese Saddle" and "Eventually Number 143."

21 *"Wodder, wodder!"*: JL, note, *Byways* file, MH.

21 *"I went a little bit"*: JL, "My Paternal Grandmother," 24.

21 *The reasons given*: "Salle d'étude," draft written for Dudley Fitts, Oct. 31, 1931, MH.

21 *at James's own request*: JL, "Salle d'étude," *Random Stories*, 117.

21 *"I was so unhappy"*: JL, "Album" and "The Day It All," MH.

21 *"Laughlin Deux"*: JL to GD, Feb. 21, 1995, MH.

22 *"Reserved and rather"*: School Records, Le Rosey, 1927–28.

22 *"Dis donc, Lowgleen"*: JL, "Salle d'étude," draft written for Dudley Fitts.

22 *"Puis-je vous"*: JL to CJB, July 16, 1982, CJB/C.

22 *Assigned to pull*: JL to Theodore Spencer, May 9, 1936?, H.

22 *"Eight days"*: Barbara Strömstad (Association Internationale des Anciens Roséens), in conversation with author, Sept. 7, 2005.

23 *"sexy"*: JL, "Looking Across at the Silvretta," *Harvard Advocate*, March 1936.

2. DISCOVERIES: THE INTELLECT

24 *a sensual epiphany*: JL to GD, Oct. 21, 1992, MH.

24 *Eaglebrook was patterned*: JL to MRL and Margaret Keyser Laughlin, July 4, 1954, MH.

24 *"though never militantly"*: JL to TM, July 12, 1947, TM/JL, 22.

24 *"parenting"*: Cynthia Zarin, "Profiles: Jaz," *New Yorker*, March 23, 1992, 44.

25 *"This is particularly hard"*: MRL to Carey Briggs, March 15, 1931, MH.

25 *"superlative star"*: Marie Edgerton to author, Feb. 7, 2002.

25 *Although nominally a Protestant*: Marie Edgerton to author, Feb. 25, 2002.

26 *Robin Hill was a cosmopolitan*: Marie Edgerton to author, Jan. 14, 2002, and March 3, 2007.

26 *Uncle Dicky, although*: Marie Edgerton to author, March 5, 2002.

26 *Boston, she said, embodied*: Carol Edgerton Thayer to author, March 20, 2008.

26 *"in thrall to her conviction"*: JL, "My Aunt," *Byways*, 135.

27 *Mlle Marie-Thérèse d'Authume*: JL to CJB, July 16, 1982, CJB/C.

27 *"Young as I was"*: JL, "The Aftermath," *Byways*, 81.

28 *"the Venerable"*: JL to Zay M. Foster, Feb. 15, 1985, MH.

28 *"You young puppies"*: JL to GD, Dec. 7, 1992, MH.

28 *"handsome but slightly"*: JL, in *New Directions in Prose and Poetry 50*, ed. J. Laughlin, Peter Glassgold, and Griselda Ohannessian (ND, 1986), 61–62.

28 *"an inch taller"*: JL to GD, Dec. 7, 1992, MH.

28 *"Fitts is a sort"*: JL to Robert Fitzgerald, 1932?, quoted in Penelope Laurans Fitzger-

ald, "'. . . And in the Bond Which Endured Between Us': Notes on the Friendship of James Laughlin and Robert Fitzgerald," *Paideuma* 31, nos. 1–3 (Spring, Fall, and Winter 2002): 148.

29 *"We save a boy's"*: George C. St. John, quoted in James B. Simpson, *Simpson's Contemporary Quotations* (1988), www.bartleby.com/63/7/2607.html.

29 *Together they motored*: JL, "The Ancestors," *Byways*, 12.

30 *"by examination"*: Shadyside Presbyterian Church Records, Pittsburgh.

30 *Howard Heinz*: JL, "For H.J.H.," address at memorial service, unpublished typescript, *Byways* file, MH.

30 *"indisposed"*: JL to GD, Dec. 6, 1993, MH.

30 *"[M]arks I hungered"*: JL, "An Old Schoolbook," *NDPP 1948*, 10:236–37.

30 *whom he asked*: Briggs to MRL, Feb. 27, 1931, MH.

30 *Fitts was happy*: JL to MacLeish, Oct. 1, 1963, Manuscript Collection, Library of Congress.

30 *During his senior*: JL to Gotham Book Mart, various dates, 1931–32, Berg.

30 *"if not too dilapidated"*: JL to Gotham, 1931, Berg.

31 *"Frances, don't you"*: Andreas Brown, interview by author, June 12, 2005.

31 *He discussed not only*: Carey Briggs to MRL, Feb. 27, 1931, MH.

31 *"He is just"*: MRL to Briggs, March 15, 1931, MH.

32 *"I was foolish"*: JL, "Record of a Growth."

32 *James resumed with Joyce*: Ibid.

33 *"the world should be"*: JL, "August 1931" Choate diary, entry for Aug. 14, 1931, MH.

33 *"lace[d] into a tub"*: JL, "Dr. Benjamin Wiesel," unpublished typescript, MH.

33 *"He alone of the family"*: HHL to Briggs, Nov. 10, 1934, MH.

33 *"Kora in / Hell and"*: JL, "Remembering William Carlos Williams," *Byways*, 144.

33 *But Fitts did have*: JL to GD, Jan. 28, 1993, *GD/JL*, 113; JL to GD, April 6, 1993, MH.

34 *He got J started*: JL, "Not-Notes," *Stolen & Contaminated Poems* (Turkey Press, 1985), 41.

34 *"This is naïveté wch"*: Dudley Fitts, Nov. 14, 1931, MH.

34 *Fitts had recently initiated*: Fitts to EP, Jan. 20, 1932, MH.

34 *"I doubt if you"*: EP to Fitts, Feb. 2, 1932, MH.

34 *"Horace laughed"*: JL, "Monotone," unpublished typescript, MH.

34 *"funny guy"*: JL to DS, July? 1938, *DS/JL*, 32.

35 *"Dear Skipper"*: JL to HHL, Nov. 1, 1931, MH.

35 *By March 1932, James*: JL, "August 1931" Choate diary, entries for March 9 and 10, 1932, MH.

35 *Among the books*: Ibid., entries for March 19–22, 1932.

35 *On the afternoon*: Ibid., entries for March 25–27, 1932.

36 *The Wallingford newspaper*: *Wallingford Daily News*, May 30, 1932.

36 *"Highest Honors"*: Certificate of admission for JL, Harvard, July 19, 1932, MH.

36 *summer reading*: JL, "Harvard—Boston—Rapallo," *Byways*, 38.

3. HARVARD, PART ONE

37 *"J.'s deserting Princeton"*: HHL to Briggs, Nov. 19, 1934, MH.

38 *"suits / Were not worn"*: JL, *Byways*, 32.

38 *"What a spread!"*: Ibid.
38 *Cousin Henry*: Ibid., 12.
38 *"nonflammable"*: Ibid., 34.
38 *Hughart relapsed*: JL to LLC, Aug. 13, 1932, MH.
38 *"the faculty"*: JL, *Byways*, 38.
39 *the Widener Library*: Ibid., 39.
39 *Joe Pulitzer was*: JL, "Wayne Andrews," Sept. 25, 1960, ND/C.
39 *Robert Lowell*: Robert Fitzgerald, *The Third Kind of Knowledge: Memoirs and Selected Writings*, ed. Penelope Laurans Fitzgerald (ND, 1993), 279.
40 *"Ole / Possum"*: JL, *Byways*, 94–95. A story that JL appropriated? Guy Davenport claimed that in another version of this story—not JL's—it was cake, not cookies, that Eliot had set out: GD to JL, Feb. 8, 1993, H.
40 *"long skoog"*: JL to Robert Fitzgerald, Jan. 1933? In Penelope Laurans Fitzgerald, "'. . . And in the Bond,'" 148.
40 *"not yet found"*: Briggs to MRL, Jan. 23, 1933, MH.
41 *"literary efforts"*: MRL to Briggs, Feb. 25, 1934, MH.
41 *"the New Englander"*: John Wheelwright, "Come Over and Help Us," *Collected Poems* (ND, 1972), 48.
42 *"Waiting & watching"*: April 2, 1933, "JL '2'" notebook, MH.
42 *"We didn't think"*: JL, "The River," *Random Stories*, 51.
42 *And when Robert Fitzgerald*: "JL '2'" notebook, MH.
42 *"having abandoned"*: Theodore Spencer, "Spencer Finds Great Change in Advocate," *Harvard Crimson*, 1933.
43 *"easily the best"*: F. O. Matthiessen, "Reviewing Current Advocate," *Harvard Crimson*, 1933.
43 *"owned half of it"*: JL to EP, Dec. 9, 1933, B.
43 *"by being as natural"*: JL to LLC, Feb. 7 and Sept. 30, 1933, MH.
43 *"I'm sorry to say"*: Fitts to JL, May 1, 1933, MH.
43 *"one of my idols"*: JL, quoted in Lyle Leverich, *Tom: The Unknown Tennessee Williams* (Crown, 1995), 471.
43 *"dear old Sherry"*: JL, interview by PLF, "James Laughlin at Meadow House," unpublished typescript, Nov. 3, 1995, private collection.
45 *"How I / Vexed her"*: JL, "The Rubble Railroad," *Byways*, 239.
45 *"I'm learning a lot"*: JL to LLC, July 21, 1933, MH.
45 *"stand behind me"*: JL to LLC, July 8, 1933, MH.
45 *"You were wearing"*: JL, "Are We Too Old to Make Love?," *Byways*, 25.
45 *During the "Liebestod" scene*: Sara Woolsey to JL, Nov. 8, 1993, H.
46 *"a river fairly blowing"*: JL, "River," 48.
46 *They were mad about*: JL to Woolsey, Oct. 12, 1991, H.
46 *Once, strangely, J tore*: Woolsey to JL, May 1992, H.
46 *"The people," he said*: JL to LLC, pmk. Munich, July 26, 1933, MH.
46 *"said to be clever"*: JL to EP, Aug. 21, 1933, B.
47 *"Visability high"*: JL, "Pound," *WIW*, 233.
47 *"Jas Loughlin Esq"*: EP to JL, Aug. 27, 1933, "James Laughlin IV/ Eliot House E-41" notebook, MH.
47 *"the bearded and cat-eyed"*: Robert Fitzgerald, *Third Kind of Knowledge*, 138.
47 *"CHARGE"*: EP typed note; pasted in "Eliot House" notebook, MH.

47 *J wrote in his notebook*: "JL '2'" notebook, MH.
48 *Zukofsky had been*: Mark Scroggins, *The Poem of a Life: A Biography of Louis Zukofsky* (Shoemaker Hoard, 2007), 133; see also Laughlin, Glassgold, and Ohannessian, *NDPP 1986*, 50: 82–84. Celia Zukofsky described the meeting—at which she was not present—in an interview after her husband's death, and Scroggins told the present author that Louis Zukofsky had often repeated essentially the same story.
48 *J departed with a copy*: JL to EP, Oct. 8, 1933, B.
48 *"without farting about"*: JL to EP, Aug. 29, 1933, B.

4. CORRESPONDENCE COURSE IN REBELLION: EZRA POUND BY SEA-POST

49 *"I like it"*: JL to LLC, Oct. 17, 1933, MH.
49 *"Yr sojourn č"*: Fitts to JL, Sept. 28, 1933, MH. Fitts favored "č" as an abbreviation for the Latin *cum*, "with."
50 *"Ezratic lingo"*: JL, *Pound as Wuz: Essays and Lectures on Ezra Pound* (Graywolf Press, 1987), 50.
50 *"American edderkashun"*: EP to JL, Oct. 26, 1933, H.
50 *"Ov all the post Abercrombie"*: EP to JL, Oct. 27, 1933, H.
50 *"When Joyce and"*: EP to JL, quoted in JL, *Pound as Wuz*, 18.
50 *"My ole farver"*: EP to JL, Oct. 27, 1933, H.
50 *"Whitehead ??"*: EP to JL, Oct. 26, 1933, H.
50 *"My language / Oriented"*: JL, *Byways*, 58.
50 *"great and lovable man"*: JL to GD, April 6, 1993, MH.
50 *"An eclectic"*: JL, autograph study notes for Epicurus, MH.
51 *"Gert the ole tub"*: EP to JL, Oct. 6, 1934, H.
51 *"debunk Stein (Toklas)"*: JL to EP, Oct. 8, 1933, B.
51 *"It takes about 600"*: EP to James Vogel, 1928, quoted in JL, *Pound as Wuz*, 42.
51 *"Go and see X"*: EP to JL, ibid.
51 *"To be watched"*: EP to JL, in "JL '2'" notebook, 1932, MH.
51 *"He seems to be settling"*: JL to EP, Oct. 8, 1933, B.
51 *"any estrangement"*: Wardwell to JL, n.d., H.
52 *No matter, she said*: Wardwell to JL, early Oct. 1933, "Eliot House" notebook, MH.
52 *Florence Codman*: JL to EP, Oct. 9, 1933, B.
52 *"I cd. be paid"*: EP to JL, Oct. 26, 1933, H.
52 *"DON'T take your"*: EP to JL, Nov. 26, 27, 1933, H.
52 *"The men who are awake"*: JL to EP, Nov. 6, 1933, B.
52 *"I don't know how"*: JL to EP, Nov. 14, 1933, B.
52 *"I think you better"*: EP to JL, Nov. 26, 27, 1933, H.
53 *"stick out Harvud"*: JL to EP, Dec. 9, 1933, B.
53 *"I need help"*: JL to EP, Dec. 9, 1933, B.
53 *"preoccupation"*: Louis Zukofsky, *Prepositions +: The Collected Critical Essays*, ed. Mark Scroggins (Wesleyan University Press, 2000), 199.
53 *"last book of thistletwit"*: JL to EP, Dec. 5, 1933, B.
53 *"neatly senile"*: JL to EP, Jan. 23, 1934, B.
53 *"EXACTLY"*: EP to JL, Feb. 3, 1934, H.

53 *"Nacherly practically NO"*: EP to JL, Dec. 24, 1933, H.

53 *"Don't go on"*: EP to JL, Feb. 12, 1934, H.

54 *"fortunately"*: EP to JL, Jan. 2, 1934, H.

54 *"Ma qvesto"*: EP, *The Cantos* (ND, 1996), 202.

54 *Pound had then lectured*: MdR, *Ezra Pound, Father and Teacher: Discretions* (ND, 1975), 123.

55 *"Write me again"*: WCW to JL, Jan. 23, 1934, *WCW/JL*, 1.

55 *Years later*: Dr. J. H. Waite, eye examination of Feb. 12, 1941, records, MH.

55 *"an every-word reader"*: JL to GD, Oct. 11, 1992, *GD/JL*, 86; JL to PLF, reported to author, Sept. 28, 2008.

55 *"the same sweet"*: JL to LLC, Dec. 25, 1933, MH.

55 *"a covey of letters"*: JL to EP, Jan. 7, 1934, B.

56 *"There is a savage young man"*: EP to Binyon, quoted in *The Selected Letters of Ezra Pound, 1907–1941*, ed. D. D. Paige (ND, 1971), 251.

56 *"Reading"*: JL to EP, Jan./Feb. 1934, B. *How to Read* was Pound's 1931 forerunner to his *ABC of Reading* (1934).

56 *"clever detail-critic"*: JL to EP, Jan. 18, 1934, B.

56 *"Good old Archie"*: JL to GD, April 4, 1993, MH.

56 *"Wms. could do the most"*: JL to EP, Jan. 18, 1934, B.

56 *"I am a little girl"*: Ibid.

56 *"I seen your squid"*: JL to EP, ca. end of Feb. 1934, B.

56 *"Writes Gilbert"*: JL to EP, Jan. 23, 1934, B.

57 *"but if you ever again advertise"*: JL to Gotham Book Mart, Feb. 21, 1934, Berg. (JL would finally come around on Canby after his article "Can We Afford Good Books?" appeared in *The Saturday Review of Literature* in 1947; Canby wondered whether large publishers who needed sales of five thousand copies would still be willing to risk the next generation of Thornton Wilders or Isak Dinesens. This was precisely the discovery and sales niche that New Directions would aspire to.)

57 *"Names have a way"*: Steloff to JL, Feb. 24, 1934, Berg.

57 *"Respected colleague"*: EP to JL, Feb. 20, 1934, H.

57 *"Yr. Eccel."*: JL to EP, Feb. 21 and 23, 1934, B.

57 *"Poetry don't sell"*: Ibid.

58 *He told his parents*: JL to HHL, Sept. 20, 1934, MH.

58 *"What wd"*: EP to JL, March 6, 1934, H.

58 *"Don't tell yr"*: EP to JL, May 25, 1934, H.

59 *"most interested"*: Steloff to JL, June 8, 1934, Berg.

59 *"he will add authors"*: Announcement on Gotham Book Mart stationery, 1934, Berg.

59 *"Shall be vurry pleesd"*: JL to EP, June 28, 1934, B.

5. "THE CHARISMATIC PYRAMID": GERTRUDE STEIN

60 *"scathing remarks"*: HHL to Briggs, Oct. 22 and 29, 1934, MH.

60 *"Nothing much to write"*: JL to MRL, July 6, 1934, MH.

60 *"I have been seeing"*: JL to EP, July 17, 1934, B.

60 *"pickin' up a bit"*: JL to EP, Sept./Oct.? 1934, B.

61 *"Torches were lighted"*: JL, unpublished typescript, MH.

61 *Many were saying*: JL to MRL and HHL, Aug. 28, 1934, MH.

61 *"I'm very much shocked"*: JL to EP, Aug. 2, 1934, B. Hitler had met secretly in Bayreuth with Theo Habicht, the Nazi leader in Austria, on July 22, 1934, and three days later the Austrian chancellor, Engelbert Dollfuss, was murdered. It became immediately clear that Habicht lacked the forces to deliver Austria to Germany, whereupon Hitler dismissed him, after sending a telegram of condolence to Dollfuss's widow.

61–62 *In mid-August, Joseph*: JL, address at the Poetry Center, Museum of Contemporary Art, Chicago, Feb. 11, 1983, unpublished tape recording, MH.

62 *"welcome invitation"*: JL to MRL and HHL, Aug. 28, 1934, MH.

62 *"Suddenly without knowing quite"*: Ibid.

62 *He exchanged gossip*: JL to MRL?, undated letter fragment, Aug. 1934?, MH.

62 *"My new passion"*: JL, diary fragment, Aug. 25, 1934, MH.

63 *"You didn't think"*: JL, at the Poetry Center, Feb. 11, 1983.

63 *"they are for a pretty"*: Janet Hobhouse, *Everybody Who Was Anybody: A Biography of Gertrude Stein* (Doubleday, 1975), 155.

63 *"No you haven't got it"*: JL, at the Poetry Center, Feb. 11, 1983.

63 *"That just ain't art"*: JL to TM, Nov. 8, 1957, Bellarmine.

63 *"I say, the kid hasn't"*: JL to MRL and HHL, Sept. 7, 1934, MH.

63 *"talking about books"*: JL, introduction to *Gotham Book Mart Catalogue 36* (Robert Alexander Press, 1936), n.p.

64 *"I like Gertrude"*: JL to MRL and HHL, Sept. 7, 1934, MH.

64 *"Miss Stein fills the car"*: JL to MRL and HHL, Sept. 7 and 10, 1934, MH.

64 *"The landscape"*: JL to MRL and HHL, Sept. 10, 1934, MH.

65 *"You see all of a sudden"*: JL to MRL and HHL, Sept. 7, 1934, MH.

65 *"certainly—practically—the most"*: JL on tape, St. Andrews College, Oct. 28, 1975.

65 *Stein told J that*: JL, interview by Daniel Bourne and Stephen Cape, *Gallery* 2, no. 4 (April 1981).

65 *"Jay, how can you read"*: JL, at the Poetry Center, Feb. 11, 1983.

65 *And when J tried to discuss*: Alice B. Toklas, *What Is Remembered* (Holt, Rinehart and Winston, 1963), 139.

66 *"a very great man"*: JL, at the Poetry Center, Feb. 11, 1983.

66 *"This is a bad thing"*: JL to MRL and HHL, Sept. 7, 1934, MH.

66 *"in a windowless"*: JL, "Paris," *Byways* file, MH.

66 *"forum or vortex"*: EP to JL, Oct. 18, 1934, H.

66 *"I suspect Gertrude"*: JL to EP, mid-Oct. 1934, B.

66 *"an impartial elucidation"*: JL to TSE, Oct. 11, 1934, H.

67 *"My LOUSY critical style"*: JL to Steloff, end of Oct. 1934, Berg.

67 *"little book"*: JL to TSE, Oct. 3, 1934, H.

67 *"I hope for original"*: TSE to JL, Oct. 10, 1934, H.

67 *"The thing to do"*: JL to Steloff, end of Oct. 1934, Berg.

67 *"This is a break"*: JL to HHL, Sept. 20, 1934, MH.

67 *Vail accepted two*: JL, "September 26," Lausanne notebook, MH.

67 *"I don't want"*: JL to HHL, Oct. 26, 1934, MH.

68 *"bloodmust"*: JL, "Danny Chinese Saddle," MH.

68 *"He sure is"*: JL to EP, Oct. 21, 1934, B.

68 *"Partial Eclipse"*: JL, *Story*, Oct. 1936, reprinted in *Random Stories*, 119–39.

68 *"dear boy"*: JL to EP, Oct. 21, 1934, B.

68 *"She is getting just"*: JL to MRL and HHL, Oct. 17, 1934, MH.
68 *"Thanx to yr machinations"*: Fitts to JL, Nov. 3, 1934, MH.
69 *"huge success"*: Fitts to JL, June 28, 1935, MH.

6. THE EZUVERSITY

70 *She sang Heine's*: JL, "'Ma' Reiss [sic] of Rapallo," unpublished typescript, *Byways* file, MH.
71 *"a marvelous educational"*: JL, *Pound as Wuz*, 165, 168–69.
71 *"Pound's mind always moved"*: JL, at the Poetry Center, Feb. 11, 1983.
71 *"Rabbit Britches"*: JL, *Pound as Wuz*, 168–69.
72 *Sometimes Pound quoted*: JL, "Pound the Teacher," *The Master of Those Who Know: Ezra Pound* (City Lights Books, 1986), 29–33.
72 *"to improve his Eye-talian"*: JL, "Pound the Teacher," *St. Andrews Review* 1, no. 1 (Fall/Winter 1970): 17.
72 *It was partly his delivery*: JL, "Pound the Teacher," *Master*, 3–4.
73 *"a great Peeeeacock"*: EP, *Cantos*, 554.
73 *"a Yiddish accent"*: JL, *Pound as Wuz*, 176.
73 *"education by provocation"*: JL, "Pound the Teacher," *Master*, 26.
73 *He worried to Uncle Dicky*: JL to G. Lister Carlisle, Nov. 29, 1934, MH.
74 *"not too ripe"*: MdR, *Ezra Pound, Father and Teacher*, 48.
74 *"grateful to Olga"*: JL to Humphrey Carpenter, Feb. 26, 1986, MH.
74 *"all that"*: JL to PLF, reported to author, April 15, 2006.
74 *"Ezra was always"*: JL to GD, March 28, 1993, MH.
74 *Flaubert and James*: JL, interview by Linda Kuehl, "Talk with James Laughlin: New and Old Directions," *New York Times Book Review*, Feb. 25, 1973.
74 *Hemingway*: JL to CJB, Oct. 2, 1982, CJB/C.
75 *"was played like"*: JL, "Pound the Teacher," 17.
75 *"Concretist"*: JL to Hugh Kenner, Dec. 1, 1971, MH.
75 *Ezra's strategy*: JL, "Pound the Teacher," 17.
75 *Ford Madox Ford said*: Humphrey Carpenter, *A Serious Character: The Life of Ezra Pound* (Houghton Mifflin, 1988), photo caption, following p. 530.
75 *"He would dive in"*: JL, St. Andrews College, Oct. 28, 1975.
75 *"carrying herself delicately"*: Iris Barry, quoted in John Tytell, *Ezra Pound: The Solitary Volcano* (Doubleday, 1987), 131.
75 *Occasionally, Pound*: JL, unpublished tape recording: JL and Robert Fitzgerald, "Education of the Poet," Guggenheim Museum, May 8, 1979, MH.
75 *"thet yr"*: EP to JL, March 16, 1934, H.
76 *"Waal, Jaz"*: JL, *Pound as Wuz*, 4.
76 *"I guess you're old enough"*: JL, St. Andrews College, Oct. 28, 1975.
76 *Pound had told Miller*: Jay Martin, *Always Merry and Bright: The Life of Henry Miller* (Capra Press, 1978), 304.
76 *he decided to spend*: JL to LLC, Dec. 20, 1934, MH.
76 *"The full moon is rising"*: Ibid.
76 *He wrote a letter*: JL to EP, ca. Dec. 22, 1934, B.
78 *"The only thing"*: JL to CJB, July 16, 1982, CJB/C.
78 *"eaten them up"*: JL to LLC, Jan. 24, 1935, MH.

78 *"The news of Robin Hill"*: JL to LLC, Dec. 30, 1934, MH.
79 *"the first track"*: JL, "Looking Across at the Silvretta."
79 *"A great deal"*: JL to EP, March? 1936, B.
79 *"I had forty-one"*: JL, *Byways* draft, MH.
79 *"in very good spirits"*: *Pittsburgh Post-Gazette*, April 9, 1935.
80 *"Don't want to seem"*: JL to EP, April 18, 1934, B.
80 *"The Living Word"*: JL, review of *Tropic of Cancer*, Lausanne notebook, 11–12, MH.
81 *"Gertrude tips"*: Ibid., 24.
81 *"Understanding Gertrude"*: JL, "Understanding Gertrude Stein," June 17, 1935, ibid., 30, MH.
81 *"parallel trends"*: JL, Arrow Editions, advertising copy in *NDPP 1936*.
81 *"ALL" literature in English*: JL, Lausanne notebook, 37, MH.
81 *"No artist needs"*: Gertrude Stein, *The Autobiography of Alice B. Toklas* (Modern Library, 1993), 319.
82 *"MURDER"*: JL to EP, June 25, 1935, B.
82 *"Mr. Eliot on Holy"*: JL, "Mr. Eliot on Holy Ground," typed manuscript, bound and illustrated, MH; published in *New English Weekly*, July 11, 1935, 250–51.
82 *"As criticism from"*: TSE to JL, Jan. 3, 1936, H.
82 *"Gertrude told me"*: JL to Robert Fitzgerald, quoted in Penelope Laurans Fitzgerald, "'. . . And in the Bond,'" 155.
83 *"had so branded"*: JL, "Melody with Fugue," *Random Stories*, 27. Originally published in *Story*, Oct. 1934.
83 *"He had the sense"*: EP to WCW, March 1, 1938, *Pound/Williams: Selected Letters of Ezra Pound and William Carlos Williams*, ed. Hugh Witemeyer (ND, 1996), 191.
83 *"The diploma"*: JL, "Pound the Teacher," *St. Andrews Review*, 18.
83 *"do something about"*: HC, "A Chronicle of New Directions," unpublished typescript, June 18, 1961, 4, ND/C.
83 *"time for me"*: Kuehl, "Talk with James Laughlin."
83 *"to print books"*: JL, "Taking a Chance on Books," *New York Times*, Feb. 28, 1993.
83 *"this worthy"*: EP, quoted in Roger Eliot Stoddard, "The Harvardian," *Paideuma* 31, nos. 1–3: 94.
84 *"a genius and"*: JL, "A Portrait of Ezra Pound," *University Review* 6, no. 2 (Dec. 1939): 118.
84 *"The tale of the perfect"*: EP, *Cantos*, 174.
84 *"Boss, do you know"*: JL to EP, June 28?, 1935, B.
84 *"I don't get very"*: JL to EP, July 2, 1935, B.
84–85 *Lola Avena was wearing*: JL, "In Another Country," *CP*, 155–59.
85 *"[A]upres de ma blonde"*: JL to EP, before July 15, 1935, B.
85 *"another literary white hope"*: Stein to Wilder, ca. July 17, 1935, *The Letters of Gertrude Stein and Thornton Wilder*, ed. Edward M. Burns and Ulla E. Dydo with William Rice (Yale University Press, 1996), 38.
85 *"You picked a gentian"*: JL, "The Bavarian Gentian," *CP*, 655.
85 *"the tallest young man"*: MdR, *Ezra Pound, Father and Teacher*, 79–81.
86 *"CHRIST"*: JL to EP, Aug. 24, 1935, B.
86 *"Boss, keep"*: Ibid.

86 *And so J sailed*: JL, "Pound Seminar," unpublished cassette audiotape, March 18, 1982, Simon Fraser University, Vancouver, B.C., MH.

7. NEW DIRECTIONS: FROM POET TO PUBLISHER

87 *"He is a very nice"*: JL to EP, Sept. 22, 1935, B.

87 *"Pound has never"*: JL, "Pound's Prose," unpublished manuscript, B.

88 *"W. C. Williams, MD"*: JL, "Remembering William Carlos Williams," *Byways*, 143.

88 *"a noncutaneous"*: Ibid., 145.

88 *"grand talk"*: JL to EP, Sept. 22, 1935, B.

88 *"stuff that busts"*: JL to WCW, Sept. 20, 1935, *WCW/JL*, 3.

88 *"like / White flowers"*: JL, "Remembering William Carlos Williams," *Byways*, 149.

89 *"If you really start"*: EP to JL, unpublished manuscript, 1935, H.

89 *"Grandfarver's head"*: EP to JL, Sept.? 1935, H; JL, "The Hairs of My Grandfather's Head," *CP*, 49.

89 *"Dear Jas"*: EP to JL, Oct. 18, 1935, H.

89 *"The vice regent"*: EP to JL, Nov. 26, 1935, H.

90 *"Adolph is NOT"*: EP to JL, Dec. 3, 1935, H.

90 *"With usura hath"*: EP, Canto 45, *Cantos*, 229–30.

90 *"the achieved Eliotic"*: EP to JL, Sept. 23, 1935, H.

90 *"A remarkable"*: JL to EP, ca. Oct. 1935, B.

90 *"The great new direction"*: JL, "New Directions," *New Democracy*, Nov. 1, 1935, 81.

91 *"I wish I thought"*: TSE to JL, Nov. 22, 1935, H.

91 *"Don't say"*: JL to TSE, Dec. 10, 1935, H.

91 *On Moore's urging*: JL, untitled memoir in Gary Fountain and Peter Brazeau, *Remembering Elizabeth Bishop: An Oral Biography* (University of Massachusetts Press, 1994), 80.

91 *"It is just awful"*: JL to EP, Sept. 22, 1935, B.

91 *"Eliot House is"*: JL to TSE, before Nov. 22, 1935, H.

91 *"A Natural History"*: JL, originally published in *Harvard Advocate*, Sept. 1935, reprinted in *Random Stories*, 105–10.

91 *"Your piece had"*: Fitts to JL, Oct. 23, 1935, MH.

92 *"crudely written"*: *Harvard Crimson*, Oct. 22, 1935.

92 *"A Natural History is not"*: JL, quoted in the Pittsburgh *Bulletin Index*, Nov. 7, 1935.

92 *"dillettantish"*: "Banned: A Laughlin Finds Plipping Turtle Eggs Taboo" [Pittsburgh newspaper cutting], Oct. 1935.

92 *"serious, gifted"*: Editors, *Bulletin Index*, Nov. 7, 1935.

92 *J's father drove*: JL to LLC, Oct. 8, 1935, MH.

92 *"He said that"*: JL to CJB, Aug. 5, 1982, CJB/C.

93 *"conversing with all"*: JL to MRL, Nov. 14, 1935, MH.

93 *"I have a new"*: JL to LLC, Nov. 18 and Dec. 4, 1935, MH.

93 *"The feeling of satisfaction"*: JL to MRL, Nov. 14, 1935, MH.

93 *"still very shy"*: JL to LLC, Nov. 7, 1935, MH.

94 *"It hurt like all hell"*: JL to HC, April 27, 1961, H.

94 *"of course, in a fit"*: JL, note, *Byways* file, MH.

94 *"keep the boy"*: HHL to MRL, Jan. 13, 1936, MH.

94 *"considerably upset"*: HHL to MRL, ca. Jan. 21, 1936, MH.

94 "swaddled": JL to HC, April 27, 1961, H.
94 "lateral processes": JL to EP, ca. March 1, 1936, B.
94 "Don't let them vertebs": EP to JL, Feb. 15, 1936, H.
94 "Ezra thinks": JL to TSE, Feb. 25, 1936, H.
94 "but it is up to you": TSE to JL, March 9, 1936, H.
95 "No real literature": EP to JL, Jan. 6, 1936, H.
96 "pretty, charming": JL to EP, March 8, 1936, B.
96 "Cant have you": EP to JL, March 22, 1936, H.
96 "I'se a gwine": JL to EP, April 3, 1936, B.
96 The most startling rumor: JL to Romanos, Dec. 25, 1991, MH.
96 "Can you print": JL, at the Poetry Center, Feb. 11, 1983.
96 "Salute del amico": JL to MdR, Sept. 7, 1936, MdR/C.
96 "The anthology": JL to Steloff, Aug.? 1936, Berg.
96 "muscling in on": JL to EP, Aug. 28, 1936, B.
97 "delightful tale": Kuehl, "Talk with James Laughlin."
97 "the first American": JL, foreword to Montagu O'Reilly [Wayne Andrews], Pianos of Sympathy (ND, 1936), n.p.
97 it was through him: Kuehl, "Talk with James Laughlin."
97 he incited J: JL, afterword to Wayne Andrews, The Surrealist Parade (ND, 1990), 157.
97 "Pianos Cards": JL, Pianos of Sympathy and NDPP 1936 notebook, H.
98 Zukofsky copied: Zukofsky to JL, Sept. 23, 1936, H.
98 J spent most: JL to EP, Oct. 1?, 1936, B.
98 "emphasis of leadership": JL, preface to NDPP 1936, 1:n.p.
99 "Didn't quite pay": JL to EP, Aug. 2, 1937, B.
99 "My own political": JL to KB, April 9, 1970, H.
99 by cutting in half: JL to EP, July 28, 1936, B.
100 "as a flagstaff": JL to EP, Oct. 8, 1936, B.
100 Sylvia Beach: Noel Riley Fitch, Sylvia Beach and the Lost Generation (Norton, 1983), 378.
101 "Latest Books Received": New York Times, Nov. 22, 1936.
101 "night watchman": "Notes on Contributors," NDPP 1937, 2:n.p.
101 "gradecrossing": "Notes on Contributors," NDPP 1938, 3:n.p.
102 "inveterate gift": Reed Whittemore, William Carlos Williams: Poet from Jersey (Houghton Mifflin, 1975), 310.
102 "Dear God": WCW to JL, Oct. 27, 1936, WCW/JL, 5.
102 "It sure was a bolt": WCW to EP, Nov. 6, 1936, Selected Letters of Ezra Pound and William Carlos Williams, 183.
102 "It does me good": JL to EP, Nov. 3, 1936, B.
103 "Bill, do you want": Whittemore, William Carlos Williams, 306. The poet's son William Eric Williams and the distinguished Williams scholar Emily Wallace are among those who maintain that W. C. Williams's alleged infidelities existed mainly in his mind and in his verse. He loved women, yes, as he loved all humanity, and he saw and described beauty, in spirit and in body, where others might have seen only the overworked and undervalued poor whom he served as a physician. See William Eric Williams, William Carlos Williams: An American Dad, ed. Emily Mitchell Wallace (ND, publication forthcoming).
103 "That an occasional": JL, "Remembering William Carlos Williams," Byways, 153.

8. AMATEUR PUBLISHER, AMATEUR SKI IMPRESARIO

104 *"West great place"*: JL to EP, Dec. 18, 1936, B.

104 *When J made himself ill*: JL to MRL and HHL, Dec. 22?, 1936, MH.

105 *"simply wonderful"*: JL to MRL and HHL, Jan. 3, 1937, MH.

105 *"The Portland Rose"*: JL to MRL and HHL, Jan. 14, 1937, MH.

105 *"Thank God"*: WCW to JL, March 4, 1937, H.

105 *"a very superior person"*: JL to MRL, March 8?, 1937, MH.

105 *"Catullus seems to me"*: JL to EP, Feb. 1937, B.

105 *"vurry good eggzesize"*: EP to JL, Feb. 28, 1937, H.

105 *"about 85 times liver"*: JL to EP, March 24, 1937, B.

105 *"thinks that she wants"*: JL to MRL, March 8?, 1937, MH.

105 *"i dare say i"*: JL to MRL and HHL, Sunday, Feb. 28?, 1937, MH.

106 *"I begin to think"*: JL to MRL, April 28, 1937, MH. In 1923, Pound had signed "Hiram Janus" to his translation of Édouard Estaunié's *Call of the Road*. Given his fascination with all things Poundian and with doubles, it is likely that JL christened his alter ego after Ezra's Hiram.

106 *"toughest anti-union"*: David H. Wollman and Donald R. Inman, *Portraits in Steel: An Illustrated History of Jones & Laughlin Steel Corporation* (Kent State University Press, 1999), 114.

106 *"'save' Father"*: JL to MRL and HHL, Jan. 14, 1937, MH.

106 *"I was terribly pleased"*: JL to MRL, April 28, 1937, MH.

106 *"BIG spiel"*: JL to EP, April 27, 1937, *EP/JL*, 80.

106 *"You've done a fine"*: WCW to JL, May 31, 1937, *WCW/JL*, 7.

106 *"To the editor"*: JL, "White Mule and New Directions," afterword to WCW, *White Mule* (ND, 1937), 293.

107 *"This is a rare"*: WCW to JL, May 31, 1937, *WCW/JL*, 7.

107 *"SHIT floating"*: JL to EP, April? 1937, B.

107 *"genuine aristocrat"*: "Duncan Phillips" (obituary), *New York Times*, May 12, 1966.

107 *"just as smart"*: JL to MRL, April 28, 1937, MH.

107 *The brochure proclaimed*: JL, New Directions brochure, April 1937, MH.

108 *"I'm having very bad moments"*: JL to MRL, April 28, 1937, MH.

108 *"about decided"*: JL to MRL, April 29, 1937, MH.

108 *"I thought I was"*: WCW, quoted in Paul Mariani, *William Carlos Williams: A New World Naked* (McGraw-Hill, 1981), 404.

109 *"The Dartmouth boys"*: JL to MRL and HHL, June 4, 1937, MH.

109 *"Brobdingnagian Laughlin"*: David Bradley, quoted in *The Man on the Medal: The Life and Times of America's First Great Ski Racer*, photographs by Dick and Margaret Durrance, text by John Jerome (Durrance Enterprises, 1995), 41.

109 *"a wonderful person"*: JL to family, July 29, 1937, MH.

109 *J and Dick were able*: Jerome, *Man on the Medal*, 42, 45.

109 *They paused en route*: JL to family, July 29, 1937, MH.

109 *"Watching him race"*: Steven Bradley, quoted in "Dick Durrance," Associated Press obituary, June 14, 2004.

109 *"just too lovely"*: JL to MRL, June 29, 1937, MH.

110 *"like Seattle"*: JL to family, July 10, 1937, MH; JL to EP, Aug. 2, 1937, B.

110 *"no wealth at all"*: JL to family, July 10, 1937, MH.

110 *"naturally I enjoy"*: JL to family, July 18, 1937, MH.

110 *"not a source of envy"*: Ibid.

110 *"though not thanks"*: JL to family, July 29, 1937, MH.
110 *"The first time I've not"*: Ibid.
110 *"These years"*: JL to family, Aug. 2, 1937, MH.
111 *"such damn beautiful writing"*: JL to EP, Aug. 2, 1937, B.
111 *"intellectual empire"*: JL to MRL, Aug. 8, 1937, MH.
111 *Australia, J thought*: JL to family, Aug. 12, 1937, MH.
111 *The rounded mountains*: Ibid.
111 *"illumination"*: Ibid.

9. ENTER KENNETH REXROTH AND DELMORE SCHWARTZ

113 *Among the spectators*: JL to MRL and HHL, Sept. 1, 1937, MH.
113 *"SECOND VICTORIAN"*: JL to MRL, cable, 9:44 a.m., Aug. 16, 1937, MH.
113 *"liberally sprinkled with"*: JL to A. Warren, Nov. 2, 1972, ND/C.
113 *His injuries were*: JL to MRL and HHL, Sept. 1, 1937, MH.
113 *"Now that is the 2nd time"*: Bertha Kaler to JL, Oct. 26, 1937, MH.
114 *"feeling fine"*: JL to MRL, cable, 10:00 a.m., Aug. 18, 1937, MH.
114 *"the richest man"*: JL to MRL and HHL, Sept. 1, 1937, MH.
114 *He was developing*: JL to MRL and HHL, Sept. 4, 1937, MH.
114 *"It looked fine"*: Ibid.
114 *"Welcome home"*: WCW to JL, Sept. 13, 1937, WCW/JL, 9.
114 *"I dare say"*: JL to MRL and HHL, Sept. 4, 1937, MH.
114 *"collected shorter prose"*: WCW to Zukofsky, July 18, 1937, *The Correspondence of William Carlos Williams and Louis Zukofsky*, ed. Barry Ahearn (Wesleyan University Press, 2003), 259.
114 *"pride and satisfaction"*: JL to MRL and HHL, Sept. 4, 1937, MH.
114 *"I certainly have luck"*: JL to MRL and HHL, Sept. 13, 1937, MH.
115 *"the throwing of an image"*: EP, *ABC of Reading* (ND, 1951), 52, 56.
115 *"unbearably cranky"*: JL, "The Old Bear: Kenneth Rexroth," *Byways*, 215.
115 *"a man who looked"*: Linda Hamalian, *A Life of Kenneth Rexroth* (Norton, 1991), 92.
116 *"chipmunks and bears"*: KR, *An Autobiographical Novel*, ed. Linda Hamalian (ND, 1991), 377.
116 *"It was a masterful"*: JL, "Old Bear," 217.
117 *"ski touring"*: KR, *Autobiographical Novel*, 458.
117 *He eliminated punctuation*: JL to Diana Stoll, Dec. 8, 1994, private collection.
117 *"Verse usually has"*: EP, *ABC of Reading*, 201.
117 *"the typewriter was"*: JL, interview by Charlie Rossiter for the New York State Council of the Arts, 1997.
117 *"The point of the screwball"*: JL to Romanos, Dec. 25, 1991, MH.
118 *"like those rabbits"*: JL, "I Follow My Beard," in "More Natural Things," *NDPP 1938*, 3.290.
118 *When readers complained*: JL to Stoll, Dec. 8, 1994, private collection.
118 *"the most artificial"*: JL, "Education of the Poet," MH.
118 *"impassive snow peaks"*: KR, "Incarnation," *Complete Poems*, ed. Sam Hamill and Bradford Morrow (Copper Canyon Press, 2003), 228–29.
119 *"You would want"*: JL to family, Aug. 12, 1937, MH.
119 *"I exerted"*: JL to MRL, Oct. 8, 1937, MH.
119 *he would always insist*: Reported to author by PLF, June 6, 2004.

119 *"Father seems to be"*: JL to MRL, Nov. 2, 1937, MH.
119 *"my greatest pleasure"*: JL to MRL, Nov. 7, 1937, MH.
119 *"As an editor"*: JL to DS, Oct. 11, 1937, *DS/JL*, 2.
120 *"No I didn't"*: JL to DS, Oct. 18, 1937, ibid., 3.
120 *"so amiably"*: DS to JL, Oct. 19, 1937, ibid., 4.
120 *"I'm sorry"*: JL to Saroyan, Oct. 11, 1937, *Paideuma* 31, nos. 1–3: 70–71.
120 *libel suit*: WCW to JL, Nov. 8, 1937, *WCW/JL*, 10. In his short story "The Five Dollar Guy," Williams had carelessly left in the real name of one of the principals who initiated a suit; they settled out of court.
120 *"a regular commercial"*: WCW to JL, Nov. 19, 1937, *WCW/JL*, 12.
120 *"You are the cornerstone"*: JL to WCW, Nov. 29, 1937, ibid., 13–16.
120 *Bill capitulated*: WCW to JL, Dec. 4, 1937, ibid., 17.
120 *Williams was more deeply*: Mariani, *William Carlos Williams*, 407.
121 *"special contributors"*: JL to Cummings, Oct. 4, 1937, H. JL paid him $35 for seven poems.
121 *"a hell of a licking"*: JL to Zukofsky, Oct. 24, 1937, H.
121 *In his preface*: JL, preface to *NDPP 1937*, 2:n.p.
122 *there was a fierce*: James F. Murphy, *The Proletarian Moment: The Controversy over Leftism in Literature* (University of Illinois Press, 1991), 166–69.
122 *"most striking"*: James Joyce, quoted in James Atlas, *Delmore Schwartz: The Life of an American Poet* (Farrar, Straus and Giroux, 1977), 196n.
122 *"editorial pigsties"*: JL, preface to *NDPP 1937*, 2:n.p.
122 *"NO my dear boy"*: EP to JL, Jan. 13, 1938, H.
122 *"Yr displeasure received"*: JL to EP, ca. Jan. 23, 1938, B.
122 *"in most parts"*: EP to JL, April 15, 1938, H.
122 *The issue also displeased*: WCW to JL, Jan. 23, 1938, *WCW/JL*, 25–26.
123 *"Suspect ole Bill's"*: EP to JL, Nov. 13, 1938, B.
123 *"management of sales"*: WCW to JL, Jan. 29, 1938, *WCW/JL*, 28–29.
123 *"I guess I just don't"*: JL to WCW, March 17, 1939, ibid., 38.
123 *Then he suffered*: Marie Edgerton to author, Jan. 28, 2002.
123 *When it was clear*: Bayard Dodge to MRL, Jan. 2, 1938, MII.
123 *"mussed it up"*: JL to Rod Symes, July 9, 1938, MH.

10. DEATH, MARRIAGE, AND LOVE CONSIDERED AND RECONSIDERED

124 *"I raised him"*: JL, "Ave Atque Vale," *CP*, 684.
124 *"He expected so much"*: Marie Edgerton, telephone conversation with author, Dec. 1, 2001.
124 *"My rev Papa is deceased"*: JL to EP, Jan.? 1938, B.
125 *"I have more money"*: JL to WCW, Jan. 21, 1938, *WCW/JL*, 23.
125 *"Your list leans"*: Dahlberg to JL, Dec. 6, 1938, H.
125 *"I can only do"*: JL to DS, Jan. 23, 1938, *DS/JL*, 10.
125 *"I am thoroughly sentimental"*: JL to DS, March 7, 1938, ibid., 25.
126 *"soak off the 3¢"*: JL to DS, Aug. 4, 1938, ibid., 34.
126 *"I would like to"*: JL to DS, Jan. 23, 1938, ibid., 10.
126 *"bilge about skiing"*: JL to DS, Dec. 16, 1938, ibid., 45.

126 "*New Directions takes*": JL to EP, March? 1938, B.
126 "*Wish you'd tell me*": Fitts to JL, Feb. 1938, MH.
126 *Fitts appears*: Fitts to JL, Jan.? 1938, MH.
126 "*a vice or a virtue*": JL to MRL, Feb.? 1938, MH.
127 "*Please don't*": JL to MRL, 1938?, "MRL Scrapbook" file, MH.
127 *Martha Gellhorn*: JL, March 23–28, 1938 trip diary/calendar, MH.
127 "*I think she is*": JL to MRL, pmk. March 29, 1938, MH.
128 *J and Phoebe*: JL to KB, Aug. 30, 1938, H.
128 *They spent their last*: JL to family, April 25, 1938, MH.
128 "*invasion*" *of Austria*: JL to family, May 17, 1938, MH. During 1938–39, Roosevelt
       would attempt, with little success, to persuade other countries to accept Jewish
       refugees from the Reich, especially to resettle them in Latin America and Africa.
       Preoccupied with the Depression, with American isolationist, xenophobic, and
       anti-Semitic sentiments, and latterly with the war, he did not make dealing with
       the plight of European Jews a priority, and for this he has been justly criticized.
128 *He skied through*: JL, April 25, 1938 trip diary, MH.
129 "*Good & weak*": JL, April 29, 1938 trip diary, MH.
129 "*writing well*": JL, May 1, 1938 trip diary, MH.
129 "*like a ten tun*": JL to MRL, May 3, 1938, MH.
129 "*Plans for taking*": JL, May 1 and 3, 1938 trip diary, MH.
129 "*snuggle bunnied*": JL, May 3, 5, 7, 8, 12, and 13, 1938 trip diary, MH.
130 "*Look after her*": JL to Elias Clark (Yale Law School), Oct. 14, 1969, MdR/C.
130 *He said specifically*: JL to MdR, Nov. 3, 1969, MdR/C.
130 "*taken over the business*": JL, May 18, 1938 trip diary, MH.
130 "*I trust if I*": JL to MRL, May 3, 1938, MH.
130 "*Import Gammy*": JL to MRL, May 7, 1938, MH.
130 "*It is somehow*": JL to MRL, May 19, 1938, MH.
130 *J had considered returning*: JL to MRL, May 19, 1938, MH.
131 "*I should like you*": Thomas to JL, March 28, 1938, *Dylan Thomas: The Collected
       Letters*, ed. Paul Ferris (Macmillan, 1985), 284–85.
131 "*without these bloody*": Thomas to JL, April 25, 1938, ibid., 291.
131 "*His books won't*": JL to MRL, May 3, 1938, MH.
131–132 "*I feel nothing at all*": JL, May 22, 1938 trip diary, MH.
132 *J moved into*: JL, May 23–27, 1938 trip diary, MH.
132 "*And after we had*": JL to GD, March 28, 1993, MH. Unpublished poem draft.
132 "*I called ceremoniously*": JL to EP, June 4, 1938, B; some details from JL to Anthony
       J. F. O'Reilly, April 28, 1985, H.
133 *he saw John Berryman*: Berryman to JL, Aug. 2, 1938, CJB/C.
133 "*Pigiron duke*": Thomas to John Davenport, Aug. 31, 1939, *Collected Letters*, 322.
133 *While reiterating to J*: JL to Thomas, July 27, 1938, ibid., 316.
133 "*disagreement*": Thomas to Davenport, Aug. 24, 1938, ibid., 318–19.
133 "*his disgusting idea*": Thomas to Davenport, Aug. 31, 1939, ibid., 322.
133 "*the little tyke*": Thomas to David Higham, March 4, 1939, ibid., 360.
133 "*it's settled now*": Thomas to JL, Sept. 15, 1939, ibid., 412.
133 "*filthy contract*": Thomas to Laurence Pollinger, late July 1940, ibid., 459–60.
133 "*I like drinking*": Thomas to Treece, June 16, 1938, *Selected Letters of Dylan Thomas*,
       ed. Constantine FitzGibbon (ND, 1967), 201.

133 *"superb—a powerful engine"*: JL to EP, June 6, 1938, B.
134 *"composition cost"*: Zukofsky to JL, June 24, 1938, H.
135 *"artistic work"*: JL to MRL, pmk. March 29, 1938, MH.
135 *"American Aristocracy"*: JL to MRL, June 20, 1938, MH.
135 *"I want so much"*: Ibid.
135 *"as he does to"*: JL to MRL, Aug. 18, 1938, MH.
135 *"militaristic imperialism"*: JL, *NDPP 1938*, 3:171.
136 *"Last night as I lay"*: Tasilo Ribischka [JL], "The Messianic Blues," ibid., 3:284.
136 *"What it does try"*: JL, preface to ibid., 3:n.p.
136 *J was coming to view*: Stanley Moss to author, Dec. 5, 2006.
136 *He did not want*: JL, preface to *NDPP 1938*, 3:n.p.
136 *In his preface*: Ibid.
137 *"parallel movements"*: Ibid.
137 *"wholly conventional"*: Tate to JL, Dec. 15, 1938, H.
137 *"every store"*: JL to DS, Feb. 26 and March 7, 1938, *DS/JL*, 19, 25.
137 *"Sold every shop"*: JL to MRL, Sunday, Oct. 16?, 1938, MH.
137 *"Reverend Gent"*: JL to Fitts, Oct. 23, 1938, MH.
138 *"Norfolk is a beautiful"*: Mary Barnard, *Assault on Mount Helicon: A Literary Memoir* (University of California Press, 1984), 140.
138 *"things busted loose"*: JL to MRL, Oct. 20, 1938, MH.
139 *J telephoned "all"*: Ibid.
139 *"deb party"*: JL to MRL, Oct. 16?, 1938, MH.
139 *"get some use"*: Ibid.
139 *"It probably won't be long"*: Ibid.
140 *What a "misery"*: Ibid.
140 *"quite cheap"*: JL to MRL, Oct. 11?, 1938, MH.
140 *"a successful, conventional"*: Ibid.
141 *"terribly depressed"*: JL to MRL, Oct. 23, 1938, MH.
141 *"as I smashed hell"*: JL to DS, Oct. 29, 1938, H.
141 *He asked Kay*: JL to KB, Jan. 15, 1939, H.
141 *"For heaven's sake"*: KB to JL, Dec. 10, 1938, H.
141 *"He is without any"*: JL to EP, Oct. 29, 1938, B.
141 *"This tellink"*: EP to JL, Dec. 12, 1938, H.
141 *"Our hero"*: Cummings to JL, Feb. 1, 1939, H.
141 *"I don't think"*: HM to JL, May 31, 1938, *HM/JL*, 10.
141 *"ill-advised criticism"*: HM to JL, June 8, 1938, ibid., 12–13.
142 *"very much impressed"*: JL to HM, Oct. 31, 1938, ibid., 17.
142 *"I am very glad"*: HM to JL, Oct. 19, 1938, ibid., 14–15. At the Munich conference of September 29, 1938, Czechoslovakia was forced to cede the Sudetenland to Germany.
142 *J wasn't sure, but*: JL to MRL, Nov. 15?, 1938, MH.
142 *"Dithyrambic Sex"*: *Time*, Nov. 21, 1938, 69.
143 *"Why does Nude Erect"*: EP to JL, Jan. 23, 1939, H.
143 *"vurry neat"*: EP to JL, Jan. 31, 1939, H.
143 *His first concern*: JL to DS, Nov. 25, 1938, *DS/JL*, 42.
143 *Williams's signature "property"*: JL to DS, March 6, 1938, ibid., 24.
143 *"You were right"*: JL to MRL, Dec. 6?, 1938, MH.

144 *"this girl is a Lowell"*: Ibid.
144 *"Diana, why are you"*: JL to CJB, Oct. 2, 1982, CJB/C.

II. THE WORLD AT WAR

145 *"rolled out"*: JL to TSE, Feb. 8, 1939, H.
145 *"Coriolanus Old and New"*: JL to DS, Thursday, [Feb.–March?] 1939, *DS/JL*, 52.
145 *"once pupil"*: Rand to JL, Nov. 10, 1939, MH.
145 *"pretty still-born"*: JL to WCW, March 17, 1939, *WCW/JL*, 39.
146 *"the old doctor"*: DS to JL, Nov. 21, 1939, *DS/JL*, 81.
146 *"until my mother dies"*: JL to DS, April 27, 1939, ibid., 63.
146 *"with glowing words"*: Miriam Patchen, "Kenneth and Miriam Patchen's Early Days at New Directions," "A Festschrift in Honor of James Laughlin," ed. Bradford Morrow, *Conjunctions* (Winter 1981–82): 253–56.
146 *"It was a definite"*: JL interview by Richard Ziegfeld, "The Art of Publishing," *Paris Review* 89 (Fall 1983): 167.
147 *"If you want to see"*: JL to WCW, March 24, 1939, in *WCW/JL*, 43n.
147 *"I'm glad you like"*: WCW to JL, March 26, 1939, ibid., 40–41.
147 *"get an effect"*: JL to WCW, April 24?, 1939, ibid., 45–46.
147 *"a terrible catastrophe"*: JL to KB, April 6, 1939, H.
147 *"What the Butler Heard"*: JL, published in *Fantasy* 3 (1939), and in *Random Stories*, 83–100.
148 *"abandoned fiction"*: JL to GD, Nov. 30, 1990, *GD/JL*, 66.
148 *"in spite of her prejudices"*: JL to DS, April 19, 1939, *DS/JL*, 58.
148 *"Dearest Mums"*: JL to MRL, Tuesday, Dec. 6?, 1938, MH.
148–149 Generously, Henry said: HM to JL, April 23, 1939, *HM/JL*, 20.
149 *"waiting for some cash"*: JL to HM, May 7, 1939, ibid., 21–22.
149 *"I urgently counsel"*: JL to EP, April? 1939, B. The phrase "¡Arriba España!" that so infuriated Williams forms the last line of "Cara al Sol," the Falangist battle anthem composed in 1935 to counter the appeal of the national anthem of the Second Spanish Republic.
149 *J himself was "all for"*: JL to DS, April 27, 1939, *DS/JL*, 64.
149 *"Latest development"*: JL to EP, April? 1939, B.
150 *"Auden I just"*: JL to DS, [June?] 1939, *DS/JL*, 66.
150 *"Not megalomania"*: MdR, *Ezra Pound, Father and Teacher*, 124.
150 *dollar library*: JL to EP, before Feb. 4, 1939, B.
150 *"The reds or pinks"*: EP to JL, Feb. 9, 1939, H.
150 *"IF you come"*: JL to EP, after March 22, 1939, B.
150 *"Welcome, Deified Sir"*: JL to EP, April 18, 1939, B.
150 *"GIVE ECONOMIC"*: Munson to EP, quoted in J. J. Wilhelm, *Ezra Pound: The Tragic Years, 1925–1972* (Pennsylvania State University Press, 1994), 146.
151 *"The man is sunk"*: WCW to JL, June 7, 1939, *WCW/JL*, 49.
151 *"Wot price yr comin"*: EP to JL, early May? 1939, H.
151 *"My connection"*: JL to DS, April 27, 1939, *DS/JL*, 63–64.
151 *"strictly non-political"*: JL to EP, April 26?, 1939, H.
151 *"Letter to Hitler"*: JL to DS, April 27, 1939, *DS/JL*, 63.
151 *"They all expected"*: JL to KB, June 9, 1939, H.

151 *How little Ezra*: Noel Stock, *The Life of Ezra Pound* (North Point Press, 1982), 365.
152 *"father of modern"*: JL, "Portrait of Ezra Pound," 111–19.
152 *"Well Harvard"*: JL to KB, June 9, 1939, H.
153 *"your refusal to print"*: KB to JL, Aug. 8, 1939, H.
153 *"if I could be"*: JL to DS, Sept. 21, 1939, *DS/JL*, 77.
153 *"attack on Academic"*: JL, preface to *NDPP 1939*, 4:xxii.
153 *"I'll take twenty-five"*: Andreas Brown, interview by author, Feb. 9, 2006.
154 *"shy, nice boy"*: Kuehl, "Talk with James Laughlin."
154 *"You and Geo Tinkham"*: EP to JL, Sept. 17, 1939, H.
154 *"And as fer wot"*: EP to JL, Nov. 24, 1939, H.
155 *"The remaining English"*: JL to TSE, Feb. 8, 1939, H.
155 *"the New & Improved"*: JL, preface to *NDPP 1939*, 4:xiii–xv.
155 *"Let us oppose"*: Ibid., xxii.
155 *"journalese"*: Ibid., xvi–xvii.
156 *"This was excellent"*: JL to Robert Maynard Hutchins, April 3, 1952, H.
156 *"proved vitality"*: "Books: Talking & Doing," *Time*, Dec. 25, 1939.
156 *"fairly good"*: Quoted in Atlas, *Delmore Schwartz*, 170.
156 *"an expert"*: DS to JL, June 30, 1939, *DS/JL*, 71.
157 *"Lawrence's heir"*: Dust jacket for Henry Miller, *The Cosmological Eye* (ND, 1939).
157 *"one of the really"*: JL, preface to Miller, *Cosmological Eye*, vii–ix.
157 *"noisome,"* sometimes: Ralph Thompson, "Books of the Times," *New York Times*, Nov. 21, 1939.
157 **"Miller too much"**: EP to JL, Nov. 24, 1939, H.
158 *"the whole Laughlin tribe"*: *Portrait of Delmore: Journals and Notes of Delmore Schwartz, 1939–1959*, ed. Elizabeth Pollet (Farrar, Straus and Giroux, 1986), 9.
158 *"eastern seaboard liberals"*: Atlas, *Delmore Schwartz*, 157.
158 *"great disfavour"*: JL to EP, Nov. 26, 1939, B.
159 *"bleak" for Ezra*: JL to EP, Dec. 5, 1939, B.
159 *"I think I can"*: Ibid.
160 *"All right"*: EP to JL, Jan. 10 and 11, 1940, *EP/JL*, 111–12.
160 *"Inasmuch as the Jew"*: EP, "The Regional," *New Age,* Nov. 6, 1919, 16.
160 *"I do NOT"*: EP to JL, Jan. 18, 1940, H.
160 *"How about giving"*: JL to EP, Feb. 5, 1940, B.
160 *"I shall NOT"*: EP to JL, Feb. 24, 1940, H.
161 *"All right"*: EP to JL, March 27, 1940, B.
161 *"I am satisfied"*: JL to EP, April 25, 1940, H.
161 *"Names have a way"*: Steloff to JL, Feb. 24, 1934, Berg.
161 *The money came*: Barnard, *Assault on Mount Helicon*, 157.

12. WORLDS APART: BOOKS AT CAMBRIDGE, SKI LIFTS AT ALTA

162 *"That son of a bitch"*: DS to JL, ca. Feb. 1940, *DS/JL*, 97.
163 *"for daring to publish"*: Thomas Mann to JL, *NDPP 1940*, 5:583.
163 *"a modern"*: Dust-jacket notes, *Goethe's Faust*, trans. C. F. MacIntyre (ND, 1941). During some of his time out west in 1941, JL involved himself in the *Faust* project. MacIntyre's translation had to be drastically rewritten, "mostly by me," he told EP.

163 *"any time you need"*: HM quoting JL in this phrase; following passages HM to JL, March 4, 1940, *HM/JL*, 33–35.
163 *"One would think"*: HM to JL, Friday, April 1940, ibid., 36.
163 *"Better drop"*: HM to JL, April 17, 1940, ibid., 37.
163 *"suitable for publication"*: JL to HM, July 3, 1940, ibid.
164 *"a little piece"*: JL to EP, April 25, 1940, B. Averell Harriman had bought the 3,888-acre Brass Ranch in 1936 for about $4 an acre and had opened the Sun Valley Lodge on the property in December 1939.
164 *"as a ski resort"*: Jerome, *Man on the Medal*, 72.
165 *Dick had thought out*: Ibid., 72–75.
165 *"another useless"*: JL, "The Mountain Afterglow," *Some Natural Things* (ND, 1945), 10.
165 *"I have acquired"*: JL to EP, Aug. 32 [sic], 1941, B.
166 *"There is joy"*: JL to TSE, April 1, 1940, H.
166 *"most interesting"*: TSE to JL, April 1, 1940, H.
166 *"the olde Eliotic serpent"*: EP to JL, Sept. 18, 1939, H.
167 *"Nobody can SUMMARIZE"*: EP to JL, Feb. 24, 1940, H.
167 *J using his father's*: JL to PLF, ca. 1990, ND/C; "HH is JL (not Handspring but my father's initials)."
167 *"as it contained"*: JL to EP, Aug. 32 [sic], 1941, B.
167 *he felt that he must*: JL, *Remembering William Carlos Williams* (ND, 1995), 16.
168 *"Blackmur"*: JL to TSE, April 1, 1940, H.
168 *"earnest young people"*: Ibid.
168 *"yet not pedantic"*: JL to Robert Greer Cohn, Aug. 21, 1958, H.
168 *"a proper city book"*: Thomas to JL, April 15, 1940, *Collected Letters*, 450.
168 *"I somehow feel"*: Bishop to Moore, Dec. 15, 1939, *Elizabeth Bishop: One Art: Letters*, ed. Robert Giroux (Noonday Press, 1995), 86.
169 *"As to Jay"*: Porter to Breit, March 3, 1942, Deering Library, Northwestern University.
169 *"raised to glory"*: JL, quoted in Barnard, *Assault on Mount Helicon*, 181, 313–14.
169 *"just no good"*: DS to JL, Sept. 19, 1939, *DS/JL*, 75.
169 *"It struck me"*: JL to DS, Sept. 21, 1939, ibid., 77.
169 *"bores me stiff"*: DS to JL, June 8, 1941, ibid., 128.
169–70 *"The man is"*: DS to JL, April 2, 1940, ibid., 98.
170 *"What about not rushing"*: DS to JL, Sept. 1940, ibid., 117.
170 *"As for your advice"*: DS to JL, [Oct.?] 1940, ibid., 118–19.
170 *"good money"*: Carpenter, *Serious Character*, 587.
170 *"on distinct understanding"*: DP to JL, Oct. 31, 1945, *EP/JL*, 140.
171 *"Ezra Pound speaking"*: *"Ezra Pound Speaking": Radio Speeches of World War II*, ed. Leonard W. Doob. Contributions in American Studies 37 (Greenwood Press, 1978), xi.
171 *"Johnnie Adams"*: Ibid., 390–91, 393.
171 *"yr. politics"*: JP to EP, April 9, 1941, *EP/JL*, 130.
171 *"Lisl as transfer"*: JL, autograph note, *Byways* file, MH.
171 *Kenneth taught him*: JL to CJB, July 28, 1982, CJB/C.
172 *"my extremities became"*: JL to DS, Wednesday [April?] 1941, *DS/JL*, 140.
172 *"Rexroth's poetry"*: JL to DS, June 16?, 1941, ibid., 107.

172 *"Is it really true"*: KR to JL, Dec. 28, 1941, *KR/JL*, 23.
172 *"No ideas but"*: KR, *The Alternative Society: Essays from the Other World* (Herder and Herder, 1970), 60.
172 *"Honey Bear"*: KR to JL, July 31, 1950, *KR/JL*, 156.
173 *"love love huntress"*: JL, "The Hunting Dog," *Some Natural Things*, 31.
173 *"soul dripping out"*: JL to GD, March 16, 1993, MH.
173 *"a very sweet"*: JL, interview by PLF, "James Laughlin at Meadow House," private collection.
173 *"steadfastness of purpose"*: JL to H. Firstenberg, Sept. 23, 1948, ELC/C.
173 *"get the feel"*: "The Book Jackets of Alvin Lustig," *Print*, Oct. 1956, 54.
174 *She had attended*: Janet Quinney Lawson, interview by author, July 2001.
174 *"really loved"*: Jerome, *Man on the Medal*, 82.
174 *"You've got to keep"*: JL, quoted in *Alta Ski Area* newsletter (Winter 1998–99), n.p.
174 *"was very quiet"*: Durrance, quoted in Jerome, *Man on the Medal*, 82.
175 *From the first*: Ibid., 79.
175 *Soon a pair of wings*: Ibid., 76–79; Alta Lodge Guest Book.
175 *He served one*: *Man on the Medal*, 79.
175 *"sweet guy"*: JL to Robert Maynard Hutchins, Jan. 10, 1954, H.
176 *"No, J was the boss"*: Red Altum, interview by author, July 2001.
176 *"Yessir they're all named"*: JL, "Go West Young Man," *Some Natural Things*, 22–23.
176 *"the future of free"*: JL, dedication, *NDPP 1940*, 5:n.p.
176 *"recantation"*: JL, preface to ibid., 5:xiii–xxi.
177 *"bogs down"*: JL to DS, [before May 30, 1941?], *DS/JL*, 101–2.
177 *"if the plates"*: Ibid., 102.
177 *"to tell me"*: JL to DS, Monday [June 16?, 1941], ibid., 108.
177 *"if you approve"*: JL to DS, [before June 3, 1941], ibid., 105.
177 *"Just no zip to him"*: JL to DS, Monday [June 16?, 1941], ibid., 107.
177 *"Waaal, as to my"*: EP to JL, Jan. 17, 1941, H.
178 *Then, at least twice*: Emily Mitchell Wallace, "The Last Diplomatic Train from Rome in 1942: Ezra Pound's Passport and His Kafkaesque Nostos," Centro Studi Americani Palazzo Antici Mattei, Rome, July 3, 2009, unpublished typescript. The train left for Lisbon on May 13, 1942.
178 *"HOME, where"*: JL to EP, 1941?, *EP/JL*, 134.
178 *"Wot do you"*: EP to JL, Sept. 17, 1941?, ibid., 134.
178 *"Dr. Ezra Pound"*: Quoted in Doob, introduction to Ezra Pound, *"Ezra Pound Speaking,"* xiii.
179 *last diplomatic train*: Several individuals have asserted that Pound was denied permission to board the last diplomatic train to leave Rome on May 13, 1942, well after the United States entered the war, among them the journalist Reynolds Packard (*Rome Was My Beat*) and Nancy Horton, an American who spoke to Pound before herself leaving Italy on that same train. Others have asserted that he did not make a serious attempt to repatriate, but U.S. consular records show that he applied for and received passport extensions valid for travel to the United States at least five times between December 4, 1939, and July 12, 1941. For an award-winning summation of the controversy over Pound's attempts to leave Italy in 1941–42, see Jonas Doberman, "The Treason Debate: Ezra Pound and His Rome Radio Broadcasts," *Concord Review* (2000), 45–66.

179 *"our nation's defense"*: "Skiing Hailed as Aid to Defense," *New York Times*, Nov. 29, 1941.
180 *"They broke a lot"*: *Man on the Medal*, 81.

13. REAL BUTTERFLIES AND METAPHORICAL CHESS: VLADIMIR NABOKOV

181 *"by far the best"*: Nabokov to JL, Feb. 10, 1941, Vladimir Nabokov, *Selected Letters, 1940–1977*, ed. Dmitri Nabokov and Matthew J. Bruccoli (Harcourt Brace Jovanovich, 1989), 37.
182 *"novator"*: Nabokov to JL, Jan. 24, 1941, ibid., 34.
182 *"Very elegant"*: JL to EP, Aug. 32 [sic], 1941, B.
182 *"The financial question"*: Nabokov to JL, July 4, 1941, Berg.
182 *"Nabokoff"*: JL to Nabokov, July 21, 1941, Berg.
182 *"Mr. Laughton"*: Nabokov to JL, July 30, 1941, Berg.
184 *"a little masterpiece"*: *New York Herald Tribune*, Jan. 25, 1942.
184 *"a reviewer's nightmare"*: Randall Jarrell, *Partisan Review* 9, no. 7 (July–Aug. 1942): 345–47.
185 *"That is why I started"*: WCW, *Autobiography* (Random House, 1951), 390–91.
185 *"He was funny"*: JL to Patchen, Feb. 11, 1941, H.
185 *"Any art is most"*: JL to KR, June 1941, *KR/JL*, 18.
185 *"in a nice way"*: JL to DS, May 9, 1941, *DS/JL*, 123.
186 *blaming Schwartz*: DS to JL, Aug. 22, 1941, ibid., 148.
186 *"set the high literary"*: JL to DS, May 19, 1941, ibid., 123–25.
186 *"There certainly has not"*: DS to JL, Sept. 10, 1941, ibid., 154.
186 *"It is a symbol"*: DS to JL, Sept. 14, 1941, ibid., 155.
186 *"as soon as possible"*: DS to JL, July 1 and 26, 1941, ibid., 141–43.
186 *"gulps of argument"*: Atlas, *Delmore Schwartz*, 143.
186 *"talking pessimistic"*: Harry Levin, *Memories of the Moderns* (ND, 1982), 159; Mrs. Harry Levin, interview by author, 2001.
187 *"with the ski hotel"*: DS to JL, Dec. 16, 1941, *DS/JL*, 161.
187 *Delmore's ill temper*: Atlas, *Delmore Schwartz*, 197.
187 *"bend every effort"*: DS to JL, Sept. 10, 1941, *DS/JL*, 154.
187 *"But if I am"*: WCW to JL, June 16, 1941, *WCW/JL*, 63.
187 *"thrown Laughlin"*: WCW to Zukofsky, Aug. 26, 1941, *Correspondence of William Carlos Williams and Louis Zukofsky*, 286.
187 *"You're too busy"*: WCW to JL, Sept. 3, 1941, *WCW/JL*, 65.
187 *"about twenty books"*: JL, quoted in *Paideuma* 31, nos. 1–3: 94.
187 *"one of the most"*: JL, "Merton" draft, 11, CJB/C.
188 *"rather wonderful"*: JL to TM, June 7, 1960, Bellarmine.
188 *"any Brecht"*: JL to DS, ca. March? 1941, *DS/JL*, 135.
188 *"I shall have nothing"*: Durrell to HM, after Feb. 6, 1940, *The Durrell Miller Letters, 1935–80*, ed. Ian S. MacNiven (Faber, 1989), 133.
188 *"I harbor a deep"*: HM to JL, Jan. 19, 1943, *HM/JL*, 38.
188 *"pointless"*: DS to JL, July 27, 1942, *DS/JL*, 175–76.
188 *"one of the world's"*: DS to JL, Sept. 4, 1941, ibid., 152.
189 *He asked J*: DS to JL, Dec. 16, 1941, ibid., 158.

189 *"Dear Mr. Laughlin"*: DS to JL, Jan. 7, 1942, ibid., 164–65.
189 *"make one more effort"*: DS to JL, early 1942, ibid., 169.
189 *"I suggest that you"*: DS to JL, Jan. 17, 1942, ibid., 170.
190 *"What a fine writer"*: DS to JL, Jan. 31, 1942, ibid., 172–73.
190 *"Oh well, Jim"*: WCW to JL, Jan. 23, 1942, *WCW/JL*, 68.
190 *"I congratulate you"*: Nabokov to JL, April 9, 1942, Berg.
191 *"I go in the army"*: JL to TSE, April 22, 1942, H.
191 *"rejected for training"*: Order to Report for Induction, local board no. 31, Norfolk, Conn., May 2, 1942, MH.
191 *"I'd managed"*: JL, "The Rubble Railroad," *Byways*, 226.
191 *profit margin of J&L*: Wollman and Inman, *Portraits in Steel*, 116–17.
192 *"Babylon is too pleasant"*: JL to DS, Jan. 1945, *DS/JL*, 236–37.
192 *"I am plodding"*: Nabokov to JL, Sept. 21, 1942, Berg.
192 *"so abominably botched"*: Nabokov to JL, July 16, 1942, *Letters*, 41.
192 *Isabel Hapgood*: JL to DS, Nov. 28, 1949, *DS/JL*, 251.
192 *"I wouldn't attack"*: JL to Nabokov, Nov. 18, 1942, Berg.
192 *"Gogol through"*: Nabokov to JL, May 26, 1943, *Letters*, 45.
193 *"most engaging"*: JL to family, Feb. 25, 1943, MH.
193 *"little fellow"*: JL, quoted in Leverich, *Tom*, 471n.
193 *"I hope we get"*: TW to family, Dec. 6, 1942, TW, *Selected Letters*, vol. 1, *1920–1945*, ed. Albert J. Devlin and Nancy M. Tischler (ND, 2000), 424.
193 *"we became almost"*: JL, quoted in Leverich, *Tom*, 471n.
194 *About a week*: JL, interview by PLF, "James Laughlin at Meadow House," 1, private collection.
194 *"even if you advised"*: TW to JL, Dec. 15, 1942, H.
194 *"I am very excited"*: JL to TW, Jan. 20, 1943, H.
195 *"a genuine rapport"*: TW to Andrew J. Lyndon, March 1943, TW, *Selected Letters*, 1:431.
195 *"You had to see"*: JL, interview by PLF, "James Laughlin at Meadow House," private collection.
195 *"The kid has it"*: JL to WCW, Dec. 1942, *WCW/JL*, 81.
195 *"As my first real"*: TW to JL, July 23, 1943, H.
195 *"snow-covered"*: TW to JL, Dec. 20, 1943, H. *You Touched Me!* would open at the Cleveland Play House on October 13, 1943.
195 *"It would be dreadful"*: TW to JL, April 14, 1944, H.
196 *"My GAWWWWD"*: JL to DS, before Dec. 16, 1942, *DS/JL*, 197–98.
196 *Fred Speyer, after twice*: Alta Ski Area newsletter (Winter 1998–99).
196 *"into glorious sunlight"*: JL to family, Feb. 17, 1943, MH.
197 *"a nice little profit"*: JL to family, Feb. 25, 1943, MH.
197 *"tendency"*: Ibid.
197 *"My wife is eating"*: JL to DS, ca. Nov. 1942, *DS/JL*, 189.
197 *Wartime restrictions*: JL to WCW, Jan. 22, 1943, *WCW/JL*, 85n.
198 *"Jimmy"*: Barnard, *Assault on Mount Helicon*, 198–99.
198 *Soon Williams was sounding*: Mariani, *William Carlos Williams*, 478, 479, 481.
198 *"small sheaf"*: JL, "Thomas Merton and His Poetry," *Random Essays: Recollections of a Publisher* (Moyer Bell, 1989), 3.
198 *"vividness of language"*: JL, "Thomas Merton," typed draft, 2, CJB/C.
198 *"verbally colorful"*: JL, "Thomas Merton and His Poetry," 3.

199 *"just a sea of bloom"*: Ibid.
199 *"And Nabokov told me"*: JL, "The Movements," *The Music of Ideas* (Brooding Heron Press, 1995), 13.
199 *"If it hadn't been"*: Donald Hall, "Ezra Pound Said Be a Publisher," *New York Times*, Aug. 23, 1981; other accounts of the adventure in Stacy Schiff, *Véra (Mrs. Vladimir Nabokov)* (Modern Library, 2000), 127; and JL to GD, Dec. 7, 1992, MH.
200 *"He didn't want any"*: JL to GD, Dec. 7, 1992, MH.
200 *Still, Nabokov seemed*: Brian Boyd, *Vladimir Nabokov: The American Years* (Princeton University Press, 1991), 63–64.
200 *"Naturally it is now"*: JL to TSE, Aug. 18, 1943, H.
200 *"our old friend"*: JL to TSE, Nov. 17, 1943, H.
201 *Unbeknownst to his American*: Carpenter, *Serious Character*, 626–29.
201 *"Müde"*: MdR, *Ezra Pound, Father and Teacher*, 185–87.

14. TENNESSEE WILLIAMS TRIUMPHS

202 *"He really is more"*: JL to LLC, Aug. 12, 1943, MH.
202 *"pretty good shape"*: JL to LLC, pmk. Sept. 23, 1943, MH.
202 *"It has been very interesting"*: JL to LLC, Oct. 15, 1943, MH.
203 *Delmore issued*: DS to JL, ca. Oct. 1943, *DS/JL*, 222–25.
203 *Instead of only two*: DS to JL, Nov. 20, 1943, ibid., 228.
203 *"a quality of horror"*: TSE, introduction to Djuna Barnes, *Nightwood* (ND, 1946), xvi.
203 *"He made a profuse"*: HM to Durrell, May 5, 1944, *Durrell-Miller Letters*, 165–66.
203 *J changed his mind*: JL, publishing reconsideration, July 7, 1944, *HM/JL*, 49n.
203 *"a bit too earthy"*: TW to Donald Windham, Nov. 23, 1943, postscript, Dec. 1, TW, *Selected Letters*, 1:121.
203 *"beautiful job"*: TW to Wood, Nov. 30, 1943, ibid., 1:500–501.
204 *"I am crazy"*: TW, entry dated Oct. 6, 1943, *Notebooks*, ed. Margaret Bradham Thornton (Yale University Press, 2006), 391.
204 *"relatively few close"*: R. C. Lewis, "A Playwright Named Tennessee," *New York Times Magazine*, Dec. 7, 1947, reprinted in *Conversations with Tennessee Williams*, ed. Albert J. Devlin (University Press of Mississippi, 1986), 29.
204 *"Laughlin is a rara avis"*: TW to Wood, Sept. 14, 1943, TW, *Selected Letters*, 1:482–83.
204 *"He is a terribly"*: TW to Windham, Nov. 23, 1943, postscript, ibid., Dec. 1, 121.
204 *"provided that they wear"*: JL to HM, Sept. 20, 1956, *HM/JL*, 126.
204 *"I wonder whether"*: Nabokov to JL, Dec. 8, 1943, Berg.
204 *"I would like"*: JL to Nabokov, Dec. 15, 1943, Berg.
204 *"PLEASE DO NOT START"*: Nabokov to JL, telegram, Dec. 22, 1943, Berg.
204 *"It seems to me"*: JL to Nabokov, Dec. 22, 1943, Berg.
204 *Nabokov made a counterproposal*: Nabokov to JL, Jan. 3, 1944, Berg.
205 *"Please just put it down"*: JL to Nabokov, Jan. 11, 1944, Berg.
205 *it was Doubleday*: Boyd, *Vladimir Nabokov*, 66.
205 *"Rarely is the graphic"*: Lustig, quoted in preface to *Bookjackets by Alvin Lustig for New Directions Books* (Gotham Book Mart Press, 1947), n.p.
206 *His concern was*: Alvin Lustig to JL, Jan. 9, 1948, H.
206 *"swearing a blue streak"*: Margaret Keyser Laughlin to MRL, Feb. 22, 1944, MH.
206 *"I am to feed"*: JL to LLC, May 12, 1944, MH.

206 *"the most talented"*: JL to Felicia Greffen (executive secretary, American Academy and Institute of Arts and Letters), Feb. 14, 1944, quoted in Leverich, *Tom*, 536.

207 *her drinking was noticed*: Frank "Buck" Sasaki to author, Oct. 14, 2009.

207 *two printers quit*: TW to Windham, July? 1944, TW, *Selected Letters*, 1:143.

207 *"inexpensive righteous sentiments"*: DS, "Delights and Defects of Experiment," *Nation*, Oct. 21, 1944, 476, 478.

207 *"I am personally"*: JL, "Editor's Notes," *NDPP 1944*, 8:xvi.

207 *"a really nasty"*: JL to Daniel Javitch, March 11, 1995, MH.

208 *"Bucko, what d'you think?"*: Sasaki to author, Oct. 14, 2009.

208 *"rolling right up"*: JL to Nabokov, March 1944, Berg.

208 *"I cant tell you"*: KR to JL, Dec. 1944, *KR/JL*, 40.

208 *"new play"*: TW to JL, Oct. 1944, H.

208 *"I doubt it"*: TW to JL, Nov. 1, 1944, H.

208 *Tennessee nervously calculated*: Leverich, *Tom*, 299, 556–61.

208 *"was really something"*: JL, interview by PLF, "James Laughlin at Meadow House," 4, private collection.

208 *"There was a radiance"*: TW, "Creator of 'The Glass Menagerie' Pays Tribute to Laurette Taylor," *New York Times*, Dec. 15, 1945.

209 *"There was young"*: TW, *The Glass Menagerie*, Centennial Edition (ND, 2011), 62.

209 *"I need not tell"*: TW to JL, Feb. 6, 1945, H.

209 *"not shown one spark"*: TW to Wood, ca. Feb. 5, 1945, TW, *Selected Letters*, 1:545.

209 *"JAY!"*: TW to JL, ca. March 1945, H.

210 *"The check for"*: TW to JL, June 6, 1943, H.

210 *"must be one of those"*: Randall Jarrell, "Poetry in War and Peace," *Partisan Review* 12, no. 1 (1945): 123–24.

210 *"wonderful romantic poet"*: JL, *Partisan Review*, quoted in *KR/JL*, 123n.

210 *"sublimating" his urge*: JL to DS, Sept. 21, 1944, *DS/JL*, 232.

210 *"I feel more"*: JL to LLC, Jan. 7, 1945, MH.

15. NORFOLK: THE EASTERN SEABOARD RECLAIMS J

211 *"So excited about"*: JL to LLC, May 19 and June 1, 1945, MH.

212 *"Norfolk is the only"*: JL to LLC, Feb. 2, 1946, MH.

212 *"a southern cavalier"*: JL to EP, Dec. 5, 1939, B.

212 *"Paidean Polyp"*: JL to Creekmore, May 2, 1947, H.

212 *"I had terrible fights"*: JL, quoted in Paul Wilner, "The Poet-Publisher Who Outgrew a Stable," *New York Times*, July 15, 1979.

213 *"ex-Fascist convicts"*: MdR, quoted in Carpenter, *Serious Character*, 641. Dorothy Pound, also quoted by Carpenter in the same place, said they were "vicious Italian Communists." According to Mary, who spoke with various Sant'Ambrogio inhabitants, one of the men was later accused of manslaughter and killed, and the other was imprisoned for theft.

213 *Ezra slipped*: Three of the most reliable accounts of Pound's arrest are in general agreement on the facts: Massimo Bacigalupo, "L'arresto di Ezra Pound," *Letteratura—Tradizione* 42 (May 2008): 2–6; C. David Heymann, *Ezra Pound: The Last Rower: A Political Profile* (Viking, 1976), 154–55; MdR, *Ezra Pound, Father and Teacher*, 241.

213 *"many spiteful enemies"*: JL to EP, Sept. 4, 1945, Lilly.

213 *"No one would be"*: MacLeish, quoted in www.spartacus.schoolnet.co.uk/USA macleish.htm, accessed Feb. 27, 2009.

214 *Julien Cornell*: JL to EP, Sept. 4, 1945, *EP/JL*, 138.

214 *"What I think is"*: TSE to JL, Oct. 11, 1945, H.

214 *"owing to insufficiency"*: JL to DP, Sept. 17, 1945, Lilly.

214 *"Public sentiment"*: JL to A. V. Moore, Sept. 30, 1945, Lilly.

214 *"Inside a fortnight"*: JL to DP, Nov. 4, 1945, Lilly.

215 *"that charming Silesian"*: JL to Elisabeth Mann Borgese, Jan. 9, 1961, H.

215 *disastrous 1939 attempt*: Four men had died, and only one set of remains was ever found, in 1999. Wiessner had blamed Jack Durrance for mistakes that led to the deaths. Durrance would only be exonerated in 1994, after a book based on his diary was published.

215 *"Flames poured"*: JL, "Above the City," *NDPP 1946*, 9:38; also in *CP*, 87.

215 *Nabokov asked J*: Nabokov to JL, July 13, 1945, ND/C.

216 *"feeling . . . that movie"*: Nabokov to JL, Sept. 1, 1946, ND/C.

216 *J would always be glad*: JL to Nabokov, Oct. 28, 1945, Berg.

216 *"It is a matter"*: Nabokov to JL, Dec. 13, 1945, Berg.

216 *"There will be no"*: Nabokov to JL, Sept. 1, 1946, ND/C.

217 *"I would get mostly"*: JL to MRL, Sept. 22, 1945, MH.

217 *"There is an almost"*: TW to JL, before Feb. 6, 1945, H.

217 *"If you can explain"*: JL, "The Avalanche," *Some Natural Things*, 38–39.

217 *"You have made"*: Fitts to JL, Sept. 5, 1945, H.

217 *Instead of concentrating*: JL to MRL, Sept. 22, 1945, MH.

218 *"not out of vanity"*: TW to JL, Nov. 14, 1945, *Selected Letters, vol. 2, 1945–1957*, ed. Albert J. Devlin and Nancy M. Tischler (ND, 2004), 25–26.

16. THE PRODIGAL RETURNS: EZRA IN THE DOCK

219 *"The thought of what"*: EP, "Cantico del Sole," *Instigations* (Boni and Liveright, 1920), 250.

219 *"I found the poor devil"*: Cornell to JL, Nov. 21, 1945, quoted in Julien Cornell, *The Trial of Ezra Pound* (Faber, 1967), 13–14.

220 *At some point Ezra*: MdR to JL, Oct. 19, 1969, MdR/C.

220 *"the pencilled notebooks"*: JL to Leonard W. Doob, Dec. 31, 1969, MdR/C.

220 *When Cornell next*: Cornell, *Trial*, 32.

220 *"not in condition"*: Ibid., 22–23.

220 *"Perhaps I am"*: JL to TSE, Dec. 14, 1945, H.

221 *"suffering from a paranoid"*: JL to TSE, Dec. 23, 1945, Lilly.

221 *Some later commentators*: Carpenter, *Serious Character*, 747–50.

221 *"hell-hole"*: EP, quoted in Tytell, *Ezra Pound*, 289.

221 *"color and sound films"*: EP, "March Arrivals," March 1941 radio broadcast no. 112, in Doob, "Ezra Pound Speaking," 384.

221 *"I thought they"*: JL, *Pound as Wuz*, 19–21.

221 *"the good critics"*: JL to TSE, Dec. 23, 1945, Lilly.

222 *"Their great victory"*: JL to TM, Jan. 12, 1946, *TM/JL*, 7.

222 *Williams fretted over*: JL, *Remembering William Carlos Williams*, 19–20.

222 *"if they can ever find"*: WCW to Mary Barnard, Dec. 28, 1945, quoted in Barnard, *Assault on Mount Helicon*, 217.
222 *"Dear Bill"*: JL to WCW, Dec. 29, 1945, H.
223 *Cummings—although*: JL, "E. E. Cummings," *NDPP 1986, 50*: 46; also in Cornell, *Trial*, 39. Dorothy returned Cummings's check but cashed the other two.
223 *Eight staff psychiatrists*: Tytell, *Ezra Pound*, 289–91.
223 *"belief in Fascism"*: JL to TSE, Feb. 15, 1946, Lilly.
223 *"I never did believe"*: Cornell, *Trial*, 44.
223 *When J visited him*: JL to TSE, Feb. 15, 1946, Lilly.

17. SAN FRANCISCO, ALTA, AND EZRA (AGAIN)
225 *"Dear Lorenzo"*: HM to JL, Dec. 17, 1945, *HM/JL*, 59.
225 *"You sound very happy"*: Jan. 14, 1946, ibid., 60.
225 *"the* funniest *man"*: Sylvia Abrams, interview by author, Jan. 26, 2014.
226 *"dear bill"*: JL to WCW, Feb.–April 1946, MH.
226 *"Speak to me not"*: JL to EP, Saturday, [June/July] 1946, Lilly.
226 *"Possum says"*: Ibid. In the version published with Pound's oversight in Italian during the war, the final word had been rendered "asse," axle or axis, and the Venetian printers had burned the remaining copies at the liberation "to avoid complications."
226 *"I really think"*: TSE to JL, Aug. 6, 1946, H.
226 *"who can draw chink"*: JL to EP, Saturday, [June/July] 1946, Lilly.
227 *"all damn foolishness"*: JL to TSE, March 11, 1946, H.
227 *she felt herself*: MdR to JL, Oct. 19, 1969, MdR/C.
228 *"was not so mentally"*: JL to TSE, May 22, 1946, H.
228 *"My Deeah Jas"*: EP to JL, Aug. 6, 1946, H.
228 *"the best long poem"*: Randall Jarrell, "The Poet and His Public," *Partisan Review* 13, no. 4 (Sept.–Oct. 1946): 498.
229 *"What can he do next?"*: Creekmore to DP, Sept. 27, 1946, Lilly.
229 *"that mean Laughlin"*: Thomas to David Higham, June 10, 1946, *Collected Letters*, 594.
229 *"my America-ward plans"*: Thomas to JL, Nov. 24, 1946, ibid., 606.
229 *"Je vois que"*: JL, reported to GD, Oct. 30, 1992, MH.
230 *"a place fit"*: JL to EP, Oct. 22, 1946, Lilly.
230 *"The inflation here"*: JL to EP, Sept. 5, 1946, Lilly.
230 *Barnes was not pleased*: Andrew Field, *Djuna: The Formidable Miss Barnes* (University of Texas Press, 1985), 238.
231 *"I want an edition"*: Zarin, "Profiles: Jaz," 62.
231 *J claimed*: JL to Jacques Barzun, Nov. 17, 1948, H.
231 *"Writers are the most"*: JL, quoted in Stoddard, "Harvardian," 94.
231 *"Hills are a fine"*: JL to TW, April 23, 1947, H.
232 *"keeps inserting"*: JL to TSE, Sept. 5, 1946, H.
232 *"Got a wonderful dinner"*: JL to EP, typed note on telegram, Aug. 9, 1946, Lilly.
232 *"I too would have liked"*: JL to TSE, March 26, 1948, H. *The Pisan Cantos* appeared with a blank space in Canto 81, line 43, of the 1948 first edition, but "Portagoose" was restored after Eliot's death.
232 *"rants and raves"*: JL to TSE, March 12, 1947, H.

232 "very frightened": JL to TSE, Jan. 16, 1947, H.
233 three hours: DP to JL, 1947, H.
233 "Tell Olga to": DP to JL, Dec. 24, 1947, H.
233 "king of the ward": Carpenter, Serious Character, 774.

18. GUIDE TO THE GODHEAD: TOM MERTON

234 "hit the crap tables": JL to Harry Reese, March 10, 1984, S/HR/C.
234 "I am not good": JL to TM, July 12, 1947, TM/JL, 22.
235 George Oppen was "crazy": KR to JL, Dec. 1944, KR/JL, 44.
235 "meretricious fraud": KR to JL, April 16, 1965, ibid., 238.
235 "the queen": KR to JL, Oct. 26, 1950, ibid., 165.
235 "like all reformed": KR to JL, Spring 1947, ibid., 87.
235 "nincompoop": KR to JL, Feb. 17, 1948, ibid., 96.
235 "wilted watch": KR to JL, Aug. 1945, ibid., 64.
236 "If you tell people": JL to KR, Jan. 28, 1948, ibid., 93.
236 "they will put you": KR to JL, Feb. 17, 1948, ibid., 96.
236 "The dark juice rising": KR, The Phoenix and the Tortoise (Copper Canyon, 2003),
     243.
236 "drop the philosophy": KR to JL, before Dec. 9, 1944, H.
236 "about fucking": JL to KR, Dec. 9, 1944, KR/JL, 42. In "When We with Sappho,"
     Rexroth wrote, "We lie here in the bee filled, ruinous / Orchard," and J assumed a
     reference to Yeats's "Lake Isle of Innisfree."
236 "autobiographical": TM, account in Michael Mott, The Seven Mountains of Thomas
     Merton (Harcourt, Brace, 1993), 231–34.
236 "I am sorry": TM to JL, April 6, 1947, TM/JL, 13.
237 Contrary to J's later: JL, "Thomas Merton and His Poetry," 8; also JL, "Thomas
     Merton," typed draft, 16, CJB/C.
237 "Grouchy old monks": JL, "Tom Merton," Byways, 219.
237 "He had a wonderful": JL, "Appendix: Thomas Merton," TM/JL, 376.
237 "There was a man": TM, The Sign of Jonas (Harcourt, Brace, 1953), 52–53; details of
     visit in JL, "Merton" typed draft, 5–6, CJB/C.
238 "because I was a publisher": JL, "Thomas Merton," typed draft, 8, CJB/C.
238 lunch with their common friend: JL, "Tom Merton," Byways, 222–23.
238 "I'm alive!": JL at Bloomington, Ind., 1971, reported to the author by Willis Barn-
     stone, Dec. 29, 2008.
238 "We have done": JL, "Tom Merton," Byways, 224.
238 he would decree: JL to KR, May 10, 1950, KR/JL, 147.
239 a tactically astute: Brother Patrick Hart to author, July 2009.
239 "This is where God": JL, "Merton" typed draft, 21, CJB/C.
239 "Tom had this overwhelming": JL, "Thomas Merton: A Personal Reminiscence,"
     unpublished tape recording, College of Creative Studies, UC Santa Barbara,
     1984.
239 two really good friends: JL, reported by Donald Faulkner to author, Feb. 27, 2007.
239 "The profits which": JL to TM, Feb. 8, 1950, TM/JL, 67.
239 "You are in no sense": JL to TM, Aug. 19, 1950, ibid., 75.
239–40 "I would never": JL to TM, Sept. 12, 1950, ibid., 77.

240 *"I pray for you"*: TM to JL, Oct. 3, 1950, ibid., 80.
240 *"You are not"*: TM to JL, July 2, 1947, ibid., 19–20.
240 *"my desire to increase"*: JL to TM, July 12, 1947, ibid., 22–23.
240 *"the sacramental character"*: TM to JL, July 2, 1947, ibid., 19–20.
240 *"as the children"*: JL to KR, May 16, 1945 [i.e., 1946], *KR/JL*, 57. This letter is misdated in the published text.

19. TROUBLES IN EUROPE, PUBLIC AND PRIVATE
241 *"Editorial Notes"*: JL, "Editorial Notes," *Spearhead: 10 Years' Experimental Writing in America*, ed. James Laughlin (ND, 1947), 9–11.
242 *J continued his assault*: Ibid., 12–13.
243 *"quite like this"*: Steloff to JL, 1947, Berg.
243 *"now seem to be"*: *Time*, Nov. 24, 1947.
243 *"The main thing"*: JL to DP, May 14, 1947, Lilly.
243 *"3/4th yr time slidin' down"*: EP to JL, Feb. 12, 1947, H.
243 *"irate plaint"*: JL to EP, March 10, 1947, Lilly.
243 *J met with Auden*: JL to EP, June 16, 1947, Lilly.
244 *"Whenever it is possible"*: TW to Wood, Aug. 29, 1947, TW, *Selected Letters*, 2:120.
244 *"Book business"*: JL to WCW, June 7, 1947, H.
244 *Unity spiritualist group*: JL to TM, July 12, 1947, *TM/JL*, 22–23.
244 *"very vaguely expressed"*: July 12, 1947, ibid., 23.
245 *"very quiet and sober"*: JL to DP, Nov. 24, 1947, Lilly.
245 *"wonderful maid"*: Margaret Keyser Laughlin to MRL, Nov. 24, 1947, MH.
245 *"original and striking"*: TW to JL, Dec. 29, 1947, TW, *Selected Letters*, 2:138, 139n.
246 *"a pudgy pill"*: Alvin Lustig to JL, April 1, 1948, H.
246 *value of the* Streetcar: Thomas Goldwasser Rare Books catalog no. 20, 2006.
246 *"terrific reviews"*: Susan Lustig Sill [Peck] to Alvin Lustig, Jan. 22, 1948, ELC/C.
246 *"J. & I are"*: Margaret Keyser Laughlin to MRL, Jan. 3, 1948, MH.
246 *"I must regretfully"*: JL to MRL, Jan. 6, 1948, MH.
246 *"I am behind"*: Ibid.
247 *"Simply adorable"*: JL to MRL, Jan. 8, 1948, MH.
247 *"It's all my fault"*: JL to MRL, Jan. 20, 1948, MH.
247 *She continued to plan*: JL to LLC, March 16, 1948, MH.
248 *"one of Musso's"*: JL to KR, Feb. 18, 1948, *KR/JL*, 98–99.
248 *"works at pleasing"*: JL to MRL, Feb. 22, 1948, MH.
248 *"parallelograms & squares"*: JL, "An Old Schoolbook," *NDPP 1948*, 10:237–38.
248 *His Italian trip*: JL to family, Feb. 7, 1948, MH.
248 *"Elegant simplicity"*: JL to Harry Reese, Feb. 2, 1984, S/HR/C.
248 *"My printing heroes"*: JL to Diana Stoll (*Aperture*), Aug. 9, 1994, private collection.
249 *"Now as I recall"*: JL to EP, before May 19, 1947, Lilly.
249 *"Say nothing"*: EP to JL, May 19, 1947, H.
249 *"I bet we get"*: JL to TSE, March 19, 1948, H.
249 *"at some later date"*: Creekmore to DP, Feb. 27, 1948, Lilly.
249 **"I have told that"**: EP to Creekmore, after Feb. 27, 1948, AN-3 written on margins and envelope of Creekmore to DP, Feb. 27, 1948, Lilly.

249 *"Please withdraw the appeal"*: DP to Cornell, March 13, 1948, quoted in Stock, *Life of Ezra Pound*, 421–22.
249 *"Jas, I will only come"*: JL, St. Andrews College, Oct. 28, 1975.
250 *"Except for the beauty"*: JL to Kenner, Aug. 21, 1973, MH.
250 *"my / Old friend"*: JL, "Rubble Railroad," 225, 227. The name Blechsteiner and the connection with stolen art might well have sprouted in JL's mind through the activities of Lincoln Kirstein, who, unlike Roditi, was intimately (and honorably) involved in the recovery of art looted by the Nazis. Kirstein had recovered, among some sixty-five hundred other works hidden in a salt mine at Altaussee, the "Golden Lamb" Ghent Altarpiece by Jan van Eyck. ND would publish Kirstein's *Rhymes of a Pfc.*
250 *Blechsteiner was*: JL, WIW, 253.
250 *"I was terribly distressed"*: JL to KB, Nov. 18, 1948, H.
250 *"Hard on the heart"*: JL to MdR, June 4, 1948, MdR/C.
250 *"The Austrians get"*: JL to MRL, Dec. 29, 1947, MH.
250 *"grey hungry men"*: JL, "In Darmstadt," *Report on a Visit to Germany (American Zone)* (ND, 1948), n.p. The man of privilege learning the value of food from the hunger of Germany. In one published account, J would move the date for the trip up to October 1945, but he was then in New York and Norfolk.
250 *"the aim of those"*: JL, "The Rubble Railroad," *Byways*, 233.
250 *"hardly like"*: JL to MdR, June 22, 1948, MdR/C.
250 *material held in trust*: JL to Leonard W. Doob, Sept. 8, 1969; JL to Elias Clark (Yale Law School), Oct. 14, 1969, MdR/C.

20. BOLLINGEN AFFAIR ROCKS LIBRARY OF CONGRESS

252 *"intimidated"*: KR to JL, Sept. 20, 1948, *KR/JL*, 121.
252 *"one of your justifications"*: KR to JL, Sept. 7, 1948, ibid., 120.
252 *"Stop badgering me!"*: JL to KR, Sept. 1948, ibid., 120.
252 *"terribly uneven"*: JL to TSE, Nov. 8, 1948, H.
253 *"I don't have"*: JL to KR, Sept. 28, 1948, *KR/JL*, 123.
253 *"experimental writing"*: JL, quoted in Talcott B. Clapp, "Publisher Aims at Quality, Not Sales," *Waterbury Republican*, Oct. 3, 1948.
253 *"Europe was wonderful"*: JL to KB, Sept. 15, 1948, H.
253 *"I seem to be"*: JL to EP, Oct. 27, 1948, Lilly.
254 *"the Little Horse"*: Maria Britneva St. Just, quoted in *Five O'Clock Angel: Letters of Tennessee Williams to Maria St. Just, 1948–1982* (Knopf, 1990), 7, 16.
254 *"something important"*: Ibid., 10.
255 *"I depend so much"*: TW to JL, Aug. 17, 1949, H.
255 *"lean over backward"*: JL to TW, Dec. 16, 1949, H.
255 *"terrific fires"*: JL to TW, Nov. 3, 1950, H.
255 *"I was a sounding"*: JL, interview by PLF, "James Laughlin at Meadow House," 10, private collection.
255 *"Now, please"*: JL to Lustig, Nov. 15, 1948, H.
255 *"This is, after all"*: JL to Lustig, Jan. 24, 1949, H.
255 *"I was not kidding"*: Lustig to JL, Jan. 27, 1949, H.
255 *he spent the entire*: Elaine L. Cohen, interview by author, March 17, 2006.

256 *"It was swell"*: JL to TSE, Nov. 25, 1948, H.

256 *Bollingen Prize*: By the end of 1948, the fourteen Library of Congress Fellows in American Letters included many who either were J's good friends or were known to be favorable to Pound: Eliot, Tate, Robert Lowell, Ted Spencer, Aiken, Auden, Robert Penn Warren, and Louise Bogan. The other jurors were Léonie Adams (chair), Katherine Garrison Chapin, Paul Green, Katherine Anne Porter, Karl Shapiro, and Willard Thorp.

256 *"Not as bad"*: JL to EP, Dec.? 1948, Lilly.

256 *by no means harmony*: Carpenter, *Serious Character*, 788.

256 *"Pound, in Mental Clinic"*: *New York Times*, Feb. 20, 1949.

256 *intended the destruction*: Engle, paraphrased by Hubert Creekmore to JL, March 5, 1949, H.

256 *"enormous press reaction"*: JL to TSE, March 24, 1949, H.

257 *"violations of the peace"*: Rolfe Humphries, draft introduction to EP's *Selected Poems*, quoted in *EP/JL*, 182n.

257 *"I believe E.P."*: DP to JL, March 21, 1949, *EP/JL*, 183.

257 *Pound's reputation*: JL to EP, Aug. 12 and Sept. 28, 1949, Lilly.

257 Life *magazine*: JL to EP, Sept. 9, 1949, Lilly.

257 *"Nothing since 1939"*: EP to JL, autograph note, before Sept. 26, 1950, Lilly.

257 *"overwhelmed with work"*: JL to KB, May 20, 1949, H.

257 *"stunningly well-done"*: TW to JL, April 10, 1949, H.

257 *"a strange little poem"*: JL to TW, March 30, 1949, H.

257 *"It is nice to be"*: Bowles to JL, April 7, 1949, *In Touch: The Letters of Paul Bowles*, ed. Jeffrey Miller (Farrar, Straus and Giroux, 1994), 201.

258 *"the infidel Laughlin"*: JL, "Merton" typed draft, 18, CJB/C.

258 *"vehicle of contempt"*: Robert Hillyer, "Treason's Strange Fruit: The Case of Ezra Pound and the Bollingen Award" and "Poetry's New Priesthood," *Saturday Review of Literature*, June 11 and 18, 1949.

258 *"lively but intelligent"*: HC, "Chronicle of New Directions," 67, ND/C.

258 *"monstrous systems"*: Ibid., 54.

258 *"fine editorial"*: JL to HC, Aug. 23, 1949, H.

259 *Carruth felt obliged*: HC, interview by author, 2003.

259 *"No comment"*: EP, quoted in Willam McGuire, *Poetry's Catbird Seat* (Library of Congress, 1988), 116.

259 *"Bubble Gum Award"*: EP, quoted in Heymann, *Ezra Pound*, 221.

259 *Congressman Jacob Javits*: William McGuire, *Bollingen: An Adventure in Collecting the Past* (Princeton University Press, 1989), 215.

259 *"Of course we just printed"*: Quoted by Karen Leick, "Ezra Pound v. *The Saturday Review of Literature*," *Journal of Modern Literature* 25, no. 2 (Winter 2001/2002): 19–37.

259 *"real stinker"*: JL to Bowles, Nov. 29, 1949, H.

259 *"very good book"*: Ibid.

259 *Bowles in turn*: Bowles to Gore Vidal, April 1950, quoted in *In Touch*, 218.

260 *"to try to make"*: JL to TW, Dec. 22, 1949, H.

260 *"are read on hikes"*: KR to JL, March 1, 1948, *KR/JL*, 102.

260 *"You turned it over"*: KR to JL, March 1948, ibid., 102–3.

260 *"high-handed"*: JL to KR, March 18, 1948, ibid., 104.

261 *"Are ya still alive"*: Field, *Djuna*, 20.

261 *"the most extraordinary"*: JL to LLC, July 7, 1949, MH.
261 *"something of an old"*: JL to TW, Aug. 1, 1949, H.

21. CRISES AT NEW DIRECTIONS
263 *"the significance"*: WCW, *Autobiography*, 311.
264 *no longer practice obstetrics*: Mariani, *William Carlos Williams*, 573.
264 *ultimatum*: WCW to JL, Feb. 3, 1950, *WCW/JL*, 176–77.
264 *Williams wrote stating*: WCW to JL, Feb. 9, 1950, ibid., 180.
264 *"What a magnificent kick"*: JL to WCW, Feb. 12, 1950, ibid., 181–83.
265 *"That clears the situation"*: WCW to JL, Feb. 17, 1950, ibid., 185.
265 *"Laughlin cannot"*: WCW to Zukofsky, April 10, 1950, *Correspondence of William Carlos Williams and Louis Zukofsky*, 424.
265 *advance from Cerf*: Hugh Witemeyer, ed. note, in *Pound/Williams*, 215.
265 *"As one might expect"*: JL, "World Championships at Aspen," *American Ski Annual and Skiing Journal*, 1950, 45–58.
265 *"cutey-pie"*: JL to LLC, Feb. 18, 1950, MH.
266 *"I don't see how"*: JL to Brinnin, Aug. 21, 1951, quoted in Andrew Lycett, *Dylan Thomas: A New Life* (Overlook Press, 2004), 319.
266 *"He will make"*: JL to KR, April 28, 1950, *KR/JL*, 140.
266 *However, when*: Millicent Dillon, *You Are Not I: A Portrait of Paul Bowles* (University of California Press, 1998), 190.
266 *"sad story"*: JL, interview by PLF, "James Laughlin at Meadow House," 11, private collection.
266 *"all I needed"*: Paul Bowles, interview by Jeffrey Bailey, *Beat Writers at Work*, 184.
266 *"I am too Pure"*: JL to Robert Maynard Hutchins, Feb. 8, 1953, H.
267 *J would reject*: Ellis Amburn, *Subterranean Kerouac: The Hidden Life of Jack Kerouac* (St. Martin's Griffin, 1998), 170, 210.
267 *"You know how"*: JL to Wood, April 27, 1950, ND/C.
267 *"brightest jewel"*: JL to Henry A. Laughlin, Nov. 1950, ND/C.
267 *"charmed as I was"*: Henry A. Laughlin to JL, Nov. 15, 1950, ND/C.
268 *"rolling merrily along"*: JL to Hubert Creekmore, Feb. 27, 1950, H.
268 *"henceforth Harcourt"*: Giroux to Burton [Stone], Jan. 1951, quoted in *TM/JL*, 85n.
268 *"even worse"*: TM to Burton [Stone], Jan. 27, 1951, quoted in ibid.
268 *Tom and J agreed*: JL to TM, July 9, 1951, ibid., 85–86.
269 *"It was probably"*: RMM, autograph annotation to HC, "Chronicle of New Directions," 74, ND/C.
270 *Most important*: Peter Glassgold, "Beyond Myths & Astral Bodies: ND as Wuz," *Paideuma* 31, nos. 1–3: 53.
270 *"Dear J—"*: RMM to JL, Sept. 6, 1950, H.
270 *"awful rat-race"*: JL to KB, July 28, 1950, H.

22. CRISIS AT HOME
272 *"Let's step on"*: JL, "Step on His Head," *The Wild Anemone and Other Poems* (ND, 1957), 13.
272 *"comfort and spiritual"*: JL to LLC, Dec. 3 and 4, 1950, MH.
273 *"any future outcome"*: Ibid.

273 *"social success"*: KR to JL, July 3, 1950, *KR/JL*, 149.

273 *"I am sick"*: JL to KR, Jan. 2, 1951, ibid., 171.

273 *What had ND done*: EP to JL, 1951, H.

274 *"MO-lasses"*: EP to JL, Oct. 30, 1950, H. Earlier, in a letter to JL, EP had further defined "MO-lasses": "A Molearse/ iz/ the/ hindEND ova/ MOLE," H.

274 *"Achilles"*: DP to JL, added at foot of EP to JL, [late Dec. 1950], H.

274 *"if only to break"*: Fang to JL, May 23, 1950, *EP/JL*, 205.

274 *"You could hear"*: Zarin, "Profiles: Jaz," 55.

274 *"Did you see"*: JL to EP, April 18, 1950, Lilly.

274 *"telescoped and condensed"*: JL to TW, Nov. 3, 1950, H.

275 *"I think Wms"*: KR to JL, Nov. 30, 1950, *KR/JL*, 169.

275 *"neurotic troublemaker"*: KR, quoted in Hamalian, *Life of Kenneth Rexroth*, 207.

275 *"one of / The most"*: KR, *The Dragon and the Unicorn*, in *Collected Longer Poems* (ND, 1968), 136.

275 *"Novel Shocks"*: *New York Times*, Nov. 21, 1950.

275 *"would not ban"*: JL to LLC, Jan. 2, 1951, MH.

276 *J came to dread*: Daniel Javitch, reported in conversation with author, Dec. 2004.

276 *"raising bloody hell"*: JL to Lustig, Feb. 5, 1951, ELC/C.

276 *"What I want"*: JL to Lustig, Jan. 2, 1951, ELC/C.

276 *"sweet with me"*: JL to LLC, Dec. 3, 1950, MH.

276 *"She would not"*: JL to LLC, Jan. 3, 1951, MH.

277 *"things about Margaret's"*: JL to LLC, March 10, 1951, MH.

277 *"I can't imagine"*: Margaret Keyser Laughlin to LLC, June 27, 1951, MH.

277 *"Seems like"*: HM to JL, Sept. 18, 1947, *HM/JL*, 72.

277 *"Buddhism with"*: Donald Faulkner to JL, reported to author, Feb. 27, 2007; JL to HM, April 10, 1951, *HM/JL*, 85.

278 *all-time bestseller*: JL and RMM, "Ad Book" [records], ND/C.

278 *"highbrow" writer*: JL to HM, May 2, 1951, *HM/JL*, 86.

278 *"sorely tempted"*: JL to LLC, March 10, 1951, MH.

278 *the New Classics*: The series included Barnes's *Nightwood*, Kay Boyle's *Monday Night*, Henry James's *Spoils of Poynton* and in one volume *The Aspern Papers* and *The Europeans*, a new printing of Kafka's *Amerika*, McCullers's *Reflections in a Golden Eye*; *Selected Poems* volumes by Patchen, Pound, Rukeyser, and William Carlos Williams, whose *In the American Grain* and *Paterson* also made the series, as did Pound's *ABC of Reading*; Stein's *Three Lives*, Nathanael West's *Miss Lonelyhearts* and *The Day of the Locust*, and Tennessee Williams's *Glass Menagerie*. Three British self-exiles and one war casualty were featured also: Joyce with *Exiles*, D. H. Lawrence with *Selected Poems* and *The Man Who Died*, Evelyn Waugh with *A Handful of Dust*, Wilfred Owen's *Poems*. The French list, with all the poetry produced in bilingual facing-page texts, was especially strong: Alain-Fournier's *Wanderer*, Baudelaire's *Flowers of Evil*, Flaubert's *Three Tales*, Madame de Lafayette's *Princess of Cleves* (considered the first modern novel in French), Mallarmé's *Poems*, Rimbaud's *Season in Hell* and *Illuminations*. Martin Turnell's monograph, *The Novel in France*, Apollinaire's *Selected Writings*, and titles by Camus, Cossery, Gide, Julien Gracq, Michaux, Queneau, Sartre, Valéry, and a pair of novels each by Céline and Stendhal were on the New Directions list and complemented the series yet stood outside it.

279 "a tiny little car": JL to LLC, Aug. 11, 1951, MH.
279 "I'm afraid Father": JL, "Thomas Merton and his Poetry," Random Essays, 10.
279 "The conversation": JL to Valerie Eliot, Feb. 21, 1968, ND/C.
279 "most upsetting": Margaret Keyser Laughlin to LLC, Aug. 29, 1951, MH.
279 "Glad you are": JL to HM, Dec. 17, 1951, HM/JL, 90.

23. PUBLIC SERVICE: INTERCULTURAL PUBLICATIONS AND OTHER EFFORTS

280 "cultural exchange": Robert Maynard Hutchins memo, April 13, 1953, Ford Foundation, MH.
281 "We want to begin": Hutchins to JL, Sept. 18, 1951, H.
281 Perspectives USA: JL, "Project Proposal," 1951, Ford Foundation, MH.
281 "Not even for Fords!": JL, "Magazine Project," Nov.? 1951, H.
282 "I never expected": JL to Hutchins, Nov. 13, 1951, H.
282 "the greatest": JL, "Not-Notes," 36.
282 "We are all": Hutchins to JL, Nov. 21, 1951, H.
282 "But you know me": Hutchins to JL, Tuesday [April?] 1953, H.
282 "Some of his best": JL to GD, April 10, 1987, GD/JL, 35.
283 "strange mixture": JL to Carol Bernstein Ferry, Oct. 12, 1995, quoted in James A. Ward, Ferrytale: The Career of W. H. "Ping" Ferry (Stanford University Press, 2001), 196.
283 "a great fixer-upper": JL to Harry Reese, July 16, 1986, S/HR/C.
283 "the Chintz Factory": JL to Hutchins, Jan. 20, 1952, H.
283 "FRIGHTFULLY PLEASED": Hutchins to JL, Jan. 19, 1952, H.
283 "inherently anti-intellectual": JL to Hutchins, confidential memo, Feb. 6, 1952, H.
283 "to keep an eye": JL to GD, Oct. 21, 1992, MH.
283 first overseas project: Francis X. Sutton, "The Ford Foundation: The Early Years," typescript draft, 1985, 10, MH. A version was published in Daedalus 116 (Winter 1987): 41–92.
284 J was again: JL to Hutchins, Feb. 23, 1952, H.
284 "other obligations": JL to Britneva, quoted in TW, Five O'Clock Angel, 55.
284 "I am bursting": TW to Britneva, May 27, 1952, ibid., 55–56.
284 "behind his shades": JL, interview by PLF, "James Laughlin at Meadow House," 7, private collection.
284 "She is a person": JL to MdR, Aug. 19, 1952, MdR/C.
284 "the burthen of": JL to Hutchins, Aug. 3, 1952, H.
285 "J had some kind": HC to author, Oct. 21, 2007.
285 "If you decide": KR to JL, May 3, 1952, KR/JL, 175.
285 "Slept out": JL to Hutchins, Saturday, June 5?, 1952, H.
285 Consultant in Poetry: Mariani, William Carlos Williams, 651–60; see also McGuire, Poetry's Cutbird Seat, 149–62. The fact that Williams had from the outset been outspokenly critical of Pound's Fascist leanings, and that both men were adamantly anti-Communist, counted for nothing.
286 Gertrude Huston: DS to JL, "I can hardly wait to hear Gertrude's impressions of India," Jan. 4, 1953, DS/JL, 304.
286 "The Lord Krishna": JL to Hutchins, Nov. 30, 1952, H.

286 *Alarmed by*: JL to family, Nov. 14, 1952, MH.

287 *"ominous torchlight"*: JL, "In Trivandrum," early draft of *Byways* section, in the *Contemporary Authors Autobiographical Series*, vol. 22 (Gale Research, 1996), 203.

287 *"I don't think"*: JL to family, Nov. 14, 1952, MH.

287 *"looked like Oswald"*: JL, "India" draft for *Byways*, CJB/C; other accounts by JL of the visit to Sri Atmananda have been drawn upon here: JL to CJB, Dec. 25, 1982, CJB/C; JL to GD, April 6, 1993, MH. In the later published versions of this story, for reasons unknown to the present writer, JL changed the Sri Atmananda character's name to Nalanda, the name of a famous ancient university. The historical Sri Atmananda posed essentially the same question to Joseph Campbell during his visit to India, in 1954–55, recorded in Campbell's *Baksheesh and Brahman: Asian Journals—India*, ed. Robin Larsen, Stephen Larsen, and Anthony Van Couvering (New World Library, 2002), 355.

287 *"emanation"*: JL, "In Trivandrum," *Byways*, 267–69.

287 *it was the coincidental*: "JL Record," pocket notebook, MH; Elizabeth Pound to author, e-mail, July 16, 2006.

288 *"by camel"*: JL to Deborah Pease, Jan. 26, 1990, Howard Gotlieb Archival Research Center, Boston University.

288 *"resignate"*: JL to Hutchins, Dec. 19, 1952, H.

288 *"scared to death"*: HC, interview by author, March 2, 2001.

288 *"be not to Westernize"*: JL to Hutchins, Nov. 30, 1952, H.

288 *"threat of Communist"*: JL to Carl Spaeth, April 11, 1953, Ford Foundation, PA53–227, MH.

289 *"If I didn't need"*: JL to MRL, March 6, 1953, MH.

289 *"It is what happens"*: RMM, autograph note, quoted by HC, "Chronicle of New Directions," 81, ND/C.

290 *Through the agency*: Barney Rosset, interview by author, 2005.

290 *Years earlier*: "The Way It Was / James Laughlin and New Directions," *Publishers Weekly*, Nov. 22, 1985, 28.

290 *"I just didn't recognize"*: JL, quoted in Caryn James, "Publishers' Confessions—Rejections I Regret," *New York Times*, May 6, 1984.

24. "LE CHEVALIER SANS PEUR ET SANS REPROCHE"

291 *"le Chevalier"*: Mme Mary Britneva, quoted in TW, *Five O'Clock Angel*, 65. Mme Britneva is applying to JL the tag by which the exemplary Renaissance knight Pierre Terrail, seigneur de Bayard, was widely known.

291 *"BIG NEWS"*: TW to Maria Britneva, Feb. 11, 1953, ibid., 72.

291 *"They made a very"*: JL to MRL, March 15, 1953, MH.

292 *MacGregor*: HC, in conversation with author, 2001; also in HC, *Beside the Shadblow Tree: A Memoir of James Laughlin* (Copper Canyon, 1999), 12.

292 *"undirected venom"*: RMM to HM, June 21, 1963, HM/JL, 220.

292 *"everyone felt"*: Anaïs Nin, *The Diary of Anaïs Nin, 1947–1955*, ed. Gunther Stuhlmann (1955; Harcourt Brace Jovanovich, 1974), 213.

292 *"a severe mental"*: Anonymous review, *Variety*, Feb. 25, 1953.

292 *"philosophical depth"*: JL to TW, March 26, 1953, H.

292 *"Nobody who"*: JL to TW, April 11, 1953, H.

293 "awfully 'esoteric'": JL to HC, Feb. 25, 1953, H.
293 "get it across": JL to Hutchins, April 29, 1953, H.
293 "using communists": JL to HC, Feb. 25, 1953, H.
293 "No 'Perspectives'": Robert Maynard Hutchins, "Memorandum on a Trip to Italy, April 19–May 3, 1953," H.
293 "Twitching-Unbewitching": TW, Five O'Clock Angel, 123.
294 "You make all": DS to JL, April 12, 1953, DS/JL, 320.
294 "Dear Forgetful": Paul Laughlin to JL, before June 29, 1953, H.
294 "That 'play'": JL to RMM, after Oct. 24, 1953, H.
294 Dylan was in terrible: David N. Thomas, Fatal Neglect: Who Killed Dylan Thomas? (Seren, 2008), 61–66; Lycett, Dylan Thomas, 362–67. The initial verdict that Thomas had died of "alcoholic toxicity" was not borne out by the pathologist's autopsy and by certain contemporary medical findings, as revealed in Fatal Neglect, 104–7.
295 J and MacGregor drew lots: JL, "Dylan," Poems, New and Selected (ND, 1998), 130. In later versions of this poem, JL substituted Brinnin for MacGregor.
295 by next day J: TW, Selected Letters, 2:505n.
295 "Dylan Thomas Fund": Circular appeal, TW et alia to Dear Friend, Nov. 10, 1953, ibid., 505.
295 "Will you help": JL, reported by Drue Heinz to author, March 20, 2007.
295 "The death of": JL to TM, Jan. 7, 1954, TM/JL, 102.
295 If half the people: JL to TSE, Dec. 8, 1953, H.
296 "I have missed": JL to Mary Britneva, Jan. 18, 1954, printed in TW, Five O'Clock Angel, 82, 86.
296 J spoke at length: TW to Maria Britneva, May 22, 1954, ibid., 92.
296 "so feelingly": JL to LLC, June 24, 1954, MH.
296 "Love progresses": JL to Ferry, Jan. 30?, 1954, H.
296 He sought marriage counseling: Drue Heinz, telephone interview with author, March 20, 2007.
296 "misconduct": JL to LLC, June 24, 1954, MH.
296 Tennessee began to believe: TW to Maria Britneva, Feb. 16, 1954, Five O'Clock Angel, 86–87.
297 J assured Maria: Mary Britneva to TW, Feb.? 1954, ibid., 88.
297 "Jamesie!": MRL to JL, ibid., 90n.
297 "a typical Russian": Drue Heinz, telephone interview with author, March 20, 2007.
297 "I like": JL, "The Sinking Stone," The Love Poems of James Laughlin (ND, 1996), n.p.
298 "most strange": JL to EP, March 24, 1954, MdR/C.
298 "harder to grasp": JL to KR, May 10, 1954, KR/JL, 191–92.
298 "very, very sad": Borgese to JL, May 4, 1954, H.
298 "Poor Maria": JL to Borgese, May 10, 1954, H.
298 Keene accompanied J: Keene, telephone interview with author, April 27, 2001.
299 When J and Maria finally met: Maria Britneva in TW, Five O'Clock Angel, 91.
299 "to envisage": JL to LLC, June 24, 1954, MH.
299 "She was great fun": PLF, in conversation with author, May 13, 2008.
299 "how really desperate": JL to LLC, June 24, 1954, MH.
300 "You make girls": Ibid.

300 *"timebomb"*: Nabokov to JL, Feb. 3, 1954, Nabokov, *Selected Letters, 1940–1977,* 144.
300 *"of the highest"*: JL to Nabokov, Oct. 11, 1954, ibid., 153n.
301 *"suspended as a security"*: KB to JL, May 8, 1954, H.
301 *"If your heart"*: JL, "Barstow," unpublished address on the retirement of Dr. Richard Barstow, *Byways* file, MH.
301 *The foundation felt*: Sutton, "Ford Foundation," 13.
301 *"Only the German"*: Ludovic Tournès, "La diplomatie culturelle de la Fondation Ford," *Vingtième siècle: Revue d'histoire* 76 (2002/4): 71, www.cairn.info/revue-vingtième -siècle-revue-d-histoire-2002-4-page-65.htm. Translation by author.
301 *"fill the great gaps"*: JL to TM, Dec. 14, 1955, H.
302 *"which is"*: Ibid.
302 *"This is something"*: JL to TW, Dec. 18, 1948, H.
302 *"He was really scared"*: JL, interview by PLF, "James Laughlin at Meadow House," 9, private collection.

25. MISSING A FEW BEATS

303 *"changed completely"*: Marie Edgerton to author, Feb. 1, 2002.
303 *"God-based reality"*: Carol Thayer to author, May 4, 2008.
303 *"content"*: "Lester" to LLC, Dec. 23, 1955, MH.
303 *"the help she"*: TW to JL, Dec. 3, 1954, H.
303 *"As you have gathered"*: JL to TW, Jan. 9, 1955, HRHRC.
304 *"Frankly, I am"*: JL to TW, Jan. 16, 1955, ND/C.
304 *the play, J thought*: JL to TW, March 8, 1955, ND/C.
304 *Tennessee sold*: TW to RMM, Aug. 20, 1955, ND/C.
304 *"the most applauded"*: JL to TW, April 4, 1955, HRHRC.
304 *"His sense of cadence"*: TW to RMM, Aug. 20, 1955, ND/C.
305 *"I think that we"*: TM, "CHEE$E / Joyce Killer-Diller," *The Collected Poems* (ND, 1977), 799.
305 *Elaine Lustig, in consultation*: Elaine Lustig Cohen, interview by author, Nov. 17, 2006.
306 *"Paperbacks sell"*: JL to TM, Feb. 23, 1960, Bellarmine.
307 *He always had manuscripts*: Drue Heinz, telephone interview by author, March 20, 2007.
307 *He would write*: PLF, in conversation with author, March 5, 2008.
307 *"They even had"*: JL to MRL, Sunday, Feb. 1955, MH.
307 *"What will I do"*: JL to MRL, April 1, 1955, MH.
307 *"a terribly"*: Mangan to JL, July 15, 1956, H.
308 *"sentimental curator"*: JL, "In the Museum at Teheran," *CP*, 114.
308 *"powerful impact"*: JL to DS, April 28, 1955, *DS/JL*, 348.
308 *"the Persians"*: Ibid.
308 *"I always remember"*: Drue Heinz to JL, Jan. 6, 1992, H.
308 *"Many people called"*: JL to GD, June 10, 1993, MH.
308 *He ranged widely*: Details about JL in India, 1955: Jean Joyce to JL, July 7, 1955; JL to GD, Jan. 19, 1994, and June 12, 1995, MH.
308 *"Foundationese"*: JL to Hutchins, Oct. 3, 1955, H.

308 *"Humdinger"*: Joyce to JL, July 7, 1955, MH.
309 *"I miss you, too"*: Joyce to JL, Aug. 15, 1955, MH.
309 *"cross-fertilize"*: JL to Vanessa Jackson, Aug. 21, 1987, private collection.
309 *"intensify the revitalization"*: Intercultural Publications Inc., Docket Excerpt, Feb. 23–27, 1953, Ford Foundation Archives, PA52–33, 5, MH.
309 *"Do not be put off"*: JL to Hutchins, Feb. 27, 1957, H.
310 *"enthusiasm / For Indian"*: JL, "In Trivandrum," *Byways*, 256.
310 *"South India"*: JL to TM, July 25, 1968, *TM/JL*, 349.
310 *"for no / Brahmin"*: JL, "In Trivandrum," *Byways*, 260.
310 *"The loveliest natural"*: Ibid., 270.
310 *"I've never seen her"*: JL to MRL, Aug. 22, 1955, MH.
310 *"and hope to"*: JL to TW, Sept. 2, 1955, H.
311 *"bow-tied"*: Jack Kerouac, *The Dharma Bums* (Signet, 1959), 11.
311 *"the Beat generation"*: Gary Snyder, interview by Eliot Weinberger (1996), *Beat Writers at Work*, 282.
312 *"find out what"*: Lawrence Ferlinghetti, interview by Andrew P. Madden (1998), *Beat Writers at Work*, 338.
312 *"Allen suddenly"*: JL, quoted in ibid., 344.

26. TRUMPED IN THE MARRIAGE GAME

313 *"hormones and"*: RMM to TW, April 2, 1961, H.
313 *"pains and love"*: JL to TM, Dec. 1955?, H.
313 *"a purely legalistic"*: JL to MdR, Dec. 22, 1955, MdR/C.
314 *"in fine spirits"*: Ibid.
314 *"but he never remembered"*: JL to GD, March 28, 1993, MH.
314 *J's Capitol contacts*: JL to TM, May 24, 1956, Bellarmine.
314 *J would have*: JL to Borgese, June 13, 1957, H.
314 *"really excite me"*: JL to TM, May 24, 1956, Bellarmine.
314 *"extra man"*: JL to MRL, March 1, 1956, MH.
315 *a decision she confided*: Griselda Ohannessian, in conversation with author, 2005.
315 *Ann Resor and*: JL to MRL, March 6, 1956, MH.
316 *"you will never believe"*: Santha Rama Rau, interview by author, April 2004.
316 *Within days*: Ibid.
316 *"much relieved"*: JL to MRL, March 17, 1956, MH.
316 *"The question arises"*: JL to MRL, March 6, 1956, MH.
316 *"But I guess"*: JL to MRL, March 17, 1956, MH.
317 *"It was fairly"*: JL to MRL, March 24, 1956, MH.
317 *"A very suitable"*: JL to Borgese, March 25, 1956, H.
317 *"a teddy bear"*: Griselda Ohannessian, interview by author, April 18, 2001.
317 *J bought Ann*: JL to MRL, April 17, 1956, MH.
317 *"a lot of things"*: JL to MRL, April 22, 1956, MH.
317 *"the 'problem'"*: JL to MRL, May 24, 1956, MH.
318 *"understanding"*: JL to MRL, May 20, 1956, MH.
318 *"Everything is"*: Ibid.
318 *J and Ann went*: Ibid.
318 *"All I have to give"*: Drue Heinz, telephone interview by author, March 20, 2007.

318 *Britneva had declared*: Maria Britneva to MdR, May 29, 1956, MdR/C.
318 *"not very exciting"*: JL to TM, July 20, 1956, Bellarmine.
319 *"Allevatore di giovani"*: Scheiwiller, quoted in MdR, "Bringing Up Young Publishers," *Paideuma* 31, nos. 1–3: 83.
319 *"I'm in the doldrums"*: DS to JL, July 23, 1956, *DS/JL*, 355.
319 *"smoking the peace"*: DS to JL, Feb. 11, 1963, H.
319 *"Ann and I"*: JL to TW, Jan. 22, 1957, H.
319 *"just possibly"*: *Time*, Dec. 24, 1956.
320 *"slipping away"*: JL to HC, Dec. 4, 1956, H.
320 *"Henry never liked"*: JL to Francis X. Sutton, Dec. 1, 1985, MH.
320 *"For me, I don't"*: JL to HC, Dec. 4, 1956, H.
320 *"among the best"*: Hugh Kenner, back cover blurb, Charles Tomlinson, *Selected Poems, 1955–1997* (ND, 1997).
320 *"I am very excited"*: JL to TW, Jan. 22, 1957, H.
320 *"A regular little factory"*: JL to Borgese, Dec. 2, 1956, H.

27. FADE-OUT IN BURMA, NEW DIRECTIONS REVISITED

321 *"I can't begin"*: JL to Dr. Kabir, Feb. 14, 1957, ND/C.
321 *they solved the problem*: Martin P. Levin to author, May 2008.
322 *"extremely affable"*: JL to TW, March 2, 1957, H.
322 *"figured out"*: JL to HM, Feb. 20, 1957, *HM/JL*, 128.
322 *"The vice of"*: JL to Borgese, June 13, 1957, H.
322 *"to assist at"*: "Burma," JL draft, *Byways* file, MH.
323 *"With three such"*: JL to TM, Nov. 8, 1957, Bellarmine. George Zournas told the author that J had said to Robert MacGregor that he had named his son after *him*: JL had reason to think well of all four men.
323 *"respected by"*: JL to Borgese, June 13, 1957, H.
323 *"deeply impressed"*: Mangan to JL, June 19, 1957, H.
323 *"& my love"*: JL, "Near Zermatt: The Drahtseilbahn," *Wild Anemone and Other Poems*, 35.
323 *"I think now"*: JL, "It's Warm Under Your Thumb," ibid., 14.
323 *"the New Yorker"*: JL, foreword to *Fifteen by Three* (ND, 1957), vii.
323 *"awfully sad"*: JL to TM, Aug. 23, 1958, Bellarmine.
324 *"some brand of internal"*: Edwin G. Arnold and Dyke Brown, "Indonesia and Burma," typed manuscript, Ford Foundation Archives, no. 003367 (Sept. 21, 1952), 4, MH.
324 *"Yes, this Jackson"*: JL to HM, July 19, 1958, *HM/JL*, 144.
324 *"very cute"*: JL to MRL, July 27 and Sept. 7, 1957, MH.
324 *"It is painful for me"*: JL to MRL, Sept. 7, 1957, MH.
325 *"I hate horses"*: JL to MRL, Aug. 10, 1957; JL to GD, July 12, 1993, MH.
325 *"kept us in stitches"*: JL to TM, Nov. 8, 1957, Bellarmine.
325 *"a blind alley"*: JL to KR, Nov. 29, 1957, *KR/JL*, 221.
325 *"The West Coast"*: Richard Eberhart, "West Coast Rhythms," *New York Times Book Review*, Sept. 2, 1956.
325 *"thoroughbreds"*: William Du Bois, "In and Out of Books," *New York Times*, Sept. 29, 1957.

326 *"As I wrote"*: JL to Levertov, April 11, 1955, H.
326 *"no mention"*: Lawrence Durrell, quoted in *HM/JL*, 155n.
326 *"Durrell has"*: RMM to HM, Dec. 30, 1958, ibid., 154.
327 *"We must be seers"*: Dag Hammarskjöld, address at the Museum of Modern Art, *Papers of the Secretaries-General of the United Nations*, vol. 2, *Dag Hammarskjöld, 1953–1956*, ed. Andrew W. Cordier and Wilder Foote (Columbia University Press, 1972), 374.
327 *"If the U.S."*: Editorial in *Life* magazine, Feb. 6, 1956, quoted in Cornell, *Trial*, 122.
327 *J doubted*: JL to MdR, March 7, 1957, MdR/C.
327 *"Ez's sad story"*: JL to GD, May 2, 1993, MH.
327 *A letter "organized"*: Tytell, *Ezra Pound*, 525–26; a fuller account of Pound's release, in essential agreement with Tytell, appears in Carpenter, *Serious Character*, 839–45.
327 *The president*: JL to GD, May 2, 1993, MH. Confirmed to author in interview with Helen Hauge, April 16, 2008.
327 *"terribly shaken"*: JL to Hugh Kenner, June 13, 1960, HRHRC.
328 *"I think the attraction"*: JL, quoted in Michiko Kakutani, "Two Poets: Uneasy Friendship?," *New York Times*, April 21, 1981.
328 *"All America"*: Carpenter, *Serious Character*, 848.
328 *"probably laughing"*: JL, *Pound as Wuz*, 181.
328 *"completely independent"*: KR, quoted in Barry Silesky, *Ferlinghetti: The Artist in His Time* (Warner Books, 1990), 84.
329 *"'Coney Island'"*: JL to Ferlinghetti, Dec. 2, 1956, ibid., 85.
329 *"it seems clear"*: JL, back cover blurb, Lawrence Ferlinghetti, *A Coney Island of the Mind* (ND, 1958).
329 *"I understand"*: JL to Ferlinghetti, Sept. 16, 1957, ibid., 87.
329 *"How can you"*: JL to WCW, Sept. 8, 1953, WCW/JL, 208.
329 *"J. has been occupied"*: WCW to Zukofsky, March 5, 1958, *Correspondence of William Carlos Williams and Louis Zukofsky*, 490.
330 *"very gay"*: JL, quoted in KR to WCW, Sept. 17, 1958, "A Public Letter for William Carlos Williams' 75th Birthday," typescript, H.

28. NEW DIRECTIONS TWENTY-FIVE YEARS ON

331 *"I am very"*: JL to Hutchins, Jan. 25, 1959, H.
332 *"a very pleasant"*: JL to Laurence Pollinger, March 12, 1959, ND/C.
332 *"terrible messes"*: RMM to Pollinger, Feb. 26, 1959, ND/C.
332 *"like a commodity"*: JL to TM, April 4, 1960, Bellarmine.
332 *"practically non-existent"*: JL to RMM, after Feb. 26, 1962, ND/C.
332 *"disappointing"*: Véra Nabokov to RMM, April 17, 1962, ND/C.
333 *"chief indoor hobby"*: RMM to Dionys Mascolo, April 27, 1962, ND/C.
333 *"It does them"*: JL to CJB, ca. Aug. 1982, CJB/C.
333 *Ann did not*: Helen Hauge, interview by author, April 16, 2008.
333 *"I said, that's it"*: JL to CJB, Sept. 16, 1982, second letter this date, CJB/C.
333 *"By the way"*: William Levitt, interview by author, May 2, 2001.
334 *"We swapped"*: Ibid.

334 *"What should we"*: Levitt, interview by author, May 2, 2001.

334 *"enormously busy"*: RMM to P. Lal, Feb. 6, 1959, ND/C.

334 *"transcreation"*: P. Lal, ed., *Great Sanskrit Plays in Modern Translation* (ND, 1946); Lal to author, Aug. 12, 2006; JL to RMM, Jan. 7, 1959, ND/C.

334 *J teased Professor Lal*: Lal to author, Aug. 12, 2006.

334 *"I suppose he"*: Ibid.

335 *"fairly decent" price*: JL to MdR, May 26, 1959, MdR/C.

335 *"a money pit"*: JL to Doris Blazek (lawyer for the Pound Estate), in conversation with author, June 6, 2010.

335 *If there was money*: MdR, in conversation with author, 2005 and 2010.

335 *Pound's intention*: Blazek and PLF, in conversation with author, June 6, 2010.

335 *its validity*: Blazek, in conversation with author, Feb. 15, 2011.

335 *"I have started"*: JL to MdR, March 8, 1956, MdR/C.

335 *"lovely surprise"*: JL to MdR, Dec. 7, 1959, MdR/C. JL refers to his poem "Rome: In the Café," *CP*, 117.

336 *telegram to Miller*: Barney Rosset to HM, April? 1959, quoted in *HM/JL*, 162n.

336 *"a good, and an aggressive"*: JL to HM, April 9, 1959, ibid., 162–63.

336 *"first class"*: JL to HM, June 24, 1959, ibid., 166.

336 *"Rosset's offer"*: JL to HM, Jan. 27, 1960, ibid., 173–74.

337 *"like the Light Brigade"*: JL to HM, after Feb. 8, 1960, ibid., 175n.

337 *"always reliable"*: HM to RMM, Feb. 8, 1960, ibid., 175.

337 *"very highly"*: JL to TM, Nov. 2, 1959, Bellarmine.

337 *"with the usual gusto"*: Ann Laughlin, in conversation with RMM, reported to HC, Sept. 16, 1959, ND/C.

337 *"inability to think"*: JL to MdR, Sept. 7, 1959, MdR/C.

337 *the breakdown foreshadowed*: Robert D. Gillman, MD, "Ezra Pound's Rorschach Diagnosis," *Bulletin of the Menninger Clinic* 58, no. 3 (Summer 1994): 307–22.

338 *Dr. Overholser had told*: JL to Humphrey Carpenter, Feb. 26, 1986, MH.

338 *"You are miserable"*: JL to MdR, Sept. 18, 1959, MdR/C.

338 *"which a loyal"*: Ibid.

338 *When Domenico*: MdR to JL, Nov. 1959, MdR/C.

338 *Pound was clearly*: MdR to JL, Feb. 2, 1960, MdR/C.

339 *"We're disappointed"*: JL to Borgese, Dec. 28, 1959, H.

339 *"I feel great pride"*: Levertov to JL, Jan. 4, 1960, H.

339 *"a little on"*: Levertov to JL, Aug. 10, 1960, H.

339 *"You are on"*: JL to Levertov, Aug. 24, 1960, H.

340 *"a cute little"*: JL to Borgese, March 4, 1960, H.

340 *"Ann takes these"*: JL to MdR, Feb. 18, 1960, MdR/C.

340 *"little Henry"*: JL to HM, March 15, 1960, *HM/JL*, 177n.

340 *"He can't do much"*: JL to MdR, March 8, 1960, MdR/C.

340 *"moral instruction"*: JL to Fitzgerald, Dec. 14, 1960, H.

340 *"the usual chaos"*: JL to Borgese, March 4, 1960, H.

340 *"If it weren't"*: JL to MdR, March 10, 1960, MdR/C.

340 *"TERRIBLY SORRY"*: JL to Borgese, March 18, 1960, H.

341 *"great fun"*: MdR to JL, May 12, 1960, MdR/C.

341 *"truly fond"*: JL to MdR, June 20, 1960, MdR/C.

341 *"inappropriate"*: Mott, *Seven Mountains of Thomas Merton*, 346.

341 *"quite badly"*: JL to TM, Feb. 10, 1960, Bellarmine.
341 *"so very happy"*: JL to TM, June 24, 1960, Bellarmine.
341 *"my little day's"*: TW to RMM, July 26, 1960, H.
341 *"Of course"*: Devlin, *Conversations with Tennessee*, 343.
341 *"absolutely remarkable"*: JL to Hugh Kenner, Oct. 15, 1963, HRHRC.
342 *"great excitement"*: JL to MdR, March 8 and July 19, 1960; Feb. 20, 1961, MdR/C.
342 *"much flattered"*: JL to TM, June 2, 1960, Bellarmine.
342 *"the old vim"*: JL to Kenner, July 19, 1960, HRHRC.
342 *"styling and stage"*: JL to TM, Aug. 31, 1960, Bellarmine.
342 *"never fussed about"*: JL to GD, Oct. 21, 1992, MH.
342 *"to be sure"*: JL to TM, Feb. 21, 1961, Bellarmine.
342 *"bitter letters"*: JL, "A Visit," appendix in *WCW/JL*, 270–73.
343 *"They've figured"*: Ibid., 262–63.
343 *"A problem has arisen"*: TM to JL, May 31, 1960, *TM/JL*, 154.
343 *"It is very kind"*: JL to TM, Nov. 30, 1960, Bellarmine.
344 *"I'm a little suspicious"*: TM to RMM, holograph comment on typed letter, March 4, 1961, ND/C.
344 *"A friend of ours"*: JL to TM, Sept. 12, 1961, *TM/JL*, 180n.
344 *"I have let them know"*: TM to JL, Dec. 4, 1962, ibid., 216.
344 *"Your idiom, Bill"*: JL to WCW, Oct. 11, 1960, MH.
344 *"on the right track"*: Levertov to JL, Sept. 1, 1960, H.
344–45 *"The metric is intended"*: JL to Vanessa Jackson, Jan. 2, 1983, private collection.
345 *"all that sort"*: JL to MdR, May 31, 1960, MdR/C.
345 *"in fine style"*: JL to TM, June 7, 1960, Bellarmine.
345 *"nobody works"*: JL to Borgese, Nov. 16 and Dec. 1, 1960, H.
345 *"Sexuality"*: Gill to JL, 1960?, H.
345 *"great exuberance"*: MdR to JL, Aug. 6, 1960, MdR/C.
345 *"just depressed"*: MdR to JL, Sept. 29, 1960, MdR/C.
345 *"immensely"*: MdR to JL, Jan. 19, 1961, MdR/C.
345 *Off went Ezra*: MdR to JL, May 18 and June 1, 1961, MdR/C.
346 *Since he did not*: MdR to JL, July 18, 1961, MdR/C.
346 *"revaluation of all"*: JL to Sherry Mangan, Oct. 20, 1958, H.
346 *"I personally declare"*: E. B. Ashton, introduction to *Primal Vision: Selected Writings of Gottfried Benn* (ND, 1960), vii–xxvi; see also RMM to Peter Schifferli, June 7, 1960, ND/C.
347 *"collateral probate" law*: JL to CJB, Sept. 30, 1982, CJB/C.
347 *J claimed that it was*: Emily Wallace, in conversation with author, Sept. 20, 2008.
347 *"discouraged about"*: JL to Hubert Creekmore, July 27, 1961, H.
348 *"I feel that you"*: JL to HC, Jan. 9, 1961, H.
348 *Carruth maintained*: HC, interview by author, Sept. 1, 2007.
348 *Although she apparently*: Helen Hauge, interview by author, April 16, 2008; Ann's brother, Stanley Rogers Resor, made similar comments to author, July 2001.
348 *"Too much"*: JL, entry in the *Twenty-Fifth Report of the Class of 1936*, reproduced in *Paideuma* 31, nos. 1–3: 94.

29. TENNESSEE, HENRY, AND TOM

351 *"So I shall"*: JL to MdR, June 1 and Aug. 14, 1961, MdR/C.

351 *"great swindle"*: Ibid.

351 *revolution in paperback poetry*: JL to KR, June 30, 1960, *KR/JL*, 230–31.

352 *"at my mother's"*: JL, quoted in *New York Times*, Jan. 9, 1983.

352 *Djuna was the only*: Field, *Djuna*, 22, 239.

352 *"long-short or"*: TW to JL, Sept. 24, 1962, H.

352 *"I would love"*: JL to TW, Oct. 1, 1962, H.

352 *Many years later*: PLF, in conversation with author, Sept. 8, 2008.

353 *"bad slump"*: JL to MdR, Aug. 18, 1961, MdR/C.

353 *"little hope"*: MdR to JL, Aug. 17, 19, and 28, 1961, MdR/C.

353 *"He was a dandy"*: JL to MdR, Sept. 5, 1962, MdR/C.

353 *"I feel closer"*: HM to RMM, Nov. 13, 1961, *HM/JL*, 197–98.

353 *"Well, that is"*: TM, quoted by JL to HM, Dec. 12, 1961, ibid., 198.

353 *"You and Tom"*: JL to HM, ibid., 198.

354 *"It Does Me Good"*: JL, *In Another Country*, n.p.

354 *"commission men"*: JL to MdR, May 17, 1962, MdR/C.

355 *"There is one judge"*: JL to HM, March 9, 1962, *HM/JL*, 204.

355 *"original child"*: TM, *Original Child Bomb* (ND, 1962).

355–56 *"absolutely amazing"*: JL to TM, May 11, 1962, *TM/JL*, 207n.

356 *"Sorry* Original Child*"*: TM to JL, May 10, 1962, ibid., 206.

356 *"being beastly"*: TM to JL, Nov. 2, 1962, ibid., 211.

356 *It was Merton's*: JL to Peter Leek, July 8, 1971, ND/C.

356 *"Father Abbot"*: JL, "Merton" draft, 24, CJB/C.

356 *"I must tell you"*: Robert Maynard Hutchins to JL, Feb. 11, 1960, H.

356 *"something is bound"*: JL to TM, Aug. 11, 1961, *TM/JL*, 174.

356–57 *"It is curious"*: TM to JL, Dec. 31, 1961, ibid., 194.

357 *"emotional astronauts"*: TW to JL, Sept. 24, 1962, H.

357 *"Your phrase"*: JL to TW, Oct. 1, 1962, H.

30. PUBLISHING AND WRITING: THEY NEVER GET EASIER

359 *"masterpiece"*: JL to Fitts, Dec. 3, 1963, MH.

359 *Once Dahlberg stormed*: JL to Donald Hall, *New York Times*, Aug. 31, 1981.

359 *"Again and again"*: JL to Dahlberg, Oct. 2, 1962, ND/C.

359 *yet before he consigned*: Charles DeFanti to JL, July 24, 1972, ND/C.

359 *"I've never written"*: Phil Casey, "Writing What He Must, Getting By—but Barely," *Washington Post*, June 18, 1973.

359 *"I like the damn"*: Fitts to JL, Nov. 30, 1963, MH.

360 *"He hasn't come"*: JL to TM, July 20, 1962, *TM/JL*, 210n.

360 *"Lucky guy!"*: JL to Charles Tomlinson, Sept. 27, 1962, H.

360 *"His tears are"*: KB to PLF, Nov. 18, 1987, H.

360 *"lively interest"*: WCW to JL, Nov. 11, 1962, *WCW/JL*, 253.

360 *"It was what"*: JL to MdR, March 13, 1963, MdR/C.

360 *"It was a very"*: Ibid.

360 *"A magnificent"*: EP to Floss Williams, March 1963, *Pound/Williams*, 319.

360 *"This is the one"*: Levertov to Robert Duncan, March 13, 1963, *The Letters of Robert*

Duncan and Denise Levertov, ed. Robert J. Bertholf and Albert Gelpi (Stanford University Press, 2004), 388–89.

360 *"I hope you can"*: JL to TM, March 19, 1963, *TM/JL*, 221n.

360–61 *"beyond my powers"*: JL to Kenner, Oct. 15, 1963, HRHRC.

361 *another list in January*: Typed sheet, Jan. 2, 1964, in Hugh Kenner files at HRHRC.

361 ἤλιος, ἄλιος, ἄλιος: EP, Canto 23, *Cantos*, 107. In this "authoritative" edition, "The idiot" is rendered without the exclamation point. The annotation "Derivation uncertain" refers to the lexicographer's inability to resolve the ambiguity of the Greek phrase, in which ἄλιος can mean either "sun" or "fruitless," and to EP's scorn for his inadequate scholarship.

361 *Kenner became concerned*: JL to Peter du Sautoy, Oct. 30, 1963, in Kenner files at HRHRC.

361 *"Stinkschuld"*: EP, *Cantos*, 257.

361 *now he asked Mary*: JL to MdR, March 19, 1963, MdR/C.

361 *"Italian Cantos"*: MdR to JL, Oct. 15, 1963, MdR/C.

362 *J decided to print*: JL to MdR, Dec. 12, 1963, MdR/C.

362 *"made me into"*: JL, reported in Carpenter, *Serious Character*, 882.

362 *"the new custodians"*: TW to RMM, Feb. 18, 1963, H.

362 *"Today I said to myself"*: TW to RMM, March 27, 1963, H.

362 *He had let it*: JL to GD, Dec. 15, 1992, MH.

362 *"The latest from"*: JL to KB, Feb. 24, 1964, H.

363 *"I am very sorry"*: TM to JL, Nov. 26, 1963, *TM/JL*, 234.

363 *"The whole business"*: JL to MdR, Dec. 12, 1963, MdR/C.

363 *"GREAT GRIEF"*: EP to Jacqueline Kennedy, Nov. 1963, John F. Kennedy Library.

363 *"A small museum"*: JL to CJB, Sept. 30, 1982; also JL, "Merton" draft, 12, CJB/C.

363 *"I have about 70"*: JL to GD, March 28, 1993, MH.

363 *J's most controversial*: JL to GD, July 30, 1989, *GD/JL*, 57.

364 *With the formal incorporation*: Griselda Ohannessian to Nikki Smith, Nov. 21, 1988, ND/C; PLF, in conversation with author, March 12, 2008.

364 *"sentimental feeling"*: JL to Ohannessian, ca. Aug. 19, 1988, ND/C.

365 *"One seldom has"*: Tomlinson to JL, May 12, 1964, H.

365 *"Your letter about"*: JL to Tomlinson, May 14, 1964, H.

366 *"importing the latest"*: Richard Kostelanetz, "Something Old, Something New," *Partisan Review* (Summer 1965): 476–78.

366 *"very expensive"*: JL to MdR, Sept. 9, 1964, MdR/C.

366 *J charged Mary*: MdR to JL, Sept. 17, 1964, MdR/C.

367 *it was bruited about*: Although Ezra Pound acknowledged Omar as his son, Omar's father was rumored to have been an Egyptian officer whom Dorothy met in Cairo between December 1925 and February 1926. Pound appears to have been aware from the outset that Omar could not have been his offspring. *The Ezra Pound Encyclopedia*, ed. Demetres P. Tryphonopoulos and Stephen J. Adams (Greenwood Press, 2005), 274; Carpenter, *Serious Character*, 451.

367 *Hassan El Rifai*: MdR in conversation with author, June 23, 2014.

367 *"legally sealed"*: JL to MdR, Sept. 24?, 1964, MdR/C.

368 *A good shuttle*: MdR to JL, May 4, 1965; JL to MdR, May 10 and 18, 1965, MdR/C.

368 *"seems to live"*: JL to Nicanor Parra, March 4, 1965, H.

368 *"real hostility"*: JL to Leonard Doob, Dec. 9, 1969, MdR/C.

368 *"a wonderful guy"*: JL to Parra, Dec. 28, 1964, H.
368 *"good tough"*: TM to JL, Feb. 3, 1965, *TM/JL*, 252.
368 *"and besides that"*: TM to JL, Dec. 13, 1964, ibid., 250.
369 *"sad old Ezra"*: JL to Fitts, March 24, 1965, MH.
369 *"Jas, I can't get it down"*: JL, St. Andrews College, Oct. 28, 1975.
369 *Olga suggested*: JL, "Collage for EP" (unpublished poem); JL, with L. C. Powell as "interlocutor," unpublished cassette audiotape, rec. Oct. 4, 1983, Modern Languages Auditorium, University of Arizona, Tucson, MH; JL, "(Coda)," typescript, CJB/C.
369 *"was a real"*: Dr. Giuseppe Bacigalupo, quoted in Carpenter, *Serious Character*, 882.
369 *"I did not enter"*: Ibid.
369 *Following Dante*: JL, *Pound as Wuz*, 26.
369 *"For me it's been"*: TSE, interview by Donald Hall (1959), *"The Paris Review" Interviews* (Picador, 2006), 1:81.
370 *"botch"*: EP to JL, May 22, 1965, *EP/JL*, 283.
370 *"straightened out"*: JL to MdR, Sept. 8, 1965, MdR/C.
370 *"the final break"*: MdR to JL, Sept. 15, 1965, MdR/C.
370 *"Those Beat Generation"*: JL, quoted in Gary Snyder, "Laughlin's 'Mahayana' or 'Big Spirit,'" *Paideuma* 31, nos. 1–3: 89.
370 *"gaze almost exclusively"*: Editorial note in Plimpton, *Beat Writers at Work*, 276.
370 *"life motto"*: KR, *Alternative Society*, 112.
370 *"I always enjoy"*: JL to McClure, Jan. 20, 1966, H.
370 *The play features*: Michael Grieg, "Folk Heroes in Old Rite," *San Francisco Chronicle*, Dec. 21, 1965.
372 *"The poisonous world"*: Pollet, *Portrait of Delmore*, 648.

31. CONFESSOR TO A MONK

373 *"go dead a lot"*: TM to JL, March 19, 1966, *TM/JL*, 278.
373 *"his nurse"*: Mott, *Seven Mountains of Thomas Merton*, 435.
373 *"we were getting"*: TM, *The Journals of Thomas Merton*, vol. 6, *Learning to Love: Exploring Solitude and Freedom, 1966–1967*, ed. Christine M. Bochen (Harper-Collins, 1997), 38.
373 *"Ah, so this is"*: JL, "Merton" draft, 31, CJB/C.
374 *"follow the ecstasy"*: TM, *Journals*, 6:52.
374 *"I have vows"*: Ibid., 46.
374 *Nicanor kicked him*: JL to Parra, June 11, 1981, H.
374 *"This is God's"*: TM, "Louisville Airport / May 5, 1966," *Eighteen Poems* (ND, 1985), n.p.
374 *"I always obey"*: TM, "I Always Obey My Nurse," ibid., n.p.
374 *"I realize that"*: TM, *Journals*, 6:54.
374 *"kind and tried"*: Ibid., 82.
375 *By his own admission*: TM, "Restricted Journal" entries for June 30 and July 8, 1966; also *Journals*, 6:90, 92.
375 *"We are two half"*: TM, "Evening: Long Distance Call," unpublished restricted poems, quoted in Mott, *Seven Mountains of Thomas Merton*, 454.
375 *"A tremendous psychomachia"*: JL, "Merton" draft, 32, CJB/C.
375 *"To fall in love"*: TM to JL, July 27, 1966, *TM/JL*, 291.

375 *"nothing more"*: TM to JL, Aug. 18, 1966, ibid., 293.

376 *"When I think of"*: John Hawkes, "John Hawkes and Albert J. Guerard in Dialogue," *A John Hawkes Symposium: Design and Debris* (ND, 1977), 24.

376 *"enthusiastic"*: JL, quoted in "Where Are They Now? Hippies of the '30s," *Newsweek*, May 1, 1967.

376 *"From all you have"*: TM to JL, Dec. 27, 1966, *TM/JL*, 308.

376 *"My saintly mother"*: JL to TW, Oct. 5, 1969, H.

376 *"almost made me"*: JL to Kenner, Jan. 10, 1967, HRHRC.

376 *"Mrs. N in New York"*: RMM to JL, Nov. 7, 1966, with marginal annotation by JL, ND/C.

376 *"Dear Jay"*: Nabokov to JL, Aug. 28, 1970, ND/C.

377 *"Dear V"*: JL to Nabokov, Aug. 19, 1972, ND/C.

377 *"But the worst mistake"*: Barry Miles, *Ginsberg: A Biography* (Virgin, 2000), 398–99.

377 *"Do you folks"*: Olga Rudge, in conversation with Ann Laughlin, ARL to JL, memo, Nov. 23, 1975, ND/C.

378 *"Dr. / O Autaukthon"*: JL to Fitts, April 25, 1968, MH.

378 *"very pleased"*: Denise Levertov to Florence Williams, July 31, 1968, *The Letters of Denise Levertov and William Carlos Williams*, ed. Christopher MacGowan (ND, 1998), 139.

378 *Adamantly against*: Brother Patrick Hart, in conversation with author, Sept. 11, 2009; see also TM, *The Journals of Thomas Merton*, vol. 7, *The Other Side of the Mountain, 1967–1968*, ed. Patrick Hart, OCSO (HarperOne, 1998), 343.

379 *"I suppose I must"*: JL to TM, July 25, 1968, *TM/JL*, 349.

379 *"ought to turn"*: TM, *The Seven Storey Mountain* (Image Books/Doubleday, 1970), 242.

379 *"a spontaneous notebook"*: TM to JL, Aug. 18, 1968, *TM/JL*, 354.

379 *"This seems to be"*: TM to JL, Sept. 5, 1968, ibid., 356.

379 *Tom sent J*: JL, "Merton" draft, 30, CJB/C.

379 *"be content with"*: Brother Patrick Hart, OCSO, *Thomas Merton: First and Last Memories* (Necessity Press, 1986), n.p.

379 *"If I just die"*: TM to JL, Sept. 5, 1968, *TM/JL*, 356.

380 *J flew to Europe*: JL to TM, Sept. 26, 1968, ibid., 361–62.

380 *In three days*: JL to Gary Snyder, Sept. 30, 1968, H.

380 *"Things continue"*: JL to Tomlinson, June 27, 1968, H.

381 *"Marxism and Monastic"*: JL, "Merton" draft, 41, CJB/C.

382 *With the body*: Ibid., 47, CJB/C.

382 *"It seems he was"*: JL, quoted in Ernesto Cardenal, "Coplas on the Death of Merton," *NDPP 1972*, 25:38.

32. THIS OBDURATE WORLD: THE SWORD FALLS

383 *a wild-eyed woman*: JL to CJB, July 17, 1982, CJB/C.

383 *"hold my own"*: JL, "Merton" draft, 42, CJB/C.

383 *"His death really"*: JL to M. Smith, July 25, 1970, *TM/JL*, 369–71.

384 *"Looking back"*: JL to Vanessa Jackson, Jan. 18, 1990, private collection.

384 *died a Buddhist*: Edward Rice, *The Man in the Sycamore Tree* (Doubleday, 1972), 129.

384 *"complete fabrication"*: JL to N. Smallwood, July 13, 1971, ND/C.

384 *"totally mendacious"*: JL to Darley Anderson, Oct. 17, 1972, ND/C.

384 *"I'm a Buddhist"*: JL, "Buddhism," unpublished draft from *The Way It Wasn't* files, MH.

384 *Ann might be*: J and Ann Laughlin, in conversation with PLF, ca. 1985, reported to author, 2006.

384 *"a major mystical"*: JL, "Merton" draft, 22–23, CJB/C.

385 *"personal epic"*: JL, "Thomas Merton: A Portrait," *TM/JL*, 382.

385 *"The originality"*: JL, "Merton" draft, 43–45, CJB/C.

385 *"far and away"*: JL to KB, Nov. 10, 1969, H.

385 *three notebooks and*: JL, "Merton" draft, 47–48, CJB/C.

386 *"rather difficult handwriting"*: Brother Patrick Hart to author, Oct. 29, 2011.

386 *"it was a happy"*: JL, "Merton" draft, 49, CJB/C.

386 *"looks like a three"*: JL to KB, Nov. 10, 1969, H.

386 *That afternoon J escorted*: JL to MdR, June 5, 1969, MdR/C.

386 *"now gaunt"*: JL, "Pound" typescript, 12, CJB/C.

386 *asked Pound if*: Henry Laughlin in conversation with author, July 2001.

386 *"Perhaps because he is"*: Address on the occasion of awarding an honorary doctorate to JL, June 8, 1969.

386 *"Why don't you discard"*: JL, reported in Carpenter, *Serious Character*, 901.

387 *"He . . . was very courtly"*: JL to Tomlinson, June 24, 1969, H.

387 *"I'll be lucky"*: JL to MdR, June 26, 1969, MdR/C.

387 *"the little known"*: David Thomas, *Holiday*, Nov. 1970, quoted in *Alta Ski Area* newsletter (Winter 1998–99).

387 *"how your humor"*: HC to JL, July 25, 1970, H.

387 *"Well, James"*: Parra to JL, Aug. 27, 1970, H.

387 *"I was sorry"*: JL to Parra, June 25, 1970, H.

388 *"These past weeks"*: JL to HC, Aug. 10, 1970, H.

388 *"rather shaky"*: JL to RMM, Sept. 24, 1970, ND.

388 *"I am still"*: JL to HC, Oct. 13, 1970, H.

388 *"I have always"*: JL to TM, July 3, 1956, Bellarmine.

388 *"a blather"*: JL to CJB, July 19, 1982, CJB/C.

389 *Wiesel listened carefully*: JL to CJB, Aug. 10, 1982, CJB/C.

389 *"let the collecting"*: JL to Lal, Dec. 13, 1972, ND/C.

389 *J would categorically*: JL to Dr. Daniel Romanos, Dec. 25, 1991, MH.

33. ONE TROUBADOUR REVIVES, ANOTHER DEPARTS

390 *Dr. Wiesel put him on lithium*: The first paper on the use of lithium to treat acute mania was published by the Australian psychiatrist John Cade in 1949, but it was not until 1998 that University of Wisconsin researchers discovered that lithium functioned by keeping the amount of glutamate active between brain cells at a healthy and stable level. This stabilizing effect reduced the tendency to mood swings in many sufferers from bipolar disorder. http://bipolar.about.com/od/lithium/a/010312_lithium1.htm, accessed Nov. 17, 2009.

391 *300 milligrams of lithium*: This figure was well below the target area of 450–1,200 milligrams per day for a blood level of between 0.6 and 1.0 millimoles per liter of blood for regular maintenance dosages in treating bipolar disorder. (Dr.

Wiesel consistently tried to keep the medication at the lowest feasible level to minimize side effects.) http://mentalhealth.com/drug/p30-102.html, accessed Nov. 17, 2009.

391 *Once he stood*: HC, in conversation with author, Sept. 1, 2007.

391 *"a few discreet showings"*: TM, *The Asian Journal of Thomas Merton*, ed. Naomi Burton, Brother Patrick Hart, and James Laughlin; consulting ed. Amiya Chakravarty (ND, 1973), 156.

391 *"We were having"*: Brother Patrick Hart, interview by author, Sept. 25, 2007.

392 *"'morning sickness'"*: TW to JL, April 23, 1971, H.

392 *"the new rage"*: JL to Lal, Dec 13. 1972, ND/C.

392 *"lively and often"*: Kuehl, "Talk with James Laughlin."

392 *"A great many people"*: Ibid.

393 *"For over a generation"*: KR, *American Poetry in the Twentieth Century* (1971; Seabury Press, 1973), 126.

393 *"romanticism is"*: TW, interview by David Frost, Jan. 21, 1970, in Devlin, *Conversations with Tennessee Williams*, 142.

393 *"I'm a moralist"*: TW, interview by Studs Terkel, Dec. 1961, ibid., 91.

394 *"I was rather"*: JL to Gary Snyder, Nov. 11, 1971, H.

394 *You have so much*: JL, "Dr. Benjamin Wiesel," typescript; also attached autograph note, MH.

394 *"a-tremble"*: JL to Snyder, Nov. 11, 1971, H.

394 *J was bored*: JL to Romanos, Dec. 25, 1991, MH.

394 *"Without my blackboard"*: JL to Carla Packer, March 1, 1971, ND/C.

395 *"quite remarkable"*: RMM to HM, Aug. 11, 1972, ND/C.

395 *"a remarkable job"*: Edward Rice, "The Asian Journal of Thomas Merton," *New York Times Book Review*, July 8, 1973.

395 *"very sad"*: JL to KR, Jan. 18, 1972, *KR/JL*, 253.

395 *"When you find"*: Kenneth Patchen, quoted by ND, 2008, www.ndpublishing.com/books/patchenwalkingaway.html.

395 *"so preposterous and sly"*: JL, quoted in Zarin, "Profiles: Jaz," 55.

395–96 *"a shining face"*: JL, "Mishima," in *WIW*, 181.

396 *"touchingly grave"*: TW to JL, April 23, 1971, H.

396 *"the most remarkable"*: JL to Nicanor Parra, March 28, 1972, H.

396 *a chair partially obscured*: Hugh Kenner, "Jas and Jasper," *Paideuma* 31, nos. 1–3: 73.

396 *"The Kenners' Cat"*: JL, "The Kenners' Cat," *CP*, 280.

397 *"personally read"*: JL to Robson, Aug. 24, 1972, ND/C.

397 *"Norfolk confetti"*: Emily Wallace came up with this name for Laughlin's notes while conducting her research on William Carlos Williams in the ND offices, according to PLF, in conversation with author, May 16, 2006.

397 *"sturdy volumes"*: JL to TW, Aug. 11, 1972, H.

397 *"somehow offensive"*: RMM to HM, Aug. 11, 1972, ND/C.

397 *"inject into the design"*: JL to Huston, April 30, 1973, ND/Personnel File.

397 *"I just happened to be"*: Griselda Ohannessian, interview by author, Sept. 7, 2001.

398 *"composition that"*: JL to KB, June 1, 1973, H.

398 *He saw the United States*: JL, in conversation with David Antin and Jerome Rothenberg, reported to author, Aug. 23, 2001.

398 *"By moving around"*: JL to TW, Oct. 31, 1982, H.

398 *"No, NO!!!!"*: Richard Taylor, "JL as Editor and Publisher: The Most Conscientious and Scrupulous Man I Have Ever Known," *Paideuma* 31, nos. 1–3: 100.

398 *Emerson-Thoreau Medal*: "Ezra Pound Is Focus of New Dispute," *New York Times*, July 5, 1972.

399 *"It matters"*: Reported in Daniel Javitch to JL, Nov. 11, 1972, MH.

399 *"the 'bad' Academy"*: JL to Lal, Dec. 13, 1972, ND/C. The Emerson-Thoreau was not awarded at all the year it was denied to Pound and would not be given again until Robert Penn Warren received it in 1975. The next three recipients were Saul Bellow (1977), J. T. Farrell (1979), and Norman Mailer (1989).

399 *"your own man"*: JL, "Coda" (on Ezra Pound), unpublished typescript, 12, 13, CJB/C.

399 *"The Academy"*: Reported in Javitch to JL, Nov. 11, 1972, MH.

399 *"a great blow"*: JL to Lal, Dec. 13, 1972, ND/C.

399 *"But your Jerusalem"*: JL, "Ezra Pound," *Byways* draft, typescript, CJB/C.

399 *"Quandocumquigitur"*: JL, "Coda," 12, 13, CJB/C.

400 *"great teacher"*: JL to MdR, Nov. 22, 1972, MdR/C.

400 *"With usura"*: EP, Canto 45, *Cantos* (ND, 1993), 229.

400 *"A blown husk"*: EP, Canto 115 fragment, ibid., 815.

34. DROPPING THE PILOT

401 *"You can imagine"*: JL to Hugh Kenner, Feb. 6, 1973, HRHRC.

401 *"What the devil"*: Ernesto Cardenal, "Trip to New York," *Pluriverse: New and Selected Poems*, ed. Jonathan Cohen, foreword by Lawrence Ferlinghetti (ND, 2009), 156, 165.

401 *"very lovable"*: JL to Octavio Paz, July 18, 1973, ND/C.

401 *"To Tom"*: Cardenal, "Trip to New York," 165.

402 *"natural solitude"*: JL to KB, Sept. 5, 1973, H.

402 *"a simply enormous"*: JL to TW, Oct. 3, 1973, H.

402 *"Giacomino!"*: JL, "In Another Country," *In Another Country*, n.p.

402 *"real thing"*: JL to Kenner, July 2, 1974, HRHRC.

402 *"We get down"*: JL to Rothenberg, May 18, 1974, ND/C.

402 *"I do like to"*: JL to Elizabeth Stevens, April 16, 1974, ND/C.

403 *"really wonderful"*: JL to Rothenberg, May 28, 1974, ND/C.

403 *"fat folder"*: JL to Kenner, July 2, 1974, HRHRC.

403 *In some desperation*: PLF, reported to author, June 29, 2006.

403 *between $5,000 and $6,000*: HM to RMM, June 14, 1974, *HM/JL*, 257.

404 *"He is a true autochthone"*: KR to New Directions, autograph note, undated, ND/C.

404 *"He knows"*: JL to Marjorie Perloff, Jan. 28, 1980, MP/C.

404 *"shared a cultural space"*: David Antin, in conversation with author, Aug. 23, 2001.

404 *"as a sister-center"*: Snyder to JL, Dec. 26, 1971, H.

404 *"My Old Gray Sweater"*: JL, "My Old Gray Sweater," *CP*, 303.

404 *"Finding the ceremonial"*: Gary Snyder, interview by Eliot Weinberger, *Beat Writers at Work*, 289.

404 *"Gary is one"*: JL, interview by Richard Ziegfeld for *Paris Review*, quoted from tape recording, July 19, 1982.

404 *He had not wanted*: JL to KB, Jan. 15, 1975, H.

405 *"making good progress"*: JL to Margaret Magie, Sept. 11, 1974, ND/C.
405 *"beautiful service"*: JL to KB, Feb. 10, 1975, H.

35. ON THE ROAD: PERFORMER AND POET
406 *"I have never"*: JL to HM, Dec. 11, 1974, *HM/JL*, 266.
407 *"hard digging"*: JL to Neil Baldwin, May 5, 1975, Collection Neil Baldwin.
407 *"I can't stand it!"*: Peter Glassgold, reported by Barbara Epler to author, April 7, 2007.
408 *"Hildebrand the playboy"*: Saul Bellow, *Humboldt's Gift* (Viking, 1975), 137.
408 *"Christ, I never"*: HM to Griselda Ohannessian, June 16, 1975, ND/C.
408 *"He's a complicator"*: JL to Peter Glassgold, reported to author, Oct. 19, 2005.
409 *"flood" of correspondence*: JL to Nathaniel Tarn, Feb. 23, 1975, ND/C.
409 *"I've decided on"*: JL to Neil Baldwin, May 5, 1975, Collection Neil Baldwin.
409 *"I have been invited"*: JL to H. J. Heinz III, July 20, 1975, H.
409 *"a grouchy old man"*: JL, early *Byways* draft in *Contemporary Authors Autobiographical Series* 22:173–74.
409 *"The pedants"*: JL, "Maledicti in plebe sint," unpublished typescript, MH.
409 *"If you opened"*: Wiesel to JL, May 27, 1977, MH.
409 *"A little Jewish girl"*: Dan Allman, in conversation with author, July 2008.
409 *"major flap"*: Frederick Martin to Dan Allman, ca. Dec. 13, 1978, autograph note, ND/C.
410 *"I thought the elegance"*: JL to Harry Reese, Dec. 6, 1983, S/HR/C.
410 *"as if she"*: JL, "In Another Country," *In Another Country*, n.p.
410 *"The dreams"*: Woolsey to JL, Monday, Sept.? 8, 1991, H.
410 *"It helps in old age"*: JL to Woolsey, Sept. 30, 1991, H.
410 *"This distillation"*: TW to JL, Aug. 13, 1978, H.
411 *"the greatest"*: JL, quoted in Thomas Lask, "Old New Directions," *New York Times*, Dec. 13, 1978.
412 *"Something good"*: JL to Wiesel, March 23, 1979, MH.
412 *"mental temperature"*: JL, autograph note, ca. Dec. 1984, MH.
412 *"Everything is oneiric"*: JL to Dr. Daniel Romanos, Dec. 25, 1991, MH.
412 *He arose at*: JL to CJB, Sept. 19, 1982, CJB/C.
413 *"the unique live"*: HM to Else Albrecht-Carrié, Sept. 30 and Oct. 17, 1979, ND/C.
413 *"busted trimeter"*: John A. Harrison, "A Selective List of Published Writing, 1935–1998, By and About James Laughlin," typescript draft, 3, ND/C.
413 *"Tossed to me"*: JL, *Byways*, 2.
413 *"more or less"*: JL to Diana Stoll, Dec. 8, 1994, private collection.
414 *"It's really"*: JL, *Byways*, 2.
414 *When Ginsberg denied*: JL to GD, March 7, 1985, GD/JL, 18.
414 *"There is some color"*: JL, "J. Poems file," CJB/C.
415 *"Henry Miller gone"*: JL to Martin, June 11, 1980, ND/C.
415 *"Glad to know"*: JL to Ohannessian, [July?] 1980, ND/C.
415 *"how much pleasure"*: JL to TW, March 5, 1981, H.
415 *"I just wish"*: JL to TW, Nov. 24, 1981, H.
415 *"I just talk"*: JL to Octavio Paz, April 20, 1982, ND/C.
415 *"how the words"*: JL, *Pound as Wuz*, 98.

415 *"At last the autobiographical"*: Wiesel to JL, Aug. 18, 1981, MH.
416 *He astounded J*: JL, *Pound as Wuz*, 96–97.
416 *"that thrilling"*: JL to GD, March 15, 1993, MH.
416 *"interest in French"*: JL, "Collaborators" (prose note), *The Collected Poems of James Laughlin* (Moyer Bell, 1994), xi.
416 *She read Proust*: JL to Marjorie Perloff, Sept. 2, 1984, MP/C.
416 *"She has gotten me"*: JL to CJB, Oct. 1982?, CJB/C.
416 *"Elle jette"*: JL, "Elle a la tête qui danse," *CP*, 233.
416 *"Non amet neguna"*: JL, "A Lady Asks Me," ibid., 328.
416 *"Les Vieillards"*: JL, "Les Vieillards," ibid., 231.
416 *"Will there be time"*: JL, "Lady Asks Me," ibid., 329.
417 *"distant little voice"*: JL, "The Last Caress," ibid., 453.
417 *"Je veux me"*: JL, "Je veux me grimer," unpublished typescript, CJB/C.
417 *"horrid Variety's"*: JL to Vanessa Jackson, ca. 1985, private collection.

36. LURED BY THE *APSARAS*
418 *"literary entertainer"*: JL to TW, Oct. 31, 1982, H.
418 *"J thought"*: VS, in conversation with author, March 29, 2011.
418 *Morrow had suggested*: Bradford Morrow, interview by author, Aug. 13, 2007.
419 *"I wouldn't have"*: KR, interview by Bradford Morrow, "Festschrift in Honor of James Laughlin," 67.
419 *"I think it's"*: JL, quoted in Edwin McDowell, "About Books and Authors," *New York Times Book Review*, Feb. 28, 1982.
419 *Carol Tinker summoned*: Carol Tinker, in conversation with author, May 13, 2006.
419 *Kenneth had been*: Morrow, interview by author, Aug. 7, 2007.
419 *"Happy Hollywood"*: Wiesel to ARL to JL, May 21, 1982, MH.
420 *a single casual kiss*: CJB to author, typed note, ca. July 2007.
420 *"I want to be"*: JL to CJB, July 11 and 13, 1982, CJB/C.
420 *"out of the kindness"*: JL to CJB, Aug. 8, 1982, CJB/C.
420 *An affectionate remembrance*: JL, "Dr Benjamin Wiesel," typescript draft, MH.
421 *"Oh, that's just J"*: Sandra Reese, interview by author, Jan. 4, 2009.
421 *"a learned idiot"*: JL, "A *Cento* from Gary/Ajar's *La Vie Devant Soi*," *Stolen & Contaminated Poems*, 43.
421 *"By my count"*: J. Roger Dane [JL], epigraph to "Girls as Windmills," *CP*, 341.
421 *In J's analysis*: JL, "The Doppelgaengers," ibid., 197. A widely accepted supposition was that Gary's death had been due to his depression over the suicide the preceding year of his ex-wife, the actress Jean Seberg.
421 *"obsessive need"*: JL, "*Cento* from Gary," 43.
421 *J had also placed Carol*: JL to CJB, July 13 [second letter this date] and 19, 1982, CJB/C.
421 *"our project"*: JL to CJB, July 28, 1982, CJB/C.
422 *"the Major Domo"*: JL to CJB, Aug. 12 and Sept. 12, 1982, CJB/C.
422 *"Despite all"*: JL to CJB, Aug. 16, 1982, CJB/C.
422 *"his lovely young wife"*: JL to CJB, Aug. 8, 1982, CJB/C.
422 *"esteemed husband"*: JL to CJB, Aug. 16, 1982, CJB/C.

422 *"goofy truffador"*: JL to CJB, Aug. 10 [second letter this date], 12, and 13, 1982, CJB/C.

422 *"Hosannah"*: JL to CJB, Aug. 12, 1982, CJB/C.

422 *"You were so funny"*: JL to CJB, Sept. 9 and 14, 1982, CJB/C.

423 *"Ubi sunt"*: JL to CJB, Aug. 18, 1982, CJB/C.

423 *"marvelous"*: JL to Susan Friedman, Sept. 23, 1982, ND/C.

423 *"wild surmise"*: JL to CJB, Aug. 20, 1982, CJB/C.

423 *"got a bit pickled"*: JL to CJB, Sept. 1 and 14, 1982, CJB/C.

423 *The final shove*: PLF, in conversation with author, Sept. 4, 2007; Snyder to author, March 11, 2011.

423 *"There were special"*: JL to GD, July 21, 1995, *GD/JL*, 203.

424 *"all my grandiloquent"*: JL to CJB, Sept. 27, 1982, CJB/C.

424 *"hysterical"*: JL to CJB, Sept. 29, 1982, CJB/C.

424 *"ATRA DIES"*: Ibid.

424 *J encouraged Carol*: JL to CJB, Sept. 30, 1982, CJB/C.

424 *"The archives will"*: ARL to CJB, Nov. 30, 1982, CJB/C.

425 *"Probably by now"*: JL to Jackson, Nov. 5, 1982, private collection.

425 *Although Vanessa never*: Vanessa Jackson, interview by author, Jan. 30, 2003.

425 *"I tell the birds"*: JL, "Alba," *CP*, 269.

425 *"Je te vois"*: JL, "La Luciole," ibid., 221.

425 *"Here's one from"*: Leila Laughlin Javitch, in conversation with author, Oct. 30, 2005.

426 *"I baked fresh"*: Emily Wallace, in conversation with author, Sept. 20, 2008.

426 *"You Were Asleep"*: JL, "You Were Asleep," *Love Poems*, n.p.

426 *"James, you are"*: JL to CJB, Dec. 25, 1982, CJB/C.

426 *"pretty uncomfortable"*: JL to Wiesel, Dec. 27, 1982, MH. *Heautontimorumenic*, masochistic, is apparently J's coinage from the title of a lost play by Menander; or from the Greek play translated or rewritten by Terence as *Heuton timorumenos* (Self-Tormentor); or from Baudelaire's "L'héautontimorouménos" in *Fleurs du Mal*.

426 *"In the slightly"*: JL to Dr. E. Nichols, Jan. 4, 1983, MH.

427 *"The faculty people"*: JL to Wiesel, Feb. 14, 1983, MH. Loose translations: *diachronated*, played with the changes of language over time; *nekuyas*, references to the dead (see the *Odyssey*, bk. 11); *periploi*, digressions, literally "sailing around": Herodotus and Thucydides contain passages based on *periploi*, the logbooks kept by ancient Greek captains; *polymetises*, many-sided, a stock Homeric epithet for Odysseus.

427 *There was great*: Keith Waldrop, in conversation with author, July 11, 2006.

427 *overdose of Seconal*: John Lahr, *Tennessee Williams: Mad Pilgrimage of the Flesh* (Norton, 2014), 588.

427 *Brad Morrow*: Morrow, interview by author, Aug. 7, 2007.

427 *"It was James"*: TW, typescript with autograph notations, Jan. 1983.

428 *"touched me more"*: JL, interview by PLF, "James Laughlin at Meadow House."

428 *"Tennessee / called"*: JL, "Tennessee," *NDPP 1983*, 47:180.

37. "IL CATULLO AMERICANO"

429 *"I loved him"*: JL to PLF, reported to author, Nov. 1, 2004.

429 *"How easily J cried"*: Deborah Pease, telephone interview by author, Nov. 26, 2005.

429 *"I'll call GORE"*: PLF, in conversation with author, Sept. 4, 2006.

430 *"I cannot write"*: Gore Vidal, introduction to *Tennessee Williams: Collected Stories* (ND, 1985), xxiii, xxv.

430 *"That hushed"*: JL to Marjorie Perloff, May 25, 1983, MP/C.

430 *"I know you know"*: JL to Janowitz, April 11, 1983, MH.

431 *The young woman found*: Vanessa Jackson, interview by author, Jan. 30, 2003.

431 *"Could the blackness"*: JL to Jackson, Aug. 27, 1983, private collection.

431 *"You Came"*: JL, "You Came as a Thought," *CP*, 292.

431 *He called her*: JL to GD, March 15, 1993, MH.

431 *"I knelt at"*: JL, "Una Ricordanza Tenera," *CP*, 600.

431 *"HOW would I meet"*: JL to Wiesel, March 26, 1983, MH.

432 *"priced down where"*: PLF, in conversation with author, March 14, 2011.

433 *"on the great course"*: Ibid.

433 *"this miserable affair"*: JL to Dr. David Luchs, Nov. 13, 1983, MH.

433 *she talked without letup*: JL to Wiesel, Oct. 18, 1983, MH.

433 *The "stolen" poems*: JL, "Not-Notes," 27.

433 *"where, say, Ariosto"*: JL to Harry Reese, Jan. 20, 1984, S/HR/C.

433 *"the juxtaposition"*: JL to Harry Reese, typescript, "Not-Notes," March 1984, S/HR/C.

433 *"making fun of"*: JL to Daniel Javitch, Feb. 15, 1984, MH.

433 *J was formal*: Sandra Reese, in conversation with author, Jan. 4, 2009.

434 *J resolved to stop*: JL to Dr. Daniel Romanos, Dec. 25, 1983, MH.

434 *"chiefly because"*: JL to Vanessa Jackson, Dec. 13, 1983, private collection.

434 *"This is not fear"*: JL to Luchs, Nov. 13, 1983, MH.

434 *He mentioned*: Lamm to author, e-mail, Dec. 16, 2005.

434 *"I keep too busy"*: JL to Jackson, Jan. 12, 1984, private collection.

434 *"an interminable evening"*: Ibid.

434 *"servant of the"*: Signet Society, citation for JL, April 14, 1984, MH.

435 *would veto*: Roger Stoddard, in conversation with author, 2002; confirmed to author by Emily Wallace.

435 *"I lost a day"*: JL to Harry Reese, May 13, 1984, S/HR/C.

435 *"Where this system"*: JL to Harry Reese, June 6, 1984, S/HR/C.

435 *"you are the greatest"*: JL to Harry Reese, Sept. 24, 1984, S/HR/C.

435 *"Dearest Dora"*: JL to Jackson, May 28, 1984, private collection.

435 *"The sheep are"*: Ibid.

436 *"felt a sense"*: Donald Faulkner, in conversation with author, Feb. 27, 2007.

436 *"A Leave-Taking"*: JL, "A Leave-Taking," *CP*, 339.

436 *"Lotsa Great Art"*: JL to Sandra and Harry Reese, Feb. 2, 1985, S/HR/C.

436 *"Without the Concept"*: Gustave Flaubert, *Letters, 1857–1880*, ed. and trans. Francis Steegmuller (Harvard University Press, 1982), 2:244.

437 *His son Robert*: JL to Wiesel, Nov. 14, 1991, MH.

437 *"The floor / was"*: JL, "Experience of Blood," *CP*, 685.

437 *"expiring, classically"*: JL to GD, March 7, 1985, GD/JL, 17.

437 *"I couldn't have"*: JL, "Experience of Blood," *CP*, 686.

437 *Javitch had assisted*: Javitch, in conversation with author, Oct. 2007.

437 *"in somewhat cockeyed"*: JL, "Building 520, Bellevue," *CP*, 653–54.

38. REVISION OF THINGS PAST

438 *"Ann is holding"*: JL to Harry Reese, Feb. 28, 1985, S/HR/C.

439 *"Sperm is from"*: GD to JL, March 2, 1986, GD/JL, 33–34.

439 *"remarkable"*: JL to GD, Oct. 14, 1985, ibid., 25.

439 *"ZOWIE!!"*: JL to GD, Dec. 21, 1985, ibid., 27.

439 *"I'm essentially"*: GD to JL, Oct. 10, 1992, ibid., 83.

440 *"Thank you especially"*: JL to Parra, May 8, 1985, H.

440 *Together they "perambulat[ed]"*: JL, "Preguntas sin Respuestas," CP, 354.

440 *"I don't know"*: Parra to JL, May 1985, H.

440 *"Unheimlich"*: JL to Sandra and Harry Reese, April 10, 1985, S/HR/C.

440 *For J, Chile*: Carlene Laughlin, in conversation with author, Aug. 25, 2005.

440 *"There may be"*: JL to Ohannessian and Glassgold, Jan. 4, 1985, ND/C; beginning in 1976, the Pushcart Press published annual anthologies of poems collected from many small-circulation magazines and presses.

440 *"What a book!"*: JL to Harry Reese, March 16, 1985, S/HR/C.

441 *"to make up to him"*: JL to Dr. Daniel Romanos, Dec. 25, 1991, MH.

441 *"Humor at Maine"*: JL to Sandra Reese, May 5, 1985, S/HR/C.

441 *"maybe I'll do"*: JL to Parra, Sept. 3, 1985, H.

441 *"My talk on economics"*: JL to Harry Reese, Oct. 28, 1985, S/HR/C.

441 *J cautioned Carpenter*: JL to Carpenter, Feb. 26, 1986, MH.

442 *"the lighthouse"*: JL to GD, Oct. 30 and Nov. 2, 1992, MH.

442 *"What can this be?"*: JL to Wiesel, Nov. 27, 1985, MH.

443 *"I've been rather down"*: JL to Jackson, Nov. 1985, private collection.

443 *"Finally I'm beginning"*: Flaubert, Letters, 1857–1880, 2:5, library at MH.

443 *"Under His Microscope"*: JL, "Under His Microscope," poem enclosed with JL to Harry Reese, Dec. 24, 1985, S/HR/C; CP, 366.

443 *"This is my son"*: JL to Jackson, May 8, 1986, private collection.

443 *"My Muse"*: JL, "My Muse," CP, 341–42.

443 *But Gregory didn't*: JL to Jackson, May 8, 1986, private collection.

443 *In Paris*: Details from Jackson, interview by author, Jan. 30, 2003; also JL to Marjorie Perloff, May 29, 1986, MP/C.

443 *Many of the places*: Vanessa Jackson, in conversation with author, May 26, 2007; JL, *Angelica: Fragment from an Autobiography* (Grenfell Press, 1992).

444 *"secret book"*: Jackson, interview by author, Jan. 30, 2003.

444 *"My last / word"*: JL, "Last Words," *Tabellae* (Grenfell Press, 1986), n.p.; and CP, 373.

444 *"He was on his best"*: JL to Parra, Oct. 7, 1986, H.

444 *he remained ardent*: "Angelica," in conversation with author, July 25, 2006.

445 *"That bores me"*: JL to Sandra Reese, Feb. 10, 1987, S/HR/C.

445 *"our poet of Chekhovian"*: Marjorie Perloff, jacket blurb, JL, *Selected Poems, 1935–1985* (City Lights, 1986).

445 *"linguistic philosophy"*: George Dickerson, "Essences and Sentiments," *New York Times*, Nov. 2, 1986.

445 *"To criticize a book"*: HC, "To the Editor," *New York Times*, Nov. 30, 1986.

446 *"Each of the early"*: JL, introduction to *NDPP 1986*, 50:xii.

446 *J arrived, looking*: PLF, in conversation with author, Feb. 11, 2002.

446 *"We know the scene"*: JL, "Some Voices from Canto 74," *Pound as Wuz*, 120–21.
446 *"I have this thing"*: JL, quoted in Nan Robertson, "Broadway: Sophocles per Pound," *New York Times*, Aug. 7, 1987.
447 *"the best thing"*: JL to Sandra and Harry Reese, Nov. 24, 1987, S/HR/C.
447 *"I looked down"*: JL to Jackson, Feb. 26, 1987, private collection.
447 *"57 memories"*: JL, "Jack," *CP*, 524.
447 *J discovered that*: Drue Heinz, telephone interview by author, March 20, 2007.
447 *"J's gratitude"*: ARL to Wiesel, March 25, 1987, MH.
447 *"I feel so disloyal"*: JL to Wiesel, March 25, 1987, MH.
447 *"I assure you"*: Wiesel to JL, March 27, 1987, MH.
447 *"After I'm Gone"*: JL, unpublished poem draft, CJB/C.
448 *"I don't think"*: JL to Wiesel, April 27, 1987, MH.
448 *"People are always"*: JL to PLF, reported to author, Nov. 15, 2008.
448 *"extreme distress"*: JL, autograph note, "Conversation with Dr Benj Wiesel," Hartford, May 12, 1987, medical files, MH.
448 *"so manic about"*: JL to Wiesel, May 27, 1987, MH.
448 *"the last"*: JL to Lawrence Ferlinghetti, Sept. 13, 1987, ND/C.
449 *"I have been"*: JL to GD, Oct. 27, 1987, GD/JL, 42.
449 *"Yes," he told*: JL to Sandra and Harry Reese, Nov. 24, 1987, S/HR/C.
449 *"Mr. Laughlin's clear love"*: Robert Minkoff, *NYTBR*, June 12, 1988.

39. WITNESS TO MORTALITY

450 *"extollatory"*: JL to GD, Feb. 15, 1988, GD/JL, 49–51.
450 *"a dreamy girl"*: JL to Sandra Reese, Jan. 24, 1993, S/HR/C.
450 *"You're as incurably"*: GD to JL, Feb. 24, 1988, GD/JL, 52.
450 *"James Laughlin's"*: Gary Snyder, autograph note, Feb. 1988, MH.
451 *"who never was"*: JL to Sandra Reese, Nov. 7, 1988, S/HR/C.
451 *"is making great"*: JL to Ferlinghetti, Jan. 28, 1989, ND.
451 *Friends noticed*: Bési Starkey, in conversation with author, April 11, 2008.
452 *"one of the great"*: JL, "Kay Boyle," introductory note, *NDPP 1986*, 50:48–49.
452 *"Again my thanks"*: KB to JL, May 17, 1989, H.
452 *"In the best"*: KB to JL, June 24, 1989, H.
452 *"We lost the Magritte"*: JL to Donald Faulkner, reported to author, June 3, 2005; Leila Laughlin Javitch, in conversation with author, Oct. 30, 2005.
452 *J particularly regretted*: JL to Sandra Reese, May 16, 1989, S/HR/C.
452 *Whole shelves of books*: JL to GD, April 12, 1989, GD/JL, 53; JL to Rosmarie Waldrop, June 16, 1989, ND/C; PLF, in conversation with author, June 4, 2005.
453 *This loss*: JL to Anne Carson, March 20, 1993, MH.
453 *"Dearest Strawberry"*: JL to Jackson, April 22, 1989, H.
453 *"If you all like"*: JL to PLF, ca. March 30, 1989, ND/C.
453 *"The doctors think"*: JL to Ferlinghetti, July 3, 1989, ND/C.
453 *They were now*: JL to Sandra Reese, May 16, 1989, S/HR/C.
453 *More than once*: Deborah Pease, in conversation with author, Nov. 26, 2005.
454 *Ann suggested*: JL to Sara Woolsey, Jan. 20, 1993, H.
454 *J could never*: Santha Rama Rau Wattle, interview by author, April 2004.
454 *"too much"*: JL, "Expectations," *CP*, 599.

454 *"Beautiful love"*: JL to Jackson, Nov. 13, 1989, H.
454 *Ann said*: JL to MdR, Feb. 12, 1989 [i.e., 1990], MdR/C.
454 *Leila spoke movingly*: PLF, in conversation with author, May 13, 2006.
455 *He "sort of fell"*: Rama Rau Wattle, interview by author, April 2004.
455 *"Ann's death"*: JL to GD, ca. Dec. 1989, MH.
455 *"A great thing"*: JL to Jackson, Jan. 18, 1990, private collection.
455 *"As he passes"*: JL, "The Empty Room," *CP*, 686–87.

40. THE SOMNAMBULIST
457 *"I think you"*: JL to GD, Dec. 18, 1990, *GD/JL*, 69.
457 *"I love words"*: JL, "Mr. Here & Now," *CP*, 716; enclosed with JL to GD, Feb. 6, 1993, MH.
457 *Sandra Reese responded*: Sandra Reese to JL, July 20, 1993, S/HR/C.
458 *"My dear old"*: JL to Jackson, Jan. 18, 1990, private collection.
458 *"a relief to be"*: JL to Deborah Pease, Jan. 29, 1990, Howard Gotlieb Archival Research Center.
458 *"J was a good"*: Carlene Laughlin, interview by author, Aug. 25, 2005.
458 *"A moment of happy"*: JL, "A Moment of Vanity," *CP*, 994.
459 *"Before I die"*: JL to PLF, signed note printed in *WIW*, 93.
459 *"The Poetry Society"*: JL to Jackson, Jan. 18, 1990, private collection.
460 *Plimpton spoke at length*: Deborah Pease, in conversation with author, July 25, 2006.
460 *"I was sorry"*: Wiesel to JL, May 22, 1990, MH.
460 *"You should plan"*: Wiesel to JL, Sept. 10, 1990, MH.
460 *"I take great pride"*: JL, quoted in Zarin, "Profiles: Jaz," 53–54. JL once told Deborah Pease, seriously, that he was prouder of Alta than of New Directions. Pease, telephone interview by author, Nov. 16, 2005.
461 *"What a woman!"*: Vanessa Jackson, in conversation with author, 2006.
461 *"How much of"*: JL, "Longing & Guilt," *CP*, 773.
461 *He also hinted at*: Pease, in conversation with author, July 25, 2006.
461 *"I'm not about to"*: Britneva St. Just to PLF, who reported comment to author, May 13, 2006.
461 *"Either you're going"*: Leila Laughlin Javitch to PLF, reported to author, May 13, 2006.
461 *"typical, slightly"*: VS to author, May 20, 2011.
461 *"I want you"*: PLF, in conversation with Susan MacNiven, Sept. 23, 2001.
461 *"I've been hoping"*: JL to Wiesel, Feb. 21, 1991, MH.
462 *"This is typical"*: JL, autograph note to VS, on Ohannessian to JL memo, July 1, 1993, private collection.
462 *"I've always considered"*: JL to Ohannessian, Glassgold, and PLF, Nov. 15, 1992, MH.
462 *"It might as well"*: JL to GD, Sept. 28, 1991, *GD/JL*, 74.
462 *"When we have guests"*: JL to Wiesel, July 22, 1991, MH.
462 *"To reason"*: JL, "The Movements," *CP*, 774.
462 *"to fashion separate"*: JL, "The Engines of Desire," ibid., 787.
463 *"Cinderella is not"*: JL to Woolsey, Oct. 12, 1991, and Sept. 15, 1992, H.
463 *Gertrude confessed*: HC, in conversation with author, 2003.

463 "*a sort of drifting*": JL to Woolsey, Sept. 15, 1992, H.
463 "*His Problem*": JL, "His Problem," *CP*, 776–77.
463 "*How can we make it*": JL, "The Kitchen Clock," ibid., 803.
463 "*I make myself*": Flaubert, *Letters, 1857–1880*, 2:24.
463 "*looking for classical*": JL to GD, Oct. 27, 1994, *GD/JL*, 184.
464 "*Es ist die kraenkliche*": JL to Wiesel, Sept. 9, 1991, MH.
464 "*All those cigarettes*": JL to Wiesel, Oct. 3, 1991, MH.
464 "*As you saw*": JL to Wiesel, Nov. 14, 1991, MH.
464 "*I've been doing*": JL to Drue Heinz, Nov. 23 and Dec. 14, 1991, H.
464 "*Making the pattern*": JL, "Prologue," *Byways*, 1, 3.
464 "*she was good*": JL, "The Yellow Pad," ibid., 245, 250.
465 "*really is 80% fiction*": JL to PLF, May 2, 1993, private collection.
465 "*For Peggy / this fabrication*": JL to PLF, annotation on front free endpaper, JL, *Angelica*.
465 *Pease was shocked*: Pease, telephone interview by author, Nov. 16, 2005.
465 *J wanted neither*: JL to PLF, May 2, 1993, private collection.
465 "*Imaginary events*": JL to GD, Oct. 30 and Nov. 2, 1992, MH. JL got a postmodern comeuppance for playing wild and loose with the facts when at a Pound conference an Italian scholar gave a paper on him that assumed *Angelica* to be gospel truth.
465 "*I don't want*": JL to PLF, before Feb. 1, 1991, ND/C.
465 "*a dignified person*": JL to Britneva St. Just, Feb. 11, 1991, ND/C.
465 "*total snake*": Britneva St. Just to ND, ca. Feb. 1991, ND/C.
466 *Gertrude called*: PLF, in conversation with author, July 26, 2006.
466 "*I fear I make*": JL to Sara Woolsey, Jan. 20, 1993, H.
466 "*I can't talk*": JL to VS, Feb. 15, 1992, private collection.
466 "*It Is So Easy*": JL, "It Is So Easy," *CP*, 523.
466 "*present anxieties*": JL to Dr. Daniel Romanos, Dec. 25, 1991, MH.
466 *J read Yeats*: JL to Harry Reese, Sept. 3, 1992, S/HR/C.
466 "*I loved it*": JL to Woolsey, Sept. 19, 1992, H.
466 *Part of his purpose*: Vanessa Jackson, in conversation with author, Jan. 30, 2003, and Sept. 29, 2006.
467 "*But I'm still*": JL, "Prologue," *Byways*, 3–4.
467 "*When I'm depressed*": JL to Woolsey, Sept. 15, 1992, H.
467 "*Since thou can'st not*": JL, early *Byways* draft in *Contemporary Authors Autobiographical Series*, 22:177.
467 "*pencil to pencil*": JL to GD, Dec. 15, 1992, MH.
467 "*reposition*": JL to GD, Dec. 18, 1992, MH.
468 "*They say I have*": JL, "The Departure," *CP*, 695; enclosed with JL to GD, Dec. 18, 1992, MH.

41. RACE TOWARD SELF-KNOWLEDGE
469 *J said because*: JL to GD, ca. Oct. 25, 1992, MH.
469 "*written to*": JL to GD, Nov. 9, 1992, MH.
469 "*What ravishing*": JL to Ohannessian and Glassgold, Oct. 6, 1992, included in *GD/JL*, 82.

469 *"Don't worry"*: Spring to author, Aug. 18, 2011.

469 *"A dream come true"*: JL to Ohannessian, Glassgold, and PLF, Nov. 15, 1992, MH.

469 *"If you would like"*: GD to JL, Nov. 4, 1992, *GD/JL*, 96.

470 *Guy expressed astonishment*: GD to JL, Oct. 24, 1992, ibid., 92.

470 *"I have never"*: JL to ND staff, Nov. 15, 1992, ibid., 98.

470 *"solace"*: JL to GD, Oct. 30 and Nov. 2, 1992, MH.

470 *J let it be known*: PLF, in conversation with author, May 23, 2001.

471 *"This is an important"*: JL to GD, Oct. 21, 1992, MH; "To Carthage then I came": T. S. Eliot had alluded in *The Waste Land* to this same passage from the *Confessions* of Saint Augustine, and JL echoed it in *Byways*, 83, "To Rapallo then I came."

471 *"What happened to"*: JL, "Grumpus at 78," *CP*, 520–21.

471 *"fascinated" by them*: JL to Carson, Dec. 29, 1992, MH.

471 *"a master"*: JL to Carson, March 20, 1993, MH.

471 *Carson replied*: Carson to JL, Feast of Saint Eulalia, [Feb. 12?], 1993, MH.

471 *"She not toasty"*: JL to GD, marginal annotation to copy of JL to Carson letter of June 1, 1993, MH.

471 *"always an ordeal"*: JL to GD, June 10, 1993, MH.

471 *"I call him 'Smiley'"*: Ibid.

471 *"I've developed"*: JL to GD, Feb. 1, 1993, MH.

472 *"Nobody unnnerstans"*: JL to GD, Nov. 9, 1992, MH.

472 *"I have spaghetti"*: PLF, in conversation with author, Feb. 15, 2011.

472 *"wonderful watercolors"*: JL to GD, Oct. 28, 1992, *GD/JL*, 94.

472 *"raise her spirits"*: JL to GD, Nov. 26, 1992, MH.

472 *"Nummusquanamuckqunmanit"*: JL to Rosmarie Waldrop, 1992, private collection.

472 *"The Two of Them"*: JL, "The Two of Them," *CP*, 761.

473 *"It was a kind"*: JL to GD, Feb. 1, 1993, MH.

473 *"I never pay"*: JL to Sandra Reese, July 28?, 1993, S/HR/C.

473 *"It's going to be"*: JL to Sandra Reese, Aug. 4, 1994, S/HR/C.

473 *"On bad days"*: JL to Sandra Reese, Jan. 24, 1993, S/HR/C.

473 *"langwidge"*: JL to GD, Jan. 28, 1993, MH.

473 *"eulogized"*: JL to GD, April 4, 1993, MH. In *apogeiticy* JL appears to be striving toward a coinage based on *apogæic*, far from the earth.

474 *"But is it possible"*: JL, "The Mistress of Improbability," *CP*, 781; Yeats's lines are from "The Spur."

474 *"The three P's"*: JL to GD, May 29, 1993, in *GD/JL*, 150.

475 *"her middle names"*: JL to GD, Oct. 30 and Nov. 2 and 3, 1992, MH.

475 *"Peggy—I hope"*: JL to PLF, June 1993, private collection.

475 *"The heat is"*: JL to GD, July 12, 1993, MH.

475 *"G. has been"*: JL to VS, July 8, 1993, private collection.

475 *"Now two quite"*: JL, "Remembrance," *CP*, 669.

476 *"He preserved"*: JL, "Dr Benjamin Wiesel," unpublished typescript, MH.

476 *"You see, J"*: Sandra Reese, in conversation with author, Jan. 4, 2009.

476 *"still dizzy"*: JL to Denise Levertov, Aug. 20?, 1993, MH.

476 *"Hard to believe"*: JL to Sandra Reese, Oct. 12, 1993, S/HR/C.

477 *"the <u>New Yawper</u>"*: JL to GD, Dec. 6, 1993, MH.

477 *"Not satyriasis"*: JL, "Remembering William Carlos Williams," *Byways*, 152.

477 *"To look about"*: JL to GD, May 31, 1994, MH.

477 *"Hallelujah"*: JL to GD, Jan. 5, 1994, MH.
477 *"kind and learned"*: JL, "Benignus Quam Doctus," *CP*, 756–57.
477 *"that the cause of"*: JL to GD, May 31, 1994, MH. *Nefasity* is not a recognized pathology; from the context it seems likely that J has coined a word for an infection of the kidneys or the male genital tract.

42. NUNC DIMITTIS SERVUM TUUM

478 *"Carruth has done"*: JL to GD, Feb. 12, 1994, 168.
478 *"many readers"*: Clarence Brown, "Nice Book if You Can Find It," *Trenton Times*, Dec. 9, 1993.
479 *"Beloved friend"*: JL, "Here & There," *CP*, 782–83.
479 *"She was a lively"*: JL, interview by PLF, "James Laughlin at Meadow House," 23.
479 *"I wish you"*: JL to Lahr, Dec. 15, 1994, ND/C.
479 *"wounded"*: John Lahr, "A Life in the Wings," *New Yorker*, Dec. 19, 1994, 89.
480 *"estatrix"*: JL to GD, Dec. 24, 1994, MH. Tennessee Williams's final will had named Lady Maria St. Just as his estate co-executor; JL remained a trustee of the Rose Isabel Williams Foundation, a subsidiary trust created for Tennessee's sister.
480 *"the monstrous"*: JL to GD, May 11, 1994, MH.
480 *"exhausted—and"*: JL to Anne Carson, March 20, 1993, MH.
480 *"Carruth was gloomy"*: JL to Daniel Javitch, March 11, 1995, MH.
480 *"I had been there"*: JL, "The Revenant," *CP*, 695–98.
480 *"The Music"*: JL, "The Music of Ideas," ibid., 772.
481 *"Old men fall"*: JL, "Old Men," ibid.
481 *"I can only stand"*: JL to Ohannessian, Feb. 15 and March 16, 1995, ND/C.
481 *"Ie wie nit"*: JL to GD, Feb. 21, 1995, MH.
481 *"my recent"*: JL to Sandra Reese, April 12, 1995, S/HR/C.
481 *"all penible"*: JL to Sandra Reese, May 21, 1995, S/HR/C.
482 *"silence and curiosity"*: JL to GD, April 9, 1995, MH.
482 *"Dear Mike Angular"*: JL to GD, Nov. 10, 1994, GD/JL, 185.
482 *"Some of them"*: JL to GD, Nov. 26, 1994, ibid., 186.
482 *"I think there is"*: JL to GD, Feb. 28, 1995, ibid., 194.
482 *"The MacArthur loot"*: JL to GD, March 5, 1996, quoted in ibid., 225n.
483 *"page after page"*: JL to GD, Sept. 24, 1996, ibid., 232.
483 *"little miracles"*: GD to JL, Sept. 26, 1996, ibid., 231.
483 *Gertrude took the measure*: Gertrude Laughlin to GD, Nov. 16, 1995, ibid., 219.
483 *"very shaky"*: JL to Sandra Reese, May 21 and Oct. 6, 1995, S/HR/C.
483 *"so wiggly"*: JL to Sandra Reese, April 12, 1995, S/HR/C.
483 *"until it is"*: JL, "Tennessee," *CP*, 340.
484 *"He was my friend"*: JL, interview by PLF, "James Laughlin at Meadow House," 1–30.
484 *"because they cut"*: JL to Sandra Reese, April 24, 1996, S/HR/C.
484 *Doggedly, J attempted*: JL to Sandra Reese, June 25, 1996, S/HR/C.
484 *"creaky legs"*: JL to GD, Oct. 28, 1996, MH.
484 *"I didn't know"*: Bési Starkey to author, April 11, 2008.
484 *"I wanted to tell you"*: Lawrence Ferlinghetti, "Allen Ginsberg Dying," typescript copy, ND/C.

485 *"a waiting book"*: JL to Leslie Miller, Aug. 28, 1997, ND/C.
485 *"The spaces in time"*: JL, *A Commonplace Book of Pentastichs*, ed. Hayden Carruth (ND, 1998), 83.
485 *"hobby project"*: JL to Glassgold, June 16, 1996, ND/C.
485 *"Little time now"*: JL, "Nunc Dimittis," *CP*, 925.
486 *"Gertrude's illness"*: JL to Glassgold, Aug. 28, 1997, ND/C.
486 *"She's very brave"*: JL to GD, Oct. 6, 1997, GD/JL, 242.
486 *"beseeched"*: HC, *Beside the Shadblow Tree*, 130. The book Carruth published after JL's death is, as the subtitle claims, a straight personal memoir with no pretense of being a history of ND.
486 *"Peggy—I don't"*: JL to PLF, ca. Aug. 1997, ND/C.
486 *"Peggy—I'm glad"*: JL to PLF, Oct. 22, 1997, ND/C. "McCowan" refers to Christopher MacGowan, editor of the Levertov/W. C. Williams correspondence.
487 *"No exact moment"*: JL, "Moments in Space," *CP*, 786.
487 *His mind was on*: JL, "Wheels," *Byways* file, MH.
487 *"terrible sound"*: Kathleen Basetta, interview by author, March 30, 2014.
487 *The cause of death*: Daniel Javitch, reported by PLF to author, 2009.
488 *"mors claudet"*: JL to Kenner, July 23, 1968, HRHRC.
488 *"Write on My Tomb"*: JL, "Write on My Tomb," *CP*, 186.

EPILOGUE
490 *"his unflagging intellectual"*: HC, advertising flyer for JL, *Poems, New and Selected*.
490 *"American corporate"*: Lawrence Ferlinghetti, quoted in *Beat Writers at Work*, 347.
490 *"the lengthened shadow"*: Donald Lamm, speaking at the Cooper Union, New York City, 1992.

Acknowledgments

The responsibility for carrying out James Laughlin's final wishes rested with the four trustees of his Private Literary Property Trust, consisting of his son-in-law, Daniel Javitch; Donald Lamm, past president of W. W. Norton; Griselda Ohannessian, then president of New Directions; and Peggy Fox, then vice president of New Directions. It was their decision in 1999 to authorize the writing of a biography of Laughlin that would also be the history of New Directions that he had long desired. Fox nominated me for the task, based on the example of my biography of the English writer Lawrence Durrell, published the previous year by Faber and Faber. After deciding to confirm that nomination, the trustees then granted me unlimited access to all files under their jurisdiction, including the New Directions Office Collection and Files in New York City, and they did not stipulate any control over my conclusions.

The backstory of the writing of Laughlin's life is the narrative of four close friends, a charmed circle in which I was the grateful fourth. The other three were Peggy Fox, who began working at New Directions in 1975, and her husband, Robert Sennish, my closest friend and teaching colleague, who had also known Laughlin through Peggy; and Susan MacNiven, my wife of many years, who was my constant companion in research and interviews for the first few years on the Laughlin trail. Then Robert died, followed within a year by Susan; Peggy and I, who had known each other for over twenty-five years, married, and it was due to Peggy's support, encouragement, and advice that I was able to continue work on the biography and complete it. In a very real sense, I was involved with New Directions, and, peripherally, in Laughlin's life, for more than a quarter century.

My debt of gratitude to all those I have contacted, and who have provided me with firsthand accounts, correspondence, documents, and photographs, is inestimable. My thanks extend to people in many categories, some now deceased, and include all those named below.

The Laughlin family: The biography as written would not have been possible without the generous cooperation of the primary James Laughlin family and of a number of Laughlin's cousins. My greatest thanks are owed to Laughlin's daughter, Leila, and her husband, Daniel Javitch, whose contribution began with opening Laughlin's Meadow House and his files and library to me, and continued through many conversations to a reading of my uncut manuscript. My thanks also to the Javitches' son-in-law, Gus Powell, for providing many of the illustrations for this volume; and to Laughlin's younger surviving son, Henry, and his wife, Carlene, who guided my steps not only in Norfolk, Connecticut, but also made it possible for me to experience Laughlin's Alta, Utah, ski area; and to Laughlin's firstborn son, Paul, and his wife, Marian. I thank also Ann Resor Laughlin and her siblings Helen Hauge (and her daughter Barbara) and Stanley R. Resor, as well as Laughlin cousins Michael Carlisle (and his wife, Olga), Marie Page Edgerton (and her daughters, Carol Edgerton Thayer and Leila Bonner Trismen), and Robert Laughlin. None of these placed the slightest restrictions on my research, nor did they request any textual oversight.

Norfolk, Connecticut: Kathleen Basetta, Carol Camper and John Hartje (who together helped initiate the biography project), Michelle and Star Childs, Leon Deloy, John Girolamo, Margaret and Keith Meyers, Elizabeth "Pebble" and H. David Potter, Bruce Ricker and Kate Gill, Virginia Schendler, Ann Scoville, and B. C. "Bési" Starkey.

Alta and Salt Lake City: Barbara and Red Altum, Dick Durrance, Dick Durrance II, Barbara and Alan K. Engen, Janet Quinney Lawson, William and Mimi Levitt, Connie Marshall, Allen L. Orr, Jane Blaffer Owen, Sheila and Nicholas Platt, Frank Sasaki, and Onno Wieringa.

Library and Institutional Staff: My great thanks to William P. Stoneman, Florence Fearington Librarian and head of Harvard University's Houghton Library; to Roger E. Stoddard, senior lecturer in English and now retired Curator of Rare Books; and especially to the present Curator of Rare Books and Manuscripts, Leslie Morris, who from the very first guided my way around the 1,422 boxes of material in the James Laughlin Papers and the New Directions Publishing Corporation records, and indeed made possible this study; and to many others on the unfailingly helpful staff in the Houghton Library Reading Room, including especially Thomas Ford, Bonnie B. Salt, and Melanie Wisener. The principal collections that I consulted at the Houghton were the James Laughlin Papers (MS Am 2077.2) and the New Directions Publishing Corporation Records (MS Am 2077).

Among the many librarians other than those at Houghton who provided essential help, I would like to thank especially Paul Pearson and Mark C. Meade of the Thomas Merton Center at Bellarmine University; Elspeth Healey of the Harry Ransom Center at the University of Texas at Austin; Mary Sue Presnell and Saundra Taylor at the Lilly Library, Indiana University Bloomington; Curator Isaac Gewirtz, Stephen Crook, and Philip Milito at the Berg Collection, the New York Public Library; Andrew Dancer at the Catskill Public Library; Ben Joseph and Nicholas Munagian at the Charles Deering Library, Northwestern University; Janet Kettering and Paul A. Kovach at Chatham University, Pittsburgh; Susan Plovic at the Third Presbyterian Church, Pittsburgh; Wenxian Zhang, Head of Archives, and Trudy Laframboise at Rollins College in Winter Park, Florida; Barbara Stromstad and Kirsten Stromstad Cirillo at Le Rosey School, Switzerland; Thomas M. Cangiano at Shady Side Academy; Susie Pettler and Laurel Schultz at the Shadyside Presbyterian Church, Pittsburgh; David V. Koch, Shelley Cox, Alan M. Cohn, and Golda Hankla of the Morris Library, Southern Illinois University Carbondale; the staff of the Beinecke Rare Book & Manuscript Library at Yale for providing extensive copies of material; the Howard Gotlieb Archival Research Center at Boston University, for copies of James Laughlin's letters to Deborah Pease; and the John F. Kennedy Presidential Library in Boston.

Private Collections: The following not only made available to me their collections of primary material, but also most generously shared with me their memories of James Laughlin: Carol Jane Bangs; Elaine Lustig Cohen; Dale Davis; Vanessa Jackson (and her husband, John Dougill), whose art inspired Laughlin to collaborate with her on a beautiful volume of her paintings and his poetry; Deborah Pease, for her especially thoughtful analysis of Laughlin's personality; Marjorie Perloff, scholar extraordinaire and mentor in poetry to Laughlin; Mary de Rachewiltz—legendary alike for her encyclopedic knowledge of all things pertaining to her father, Ezra Pound, and for her warm hospitality to scholars; Sandra and Harry Reese, creators of the incomparable Turkey Press; Virginia Schendler, for copies of her Laughlin correspondence and for her photographs; Vojo Šindolić, poet and major translator of American poetry in the Balkans; and Diana Stoll (Aperture).

New Directions Employees, Current and Past: Three successive presidents and publishers of New Directions—Griselda Ohannessian, Peggy Fox, and Barbara Epler—cheerfully gave me unparalleled access to information as well as working space for the years during which I sifted through the office files. Their senior staff proved equally generous. Dan Allman imparted to me his intimate knowledge of the business side of New Directions, abetted by his husband, Michael Coleman, while Laurie Callahan and Declan Spring patiently answered my many questions, both historical and technical. Peter Glassgold, formerly New Directions editor in chief and then engaged in compiling and editing Laughlin's monumental Collected Poems 1935–1997, most generously shared memories going back forty years, accounts corroborated by his publisher wife, Suzanne Thibodeau. Michael Barron was one of the earliest readers of my manuscript, charged with determining its accessibility to coming generations. Kelsey Ford must be thanked for her superlative and efficient handling of permissions. Many others in the New Directions family gave me essential assistance, including Else (Lorch) Albrecht-Carrié, Kurt Beals, Jeff Clapper, Valerie Danby-Smith Hemingway, Thomas Keith (and his partner Arturo Noguera), Elizabeth Marraffino, Frederick Martin, Semadar Megged, Erik Rieselbach, Joe Rizzo, Sylvia Frezzolini Severance, Anna Della Subin, and Jeffrey Yang, recognized poet and ND poetry editor.

My great thanks to many at Farrar, Straus and Giroux who have gone far beyond the typical author-publisher relationship to make my preparation of the final text a rewarding and even pleasurable experience—especially to Jonathan Galassi, who, long before he became my publisher, shared with me his knowledge of Laughlin's life in Norfolk; to Eric Chinski, who encouraged me from the very first and then waited with saintlike and uncomplaining patience for the manuscript finally to arrive on his desk; to my in-house editor, Miranda Popkey, who, with exemplary sensitivity, presided over and advised on the pruning of an overlong text; to Susan Goldfarb for necessary fine-tuning of my prose and much-appreciated responses to my queries; and to Ingrid Sterner for her meticulous copyediting. Rodrigo Corral and Jonathan Lippincott have my profound appreciation for producing, respectively, a jacket design and a text layout in keeping with Laughlin's exacting standards for the appearance of a fine book. And I thank the many others whose contributions are too many for individual description here: Jesse Coleman, Nicholas Courage, Katie Kurtzman, Jeff Seroy, and Stephen Weil.

Special thanks to my agent, Michael Carlisle of Inkwell, a member of the distinguished Carlisle family, related to the Laughlins, that features in this volume.

Great thanks to all those who by granting interviews; providing letters, photographs, and documents; and in so many other ways assisted me in the understanding of James Laughlin: Sylvia Abrams (lifelong friend of Laughlin's third wife, Gertrude Huston); John Allman; David Antin; Massimo Bacigalupo; Neil Baldwin; Greg Barnhisel; Lee Bartlett; Ronald Bayes; Eric Bentley; Joanne Bentley; Charles Bernstein; Bei Dao; Jacques Barzun; Dr. Martin Bax (Ambit magazine); Georges Borchardt; Kay Boyle (and her son, Ian von Franckenstein); Andreas Brown; Ernesto Cardenal; Hayden Carruth, whose sympathetic understanding of Laughlin was second to none, and who generously shared his insights with me (and his poet wife, Joe-Anne McLaughlin); Anne Carson; Patricia Cockram; Jonathan Cohen; Dr. Robert Coles; David Cooper; Robert Creeley; Robert Duncan; Guy Davenport; Carla and Richard Durante (then owners of the ancestral Laughlin home in Zellwood, Florida, to which they gave me full access); Lawrence Durrell; Ulla Dydo; Don Faulkner; Lawrence Ferlinghetti; Penelope Laurans Fitzgerald; James Forest; Forrest Gander; Allen Ginsberg; Robert Giroux; Daniel Halpern; Sam Hamill; Dosier Hammond (W. W. Norton); Brother Patrick Hart, for his unparalleled firsthand knowledge of Thomas Merton; Sophie and John Hawkes; Priscilla and Michael Heim; Drue Heinz; Suzanne and Robert Helbling; David Hinton; Jeannette and William Herrick; Eva Hesse; Boris and Georges Hoffman (Agence Hoffman); Richard M. Hunt; Donald Keene; Hugh Kenner; Stephen Kessler; Galway Kinnell; Henry Kissinger; Asha and Dr. Bachu Kothari, for twice guiding me around northern India; Michael Krüger (Carl Hanser Verlag); Paul Lacey; John Lahr; Purusottama Lal; Donald Lamm (who twice read and critiqued my entire manuscript and who, while president of Norton, initiated the seven volumes to date of Laughlin's correspondence with various authors); Herbert Leibowitz; Elena Levin (and her daughter, Marina Frederiksen); Martin P. Levin; Jill Levine; Drake McFeeley (W. W. Norton); Michael McClure; Anne H. McCormick; C. Ravindran Nambiar, for helping me experience Laughlin's favorite part of India; Javier Marías; Tony Miller; Bradford Morrow (*Conjunctions* journal); Stanley Moss; Rebecca Newth (and her husband, John A. Harrison, compilers of the essential bibliography of New Directions titles through Laughlin's death); Tommie and Frank O'Callaghan; Linda Oppen; Maria José Paz; Robert S. Phillips; John and Gene Pick; George Plimpton; Elizabeth Pollet; Elizabeth and Omar Pound; Joseph Quattrone; Alice Quinn; Gregory Rabassa; Brigitte and Siegfried Walter de Rachewiltz; Patrizia de Rachewiltz; Mikhail de Rachewiltz; Nicholas de Rachewiltz; Chuck Ralston; Erik Reece; Joan Retallack; Astrid and Barnet Rosset; Sarah and the Reverend Martin Roth, who guided me around Laughlin's Pittsburgh and provided useful help in genealogical research; Dianne and Jerome Rothenberg; Michael Schmidt (Carcanet Press); Laurel Schultz; Mark Scroggins; Anita Shapolsky; Richard Sieburth; Charles Simic; Gary Snyder; Robert Stakeley; Frances Steloff; Shirley Sterrett; Justin Swink; Tree Swenson; Carol Tinker; Brenda and Charles Tomlinson; Fiddle Viracola; Rosmarie and Keith Waldrop (Burning Deck); Emily Mitchell Wallace, whose knowledge of Pound and W. C. Williams is unequaled, and her husband, Gregory Harvey, for his informed legal insights; Santha Rama Rau Wattle; Eliot Weinberger; Doris Blazek-White; John "Jack" Wilkins; Jonathan Williams (Jargon Press); Barbara and Hugh Witemeyer; Sherrie Y. Young; George Zournas.

"They also serve who only stand and wait": Profound thanks to those who provided essential encouragement and support throughout the long progress to completion, dear friends all: Melinda Barnhardt and Henry Jud; Heinz Boeckmann; Beth and Jack Caldwell; Margaret and Steven Crockett; Jan Fergus; Karen White Fox and Michael Fox (and their daughters, Elizabeth, Susanna, and Carolyn); Monica Grage; Penelope Durrell and John Hope; Jane and Vance Johnston; Trudy Katzer; Jane Keller; Daniel Kempton; Anthea Morton-Saner (and her companion, James Rogers); Kelly Reed and Mark Dennen; Helen and William Sands; Bronwen Sennish and Arthur Albert (and their son, Nicholas Albert); Maggie Sennish (and her son, Marcus Mulligan); Linda and Albert Steier; H. R. Stoneback; Chris and Willem ten Pas; Ellen Verhagen; and Elfi and Markus Zimmermann.

Index

PERMISSIONS ACKNOWLEDGMENTS